fatima.music
left bank

POLITICS IN A
CHANGING WORLD

A COMPARATIVE INTRODUCTION
TO POLITICAL SCIENCE

FIFTH EDITION

MARCUS E. ETHRIDGE
University of Wisconsin-Milwaukee

HOWARD HANDELMAN
University of Wisconsin-Milwaukee—Emeritus

WADSWORTH
CENGAGE Learning

Australia • Brazil • Canada • Mexico • Singapore • Spain • United Kingdom • United States

Politics in a Changing World: A Comparative Introduction to Political Science, **Fifth Edition**
Marcus E. Ethridge, Howard Handelman

Executive Editor: Carolyn Merrill

Acquisitions Editor: Edwin Hill

Development Editor: David Estrin

Assistant Editor: Katie Hayes

Editorial Assistant: Jessica Chance

Marketing Manager: Amy Whitaker

Marketing Coordinator: Josh Hendrick

Project Manager: Katy Gabel

Print Buyer: Paula Vang

Permissions Editor: Mardell Glinki Schultz

Photo Manager: Robyn Young

Cover Designer: C Miller Design

Cover Image: © Photodisc

Compositor: PrePress PMG

For product information and technology assistance, contact us at
Cengage Learning Customer & Sales Support, 1-800-354-9706

For permission to use material from this text or product,
submit all requests online at **www.cengage.com/permissions**
Further permissions questions can be emailed to
permissionrequest@cengage.com

Library of Congress Control Number: 2008940893

ISBN-13: 978-0-495-57048-6

ISBN-10: 0-495-57048-6

Wadsworth
20 Channel Center Street
Boston, MA 02210
USA

Cengage Learning products are represented in Canada by Nelson Education, Ltd.

For your course and learning solutions, visit **www.cengage.com.**

Purchase any of our products at your local college store or at our preferred online store **www.ichapters.com.**

Printed in Canada
1 2 3 4 5 6 7 12 11 10 09 08

CONTENTS

PREFACE

We designed the fifth edition of *Politics in a Changing World* to provide a foundation for understanding political life and the increasingly diverse field of political science.

Although we hope the book will be helpful for those who become political science majors, its primary purpose is to introduce students from a wide range of fields to the discipline. Citizens in every walk of life—not only politicians, government officials, and political analysts—need to understand the consequences of political choices and the processes through which those choices are made.

THE CHANGING WORLD IN THE TWENTY-FIRST CENTURY

Revising a political science textbook through five editions is a wonderfully compelling way to confront the reality of political change. When we wrote the first edition, the United States had never experienced a significant terrorist attack, an elected president had never been impeached, the Institutional Revolutionary Party (PRI) still controlled Mexico, Saddam Hussein had a firm grip on power in Iraq, ethnic conflicts in southern and eastern Europe were only beginning, the "Euro" was still in the planning stage, per capita income in China was less than a quarter of what it is today, and the North American Free Trade Agreement was just about to take effect. Political scientists were only beginning to consider how international affairs would be changed by the end of the Cold War, and there was widespread optimism that genuine democracy was dawning in Russia. No one expected the party controlling the U.S. White House to gain seats in the House of Representatives in a midterm election. (That has now happened twice, in 1998 and 2002!)

Although political scientists correctly predicted few of these changes and events, the accumulated knowledge generated by the discipline helps us to make sense of them. Studies of voting behavior, the causes of war, the process of political development, and the impact of economics on politics help us understand what factors will be important as government and international relations evolve in the years to come. The increasing importance of international trade will figure in both foreign and domestic policy in nearly all countries, and the protracted state of cultural and ethnic conflict—particularly conflict involving radical Islamic Fundamentalism—will influence many of the choices governments and citizens will make. The spread of democracy throughout the world has slowed, but the trend toward greater openness in both the political and the economic spheres is firmly entrenched in many areas. Technological advances and the spread of the Internet will shape a great deal of our lives, including commerce, our expectations of privacy, and national security. Political science sheds light on all of these factors.

Politics in a Changing World focuses on the ways in which accumulated knowledge in political science helps us account for the basic changes taking place in politics, and it explores the ways in which those changes have forced political scientists to revise their concepts, theories, and ideas.

POLITICS IN DIFFERENT NATIONS

Beginning with the first edition of *Politics in a Changing World*, we have been guided by the firm conviction that politics cannot be understood fully by considering only a single country. Just as a biologist cannot hope to understand the basic elements of life by studying one species, and just as a physicist cannot hope to understand the nature of combustion by studying only one chemical compound, we cannot understand politics if we restrict ourselves to analysis of a single political system.

Thus, as in the previous editions, a key feature of the fifth edition of *Politics in a Changing World* is its separate chapters on different countries—the United States, Great Britain, Russia (and its predecessor, the Soviet Union), China, and Mexico—along with a chapter on the special problems of developing nations. Although these chapters are not intended even to summarize what is known about those governments, they allow us to give meaningful contexts to our discussions of elections, parties, legislatures, chief executives, courts, and interest groups. They also provide useful historical grounding. For example, the story of Britain's gradual development of democracy is important if we are to understand its current party system, and we need to know something about the Mexican Revolution to appreciate modern political problems and changes in that country.

Most readers of *Politics in a Changing World* are students born in the United States, and most of them have considerable knowledge about the U.S. system of government. But we believe that even a limited understanding of one's own political system is enhanced by coming to understand government and politics in other countries. Government in the United States is unique in many ways, and helping students to appreciate its special nature is one of our objectives in designing this comparative section of the book.

THE PLAN OF THE BOOK

When the discipline of political science reached its adolescence during the 1950s, leading political science departments were hotly divided between those who approached their work with advanced statistical tools and quasi-experimental research methods and those who used more traditional approaches. Over the years, that division between "empiricist-quantifiers" and "traditionalists" was largely replaced by an increasingly diverse array of distinct subfields. Some political scientists study institutions, others study individual behavior, some study ideology, and still others apply economic theories to politics. There is also a great division between those who study government in many nations and those who emphasize a single nation or area. As discussed in Chapter 1, there is now something of a backlash against quantitative analysis in the discipline, although statistics and mathematics continue to dominate political science research methods.

The divisions in contemporary political science present significant challenges for any introductory text. However, we are convinced that the diversity of perspectives, approaches, and methods in political science is beneficial. Specialists in one subfield often make good use of insights generated in other subfields. Indeed, the opportunity to bring together the diverse elements of the discipline has confirmed that impression for us, and we hope our positive feelings about political science as a discipline are communicated effectively to our readers.

We have organized the book into six parts: Fundamentals, Political Behavior, Political Institutions, Politics in Selected Nations, and International Relations. Each section contains chapters devoted to more specific topics. The Epilogue summarizes what we see as the most important prospects and challenges that will shape political change in the next decade and beyond. Part IV comprises the chapters on the United States, Great Britain, Russia, China, Mexico, and the developing world. These chapters can be read as a special unit after the more general chapters are covered, or they may be used as supplementary reading during discussions of political behavior, institutions, or international relations.

Each of the chapters devoted to specific countries contains a map to help readers understand that country's geographical context. Key terms in each chapter are introduced in boldface and are defined in the Glossary. Although the material may be organized in different ways, we have arranged the chapters to correspond to the steps that citizens typically take in approaching politics: Culture and ideology affect us first, then various options for political activity present themselves, and then we consider the institutions we wish to influence. Special issues pertaining to gender transcend the study of ideology, behavior, institutions, and political development, and so appropriate sections devoted to those issues are included in many chapters. Similarly, political economy is relevant to virtually all areas of our discipline, and readers will find that topic addressed throughout the text.

NEW TO THIS EDITION

We have included several changes and numerous updates for the fifth edition of *Politics in a Changing World*. Some of these changes bring the text up to date, and others reflect helpful suggestions from students and instructors.

Extensive Updates Throughout

The wars in Iraq and Afghanistan, and the broader tensions associated with international terrorism profoundly affect both domestic and international politics in most parts of the world. Increasingly, the U.S. and other political systems must determine the proper balance between national (and individual) security against terrorism and the protection of citizens' civil liberties. The rapidly increasing prices for oil and food have exacerbated conflicts and deepened divisions in many nations. Readers will encounter discussions of issues related to those events in several chapters.

The 2008 U.S. presidential election was historic, and we include extensive coverage of its implications for the study of voting behavior, public opinion, and the future of U.S. government. China's astounding economic growth, and Russia's increasingly disturbing departures from democratic government, are two of the most important forces that will shape international relations for decades. We include significant coverage of these subjects.

As in earlier editions, we also include accessible, brief discussions of recent political science research. For example, Chapter 6 contains a discussion of recent research on interest group strategies, new research on the impact of the International Criminal Court is included in Chapter 17, and Chapter 7 features a new box on how the size of a national legislature may influence how much it wastes tax revenue. Chapter 19 discusses the possibility of a new Cold War between Russia and the United States. These new sections are, we hope, interesting in themselves, but we included them because they also help to clarify basic concepts.

"Where on the Web?" Boxes

As in previous editions, each chapter contains a boxed display titled "Where on the Web?" listing Web sites relevant to that chapter's subject matter. The World Wide Web contains a staggering array of information ranging from official government documents and survey and election results to partisan propaganda. The resources are impressive, and they are often very current, but Web "surfers" quickly become aware that a great deal of time can be lost searching through addresses that are less useful than their titles suggest. We have sifted through a large number of Web sites to identify resources that are genuinely useful and are likely to be in place for the foreseeable future. Students and instructors are encouraged to consult those addresses for supplementary information, updates, data, and stimulating ideas.

Web-Based Instructional Guide

Wadsworth, a part of Cengage Learning, has also created a Web site exclusively devoted to the fifth edition of *Politics in a Changing World*. The site includes suggestions about new Web addresses, new articles and books, and updated information about current political events that will enrich class discussions. Students and instructors are encouraged to use this site, found at www.cengage.com/politicalscience/ethridge/pinacw6e.

ACKNOWLEDGMENTS

One of the most rewarding aspects of writing this new edition was the opportunity for each of us to explore in detail subjects beyond our current specialized interests. Nevertheless, several colleagues have provided valuable assistance in correcting errors and omissions, pointing us to helpful examples, and sharpening our arguments. Shale Horowitz, Uk Heo, Robert Eger, David Garnham, Steve Redd, and Don Pienkos generously gave their time to answer endless questions and to provide sources for us to explore. Sandee Enriquez and Kate Day helped Marc locate some highly interesting insights through their diligent research. In addition, the book reflects the suggestions of the following professors and specialists who participated in Wadsworth's rigorous review process: Christopher P. Elmore, Johnson County Community College; Vernon D. Johnson, Western Washington University; F. David Levenbach, Arkansas State University; William Miles, Northeastern University; Kul B. Rai, Southern Connecticut State University; and Paul B. Ethridge, GlaxoSmithKline, Inc.

Marc also wishes to thank Greg and Zach Cigich for their moral support.

Finally, our editor helped to guide this new edition, gently keeping us on schedule and working with us to ensure that it will be stimulating and accessible to students.

ABOUT THE AUTHORS

Marcus E. Ethridge is professor of political science and chairs the Department of Political Science at the University of Wisconsin, Milwaukee. He is a specialist in the study of American government, focusing on interest group behavior, rational-choice theory, and administrative law. His publications include *The Political Research Experience*, *Legislative Participation in Implementation*, and numerous articles in the *American Journal of Political Science*, *Political Research Quarterly*, the *Journal of Politics*, and other journals. He is completing a new book tentatively entitled *The Case for Gridlock*.

Howard Handelman is emeritus professor of political science at the University of Wisconsin, Milwaukee. He specializes in Latin American politics and the politics of developing nations. His books include *The Challenge of Third World Development* (Fifth Edition), *Üçüncü Dünyanin: Meydan Okuryan Ilerles,i* (Turkish-language edition of *The Challenge of Third World Development*), and *Mexican Politics: The Dynamics of Change*. He has contributed journal articles to the *Latin American Research Review*, *Canadian Journal of Latin American Studies*, and *Studies in Comparative International Development*, among others.

PART I

FUNDAMENTALS

Like many other disciplines, political science addresses a wide range of problems, issues, and topics, employing a diverse assortment of research approaches. Nevertheless, there are some concepts that are important to everyone interested in the field. Chapter 1 includes basic information on definitions of politics and government, an exploration of the functions of government, approaches to classifying governments, a discussion of the stakes of politics, and a brief digression regarding the different ways in which political scientists conduct research.

Chapter 2 is devoted to an overview of the most commonly discussed ideologies that influence the way we think about politics and government. Conservatism, liberalism, Marxism, and other ideologies frame debates about specific political issues, and they also figure in the way we evaluate different countries, the causes of war, and efforts to understand political change. A basic understanding of these ways of thinking about politics and government is essential for all political scientists.

RIOTING OVER FOOD IN HAITI   In April 2008, riots broke out in Haiti in response to the soaring costs of food. There was similar rioting in Bangladesh, Egypt, and other developing countries. Food shortages were caused, in part, by the increased demand for ethanol, which drove up the price of grain around the world.

© Ariana Cubillos/AP Photo

1

POLITICS, GOVERNMENT, AND POLITICAL SCIENCE

◆ Politics and Government Defined ◆ Government Functions ◆ Kinds of Governments ◆ The Stakes of Politics ◆ Politics in a Changing World ◆ Conclusion: Why Study Political Science?

The first decade of the new millennium is ending with great promise, and perhaps even greater peril. Economic growth in several parts of the world, particularly in China and India, has lifted millions out of poverty; there are signs that Iraq is becoming more stable; Pakistan, Thailand, and Chile appear to be moving toward or strengthening democracy; and science continues to produce new advances in energy efficiency, treatments and cures for diseases, and information technology.

Yet many millions of people in Africa, Latin America, Asia, and elsewhere live in terrible poverty; the AIDS crisis continues to claim thousands each year throughout the world, but particularly in parts of Africa, India, and China; Russia is becoming less democratic and increasingly antagonistic to the West (and to some of its neighbors); tensions in the Middle East remain high; armed conflict continues in Iraq, Afghanistan, the Darfur region of Sudan, and in many other places; there are increasing signs of further nuclear proliferation, particularly in Iran and North Korea; and many scientists believe that a radical restructuring of the world's industrial economies is essential if we are to avoid the catastrophic effects of global climate change.

Political decisions within and among nations will largely determine whether the future is one of expanding progress, prosperity, and an improved quality of life; or one of escalating war, worsening economic conditions, and tyranny. The way governments work (or fail to work) has tremendous effects on all of us.

At the same time, we should not lose sight of the fact that politics does not explain or determine *everything*; many of the best things in life have little or nothing to do with politics. Personal relationships, the satisfaction of learning and working, artistic achievement and enjoyment, the challenges and deep fulfillment of raising a child—we can experience all of those things without doing anything "political." Most aspects of our day-to-day lives do not necessarily involve political institutions, issues, and movements. There is much more to life than politics.

Politics and government have to do with *public* policies and *public* decision making, concerns that most people think about only occasionally. Yet political decisions do have a huge impact beyond purely "governmental" matters. Political decisions frequently affect parenting, for example. In most countries, the government determines what material children must learn in school and when they will learn it. Often the government mandates what kinds of health-related precautions parents and teachers must take to protect students and what kinds of discipline and religious training children can be given in public schools. Most governments restrict artistic expression. Sometimes these limits restrict exhibitions seen as improper in their cultures and sometimes they are intended to prevent the dissemination of ideas that may foster dissent and disloyalty.* Governments sometimes restrict political expressions that may undermine stability, or that breed ethnic or religious intolerance, raising difficult questions about how to balance basic elements of democracy (see Box 1-1).

---

* Governmental restrictions on free speech are found in modern democracies, not only in dictatorial regimes in developing countries. On February 20, 2006, an Austrian court sentenced David Irving, a British writer, to three years in prison for having written a book in 1989 that denied the existence of gas chambers in the notorious Nazi death camp at Auschwitz. And, in March 2006, the government of Afghanistan arrested one of its citizens for converting to Christianity, a crime that could lead to the death penalty for those convicted. The individual was released, following mounting international pressure, and was exiled to Italy.

Box 1-1

GOVERNMENTAL POWER AND FREE SPEECH

In October 2006, a prominent Canadian news magazine (*Macleans*), published a chapter of *America Alone*, a book by a controversial columnist named Mark Steyn. Here are a couple of excerpts:

> You may vaguely remember seeing some flaming cars on the evening news toward the end of 2005. Something going on in France, apparently. Something to do with—what's the word?—"youths." When I pointed out the media's strange reluctance to use the M-word vis-à-vis the rioting "youths," I received a ton of e-mails arguing there's no Islamist component, . . . they may be Muslim but they're secular and Westernized and into drugs and rap and meaningless sex with no emotional commitment, and rioting and looting and torching and trashing, just like any normal healthy Western teenagers.
>
> The enemies we face in the future will look a lot like al-Qaeda: transnational, globalized, locally franchised, extensively outsourced—but tied together through a powerful identity that leaps frontiers and continents. They won't be nation-states and they'll have no interest in becoming nation-states, though they might use the husks thereof, as they did in Afghanistan and then Somalia. The jihad may be the first, but other transnational deformities will embrace similar techniques. Sept. 10 institutions like the UN and the EU will be unlikely to provide effective responses.

The Canadian Islamic Congress (CIC) was very disturbed by the book and by the magazine's decision to publish a chapter from it. In 2007, the CIC filed a complaint with the Canadian Human Rights Commission, the Ontario Human Rights Commission, and the British Columbia Human Rights Tribunal. The group argued that the author and *Macleans* had engaged "in a discriminatory form of journalism that targets the Muslim community, promotes stereotypes, misrepresents fringe elements as the mainstream Muslim community, and distorts facts to present a false image of Muslims."

The Canadian Human Rights Act prohibits discrimination based on "race, national or ethnic origin, colour, religion, age, sex, sexual orientation, marital status, family status, disability and conviction for which a pardon has been granted" (Part I, Section 3). Most of the specifically prohibited acts involve discriminatory practices (separate sanitary facilities, lower wages, etc.), but Section 13 prohibits electronic communication of statements or other material "that is likely to expose a person or persons to hatred or contempt by reason of the fact

that that person or those persons are identifiable on the basis of a prohibited ground of discrimination." Under this act, one cannot defend himself or herself by arguing that the statements in question were true or that the person responsible for them sincerely believed them.

On June 27, 2008, the Canadian Human Rights Commission dismissed the complaint, explaining that while Steyn's article was "calculated to . . . offend certain readers," it was "not of an extreme nature as defined by the Supreme Court" in previous cases.[*]

Prior to the Steyn case, every "Section 13" complaint heard by the Canadian Human Rights Commission had been upheld.[†]

Steyn's defenders, and many of his critics, continue to be deeply concerned about the free speech implications of the official investigation and prosecution relating to the publication. According to Terry Glavin, a popular Canadian commentator, "The question is whether human rights tribunals can sort through the necessary cacophony of utterances and statements in a free and open society in order to police vigorous public debates for commentary that is 'likely to expose' religious, ethnic or other minority groups to hatred, contempt or discrimination. And the answer is they can't, and they shouldn't."[‡]

It has been argued that some groups make use of the Canadian Human Rights Commission to suppress speech, largely because, unlike suing for defamation, which involves substantial legal fees for the complaining parties, complaints before the CHRC are processed at taxpayer expense. "The defendant in all HRC proceedings must cover his own legal expenses but the state does not charge the complainant. This system, many have said, leaves the HRC wide open to abuse as a completely taxpayer paid (for the complainant only) weapon in political battles that would be prohibitively expensive in the legitimate court system."[§]

[*] See the Canadian Human Rights Commission's decision in *Canadian Islamic Congress v. Rogers Media, Inc.*, case number 20071008.

[†] See Astier, Henri, "Speech Row Rocks Multi-Ethnic Canada," BBC story, March 24, 2008, available at <http://news.bbc.co.uk/2/hi/americas/7273870.stm>.

[‡] Terry Glavin, "Mark Steyn: Last Straw," web commentary, December 13, 2008. Available at: http://thetyee.ca/Views/2007/12/13/MarkSteyn/

[§] Hilary White, "Mark Steyn Case Wakes Up Canadian Press to Human Rights Tribunals' Threat to Free Speech," LifeSiteNews.com story, December 19, 2007.

(Continued)

Box 1-1

GOVERNMENTAL POWER AND FREE SPEECH
(*Continued*)

Also in 2006, a Federal District Court in West Virginia heard the case *Rank and Rank v. Hamm, et al.* Nicole and Jeffrey Rank had initiated a suit for civil damages arising from their treatment and arrest prior to a speech by President George W. Bush in 2004. The defendants in the suit were several White House officials and local law enforcement officers.

On Sunday, July 4 of that year, the President gave a speech in Charleston, West Virginia. It was an official appearance, funded by taxpayers. Admission to the event was managed by the White House Office of Presidential Advance. Following its procedures, the Office set up a system in which only those with tickets could attend.

Two individuals, Nicole Rank and Jeffrey Rank, were among those who received tickets. In order to receive them, they had to submit their names, addresses, and social security numbers. They received emails stating that there was no required dress code, and there was no indication that attendees had to be supporters of a particular political party, and there was no requirement that attendees be supporters of the president.

According to the complaint, "on the evening of July 3, 2004, one of the defendants met with several members of the White House Event Staff and gave them instructions. . . . [He] told the White House Event Staff that certain categories of expression were prohibited and that Event Staff were to order any audience member found displaying a prohibited message to cover up that message or leave the event."

After Nicole and Jeffrey were admitted to the West Virginia State Capitol grounds, they "removed their outer shirts to display an expression of their disagreement with the policies of President Bush. The front of both Plaintiffs' t-shirts bore the international 'no' symbol (a circle with a diagonal line across it) superimposed over the word 'Bush.' Both shirts also displayed on the left sleeve a small photograph of President Bush with the international 'no' symbol superimposed over it, and on the right sleeve a 'Kerry' button. The message on the back of Nicole Rank's t-shirt was 'Love America, Hate Bush.'"

One of the defendants told Nicole and Jeffrey "that they could not remain on the grounds while wearing their t-shirts." They were told that their tickets had been revoked, and state troopers subsequently arrested them for trespassing and led them away in handcuffs to jail.

The Court noted that the "Presidential speech included individuals who were wearing political paraphernalia expressing support for the President and his policies and who were not arrested, asked to leave, asked to cover their political messages, or otherwise harassed by law enforcement."

The criminal charges against the Plaintiffs were subsequently dismissed in 2007. The Ranks accepted a settlement in which they received $80,000 from the U.S. Government in compensation for damages.

Some people think that attacks on free political expression only take place in developing countries and undemocratic societies. But these incidents took place in two of the most advanced democracies on the planet. In both cases, coherent arguments can be crafted to justify the respective governments' positions: The Canadian law reflected a concern for tolerance and social harmony, and President Bush's White House Advance team was apparently apprehensive about anything that would disrupt a public appearance.

However, many people feel that freedom of expression was inappropriately attacked in each of these situations. Some have argued that all governments have a tendency to do things that erode political and personal freedoms, and that freedom is a highly unnatural condition. The late Milton Friedman once wrote that "because we live in a largely free society, we tend to forget how limited is the span of time and the part of the globe for which there has ever been anything like political freedom: *the typical state of mankind is tyranny, servitude, and misery.*"* Perhaps Friedman's statement was extreme, but it is clear that freedom of expression is often fragile and that even democratic governments occasionally constrain it.

The website for the CHRC: **http://www.chrc-ccdp. ca/default-en.asp**

The chapter from Steyn's book printed in *Macleans* is available at: **http://www.macleans.ca/article. jsp?content=20061023_134898_134898&source**

The following ACLU website includes more information regarding the arrest of Jeffrey and Nicole Rank: **http://www.aclu.org/freespeech/protest/ 11462prs20040914.html**

* *Capitalism and Freedom*, 1962, Chapter 1. Online version: http://www.ditext.com/friedman/title.html

Virtually everywhere, government regulates membership in selected professions (including not only law and medicine but also plumbing, architecture, and many other fields), restricting career choices. Governments are the only organizations that may legally apply the death penalty to their citizens. And, of course, when nations decide to make war on one another, virtually all aspects of their citizens' personal lives may be drastically changed.

Why politics has such pervasive effects is itself a controversial matter. Some contend that government is extensively involved in our lives because much of what people do as individuals affects the economic opportunities of others, the environment, or public safety, and citizens demand that government take action to control those effects. Government policies in many countries restrict industrial development because of problems with pollution. Private actions often have public consequences, and many governments regulate those consequences. The nature of modern life thus accounts for a growing governmental role, as societies turn to government to safeguard widely shared interests in an increasingly complex, technological age.

There are other reasons for the growing role of government. Large numbers of citizens in many countries feel that government should be used as a tool to enforce and strengthen certain moral principles. In the United States, contending groups vigorously debate the morality (and legality) of abortion, while in some countries people argue for and against laws allowing husbands to beat their wives.* In these and many other instances, people demand government actions that reflect their moral or religious views, and many governments respond by enacting new restrictions and regulations.

Governments also apply power in pursuit of economic objectives. Sometimes this power is used to stimulate economic growth and opportunity, or to reduce economic inequality, and in other cases government power is employed to increase the wealth of individuals or groups that have gained access to government officials. The British National Health Service, established shortly after World War II, is an example of the use of government power to reduce economic inequality; various laws passed under the Somoza regime (1937–1979) in pre-revolutionary Nicaragua employed government power to maintain a privileged status for the ruling family and its allies, making inequality more severe.

In short, government can be beneficial or devastating, but its significance is growing almost everywhere. Given the potential impact of government on so much of our lives, it is important to understand how government works, how it changes, how it can be influenced, and why different forms or designs of government operate differently.

Political science is the effort to shed light on these questions through careful, systematic, and informed study.

POLITICS AND GOVERNMENT DEFINED

The study of political science requires that we define *politics, political power, influence,* and *government*—terms about which most of us have definite opinions. Consequently, political scientists have crafted definitions designed to be objective and applicable to

* A German judge in 2007 rejected a woman's petition for a speedy divorce. Her legal basis for seeking the divorce was that her husband physically beat her. The judge argued that her reasons were insufficient, because "the couple came from a Moroccan cultural milieu, in which it is common for husbands to beat their wives" (*New York Times*, March 22).

all cultures, which is why they may strike us as abstract and sterile. The scope of our concerns is broad—the terms we employ must apply to systems very different from our own if we are to discover and understand the basic elements of political life.

The definitions of two terms are particularly important: *politics* and *government*.

Politics

People commonly use the term **politics** in a negative or pejorative sense, as in "There's only one explanation for her being appointed to be the new ambassador—*politics*"; or, simply, "It's back to *politics* as usual." The idea behind this casual use of the term implies that a decision is "political" if influence or power is involved in making it. The negative connotation that often surrounds "politics" derives from the belief that decisions *should* be made objectively, on the basis of merit, quality, achievement, or some other legitimate standard. When we find that influence and power has had an effect on an important decision in government or in large organizations, most people develop a very cynical attitude, accepting the idea that "politics" is synonymous with cheating or underhanded dealing.

Here are some definitions coined by political scientists:

"Politics is the science of who gets what, when, and how."

Politics is "the authoritative allocation of values."

"Politics [is] . . . the activity by which differing interests within a given unit of rule are conciliated by giving them a share in power in proportion to their importance to . . . the whole community."

Politics is "the processes by which human efforts towards attaining social goals are steered and coordinated."

"Political science is the academic subject centering on the relations between governments and other governments, and between governments and peoples."[1]

The most basic idea contained in these definitions is that politics involves decision making among people in some large group. An isolated person on a desert island cannot meaningfully be said to act *politically*, although economists could model his or her decisions regarding the investment of time and resources and his or her consumption, historians could chronicle his or her activities, and psychologists could examine the individual's changing mental state. But a political scientist would find nothing to study in the behavior of a totally isolated person.

More important, the definitions also suggest that political decisions involve *influence* and *power*. We can thus contrast political decisions with decisions made through, say, scientific computation or religious revelation. Although some of us may wish that governments would make decisions with the same kind of precision and objectivity that a chemist uses to determine the atomic weight of an element, a key characteristic of political decisions is that they are made in less objective ways. That is what makes the study of politics so interesting, and, ironically, it is also what sometimes makes politics a "dirty" word. Political decision making involves divergent interests, ideas, and preferences, and it applies power and influence to resolve them.

Politics, then, is the process of making collective decisions in a community, society, or group through the application of influence and power.

Government

When U.S. citizens think of **government,** they normally think of the president, the Congress, governors and state legislatures, mayors, and the courts and agencies that implement programs. In primitive societies, "the government" may consist of a few individuals. Government can be a vast, multifaceted, and complex arrangement, or it can be as simple as one village chieftain or tribal council.

However, in order to qualify as a government, the system, institutions, or persons must *govern*, and to do this they must wield *authority*. Government decisions are normally more coercive than decisions made by other forces in society. For example, if the Japanese corporation that produces Lexus automobiles decides to make a different model, no one is compelled to buy it. However, if the British Parliament decides to purchase new aircraft for its navy, British citizens are compelled to purchase the new planes with their tax money.

A **government** is the people or organizations that make, enforce, and implement political decisions for a society.* Accomplishing these tasks involves the performance of certain basic *functions,* which we now explore in more detail.

GOVERNMENT FUNCTIONS

Because actual governments are so different in scale, complexity, and structure, many political scientists have found it useful to itemize the **government functions** performed, in one way or another, in all thriving political systems. Asserting that "all governments have a legislature, an executive branch, courts, and bureaucracies," would imply that a government would have to operate and be organized along the lines of governments in the U.S., France, Japan, and other developed democracies in order to qualify as a "government." This would be a limiting, and culturally biased approach. Identifying universal government *functions* helps us to appreciate that even when a government does not have institutions that seem familiar to us, it is still a government. It simply performs the basic governmental functions in different ways.[2]

Rule Making

Perhaps the most fundamental function of government is **rule making**—that is, making what are normally called *laws* or *orders* or even *constitutions.* These rules define what is legal and illegal, what actions are required, and the rights and responsibilities of citizens. In the United States, Congress (with participation by the president and sometimes the bureaucracy and the Supreme Court) performs this function; in China, the People's Congress officially makes rules (although most legislative decisions are really made by top Communist Party leaders). Councils of elders often act in this capacity in traditional societies, and the king and his advisers establish rules in the monarchy in contemporary Saudi Arabia.

---

* In the United States, *government* applies broadly to a vast array of national, state, and local institutions. In European parliamentary systems (for example, Great Britain, Italy, Norway), we may speak of "the Government" to apply specifically to the prime minister and cabinet serving at a particular point in time. Thus, when the Italians say that "the Government resigned today," they are using the term in this more restricted sense.

In some way, all governments perform the task of making rules for their citizens. Some rules apply to criminal behavior, others establish economic regulations, and still others create or change public services. A rule is simply an *authoritative act.*

Rule Execution

Rules must be enforced and carried out if they are to have impact; this is what we mean by **rule execution.** A government that proclaims laws and programs will not be very effective if it lacks the ability to put force behind its decision making. Some governments appear to have had the capacity to perform the former function without the latter. For example, many historians noted that the French Fourth Republic (1875–1940) had the ability to make rules (it had an energetic legislature) but that it had a terribly weak executive, a combination that led to protracted periods of instability. Many Latin American governments have passed social legislation in the areas of health care or agrarian reform, but they lack executive establishments capable of enforcing the law. The failure of some systems to thrive can thus be attributed partly to an inability to perform the basic function of rule execution.*

Rule Adjudication

Governments normally apply their laws to specific cases and individuals. If there is a law against murder, for example, there will be situations in which it will be necessary to determine whether a particular killing was murder, manslaughter, self-defense, or even an accident. Laws are frequently ambiguous. As a result, virtually all governments have some way of performing **rule adjudication.** Legal systems, usually with courts and judges, are established to apply and interpret laws that are made in general terms but that must have an impact at the individual level. In most modern societies, institutions for rule adjudication (courts) are at least partly distinct from the bodies that make the rules. In a tribal society or a traditional monarchy, a single governmental group may perform both functions.

Other Functions

Making, executing, and applying rules are the most basic functions of government, but other tasks must be performed for the system to operate effectively. Governments must be able to *communicate* with their citizens. People must be aware of laws if they are to obey them, and they must know about new programs if they are to participate in them. The leaders must also have some way of determining what people want, what they will support, and what they will not tolerate. Governments need some way to *recruit leaders*, perhaps through a party system or through a well-established routine of succession to the throne. It is also necessary that governments have some means of *extracting resources* (such as taxes, military service, or labor in public works projects) from their citizens.

Finally, a healthy political system has some means through which citizens come to support the basic principles and values of their government. Creating this foundation

* Students of early-twentieth-century France point out that the system was held together during periods of political instability in the executive branch during the Fourth Republic (1946-1958) by its strong, stable bureaucracy. See Michael Crozier, *The Bureaucratic Phenomenon* (Chicago: University of Chicago Press, 1964), for the classic discussion along these lines.

of involvement and awareness is referred to as the process of **political socialization**. Stable political systems also have some established ways for people to present demands for change. Interests must be expressed so that the government is able to take them into account in its decision making. Political parties, interest groups, and voting systems are some familiar mechanisms through which this function of **interest articulation** is performed.

A good political theory directs us to helpful questions. **Functionalism**, or the notion that healthy governments must perform certain basic functions, tells us what to look for in our efforts to understand and evaluate actual governments. The concept also suggests that these functions can be performed in many ways and through many different governmental organizations or processes.

KINDS OF GOVERNMENTS

There are many ways to classify governments. The kind of classification most of us probably encountered as children simply divided governments into free and unfree, or maybe even good and evil. Those concepts can be interesting to discuss, but political scientists have found it valuable to devise somewhat more precise classifications. The Greek philosopher Aristotle (384–322 BCE) constructed one of the first classification schemes, one that focused on who was in charge and in whose interests the ruler ruled. (See Box 1-2.) Many other classification approaches have been devised, some emphasizing economic systems, others reflecting legal arrangements, and still others based on wealth, culture, or even size.

An often useful approach is to classify political systems on the basis of how *developed* they are. The United States, New Zealand, and Sweden have developed political systems, whereas those in Nigeria, Chad, and Peru are termed *developing* (or, alternatively, *underdeveloped* or *less developed*). Unfortunately, the criteria for making these distinctions are often unclear. What determines whether Nigeria or the People's Republic

---

Box 1-2

ARISTOTLE'S APPROACH TO GOVERNMENTS

	Ruler Rules in Interest of:	
	Ruler	All Citizens
Type of Ruler		
One	Tyranny	Monarchy
Few	Oligarchy	Aristocracy
Many	Democracy	Polity

Aristotle's classification is remarkable for its combination of an empirically observable factor (is the ruler a single person, a small elite group, or the masses?) with a more value-laden factor (does the ruler rule in his or her own interest or in the interest of all?). Aristotle obviously felt that nations with any of these three governing systems could operate fairly or with great injustice. His categories have suggested questions for political research for centuries.

One notable feature of Aristotle's classification is the assumption that democracy is a bad form of government; this concept was also on the minds of several of the framers of the U.S. Constitution, as we discuss in Chapter 11.

of China is a developed or a developing nation? Are *political* development and *economic* development the same thing? If not, does political development require economic development? Was wealthy Kuwait on the eve of the 1990 Iraqi invasion a developed nation? (It was quite prosperous, but it had an ancient form of government.) Does Costa Rica's thriving democracy make it a developed nation (despite its poor economy)?

In their classic book, *Comparative Politics: A Developmental Approach,* Gabriel Almond and Bingham Powell offered one answer. Political systems are developed, they argued, if they can effectively carry out the functions of government outlined earlier. To the extent that they cannot, undeveloped governments are often prone to political instability, violence, and military takeovers.[3] We discuss the idea of **political development** in Chapter 15.

What Is Democracy?   Political scientists often compare governments on the basis of how democratic they are. In practice, **democracy**, like political development, is a matter of degree, and so we speak of governments being "more" or "less" democratic. The degree to which a government is democratic depends on several related factors.

First, democratic government requires adherence to the principle of *political equality.* If large segments of the population are denied political rights by virtue of their race, family heritage, economic status, or religious affiliation, then political influence is not in the hands of the people, and the government thus fails to meet a basic principle of democracy. Governments can be undemocratic with respect to this principle in many ways: by giving special political power to the upper echelons of an economic elite or a ruling family, as in El Salvador or Kuwait; by excluding significant parts of society from political life, as South Africa did until the end of *apartheid;* by concentrating power in the hands of the military, as in Nigeria and Burma; or by putting nearly all political power in the hands of a political elite, as in North Korea, Cuba, China, Nazi Germany, and the former Soviet Union.

Even if political equality is generally secure, a government is not really democratic unless there is some process or mechanism through which the people have an opportunity to express their opinions. **Popular consultation** is thus a key component of democracy. It means that the people have a real opportunity to be heard and that this opportunity takes place regularly. (A country would not be very democratic, for example, if its next general election were scheduled for a date 20 years in the future.)

Finally, democracy requires substantial adherence to the principle of **majority rule**. This principle is simple but often controversial. It means that when citizens disagree about a political decision or candidate, as they virtually always do, then the decision made or the candidate selected will be the one preferred by the larger group of people. If a minority (an elite group of landed aristocrats or an exclusive religious leadership, for example) makes political decisions over the objections of the majority of a country's people, the government would not be very democratic.

It is important to recognize, however, that majority rule can lead to the violation of other democratic norms. What if the majority votes to deny electoral rights to a religious or racial minority? Such an action would violate the principle of political equality and would be undemocratic despite the fact that it was adopted through popular consultation and majority rule. Hence, if democracy is to be preserved, the majority must not be allowed to erase fundamental minority rights; democracy implies at least some *limitation* on majority rule. The relationship between majority rule and minority rights is a sticky problem, and it is a central challenge encountered by all democratic governments. As we will see later, although the United States generally appears democratic with respect to the principles of political equality and popular consultation, several features of its Constitution limit majority rule.*

Democratic governments differ in many ways. They have widely varying degrees of government ownership of industry, their citizens engage in different levels and kinds of political participation, and they vary with respect to their economic development and the design of their institutions. Political scientists have devoted great attention, in particular, to the differences between the United States, with its divided powers and "checks and balances," and Great Britain, with its more streamlined, centralized institutions. Other scholars distinguish between *industrial democracies* (those with well-developed economies, such as Germany and France) and less economically developed democratic nations (for example, India and Venezuela), which are less able to provide fundamental services for their populations. We explore the great diversity among democratic governments in later chapters.

Nondemocratic governments also operate in many ways, but most political scientists recognize two well-established types. Both kinds effectively deny political equality, popular consultation, and majority rule, maintaining real political power in the hands of a ruling party, elite group, dictator, or family. The difference between the two types of nondemocratic regimes has to do with the government's long-term goals.

Authoritarian systems require only that citizens obey government edicts and limit their dissent. Africa, Asia, and Latin America have been replete with authoritarian governments in recent decades. Such governments may violently repress opposition groups and torture political prisoners, but ultimately the state simply insists that the people not challenge the orders of the ruling elite. The governments of Haiti and Indonesia are good current examples.

In contrast, **totalitarian systems** energetically seek to change the political thinking and the allegiance of their citizens. The governments of Nazi Germany and Stalinist Russia, for example, sought to indoctrinate their populations into the dominant ideology (fascism or communism), a phenomenon not found in authoritarian regimes. Political recruitment and indoctrination take place in totalitarian regimes largely through a ruling party that dominates public affairs and much of private life as well. Totalitarian systems attempt to politicize virtually all pursuits, including sports and art, that are less constrained in democratic and even in authoritarian societies. For example, under the leadership of Mao Zedong in the 1960s, China's "top ten" pop songs often dealt with such unexpected topics as surpassing Great Britain in steel production or resisting Western imperialism. Even as recently as 2006, the Chinese government told the Rolling Stones that they couldn't play "Brown Sugar," among several other classic Jagger/Richards tunes, when they performed in Singapore, because the song was "inappropriate."†

Although citizens have little voice in the affairs of either type of nondemocratic system, authoritarian governments often permit churches, unions, and some interest groups to retain relative independence as long as they do not challenge state authority. Totalitarian governments generally dominate and remove existing organizational features of a society in their attempt to permeate the totality of their

---

* See Dahl, Robert A., *How Democratic Is the American Constitution?* 2nd ed. (New Haven, CT: Yale University Press, 2003).
† Surprisingly, the Chinese government did allow them to play "Bitch," which they chose to open the show.

citizens' lives.* In fact, we might think of democratic, authoritarian, and totalitarian governments as ranging along a continuum; they differ in the degree of independence from government control that they allow individual citizens and groups in society. Democracies are often referred to as *pluralistic* or *liberal* because they permit the greatest diversity of political behavior and viewpoints.

It is important to understand that both democratic and nondemocratic governments can perform the basic functions of government. Both kinds of governments make, enforce, and adjudicate rules; they communicate with their citizens; and they establish some basis for political socialization. Interest articulation occurs in nondemocratic governments as well as in democracies (although smaller segments of citizens articulate a narrower range of demands in nondemocratic governments). Quite simply, whether it operates according to democratic principles or in violation of them, a government is still a government.

Nor are political systems static. Countries may change over time, moving from one form of government to another. During the 1960s and early 1970s, for example, Argentina, Brazil, Chile, and a host of other democratic governments in Latin America collapsed under the strain of internal conflicts. Repressive authoritarian regimes, such as the Pinochet dictatorship in Chile, were established throughout the region. In the 1980s, however, democracy was restored to most of the region. Some Eastern European countries (Hungary, Poland, Czech Republic) that until recently were totalitarian are now fledgling democracies. On the other hand, Sudan, Nepal, and Russia, each of which was part of the movement toward democracy in the last two decades of the twentieth century, have slipped back toward authoritarianism. Other nations—Thailand, for example—continue to straddle the line between authoritarianism and limited democracy.

Politics and government constitute the scope of inquiry and analysis for political scientists. The preceding sections describe the kinds of things that political scientists study in their efforts to contribute to our understanding. Through the scientific study of politics we attempt to find out why some forms of government work better than others, how people influence government, how governments change over time, how economic systems influence politics, and many other related matters. Ultimately, however, questions about politics and government are important because of what is at stake when governments act (or fail to act).

THE STAKES OF POLITICS

Most of the important consequences that can be traced to governmental action or inaction fall into one of five categories:

1. The allocation of resources
2. Human rights
3. The physical environment
4. Public services
5. War and peace

---

* Totalitarianism is a twentieth-century political concept. Most analysts argue that totalitarianism is possible only in countries with the technology to support mass communications, rapid transportation, and the means to engage in active, comprehensive surveillance of their citizens. Thus, all nondemocratic governments before that century were simply authoritarian. For a classic discussion, see Hannah Arendt, *The Origins of Totalitarianism* (New York: Harcourt, Brace, and World, 1966).

These are the primary "stakes" of politics, the scope of concerns in which politics makes a difference. Although some specific issues may pertain to more than one of these categories, the categories identify distinct aspects of our lives in which government and politics are critical.

The Allocation of Resources

Although politics affects many other things, it is fair to say that the majority of political decisions have to do with the **allocation of resources.**

Government power often has a tremendous impact on how wealth is distributed and on the purposes to which scarce resources are devoted. The word *authoritative* in this definition is crucial. In many countries, a considerable share of national resources is allocated through economic exchange (investing, buying, and selling). This is the normal domain of economic analysis. Some get rich, and others become poor, through the economic choices made by consumers, workers, producers, and investors. In contrast, when governmental acts allocate resources, we refer to the allocation as authoritative.

The distinction is important. When Henry Ford applied assembly-line manufacturing methods to his auto plant, manufacturing costs plummeted, prices fell, and a huge increase took place in the number of people who could afford cars. The labor of thousands of people was diverted from agricultural production and small craft activities to auto assembly. Through an economic process of exchange, a large share of national resources—both materials and labor—was allocated to the manufacture of automobiles. Yet this allocation was not *authoritative*, because the decisions creating it were made voluntarily—most importantly, by consumers. As noted above, governmental bodies allocate resources through coercive authority, not through the forces of voluntary exchanges.

New laws may also increase or decrease the proportion of taxes to be paid by the richest and the poorest citizens. These decisions involve allocations, whether they have to do with tax rates or expenditures. And such allocations are authoritative—citizens are required to make the contributions, and the expenditures are made as a matter of law.* Although resource allocation in *all* countries is affected by both economic exchange and authoritative governmental acts, the relative importance of economic and political allocations is very different in different countries. Most of the resource allocation that takes place in Taiwan, for example, is driven by economic exchange. The public sector is relatively small. In Cuba the government directly influences the bulk of resource allocation by making decisions regarding what is produced, at what prices, and with which raw materials. The forces of *both* economic exchange and government authority are important in the United States, Great Britain, Mexico, France, Italy, and most other countries. We use the term *mixed economies* to describe such societies.

Political economy is the study of how political decisions affect economic conditions. Government actions that alter the allocation of resources constitute the basic concerns of political economy. Two basic political problems dominate the field. First, government decisions can fundamentally shift the balance of resources held by the

---

* To qualify as authoritative, however, the allocation must be made under *legitimate* public authority. Resources are involuntarily "allocated" from one person to another when a burglar carries off your big screen television and MP3 player. It is coercion by *legitimate government power* that makes the allocation authoritative and thus distinctively political.

poorest and the richest segments of the population. We discuss the issues of **income distribution** in more detail in Chapter 15. At this point, however, it is important to note that nations differ dramatically with respect to how wealthy they are, and with respect to how that wealth is distributed among rich and poor. See Table 15.1.

Many things contribute to the differences among countries with respect to wealth and the equality with which wealth is distributed. Natural resources, climate, population, access to transportation, and other such factors are obviously important. However, the nature of government and the policies governments enact are profoundly important. In fact, according to Nobel laureate Douglass North, institutions "are the underlying determinant of the long-run performance of economies."[4] Table 1.1 indicates the differences among 13 selected countries with respect to per capita income, governmental corruption, infant mortality rates, corporate tax rates, and the number of days that it takes, on average, to obtain government approval to start a business.

A look at the figures quickly demonstrates that the quality of life and the workings of government vary tremendously across the world. There are dramatic differences

TABLE 1.1 DIFFERENCES AMONG GOVERNMENTS ARE ASSOCIATED WITH DIFFERENCES IN LIVING CONDITIONS

	Per capita income	Infant mortality	Corruption Score (*country rank in parentheses*)	Tax Rate (Percent of Profit)	Number of days to start a business
United States	$44,970	8	7.2 (20)	46.2	6
Japan	$38,410	4	7.5 (17)	52.0	23
France	$36,550	5	7.3 (19)	66.3	7
Russia	$ 5,780	21	2.3 (143)	51.4	29
Brazil	$ 4,730	34	3.5 (72)	69.2	152
Kazakhstan	$ 3,790	73	2.1 (150)	36.7	21
Thailand	$ 2,990	21	3.3 (84)	37.7	33
Colombia	$ 2,740	21	3.8 (68)	82.4	42
El Salvador	$ 2,540	28	4.0 (67)	33.8	26
Philippines	$ 1,420	34	2.5 (131)	N/A	58
Haiti	$ 480	117	1.6 (177)	40.0	202
Burundi	$ 100	190	2.5 (131)	278.7	43
Malawi	$ 170	175	2.7 (118)	32.2	37

NOTE: *Per capita income* is measured in 2006 U.S. dollars. *Infant mortality* is the number of deaths to persons under 5 years of age per 1,000 live births. The *corruption score* ranges from zero to 10, and higher scores indicate less corruption. The *number of days to start a business* column indicates how long, in days, it is estimated to take to obtain government licenses and other approvals needed to start a business.

SOURCES: Data on *per capita income* and *infant mortality* are from the *World Development Indicators Database*, World Bank, September 14, 2007 (worldbank.org); data on *corruption score* are from *Transparency International*, a "global organization leading the fight against corruption." This organization began its work in 1993, and bases its scores on a wide range of surveys. The World Bank material is from its *World Development Report 2006*, Table A3, available at **http://siteresources.worldbank.org/INTWDR2005/Resources/complete_ report.pdf**, its publication, *Governance Matters IV: Governance Indicators for 1996–2004*, available at **http://www. worldbank.org/wbi/governance/pubs/govmatters4.html** and its *World Development Report 2005*, Table 1, available at **http://siteresources.worldbank.org/INTWDR2005/Resources/complete_report.pdf**.

Data on the number of days needed to start a business were taken from the World Bank's *Doing Business in 2005: Removing Obstacles to Growth*, available at **http://www.doingbusiness.org/documents/DoingBusiness2005. pdf** pp. 89–91. The CIA World Factbook is available at **http://www.cia.gov/cia/publications/factbook/**.

among governments with respect to these factors. In countries where there is less governmental corruption, a more established rule of law, and more efficient approvals of business start-ups, there are lower infant mortality rates and more wealth. Culture, climate, natural resources, and other factors are extremely important, but the quality of government makes an even greater difference in the lives of citizens.

A great deal of the political conflict among people reflects different views regarding the extent to which government effort *should* be devoted to shifting the allocation of resources from one group of people to another. In developing nations, where gaps between rich and poor are often particularly sharp, conflicts between "haves" and "have nots" periodically unleash revolutionary forces (as in Nicaragua, the Philippines, and El Salvador). Extreme inequality in the distribution of income or land increases the likelihood of political instability in developing nations.

In industrial democracies, economic inequality is a less explosive issue but, nevertheless, the major parties in the United States, Great Britain, France, and Germany tend to define themselves primarily by their different positions on resource allocation. More generally, the distinction between "left" and "right" on the political spectrum is largely, although not entirely, a matter of differing positions on what government should do to alter the distribution of resources; those on the left favor more active efforts to redistribute income, whereas those on the right are either less supportive of, or hostile to, such efforts.

Governments are also heavily involved in resource allocations that, though involving large shares of wealth, do not alter the balance between rich and poor. These *intersector allocations* constitute a second set of concerns in the area of political economy. For example, import restrictions alter the allocation of resources. When a government restricts or severely taxes the importation of a particular good, the domestic manufacturers and workers who produce that good find that the demand for what they have to sell is greater (because consumers can no longer buy the imports). Domestic resources that would otherwise be devoted to the production of other goods are then devoted to manufacture of the previously imported good. The trade restriction thus changes the allocation of resources from the production of one good to another, and it increases the income of the manufacturers and workers producing the protected good.

Of course, other groups realize a net decrease in wealth. When the state restricts importation of a good, the total supply of that good is reduced, and the price charged by domestic producers goes up. People who had paid $14,000 for a car before import restrictions were in place may now have to pay $18,000 for the same car. These people have experienced a net wealth reduction of $4,000. The government has "allocated" thousands of dollars from consumers to workers and corporations involved in the auto industry by enacting the change in trade policy.

Governments also allocate resources in other ways—by adjusting interest rates, changing tax rates and exemptions, nationalizing private industries, and controlling prices and wages. Using these and many other kinds of powers, governments have a tremendous capacity to change economic conditions. Governments can make societies richer or poorer; they can foster a more equal or a less equal distribution of wealth; they can hasten or retard the development of specific industries. Perhaps there is also a connection between government policies that encourage economic freedom and the emergence of democracy. (See Box 1-3.) In short, the widely varying economic conditions among contemporary nations reflect, in large measure, the political choices made by governments.

Human Rights

Although economic issues often seem to dominate politics, many of the political issues that most sharply divide us involve governmental policies in non-economic areas. In the United States, heated debates have focused on prayers in public schools, the achievement of racial balance in public and private organizations, the right to have an abortion, and the rights of homosexuals. In India, Lebanon, Northern Ireland, and Canada, conflicts over religious or language policies have sometimes erupted in violence. Governments have a tremendous capacity both to protect and to trample on the civil liberties of their citizens.

Nearly everywhere, there is always great disagreement regarding the nature and extent of **human rights**, and even when people agree that a particular right should be respected, they often differ about when and under what conditions the right may be

---

Box 1-3

GOVERNMENTS, CAPITALISM, AND DEMOCRACY

The decline of communism at the end of the last century sparked increased interest in the connection between capitalism and democracy. Ardent advocates of capitalism have long argued that the economic freedoms of capitalism inevitably lead to political freedoms, and that a nation that enjoys genuine political freedom will always construct and maintain a market economy.[5] Although cases can be found to support this argument, the actual record is not so clear.

Historically, the rise of liberal democracy (competitive elections with guaranteed civil liberties) evolved first in Britain and then spread to other parts of Western Europe and the United States at the same time that capitalism was emerging as the new economic system. The tendency of these political and economic systems to develop simultaneously was far from coincidental. As scholars from Karl Marx onward have recognized, it was the rising class of capitalist entrepreneurs and businessmen—often known as the bourgeoisie—who mounted the first major challenges to the political and economic power of the feudal or semi-feudal aristocracy that had previously dominated Europe. The bourgeoisie became the most powerful voice for parliamentary government, wider citizen participation in politics, and notions of guaranteed individual liberties.

In general, capitalism tends to produce democracy because the existence of an independent bourgeoisie in a capitalist society creates centers of economic power independent of the government and makes it easier for political pluralism to flourish. For example, the students who organized China's short-lived democracy movement in 1989 were partly financed by the country's new class of independent businessmen. In a classic study, a leading scholar of political and economic development nicely summed it up by exclaiming "no bourgeoisie, no democracy!"[6]

However, not all capitalist countries are democratic and not all democracies are purely capitalist. From the 1960s through the 1980s, a number of East and Southeast Asian countries became models of capitalist economic development, with very high levels of growth, while at the same time maintaining relatively repressive dictatorships. These countries included South Korea, Taiwan, Singapore, Indonesia, and Malaysia. From 1973 to 1990, Chile's president, General Augusto Pinochet, imposed one of Latin America's more brutal regimes. But, at the same time, led by U.S.-trained economists, the country developed what Nobel Prize–winning economist (and champion of unfettered capitalism) Milton Friedman hailed as one of the world's purest capitalist systems. Moreover, China today seems to be developing an essentially capitalist economy within the confines of an authoritarian, communist political system.

Examples of democracies that are not capitalist are harder to find, and it probably is true that no modern democracy has existed without some elements of capitalism. It should be noted, however, that a number of Western European countries have thrived under highly developed democratic political systems and mixed economic systems that combine elements of capitalism and socialism. Norway, Sweden, Denmark, Finland, and Iceland have some of the highest standards of living in the world, socialist welfare systems, and highly

appropriately abridged. A great deal of political conflict thus involves disputes regarding human rights.

Although issues of human rights can be approached in many ways, two kinds of rights can be distinguished according to how they relate to government. Some rights correspond to limits on government power and are thus called *negative rights*. Examples include the right to free expression, to religious freedom, to a fair trial before punishment, to travel, and so on. They are called negative rights because we enjoy them when government is *prevented* from certain actions. We have freedom of the press, for example, to the extent that the government is *not* free to limit what can be written, printed, or broadcast. In contrast, *positive rights* require governmental action. For example, if we feel that every person has the right to a job or to health care, the government must take steps to provide them to people who are unable to obtain private employment or to pay their own medical bills.

---

democratic politics. It could be argued that in the last years of the Soviet Union (see Chapter 13), President Mikhail Gorbachev's political reforms in the 1980s produced a country that was moderately democratic (competitive elections, multiple parties, a fairly free press, religious tolerance) with an economy that was still primarily state controlled (communist).

Many of these exceptional cases have proven to be transitory. Chile, Taiwan, and South Korea have all democratized. But change is rarely steady or uninterrupted. Russia's totalitarian political system first became authoritarian (after Stalin's death) and then, when the communist economic and political system collapsed, it moved toward capitalism and democracy in the 1990s. Today, capitalism in Russia seems more secure, although it is undermined by corruption and organized crime. But Vladimir Putin (first as president and then as prime minister) turned the country away from democracy. Similarly, although China has moved very effectively toward a largely capitalist economy, and although political controls and repression have diminished in many respects, the country remains quite authoritarian. Experts are still divided as to when, if at all, real democracy will emerge there. Still, although capitalist societies can be authoritarian, at least for a substantial number of years, and although Scandinavia's mixed economies coexist very smoothly with democracy, there is no question that in the long run capitalist economic systems and democratic political systems seem to reinforce each other. It should also be noted that the wealth creation that characterizes capitalism may itself undermine democracy. Kevin Phillips, a controversial social critic often seen on public television in the United States, argued along these

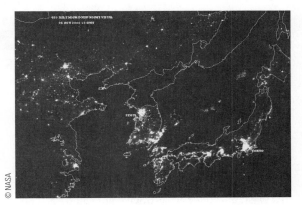

© NASA

THE LIGHTS ARE OUT   This nighttime satellite photo provides a striking visual indicator of how different forms of government can create very different living conditions. Although the cities of Seoul, South Korea, Beijing, China, and Tokyo, Japan are very obvious, North Korea is almost completely dark. It is estimated that 22 million people live there.

lines in a 2002 book.[7] He states that U.S. capitalism has led to a concentration of wealth that is much more pronounced than in earlier periods, and that it threatens the egalitarian conditions that were in place during the Founding period. If the wealthy become too powerful, according to Phillips, the political system will be less democratic.

In short, there is clearly an important connection between capitalism and democracy, but it is far too simple to claim that one always produces or requires the other.

Both negative and positive rights are contained in the United Nations Universal Declaration on Human Rights and in the U.S. Bill of Rights. (See Box 1-4.) We explore controversies about human rights in our discussions of ideology in the next chapter.

A special set of human rights issues involves the treatment of women. The rights of women are severely restricted in many political systems, most notably under the infamous Taliban regime in Afghanistan, which was quickly toppled in 2001 by a coalition of forces led by the United States. Taliban policies and laws provided for physical beatings if women failed to observe a wide range of clothing requirements, and these punishments were regularly carried out. Women face restrictions on reproductive choices in China, many Latin American countries, and much of Africa. Although most factors affecting gender equality stem from cultural influences, government policies play a major role in reinforcing or reforming them.

Human rights are important in the stakes of politics because people care deeply about them. In some cases, one person's freedom injures another citizen (as when a

---

Box 1-4

FOUR STATEMENTS OF HUMAN RIGHTS

I. THE MAGNA CARTA (THE GREAT CHARTER) [EXCERPTS]

Signed by King John of England in 1215.

—No bailiff for the future shall, upon his own unsupported complaint, put anyone to his "law," without credible witnesses brought for this purpose.

—No freemen shall be taken or imprisoned . . . or exiled or in any way destroyed, nor will we go upon him nor send upon him, except by the lawful judgment of his peers or by the law of the land.

—We will appoint as justices, constables, sheriffs, or bailiffs only such as know the law of the realm and mean to observe it well.

—Wherefore we will and firmly order that the English Church be free, and that the men in our kingdom have and hold all the aforesaid liberties, rights, and concessions, well and peaceably, freely and quietly, fully and wholly, for themselves and their heirs, of us and our heirs, in all respects and in all places forever, as is aforesaid. An oath, moreover, has been taken, as well on our part as on the art of the barons, that all these conditions aforesaid shall be kept in good faith and without evil intent. Given under our hand—the above named and many others being witnesses—in the meadow which is called Runnymede, between Windsor and Staines,

on the fifteenth day of June, in the seventeenth year of our reign.

II. THE UNITED STATES BILL OF RIGHTS [EXCERPTS]

Adopted in 1791.

Amendment 1. Congress shall make no law respecting an establishment of religion, or prohibiting the free exercise thereof; or abridging the freedom of speech, or of the press. . . .

Amendment 2. A well-regulated militia being necessary to the security of a free State, the right of the people to keep and bear arms shall not be infringed.

Amendment 4. The right of the people to be secure in their persons, houses, papers, and effects, against unreasonable searches and seizures, shall not be violated. . . .

Amendment 5. No person . . . shall be compelled in any criminal case to be a witness against himself, nor be deprived of life, liberty, or property, without due process of law. . . .

Amendment 8. Excessive bail shall not be required, nor excessive fines imposed, nor cruel and unusual punishment inflicted.

restaurant owner exercises the "freedom" to deny service to African-Americans). Citizens are divided in many countries with respect to whether abortion should be legalized. Much of the disagreement has to do with a conflict, in the eyes of many citizens, between the right to privacy and the right of the unborn to live. There is often a basic moral conflict between the rights of those accused of crimes and the right of society to be safe from criminals.

In short, people disagree about human rights on many levels, and government action is often demanded either to secure or to modify those rights. Human rights even figure in foreign policy issues. In the United States, the government has been criticized for its present or past affiliation with regimes that have poor records on human rights, for the fact that capital punishment is used in many states, and for the violent suppression of civil rights activists in the 1950s and 1960s. One of the justifications that the George W. Bush administration gave for its military action against Iraq was that country's horrendous human rights abuses, including mass murder and the use of chemical weapons against its citizens. In the 1990s,

III. THE UNITED NATIONS UNIVERSAL DECLARATION ON HUMAN RIGHTS [EXCERPTS]

Adopted and Proclaimed by the General Assembly Resolution 217 A (III) of December 10, 1948.

Article 1: All human beings are born free and equal in dignity and rights.

Article 2: Everyone is entitled to all the rights and freedoms set forth in this Declaration, without distinction of any kind, such as race, color, sex, language, religion, political or other opinion, national or social origin, property, birth, or other status.

Article 3: Everyone has the right to life, liberty, and the security of person.

Article 4: No one shall be held in slavery. . . .

Article 18: Everyone has the right to freedom of thought, conscience, and religion. . . .

Article 23: Everyone has the right to work,. . .to just and favorable conditions of work and to protection against unemployment.

Article 26: Everyone has the right to education. Education shall be free. . . .

IV. THE CHARTER OF FUNDAMENTAL RIGHTS OF THE EUROPEAN UNION [EXCERPTS]

Adopted on December 7, 2000

Article 8, Section 1: Everyone has the right to the protection of personal data concerning him or her.

Article 9: The right to marry and the right to found a family shall be guaranteed in accordance with the national laws governing the exercise of these rights.

Article 11, Section 1: Everyone has the right to freedom of expression. This right shall include freedom to hold opinions and to receive and impart information and ideas without interference by public authority. . . .

Article 11, Section 2: The freedom and pluralism of the media shall be respected.

Article 13: The arts and scientific research shall be free of constraint. Academic freedom shall be respected.

Article 17, Section 1: Everyone has the right to own, use, dispose of and bequeath his or her lawfully acquired possessions. No one may be deprived of his or her possessions, except in the public interest and in the cases and under the conditions provided for by law, subject to fair compensation being paid in good time for their loss. The use of property may be regulated by law in so far as is necessary for the general interest.

Article 21: Any discrimination based on any ground such as sex, race, colour, ethnic or social origin, genetic features, language, religion or belief, political or any other opinion, membership of a national minority, property, birth, disability, age or sexual orientation shall be prohibited.

The homepage for the EU's Charter may be found at: **http://www.europarl.europa.eu/charter/ default_en.htm**

some critics urged the U.S. government to act more forcefully against the Chinese government for its massacre of students at Tiananmen Square in 1989. Especially when a concern for human rights conflicts with other national interests, such as international trade, political decision making becomes very difficult. How human rights should be defined and respected are issues that are very much at stake in political life.

The Physical Environment

Governments play a special role with respect to issues of environmental protection. Most goods and services can be produced entirely through private efforts because investors know that they can be paid for what they produce. But clean air and water, the elimination of toxic wastes, and protection of the natural beauty of the wilderness are "goods" that profit-seeking firms are not necessarily motivated to preserve. If we are to have environmental protection, most people feel that the government must act.

Protection of the environment thus depends almost entirely on governmental action. The continuing controversy over the "greenhouse" effect (the idea that Earth's climate is becoming warmer because of various pollutants entering the atmosphere and because of the destruction of rain forests) is only the most spectacular illustration of the stakes involved—and of the inability of any institution except government to do anything about it.

Although virtually everyone favors protection of the environment, people differ greatly about the priority that environmental protection should be given and about who should pay for it. Should Brazil limit farming in rain forest regions if it means that destitute people in that area will have less food? Should auto makers be forced to produce more electric and hybrid cars, even if it means that consumers will be denied some of the choices they would like to have? Does the use of ethanol as a supplement for gasoline drive up the cost of food in poor countries? In the long run, the quality of human life will be crucially affected by what governments do and fail to do concerning environmental protection.

Public Services

Governments do more than govern. People also look to government for important services—most notably, public education, public transportation, cultural amenities such as museums and libraries, and "infrastructure" support (road repair, street sweeping, and so forth). Although most people accept the need for government to play a role in providing these services, considerable controversy surrounds the scope and nature of this role.

For one thing, public services cost a great deal of money. Paying for them requires taxes, and some taxpayers are reluctant to support the provision of these services. Even the richest of nations can never afford to pay for all desirable services. The problem has not yet been solved. The Federal Highway Administration's 2005 "Report Card" estimated that eliminating problems with bridges alone would cost $9.4 billion annually for 20 years, and that another $10 billion would be needed over the next dozen years to refurbish non-federal dams. The 2007 "National Traffic Signal Report Card" concluded that traffic "congestion causes the average peak-period traveler an extra 38 hours of travel time and an additional 26 gallons of fuel, amounting to a cost of $710 per traveler per year."* Where will the money to fix these problems come from, and what other critical services (education, health care, defense) will be cut? In poor nations, with greater needs and far fewer resources, the choices are yet more difficult.

Provision of public services is also controversial because it can be a way to redistribute income or opportunities. An extensive public education system, such as that in the United States, increases opportunities for poorer children. In South Africa, where secondary education for blacks was limited, or in Colombia, where most secondary schools are private, education reinforces societal inequalities. Similarly, in all countries decisions about where to build roads may be determined by economic development priorities or by political influence. Some win, and others lose.

The government role in provision of public services thus relates to issues that transcend the often mundane concerns of road construction and water utilities. Basic political choices in these areas affect us, since much of the productivity of society depends on the quality of public services.

War and Peace

"War," according to Karl von Clausewitz, is "a real political instrument, a continuation of political commerce . . . by other means."[8] Although a war might be started through some terrible accident, and although military leaders can start wars by taking sudden actions on their own, most wars begin as a result of deliberate policy choices made by political leaders. Those choices may be rational or irrational, well informed or grounded in miscalculation. (Saddam Hussein certainly miscalculated when he believed, in 1990, that he could invade and hold Kuwait. And, the U.S. government acted, in part, on faulty intelligence about Iraq's weapons of mass destruction program when it invaded that country in 2003.) The monumental consequences of war make questions of war and peace a central reason for concluding that politics matters.

We discuss several approaches to understanding the causes of war in Chapter 17. For now, it is important simply to appreciate Clausewitz's notion that war is a "political instrument." Wars can erupt when governments are moved to pursue a moral purpose, when they seek material gain, when they are anxious about their security, or when domestic pressures move them into conflict. In short, the same sets of conflicting passions, interests, and needs that influence political decision making in general are often involved, in one way or another, in the causes of war.

It is important to appreciate the extent to which government action can make a difference in each of the five areas we have outlined. Governments can help provide a basis for economic growth and opportunity, or they can condemn the vast majority of their citizens to poverty and hopelessness. They can plunge their citizens into devastating military conflicts, or they can contribute to peace. Governments can secure or destroy basic rights, protect or savage the environment, and provide or not provide needed public services.

A disinterested extraterrestrial observer, looking at Earth for the first time, would probably be startled by the vast range of conditions in which humans live throughout the planet. Different political choices, made by various kinds of governments, account for much of the diversity in the quality of human life. Perhaps that is why Aristotle

---

* See the "Infrastructure Report Card, 2005," issued by the American Society of Civil Engineers, available at www.asce.org/reportcard/2005/. Also see the "National Traffic Signal Report Card," available at http://www.ite.org/reportcard/.

referred to politics as the "master science"—political choices have effects, direct and indirect, on virtually everything.

POLITICS IN A CHANGING WORLD

The past quarter-century has been a period of especially momentous changes in political life. Many years from now, historians will write about the fall of communism in the early 1990s, noting that this event marked the end of the Cold War and the beginning of an era in which one country, the United States, became the world's only superpower. For nearly 50 years, virtually every incident, alliance, and issue involving foreign policy had been affected by intense rivalry between the communist and non-communist blocs, and millions saw Marxist-Leninist ideology as a worthy alternative to democratic government. Beginning in 1989, all of this changed. People around the world were transfixed by pictures of German youth triumphantly climbing and dismantling the Berlin wall, the sounds of Romanian crowds challenging their nation's dreaded secret police (the *securitati*), and the dignity of Lech Walesa and Vaclav Havel as they led the governments of Poland and Czechoslovakia. The end of communism changed the world in profound ways.

Perhaps the changes in Eastern Europe that began in the late 1980s were but part of a worldwide movement toward democracy. In Latin America, the same period witnessed the restoration of elected civilian governments in such erstwhile rightist military dictatorships as Argentina, Brazil, Chile, Paraguay, and Uruguay. In 1986, a popular uprising toppled the corrupt Marcos dictatorship in the Philippines, while elsewhere in Asia, authoritarian governments in South Korea and Taiwan moved toward limited democracy. Changes during this period in Africa were not limited to Mandela's success; elsewhere in that continent, a number of single-party regimes tentatively began to recognize opposition-party activity.

There are reasons to believe that the democracy movement is continuing. A Harvard-trained banker, Ellen Johnson-Sirleaf, was elected as President of Liberia in January 2006. She is the first woman to serve as head of state of any African country, and the election itself was widely regarded as a legitimate exercise of democracy. During the same month, the voters of Chile elected that country's first female head of state (Michelle Bachelet). If the overthrow of Saddam Hussein leads to a new era of peace and democratization in the Middle East (the outcome is currently far from certain), political scientists and historians will look back on this event as another critical moment in world history.

The long-term trend is difficult to deny. As recently as 1977, Freedom House classified only 43 countries as "free," and another 48 as "partly free," while 64 countries were "not free." In 2007, 90 countries were "free," and the number of "not free" countries had declined to 43.[9] Nevertheless, serious problems threaten the further spread of democracy. Some contemporary analysts fear that the U.S. actions in Iraq and Afghanistan have only aggravated the tensions in the region, prompting an escalation of violence and instability that will become increasingly severe in years to come. At the time of this writing, the Iranians appear to be well on their way to developing nuclear weapons that can be deployed on missiles capable of reaching Israel, India, and parts of Europe. North Korea remains dangerous and unpredictable.

The European Union, Japan, Korea, China, and the United States are still working through the uncertain waters of economic globalization, making it very difficult to predict even near-term developments in politics and economic policy. Given much of Africa's extremely low literacy rates, low gross national product (GNP) per capita, and lack of democratic traditions in national government, the prospects for democratization there seem limited. The futures of Cuba and China are far from clear, although many experts feel that democratic pressures will be hard to resist in the long run. Countries in East Asia, South America, and Eastern Europe (with some still authoritarian and others only marginally democratic) tend to offer better hopes for greater democracy. Even in those more developed countries, deeply rooted class tensions (as in Peru or Colombia) or ethnic hostilities (Bosnia, Sudan, Malaysia) undermine democratic forces.

In short, it is not entirely clear that a rosy democratic future stands before us. There is currently much instability among and within many nations. Furthermore, democracy does not solve all societal problems and in some cases may even open a Pandora's Box of new conflicts. In much of Eastern Europe, totalitarian rule held down a host of bitter ethnic rivalries: Serbs against Croatians and Bosnians in the former Yugoslavia; Azerbaijanis against Armenians in the Soviet Union; Bulgarians against the Turkish minority in Bulgaria. Although the governments in these examples are probably semi-democratic at best, it is clear that the tenuous steps that have been taken in that direction have not produced a stable order. The weakening of harsh authoritarian controls has unleashed intense ethnic nationalism, often leading to bloodshed. The march toward stable democracy, if it is under way at all, is neither irreversible nor universal.

The knowledge and understanding accumulated through generations of political science research suggest that the growth of democratic government is rooted in societal forces more fundamental than the actions or vision of particular leaders, or the fallout from single events. Most political scientists conclude that economic growth creates greater social and political diversity as well as heightened political participation and awareness; that all governments need some degree of popular support; and that governments cut off from the pressures of competitive political influences are inherently unstable in the long run. Building on this understanding and related ideas, several leading political scientists and political economists anticipated the breakdown of communist rule as long ago as 1960.[10]

Political science thus presents no clear or universally accepted vision of the future of politics in our changing world. However, there is some basis for predicting that economic growth will create democratic tendencies. Research indicates that countries with annual GNPs of under $1,000 per year and literacy rates below 50 percent are very unlikely to achieve democracy. Higher levels of economic development, accompanied by a reasonably equitable income distribution, accelerate literacy and the spread of information through newspapers, books, and broadcast media. Together, these conditions produce a more politically informed public, capable of holding elected officials accountable. Opinion surveys suggest that more educated populations are more likely to support democratic values.

It is clear that we are living in an era in which political life is both extremely important and highly volatile. As economic growth spreads (unevenly) through the world, and as nations become increasingly interdependent, we will find that the old conflict between communists and anticommunists has been replaced by a more complex pattern of economic, ethnic, and religious relations. The task of political science is to bring sound scientific inquiry to these problems.

Approaches to Political Understanding

"The word politics, sir," said Mr. Pickwick, "comprises in itself, a difficult study of no inconsiderable magnitude."

Charles Dickens, *The Pickwick Papers*, 1837.

The preceding sections present the scope of our concerns and explore why they are worth studying. It is important to understand, however, that political scientists approach their discipline in a variety of ways. More than most fields of study, political science is eclectic: It borrows from other fields to forge its own identity. Although political science enjoys a healthy diversity, it is also one of the most fragmented of academic disciplines.

The first effort to study political life was as a subtopic of *philosophy*. Those studying politics in this manner focus on questions pertaining to the origins of government, the problem of human rights and justice under law, the idea of a "just war," and other basic philosophical concerns. It is important to emphasize, however, that political philosophy includes several very different approaches. Most scholars claim that the field began in ancient Greece with Plato (427–347 BCE) and his student Aristotle. Essential elements of **classical political philosophy** include a distrust of democracy and an emphasis on the problem of designing a political community in accordance with principles of justice. **Modern political philosophy**—beginning with Machiavelli (1469–1527), Hobbes (1588–1679), Locke (1632–1704), and Rousseau (1712–1778)—is distinguished by its emphasis on individualism and its rejection of Plato's search for an ideal state order. Both classical and modern political philosophy includes a wide range of more specific perspectives.

The study of *law* was a second major influence on political science. Legal scholars study different approaches to interpreting laws and principles pertaining to how courts operate. Legal analysis is also relevant to questions about the powers of governmental institutions and their procedures. Much of political science through the first quarter of the twentieth century was influenced by legal thinking, and the term **formal-legal analysis** was used to describe pre–World War II political science. During this period, political scientists devoted themselves to issues of constitutional design and formal governmental institutions.

At the beginning of the twentieth century, some political scientists began to criticize philosophical and legal approaches to understanding politics. They argued that we could not fully account for policy choices by considering ethical concerns or legal powers and rights alone. Instead, we should observe actual political *behavior*. The "behavioral revolution" took root and, by the 1960s, was firmly established as the mainstream of the discipline. Perhaps the first shot in this revolution was fired in 1908 by Arthur Bentley in *The Process of Government*, an important book that argued persuasively for the observation of behavior in political research.[11] In political science, this approach is known as **behavioralism**.

The behavioral approach to political science necessitated borrowing skills from other disciplines. When we observe behavior—in the form of voting, political demonstrations, voicing opinions, and so on—we usually need to quantify it. How many people voted in the last election, and what caused them to vote as they did? What kinds of people participated in the demonstrations? Analyzing data in a quantified form requires that political scientists have some familiarity with *statistics*. The emphasis on statistical analysis is readily apparent to students exploring political science journals for the first time. Political research often (although not always) involves the use of basic and even highly advanced statistical tools as scholars try to discover and identify patterns in the behavior they observe.

Contemporary political science also owes a great deal to *history* and *sociology*. These disciplines suggested basic questions for political science research. If we are attempting to find out why poor people vote less regularly than rich people, for example, research from sociology is helpful in that it identifies important influences on the behavior of people in different segments of society. Historical knowledge provides an essential context for exploring political changes in both domestic and international relations.

Particularly in the past twenty years or so, political scientists have increasingly drawn from *economics* in their work. (See Box 1-5.) Some have applied the economic concept of the rational, self-interested person in analysis of everything from voting to group membership. The rational choice school is controversial within the discipline because many political scientists believe that it oversimplifies human motivations. But there is general agreement on the relevance of economic concepts and tools in the study of political behavior.

Perhaps in reaction to the dominance of the behavioral method and the increasing influence of approaches using economic theory, a significant number of political scientists now argue that there is an important place for less-mathematical research methods. This way of thinking is sometimes termed "postmodernism" or "postbehavioralist interpretivism." Although it is not an approach given to clear definition, its adherents share a conviction that the behavioralists and the rational choice analysts have allowed mathematical rigor to displace the politics in political science. Numbers can tell us some things, but they cannot reveal the whole sense of what is critical about political issues and events, and methods steeped in mathematics may even obscure or distort the essential political nature of the things they do measure, according to postmodernists.

Political scientists thus attempt to understand politics and government by using a wide range of approaches to study. Sometimes, the differences among political scientists with respect to their research methods can become rather heated, and a number of essays have been published attacking and defending various approaches. (See the list of suggested readings at the end of this chapter for some good examples.) We may hope that the decades-long debate over research methods in political science will prove to be useful in moving the discipline to refine and strengthen its ability to produce genuine understanding.

CONCLUSION: WHY STUDY POLITICAL SCIENCE?

Political science encompasses a wide variety of approaches. Sometimes the diversity is enriching and stimulating, but it must be acknowledged that political science is also a highly divided discipline. Some are quite vocal in disparaging the efforts of colleagues who use different tools or methods. Disagreements can be healthy, however, even when they are heated. The diversity and the energy that political

---

Box 1-5

"RATIONAL CHOICE" IN POLITICAL SCIENCE

Political scientists are hotly divided over the role of "rational choice" theory in their discipline. Drawn largely from economic theory, the rational choice approach begins with the assumption that individuals seek to maximize "utility" with their choices and behaviors. This assumption is rarely controversial in economics, where it is used to construct models pertaining to buying and selling oranges, computers, and "widgets," but some political scientists apply it to politics and government. For example, using rational choice logic, one analyst argued that party leaders should be expected to shape their ideological positions in ways that appeal to voters in the center of the ideological spectrum, where the party can "maximize" its votes, just as a retailer shapes a marketing campaign to maximize customers.

Although this example is hardly controversial, other applications are much more contentious. For example, some have used rational choice to construct theories of bureaucratic behavior, predicting that bureaucrats will have a natural urge to expand their agencies in order to increase their personal wealth. We will explore one of the most famous rational choice ideas in Chapter 6 (Interest Groups). It holds that people will not willingly participate in collective political efforts because the rational person will realize that one person's contribution is inconsequential and because non-contributors will receive as much benefit from the group's success (if any) as contributors. Political scientists have also used rational choice logic in understanding the emergence of democracy in developing countries.[12]

Advocates of rational choice contend that the approach opens new avenues for understanding political institutions and individual behavior. Others insist that it oversimplifies motivations, that it contains a conservative ideological bias, and that it has not produced any meaningful predictions that could not be derived from other approaches. In a book provocatively entitled *Pathologies of Rational Choice Theory*, two members of the Yale Political Science Department argue essentially that rational choice theory has been a failure.* This volume prompted the publication of *The Rational Choice Controversy*, by another Yale political scientist, which includes essays both criticizing and defending rational choice theory.†

The dispute has become even more heated in the last few years. A full-fledged "movement" in political science, termed by its leaders the *Perestroika* revolt, emerged when a number of political scientists rebelled against the use of mathematical models and

*Donald P. Green and Ian Shapiro, *Pathologies of Rational Choice Theory* (New Haven: Yale University Press, 1994).

†Jeffrey Friedman, ed., *The Rational Choice Controversy* (New Haven: Yale University Press, 1996).

---

scientists bring to their work reflect the deep interest they share in their subject. These are also reasons that political science is fascinating and so involving. The primary answer to the question "Why study political science?" is simply that it helps us understand the problems and issues that define public affairs. Studying political science is also an excellent foundation for careers in law, government, public administration, and other areas, but the most fundamental justification is that it helps us to become more effective participants in the civic life that increasingly affects our future. The passion for political understanding, shared among professionals and amateurs alike, is nicely captured in the following statement by a pioneering political scientist:

> No one can deny that the idea is fascinating—the idea of subduing the phenomena of politics to the laws of causation, of penetrating to the mystery of its transformations, of symbolizing the trajectory of its future. . . . If nothing ever comes of it, its very existence will fertilize thought and enrich imagination.[13]

rational choice thinking, arguing that they made the profession's journals irrelevant and unreadable. Political science would be better served, say *Perestroika's* supporters, if researchers would emphasize social and political reality instead of abstract models borrowed from economics and the natural sciences, where they make more sense.*

The Perestroika movement emerged formally at the 2001 Annual Meeting of the American Political Science Association in San Francisco. A story on the meeting in the *Chronicle of Higher Education* included the following quotations from two noted political scientists:

"I'm not very proud of being a political scientist, and I'm not very proud of political science . . . because we are not as useful as we could be," said Rogers M. Smith, a political theorist at the University of Pennsylvania, to cheers and laughter. He called on his audience to create a "critical gadfly profession" that will be "dangerous and troublesome and no longer trivial in the world."

"I've felt since the late 1980s that the discipline was in trouble," said John J. Mearsheimer, a professor of international relations at the University of Chicago.

*See Kristen Renwick Monroe, *Perestroika! The Raucous Rebellion in Political Science* (New Haven: Yale University Press, 2005).

He concluded that there is "a hegemonic threat out there" from rational-choice scholars*

In addition to arguing that rational choice theory has distracted political scientists from the generation of productive research, some critics worry that introducing students to rational choice ideas—with their emphasis on self-interested motives—tends to undermine the development of a civic consciousness among students and teachers. These critics point to a 1993 study that found that "economics professors are more likely to refrain from donations in support of public goods . . . [and] that economics students less frequently invoke conceptions of fairness, and behave more often with aggressive self-interest in experimental games. . . ."†

On the other hand, a growing segment of the discipline remains convinced that understanding everything from voting to bureaucracies to elections requires a keen grasp of the choices that rational people make in pursuit of their interests. This debate will figure prominently in the future development of political science.

*D.W. Miller, "The Perestroika Movement," *Chronicle of Higher Education*, September 21, 2001 (available at **http://www.btinternet.com/~pae_news/Perestroika/Miller.htm**).

†See Robert Abelson, "The Secret Existence of Expressive Behavior," in *The Rational Choice Controversy*, Jeffrey Friedman, ed. (New Haven: Yale University Press, 1996), pp. 25–36. The study Abelson refers to is Frank, Robert H., Thomas Gilovich, and Dennis T. Regan. 1993. "Does Studying Economics Inhibit Cooperation?" *Journal of Economic Perspectives*, Vol. 7, pp. 159–171.

 # WHERE ON THE WEB?

http://www.aclu.org/

The website for the American Civil Liberties Union. Founded in 1920, the ACLU has worked in both political and legal arenas for the protection of Americans' civil liberties. Some of its stands have made the organization increasingly controversial in recent decades.

http://www.apsanet.org/

The home page of the American Political Science Association provides information about important publications in political science, career opportunities, internships, and other resources.

http://www.icpsr.umich.edu/

Housed at the University of Michigan, this site is the home page for the Inter-University Consortium for Political and Social Research. It provides a great deal of useful information for anyone interested in advanced political science research and data.

http://www.freedomhouse.org/

Eleanor Roosevelt founded Freedom House in 1941, an organization dedicated to opposing "tyranny around the world, including dictatorships in Latin America, apartheid in South Africa, Soviet domination of Central and Eastern Europe, and religiously-based totalitarian regimes such as those governing Sudan, Iran and Saudi Arabia."

http://www.ucis.pitt.edu/cwes/index.html/

The home page of the Center for Western European Studies at the University of Pittsburgh provides useful information about European politics and economics.

http://www.worldbank.org/

The home page of the World Bank offers data and links to publications regarding economic development and global poverty issues.

http://www.brook.edu/

The Brookings Institution—the nation's oldest think tank—defines itself as "A private, independent, nonprofit research organization seeking to improve the performance of American institutions and government programs and policies." The site lists Brookings studies and personnel.

http://www.cato.org/

The Cato Institute, another think tank, states on its home page that it "promotes public policy based on individual liberty, limited government, free markets, and peace."

http://www.apsanet.org/~psa/

This is the home page of Pi Sigma Alpha, the national Political Science Honor Society for undergraduate and graduate students majoring or minoring in political science.

◆ ◆ ◆

Key Terms and Concepts _____

allocation of resources
authoritarian systems
behavioralism
classical political philosophy
democracy
formal-legal analysis
functionalism
government
government functions
human rights
income distribution

interest articulation
political development
political economy
political socialization
politics
popular consultation
rule adjudication
rule execution
rule making
totalitarian systems

Discussion Questions _____

1. What are the most basic functions of government? Explain why a political system cannot be stable and effective unless each of these functions is performed.
2. What is the difference between "positive" and "negative" human rights?
3. If politics means "the application of influence and power in making public decisions," does this mean that politics is underhanded?
4. How are free markets and democracy related to each other?

Notes _____

1. These definitions are adapted from Harold Lasswell, *Politics: Who Gets What, When, and How* (New York: McGraw-Hill, 1936); David Easton, *The Political System*, 2nd ed. (New York: Knopf, 1971); Bernard Crick, *In Defense of Politics*, 2nd ed. (Chicago: University of Chicago Press, 1972); Karl Deutsch, *The Nerves of Government* (New York: Free Press, 1963), and from the Glossary on the "About Economics" Web site, **http://economics.about.com/od/economicsglossary/g/political.htm.**
2. Much of this discussion is drawn from a basic, pioneering work that still influences contemporary political analysis. See Gabriel Almond and G. Bingham Powell, *Comparative Politics: A Developmental Approach* (Boston: Little, Brown, 1966).
3. Ibid.
4. North, Douglass C., *Institutions, Institutional Change and Economic Performance* (Cambridge: Cambridge University Press, 1990), p. 107.
5. One of the most widely read books making this argument is *Free to Choose*, by Milton and Rose Friedman (New York: Harcourt Brace Jovanovich, 1980).
6. Barrington Moore, Jr., *Social Origins of Dictatorship and Democracy: Lords and Peasants in the Making of the Modern World* (Boston: Beacon Press, 1967). For an important refinement of Moore's work, see Dietrich Rueschemeyer, Evelyn Huber Stephens, and John Stephens, *Capitalist Development and Democracy* (Chicago: University of Chicago Press, 1992).
7. Phillips, Kevin, *Wealth and Democracy: How Great Fortunes and Government Created America's Aristocracy* (New York: Broadway Books, 2002).
8. This famous quote is from *On War*, bk. 1, chap. 1, as translated by J. J. Graham (New York: Barnes & Noble, 1956), p. 23.
9. See "Freedom in the World: 2008," Freedom House, at **www.freedomhouse.org.**
10. A famous statement of this idea can be found in W. W. Rostow, *The Stages of Economic Growth* (Cambridge: Harvard University Press, 1960).
11. Arthur Bentley, *The Process of Government* (Cambridge: Harvard University Press, 1906). Several decades later, David Truman wrote the similarly titled *Governmental Process* (New York: Knopf, 1958), a book that extended and applied Bentley's approach.
12. See Barbara Geddes, "The Uses and Limitations of Rational Choice," in *Latin America in Comparative Perspective*, ed. Peter H. Smith (Boulder, Colo.: Westview, 1995), pp. 81–108.
13. Quoted in David Easton, *The Political System*, 2nd ed. (New York: Knopf, 1971), p. viii.

For Further Reading _____

Abouharb, M. Rodwan, and David Cingranellli. *Human Rights and Structural Adjustment*. New York: Cambridge University Press, 2008.

Arendt, Hannah. *The Origins of Totalitarianism*. New York: Harcourt, Brace, and World, 1966.

Beem, Christopher. *The Necessity of Politics*. Chicago: University of Chicago Press, 2002.

Bentley, Arthur. *The Process of Government*. Cambridge: Harvard University Press, 1906.

Easton, David. *The Political System: An Inquiry into the State of Political Science*. 2nd ed. New York: Knopf, 1971.

Farr, James, John S. Dryzek, and Stephen T. Leonard. *Political Science in History: Research Programs and Political Traditions*. New York: Cambridge University Press, 1995.

Finifter, Ada W. *Political Science: The State of the Discipline III*. Washington, DC: American Political Science Association, 2002.

Friedman, Jeffrey, ed. *The Rational Choice Controversy*. New Haven: Yale University Press, 1996.

Green, Donald P., and Ian Shapiro. *Pathologies of Rational Choice Theory*. New Haven: Yale University Press, 1994.

Held, David. *Models of Democracy*. 3rd ed. Palo Alto, CA.: Stanford University Press, 2006.

Huntington, Samuel P. *The Third Wave: Democratization in the Late Twentieth Century*. Norman, OK: University of Oklahoma Press, 1991.

Landman, Todd. *Protecting Human Rights: A Comparative Study*. Chicago: University of Chicago Press, 2005.

Lowi, Theodore J. *The End of Liberalism*. 2nd ed. New York: Norton, 1979.

Morris, Irwin L., Joe A. Oppenheimer, and Karol Edward Soltan, eds. *Politics from Anarchy to Democracy: Rational Choice in Political Science*. Palo Alto, CA.: Stanford University Press, 2004.

Page, Benjamin I., and James R. Simmons. *What Government Can Do.* Chicago: University of Chicago Press, 2000.

Phillips, Kevin. *American Theocracy: The Peril and Politics of Radical Religion, Oil, and Borrowed Money in the 21st Century.* New York: Penguin, 2007.

Schmidt, Diane E. *Writing in Political Science: A Practical Guide.* 3rd ed. New York: Pearson Longman, 2005.

Walzer, Michael. *Thinking Politically: Essays in Political Theory.* New Haven, CT: Yale University Press, 2007.

Warren, Robert Penn. *All the King's Men.* New York: Harcourt, Brace, 1946.

Cartoonists on the Left and Right find it quite easy to skewer their ideological opponents, and, while they use large measures of invective and humor, their attacks often relate to real aspects of the ideological differences between liberals and conservatives.

2

IDEOLOGIES: IMAGES OF POLITICAL LIFE

◆ Liberalism and Conservatism ◆ Capitalism ◆ Marxism
◆ Socialism ◆ Other Ideologies ◆ Conclusion: Ideology
Shapes Political Community and Political Conflict

Each of us thinks about politics in a unique way. Our views of political issues, controversies, and values are expressions of our personalities and backgrounds. Some of us want government to control more of the economy, while others feel that markets should be less regulated. Some of us think most about domestic social problems, others focus on ethical concerns, and still others think about foreign affairs or legal concepts. Some advocate radical change, and others seek to preserve traditions.

Nevertheless, despite the individualized nature of political orientations, we can identify certain well-established *ideologies* that describe patterns of political thinking among large numbers of people. An **ideology** is a more or less coherent system of political thinking. The most elaborate and complete ideologies, such as Marxism, contain a vision of justice, an identified adversary, a plan for attaining an ideal society, and a conception of good government. Less elaborate ideologies are simply "approaches" based on assumptions regarding the kinds of policies that work best.

Understanding the most important ideologies is useful in two ways. First, the nature of the prevailing ideology that exists in a society affects the way its government works. It will influence the way citizens participate in politics, how the government makes decisions, and what people expect from government. The articulation of interests; the making, adjudication, and execution of rules; the way that people are socialized into political life—all these things are dramatically affected by the ideology that prevails among a nation's citizens. The dominant ideology in North Korea, for example, provides a foundation for widespread deference to state authority in social, economic, and even personal affairs, whereas the strong elements of **individualism** and **capitalism** in Australia produce a very different kind of politics. Second, the degree of ideological *consensus* in a political system has an important influence on its stability. If a society experiences severe ideological conflict (as Nicaragua did in the 1980s), political life is often violent and unstable, whereas a general ideological consensus contributes to a relatively settled political order, as in Britain or Japan.

In addition to helping us understand the behavior of citizens and governments, studying ideologies helps us to decide for ourselves how we feel about political issues. Many of us have a fairly good idea about the differences between **liberalism** and conservatism, and we may know something about Marxism, **socialism**, or other ideologies. But even a brief analysis of the basic principles of these ideologies may help us understand our own political thinking. An individual may find that his or her positions on affirmative action, abortion, and arms control, for example, are manifestations of a political perspective that shapes the development of many other political opinions.

The following sections discuss ideologies that vary considerably with respect to their coherence and comprehensiveness. By some strict definitions, some of them do not fully qualify as "ideologies" at all. In keeping with familiar usage, however, and because of their great practical importance, we discuss each of them here.

LIBERALISM AND CONSERVATISM

Most Americans think of themselves, to some degree, as either liberal or conservative—even people who are generally uninterested in politics. Although being a "liberal" or a "conservative" does not require a consistent adherence to a comprehensive system of thought, there is a meaningful contrast between these ways of thinking about politics.

JOHN LOCKE (1632–1704), one of the foundational philosophers of liberalism.

Portrait of John Locke (1632-1704) (see also 1419), Kneller, Sir Godfrey (1646-1723) (after)/Private Collection, © Philip Mould Ltd, London/Bridgeman Art Library

Liberalism

Liberalism has a long and complex history. Some analysts contend that the first important statement of liberalism was contained in the writings of the British political philosopher John Locke (1632–1704), whose ideas influenced the American Declaration of Independence. Perhaps the core idea of Lockean liberalism is simply the recognition that there is a sphere of individual rights that government should respect and leave untouched.

The widespread acceptance of this idea for generations in the U.S. makes it seem obvious to contemporary Americans. However, it is important to realize that other ways of thinking about politics—particularly the classical political philosophy of Plato and Aristotle—attributed no special status to individual rights. An individual's place, and his or her rights, were to be defined with respect to the nature of the social order. Liberalism *begins* with the idea that individual rights come first. Government power is then built around them, so to speak.

Modern liberalism has evolved in ways that have transformed and extended Locke's ideas. Modern liberals oppose the application of state power to enforce conventional moral, religious, or traditional standards of behavior. In this respect, they carry forward a basic component of Lockean liberalism. When some politician or group proposes a law banning abortion or prohibiting flag burning, liberals unite in opposition. In such instances, liberalism advocates the security of individual choices over the state's (or the majority's) demands for the continuation of a single set of values. Liberalism thus emphasizes *tolerance*.

Yet modern liberals advocate the expansion of government authority to counteract corporate economic power and to create social conditions that improve the opportunities for people to engage in a full, satisfying life. This is not necessarily a contradiction, although conservatives often claim that it *is* inconsistent to be simultaneously opposed to state power and also supportive of expanding that power. The consistency is in the liberal's commitment to freeing the individual from forces that interfere with personal advancement and growth. Thus, liberals want to keep the state from enforcing moral conformity, but they support aggressive *government intervention* to provide disadvantaged individuals a way out of the economic and social conditions that condemn them to a bleak, limited future.

Modern liberals see many of society's problems as being rooted in negative social conditions. Again, we can see the common thread running back to the initial concerns of liberal thinking. If, as liberals believe, individuals need to be free both from the restrictions of antiquated traditions *and* from the restrictions created by poverty in order to prosper and develop, it is logical to suppose that many people will fail to thrive when economic distress, racial discrimination, and religious intolerance frustrate their hopes. Poor people turn to crime, teenagers become pregnant and drop out of school, and rates of drug addiction reach epidemic proportions, say liberals, because social conditions deny those people real opportunities.

Although the range of identifiably "liberal" policy positions is quite wide—including everything from advocating gay rights to supporting labor unions to demanding national health plans—modern liberalism is not simply a patchwork quilt of ideas. Its precepts are held together by a faith in the ability of all people to prosper and grow. Liberal policies are thus designed to preserve the rights of individuals and to expand opportunities when social conditions dampen them.

Conservatism

The core features of conservative thinking are notoriously difficult to define. Many capsule definitions begin with the conservative's preference for preserving society's political, social, and economic traditions, thus seeing conservatism as nothing more than support for the status quo. (One of contemporary American conservatism's elder statesmen, the late William F. Buckley, gave support to this view of conservatism when he famously stated that the role of the conservative is simply to "stand athwart history, yelling Stop!"). A second often heard claim is that conservatism is based on the belief that human reason is limited and that we cannot solve social and political problems. Neither of these views gives us a complete view of conservatism.

The most fundamental element of **conservatism** is support for the idea that *traditional values strengthen society*. Although there is considerable variety among conservatives with respect to which values are emphasized and for what purposes, most conservatives feel that humans have natural tendencies toward greed, promiscuity, aggressiveness, and sloth, and that the best way to inhibit those tendencies is through strong traditional values. Churches, schools, and even the state should act to preserve those values, according to conservative thinking, even at the expense of some freedoms.

Sir Edmund Burke (1729–1797) is often considered the father of conservative thinking, particularly in light of his 1790 essay, "Reflections on the Revolution in France."* While liberals applauded the revolution's goals of "Liberty, Equality, and Fraternity," Burke was appalled by the revolution's violent attacks against the aristocracy

* The text of this classic essay may be found at the Web site of the Constitution Society: http://www.constitution.org/eb/rev_fran.htm

and the church. He argued that the "customs and traditions" that define the character of a society are essential in preserving stability, culture, and progress. Burke felt that the French revolutionaries were bent on the destruction of French culture, and that their success in doing so would create disorder, injustice, and a lower quality of life for all.

A particularly controversial aspect of Burke's thinking was his acceptance of *class distinctions*. He argued that society is better off with its aristocratic heritage intact, even if it perpetuates vast differences between the rich and the poor. Thus, Burke felt that the trappings of class distinctions, including attendance at different churches for upper- and lower-class citizens, differences in clothing and accents, deferential forms of address to one's "betters," among other things, are traditions that make society work. When people know and accept their places in society, order and stability are possible. Perhaps reflecting that kind of thinking, all Conservative British prime ministers until the 1970s had aristocratic roots.

In its modern form, conservatism has two identifiable branches. One focuses on the moral sphere. According to this aspect of conservative thinking, a good society is one in which people place greater value on "self-restraint" than self-expression and pleasure. Conservatives are thus more inclined than liberals to support, for example, restrictions on obscene artistic expressions, marijuana use, same-sex marriages, and strict discipline in schools.

Consequently, conservatives often look to *erosions* of traditional moral values as the primary cause of social ills, while modern liberals are apt to blame poverty or racism. "Bad conditions do not cause riots, bad men do" is a commonly heard conservative refrain. Similarly, many conservatives argue that unwanted teenage pregnancies do not occur as a result of poverty, racism, or inadequate sex education, but as a result of the erosion of traditional morality. In fact, conservatives often contend that public school sex education contributes to the perception that sexual behavior has nothing to do with values. In a wide variety of contexts, conservatism looks to moral standards as a guide to behavior and claims that liberals, in their emphasis on tolerance, erode the force of those moral standards, producing disorder, hopelessness, crime, and poverty.

A second identifiable branch of conservatism focuses on economic concerns. Conservatives who emphasize economics may become indistinguishable from capitalists in their policy positions (see the following section). Free-market economics is not supported wholly by all conservatives, but it is not a coincidence that many conservatives blend a traditional perspective on moral issues with support for the free market. A common thread linking "traditional values" conservatism and "economic" conservatism is support for the work ethic as a traditional value. Conservatives claim that they defend the work ethic by maintaining an economic system that rewards initiative, talent, and hard work while penalizing idleness. Conservatives feel liberals interfere with the market's ability to allocate resources by enacting policies that restrict initiative and allocate rewards on the basis of need or simply to produce a more equal distribution of wealth.

American and European conservatives tend to place differing amounts of emphasis on economic freedoms. A strong communitarian perspective is often present among European conservatives, whereas many American conservatives embrace individualism more firmly. William Bennett, a former Secretary of Education who gained national fame with his successful volume *The Book of Virtues*, is an exception among modern American conservatives, emphasizing social values much more than free-market liberties.*

The Policy Relevance of Liberal and Conservative Ideologies

In most industrialized democracies, policies typically reflect a mixture of conservative and liberal thinking. Perhaps the best illustration of this is the changing size and scope of the welfare state. Liberal administrations often expand the welfare state, while conservatives restrain the growth of social programs. A comprehensive study of U.S. income distribution policies after World War II confirmed this general impression: "When the Democrats are at average or above-average congressional strength . . . transfer spending . . . tends to trend upward. . . ."[1] The rate of growth in social programs in this country thus reflects the ever-changing competition between liberal and conservative political influence.

An important 2005 article in the *American Journal of Political Science* provides further confirmation that liberalism and conservatism have real policy consequences. Political scientist Nathan Kelly measured inequality in the U.S. by calculating the ratio of the average income of the richest 20 percent of the population to the average income of the poorest 40 percent. This ratio changes somewhat from year to year, ranging from about 1.7 to over 2.3. Figure 2.1 shows what happened to inequality in the years following the "Great Society" anti-poverty programs enacted in the 1960s. These programs, including Medicare and Medicaid along with several others, represented a major thrust of liberalism in public policy. The impact was a marked reduction in inequality.

FIGURE 2.1   THE EFFECT OF IDEOLOGY ON INCOME INEQUALITY IN THE U.S.

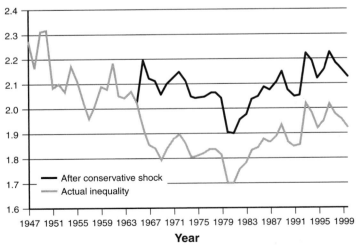

SOURCE: From Kelly, Nathan J. 2005. "Political Choice, Public Policy, and Distributional Outcomes," *American Journal of Political Science*, Vol. 49 (October): p. 877. Reprinted by permission of Blackwell Publishing Ltd.

* See William J. Bennett, *The Book of Virtues* (New York: Simon and Schuster, 1993). Bennett's conservative themes are also apparent in *America: The Last Best Hope, Volumes I and II* (Nashville, TN: Thomas Nelson, 2007).

After 1965, the two lines diverge on the graph. The lower line depicts what actually happened to inequality levels following the "Great Society" programs, and the upper line demonstrates the inequality levels that would have existed if policy changes in 1965 had embodied conservative ideology instead of liberal ideology. While Kelly's approaches to measuring these factors may be open to debate, the study provides striking confirmation that ideology affects people in a concrete way.

Of course, when policy disputes emphasize moral concerns, it is difficult to make decisions that reflect some measure of both liberal and conservative ideology. Opposing perspectives on abortion severely divide several societies, including the United States. Many proponents of abortion rights tend to view any restriction, even laws requiring parental notification or limits on public funding of abortions, as invasions of a fundamental right. Some of those opposing abortion argue that virtually any abortion, even an abortion to save the woman's life or an abortion sought by victim of rape or incest, constitutes murder. The U.S. Supreme Court essentially removed this issue from the legislative process with its 1973 *Roe v. Wade* decision, and it is fair to say that many state legislators were glad that they were spared the necessity of taking an

---

Box 2-1

CONSERVATIVES AND LIBERALS: HAS THE WORLD WIDE WEB CREATED A NATION OF ISOLATED IDEOLOGICAL EXTREMISTS?

If the differences between conservatives and liberals seem greater than ever before, it is probably due to major changes in mass communication. The expansion of cable television, the growth of the World Wide Web, and the end of the "fairness doctrine" in the U.S. are three developments that have taken place in roughly the same time period, and, taken together, they have arguably created a more heated debate between liberals and conservatives throughout the world.

Until the mid-1980s, citizens read newspapers and magazines, and they watched three or four television networks. There was very little political content on radio stations, and, at least in the U.S., all broadcasters dampened their coverage of controversial political issues so that they would not run afoul of the "fairness doctrine."* Liberals and conservatives got most of their information from the same sources. Today, we can choose to watch Ann Coulter or Keith Olbermann on television, to read dailykos.com or rushlimbaugh.com on the Web, and to listen to Air America or Sean Hannity on the radio. What has been the effect of having so many decidedly conservative and decidedly liberal news and opinion sources on the nature of modern democracy?

The following figure presents an arresting illustration of "conservative" and "liberal" communication patterns on the Internet.[†] Clearly, conservatives primarily link to other conservative sites, and liberals do the same, although the concentration of lines between the two nodes indicates a fair amount of conservative-to-liberal and liberal-to-conservative linking.

* The Federal Communications Commission established the "fairness doctrine" in the 1960s by administrative rule. Under the doctrine, the FCC could find that a licensed broadcaster had not been serving the public interest if the content of its programming did not present "balanced coverage of various and conflicting views on issues of public importance." In 1986, the Commission repealed the fairness doctrine, making it possible for broadcasters to air programs that were clearly conservative or liberal in nature. It is often argued that the fairness doctrine was an unconstitutional infringement on freedom of the press, but some Americans and some members of Congress have recently expressed interest in reinstating it.

[†] This figure is taken from Adamic, L. A., and N. Glance, "The Political Blogosphere and the 2004 U.S. Election: Divided They Blog." *WWW 2005 Conference's 2nd Annual Workshop on the Weblogging Ecosystem: Aggregation, Analysis, and Dynamics*, 2005. http://www.blogpulse.com/papers/2005/AdamicGlanceBlogWWW.pdf

(Continued)

Box 2-1

CONSERVATIVES AND LIBERALS: HAS THE WORLD WIDE WEB CREATED A NATION OF ISOLATED IDEOLOGICAL EXTREMISTS?
(Continued)

FIGURE 2.2   THE POLITICAL BLOGOSPHERE IN THE 2004 U.S. PRESIDENTIAL ELECTION

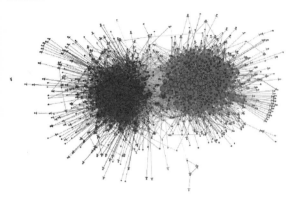

NOTE: The dots on the left represent liberal sites (blogs and news sources) and those on the right represent conservative sites. The size of each dot corresponds to the number of other sites that link to that site. The straight lines represent linkages.

If stable, healthy democracy requires that citizens share exposure to some unifying ideas, and that people read, hear, and see ideas presented from perspectives other than their own, the explosion of divisive Internet, radio, and cable television outlets may be a cause for concern. When virtually all British citizens got their news from the BBC, and when most U.S. citizens watched Dan Rather or Peter Jennings each night, it made sense to speak of a shared foundation on which citizens developed their political demands and preferences. At least to some degree, these outlets included an assortment of political perspectives. Today, anyone with an ideological identification can seek news and opinion outlets that confirm and strengthen his or her views, and few of these outlets present the "other" side.

Legal theorist and social philosopher Cass Sunstein expressed his concerns in a book written a few years ago, entitled *Republic.com*. He argues that the new system of mass communications has given citizens the power to "filter" the information they receive, a power that may not be a positive thing for democracy:

"... from the standpoint of democracy, filtering is a mixed blessing. ... In a heterogeneous society,

such a system requires something other than free, or publicly unrestricted, individual choices. On the contrary, it imposes two distinctive requirements. First, people should be exposed to materials that they would not have chosen in advance. Unanticipated encounters, involving topics and points of view that people have not sought out and perhaps find irritating, are central to democracy and even to freedom itself. Second, many or most citizens should have a range of common experiences. Without shared experiences, a heterogeneous society will have a more difficult time addressing social problems and understanding one another."*

Sunstein's argument is persuasive, and most of us can point to plenty of recent examples of divisive political rhetoric that generate more heat than light. However, a 2008 study explored changes over time with respect to "cross-ideological" discussions on the Internet, and while the researchers found that people tend to communicate most often with persons sharing their political views, they found that this pattern had not become more pronounced over time: "Over the ten-month span included in our data set, we find no evidence that conservative or liberal bloggers are addressing each other less at the end of our time period than at the beginning."† Most of the discussions between conservatives and liberals were classified by the researchers as "straw-man" arguments that do not contribute to substantive debates, but even these discussions increase awareness of opposing points of view.

Passionate arguments between conservatives and liberals (and among proponents of other ideologies) have been going on since Aristotle's time, and they will doubtlessly continue. It is probably too early to conclude that the Internet, cable television, and talk radio have transformed political discourse in modern countries, but there is no denying that it is far easier to find heated, "over-the-top" ideological material than it once was.

* See Cass R. Sunstein, *Republic.com* (Princeton, N.J.: Princeton University Press, 2001). This excerpt was published in the Boston Review at bostonreview.net.

† Eszter Hargittai, Jason Gallo, and Matthew Kane, "Cross-ideological Discussions Among Conservative and Liberal Bloggers," *Public Choice*, Vol. 134 (2008), pp. 67–86.

official stand.* Following the 2008 decision by the California Supreme Court striking down state laws prohibiting same-sex marriages, an especially heated fight between liberals and conservatives continues to rage over this issue as well.

Liberals and conservatives often clash on college campuses. In recent years, many colleges and universities have seen passionate debates over the "Academic Bill of Rights," a controversial proposal by a leading conservative advocate. Some conservatives believe that the devotion to **multiculturalism** in nearly all major universities has itself become a source of intolerance. They claim that conservative students and faculty are denied the right to express and hear conservative criticisms of multiculturalism, and that campuses are becoming centers of oppression. The Academic Bill of Rights was designed to "protect students and professors from political bias." Here are a few key passages from the proposal, which has been considered by several state legislatures:

. . . All faculty shall be hired, fired, promoted and granted tenure on the basis of their competence and appropriate knowledge in the field of their expertise and, in the humanities, the social sciences, and the arts, with a view toward fostering a plurality of methodologies and perspectives.

. . . Students will be graded solely on the basis of their reasoned answers and appropriate knowledge of the subjects and disciplines they study, not on the basis of their political or religious beliefs.

. . . Exposing students to the spectrum of significant scholarly viewpoints on the subjects examined in their courses is a major responsibility of faculty. Faculty will not use their courses for the purpose of political, ideological, religious or anti-religious indoctrination.

Is the Academic Bill of Rights a statement of liberal or conservative principles? The passages excerpted above are certainly consistent with the ideas of tolerance for diversity and dissent that are core aspects of liberalism. However, many academics have argued that, if implemented in law, it would be used to stifle the discussion of leftist views in social science and humanities classes. Some professors would be concerned that they might not be able to cover the other side adequately, thereby making them vulnerable to disciplinary action. The safest course would be to avoid controversy altogether. If the Academic Bill of Rights were fully implemented, it is difficult to say whether it would restore diversity and tolerance, as David Horowitz and his supporters claim, or whether it would usher in a new era of inhibited political discussion on college campuses.

The full text of the Academic Bill of Rights is available at www.studentsfor academicfreedom.org/.

CAPITALISM

Capitalism refers both to an economic system and to an ideology. As an economic system, capitalism may be defined by its reliance on *economic exchange* and *private ownership* to allocate society's resources. A capitalist system is one in which

---

* On April 18, 2007, the U.S. Supreme Court held that the federal "Partial Birth Abortion Ban Act of 2003" was constitutional (see *Gonzales v. Carhart*). Many observers, along with the four dissenters on the Court, noted that the decision reflected a change in the ideological composition of the Court following the appointment of Justice Samuel Alito to replace retired Justice Sandra Day O'Connor.

profit-seeking behavior, not governmental decision making, determines what happens in the economy. Capitalist ideology provides philosophical and analytical support for such a system.*

Capitalism, like liberalism and conservatism, is not a complete ideology. It does not contain an explicit view of human history, it does not identify a specific adversary, and it does not present a picture of some future state of perfect human development. Some capitalist thinkers certainly have views on such matters, but their positions are not intrinsic to capitalist thinking. Nevertheless, capitalism is a powerful ideology, one that continues to exert considerable influence on political movements and on policy making.

The Elements of Capitalist Ideology

There are two identifiable elements in capitalist ideology. First, capitalism places a heavy emphasis on individualism. Whereas socialists focus on communal values and needs, those drawn to capitalism tend to emphasize individual accomplishments and talents and the private sphere of life. Advocates of capitalist ideology typically believe that the general good is best served when each individual seeks his or her economic self-interest. Adam Smith stated this idea in 1776 in his landmark treatise *An Inquiry into the Nature and Causes of The Wealth of Nations*: "[An individual who] intends only his own gain [is] led by an invisible hand to promote an end which was no part of his intention. . . . By pursuing his own interest he frequently promotes that of the society more effectually than when he really intends to promote it."[2] Factories are built, jobs are provided, and wealth is generated—all as the result of free individuals seeking profits in a free marketplace.

Second, capitalist thinking is often associated with *distrust of government control* of social resources. The capitalist sees central bureaucracies as inherently wasteful and inefficient, whereas the market, with its multitude of individual decisions driven by self-interest, is rational and productive. Government decisions are driven by the vague, ill-informed, and misguided motivations of leaders, not by the precise incentives of profit seeking. Thus, those favoring a capitalist economy point with great satisfaction to the vast differences between what used to be East Germany and West Germany. Two states with essentially similar people, a similar culture, and the same climate had very different economic growth rates and conditions between 1947 and 1990. In 1988, before German Unification, the gross domestic product (GDP) per capita was $18,480 in West Germany and only $11,860 in East Germany. An even starker contrast exists today between North and South Korea. The GDP per capita is over $24,600 in South Korea but only $1,900 in North Korea. Differences of this magnitude reflect the tremendous impact of ideology on the lives of people.[3] (Also, see the night-time photo of North and South Korea in Chapter 1.)

Policy Implications of Capitalist Ideology

Believing in individualism and free-market economics does not require one to favor the elimination of government's role in society. If it did, capitalist ideology would

---

* The French phrase *laissez faire*, meaning "leave alone," is commonly employed to designate the essence of what we here term *capitalist* ideology. In fact, some economists say that capitalism is not a "system" at all, but simply a description of what happens when no system is imposed on free individuals, as long as basic property rights and freedoms are protected.

have little practical relevance to real-world politics. Capitalist ideas can find their way into policy making in less radical ways.

For example, political leaders who support capitalist ideology often advocate tax policies that de-emphasize the goal of economic equality. Proportional tax rates take the same percentage of income from each citizen, regardless of income, whereas progressive systems take an increasing percentage from wealthier citizens. The rich pay more taxes than the poor under both approaches, but progressive taxes are slanted more toward the advantage of the poor. Capitalists claim that steeply progressive taxes stifle the initiative of talented people (since economic success is "penalized" by placing high earners in a higher tax bracket).

Capitalist thinking similarly supports policy choices that emphasize or strengthen private production of goods and services and that give consumers a wider range of choices. (See Box 2-2.) During the Reagan administration (1981–1989), some significant changes along those lines were made in the United States, resulting in a considerable increase in what is called *contracting out* for public services. The current trend in many Latin American societies is also toward greater privatization of state enterprises. In this arrangement, private contractors submitting the lowest qualified bid provide services previously provided by public employees. Capitalist ideology welcomes this approach as a way to harness the power of competition.

Capitalists similarly support **deregulation**. The distrust of purely profit-driven decisions has, in most industrialized nations, led to an extensive framework of regulations that restrict pricing decisions and require safety measures for workers, consumers, and the environment. Capitalist ideology supports the removal of many such regulations, both because the capitalist wants to rely on individual choice as a way to keep prices low and product quality high, and because they distrust government power. Critics of capitalist thinking doubt that free-market forces would induce private enterprise to control pollution emissions, properly dispose of hazardous waste, or install sufficient safety protection in automobiles or in the workplace.

MARXISM

Strictly speaking, Marxism is the set of ideas derived from the German philosopher Karl Marx (1818–1883). In contrast to liberalism and conservatism, Marxism is an elaborate, detailed system of thought. It is therefore arguably the most complete example of an ideology. Marxism incorporates an interpretation of history, the identification of an adversary, a plan for the future, and a conception of the just society. Marx was convinced that everything important in society, even the way people *think,* could be accounted for through the impact of class struggles: "It is not the consciousness of men that determines their existence, but, on the contrary, their social existence determines their consciousness."[4] Marxism still exerts a strong political influence in today's changing world.

The essence of **Marxism** is *the belief that economic conflict between a ruling class and an exploited lower class is the driving force in social and political life.* The elements of this definition require some elaboration.

Economic Exploitation and Economic Determinism

Marxism begins with the idea that people are divided into social classes, one of which suffers severe exploitation by the other. Although many other thinkers focused on

---

Box 2-2

IDEOLOGY AND THE CONTROVERSY OVER "SCHOOL CHOICE"

Many analysts and citizens agree that American public schools have deteriorated during the last 30 years. Since the early 1960s, scores on college entrance exams have dropped, and professors regularly complain that basic writing and math skills are lacking among high school graduates. One controversial solution, often simply termed "school choice," is remarkable for how closely it reflects capitalist thinking.

Parents and students have always had a choice about whether to attend a public school or a private or parochial school. The controversial aspect of school choice is that the state or school district would be required to give some of the tax funds that the public school would expend in educating the student to a private or a parochial school if the student and his or her parents choose to attend such a school. (The details of these proposals vary widely, but most provide a voucher to parents that can be used to help pay tuition.)

Capitalist ideology strongly supports school choice. Proponents of the policy often point out that vigorous competition among universities has made American higher education the envy of the world, whereas the traditional system of public elementary and high schools is the closest thing in America to a purely socialist arrangement, producing inefficiencies and low-quality service. According to this point of view, when a school's administrators know that students and parents dissatisfied with their school can choose a competing school, they will make their schools better, just as Toyota's fear of losing business to Honda makes them work hard to produce innovations and high-quality goods.

Opponents of school choice argue that the capitalist assumptions break down in this context. Even with taxpayer funds in the form of vouchers, the poorest parents often will not be able to afford the additional amount needed to pay tuition at the best private schools; therefore, public schools will overwhelmingly become populated by students from poor families, who are more likely to have academic difficulties. Opponents also feel that public education provides a setting in which widely shared values can be instilled in students and that society will become more fragmented without the common denominator of public school experience.

In June 2002, the U.S. Supreme Court handed down a landmark decision upholding the constitutionality of a voucher program in Ohio that used taxpayer funds to pay for education in private and parochial schools. Since most private schools in the United States have a religious affiliation, one of the most controversial aspects of school choice programs is the fact that most of them permit parents to use taxpayer funds for tuition at religious schools. Some argue that this violates the First Amendment's prohibition of the establishment of a state religion. However, in *Zelman v. Simmons-Harris et al.*, the Supreme Court concluded that the Ohio program was constitutional, primarily because it allowed the parents (and not a state official) to decide which schools would receive the state money. The decision was a very close one, and this issue will continue to divide liberals and conservatives for many years.

See John E. Chubb and Terry M. Moe, *Politics, Markets, and America's Schools* (Washington, DC: Brookings Institution, 1990), for a foundational argument favoring school choice; and see Kenneth J. Meier and Kevin B. Smith, *The Case against School Choice* (Armonk, NY: Sharpe, 1995), for a widely-cited opposing view. More recent sources include William G. Howell and Paul E. Peterson, *The Education Gap: Vouchers and Urban Schools*, rev. ed. (Washington, DC: Brookings Institution Press, 2006), and Herbert J. Walberg, *School Choice: The Findings* (Washington, D.C.: Cato Institute, 2007).

---

this problem before and after him, Marx's analysis of the problem was fundamentally different. Conventional leftists like Representative Maxine Waters (Democrat from California) and Senator Richard Durbin (Democrat from Illinois) argue that selfishness and shortsightedness among those in power are the ultimate causes of poverty and economic oppression. Better policies enacted by a more generous set of leaders would produce a fairer distribution of wealth.

Marx rejected this line of reasoning. He argued that economic forces largely *determine* ideas and political movements, and that these forces constitute the real source of everything in political life. In Marx's view, poor people are exploited not because some people are greedy or because people do not fully appreciate the social costs of poverty, but because *the economic structure of capitalist society makes exploitation of the poor inevitable.* According to his concept of **economic determinism**, human history is the process of economic forces pushing society from one stage of development to another, until the inevitable end point (communism) is reached.

The Stages of Prehistory

The distinguishing feature of the first human societies, according to Marx, was the sharing of the basic resources of life. The first "stage" of "prehistory," **primitive communism** (or **communalism**), was the economic system that existed before the evolution of private property, slavery, or classes. Small bands of humans lived together in joint control over the land, wildlife, and food supplies. While this image has long been described by anthropologists, Marx's distinctive idea was that the communal nature of such societies was created by an economic fact. It was not simply that no person had yet discovered self-interest; *communal society existed because the primitive level of agricultural productivity made land ownership and slavery economically impossible.*

Why would this be true? Since each person could produce only enough to stay alive, a slave would have had to consume everything that he or she produced, leaving nothing for a master to save or consume. Because nearly all one's time was spent gathering food, it was also impractical to devote resources to defending a territory. Ownership of land and exploitation of others simply did not make economic sense. Humans shared resources in primitive society entirely because the low state of productivity made any other arrangement impractical.

Feudalism arose when agricultural productivity advanced. As some people found that they could produce more than they and their families consumed, some of them hired soldiers (fed with food not needed by the owners) to defend estates. Land ownership produced power, since large acreages could support armed strength. Feudalism thereby created the first *class* divisions: in one group were those who owned the land, and in the other were those who worked on it.

Capitalism emerged as a consequence of further economic development. Greater farm productivity made resources available for enterprises other than agriculture, and people acquired power through their ownership of *capital.* They invested that capital in factories, hiring workers to trade their labor for wages. The "surplus value" created by the workers was then taken by the capitalists, who used it to add to their wealth and power.

A core idea of Marxism holds that capitalism contains flaws (Marxists call them "contradictions") that make its demise inevitable. Capitalists would eventually have to compete aggressively with one another, forcing them to exploit workers ever more severely. Wages would drop, work hours would increase, and work conditions would deteriorate. And, unlike the exploited serfs under feudalism who lived in isolation across huge farms, the increasingly exploited workers under capitalism (the "proletariat") lived and worked together in large numbers in factory settings.

This was a fatal "contradiction" of capitalism, entirely created by the *economic facts* regarding industrial production: Masses of workers would be exploited with increasing cruelty at the same time that they were brought into close contact with one another to work in factories, thereby becoming a potentially powerful political force. The downtrodden workers would achieve a sense of class consciousness, realizing their common bond and their common capitalist class enemies. Capitalism would have to fall.

The resulting system would be the fourth stage: *socialism*. Under the new system, workers would be paid fairly, industrial production would be driven by the real needs of the vast majority of people, and, most important, there would no longer be a ruling class. Eventually, productivity would increase to the point at which all the real needs of society could be satisfied without government help, and there would be enough of everything for everyone, making economic "scarcity" a thing of the past. "True" history would begin as *communism* emerged from human pre-history, and the state would "wither away" with no class conflict to resolve.

The Political Relevance of Marxist Ideology

In discussing how Marxism has affected government and politics, it is essential to remember that Marx himself was primarily an economic philosopher and his main contribution was the development of a theory. The real "founding father" of communism—and of the first communist system, the Soviet Union—was Vladimir Ilyich Ulyanov, better known as Lenin (1870–1924). Hence, we usually speak of the guiding ideology of communist systems as "Marxism-Leninism."*

Lenin developed the idea of the Communist Party as the "vanguard of the proletariat," a firmly organized unit that could understand the needs of the working class even when workers themselves were confused or misled. Lenin emphasized measures to ensure the expansion of the party's exclusive position of power. In fact, much of what is distinctive about actual communist political systems derives from Lenin's ideas regarding party organization and control. Communist systems share at least two characteristics that are a result of Marxist-Leninist ideology.

First, the premise that political conflict is essentially a conflict between workers and those who exploit them leads to restrictions on political diversity. Competitive political party systems are illegitimate in Marxist-Leninist thinking because only the Communist Party is believed to have the true interests of the people (that is, the working class) at heart. Until very recently, countries dominated by Marxist-Leninist thinking have all been one-party states. Only after the influence of Marxism receded have competitive electoral processes been established in formerly communist countries.

Second, communist governments have frequently used the idea of class conflict as the intellectual justification for repressing political, religious, and artistic expression. Drawing on Marx's contention that "religion is the opium of the people," Marxist governments in Europe and elsewhere have restricted religious freedom, viewing the Orthodox and Catholic churches as distracting the working class from its true political interests. In 2008, Freedom House included Cuba and North Korea, both Marxist nations, among the eight most repressive regimes on earth.[†]

---

* Similarly, Chinese communism is sometimes termed "Marxism-Leninism-Maoism" because of the importance of Mao Zedong's influence on that version of the ideology. In addition to Lenin and Mao, Fidel Castro, Chè Guevara, and others adapted and altered Marxist concepts in the course of revolutionary movements. We outline the most crucial of the extensions of Marxism in discussing Russia and China (Chapters 13 and 14).
† See the "Worst of the Worst: The World's Most Repressive Societies," Freedom House, 2008, available at http://www.freedomhouse.org/template.cfm?page=70&release=661.

Although precise data are often lacking, there is some evidence that Marxist revolutions in underdeveloped nations have produced greater economic equality and more social welfare programs for the poor. For example, whereas most of Latin America is characterized by great income disparities between rich and poor, the Cuban Revolution created far greater economic equality as well as the region's most extensive educational and health-care programs. Proponents of Marxism like to note that Cuba has the highest literacy rate, lowest infant mortality, and longest life expectancy of any nation in Latin America. Comparisons favorable to Marxism are more difficult to find in the developed world; pre-1990 Germany was divided into a communist side with a low standard of living (with a somewhat more equal distribution of income), terrible pollution problems, and other difficulties, and a capitalist side with such superior economic and social conditions that a wall had to be built to prevent migration from East to West.

SOCIALISM

Socialism is a much more generalized ideology that actually predates Marxism. Although many socialists, particularly in years past, have shared many Marxist beliefs, others have not. Socialism shares with Marxism a deep concern about the divisive effects of private property, and it too is driven by a hope that greater social and economic equality can be achieved. Some socialists would even agree that the best way to make progress is to work toward a revolution, although socialist ideology does not require such a position. Once we get beyond the basic problem of social inequality, it becomes clear that *socialism* is a term applied to a rather diverse range of approaches to politics.

Socialism: A Confusing Political Term

The term socialism is used in many different ways, creating enormous confusion. Marx used the term specifically, to mean the stage of "prehistory" subsequent to the fall of capitalism and before the "withering away of the state" under communism. Marxist regimes in the former Soviet Union, China, Cuba, and Eastern Europe have referred to themselves as socialist in that sense, because the state has not withered away, nor has it given direct control over the means of production to the workers.

In twentieth-century Western Europe, however, socialism took on a far different meaning. Competing socialist and communist political parties, often sharply antagonistic toward each other, developed in nations such as France and Italy. The communist parties (with the notable exception of the Italian communists) generally accepted the political supremacy of the Soviet Union and its authoritarian political system. In contrast, most socialist parties throughout Western Europe were highly critical of the Soviet Union and strongly committed to democratic principles.

At one time or another during the past two decades, socialist political parties have governed Great Britain, France, West Germany, Greece, Spain, Portugal, Sweden, Norway, and other Western European democracies. Even in the United States, a few cities have had socialist mayors, and Vermont now has a socialist congressman (though he is officially listed as an Independent). These leaders—as well as former French President François Mitterrand, former West German Prime Minister

Willy Brandt, and other Western European socialist politicians—have a different view of socialism from that associated with the leaders of China and North Korea. Indeed, Brandt and many Western European socialist leaders were noted for their strong attacks on Soviet foreign policy and for their support of democratic political rights. In this discussion, then, we are considering socialism as an identifiable ideology that can be distinguished from Marxism. In its most moderate forms, European-style socialism is referred to as *social democracy.*

Fundamental Elements of Socialism

The core idea of socialism is the assumption that a just society requires purposeful social action, or, to put it negatively, that actions based on *private interests* prevent the achievement of a fair society. Socialists focus on the potential for *community* and *public interest,* opposing what they see as an excessive emphasis on profit seeking and self-interest in other approaches to political life. Clearly, the most important fault socialists find in capitalist systems is social and economic inequality, but the creation of greater equality is not their only goal. Socialists also want to establish a greater public role to counter the forces dividing society and the selfishness unleashed by private interests.

Nowhere is this sentiment more wonderfully captured than in the following statement by French philosopher Jean-Jacques Rousseau (1712–1778):

> The first man, who after enclosing a piece of ground, took it into his head to say, *this is mine,* and found people simple enough to believe him, was the real founder of civil society. How many crimes, how many wars, how many murders, how many misfortunes and horrors, would that man have saved the human species, who . . . should have cried to his fellows: Beware of listening to this impostor; you are lost, if you forget that the fruits of the earth belong equally to us all, and the earth itself to nobody![5]

Beyond their general agreement with this sentiment, socialists are a diverse lot. The person generally regarded as the first to use the term *socialism* was a British industrialist named Robert Owen (1771–1858). He supported the free-market system in most respects, although he advocated the establishment of state schools and supported the idea, radical for its time, that children under 12 years of age should not be permitted to work a full (thirteen-hour) day. Although one does not have to be a socialist to agree wholeheartedly with those reforms, they do embody the essence of socialism: The force of the public interest must be brought to bear as a restraint on the forces of private interest.[6]

For most socialists, profit-motivated behavior is less fair and even less efficient than public decision making, and thus socialists favor public ownership of much industrial production. Democratic socialist governments in Western Europe have taken control only of certain key industries, such as steel, electric power, or railroads. Socialists believe that public ownership will produce equitable prices and wages along with safe working conditions and safe workplaces. Moreover, consumers will obtain reliable products and services. It should be noted, however, that in practice, European socialist parties in countries such as France and Spain have recently become far more skeptical about the value of state ownership in the economy. Still, they continue to believe that the state should be able to allocate scarce resources to where they are most needed, not simply to where the market demands them.

Democratic Socialism and Marxism

It is often argued that democratic socialism and Marxism share a common view of social injustice but that they diverge with respect to what should be done about it. Marxists (especially those who accept Lenin's ideas) typically advocate revolution, whereas democratic socialists believe in working for change through democratic political channels. Although some people who consider themselves Marxists would not agree, most Marxists assume that political decision making in a capitalist societies is inevitably driven by the interests of an elite ruling class.

Most Marxists reject the idea that capitalists can be "voted out" of power, and they therefore distrust elections.* (An important exception to this generalization was the Marxist-Leninist Sandinista Party in Nicaragua, which allowed elections in which opposition parties voted it out of power in 1984.) In contrast, democratic socialists work for progressive policies and programs in hopes of creating greater equality of economic conditions and opportunities and bringing communal interests to bear on social choices.

Perhaps the most important aspect of this divergence has to do with the problem of democracy itself. Democratic socialists accept the idea of democracy as a *process*. When people are able to express their views and choose among competitive parties, socialists expect to be able to achieve their objectives. Many Marxists define democracy as an *outcome*—namely, a just distribution of wealth. Democracy, for a Marxist, thus requires the elimination of class divisions; as long as class differences exist, the democratic process is empty, misleading, and doomed to fail.

The Political Relevance of Socialist Ideology

Despite the diversity among those who support socialism, there is an identifiable pattern of policy choices associated with this ideology. First, as noted earlier, socialist systems usually have adopted some degree of *public ownership* of banking, communications, transportation, and steel production, among other industries, to ensure that allocations are in the public interest.

Second, socialist governments usually *regulate private industries* extensively. A distrust of profit-driven decision making leads to government requirements regarding worker safety, equity in compensation of employees, consumer safety, and environmental protection. Although all modern governments have adopted at least some regulatory initiatives, socialist ideology is associated with more extensive and more comprehensive regulation of private industry.

Third, socialist countries have *large, expensive welfare systems*. The government sector of the economy employs a large proportion of the workforce in implementing programs for social security, education, income maintenance, and health care. Many socialists contend that a basic income and adequate medical care are fundamental human rights, not simply advantages that those with good fortune can enjoy. Along with a large **welfare state** (an extensive array of government programs in housing, health

---

* Many contemporary Marxist political thinkers and intellectuals, particularly in Europe, strongly support democratic principles, arguing that there is no necessary contradiction between Marxist theory and democracy. However, the record of Marxist regimes in practice has not been tolerant of opposing points of view.

care, and education), socialist ideology generally leads to higher public spending relative to the size of the economy. For example, socialist thinking has long influenced politics in Sweden, and government spending there is quite high, but it is much lower in less-socialist Paraguay.

The high taxes and extensive welfare state associated with socialist ideology are also linked to a fourth policy implication of socialism: *redistribution of income*. Socialists, as discussed earlier, are often drawn to their ideology by a concern for the plight of the poor and by a corresponding discomfort at the opulence of the rich. Socialists contend that taking from the rich does not rob them of anything they genuinely need (since they have enough left to provide for themselves), but that it does make the difference between stark poverty and a minimally acceptable standard of living for the poor. Hence, not only do socialist systems have high taxes, but their tax systems also take a larger proportion of taxes from those with high incomes. (See Box 2-3.)

Despite the socialist emphasis on income equality, it is not always true that socialist systems as a whole are strikingly more egalitarian than other systems. Some comparisons suggest that socialism leads to greater equality—for example, largely socialist Sweden has greater income equality than France. Yet capitalist South Korea and Taiwan both have very high income equality, approaching a distribution of wealth similar to that in China.

In a controversial empirical study, two prominent political scientists attempted to determine the effect of socialism on economic equality. Although individual comparisons can be found to support the idea that socialist ideology promotes greater equality, the results of this study supported the idea that *higher levels of economic development are, in general, associated with greater equality* and that the degree to which the country adopts socialist policies makes little difference.[7] For example, on the "Gini Index" measure of income inequality (in which a score of zero indicates perfect equality and a score of 100 indicates perfect inequality), China's score of 46.9 is considerably higher than the U.S. score of 40.8, and South Korea's 31.6 score indicates greater equality than in Mexico, which received a score of 46.1.[8] Obviously, there is no simple explanation for differences among nations with respect to income inequality.

Fifth, socialist ideology usually favors *public service delivery* over private services. Support for public education is actually widespread in most industrialized countries, but public education is especially central to socialist thinking. Reliance on private institutions to provide educational services would be contrary to socialist principles both because, according to socialists, it would foster elitism and because a public educational institution is the most effective way to instill communal, shared ideals in the citizenry. Socialists favor public over private service delivery in other areas, of course, including most municipal services (public safety, road building and repair, garbage collection, prison administration, and many others). The public role in these areas allows the government to make policy choices in accordance with community purposes, and, as an additional socialist benefit, it enables government to provide employment opportunities to those who may not be able to obtain private jobs.

OTHER IDEOLOGIES

Most contemporary political systems make policies that, in varying degrees and mixtures, reflect the ideologies already discussed. Still other ideological strains can be identified, however, and although they have not been as pervasive, these other

---

Box 2-3

THE "THIRD WAY"

In the 1980s, left-leaning parties with socialist sympathies suffered declining support in several Western nations, particularly after the fall of communism in the Soviet Union. Ronald Reagan and Margaret Thatcher became two of the world's most powerful leaders, and their support of most principles of capitalist ideology was a central part of their approaches to government. Supporters of movements toward greater socialism concluded that their parties needed to change their message in order to return to power.

British Prime Minister Tony Blair successfully advocated a "Third Way," blending substantial state activism in education, welfare, public transportation, and other areas with a strong dose of economic prudence and traditional management principles. His good friend Bill Clinton won two elections quite handily in the 1990s by using this approach in his campaigns. For both Blair and Clinton, the "Third Way" meant being tough on crime and generally friendly toward business, while supporting most feminist and minority concerns and maintaining a strong role for the state in providing social services.

The precise meaning of the "Third Way" is open to dispute. Some observers claim that it had no new substance, and that it was simply an attempt by traditional left-leaning politicians to disguise their more liberal policy positions to get votes from moderate citizens. However, at least with respect to Blair and Clinton, it is arguable that they forged a combination of policy positions that was genuinely distinctive. For example, Bill Clinton publicly supported the death penalty, he signed the "Defense of Marriage Act," he instituted a "don't ask, don't tell" policy regarding homosexuals serving in the armed forces, and his most important achievements as president were gaining U.S. ratification of the North American Free Trade Agreement (NAFTA) and his decision to sign a Republican-sponsored welfare reform

plan. A very high percentage of liberal Democrats opposed those policy positions. Although the death penalty is not a significant issue in Britain, Tony Blair has frequently supported free-trade policies. At the same time, both Clinton and Blair supported trade unions, affirmative action programs, and expansions of national health insurance, policy positions strongly supported by those on the left. In 2007, Nicolas Sarkozy was elected president of France, and has worked to moderate some of that country's most elaborate and expensive economic policies while maintaining much of the welfare state.

George W. Bush moved toward some of the same middle ground. While much of his party's base remained solidly conservative and opposed to any kind of activist government policies, he expanded the U.S. welfare state more than any president since Lyndon Johnson in the 1960s. With an increased public role in education and in providing prescription drug benefits to older Americans, Bush's policies may be seen as attempting to graft some conservative principles onto "big government" programs. According to political scientist Jonathan Rauch, Bush's ideas embodied a much stronger government role than conservative Republicans traditionally accepted: "government curtails freedom not by being large or active but by making choices that should be left to the people. . . . If he needs to expand government to deliver more choices—well, he can live with that."*

The leading books on this subject are by Anthony Giddens, the sociologist who coined the term: *The Third Way* (London: Polity Press, 1998), *Beyond Left and Right* (Polity Press, 1994), and *The Third Way and Its Critics* (Polity Press, 2000).

* Jonathan Rauch, "The Accidental Radical," *National Journal*, July 25, 2003, http://www.nationaljournal.com/about/njweekly/stories/2003/0725nj1.htm

---

ideologies have exerted considerable influence on policy decisions, important political movements, or both.

Feminism

Feminism actually applies to two rather different sets of ideas. On one hand, feminism is the demand that females should enjoy the same rights and responsibilities enjoyed by males and that laws and practices placing females in a lower status are unfair, foolish, and wasteful. This type of feminism is largely a statement of basic liberal principles specifically applied to the rights of women. On the other hand, feminism also refers to an approach that attempts to identify special feminine (and masculine) qualities, usually arguing that feminine qualities have not been fully appreciated and that masculine qualities have dominated and distorted social and cultural development.

The first variety of feminism is a widespread, sustained movement that focuses on opening opportunities for women with respect to voting and other civil rights and the removal of gender restrictions in various occupations and in the armed services. For example, a woman may not legally drive a car in contemporary Saudi Arabia, and the former Taliban government of Afghanistan prevented women from obtaining education and mandated severe beatings for women who appeared in public without the *burkas* that covered them literally from head to toe.

Although the policies of the Taliban regime constituted what was perhaps the most extreme restrictions on women's rights, it is important to note that women were denied the vote in virtually all democracies until the early 1900s. In its simplest forms, feminism is a demand that these kinds of inequities be removed. Often, feminists argue that removing legal or even constitutional restrictions is not enough; there must be representation of women where traditions and "old boy" networks effectively exclude them, even when laws officially open the doors to all applicants. Hence, feminists have fought for the appointment of more women to leadership positions in government, universities, and professions historically considered beyond their reach (firefighting, science teaching, space programs).

Feminism also embraces noneconomic policies. The abortion issue occupies a central place among feminist policy demands in the United States, and it is related to the status of women in several ways. Most feminists argue that laws restricting abortion lead women to obtain dangerous illegal abortions, and they note that men are not subject to any parallel restriction. More fundamentally, they see abortion restrictions as a violation of privacy. In Africa, many feminists battle against forced female circumcision, a painful procedure designed to minimize women's enjoyment of sex.

Relatedly, feminists argue that the burdens of childrearing fall disproportionately on women and that the government should act to eliminate this disparity. In many industrialized democracies, taxpayers provide day-care services to any woman needing them, and many feminists argue that this policy should be widely adopted. Without such a policy in place, most men are able to advance their careers while many women are forced to compromise theirs, inevitably falling behind. State-sponsored child care is one way to spread the burden of this essential social function equally between the sexes. (In Cuba, the nation's Family Code requires both spouses to share equally in housework, although it is not clear that the provision is well enforced.)

Senator Hillary Clinton's historic campaign to become the Democratic Party's 2008 nominee for the U.S. presidency was a very conspicuous indicator of how successful this first type of feminism has been. Although she did not win, millions of Democrats voted for her, including people of both genders, all ethnicities, and in different socioeconomic circumstances. She won important primaries in Ohio, Texas, and California, among many others, and while female voters preferred her virtually everywhere, nearly half of all males in many Democratic primaries voted for her as well. (A majority of men voting in the Ohio, Kentucky, and West Virginia primaries voted for Clinton, for example.) This level of success for a female candidate demonstrates that the mainstream feminists' demands for equality have produced important changes, even if full gender equality remains a challenge.

The second variant of feminism (sometimes termed "radical" or "gender" feminism) generally supports those and other efforts to achieve social and economic equality, but it focuses more on the *differences* between the sexes. Some of these feminists contend that females have greater humanism, are more pacifist, and have a broader ability to nurture than males do, and that these characteristics stem from fundamental biological differences.[9] According to these feminists, the fact that men continue to hold dominant positions in corporations, government, and education suggests that the nature of private and public life is driven by the "male" traits of competition and individualism. Identifying essential feminine characteristics helps us to see that society would become more peaceful, more humane, and more community-oriented if females achieve equal status.

Both strands of feminist thinking will likely grow in importance in the years ahead. At least in the industrial democracies, women have become influential players in national leadership positions, and feminists have acquired a strong voice in academic and policy-making circles. Although it is important to note that feminism embodies a very diverse set of ideas, this ideology will have considerable impact on virtually all areas of public policy in future decades.

Libertarianism

The basic feature of libertarian ideology is its insistence on *liberty* from government control. The movement thus shares some of the views of both liberalism and capitalism. Libertarians oppose laws restricting abortion or the freedoms of religion and expression. They also oppose the military draft, restrictions on drug use, occupational-safety legislation, and most pollution-control laws. They support an isolationist foreign policy, primarily because an active foreign policy usually requires extensive preparations for war, which interfere with personal freedom on many levels.

Libertarians differ sharply, however, with the modern liberals' support of government as a force to create or maintain better conditions for the poor and disadvantaged. For example, most libertarians oppose the minimum wage law. If a person wants to sell his or her labor for $4 per hour, and if an employer wants to buy it at that price, libertarians believe that government has no right to interfere. Moreover, they contend the government has no right to force people to use seat belts in a car or to wear helmets while riding motorcycles. Libertarians disagree with conservatives regarding laws that criminalize marijuana, prostitution, or obscenity.

Thus, both Left and Right are attracted and repelled by **libertarianism**. Both liberals and conservatives support the ideal of privacy in different ways, but each also advocates principles regarding the public interest, and each contains some idea of "civic virtue." Liberals suggest that the public interest requires certain activist social policies, and conservatives argue that the public interest demands the support of traditional values that nurture and preserve culture. In very different ways, then, both liberalism and conservatism advocate an activist government. In contrast, libertarianism will probably always be a limited movement because its ideas cannot incorporate any positive idea of the public interest.

Environmentalism

A great number of people, primarily in developed societies, are deeply concerned about the physical environment, and some of them approach politics and government largely through those concerns. There are many interest groups and at least one well-known political party, the Green Party, for which environmental issues are central. At the beginning of the twenty-first century, **environmentalism** has become large and influential enough to be considered an ideology.

For most people, environmental issues are simply one important issue, to be considered and debated alongside other issues, such as poverty, national defense, economic security, and education. But quite a few citizens in the United States, Western Europe, Japan, and elsewhere are convinced that current threats to the environment are so critical that virtually every policy decision should be made on the basis of its potential impact on the environment. These people are interested not only in specific pollution control plans but also in the globalization of the economy, public transportation, public management of housing patterns, and foreign aid programs, among many other kinds of policies.

The environmental movement focused on fairly specific policy objectives a few decades ago. The publication of Rachel Carson's *Silent Spring* was a landmark event, depicting how pesticides such as DDT had devastated several endangered bird species.[10] Serialized in 1962 in *The New Yorker,* Carson's book eventually led to restrictions on pesticide use. Environmentalists were also key players in the development of regulations on automobile emissions. However, the more recent issue of "global warming" has produced an even more contentious debate, largely because the actions proposed to address the issue would arguably shake the foundations of industrial society.

There is a worldwide movement focused on the issue of global climate change.* In 2007, former Vice President Al Gore, Jr., received an Academy Award for his documentary, *An Inconvenient Truth,* which makes the case for the idea that global warming is caused largely by human activity and that the world's oceans will rise to catastrophic levels in several decades. The film, along with the book it was based on, many other books, speeches, Internet sites, and essays, has helped to make climate change one of the leading issues of the new century. (There is even an Italian opera version of *An Inconvenient Truth* being written for production in Milan in 2011.) Gore also received the Nobel Peace Prize in the same year, also for his work in publicizing the global warming issue. Many scientists and laypersons believe that storms of all kinds will become more severe, droughts will kill millions, and coastal cities will be flooded, and that these tragedies can be averted by controlling industrialization.

However, the issue remains controversial. In October 2007, a British citizen went to court to challenge the public school system's decision to show Gore's film to students. The court ruled that it contains a number of factual errors and misrepresentations, and insisted that the film be presented in classes as "a political work." Several scientists remain unconvinced that human activity is a significant influence.† Others are convinced that humankind can avoid profoundly damaging impacts by making radical changes in the way we use energy. Given the high stakes involved, and the difficulty of constructing definite scientific projections, climate change will be a major political issue for years.

---

* The U.S. Environmental Protection Agency maintains a Web site with a wealth of resources on climate change: http://www.epa.gov/climatechange/.
† Perhaps the most widely cited critic of the climate change concept is Richard Lindzen, a professor of meteorology at the Massachusetts Institute of Technology.

With the demise of communism, a great deal of political energy that was previously expended on class-based revolutionary struggle and other such issues is now being devoted to environmental problems. Left-leaning parties in industrialized countries have incorporated environmental concerns into their platforms, but it is fair to say that environmentalism transcends traditional party lines. In the United States, for example, a substantial number of upper-class voters, many of whom support the Republican Party, have become ardent advocates for environmental preservation, especially wilderness protection. The environmental debate will doubtlessly grow in importance in the years to come.

Fascism

As an ideology, **fascism** is short on intellectual content and long on emotion. All ideologies have an element of emotional appeal, of course; people have been known to wax sentimental over socialism, Marxism, and even capitalism. But fascist thinking seems to thrive on emotion. Fascism is aimed more at the heart than at the mind.

The components of fascism vary with culture and the particular historical context in which it takes root. However, all fascist thinking includes an extreme belief in *political obedience,* a pathological *distrust of foreigners,* and the conviction that *progress is possible only through conquest and war.* The following "Commandments of the Fascist Fighter" capture the essence of fascist ideology: "Whoever is not ready to give himself body and soul for his country and to serve . . . without discussion, is not worthy. . . . Discipline is not only a virtue of the soldiers in the ranks, it must also be the practice of every day. And thank God every day for having made you Fascist and Italian!"[11] Although those statements were written to inspire Benito Mussolini's Fascist movement in Italy in the 1930s, they reflect the general character of fascism: slavish obedience, an appetite for war, and extreme nationalism.

The policy content of fascist ideology is vague, except that it always supports a large military establishment and a sense of "supernationalism." In addition, fascist distrust of foreigners typically promotes racist or ethnic divisions, as when Hitler targeted the Jews as enemies of German culture, when ultra-rightists in South Africa attacked blacks, or when Iraq's Saddam Hussein effectively designated the Kurds as a group to be eliminated. In Europe, where the ideology originated, fascism was historically associated with anti-Semitism and has retained that feature in almost all settings. Fascism clearly rejects the liberal's notion that all people have equal rights that should be protected and enhanced. But fascism does not speak directly to questions regarding economic systems or many specific problems of social policy.

Some have argued that fascism is simply an extreme form of conservatism, since it is primarily driven by a fanatical attraction to the traditions of the dominant culture. Historically, extreme conservatives in Europe and Latin America have on occasion joined forces with fascist movements. Fascism, however, usually destroys the institutions from which the customs and traditions of a society derive. Whereas conservatives often support traditional religious values, fascists usually permit only a state-approved version of religion (or no religion at all) to exist as a source of influence. Fascists also dominate business and economic enterprise, subordinating those private affairs to the needs of the state. Even extreme conservatism thus breaks with fascism;

the elimination of all pillars of traditional society is necessary for fascists but abhorrent to conservatives.*

Given their emphasis on supernationalism and military might, it is not surprising that fascist governments have often brought their countries to disastrous wars. Although people may quibble over which countries may fairly be considered fascist, Hitler's Germany, Mussolini's Italy, and Saddam Hussein's Iraq were arguably fascist states, and all were thoroughly defeated in war.

Islamic Fundamentalism

We normally don't think of religions as political ideologies, and Western religions generally have restricted themselves to the spiritual realm, at least in modern times. But, it should be noted that the Catholic Church has been closely linked to important Christian Democratic political parties in Europe and Latin America and those parties have, in turn, based their ideologies substantially on church teaching. And, the so-called "Christian Right" of American Protestantism has been closely linked to the conservative wing of the Republican Party and other conservative movements. Similarly, leftist politicians such as Jesse Jackson and Al Sharpton have used their religious backgrounds as a base of political support in the Democratic Party.

In the Islamic world there has always been a far closer link between politics and religion. For example, in the Turkish Empire that dominated the Middle East for several centuries, the Caliph was both the temporal ruler of the empire and the top official of the Muslim religion. Today in the Muslim world (stretching from Indonesia to Turkey), there are some countries in which there is a very close linkage between the political and the religious systems (Saudi Arabia and Iran, for example) and others in which there is more of a separation of church and state (Egypt and, especially, Turkey). Adherents of Islam themselves vary from very secular Muslims to fundamentalists who believe that the Koran, the Muslim holy book, must be interpreted literally and that government laws and policies should reflect traditional Islamic values in all aspects of human life.

Just as fundamentalists are a minority of Christian believers in the Western world, Islamic fundamentalists are a minority in the Middle East and other parts of the Muslim world. Moreover, even within the fundamentalist minority, most reject violence and some (including the Saudi royal family) are strongly pro-Western.

Despite their minority status, adherents of fundamentalist beliefs and militant (violent) fundamentalist Islam have multiplied recently in the Middle East and other parts of the Islamic world (most notably in Afghanistan and Pakistan). Militant **Islamic fundamentalism** has the qualities both of a political ideology and of a religious theology. It envisions an ideal political system in which political leaders are inspired by the Koran, in which Western and other non-Islamic values are largely purged from society, and in which citizens are required to live according to traditional Islamic codes. In February 2006, Abdul Rahman, a citizen of Afghanistan who had converted to Christianity, was on trial for his life because of his religious beliefs. U.S. Secretary of

---

* In a highly controversial book, *Liberal Fascism: The Secret History of the American Left, From Mussolini to the Politics of Meaning* (New York: Doubleday, 2008), author Jonah Goldberg argues that fascism arose not from conservative thinking, but from socialist concepts. The many reviews and commentaries on this inflammatory volume may shed more light on the nature of ideology than the book itself does.

© ISNA/AP Photo

IDEOLOGY AND LEADERSHIP   Iranian President Mahmoud Ahmadinejad speaks during a conference on Wednesday October 26, 2005 in Tehran entitled "The World without Zionism." He has said that Israel should be "wiped off the map."

State Condoleezza Rice and others put considerable pressure on the government of Afghanistan, and Rahman was finally released. This incident illustrates the conflict between Islamic fundamentalism and the most basic freedoms associated with democracy.

In some cases, the spread of fundamentalist Islamic beliefs has been driven by bitterness against corrupt and repressive governments (Egypt, Pakistan, Iran, and others), and often this bitterness was extended to the United States and other Western nations. For example, the first Islamic revolution took place in Iran, where the Shah (emperor) had been closely linked to the U.S. Following the revolution, the fundamentalist clergymen who ruled Iran referred to the United States as "the great Satan." Moreover, because Islamic fundamentalist movements were often among the first to risk protesting against those unpopular governments and were willing to go to jail or to die for their political principles, many Muslims came to identify the Islamic fundamentalist movement with real democracy. In many contexts, fundamentalist movements have successfully linked Israel with Western modernization and have used Arab enmity toward Israel to appeal to their countrymen.

The influence of Islamic fundamentalism is apparent in both the domestic and the foreign policies of several nations, and it motivates important political movements that challenge the governments of countries not officially run by fundamentalists. Some contend that this way of thinking is on the wrong side of history, with its anti-modern, anti-democratic features, but others see it as a force that will grow for decades to come. At least for the present, Islamic fundamentalism is an ideology that demands our attention.[12]

Anarchism

The idea of a society without government, or **anarchism**, appears in many different contexts. Some religious traditions contain elements of anarchism in their belief that secular influences (such as government) should be limited or are unnecessary. Some early socialists believed that once private property was eliminated, a common bond would develop among all people, making government obsolete. Serious anarchists consistently paint an idealized picture of human society, one in which community and sharing replace individual interests and competition. In such a world, government becomes a useless relic and is soon discarded.*

More radical anarchists work to destroy government by force and violence. Although usually motivated by some particular concern, violent anarchists put their energy more into destruction than into creating a new order or demanding innovative policies. As an ideology, anarchism is thus profoundly limited, both in practical and in philosophical terms.

CONCLUSION: IDEOLOGY SHAPES POLITICAL COMMUNITY AND POLITICAL CONFLICT

Any overview of ideology will necessarily omit some perspectives or movements that some people consider important. The New Left, certain racially based movements, extreme religious sects, and other approaches to politics also could have been discussed as examples of ideologies. The ideologies considered here are those with the greatest political significance.

Most people are not, strictly speaking, ideologues. The typical citizen rarely thinks about politics in the systematic, philosophical manner characteristic of ideology. Moreover, when most people consider fundamental political principles, they often combine aspects of different ideologies in their thinking. Some people with strong socialist impulses, for example, are also favorable toward certain aspects of capitalism.

Nevertheless, although only a small percentage of citizens are ideologically inclined, appreciating the elements of existing ideologies is a necessary part of learning the language of political life.

 WHERE ON THE WEB?

http://www.sosig.ac.uk/roads/subject-listing/World-cat/polideol.html
Includes links to dozens of other sites relevant to the main ideologies discussed here.

http://www.swif.uniba.it/lei/filpol/filpole/homefpe.htm
An Italian site (in English) that provides a great amount of material related to political philosophy.

http://www.conservative.org
The Web page of the American Conservative Union; includes ratings of members of Congress as measured by the extent to which they vote in accordance with conservative principles.

* Some of the counterculture leaders of the 1960s in the United States and Western Europe articulated heartfelt notions along these lines. In a highly euphoric state, many interpreted the famous Woodstock festival, in which 300,000 people lived together for three days of "peace, love, and music," as confirmation that people could live together without government if they only had the right frame of mind.

http://adaction.org/

The Web page for the Americans for Democratic Action, "the nation's oldest liberal political organization." The ADA is perhaps best known for its rating of members of Congress as measured by the extent to which they vote in accordance with liberal principles.

http://www.thefire.org/

As stated on its Web page, the Foundation for Individual Rights in Education is a "nonprofit educational foundation devoted to free speech, individual liberty, religious freedom, the rights of conscience, legal equality, due process, and academic freedom on our nation's campuses."

http://cc.org/

The Web page of the Christian Coalition, a conservative religious organization with significant political activities in the United States.

http://www.now.org

The Web page of the National Organization for Women, a liberal/feminist political organization based in the United States.

http://www.cwfa.org/

The Web page of the Concerned Women for America, a conservative women's group based in the United States.

http://www.marxists.org/

The "Marxists Internet Archive" contains a great deal of information about Marx, Marxism, and contemporary Marxists.

http://www.mises.org/

The homepage of the Ludwig von Mises Institute, the "research and educational center of classical liberalism, libertarian political theory, and the Austrian School of economics." The organization works to advance the intellectual tradition of Ludwig von Mises (1881–1973). Many modern libertarians have been influenced by the Austrian School.

◆ ◆ ◆

Key Terms and Concepts _____

anarchism
capitalism
communalism
communism
conservatism
deregulation
economic determinism
environmentalism
fascism
feminism
feudalism
ideology

individualism
Islamic fundamentalism
liberalism
libertarianism
Marxism
multiculturalism
primitive communism
postmodernism
socialism
welfare state
Third Way

Discussion Questions _____

1. Give two examples of policy choices or positions associated with liberal and conservative ideology.
2. What is the role of economic analysis in Marxist ideology?
3. Is feminism one ideology or two?
4. What do you think makes some people more rigid than others in their adherence to an ideology?

Notes ──────────

1. See Douglas A. Hibbs, Jr., and Christopher Dennis, "Income Distribution in the United States," *American Political Science Review* 82 (June 1988): 482, 485. A more recent study confirms the pattern, particularly with respect to taxation policy. See Carla Inclan, Dennis P. Quinn, and Robert Y. Shapiro, "Origins and Consequences of Changes in U.S. Corporate Taxation: 1981–1998," *American Journal of Political Science* 45 (January 2001): 179–201.

2. Adam Smith, quoted in Milton Friedman and Rose Friedman, *Free to Choose* (New York: Harcourt Brace Jovanovich, 1980), p. 2.

3. Figures for Germany are taken from Michael J. Sullivan, ed., *Measuring Global Values* (New York: Praeger, 1991), p. 102; and figures for North and South Korea from the *CIA World Factbook,* https://www.cia.gov/library/publications/the-world-factbook/

4. Karl Marx, "A Contribution to the Critique of Political Economy, Preface," in *Marx and Engels: Collected Works,* vol. 29, *Marx: 1858–1861* (New York: International Publishers, 1987), p. 263.

5. Jean-Jacques Rousseau, *The Social Contract and Discourse on the Origins of Inequality,* bk. 1 [1762] (Harmondsworth, England: Penguin, 1968).

6. See Robert Owen's collection of essays titled *A New View of Society* (London: Cadell and Davies, 1813).

7. Thomas R. Dye and Harmon Zeigler, "Socialism and Equality in Cross-National Perspective," *PS: Political Science and Politics* 21 (Winter 1988): 45–56.

8. Data from the 2007–2008 *Human Development Report,* World Bank, available at http://hdrstats.undp.org/indicators/147.html

9. See, for example, Lynne Segal, *Is the Future Female?* (New York: Peter Bedrick, 1988); Adrienne Rich, *Of Woman Born* (London: Virago, 1977); Susan Griffin, *Rape, the Power of Consciousness* (San Francisco: Harper and Row, 1986); Andrea Dworkin, *Pornography: Men Possessing Women* (New York: Putnam, 1981); Nancy J. Hirschmann, "Freedom, Recognition, and Obligation: A Feminist Approach to Political Theory," *American Political Science Review* 83 (1989): 1227–1244; and Mary L. Shanley and Carole Pateman, *Feminist Interpretations and Political Theory* (College Park: Penn State Press, 1991). For a controversial and very different view, see Christina Hoff Sommers, *Who Stole Feminism? How Women Have Betrayed Women* (New York: Simon & Schuster, 1994).

10. Rachel Carson, *Silent Spring* (New York: Mariner Press, 1994; originally published 1962).

11. Cited in Roy C. Macridis, *Contemporary Political Ideologies,* 2nd ed. (Boston: Little, Brown, 1983), p. 204.

12. A new book on Islamic fundamentalism provides excellent historical background and informed analysis. See Mansoor Moaddel, *Islamic Modernism, Nationalism, and Fundamentalism.* Chicago: University of Chicago Press, 2005.

For Further Reading ──────────

Anderson, Charles W. *Pragmatic Liberalism.* Chicago: University of Chicago Press, 1990.

Burke, Edmund. *Reflections on the Revolution in France.* Chicago: Henry Regnery, 1955.

Carson, Rachel. *Silent Spring.* New York: Mariner Press, 1994. Originally published 1962.

Crick, Bernard. *In Defense of Politics,* 2nd ed. Chicago: University of Chicago Press, 1972.

Critchlow, Donald. 2007. *The Conservative Ascendancy: How the GOP Right Made Political History.* Cambridge, MA: Harvard University Press.

Dworkin, Andrea. *Pornography: Men Possessing Women.* New York: Putnam, 1981.

Euben, Roxanne L. *Enemy in the Mirror: Islamic Fundamentalism and the Limits of Modern Rationalism.* Princeton, NJ: Princeton University Press, 1999.

Harrison, Lawrence E. 2006. *The Central Liberal Truth: How Politics Can Change a Culture and Save It From Itself.* New York: Oxford University Press.

Hashmi, Sohail H. *Islamic Political Ethics: Civil Society, Pluralism, and Conflict.* Princeton, NJ: Princeton University Press, 2002.

Hirsch, H. N. *A Theory of Liberty.* New York: Routledge, 1992.

Hitler, Adolf. *Mein Kampf.* Translated by Ralph Manheim. Boston: Houghton Mifflin, 1943.

Jumonville, Neil, and Kevin Mattson, eds. 2007. *Liberalism for a New Century.* Berkeley: University of California Press.

Kelly, Nathan J. 2005. "Political Choice, Public Policy, and Distributional Outcomes," *American Journal of Political Science,* Vol. 49 (October): 865–880.

Kirk, Russell. *The Portable Conservative Reader.* London: Penguin, 1982.

Knight, Jack, and James Johnson. 2007. "The Priority of Democracy: A Pragmatist Approach to Political-Economic Institutions and the Burden of Justification," *American Political Science Review*, Vol. 101 (February): 47–61.

Lenin, V. I. *State and Revolution.* New York: International Publishers, 1932.

———. *Imperialism: The Highest Stage of Capitalism.* New York: International Publishers, 1939.

Linebaugh, Peter. *The Magna Carta Manifesto: Liberties and Commons for All.* Berkeley: University of California Press, 2008.

Meyer, Alfred G. *Leninism.* New York: Praeger, 1957.

———. *Communism,* 4th ed. New York: Random House, 1984.

Mill, John Stuart. *On Liberty and Considerations on Representative Government.* Fair Haven, NJ: Oxford University Press, 1933.

Moaddel, Mansoor. *Islamic Modernism, Nationalism, and Fundamentalism.* Chicago: University of Chicago Press, 2005.

Pettit, Philip. *Contemporary Political Theory.* New York: Macmillan, 1991.

Rahe, Paul. A. 2008. *Against Throne and Altar: Machiavelli and Political Theory Under the English Republic.* New York: Cambridge University Press.

Roy, Oliver. *The Failure of Political Islam.* Cambridge: Harvard University Press, 1998.

Sandel, Michael J. *Justice.* New York: Oxford University Press, 2007.

Shapiro, Ian. *The State of Democratic Theory.* Princeton, NJ: Princeton University Press, 2003.

Susser, Bernard. *Approaches to the Study of Politics.* New York: Macmillan, 1992.

Thiele, Leslie Paul. *Thinking Politics,* 2nd ed. New York: Chatham House, 2003.

Wolin, Sheldon S. *Politics and Vision,* expanded edition. Princeton, NJ: Princeton University Press, 2006.

PART II

POLITICAL BEHAVIOR

A society's beliefs, values, and resulting behavior shape the way its political system works and affect its prospects for the future. Nearly all political systems have an identifiable political culture—sometimes several *conflicting* political cultures, as explored in Chapter 3. Political culture influences what people expect from politics, what kind of role they feel they should have in government decisions, and the rights they demand. Chapter 4 focuses on elections and public opinion. Elections are increasingly common in political life everywhere, but the behavior of voters in different countries varies dramatically. Some people choose not to vote, and those who do are influenced by a number of important factors that help us predict voter choices. Finally, Chapters 5 and 6 address political parties and interest groups. Parties and interest groups provide the population with additional opportunities for political participation, and understanding their impact on political systems is a central problem in political science.

SPREADING FUNDAMENTALIST CULTURE   A boy awaits classes in front of a *madrasa*, or Islamic school, outside of Peshawar, Pakistan, a city largely populated by Afghan refugees at that time (2001). Many of the fundamentalist *madrasas* for refugees were funded by the Saudi government. Subsequently, many of their graduates became Taliban activists.

3

POLITICAL CULTURE AND SOCIALIZATION

◆ Political Culture: Origins of the Concept ◆ Agents of Political Socialization ◆ Classifying Political Cultures ◆ The Evolution of Political Cultures ◆ The Utility of Political Culture

For many people, one of the most exciting and interesting aspects of foreign travel is the opportunity to observe and interact with cultures that are very different from their own. For example, it is impolite to shake somebody's hand in Bangkok, where people are accustomed to greeting others by holding their own palms together at chest or face level (with that exchange initiated by the person of inferior social status). A visitor to Saudi Arabia and Pakistan soon notes that these cultures assign women far more restrictive behavior, employment, and dress than in the West. Other cultural values are less immediately obvious. Indians and Colombians are more likely than Canadians are to judge people based on their caste or class origins. Survey research reveals that the percentage of the population that believes that "most people can be trusted" is much higher in the United States and Britain than in Chile or Romania, but substantially lower than in Sweden or Finland.[1]

People coming from different cultures may hold dissimilar views regarding the value of voting in national elections, their willingness to live near people of different races or ethnicities, the level of free speech they would allow political dissidents, and a host of other politically relevant issues. Nations or regions also vary in the extent to which their populations follow politics or are informed about key political leaders and institutions.

A **political culture** is defined as "a people's predominant beliefs, attitudes, values, ideals, sentiments, and evaluations about the political system of its country, and the role of the self in that system."[2] It includes a society's level of political knowledge as well as its evaluations of the political system and its institutions. But it also encompasses attitudes toward family, neighbors, religion, and other values and feelings that shape and influence people's political outlook.

Political cultures vary both between and within individual nations. For example, Russians are more skeptical than Australians about the advantages of democracy. The French are more inclined to follow politics than are the citizens of Bhutan. Southern Italians tend to be more suspicious of elected officials than northerners are. While these differences are surely important, political scientists disagree about how well we can actually measure differences between political cultures, what the relationship is between political culture and political behavior, and what limits a nation's political culture imposes on its political system. In short, for many years scholars have debated the question, "Does political culture matter?" Or, perhaps more precisely, "How much does political culture matter?"[3]

Those who believe in the importance of political culture argue that cultural values affect vital issues, such as the likelihood of a specific country or a region establishing or maintaining democracy. Thus, for example, many political scientists argue that the reason so few Muslim nations are democratic is that many Islamic cultural values contradict democratic standards. Specifically, they point to Islam's merger of Church and State and the limits many Islamic nations put on women's political and social participation (see Box 3-3).

Gabriel Almond, one of the first scholars to study political culture cross-nationally, noted that "political culture affects governmental structure and performance—constrains it, but surely does not determine it."[4] But scholars still debate the degree of influence culture has over political behavior. Similarly, they disagree about how extensively a nation may change its own or some other political culture in a relatively short period of time. "Culturalists" point to elements of German and Japanese political culture that they feel contributed to the rise of militarism and authoritarianism in both countries in the years leading up to World War II. Critics, pointing to the great cultural shift in those two countries *after* the war, argue that political culture is more malleable than culturalists admit, and insist that new political institutions (such as competitive elections) can change popular attitudes and values relatively quickly. Today, the United States' efforts to democratize Iraq depend heavily on the extent to which it can help Iraqis to develop a democratic political culture.

In discussing a political culture or subculture, the unit we analyze may be a country, a portion of a country, a continent, or a religion. Thus, we may speak about European political culture (assuming that the region has important common values that are distinguishable from those of other continents or regions), Irish political culture (presumably different from, say, Italy's), and Irish Catholic political culture (as opposed to Irish Protestant political values). Similarly, there may be values in American political culture—including a belief in equality of opportunity and a pragmatic (rather than ideologically determined) approach to solving political problems—that distinguish it from Colombian or Indian culture. At the same time, although Americans share many common values, the country also encompasses distinct Southern, Midwestern, Evangelical, and Chicano **political subcultures,** each with its own distinguishing characteristics.

We study political culture because it helps us understand political life. For example, why do different ethnic groups cooperate reasonably well in Switzerland but not in Bosnia or Lebanon? Why are Russians more inclined than Canadians to support an all-powerful political leader? Why has political corruption been a serious and long-standing problem in Mexico but not in Chile? Political culture may provide at least partial answers.

Although ideology (Chapter 2), political culture, and public opinion (Chapter 4) all explain how people feel about politics, they are distinct concepts. Ideologies reflect *intellectual efforts*—often identified with political philosophers, such as Locke or Marx— to achieve an ideal society. In contrast, political culture encompasses the actual *values, attitudes, and beliefs* that most people hold in a society. Thus, although many Americans lack a well-defined ideology, their political knowledge (or lack of interest), attitudes, and values contribute to their society's political culture.

Even though political culture and public opinion both measure people's feelings, they also are distinct concepts. Public opinion reflects short-term outlooks, such as how French citizens rate their president or what Americans want government to do about high gas prices. Such opinions normally vary considerably within a country and may change from month to month. For example, shortly after the 2003 U.S. invasion of Iraq, over 70 percent of Americans polled by the Pew Research Center supported that intervention. By early 2005, however, a growing majority said that the invasion had been a mistake.[5] Political culture, on the other hand, measures a society's more deep-seated values, such as what role people feel organized religion should play in politics or how tolerant citizens are of people holding very different political views— attitudes that are more deeply held and slower to change than public opinion. But as we will see, political cultures are not entirely static. They do change over time, and sometimes that change can be accelerated.

POLITICAL CULTURE: ORIGINS OF THE CONCEPT

Decades ago, as political scientists expanded their understanding of other political systems, they realized that institutions such as political parties or national legislatures operate differently from one society to the next, even when they are structured in similar ways.

Moreover, they observed that particular forms of political behavior, such as voting, often have different meanings for, say, Mexicans or Russians than for Icelanders or Costa Ricans. So merely studying political parties, the bureaucracy, or interest-group membership does not afford a full understanding of a nation's political processes. We also need to consider the cultural foundations upon which political systems operate.

Just as anthropologists and psychologists once analyzed the "national character" of countries such as Germany or Japan, political scientists today analyze political cultures, asking questions such as these: Do Chinese citizens value a free press as much as the Swiss do? Do South Africans trust their fellow citizens? Do Kenyans feel that they can influence their political system? Answers to such questions offer important insights into the nature of various political systems and help us predict change.

It is also important to recognize, however, that *within a single nation there is usually a degree of cultural diversity.* When we describe the Nigerian and Indian political cultures in a certain way, we are not claiming that *all* Nigerians and *all* Indians have the same beliefs. We are merely identifying certain distinctive national patterns while acknowledging substantial variation within each country's borders.

Moreover, not only do *individuals* in any society vary in their political values, but *groups* within a society also often have distinctive political orientations. As we have seen, any political culture may include a number of political subcultures. In the United States, for example, there is a national political culture encompassing our society's general political value system. There are, however, also distinctive political subcultures in different regions of the country, and among African-Americans, Hispanics, Whites, Catholics, Jews, Muslims, and Southern Baptists. A healthy political system, which both respects diversity and imposes broad guidelines on everyone, can accommodate such differences. If, however, regional, religious, ethnic, or other subcultures become so different that no discernible "national" culture seems to exist—as still seems true in Iraq among its Shi'ite, Sunni, and Kurd populations—political stability is likely to be threatened.

In studying various groups in society, political scientists need to ascertain which attitudinal or behavioral differences grow out of diverse cultural patterns and which simply reflect different realities. For example, survey research reveals that poor Mexicans have less confidence in their country's legal system than do their middle- or upper-class counterparts and they are also less likely to sign political petitions.[6] Are these attitudes a reflection of a distinct working-class political culture? In other words, do poor Mexicans have less trust in the courts or less confidence in their ability to influence politics because they often grew up in authoritarian families, where the fathers' views went unchallenged, or because they were never taught to participate in politics? Or, more likely, do their attitudes simply mirror the harsh reality that Mexican government officials (including judges) are less likely to give poor citizens a fair hearing?

Of course, change in objective conditions can produce changes in political culture, which in turn lead to changes in the way the government works. As the educational levels of South Koreans and Mexicans rose in the last decades of the twentieth century, and as more of them entered the middle class, their political values changed. As citizens of these countries became more educated, affluent, and urban, they began to demand a more open political system, forcing their authoritarian governments to democratize.

Historical factors—particularly dramatic events such as wars, revolutions, and economic depressions—can also alter a nation's political culture. For example, the Great

Depression of the 1920s and 1930s convinced many Americans and Europeans of the need for greater government intervention in the economy (guaranteeing bank savings, for example, and providing Social Security). Such historical events often continue to influence the political behavior and the political system long after they are over. From World War II through the 1970s, the role of government (as measured by its percentage of the GNP) grew substantially in Europe and the U.S., as citizens, many of whom grew up in the depression, sought the protective blanket of government social welfare programs. Since the 1970s, however, new generations of voters have emerged who were raised in the growing prosperity of the 1950s–1970s and who are less concerned about having a government safety net, at least until the 2008 financial crisis.

Even more profoundly, the Nazi era had an enduring impact on German political culture. In their landmark study of political culture, Gabriel Almond and Sidney Verba discovered that in the decades after World War II, even though West Germans were more likely than Mexicans to expect fair treatment from local government officials, they were less proud of their political institutions. Moreover, despite their higher educational level, Germans felt less obligated than did Mexicans to participate in local politics. The Germans' more negative view of government probably reflected a wariness stemming from their country's Nazi past. Mexicans, in contrast, although critical of specific government behavior, expressed general pride in their political system, reflecting the stability and nationalism that emerged from their 1910 revolution.[7] Since that study was completed, further historical changes have made Germans far more confident of their democracy. But even today, Germany's political culture remains influenced by events that occurred more than 60 years ago. For example, most Germans oppose foreign military involvement because of their country's suffering in World War II and the international notoriety that Nazi brutality had brought them. Thus, Germany refused to join U.S. and British troops in Iraq and, although the country has deployed over 3,000 troops to Afghanistan, it has limited their service to the northern part of the country where fighting is less intense than in the south. Even so, opinion polls indicate that most Germans want those troops removed.

Political culture is a simple concept, but it can easily be misunderstood. The fact that we may characterize a given nation's culture in some way should not lead us to underestimate the importance of diverse subcultures within it. Similarly, the fact that political culture may be an explanatory factor should not lead us to overlook the possibility that objective conditions within a country may be responsible for behavior often attributed to culture.

AGENTS OF POLITICAL SOCIALIZATION

How do individual citizens in any country acquire the values and feelings that constitute their political culture? **Political socialization** is the process of shaping and transmitting a political culture. It involves the transfer of political values from one generation to another and usually entails changes over time that lead to a gradual transformation of the culture.[8]

Agents of political socialization are individuals, groups, or institutions that transmit political values to each generation. Obviously, the importance of specific socialization agents differs from culture to culture and from individual to individual. Nevertheless, the following agents are important in virtually every society.

The Family

As in so many other aspects of life, the family is the first, and frequently the most important, source of political values. For example, in the United States and Japan, people tend to vote for the political party their parents supported.[9] But the political influence of family goes far beyond the development of partisan identification. In Argentina or Russia, many young people at the dinner table repeatedly hear their parents complain about corrupt politicians and, as a consequence, often become cynical about political participation. Meanwhile, in the Netherlands, parents may depict political involvement as a nobler calling.

Because the family exerts its influence from such an early age, when people are most impressionable, some political scientists view the family as the most critical agent for transmitting broad moral and political values during a person's formative years. "Other individuals may have profound influence on a person's political outlook, but none of them is typically credited with as much influence as the child's parents."[10] As people advance toward middle age, however, they are more prone to develop some values and orientations that are distinct from those of their parents.[11]

Family impact seems to be greatest in cultures such as our own, where people often discuss politics at home. In nations such as France (where there are fewer political conversations at home) or China (where the state, at least until recently, has played a dominant role in the socialization process), the family may have less political importance.

Education

From their kindergarten days making Thanksgiving decorations, through high school civics and college political science courses, most American students acquire important political values from the educational system: patriotism, the importance of voting, or the value of constitutional rights, for example. In communist nations such as Cuba, schools have been an important agent for socializing youth into the values of Marxism-Leninism. Similarly, during the long struggle to free Afghanistan from Soviet occupation, the Saudi government established schools in Afghanistan and in the many Afghan refugee camps across the border in Pakistan. Those schools taught a fundamentalist version of Islam, called Wahhabi and helped give birth to the Taliban, the army of religious extremists that eventually seized control of Afghanistan after the Afghans had ousted the Soviets from their country. The Taliban subsequently hosted Osama bin Laden and al-Qaeda at the time of the 9/11 attack. Today it battles U.S. and NATO troops in Afghanistan and has spread its insurgency into neighboring Pakistan.

Peer Groups

Although family and school are the most influential early influences on political values, the socialization process continues into our adult years. As people grow older, their political values are influenced by their friends and co-workers. During adolescence, peers compete with parents and teachers as the most important source of values.[12] The impact of friends and co-workers seems to be especially strong in economically developed societies, where the influence of family elders, kinship groups, or religion is weaker than in Third World nations. As we will see (Box 3-1), even membership in social clubs and bowling leagues may influence the political culture.

Box 3-1

SOCIAL CAPITAL, TRUST, AND BOWLING ALONE

From his extensive study of Italian politics over a 20-year period, Robert Putnam and his associates concluded that there were marked differences in the quality of performance by the country's regional governments and that those disparities could be linked to cultural and historical factors. Regional governments were more effective and better able to stimulate economic growth in northern Italy than in the south. Furthermore, Putnam found that these differences in political and economic performance reflected the degree of civic engagement by each region's citizens, including their interest in furthering the good of the community rather than just the welfare of their families and friends.

People in the northern, more civic-minded regions were more likely to belong to local associations, ranging from sports clubs to associations of bird watchers, causing them to interact with others in their community and to work cooperatively with them. A region's "**social capital**" was a measure of the density of associational involvement in a town, region, or country and the norms and social trust that these group activities produced.[13]

Regions or communities with high levels of social capital, according to Putnam's research, produced citizens who were more law abiding and more trustful of their neighbors, including those whom they did not know very well. These attitudes, in turn were conducive to effective democratic government. But not all involvement in clubs, associations, or groups produces social capital, argued Putnam. Relationships between members must be "horizontal"—between relative equals. If, however, relationships are "vertical"—with a top-down, hierarchical structure like the Mafia in Sicily—such group membership does not build social capital. Since Russia, Romania, and other post-communist nations had no network of *independent* clubs and groups (all were previously under government control), social capital and, hence, trust, is very low in those nations.

In his best-selling book, *Bowling Alone*, Putnam notes that the United States has always enjoyed a dense network of groups, clubs, and associations. But while it still compares well with many other nations, "the vibrancy of American civil society has notably declined over the past few decades."[14] For example, more and more Americans have preferred to "bowl alone" or with a small number of friends and family members,

while they have been less inclined to bowl in leagues, where they could network with people whom they don't know as well. Thus, between 1980 and 1993, the number of bowlers in the U.S. increased by 10 percent, but the number of people in bowling leagues *decreased* by 40 percent (and that decline continued into the twenty-first century). There have been similarly sharp declines in the past 30 to 50 years in the number of Americans belonging to parent-teacher associations (PTAs), the League of Women Voters, the Red Cross, the Shriners, and the Masons, as well as fewer adult volunteers for the Boy Scouts. Putnam maintains that all of these changes reflect a broader decline in social engagement.

It is true that some organizations have increased their membership greatly during this period, including the American Association of Retired Persons (AARP) and the National Organization for Women (NOW). But unlike the associations just mentioned, with sharply declining memberships, these expanding organizations involve little or no face-to-face contacts between members. And despite gains by some groups, total membership in associations declined by almost 30 percent from 1967 to 1993, a trend that has continued since.

The reasons for the decline in groups such as the PTA and bowling leagues are complex and varied: many people are busier with their careers; watching television and DVDs, playing video games, surfing the Web, and other relatively solitary activities have become more prevalent; and traditional families, which are often the hubs of associational activity (Boy Scouts, PTA) have been weakened by rising divorce rates and the increased numbers of people who elect to postpone or avoid marriage.

Whatever the reasons (and there are others), Putnam argues that America's stock of social capital has eroded, a decline that has significant social and political consequences. During the past 40 years or so, as fewer people have joined associations that bring them into contact with new people, as people less frequently invite neighbors to their homes for dinner, and as the percentage of Americans attending church has declined modestly since the 1950s, the percentage of people who give to charity and the share of total

(Continued)

Box 3-1

SOCIAL CAPITAL, TRUST, AND BOWLING ALONE
(Continued)

national income given to charity has also declined. It is equally disconcerting that during the last decades of the twentieth century, the percentage of people who had worked for a political party fell 42 percent, the proportion of those who had attended a political rally or speech declined by 34 percent, and the percentage who had written to their congressman or senator fell by 23 percent. At the same time Americans have become less trustful of each other. Moreover, states with the highest social capital (such as South Dakota, Minnesota, and Vermont) tend to have significantly higher rates of compliance with tax laws (i.e., lower rates of criminal charges brought by the IRS), higher levels of tolerance for racial and gender equality, and lower mortality rates (people who belong to clubs have a higher life expectancy than those who don't) than do states with the lowest levels of social capital (Nevada, Mississippi, and Georgia). They also have school systems that are more effective. These findings suggest to Putnam and others that the growing tendency of Americans to "bowl alone" and reduce social contacts with co-workers or neighbors is troublesome for American democracy and civil society.

A recent book by Russell J. Dalton discusses a somewhat related phenomenon in 18 advanced, industrial democracies. Data from the World Values Survey and the Eurobarometer shows that in 16 of those 18 nations there has been a clear decline in citizen support for and trust in their country's political institutions (such as Parliament or Congress). Such declines were frequently not related to government performance or contemporary events. For example, in the United States:

> In ... 1966, with the war in Vietnam raging and race riots in Cleveland, Chicago, and Atlanta, 66 percent of Americans *rejected* the view that "the people running the country don't really care what happens to you." In ... 1997, after America's cold war victory and in the midst of the longest period of peace and prosperity in more than two generations, [only] 57 per cent of Americans *endorsed* the same view.[15]

Similar declines in support for government, the courts, and other government institutions took place in almost all advanced democracies during those three decades (and continued into the twenty-first century). For example, the percentage of Swedes who expressed confidence in their parliament declined from 51 percent in 1986 to 19 percent in 1996. Despite growing public distrust of government, the level of support for democracy as the best form of government has remained high (or even risen) in all 18 nations, ranging from a high of 99 percent support in Denmark and 97 percent support in Iceland, Austria, and West Germany to a low (within this group) of 78 percent in Britain and 86 to 87 percent in the Netherlands and the U.S.[16] Still, Dalton and others argue that if distrust of government and negative evaluations of government institutions continues to grow, this trend could well undermine democracy.

Thus, for example, since growing cynicism about government is associated with reduced participation in politics, a vicious cycle can develop whereby politicians, who are less closely scrutinized by a "turned-off" citizenry, become less responsible to the voters and generate further political apathy. Furthermore, survey research across these nations indicates that citizens who express lower trust in and support for the political system reveal a somewhat greater willingness to cheat on their tax payments and to break the law more generally. They are also less willing to fulfill civic duties such as sitting on juries.[17] All of these data suggest that growing alienation from the political system should be a cause for concern.

Survey data also indicate that dramatic events such as corruption scandals in Italy and Japan, or Watergate and the Vietnam War in the United States, did not fully account for this increased political distrust. Although there are multiple causes of greater political dissatisfaction, ironically it appears that two important reasons are increased educational levels and growing concern for "post-material" issues such as protecting the environment and promoting gender equality (see Box 3-5 on post-materialism). The evidence suggests that post-materialists (those more concerned about issues like those just named rather than in their own material interests) and more educated citizens are more likely to have higher expectations of government. Consequently, they are more disappointed with the political system if it fails to meet those standards. At the same time, post-materialists (who are generally more educated) express the highest level of support for civil liberties such as free speech.

The Media

In advanced industrialized societies, people receive much of their political information and many of their political values from the mass media. Newspapers, news magazines, and especially radio and television play an increasingly important role in transmitting political culture. In some countries young children and adolescents typically spend several hours daily in front of the television set. One study of nearly two thousand American high school seniors concluded that the mass media equaled parents in importance as an agent of political socialization.[18] In recent years, U.S. radio talk shows have become a potent influence on adults' political values. The Internet is now also a major source of political ideas and values, particularly among young adults (see Box 3-2). Even in developing nations radios are fairly universal, and in many Third World countries increasing numbers of people have access to television. Well aware of television's potential for shaping political values, the Cuban government has supplied a free television set to most recipients of public housing. The spread of television in many societies has tended to homogenize political culture—that is, to reduce regional or urban-rural differences. Laurence Wylie's classic study of small-town France several decades ago indicated that villagers were quite suspicious of outsiders and distrusted national politicians.[19] Subsequent research indicated that, more generally, the French tended to close themselves off from influences outside their extended family and were less likely than other Western Europeans or Americans to join political organizations.[20] In recent decades, however, the spread of television has helped break down regional and urban-rural cultural differences.[21] Survey research indicates that the French are far less distrustful today than they were two or three decades ago of people outside their circle of friends and family.[22]

Business and Professional Associations, the Military, Labor Unions, and Religious Groups

Unlike schools, these organizations are all examples of "secondary groups"—organizations that people join for a common goal. Like the family, schools, and the media, their primary role is not to influence political values. Yet each of these groups may exert substantial political influence over its members. That influence may be direct, as when business groups distribute material to their members criticizing government intervention in the economy. Or it may be indirect, as when the leaders of a religious group promote patriarchal (male-dominant) family values. Traditionally, the Catholic Church in Latin America and parts of Europe, Judaism in Israel, as well as Islamic religious institutions in the Middle East, North Africa, and parts of South Asia have exercised an especially strong influence over those regions' political cultures. In Israel, which has nearly universal military service for young men and women, the armed forces have effectively integrated generations of young immigrants into the nation's political culture. The military often plays a similar role in the Third World, socializing recruits into national values.

Voting patterns in countries such as Chile and Italy illustrate the influence of secondary groups. In both countries, men generally have been more likely than women to support leftist political parties, while women have been more likely to support the Christian Democratic Party or other centrist or right-wing parties. A major cause of that gender gap has been the influence of two agents of

---

Box 3-2

Is the Spread of Information Technology Helping or Hurting Political Participation?—Generation Y

Over the past few decades in the United States and a number of other Western democracies, interest and participation in national politics seem to have declined. The most dramatic evidence is the fall in voter turnout (the percentage of eligible voters who actually vote) over the past 50 years in countries such as the United States, Great Britain, France, Italy, Portugal, Finland and the Netherlands.[23] There are many reasons for this trend, and they vary from country to country. For example, voter turnout dropped sharply—and not surprisingly—when the Netherlands abolished a legal requirement to vote. However, many political scientists have suggested that broad voter apathy or even antipathy toward politics and politicians plays a role. Numerous opinion surveys indicate that voters in Western democracies have become more negative about the political process, more cynical about government, and more suspicious of political leaders. At the same time, people are losing faith in the political parties, causing the level of party membership to fall significantly.

Most political analysts are concerned about these trends. If many people are tuning out politics and voter turnout is declining, then election results might only be reflecting the views of portions of the population who vote more regularly (older voters, more affluent voters), while inadequately representing others who don't (younger voters, minority groups, the poor). Furthermore, if the public is disinterested in politics, elected officials are likely to be less accountable to their constituents. These concerns are most acute regarding younger citizens (aged 18–25), the demographic group that has been least likely to vote, join a political party, or follow politics.

These issues point to the importance of political socialization and the creation of a participant political culture. The way in which young adults are

socialized and the values they develop may follow them throughout their lives. The evidence suggests that in the United States and countries such as the United Kingdom, Italy, and Ireland, as newspaper circulation and television news audiences decline, the influence of **information and communications technology (ICT)** has surged.[24] ICT—particularly the Internet, but also texting and podcasting—has been of particular importance to younger citizens. These technologies provide young adults with an enormous and growing portion of their political information and values. In fact, Barack Obama first announced who his running-mate would be in text and e-mail messages. Furthermore, the share of the population in developed democracies who participate in the digital revolution will only grow over the years.

Some scholars argue that ICT offers tremendous opportunities for mobilizing political participation and overcoming voter apathy. Others question how much these new technologies will contribute to a more participatory political culture and even see potential dangers in digital forms of political socialization. The first group argues that if political leaders and commentators wish to reach the **"Generation Y,"** also known as "Echo Boomers" or "the Millennium Generation" (those born roughly between 1978 and 2000 who are coming of age in the early decades of the twenty-first century) they need to communicate with them through their media of choice—the Web, podcasts, and the like. At the same time, these so-called **"techno-enthusiasts"** insist, ICT has substantial advantages as an agent of political socialization. Unlike television, radio and the press, which only allow one-way (top-down) communications between politicians and the public, the Internet and text messaging allow young citizens to communicate with their political leaders and with each other.

---

socialization—labor unions and the church. Since men are more likely than women to work in factories or other sites where labor is well organized, they are more likely to belong to unions. In both Chile and Italy unions tend to support the Left. In contrast, more women than men are devout Catholics. Consequently they were more influenced by the Christian Democratic or other Center-Right orientations of most parish priests.

ICT supporters argue that this allows Generation Y and future generations to develop a more participatory view of democracy. Furthermore, these analysts maintain that it will raise levels of participation eventually. Studies have also found that members of Generation Y are more receptive than their elders were to opinions and information from friends and peers and are less likely to follow the views of "experts." All of these factors, the techno-enthusiasts argue, are producing higher levels of political involvement among young adults.

Critics of that perspective have marshaled a number of arguments. They point out that during the first decade or so after the explosion of Web usage in the United States, voter turnout among those aged 18–24 continued to fall and continued to lag far behind participation by older voters. Thus, in the 2000 presidential election (Bush vs. Gore), turnout among citizens aged 25 and older was 63 percent (itself a low figure when compared to most European nations), while among people aged 18–24 a mere 36 percent managed to vote, close to a record low. Looking at the data somewhat differently, in the 1972 presidential election, young voters cast roughly one-seventh of the total vote (14.2 percent). By the 2000 election (the first presidential election for Generation Y), after nearly three decades of steady decline, that age group contributed only 1/13th of the total votes (7.8 percent).[25] This seemed to suggest that expanded use of the Internet in the 1990s did not increase political participation by young citizens. Small wonder that critics argued that "the Internet [merely] reinforces existing trends. It may be more than a blip, but it falls far short of being a revolution."[26]

It is possible, however, that these critics spoke too early. More recent evidence indicates that Generation Y's political participation and civic involvement are now on the rise. For example, surveys by the U.S. Government's Corporation for National and Community Service revealed that volunteerism by college students increased by 20 percent between 2002 and 2005. Similarly, between the 2000 and 2004 presidential elections,

turnout among young adults (18–24) jumped sharply—from 36 percent to 47 percent—reaching one of the highest rates since 1952. Young voter turnout in 2006 (including congressional elections) was also up from recent mid-term (non-presidential) elections and was among the highest in recent decades. Finally, in 2008 the rate of young voter participation in the first 39 state primaries and caucuses increased phenomenally, more than doubling the 2004 turnout.[27] Supporters of Barack Obama have provided the lion's share of that turnout. They not only have voted in huge numbers but have been key participants in his grassroots organization. The Internet, particularly YouTube has played an important tool in that mobilization.

In short, there is considerable recent evidence to support the techno-enthusiasts belief that ICT has been a positive socializing agent in promoting political participation among younger voters. Skeptics worry that, while political communication through such social networks as MySpace and Facebook has its value, young citizens may be overly prone to accept their peers' opinions at the expense of input from older experts. They believe that expert analyses of the candidates in outlets such as PBS's *News Hour with Jim Lehrer* or in the *Los Angeles Times* or *Washington Post* are far more informative than opinions expressed on MySpace. Others fear that Web-based political socialization puts greater stress on personality and charm than on issues. For example, some maintain that Barack Obama's meteoric rise to national prominence had more to do with his charisma and oratory skills than with his initially ill-defined policy prescriptions. Obama's ICT outreach is symbolized by people such as at Chris Hughes, the 24-year-old cofounder of Facebook, who left that company in 2007 to work full-time on Obama's media campaign. Finally, many critics agree that ICT is having a powerful influence on political socialization and participation, but worry about the "digital divide" separating those who have the resources and skills to access ICT and those, particularly the poor, who do not.

CLASSIFYING POLITICAL CULTURES

Survey research on culture (including political culture) has produced a gold mine of information that can be invaluable at cocktail parties or in trivia games. We know, for example, that among western and southern Europeans, the Irish are most prone to feel that divorce can *never* be justified, whereas the Danes and the French are most likely to accept it. The Netherlands and Denmark have the highest percentage of respondents who said that they were "very happy," while Portugal and Greece have the lowest.[28] Although such facts are interesting, what do they tell us about the political process? How do different cultures cause their governments to behave differently?

When Almond and Verba wrote their landmark study of political culture, *The Civic Culture*, they did more than merely describe the political knowledge, values, and beliefs of the five countries that they had studied (the United States, Great Britain, West Germany, Italy, and Mexico). Beyond that, they examined which political values are most compatible with democracy. As many Third World nations have found, simply copying political institutions from the West is not enough to produce stable democracy. "A democratic form of participatory political system requires as well a political culture consistent with it."[29]

Much of the subsequent research on political culture has examined the compatibility of a nation's values with desired political goals. For example, this book's discussions of politics in selected nations (Chapters 11 to 17) note that political values in the United States and Great Britain support democratic practices and institutions better than the political cultures in Russia and China do. Indeed, both of the latter countries have held authoritarian values that long preceded the rise of communism.

Similarly, political scientists have often examined the relationship between political culture and political stability. If people distrust one another or if they are sharply divided along class, racial, religious, or ethnic lines, their prospects for political stability in that society diminish. Northern Ireland, Lebanon, Rwanda, Bosnia, and Iraq come to mind. In turn, a nation clearly needs some level of stability in order for democracy to take hold. On the other hand, China's political cultures and Mexico's until recently may have placed so high a value on stability that many citizens rejected democratic protests (such as Tiananmen Square) because they feared that they would create disorder.

As we have noted, the core values of a political culture change more slowly than public opinion does. For example, American support for the war in Iraq declined sharply in only two years after the invasion. Similarly, candidates for office may start their campaigns with wide public support only to see that support evaporate by Election Day. Basic cultural values, however, normally take years or even generations to change. More than half a century ago, European sociologist Gunnar Myrdal noted "an American dilemma," a disconnect in U.S. political culture between its commitment to the fundamental equality of all citizens and its persistent racial prejudices.[30] Even though American racial attitudes have changed significantly since that time and institutionalized racism has been greatly reduced, racial prejudice continues to linger in our culture. Barack Obama's success in the Democratic primaries and caucuses showed how much American racial attitudes have changed. But the significant minority of White voters in states such as Mississippi, Pennsylvania, and West Virginia who admitted to pollsters that they would not vote for a Black presidential candidate (or, more tellingly, the higher percentage of respondents who said that their friends wouldn't) indicated that elements of racism persist in U.S. political culture.

Cultural differences often also explain divergent policy outcomes in different countries. For example, American political culture has historically placed a greater value than European culture does on individuality and the right of individual citizens to be protected from government intervention. On the other hand, the French,

Germans, Swedes, and other Europeans place greater emphasis than Americans do on government's obligation to provide help to society's disadvantaged citizens. Those cultural differences have remained fairly constant for at least 70 years. Consequently, Western Europeans have been more likely than Americans to support extensive social welfare programs and to accept the tax burden that those programs entail. Western European nations also enforce tighter gun controls than the United States does.

Still, over time *political cultures do change!* Sometimes those changes are the result of conscious government or societal planning as, for example, the concerted efforts after World War II by the schools, mass media, labor unions, and other agents of political socialization in both Germany and Japan to erase fascist and ultra-nationalistic sentiments and to create a more democratic political culture. (See the discussion of political resocialization, later in this chapter.) At other times, more gradual social and economic changes alter the political culture. In Mexico during the last half of the twentieth century, the spread of education and literacy, expansion of the broadcast media, and rapid urbanization created a better informed and more participatory political culture.

Political scientists have categorized various kinds of political cultures. We define some of them next and briefly refer to others. These are not necessarily mutually exclusive categories. For example, many societies have both a democratic and a participatory political culture (see below).

Democratic Political Culture

Although the cultural prerequisites for democracy are quite varied and not always fully understood, certain attitudes clearly are helpful. Democracy is most likely to emerge and endure in societies that tolerate diverse points of view, including unpopular or dissenting opinions. When the U.S. Supreme Court ruled that individuals have the right to burn the American flag as an expression of free speech, it took this principle beyond the point that many Americans thought reasonable. Despite some initial outrage, however, Congress chose not to introduce a constitutional amendment to ban flag burning. On the other hand, in Iranian political culture there is no such tolerance for somebody who defiles or mocks the Koran.

As democratic values become more firmly entrenched in a country's political culture, a nation can more easily tolerate antidemocratic political actors. Nations struggling to establish or stabilize democracy in a formerly authoritarian setting, however, may believe that initially it is necessary to exclude political parties and groups that do not accept democratic principles. For that reason, postwar West Germany barred the Nazi Party from political participation in elections. In 1992, following a series of neo-Nazi attacks on immigrants, the German parliament, mindful of the country's history, restricted the speech rights of hate groups.

Other important components of a democratic political culture include "moderation, accommodation, restrained partisanship, system loyalty, and trust."[31] Survey research indicates that levels of trust (in one's fellow citizens and in government) are very low in Russia and many other former communist nations in Eastern and Central Europe. When that happens, people are more likely to support repression of fellow citizens with unpopular points of view, more likely to evade taxes, and less likely to extend business credit, thereby inhibiting both democracy and economic growth.

Authoritarian Political Culture

Despite the growing strength of democratic values worldwide, most political cultures have some authoritarian strains. In the developing world, only a few nations—such as Costa Rica and India—have long-established democratic traditions. And even in India, where competitive elections and parliamentary government have been the norm, most of the population lives in villages, where the caste system, domination by powerful landlords, and local political machines create undemocratic conditions.

What do we mean when we describe Malaysia, Russia, and Iran as having authoritarian political cultures or subcultures? The phrase suggests that both the leaders of the country and much of the population reject either majority rule or minority rights. In particular, authoritarian political cultures are less tolerant of dissenters and of ethnic or religious minorities. In Iran, for example, Islamic fundamentalism denies the legitimacy of other religions (such as Baha'i) or opposing political viewpoints. In both communist North Korea and capitalist South Korea, many citizens believe that journalists have no right to publish material that contradicts the country's prevailing political ideology or that potentially destabilizes society. Similarly, Guatemalan political culture features *caudillaje,* a set of values that makes the pursuit of power the "referent for life's activities." These values support political leaders with "manipulative, exploitative, and opportunistic" personalities.[32]

Authoritarian political cultures stress the importance of stability and order. The rough-and-tumble of democratic competition may seem threatening to that order. In Russia, many citizens felt threatened by the crime and economic disarray that followed the collapse of communism, leading voters to overwhelmingly support President (now Prime Minister) Putin in spite of his repeated assaults on democratic institutions. When asked if they approved or disapproved of strong authoritarian leaders, respondents in countries such as Denmark, the Netherlands, Spain, and Iceland overwhelmingly disapproved, while Tanzanians, Jordanians, Nigerians, and Romanians were far more likely to approve.[33] Many authoritarian cultures support traditional authority structures and hierarchy. For example, women may be socialized to unquestioningly obey their husbands. Similarly, authoritarian political cultures believe that the nation's leaders know what is best for society and should be obeyed. Some Mexican anthropologists argued that their country's children had been raised to unquestionably accept their own father's authority. Consequently, when they grew up, they generally transferred that obedience to the nation's president and to other authority figures.[34] In the Soviet Union many people had a paternalistic view of the ruling, communist ("vanguard") party, which claimed to know with scientific certainty what was good for the people (see Chapter 13). That acceptance of government authority also prevails in the authoritarian cultures of Confucian (and capitalist) Singapore and Muslim Saudi Arabia.

In recent years, a debate has raged among scholars (and some political leaders) as to whether democratic values can readily flourish in Islamic or East Asian cultures. Some have argued, for example, that there are aspects of Islamic and Confucian values that are incompatible with democratic norms (see Box 3-3). In some cases political leaders, such as the former long-time prime minister of Singapore, have used such arguments to justify nondemocratic practices in their own countries. Others, however, find such arguments ethnocentric if not racist. They object strenuously to the idea that Muslims in, say, Malaysia, or Confucians in Singapore are somehow culturally predisposed to reject democracy.[35]

Box 3-3

ISLAM AND DEMOCRACY

The relationship between a society's dominant religious beliefs and its political attitudes and behavior has been the subject of sharp debate. Historically, Protestant countries were most liable to nurture democracy, Islamic countries least likely. In the late 1980s, noted political scientist Samuel Huntington wrote *The Clash of Civilizations and the Remaking of World Order*, a book that reached a wide readership and inspired substantial controversy. In it he argued that there were nine primary civilizations in the world today, which could be distinguished primarily (but not exclusively) by their religion.[36] These included the Christian, Christian Orthodox (Russian and Greek), Muslim, Hindu, and Sino-Confucian cultures. He predicted that future international strife would not center on conflict between ideological blocs (as in the Cold War), but rather between clashing civilizations. He predicted that future conflict would pit Western political culture against Islamic and Confucian civilizations.

In one of Huntington's most controversial statements, he warned that "the problem for the West is not [just] Islamic fundamentalism, it is Islam." Islamic civilization, he argued, is culturally opposed to Western democracy. Not surprisingly, other scholars have strongly challenged that assertion, noting, for example, that Muslims have a wide range of political attitudes and that it made little sense to lump them all together as undemocratic.[37] But several years later, when al-Qaeda carried out its September 11 attacks, Huntington's critical view of Islam gained new support. Prompted by Huntington's work and growing Western suspicion of Islam, a number of scholars have systematically examined the proposition that Islamic culture creates barriers to democracy.

Alfred Stepan and Graeme Robertson recently compared the extent of free and fair elections (electoral democracy) in 47 nations with Muslim-majority populations, separating them into two groups: 16 Arab countries and 31 non-Arab states.[38] Specifically, they wanted to see what percentage of the countries in each group had been able to sustain electoral democracy for at least five consecutive years during the period from 1972 to 2000. They found that while not a single Arab state had met that standard, 8 of the 31 non-Arab Muslim countries had. This suggests that it may be *Arab* history and culture rather than *Islamic* culture that create obstacles to democracy.

But even *non-Arab* Islamic countries still have a lower rate of electoral democracy than non-Islamic countries do. Were Islamic beliefs responsible for that gap? Like other critics of the *Clash of Civilizations*, Stepan and Robertson suggested that this "democracy gap" was attributable to factors other than religion. Might the poorer democratic performance of Muslim countries be caused by their poverty rather than their cultures? We know that very poor countries (with per capita incomes below $1,500) are relatively unlikely to sustain democracy, while countries with average incomes exceeding $5,500 annually are far more likely to maintain it. Hence, any very poor countries that have had a sustained period of electoral democracy were called "overachievers," while any relatively "affluent" states that were unable to maintain free and fair elections were labeled "underachievers."

By those standards, the authors found that half of the Arab countries (including Libya, Kuwait, and Saudi Arabia) had been "underachievers" over the previous 30 years while none had been "overachievers." But among 29 non-Arab, Muslim countries, one-fourth of them (including Albania, Bangladesh, and Nigeria) were overachievers and none were underachievers. Looking at it from a different angle, the authors studied the 38 *poorest* countries in the world (including 1 Arab country, 15 non-Arab predominantly Muslim states, 10 predominantly Christian countries, and 12 with other religions). As expected, most of these countries lacked a record of sustained electoral democracy, but almost one-third of them had exceeded expectations. How did the record of the poor, non-Arab, Muslim nations compare to that of poor non-Muslim countries? While 30 percent of the predominantly Christian nations had overachieved, 33 percent of the non-Arab Muslim countries and 33 percent of the countries with other religions did so as well. In short, two factors seemed to inhibit democracy in many developing countries—extreme poverty and Arabic culture. Islamic beliefs in themselves seemed to present no independent barrier to democracy.

Rather than comparing the past political *performance* of Muslim and non-Muslim countries, Pippa Norris and Ronald Inglehart compared the contemporary attitudes toward democracy of citizens in Muslim and non-Muslim countries.[39] Drawing on survey research

(Continued)

Box 3-3

ISLAM AND DEMOCRACY
(Continued)

findings for 43 countries of all types, they examined citizens' attitudes. To make sure that any differences they found between religious groups were not caused by other factors, they statistically controlled for the level of economic and political development in each country and for the individual respondents' age, gender, education, income, and strength of religious belief.

Once all those factors were controlled, the surveys showed that citizens of Islamic countries are as supportive of democracy as Westerners are. By contrast, the populations of Eastern and Central Europe (the former communist bloc) and of Latin America were less supportive. There is a cultural gap between Muslim nations and the West, they found—not in their attitudes toward democracy, but rather in the Muslim population's more conservative *social* values toward gender equality and sexual liberalization.

In fact, countries with certain dominant religions are more likely than others to be democratic *even when we statistically control for educational or income differences that are known to affect the likelihood of democracy*. In other words, when we compare countries of comparable educational and income levels with one another, Protestant nations are most likely to be democratic and Islamic nations are least likely. Some scholars have argued that Protestantism emphasizes individuality, which contributes to democratic government, whereas Islam believes in a merger of church and state that retards democratic development.

Although there is likely some truth to these assertions, and although the statistical correlations cannot be denied, it is important to keep in mind our previous assertion that *though cultures are generally slow to change, they can and do change!* Historically, Catholic countries in the West have been less hospitable to democracy than Protestant nations. Not long ago, Spain, Portugal, Brazil, Mexico, and a large percentage of other Catholic nations had authoritarian regimes. Some analysts attributed this to the hierarchical nature of the Catholic Church and its belief in papal infallibility in matters of faith. But in the Third Wave of democratization, starting in the early 1970s, Catholic countries in Europe and Latin America were among the most important players. Indeed, the Third Wave started in the Catholic nations of Portugal and Spain. Similarly, culture and religion allegedly explained why, at one time, Confucian South Korea and Taiwan remained authoritarian despite their relatively high income and educational levels. Today, however, both have become democracies. These examples suggest that religious and other cultural traditions may inhibit democratization for a period of time, but they do not make democratic change *impossible*.

Thus, when some political scientists say that a country such as Russia or Pakistan lacks important elements of a democratic political culture, they often point to important cultural hurdles impeding those countries' transitions to democracy. However, that does not mean that those hurdles are permanent or that authoritarian cultural values cannot be changed. Surveys in contemporary Russia, for example, indicated that younger citizens—partly or wholly socialized since glasnost (the Soviet Union's political opening in the late 1980s) and the fall of communism—are more inclined to support democratic values than older Russians are. On the other hand, it is certainly possible that countries that have endured long periods of ineffective or corrupt rule by a democratic government may see democratic values diminish.

Consensual and Conflictual Cultures

We can also classify political cultures according to their degree of consensus or conflict over crucial political issues. In **consensual political cultures**—such as Great Britain, Japan, and Costa Rica—citizens tend to agree on basic political procedures (for example, the legitimacy of free elections) and on the general goals of the political system. **Conflictual political cultures**—in nations such as Rwanda, Bosnia, and Guatemala—are highly polarized by fundamental differences over those issues. In Central America during the 1980s, deep ideological divisions between left-wing and right-wing political subcultures brought El Salvador, Guatemala, and Nicaragua to civil war. Nepal's deep economic divisions gave life to a bloody civil war between Maoist guerrillas and the government. Following the abdication of that country's unpopular king and the Maoists' entry into the democratic electoral process, the country is now, hopefully, moving toward a consensual culture.

Ethnic, religious, or racial divisions may also polarize countries. The people of Bosnia have been violently divided by ethnic nationalism pitting Muslims, Serbs, and Croats against one another. Similarly, in Lebanon, militias representing various Christian and Islamic denominations have decimated one another for years. In 1994, Hutus in Rwanda massacred perhaps 800,000 of their Tutsi countrymen. Obviously, relatively homogeneous cultures (which share a common language, religion, and ethnicity) are more likely to achieve a consensual political culture than are nations that are multiracial or multicultural. Thus, it is much easier to achieve political stability and consensus in Denmark or Japan than in India (a nation split into three major religions and dozens of languages) or Rwanda. Nevertheless, Canada, Switzerland, and the United States demonstrate that some heterogeneous societies have developed consensual cultures despite the obstacles.

Other Cultural Classifications

Along with the classifications we have already mentioned, political scientists have a host of other classifications of political cultures. Observers of Cuban, North Korean, and Chinese politics have often spoken of those countries' revolutionary or Marxist political cultures. Some authors write of countries with a capitalist political culture, indicating that the values are congruent with a free-market ideology. And as we have seen, still other scholars have focused on religion as the central component of political values in a specific region or nation. They speak of a Confucian political culture in China, Taiwan, Korea, and Singapore; a Hindu culture in the Indian subcontinent; and an Islamic political culture in Iran and Algeria. Finally, a number of political scientists have argued that geographic regions have distinct values and orientations that define a Latin American, African, or Mediterranean political culture.

All these classifications are reasonable if they capture a distinctive set of political values and attitudes that characterize a society or region and distinguish it from other political cultures. Thus, the label "Islamic political culture" is scientifically meaningful only if it describes important political values that are common to most Muslims and are distinct from non-Muslim values. If the classification does not do both things (identify common values and attitudes of one culture *and* distinguish those from other cultures), then it is not useful.

THE EVOLUTION OF POLITICAL CULTURES

Political cultures may reflect a balance of *stable* values that have endured for centuries, *gradual changes* in beliefs that transpire over many years, more rapid value changes resulting from socioeconomic or political development (such as greater education), and dramatic events (such as war or revolution). Thus, although all cultures change (some more rapidly than others), the cultural foundations of political systems are not transformed overnight. Like all value systems, traditional beliefs may serve as anchors of stability in an otherwise confusing world or may be impediments to progress. Hindu political culture has supported the caste system, limiting the opportunities available to many Indian citizens and contributing to hierarchical political values. On the other hand, many experts argue that Hinduism's separation of church and state and its lack of church hierarchy help explain why India, despite its abysmal poverty and relatively low literacy rate, has been such a stable democracy.

Because all political cultures change, our understanding of individual societies needs to be constantly reexamined. Clearly, neither Nigerians nor Spaniards nor Americans believe the same things today that they did twenty or thirty years ago. Sometimes, substantial cultural changes are the unintended consequence of rapid urbanization, economic modernization, or increased education. At other times, however, cultural change occurs through **political resocialization**, a conscious effort by government leaders to transform their society's political culture. And sometimes, cultural change is a byproduct of both conscious and unconscious factors.

Of course, in recent decades some aspects of American political culture also have undergone change. In 1959, Almond and Verba found that Americans had more confidence in their political institutions than did citizens in any of the other four countries they had studied. However, that confidence eroded during the late 1960s and the 1970s as a result of the assassinations of President Kennedy and Martin Luther King, an unpopular war in Vietnam, and the Watergate scandal, which almost led to the impeachment of President Richard Nixon. Although the Reagan presidency, the Gulf War, and even the September 11 terrorist attacks all rekindled national pride, public opinion polls indicate that Americans currently have less faith than they once did in political institutions, such as Congress.

More dramatic changes sometimes occur in countries where the government deliberately tries to transform the political culture. Such efforts are always difficult and are sometimes disastrous. Just as it is hard to "teach an old dog new tricks," it is difficult to change long-standing cultural traditions rapidly. These attempts are most likely to take place when a war, a revolution, or other upheaval has radically altered the political system or the government's political ideology. In our analysis of Chinese politics in Chapter 14, we discuss how Mao Zedong's government conducted political campaigns to create mass commitment to volunteer labor, social equality, and other revolutionary values.

Following the Cuban Revolution, the government introduced a massive adult literacy campaign and created neighborhood political units, called Committees for the Defense of the Revolution (CDRs), throughout the nation. The literacy campaign used reading primers with overtly political messages about the benefits that Fidel Castro had brought to the island. CDRs stressed the value of hard work and individual sacrifice for the good of society, while advocating racial, class, and sexual equality. School curricula stressed similar values. Richard Fagen's study of Cuban revolutionary culture suggested

READING AND POLITICS   Cuba's adult literacy program was designed both to achieve universal adult literacy and to inculcate students with revolutionary values. A volunteer in the program is shown here.

a number of impressive results. Surveys of high school students indicated that boys were developing less sexist attitudes toward females. Violent crime rates diminished and poor Cubans became more confident that they could get ahead through study and hard work.[40] In short, the Cuban government had seemingly used education and mass mobilization to reduce prejudice, fatalism, and other pre-revolutionary values.

Yet, the radical transformation of any political culture has its costs. Although Cuban crime rates declined, visits to psychiatrists rose as many Cubans were told at CDR meetings that their pre-revolutionary values were wrong. The introduction of feminist concerns into a *macho* political culture improved sexual equality (husbands, for example, were pressured to do housework, and women were encouraged to enter the labor force) but likely also contributed to a sharp rise in the country's divorce rate.

Other studies have suggested that rapid, government-directed cultural transformations sometimes have been more apparent than real. Although revolutionary activists in Cuba readily mouthed the "correct" political slogans, some of them privately felt or acted differently. For example, one study of a Havana slum found that CDR leaders in that neighborhood were using the organization as a front for gambling and prostitution operations.[41] Other evidence from Cuba, Nicaragua, and Eastern Europe suggests that although many people accepted at least some revolutionary values, others just went through the motions or feigned a cultural transformation for the sake of personal advancement (see Box 3-4).

Box 3-4

TRANSFORMING EASTERN EUROPEAN POLITICAL CULTURE AFTER THE FALL OF COMMUNISM

Between 1989 and 1991, much to the world's surprise, communist regimes collapsed, first in Eastern and Central Europe (including East Germany, Poland, Hungary and Bulgaria), and subsequently in much of the Soviet Union (including Russia, Latvia, and Estonia). An obvious concern was whether or not these countries' political cultures would accept democratic values after 45 to 75 years of communist-directed political socialization. Lucian Pye, one of the leading pioneers of political culture research, argued that this change represented the greatest transformation of political cultures since the nations of Africa, Asia, and the Middle East shed colonialism from the 1940s through the 1960s.[42] Would Eastern/Central Europeans readily adopt democratic values? Would certain countries have an easier time than others developing a democratic political culture?

In 1996 a multinational survey of political attitudes revealed some important differences and a few surprising similarities between the political cultures of mature, Western democracies and those of post-communist societies. Drawing on data from that survey, Jacobs, Muller, and Pickel examined three mature democracies—the United States, Britain, and the former West Germany (now the western part of a united Germany)—and eight post-communist countries—Bulgaria, the Czech Republic, the former East Germany, Hungary, Latvia, Poland, Russia, and Slovenia.[43]

TABLE 3.1   SUPPORT FOR DEMOCRATIC POLITICAL VALUES

Country	Satisfied with Democracy (Percent)	Support Free Speech Even By Extremists (Percent)	Resistance to Democracy Index (RTDI)
United States	72	67	0.641
(former) West Germany	83	64	0.721
Britain	70	59	0.763
Czech Republic	48	64	1.114
(former) East Germany	60	64	1.144
Bulgaria	45	54	1.145
Slovenia	49	64	1.231
Poland	57	47	1.316
Latvia	42	31	1.329
Hungary	23	42	1.436
Russia	18	43	1.705

SOURCE: Jurgen Jacobs, Olaf Muller, and Gert Pickel, "Persistence of the Democracies in Central and Eastern Europe," in *Political Culture in Post-Communist Europe*, eds. Detlef Pollack et al. (Burlington, VT: Ashgate Publishing, 2003), pp. 96 and 99.

Respondents were asked to evaluate how well democracy had been working in their own country and choose one of the following alternatives: 1) It works well and there is *no need for change* 2) It works well but there is a need for *a little change* 3) It doesn't work and there is a need for *much change* or 4) It doesn't work and there is a need for *total change*.

Column 1 Table 3.1 shows the combined percent of the population who felt democracy was working either perfectly well or pretty well, seeing little or no need for change. In the three Western democracies the number desiring little or no change ranged from 70 percent (Britain) to 83 percent (Western Germany). Of the post-communist nations, only Eastern Germany (60 percent) and Poland (57 percent) had anywhere close to those rates of satisfaction with democracy. Within the remaining post-communist countries, satisfaction with democracy was considerably lower, ranging from only 18 percent in Russia to 49 percent in Slovenia (formerly part of Yugoslavia).

A second survey question asked respondents whether they felt that their government should deny the right of free speech to people with "extremist" political views. Their responses measured their willingness to tolerate unpopular political opinions, a key component of a democratic political culture. Column 2 shows the percentage of people in each country who fully supported free speech, even for those with extreme views. Perhaps because some respondents may have associated the term "extremist views" with advocacy of violence, at least one-third of those polled in all 11 countries believed in denying free speech rights to extremists. As expected, citizens of mature democracies generally supported free speech (even for "extremist" viewpoints) more broadly than their post-communist counterparts did. Americans were most committed to free speech (67 percent), even for people with extremist viewpoints. The former West Germany (64 percent) and Britain (59 percent) were only slightly less tolerant. As expected, respondents in several post-communist countries were much less likely to extend free speech that far—Latvia (only 31 percent), Hungary (42 percent), Russia (43 percent), and Poland (47 percent). On the other hand, in three post-communist states—the former East Germany, the Czech Republic, and Slovenia, support for free speech was as high as in the three Western democracies (in fact, higher than in Great Britain).

Finally, the third column in the table presents the most comprehensive indicator of support for democratic values and attitudes. Each country was rated on a "Resistance to Democracy Index (RTDI)," an index that combined 16 variables measuring how *opposed* respondents were to democratic values. A *lower* RTDI score in column 3 indicates that that people in that country were less wary of democracy or, better put, that they had a *more democratic* political culture. As expected, the three mature Western Democracies had the lowest RTDI scores (i.e., they has the strongest democratic political culture), well ahead of any post-communist nation. Of the eight post-communist countries, the Czech Republic, the former East Germany, Bulgaria, and Slovenia had relatively stronger democratic political cultures. Poland and Latvia came next, while Hungary and, especially, Russia least supported democratic values.

Some of these results conform to existing theories about political culture and political socialization, but other findings were unanticipated. Not surprisingly, two of the three countries with the highest resistance to democracy (RTDI)—Latvia and Russia—were previously part of the Soviet Union and had little historical experience with democracy. At the other end of the spectrum, however, Eastern Germans and Czechs had

some of the strongest democratic values even though they had endured intense political socialization and indoctrination under two of Central Europe's most repressive communist regimes. In the East German case, the explanation seems to be that after the fall of its communist government, the country was quickly reunited with West Germany, one of the world's wealthiest nations, with a strong commitment to democratic values developed in the post-Nazi era. West Germany was able to subsidize the former East Germany's economy and soften the painful transition to capitalism that other post-communist countries endured. In the Czech case, the explanation may lie in its precommunist past. The country had been the more modern part of Czechoslovakia (before that country broke up into the Czech Republic and Slovakia), a nation that had enjoyed Central Europe's strongest democratic tradition prior to the Nazi occupation during World War II and the subsequent Soviet takeover (1948). In 1968, a reformist communist government, with considerable public support, broadened civil liberties before Soviet troops invaded the country and crushed Czechoslovakia's limited attempts at democratization. Finally, Czechs united behind the "Velvet Revolution" of 1989, a peaceful pro-democracy protest movement that toppled the communist regime. Thus, as of the mid-to-late 1990s, post-communist political cultures in both countries seem to have been shaped more by events before the advent of communism (the Czech Republic) or after the collapse of communism (East Germany) than by the decades of communist political socialization.

Perhaps the most surprising finding in this survey was Hungary's very negative attitude toward democracy and democratic values. That country had enjoyed one of Central Europe's highest levels of economic development and the region's least repressive communist regime. So Hungary's unexpectedly high Resistance to Democracy Index may have less to do with its political culture under the communists than with events preceding and following the fall of communism. Perhaps Hungary's reformist government in the last years of communism and the relatively smooth transition to democracy had raised unrealistic hopes among Hungarians; hopes that were confounded by the country's very difficult economic transition to capitalism in the early 1990s.

All of this suggests that political culture may have a less enduring and significant impact than many of its champions suggested, at least in the European post-communist experience. With the apparent exception

(Continued)

Box 3-4

TRANSFORMING EASTERN EUROPEAN POLITICAL
CULTURE AFTER THE FALL OF COMMUNISM
(*Continued*)

of Russia (and the perplexing case of Hungary), decades of communist political socialization did not seem to impede those countries' rapid absorption of democratic or semi-democratic political values in less than a decade. In many—perhaps most—countries, mass attitudes toward democracy seemed to be influenced primarily by how painful their economic transition to capitalism was.* In Germany and the Czech Republic that economic transition went relatively smoothly, while Russians endured a decade of terrible economic suffering (see Chapter 13).

* During that economic transition there was a gap between the end of communist-era benefits and the beginning of capitalist gains. Prices soared as post-communist governments stopped subsidies for food, rent, and other consumer goods. They also terminated free health care and guaranteed employment. For more details, see the discussion of Russia's economic transformation in Chapter 13.

Finally, we ask how well the different levels of support for democracy (as shown in Table 3.1) predicted each nation's subsequent political development. Did post-communist countries with more democratic political cultures (as of the mid-1990s) more effectively achieve and maintain democratic government than did those with seemingly less democratic commitment? Clearly Russia's high RTDI helps explain why most citizens were not troubled by President Putin's authoritarian measures (2000–2008) as long as he presided over an economic recovery (Chapter 13). On the other hand, other post-communist nations, with weak democratic cultures (Hungary, Latvia, and Poland), were subsequently able to consolidate democracy as effectively as the countries with stronger democratic values did. So in this case, at least, political culture did not predict well a country's chances of consolidating democracy.

Postmaterialism and Cultural Change

We have seen that cataclysmic events such as Germany's defeat in World War II, the collapse of Soviet communism, or the Cuban revolution may dramatically change that society's political culture. But other cultural transformations may occur more gradually as the result of broad social and economic developments. The phenomenon of **postmaterialism** is one of the most significant examples of such a cultural transformation. During the quarter century following World War II, North American and Western European living standards improved at a historically unparalleled rate. Drawing on data from Western Europe and other economically advanced areas, Ronald Inglehart argued that modernization and economic growth substantially altered the political culture of these advanced industrial democracies.[44]

He noted that most people who grew up during the expanding prosperity of the postwar period (1945 through the early 1970s) felt more economically secure than their parents and grandparents, many of whom had suffered through the Great Depression or the ravages of World War II. Having enjoyed relative economic security during their formative years, postwar generations tended to be less preoccupied than their elders were with economic stability and growth and to be more concerned about issues such as environmental protection and military disarmament.

Based on their responses to survey questionnaires, individuals in advanced industrial democracies may be classified as materialists, postmaterialists, or a combination of the two subcultures. Materialists, still the largest portion of the population, tend to make political decisions based on economic self-interest. Thus, most middle-class materialists would oppose higher taxes, even as poorer materialists would tend to favor expansion of social welfare programs. In addition, materialists are especially concerned about domestic law and order, a strong national defense, maintaining a stable economy, and controlling inflation.

In the decades since Inglehart developed his theory, the number of postmaterialists has gradually increased in most of the world's industrialized democracies (see Table 3.2). Although they are sympathetic to many of the materialists' concerns (hardly anybody, after all, likes street crime, inflation, or economic instability), post-materialists put those goals lower on their political agenda than materialists do. At the same time, they are more concerned than materialists are about "moving toward a society where ideas count more than money," as well as "moving toward a friendlier, less impersonal society," protecting the environment, increasing grassroots participation in politics and at the workplace, and defending free speech and other civil liberties.[45] Postmaterialists tend to be more liberal on social issues such as divorce, abortion, and homosexual marriage. They are also more sympathetic to feminist concerns, more committed to disarmament, and less religiously conservative (see Box 3-5).[46]

Postwar Germany provided an excellent example of what Inglehart calls "culture shift" and the expansion of postmaterialist culture. Over the years, various national surveys asked Germans which of the following four freedoms they felt was most important to them: freedom of speech, freedom of worship, freedom from fear, or freedom from want. In the years after World War II, when the German economy was still in shambles, respondents were most likely to select "freedom from want." By 1959, however, as Germans felt more economically secure, they chose freedom of speech more often than the other three choices combined.[47]

As the number of postmaterialist voters in Western Europe and the United States grew, Inglehart argues, pocketbook issues played a declining role in elections, and social class diminished as a determinant of voting.[48] As we will see in Chapters 4 and 5, working-class voters have been historically more likely to support left-of-center parties in Europe and the United States, whereas the middle and upper classes have tended to vote for more conservative candidates. That relationship continues, but in recent decades the correlation between class and party ideology has weakened. Today, many middle-class postmaterialists vote for left-of-center candidates (attracted by their position on issues such as the environment or civil liberties) and increasing numbers of workers vote for conservative candidates (often based on their conservative religious and social values).

Using extensive European survey data over the past few decades, Inglehart and Russell Dalton noted that the number of people in the postmaterialist political culture has grown steadily as young people raised in postwar affluence have entered the political system and as older materialists have died or retired from politics. That trend helps explain the growth of ecologically oriented Green parties in Western Europe and suggests that issues such as the environment will become increasingly important. If postmaterialist culture continues to grow, liberal parties that stress disarmament, feminist issues, and the environment are likely to benefit, whereas conservative and religiously affiliated parties (such as the German Christian Democrats) could lose ground. At the same time, however, as Western Europeans became more economically secure and postmaterialist culture expanded, class divisions diminished and voters became less attracted to the welfare-state programs once endorsed by the Continent's leftist political parties. As a result, a traditional Marxist party, the French Communist Party—unable to adapt to changing public attitudes—saw its proportion of the vote decline from more than 25 percent in the late 1940s to less than 5 percent today. The French and German socialist parties, perhaps as a response to spreading postmaterialism, have largely abandoned Marxist economics and have increasingly stressed social issues in their campaigns. By expanding beyond its traditional electoral base of workers and teachers, and by attracting the support of middle-class postmaterialists, the French Socialist Party became the nation's largest party in the 1980s and the early 1990s (though they have faded badly since).

Inglehart's theories have greatly influenced the study of political culture in advanced industrial democracies. However, since the 1990s, chronic unemployment in Europe, and the recent world-wide financial crisis may slow that growth. In Europe, especially, high unemployment rates over an extended period have contributed to support for France's neofascist National Front Party and for neo-Nazi skinhead activity in Austria and Germany. These groups express views that are quite the opposite of postmaterialist beliefs.

Box 3-5

POSTMATERIALISM IN WESTERN EUROPE AND THE UNITED STATES

For the most part, the number of postmaterialists has grown fairly steadily in developed Western nations during the past 35 years. Yet, not surprisingly, concerns over materialist issues such as the state of the economy remain strong. Survey data on five such nations from 1973 to 2007 (Table 3.2), show a general upward trend in postmaterialism, particularly in Western Germany, Norway and Britain. But, in the United States and Spain—for which there are only limited data—fell significantly in the 1990s. And, Western Germany, which had experienced the most dramatic surge in postmaterialism from 1973 to 1999, saw a substantial decline from 1999 to 2007.

It is too soon to know how the 2008 financial meltdown and the looming recession will affect the future values of today's youth (currently roughly aged 14-21). But, with economic insecurity at its highest level since the Great Depression of the 1920s and 1930s, materialist values may stage a comeback in future years as a new generation of voters enters the political arena.

TABLE 3.2   THE GROWTH OF POSTMATERIALIST VALUES IN INDUSTRIALIZED DEMOCRACIES (IN PERCENTAGES)

Country	1973	1990	1999	2007
United States	—	31	23	—
Germany (West)	13	36	43	30
Great Britain	18	19	—	25
Norway	—	17	20	26
Spain	—	37	29	—

Russell J. Dalton, *Citizen Politics*, 5th ed. (Washington, D.C.: CQ Press, 2008), p. 86. Copyright © 2008 CQ Press, a division of SAGE Publications, Inc. Reprinted by permission.

CONCLUSION: THE UTILITY OF POLITICAL CULTURE

Some years ago, Harry Eckstein, a leading political scientist, argued that political culture theory had been one of the two most important developments in political theory during the previous 40 years. (We discuss the other development, rational choice theory, in Chapter 6).[49] Culturalist theories have enabled us to progress beyond the study of government institutions in order to understand more fully how politics differs in nations throughout the world. After a period of some disuse, cultural approaches to understanding politics have experienced a revival in recent years, examining such subjects as the prospects for democracy in Eastern Europe and the Middle East, and the relationship of religious values to political beliefs.[50]

Like any important theory, however, cultural explanations of politics have not been without their critics. One significant criticism is that survey research on political values and beliefs sometimes uses questions that are not meaningful in other cultures or are translated into terms that have different meanings in different languages. To some extent, that problem can be addressed by more careful translation and greater concern for cultural differences.

A more subtle criticism of much of the political culture research is that it has implicit cultural and ideological biases. Carole Pateman has argued that *The Civic Culture* was based on the erroneous assumption that British–American-style democracy is the ideal form of government and consequently that political cultures throughout the world should be judged by the degree to which they support that form of democracy.[51] Richard Wilson goes a step further by arguing that all political cultures consist of widely held (or inculcated) values that justify their political system.[52] Thus, both British and Chinese schoolchildren are politically socialized to support their own system.

Perhaps the most telling criticism of political culture theory is that too often it is vague and imprecise and that it frequently fails to explain or predict important political changes.[53] For example, we noted earlier the frequent assertion that Latin America has an authoritarian political culture. Yet that assertion fails to explain why Costa Rica has been able to establish a stable democratic order or how Venezuela—historically one of the least democratic nations in South America—was able to transform itself in the late 1950s into one of the region's most stable democracies and then regressed to a limited form of democracy in the 1990s. Similarly, there do not appear to be any identifiable cultural traits that explain why India has been democratic for almost all of the 60 years since its independence, yet none of its neighbors in South Asia have enjoyed a comparable record.

Too often, analysts use culture as a "second-order" or residual explanation.[54] In other words, if political scientists cannot explain why Indian and Pakistani politics are so different or why Canadians have less political violence than Americans, they simply chalk it up to culture. Thus, political culture frequently becomes a fallback explanation for anything that political scientists have been unable to explain by other means. In other words, when scholars are unable to explain differences between two political systems, they often assume that the explanation lies in their political cultures.

These criticisms indicate that some culturalist research and some culturalist explanations are weak. Surely, political scientists must be careful not to overstretch these theories or to use their own political values as measuring sticks for evaluating other cultures. These criticisms notwithstanding, most political scientists recognize the substantial value of political culture theory when it is carefully and prudently applied.

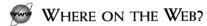

WHERE ON THE WEB?

http://www.columbia.edu/acis/eds/dset_guides/eurobar.html
Provides information on the Eurobarometer, the most comprehensive survey of European public opinion.

http://www.socialstudieshelp.com/APGOV_Political%20Culture.htm
Offers a discussion of U.S. political culture.

http://www.pitt.edu/~redsox/polcul.html
This survey by the University of Pittsburgh gives you a feel for the kinds of questions that go into a political culture study in the United States.

http://www.afrobarometer.org/
The Home Page of Afrobarometer—the most comprehensive source of contemporary survey research on African political attitudes—offers links to papers and to data.

http://www.latinobarometro.org/
The Home Page of Latinobarómetro, the most comprehensive source of contemporary survey research on Latin American political attitudes. Click on "English" to change from the Spanish page, which will first appear. Links to articles and data.

Key Terms and Concepts _____

agents of political socialization
conflictual political cultures
consensual political cultures
Generation Y
Information and Communications Technology (ICT)
political culture

political resocialization
political socialization
political subcultures
postmaterialism
social capital
techno-enthusiasts

Discussion Questions _____

1. Discuss the ways in which a society transmits its political values to its members, particularly to new generations. What are the principal agents of political socialization in the United States, and how might their role in the United States differ from their role in socioeconomically underdeveloped nations?
2. Compare the primary characteristics of a democratic political culture with those of an authoritarian political culture. When analysts characterize countries such as Russia or Egypt as having an authoritarian or semiauthoritarian political culture, what does that say about those countries' chances of ever becoming democratic?
3. How do Information and Communication Technologies (ICT), such as the Internet or text messaging, affect political socialization in developed democracies? What are the advantages and disadvantages of ICT as a socializing agent?
4. Even in societies that favor a separation of church and state, organized religions play important roles as agents of political socialization. Discuss ways in which political socialization through institutionalized religion can play a positive role in establishing political stability and democracy. Then discuss the ways in which such socialization can play a negative role.
5. How enduring was the influence of communist political culture in East/Central Europe? Which countries in those regions have embraced democratic values more extensively and quickly and which have lagged behind? Explain some of these differences between post-communist countries.

6. Discuss Inglehart's notion of postmaterialism. Specifically, in which countries (or kinds of countries) did postmaterialist values develop? Which types of people are most likely to be postmaterialists? What values distinguish postmaterialists from other people? What are the political consequences of postmaterialist values?
7. What evidence is there to support the claim that Islamic political cultures are less receptive to democracy? What evidence suggests that this argument is untrue?
8. What is the basic argument that Robert Putnam presents in *Bowling Alone*? What are the dangers of a loss of social capital?

Notes ——————

1. World Values Survey data in Ronald Inglehart, *Modernization and Postmodernization: Cultural, Economic, and Political Change in 43 Societies* (Princeton, NJ: Princeton University Press, 1997), p. 174.
2. Larry Diamond, "Introduction: Political Culture and Democracy," in *Political Culture and Democracy in Developing Countries*, ed. Larry Diamond (Boulder, CO: Lynne Rienner, 1993), pp. 7–8.
3. Richard J. Ellis and Michael Thompson, eds. *Culture Matters: Essays in Honor of Aaron Wildavsky*. (Boulder, CO: Westview, 1997).
4. Gabriel Almond, "The Study of Political Culture," in *A Divided Discipline: Schools and Sects in Political Science*, ed. Gabriel Almond (Newbury Park, CA: Sage, 1990), p. 144.
5. Scott Keeter, "Trends in Public Opinion about the War in Iraq, 2003–2007," Pew Research Center for the People and the Press (March 15, 2007), http://pewresearch.org/pubs/431/.
6. Data from the World Values Survey cited in Frederick C. Turner, "Reassessing Political Culture," in *Latin America in Comparative Perspective*, ed. Peter H. Smith (Boulder, CO: Westview, 1995), p. 202.
7. Gabriel Almond and Sidney Verba, *The Civic Culture* (Boston: Little, Brown, 1965).
8. Richard Dawson and Kenneth Prewitt, *Political Socialization* (Boston: Little, Brown, 1969), p. 27.
9. Akira Kubota and Robert Ward, "Family Influence and Political Socialization in Japan," in *Comparative Political Socialization*, eds. Jack Dennis and M. Kent Jennings (Beverly Hills, CA: Sage, 1970), pp. 11–46.
10. Paul Allen Beck and M. Kent Jennings, "Family Traditions, Political Periods, and the Development of Partisan Orientations," *Journal of Politics* 53, no. 3 (August 1991): 743.
11. Ibid., 742–763.
12. James Coleman, *The Adolescent Society* (New York: Free Press, 1961).
13. Robert Putnam with Robert Leonardi and Raffaella Nanetti, *Making Democracy Work: Civic Traditions in Modern Italy* (Princeton, NJ: Princeton University Press, 1993).
14. Robert Putnam, "Bowling Alone: America's Declining Social Capital," *Journal of Democracy* 6, no. 1 (1995): 65; Robert Putnam, *Bowling Alone* (New York: Simon and Schuster, 2000).
15. Russell J. Dalton, *Democratic Challenges, Democratic Choices* (New York: Oxford University Press, 2004), p. 191.
16. Ibid, p. 42.
17. Ibid, pp. 165–171.
18. M. Kent Jennings and Richard Niemi, "The Transmission of Political Values from Parent to Child," *American Political Science Review* 62 (March 1968): 169–184.
19. Laurence Wylie, *Village in the Vaucluse* (Cambridge: Harvard University Press, 1974).
20. Michael Crozier, *The Stalled Society* (New York: Viking, 1973).
21. John Ardagh, *France in the 1980s* (New York: Penguin, 1982).
22. William Safran, *The French Polity* (New York: Longman, 1991), pp. 47–48.
23. Richard Rose, "Voter Turnout in the European Union Member Countries," in *Voter Turnout in Western Europe Since 1945: A Regional Report*, eds. Rafael López Pintor and Maria Gratschew (Stockholm, Sweden: International IDEA, 2004).
24. Brian D. Loader, ed. *Young Citizens in the Digital Age: Political Engagement, Young People, and the New Media* (London and New York: Rutledge, 2007).
25. Mark Hugo Lopez, Emily Kirby, and Jared Sagoff, "The Youth Vote 2004" (The Center for Information and Research on Civic Learning and Engagement, 2005), http://www.civicyouth.org/PopUps/FactSheets/FS_Youth_Voting_72-04.pdf.
26. Doris Graber, "Mediated Politics and Citizenship in the Twenty-First Century," Vol. 55 (2004), 568, quoted in Loader, *Young Citizens*, p. 31.
27. Data on volunteerism cited in Sharon Jayson, "Generation Y Gets Involved," *USA Today* (October 23, 2006), http://www.usatoday.com; Data on the 2000 and 2004 presidential elections come from Lopez, Kirby, and Sagoff, "Youth Vote 2004." Data on the 2006 election come from The Pew Charitable Trust, "Young Voter Turnout Up for the Second Election in a Row," http://www.pewtrusts.org/news_room_detail.aspx?id=20306; Data on the 2008 primary and caucus turnout come from Rock the Vote, "Young Voter Turnout, 2008 Primaries and Caucuses," http://www.blog.rockthevote.com/.

28. Ronald Inglehart, *Culture Shift in Advanced Industrial Society* (Princeton, NJ: Princeton University Press, 1990), pp. 197, 449.
29. Almond and Verba, *Civic Culture*, p. 3.
30. Gunnar Myrdal, *An American Dilemma* (New York: McGraw-Hill, 1962; Twentieth Anniversary Edition).
31. Diamond, "Introduction: Political Culture and Democracy," in *Political Culture and Democracy*, p.5.
32. Glen C. Dealy, *The Public Man: An Interpretation of Latin America and Other Catholic Countries* (Amherst: University of Massachusetts Press, 1977), pp. 34–35; and Roland Ebel, "Guatemala: The Politics of Unstable Stability," in *Latin American Politics and Development*, eds. Howard J. Wiarda and Harvey F. Kline (Boulder, CO: Westview, 1990), pp. 508–509.
33. World Values and European Values surveys 1995–2001 as cited in Pippa Norris and Ronald Inglehart, *Sacred and Secular: Religion and Politics Worldwide* (New York: Cambridge University Press, 2004), p. 147.
34. Turner, "Reassessing Political Culture," p. 209.
35. For arguments on both sides of this issue, see Samuel P. Huntington, "The Clash of Civilizations," *Foreign Affairs* 72, no. 3 (Summer 1993): 22–49; Donald Emerson, "Singapore and the Asian Values Debate," *Journal of Democracy* (October 1995): 95–105; Mohamed Elhachmi Hamdi, "The Limits of the Western Model," *Journal of Democracy* (April 1996): 81–85; Adrian Karatnycky, "Muslim Countries and the Democracy Gap," *Journal of Democracy* (January 2002): 99–112.
36. Samuel Huntington, *The Clash of Civilizations and the Remaking of World Order* (New York: Simon and Schuster, 1996).
37. For one of the many challenges to Huntington, see Mark Tessler, "Do Islamic Orientations Influence Attitudes toward Democracy in the Arab World?" *International Journal of Comparative Sociology* 43 (2003), no. 3–4: 229–249; Shireen T. Hunter, *The Future of Islam and the West: Clash of Civilizations or Peaceful Coexistence?* (Westport, CT: Praeger, 1998).
38. Alfred Stepan and Graeme B. Robertson, "An 'Arab' Rather than a 'Muslim' Electoral Gap," *Journal of Democracy* 14, no. 3 (July 2003): 30–44.
39. Norris and Inglehart, *Sacred and Secular*, pp. 133–155.
40. Richard Fagen, *The Transformation of Cuban Political Culture* (Stanford, CA: Stanford University Press, 1969).
41. Douglas Butterworth, "Grass Roots Political Organization in Cuba: The Case of the Committees for the Defense of the Revolution," in *Latin American Urban Research*, vol. 4, eds. Wayne Cornelius and Felicity Trueblood (Beverly Hills, CA: Sage, 1974).
42. Lucian W. Pye, "Culture as Destiny," in *Political Culture in Post-Communist Europe*, eds. Detlef Pollack et al. (Burlington, VT: Ashgate Publishing, 2003), pp. 3–16.
43. Data in this box come from Jurgen Jacobs, Olaf Muller, and Gert Pickel, "Persistence of the Democracies in Central and Eastern Europe," in *Political Culture in Post-Communist Europe*, pp. 96–99. They drew their data from a much larger collection of countries surveyed by the International Social Survey Program (ISSP).
44. See, especially, Ronald Inglehart, *Culture Shift in Advanced Industrial Society*; Ronald Inglehart, *The Silent Revolution: Changing Values and Political Styles among Western Publics* (Princeton, NJ: Princeton University Press, 1977); and Inglehart, *Modernization and Postmodernization*.
45. Inglehart, *Culture Shift*, pp. 74–75.
46. Inglehart, *Modernization and Postmodernization*, pp. 276–292.
47. Inglehart, *Culture Shift*, p. 71.
48. Inglehart, *Modernization and Postmodernization*, pp. 240–243.
49. Harry Eckstein, "A Culturalist Theory of Political Change," *American Political Science Review* 82, no. 3 (September 1988): 789–804.
50. Some of the many interesting works include Nicolai N. Petro, *The Rebirth of Russian Democracy: An Interpretation of Political Culture* (Cambridge: Harvard University Press, 1995); Daniel Price, *Islamic Political Culture, Democracy, and Human Rights: A Comparative Study* (Westport, CT: Praeger, 1999); Norris and Inglehart, *Sacred and Secular*.
51. Carole Pateman, "The Civic Culture: A Philosophical Critique," in Almond and Verba, *Civic Culture Revisited*.
52. Richard W. Wilson, *Compliance Ideologies: Rethinking Political Culture* (New York: Cambridge University Press, 1992).
53. Paul Warwick, *Culture, Structure or Choice* (New York: Agathon, 1990), pp. 3–24.
54. David Elkins and Richard Simeon, "A Cause in Search of Its Effect, or What Does Political Culture Explain?" *Comparative Politics* (January 1979): 127–145.

For Further Reading ⎯⎯⎯⎯

Almond, Gabriel, and Sidney Verba. *The Civic Culture.* Boston: Little, Brown, 1965.

Cheney, Kristen E. *Pillars of the Nation: Child Citizens and Ugandan National Development.* Chicago: University of Chicago Press, 2007.

Dalton, Russell J. *Citizen Politics.* 5th ed. Washington, D.C.: CQ Press, 2008.

⎯⎯⎯. *Democratic Challenges, Democratic Choices.* New York: Oxford University Press, 2004.

Inglehart, Ronald. *Culture Shift in Advanced Industrial Society.* Princeton, NJ: Princeton University Press, 1990.

⎯⎯⎯. *Modernization and Postmodernization: Cultural, Economic, and Political Change in 43 Societies.* Princeton, NJ: Princeton University Press, 1997.

Loader, Brian D., ed. *Young Citizens in the Digital Age: Political Engagement, Young People and New Media.* London and New York: Routledge, 2007.

Lomnitz, Larissa Adler and Ana Melnick. *Chile's Political Culture and Parties.* Notre Dame, IN: Notre Dame University Press, 2000.

Norris, Pippa, ed. *Critical Citizens: Global Support for Democratic Government.* Oxford and New York: Oxford University Press, 1999.

⎯⎯⎯ and Ronald Inglehart. *Sacred and Secular: Religion and Politics Worldwide.* Cambridge, England: Cambridge University Press, 2004.

Pollack, Detlef et al, eds. *Political Culture in Post-Communist Europe.* Burlington, VT: Ashgate Publishing, 2003.

Putnam, Robert D. *Bowling Alone: The Collapse and Revival of American Community.* New York: Simon & Schuster, 2000.

⎯⎯⎯, ed. *Democracies in Flux: The Evolution of Social Capital in Contemporary Society.* New York: Oxford University Press, 2002.

Wilson, Richard W. *East Asian Political Culture.* Piscataway, NJ: Transaction Periodicals Consortium, 2002.

Wiseman, Nelson. *In Search of Canadian Political Culture.* Vancouver, British Columbia: University of British Columbia Press, 2008.

Senators John McCain and Barack Obama meet for the first
Presidential Debate at the University of Mississippi on September 26, 2008.

4

PUBLIC OPINION AND ELECTIONS

◆ Influences on Public Opinion and Voting Choice ◆ Voter
Turnout ◆ Belief Systems ◆ The Electoral Process and
Campaign Money ◆ Electoral Systems ◆ Public Opinion
Polling ◆ Conclusion: Elections and Public
Opinion—The People's Voice?

People participate in politics in many ways. They write to government officials, join political parties and interest groups, take part in demonstrations (violent and non-violent), and discuss politics with relatives and friends. When governments attempt to suppress political involvement, creative people participate in politics in more subtle ways, perhaps by creating literature or music or films containing political messages. In some countries, most notably in the Middle East, Latin America, and parts of Eastern Europe, church-related activities constitute an important setting for political involvement.

Nevertheless, the act of *voting* occupies a central place in political behavior. Elections are a direct and generally accepted approach to popular consultation and are a basic component of democratic government. By selecting one candidate or party over another, citizens express preferences regarding who should govern them and which government policies should be adopted or changed. Apart from voting choices, *public opinion* itself is an important aspect of political behavior. By studying voting and public opinion, we are able to understand a great deal about politics, at least in democracies.

Of course, non-democratic political systems hold elections as well, with the voters often given a "choice" of a single slate of candidates. Such single-party elections are held in China, Vietnam, North Korea, and most African nations. They were the norm, until recently, in the former Soviet Union and Eastern Europe. Other nations have held elections in which weak opposition parties have been permitted to nominate candidates but have not been given an opportunity to win. In Nicaragua, for example, before the *Sandinista* revolution (1979), the Somoza dictatorship regularly staged such elections. In Mexico, the Institutional Revolutionary Party (PRI) controlled both houses of Congress for 70 years, until July 1997, and it held the presidency until July 2000, when Vicente Fox, the National Action Party (PAN) candidate was elected (see Chapter 16). Because of the obvious predictability of rigged elections, they tell us little about public opinion or electoral behavior. Hence, this chapter focuses on elections in democratic systems.

The study of public opinion and voting focuses primarily on factors that influence how citizens vote and why people hold different views on policies and candidates. Researchers are also interested in the strength and distribution of opinions. Analysts want to know what kinds of people support each political party, how the rich and poor or people of different religions differ with respect to opinions and voting choices, how economic conditions and foreign policy crises affect elections, and how a candidate's personality or character amplifies or restricts his or her support. Our understanding of many kinds of political activity is built mainly on information regarding these matters. And, as a practical matter, the study of voting and public opinion is crucial to strategists who manage campaigns and allocate scarce campaign funds.

In this chapter, we discuss six important problems: factors influencing the direction of public opinion and voting choices, factors affecting voter turnout, the development of belief systems, campaign financing, electoral laws and procedure, and public opinion polling.

INFLUENCES ON PUBLIC OPINION AND VOTING CHOICE

In our discussion of political culture (Chapter 3), we noted the major agents of political socialization—family, education, friends, religious and social groups, and the media—and analyzed their impact on political culture. In this section, we shift our focus to consider the determinants of *specific* political opinions and voting choices: What led some American Democrats to support Hillary Clinton in 2008, while others supported Barack Obama? How can we explain the choices of some British citizens to oppose U.S. action against Iraq much more avidly than others?

Orientations to Politics: How Citizens "Filter" Political Information

In a modern industrial democracy, citizens are flooded with complex and detailed information about political issues, national events, and candidates. People need to interpret that information before it will affect their opinions or votes. Political scientists have identified two important ways in which people "filter" political information, helping them to develop their preferences and their votes: party identification and ideology.

Party Identification   Imagine that your instructor asks you to guess which way a randomly selected fellow student (with whom you are not acquainted) voted in the 2008 presidential election. If you guess correctly, you will win an all-expenses-paid spring break in Cancun. Before guessing, the instructor tells you that you can ask the student *one* question to help you guess. What question should you ask?

Political scientists would not hesitate—if they had to guess which way a given citizen voted in a democratic country's national election, and if they could only have one piece of information to help them guess correctly, they would want to know the person's **party identification**. A citizen who clearly identifies with a particular political party (Democratic or Republican in the U.S., Conservative or Labour in the UK, and so on) will nearly always develop opinions consistent with the party's policy goals and vote for the party's candidates. Even when it is relatively weak, party identification affects people's political opinions.

In the U.S. presidential election of 2008, John McCain won 46 percent of the popular vote, and Barack Obama won 53 percent. A student with a rudimentary grasp of probability theory would therefore guess that a randomly chosen person voted for Obama, and the guess would be incorrect 47 percent of the time. However, you would have a very good chance of making an accurate guess about that randomly selected voter's choice with information on his or her party identification. In 2000, fully 86 percent of voters identifying themselves as Democrats voted for Al Gore, and 91 percent of Republicans voted for George W. Bush. In 2004, 89 percent of Democrats voted for John Kerry, while 93 percent of Republicans voted for George W. Bush. And, in 2008, 89 percent of Republicans voted for John McCain while 89 percent of Democrats voted for Barack Obama.*

A renowned American political scientist, V. O. Key, Jr. (1908–1963), observed in 1952 that "the time of casting a ballot is not a time of decision for many voters; it is merely an occasion for the reaffirmation of a partisan faith of long standing."[1] The voter begins with the belief that one party supports his or her interests and simply chooses the candidate nominated by that party. Thus, according to Key, the typical voter rarely evaluates candidates objectively. A person may not immediately know anything about, say, Jim Bunning (Republican senator from Kentucky) or Herb Kohl (Democratic senator from Wisconsin), but upon discovering each politician's party affiliation, most

---

* Data from CNN exit poll, available at www.cnn.com/POLITICS/

people will quickly develop a strong opinion. If a voter identifies with the candidate's party, he or she almost always concludes that the candidate favors the right proposals.

Party identification even influences the way people evaluate a politician's character. The Watergate scandal (1972–1974) produced a wide range of opinion about the nature and significance of actions taken by Richard Nixon and his advisers, and many people formed their opinions under the influence of partisan identification. Republicans were far more likely than Democrats to conclude that Richard Nixon's illegal activities were excusable or unimportant.

Bill Clinton's second term (1997–2001) was marked by the scandal surrounding his testimony about his relationship with intern Monica Lewinsky in a sexual-harassment lawsuit brought by former Arkansas state employee Paula Jones. Although polls regularly indicated that nearly all Americans disapproved of his behavior, most of those identifying with the Democratic Party concluded that Clinton's behavior was a personal issue, whereas Republicans argued that he was guilty of multiple felonies, particularly perjury and obstruction of justice. Party identification even influences how people interpret news about the economy. In June 2008, a CBS/*New York Times* poll reported that 34 percent of Republicans, but only 9 percent of Democrats, felt that the economy was "very" or "fairly" good, and 64 percent of Republicans, but 89 percent of Democrats, felt that the economy was "fairly" or "very" bad.[2]

The stronger an individual's identification with a particular party, the greater the likelihood that party identification will influence that person's policy views and voting choices. A recent U.S. study of the impact of character on voter judgments confirmed that "partisan bias promotes reliance on impressions of character weakness." In other words, "the more strongly people identify with the party" opposing the candidate, the more their negative impression of the candidate's character influences their impressions of his or her overall performance.[3]

Why does party identification play such a role? For one thing, people get much of their political information from parties or from advertisements paid for by parties, and information is always presented in ways that show the party's position to full advantage. Few of us have the time or the inclination to unearth detailed information independently; parties collect and digest the raw data regarding government and politics, presenting it to their supporters (and potential supporters) in an intelligible way.

Considerable, though not uncontested, evidence suggests that the influence of party identification has diminished in contemporary industrial democracies, particularly in Western Europe and the United States. A study of 21 Western nations concluded that party identification has steadily declined in 19 of them, including the United States, Britain, France, Germany, Sweden, Austria, and Italy.[4] Moreover, a study of Venezuela found that party identification there has become less stable in recent elections, making it difficult for a winning party to be assured of holding onto its electoral majority.[5] Where identification is weaker, it has less impact on political behavior, and its impact may be less secure.

Perhaps the most dramatic evidence of this change is the ticket splitting that has become so apparent in the United States. In national elections in the early part of the twentieth century, majorities of voters in over 90 percent of the voting districts chose candidates from the same party for both presidential and congressional races. During the 1980s, majorities of voters in more than one-third of the districts selected a presidential candidate from one party and a congressional candidate from another.[6]

Ticket splitting continues in this century. In 2004, 41 of the House districts won by George W. Bush elected Democrats to Congress, and 18 of the House districts that John Kerry won elected Republicans to Congress. Clearly, although party identification remains an important influence on voting choices and opinions, other factors are also important, leading many citizens to oppose their chosen parties with some of their votes.

Of course, party leaders in power can take steps to increase their support among voters. Parties tend to become identified with certain policies over a long period of time, and some of these policies have a negative impact on their support among the general public. In the U.S., many voters associate the Democratic Party with public welfare programs, and—rightly or wrongly—this association has been exploited by the Republican Party. A 2007 study explored the idea that President Clinton, along with many important Democrats in Congress, enacted welfare reform in an effort to "free the party of a significant electoral liability." Although the evidence is mixed, the data suggest that, following the 1996 legislation reforming welfare (and essentially ending it as a federal entitlement), the Republican Party largely lost its advantage over the Democratic Party on the welfare issue.[7]

The researchers compared survey results over a thirty-year period. Voters were asked whether welfare policy was a "reason to like" or a "reason to dislike" each of the parties. In 1982, the percentage of respondents reporting that welfare policy was a "reason to like" the Republicans was 20 percent higher than the percentage of respondents who said that welfare policy was a reason to like the Democrats, but neither party had an advantage on this issue after 2000. Party identification clearly affects the choices voters make, but once in power, parties may be able to affect the support they enjoy by changing policies.

Ideology   The most significant influence on political opinions after party identification is *ideological orientation*. As discussed in Chapter 2, we often speak of a person's being liberal or conservative, suggesting a predisposition to interpret political issues from a particular viewpoint. As with party identification, ideological orientations shape voters' opinions. Conservatives tend to discount allegations of impropriety on the part of conservative politicians, and liberals tend to do the same with liberal politicians. Moreover, someone may hear of a specific issue or policy question on which he or she is initially undecided. If this person considers himself or herself a "liberal," and then finds out which side is the "liberal" side, he or she will tend to support that position (unless other influences operate in the opposite direction). Of course, conservatives act this way as well.

Thus, liberals vote for liberal candidates and conservatives vote for conservative candidates. In 2004, conservatives rated George W. Bush nearly twice as highly as liberals did. Liberal and conservative votes followed the same pattern in 2008, as 88 percent of liberals voted for Barack Obama, and 78 percent of conservatives voted for John McCain.

In short, if we want to understand how to account for the public's opinions on candidates or issues, it is useful to begin with party identification and ideological orientation. These general frameworks often determine how citizens make their specific political choices. Although most voters occasionally disagree with their party or with ideologically similar friends about some issue or candidate, predictions about a person's vote are likely to be much more accurate if we have firm data about that person's partisan and ideological orientations.

Sources of Party Identification and Ideological Orientation

Where do these important influences on vote choice and public opinion come from? (Almost no one thinks they are determined by our DNA.) People develop their party identification and ideological orientation through the influence of family, education, work groups, religious affiliation, the media, unions and professional associations, and other important relationships. Despite the individualized nature of this process, however, some general patterns can be identified.

Socioeconomic Status (SES)   For some time, social scientists have discussed the importance of **socioeconomic status**, or SES. A person's SES is determined by income, education, and job status. (Successful neurosurgeons and certified public accountants with leading firms have "high" SES; the typical migrant farm laborer has "low" SES.) Political scientists, sociologists, and campaign strategists have noted a strong relationship between SES and partisan and ideological orientations, at least among people in industrialized democracies.

Simply put, people with high SES tend to support conservative parties and ideology, and low-SES people tend to support leftist parties and ideology. This relationship has been observed in many countries and over a long period of time. A classic study of U.S. public opinion found that in 1964 nearly 50 percent of self-identified "working-class" respondents identified themselves as "completely liberal," compared with only 20 percent of respondents from higher classes.[8] The same pattern was evident in recent presidential elections. In both 1992 and 1996, Democrat Bill Clinton received 59 percent of the votes cast by citizens with annual incomes under $15,000. Wealthier voters found him and his party far less appealing. Clinton received only 35 percent of the votes cast by people with household incomes over $75,000 in 1992, and only about 40 percent of the votes from this group in 1996. In 2004, Democrat Kerry beat Republican Bush 63 percent to 36 percent among the lowest income group, while Bush won handily among those making $200,000 or more, 63 percent to 35 percent. And, in 2008, Democrat Barack Obama only received 49 percent of the vote from those with incomes above $100,000, but he received 55 percent from those with incomes below $100,000. The tendency for SES to influence partisan and ideological orientation is also regularly found in Great Britain, France, Germany, Sweden, and many other democratic political systems.

Two important facts must be noted about this relationship. First, the relationship between SES on the one hand, and ideology or party identification on the other, is valid only in the *aggregate*. A thousand randomly selected wealthy Britons will include more Conservatives than will a thousand randomly selected blue-collar workers. One will also find more Democratic Party supporters among a thousand randomly selected American blue-collar workers than among a thousand wealthy Americans. There will obviously be many exceptions.

Second, the impact of SES has been declining in the United States and Europe over the past five decades. In the United States and Great Britain, as working-class voters have become more economically comfortable (particularly as they have become homeowners), many have become less attached to the economic policies of the Democratic and Labour parties. Substantial numbers of them voted for Ronald Reagan and George Bush in the United States and for the Conservative Party in Great Britain.

*Data from CNN exit polls, available at www.cnn.com/POLITICS/

At the same time, increasing numbers of high-SES citizens are drawn to leftist parties and candidates who advocate more vigorous environmental regulation. Both trends run counter to the traditional relationship between SES and opinion/voting choice.

In the previous chapter, we discussed Ronald Inglehart's evidence of a "culture shift" associated with the rise of what he terms post-materialist values in the industrial democracies of Europe and North America.[9] As societies move beyond struggles over industrial and economic policy, political issues become immersed in other matters, and the impact of SES on party and ideology is less straightforward.

Figure 4.1 shows how the political effect of SES changed in four democracies during the second half of the twentieth century. The vertical axis is the "Alford Class Voting Index," which is simply the "difference between the percentage of the *working class* voting for the left and the percentage of the *middle class* voting left."[10] Thus, where the curves are in the upper part of the graph, it indicates that the influence of SES on vote choice was very strong—that the percentage of *working-class voters* who voted for leftist parties was much higher than the percentage of *middle-class voters* who chose such parties. Where the curves are in the lower part of the graph, there was little difference between lower and middle classes with respect to their support for leftist parties. In 1948, 75 percent of Swedish working-class voters favored the Socialist Party, whereas only 25 percent of middle-class Swedes did the same (producing a difference

FIGURE 4.1   The Decline of "Class-Based" Voting

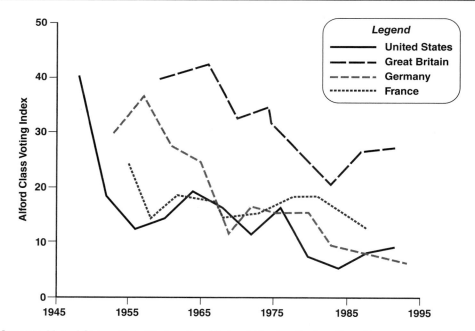

SOURCES: United States, 1948–92, American National Election Studies. Great Britain, 1959, Civic Culture Study; 1964–92, British Election Studies. Germany, 1953–94, German Election Studies. France, 1955, MacRae (1967, 257); 1958, Converse and Dupeux study; 1962, IFOP survey; 1967, Converse and Pierce study; 1968, Inglehart study; 1973–88, Eurobarometer studies. Reprinted from Russell J. Dalton, *Citizen Politics* (Chatham, NJ: Chatham House, 1996) p. 172. Reprinted by permission.

score of 50 points). The 1948 presidential election in the United States between Harry Truman and Thomas Dewey produced almost as big a gap, with working-class voters 45 points more favorable to Truman than middle-class voters were.

However, the figure reveals a fairly sharp drop in the relationship between class and vote during the second half of the twentieth century in the United States and in three countries in Western Europe. In the 1972 U.S. presidential race (Democrat George McGovern versus Republican Richard Nixon), for example, there was virtually no difference in the percentages of working-class and middle-class voters favoring the liberal candidate. Among the countries in Figure 4.1, Britain retains the strongest relationship between class and voting preference, whereas in the United States and Germany that linkage is quite low. A recent study of public opinion in Russia presents further evidence suggesting that the traditional relationship between SES and political attitudes is not as simple or as strong as it once was. According to Ada Finifter, the belief that the individual—not the state—is primarily responsible for a person's well-being (a basic axiom of conservatism) is not strongly related to the respondent's level of education in Russia.* Contemporary Russian public opinion thus does not confirm the traditional pattern of high-SES conservatism.

A recent study by three European political scientists concluded that "the decline of the relationship between class and voting behavior has been caused by a . . . decrease in the tendency of the well educated to vote for parties on the right and a decrease in the poorly educated to vote for parties on the left."[11] Their analysis of the data attributes this change to the rise of "cultural" issues, and the authors argue that, apart from the voting choices influenced by these factors, there is still an underlying tendency for SES to play its established role (i.e., high SES citizens vote for conservatives, low SES citizens vote for liberals). "Class voting" still exists, they argue, but its effects are often obscured by "cultural voting."

As discussed in Chapter 3, the reasons for the declining importance of SES are complex, but they have to do with the increasing economic security and accumulated property on the part of lower-income voters and the increasing concern for non-economic values (for example, environmental protection) among the more affluent. Thus, more low-SES voters are drawn to conservative parties than in earlier decades, and more high-SES voters support liberal parties. The traditional pattern—high-SES conservatives and low-SES liberals—becomes weaker.

Despite the contemporary erosion of the relationship between SES and party/ideological orientations, this basic feature of modern politics is far from obsolete. Liberal candidates generally do not spend a major share of their time or money campaigning in the wealthier suburbs of British or Australian cities, for example, and conservative Republicans rarely hold rallies in low-income urban neighborhoods in the U.S. These strategies (and many others) are based on the widely recognized relationship between SES and partisan and ideological orientations. SES remains the best single predictor of a person's party and ideology, even though such predictions are less secure than they used to be.

Gender Beginning the 1980s, political scientists and journalists noted that the distribution of opinion among women and men was conspicuously different in many industrialized democracies. Polls show that women are likely to be somewhat more

* See Ada W. Finifter, "Attitudes toward Individual Responsibility and Political Reform in the Former Soviet Union," *American Political Science Review* 90 (1996): 138–152. The study also reported results from 39 other countries, suggesting that educational level is only weakly related to conservative views on this issue.

liberal than men on foreign policy, domestic spending priorities, and several other policy issues. Hence, analysts now often speak of a **gender gap**, suggesting that gender is an increasingly important influence on opinion formation and voting choices.

Figure 4.2 shows the influence of gender on political attitudes in a large array of countries, including both industrial and developing nations. The data are from a survey in which respondents were asked if they think that the government or private industry should be given increased influence in society. Those favoring private industry were judged to be "right-wing," and those favoring a stronger government role were judged to be "left-wing." When the bar on the figure corresponding to a given country is on the left side, it indicates the degree to which women in that country are more liberal than men.[12] When it is on the right side, it indicates the degree to which women are more conservative than men. The data show that the tendency for women to be more liberal than men is almost universal, at least since the 1990s.

The idea that men and women approach politics differently is not new. In the early years of the twentieth century, in both the United States and Great Britain, supporters of voting rights for women argued that the political impact of such a reform would be dramatic. Wars would be avoided, there would be less corruption, and family values would be strengthened if women were allowed to vote. Early empirical work suggested that those predictions were wrong. In the 1960s, Almond and Verba's *The Civic Culture* concluded that "women differ from men . . . only in being somewhat more . . . apathetic, parochial, conservative, and sensitive to the personality, emotional, and aesthetic aspects of political life and electoral campaigns."[13]

Things have certainly changed since *The Civic Culture* was published. In the United States, women are clearly more supportive of the Democratic Party than are men, and they adopt somewhat more liberal positions on policy. Women are less sympathetic to large defense expenditures than men are, and, in general, women are less "hawkish." As a group, women were more hesitant about entering the 1991 Gulf War and the 2003 invasion of Iraq, and are also more likely than men to see a need for state intervention in the economy for health care and education.

Nevertheless, the extent to which the sexes hold different opinions is often exaggerated. For example, although female voters in the United States have been more sympathetic than males to Democratic presidential candidates in recent years, women as a group still favored Ronald Reagan over Jimmy Carter in 1980 and over Walter Mondale in 1984, and they were evenly split between George Bush and Michael Dukakis in 1988. Table 4.1 also shows that both men and women preferred Clinton to Bush in 1992, although the margin among women was considerably larger. Beginning in 1996, majorities of U.S. men and majorities of U.S. women preferred different candidates. In 1996, men slightly favored Dole (44 to 43 percent), whereas women clearly favored Clinton (54 to 38 percent); in 2000, men favored Bush (53 to 42 percent), whereas women favored Gore (54 to 43 percent); and in 2004, men favored Bush (55 to 44 percent), whereas women favored Kerry (51 to 48 percent). In 2008, men were almost evenly split between the candidates, 49 percent for Obama and 48 percent for McCain, but women favored Obama by a strong margin of 56 percent to 43 percent.

What has caused this conspicuous difference in political opinions? Many observers (and nearly all journalists) attribute the gender gap in the U.S. to the success of the feminist movement. By raising women's "consciousness," feminist organizations have made women see that their interests demand leftist policies, according to this view. Moreover, as women have entered the workforce in greater proportions, their

FIGURE 4.2   THE POLITICAL GENDER GAP AROUND THE WORLD

The lengths of the bars indicate the gender gap for each country. When the bar is to the left of the zero line, it indicates that women are more supportive of left-wing ideologies than men are; for the few countries in which the bar is to the right, it indicates that women are more supportive of right-wing ideologies than men are.

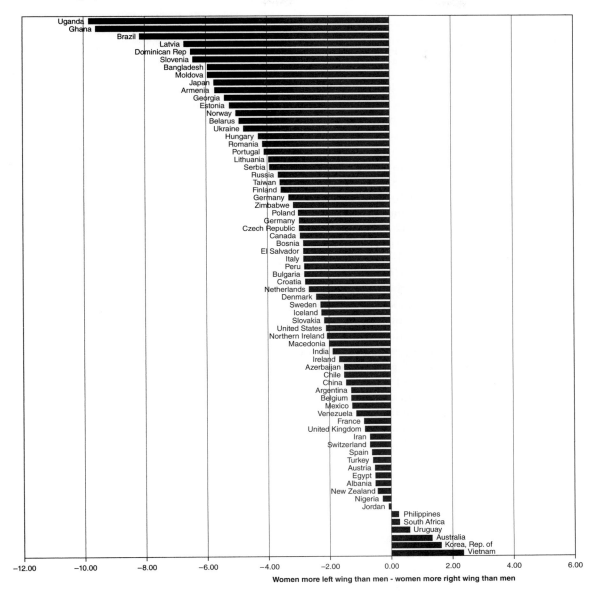

SOURCE: Ronald Inglehart and Pippa Norris, *The Rising Tide: Gender Equality and Cultural Change Around the World* (Cambridge, UK: Cambridge University Press, 2003), p. 82.

TABLE 4.1   ELECTORAL RESULTS FROM RECENT U.S. PRESIDENTIAL ELECTIONS, BY GENDER (PERCENT)

	1988		1992			1996		2000		2004		2008	
	Bush	Dukakis	Clinton	Bush	Perot	Clinton	Dole	Bush	Gore	Bush	Kerry	McCain	Obama
Men	57	41	41	38	10	43	44	53	42	55	44	48	49
Women	50	49	48	37	7	54	38	43	52	48	51	43	56

SOURCE: Exit poll data. *New York Times* on the Web at www.nyt.com. Results for the 2000, 2004, and 2008 elections are from the CNN exit polls, available at www.cnn.com/POLITICS/

traditional roles have all but vanished. Many women thus have acquired a pronounced feminist perspective regarding such issues as child care, nuclear disarmament, and abortion. Perhaps the modern gender gap has been created by the fact that the remaining vestiges of traditional gender roles seem increasingly antiquated and unfair in modern life.

However, an important study in the *American Journal of Political Science* evaluated data on U.S. elections beginning in the 1950s and concluded that the "gender gap is the product of the changing partisanship of *men*."[14] In other words, the observed differences between male and female voters have grown not because women have deserted the Republican Party *but because many men have deserted the Democratic Party.*

Figure 4.3 sheds some light on changes over time with respect to gender and political attitudes. In the 1950s, majorities of both men and women identified with the Democratic Party. Beginning in the 1980s, however, women remained generally unchanged in their party allegiance, while men substantially drifted to the Republicans. The Democratic Party has thus been damaged by the gender gap: the last time a majority of non-minority males voted for a Democratic presidential candidate was 1964, and the Republican "revolution" of 1994 was often attributed to the fact that many male voters had left the Democratic Party. The pattern has continued. In 2008, a Rasmussen Report found that 47% of U.S. women identified with the Democratic Party, compared to just 36% of U.S. men.[15]

As political scientists have worked to understand the influence of gender on vote choice and public opinion, they have recently focused on the importance of *marital status*. In several recent U.S. elections, the gap between married and non-married voters has actually been greater than the gap between men and women. For example, in the 2004 election, married voters were considerably more supportive of the Republicans over the Democrats (36 percent to 28 percent), while non-married voters preferred the Democrats (36 percent to 24 percent). Married women support the Republican Party almost as strongly as married men do, but non-married women are nearly twice as supportive of the Democrats as they are of the Republicans.[16]

The gender gap is the subject of a great deal of contemporary research in psychology and sociology. Some analysts emphasize that more women than men are primary caregivers to both children and the elderly and that these experiences generate concern for social programs advocated by liberal parties. Others contend that the root of the gender gap is deeper, having to do with the differences between the way male and female infants relate to their mothers. According to this controversial argument, the male child has a greater need to emphasize his separateness from the mother, leading men to be more aggressive and competitive, eventually becoming more supportive of defense spending and less drawn to social welfare efforts.[17]

FIGURE 4.3   THE SOURCE OF THE "GENDER GAP"

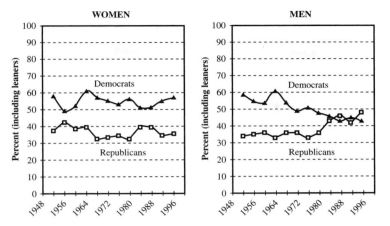

SOURCE: From Karen M. Kaufmann and John R. Petrocik, "The Changing Politics of American Men: Understanding the Sources of the Gender Gap," *American Journal of Political Science*, Vol. 43 (1999). Reprinted by permission of Blackwell Publishing Ltd.

Other Influences on Party Identification and Ideological Orientation   Several other factors influence partisan and ideological orientation. In many countries, *race* continues to be critical, often overriding the effects of party or ideology. Most observers of U.S. politics are aware, for example, that fewer than 8 percent of African Americans have voted for Republican presidential candidates in recent elections. Race and ethnicity are also profoundly important factors in elections in Israel, where Sephardic Jews (those descended from Jews in Spain, Portugal, the Middle East, and North Africa) are traditionally more supportive of the conservative Likud Party, while Ashkenazi Jews (Jews of European origin) are more likely to vote for leftist parties.

Religion remains a major political influence in some countries. French and Italian citizens who regularly attend church have more conservative beliefs than those who do not.[18] Voters in different *regions* of some countries approach politics in distinctive ways, revealing modern echoes of ancient conflicts.

Psychological factors constitute a rather different (and often questioned) influence on partisan and ideological orientations. A famous U.S. study in the 1950s concluded that people who held conservative beliefs tended to have psychological traits that were different from liberals. People suffering from significant anxiety, for example, supposedly developed an aversion to change and thus chose to support conservative leaders and parties.[19] Although the methods and data used in that study were widely criticized, many analysts feel that psychology and political attitudes are related.

Candidate Evaluation: A Confounding Element in Public Opinion

Citizens do not always form opinions or make their voting choices on the basis of party identification and ideological orientation. It is well established that people often react strongly to the personality, style, or "charisma" of a particular candidate. Such

© Karim Sahib/AP Photo

VOTING IN IRAQ, 2005   Iraqi Industry Minister Hajim al-Hassani, a Sunni Arab, casts his vote at the National Assembly session in Baghdad, Iraq, Sunday April 3, 2005. Iraqi lawmakers elected al-Hassani as parliament speaker Sunday, ending days of deadlock and moving forward on forming a new government two months after the country's historic elections.

reactions, positive or negative, can influence not only a person's vote but also his or her opinions regarding policies and political controversies.

This simple, obvious fact often makes public opinion and voting behavior unpredictable. The influence of **candidate evaluation** was extensively discussed in the United States in the 1980s when Ronald Reagan persuaded large numbers of Democratic Party identifiers to vote for him. Democratic Party leaders claimed that most of those voters really supported their policies but were deluded into voting for Reagan by his winning personality and his professional actor's gifts for communication. Similarly, many political analysts argued that Robert Dole lost in 1996 in part because his dour personality (at least on television) made him less appealing than Bill Clinton. In Britain, Labour Party leader Tony Blair used his John Kennedyesque appeal to become the longest serving British Prime Minister (1997–2007). On the other hand, Stephen Harper, whose Conservative Party won a 2006 election in Canada, is generally considered rather introverted and has a reputation for stiffness in public appearances. Many consider Barack Obama to be the most charismatic U.S. politician in decades, and his ability to inspire citizens was a factor in 2008, as were some nagging questions about the persons he was associated with early in his career. While candidate personality and appeal may matter, other things obviously can overwhelm their effects.

Generally speaking, candidate evaluation can be especially important in elections in which the mass media figure prominently and when highly paid consultants successfully manipulate a candidate's "image." Candidate evaluation presents a problem for political analysis, however, because it is so unpredictable. Since citizens can be influenced by factors as changeable as the prevailing image of a candidate's personality, predictions of electoral results on the basis of partisan identification and ideological orientation will often be wrong.

The Impact of Mass Media

In most countries, the mass media, especially newspapers and television, influence voters significantly. The media can amplify or undercut support for a specific candidate; over time, they may even influence deep-seated ideological and partisan attachments. Questions pertaining to the actual workings and effects of the media in these matters are thus critical to the study of public opinion and electoral behavior.

At the outset, it is vital to recognize that not all countries have the same mass media influences. Americans (as well as French and British citizens) rely heavily on television for their political information. According to BBC Tokyo Bureau Chief William Horsley writing in the 1980s, Japanese voters avidly read newspapers, which "play the role of the constructive critic of the government."[20] In rural areas of the developing world, radio has a great influence. In virtually all societies, however, mass media of some form exert an influence on public opinion.

Gauging the impact of the media on opinions and voting choices is difficult because it is so hard to separate the influence of the media from the influence of party affiliation, family and peer groups, and other organizational relationships. The most difficult questions have to do with the bias allegedly created by broadcasters and newspapers in democratic societies. There is an intriguing symmetry to the charges of bias; nearly always, activists and politicians on *both* the right and the left present charges that the media slant the news. Richard Nixon was strident in his repeated attacks against media bias. He often claimed that the media "kicked him around," and revelations during the Watergate period indicated how much he resented the media. (Nixon had an "enemies" list that included correspondent Daniel Schorr and other journalists.)

Although not as aroused as Nixon was by the media, virtually every president has argued that journalists are unfair. Bill Clinton's scandals were thoroughly covered in both broadcast and print media, and the subject matter involved enabled reporters and news anchors to keep their readers and audiences continually interested. Mere weeks prior to the 2004 election, former CBS News Director Dan Rather presented a very critical report about George W. Bush's National Guard Service, although the documents that figured prominently in the story were almost certainly forged. In 2008, Bill Clinton complained bitterly about the media's treatment of Senator Hillary Clinton's campaign to become the Democratic Party's presidential nominee, claiming that the press was sexist and profoundly biased toward Senator Barack Obama.

Beyond bias, the most troubling political problem associated with the media has to do with the tendency to oversimplify and distort serious political issues, thereby degrading political discourse. (See Box 4-1.) Television seems particularly susceptible to damaging manipulation, but sophisticated campaign managers are often creative in achieving the same effects in other contexts. One famous example of an oversimplifying, emotional political advertisement occurred during the 1964 U.S. presidential race, when Democrat Lyndon Johnson's campaign ran a television spot—designed to discredit Republican candidate Barry Goldwater—showing a little girl playing with a flower. A narrator spoke in ominous tones about Goldwater's allegedly "warmongering"

THE EFFECT OF THE MEDIA ON POLITICAL TOLERANCE

"Do we really believe that ALL red-state residents are ignorant fascist knuckle-dragging NASCAR-obsessed cousin-marrying road-kill-eating tobacco-juice-dribbling gun-fondling religious fanatic rednecks; or that ALL blue state residents are godless unpatriotic pierced-nose Volvo-driving France-loving left-wing Communist latte-sucking tofu-chomping holistic-wacko neurotic vegan weenie perverts?" This question, posed by humorist Dave Barry in December 2004, is perhaps less of an exaggeration of the way Americans view their ideological opposites than we would like to think.*

In an important recent article in the American Political Science Review, Diana Mutz examined findings from a series of experimental studies, concluding that contemporary television news coverage in the U.S. tends to make people less tolerant of candidates and issue positions they oppose: "The 'in-your-face' intimacy of uncivil political discourse on television discourages the kind of mutual respect that might sustain perceptions of a legitimate opposition." Vehement and even violent disagreements are nothing new in political life, but there are indications that television coverage of politics on 24-hour news channels during the last two decades has intensified "citizens' negativity toward those people and ideas that they dislike."[21]

Tolerance for dissenting opinions is a fundamental component of stable democracy. If television coverage of politics leads a large share of the population to become less tolerant of political opposition, it could lead to some real problems in the future. On the other hand, a highly mobilized public can be a healthy characteristic of democratic society, even when debate is heated and passionate. Despite Dave Barry's very funny caricature, there are few signs of a basic breakdown of democratic political culture in the U.S. (or in other countries with access to our news channels), but the rhetoric is sometimes striking.

* Dave Barry's rhetorical question was quoted in Mutz, Diana C., "Effects of 'In-Your-Face' Television Discourse on Perceptions of a Legitimate Opposition," *American Political Science Review*, Vol. 101 (November 2007), p. 621.

policy proposals, and then the girl looked up as a mushroom cloud rose from an atomic bomb. Although the commercial aired only once, it demonstrated the power of television to use emotion in influencing voters. In 2004, perhaps the most controversial ads on television were those run by the Swiftboat Veterans for Truth, a group claiming that Democrat John Kerry had misrepresented his combat record in Vietnam. The 2008 U.S. presidential race was memorable for television (and YouTube) coverage of fiery sermons by Reverend Jeremiah Wright, a former pastor and friend of Senator Barack Obama. In all these cases, the mass media treated important and complex issues in ways that were arguably emotional and manipulative while making little contribution to rational analysis.

It is thus ironic that a recent study concluded that "political advertising [in the United States] contributes to a well-informed electorate."[†] Researchers found that U.S. respondents who paid attention to paid political advertisements had more information about the candidates' issue positions than those who only read newspapers and watched television news. Apparently, campaign commercials transmit at least some real information along with the "sound bites."

Contemporary democracies vary with respect to regulation of political advertising. Paid political advertisements are permitted in Australia, Canada, and Japan, but have been prohibited in Great Britain, Sweden, Italy, India, France, and Germany,

† See Craig Leonard Brians and Martin P. Wattenberg, "Campaign Issue Knowledge and Salience: Comparing Reception from TV Commercials, TV News, and Newspapers," *American Journal of Political Science* 40 (1996): 172–193.

among other countries. The Bipartisan Campaign Reform Act of 2002, signed into law by President Bush on March 27, 2002, regulates contributions and some issue ads in the United States, and we will discuss this legislation in detail in Chapter 11. Most of the countries that prohibit paid ads reserve free broadcast time for parties, typically allocated to each in proportion to its voting strength. The objective is to ensure that broadcast media will bring information to voters while minimizing the chances that money and clever tactics will manipulate the voters. However, in many Third World countries, one party often has much more money for media advertising than others, giving it a distinct advantage.

Perhaps the most critical factor is the *diversity* of mass media; if no single voice controls newspapers and broadcasting, it is much more difficult to produce significant shifts in support and opposition through the media. A state-controlled or censored press—such as has existed in Chile, Vietnam, China, and elsewhere—is clearly an influential tool. Television, radio, and newspapers in these countries are used to generate support, direct citizens, and retain power. Yet the demise of repressive regimes in Eastern Europe, Chile, and elsewhere suggests that the power of state-owned media to control public opinion has its limits. Where the press is free and open, some alternative spokesperson will find an outlet to criticize the government or the ruling party, and some people will listen. The impact of the media is substantially blunted when real media diversity exists, and it is greatly multiplied when all media are in the hands of one ruling party or group.

A particularly controversial news source was added to the international mix of media outlets in 2006. In that year, Al Jazeera launched "Al Jazeera International," a 24-hour English language news and current affairs channel. (There is also a Web version of Al Jazeera, at http://english.aljazeera.net/English.) With little competition in the Middle East, the question of Al Jazeera's political influence in these unsettled countries is profoundly important. U.S. government officials have argued that Al Jazeera's news coverage is anti-American, anti-Israeli, and that it gives implicit support to al-Qaeda and other terrorist organizations.

Dr. Walid Phares, a professor of Middle East Studies and comparative politics at Florida Atlantic University, stated that Al Jazeera misrepresented a pro-democracy demonstration in central Baghdad. In December of 2003, some 20,000 men and women marched through the streets shouting *"La' la' lil irhab. Na'am, na'am lil dimurcratiya."* ("No, no to terrorism. Yes, yes to Democracy!"). Instead of reporting that a significant demonstration had taken place that supported the U.S. and coalition activities, the Al Jazeera coverage stated that about half that many people marched and that they "were 'expressing views against *what they call* terrorism.'"* James Morris, of the Institute of Arab and Islamic Studies at the University of Exeter in Britain, concluded that the network is simply "Osama bin Laden's loudspeaker."

The network's defenders claim that it is often criticized by radical Islamic fundamentalists as serving as a mouthpiece for the West, and that it simply presents both sides of all issues. They also point out that errors in translating their stories into English have been responsible for some of the apparent bias in the stories Al Jazeera broadcasts. In any case, this controversial news outlet will probably have a significant degree of influence as conflict within the Islamic world continues.

* The Phares essay is available at http://frontpagemag.com/Articles/Read.aspx?GUID=B8515BAE-52A2-4B96-A6B8-B2CD4161D804.

Perceptions of the Government's Economic Performance

Significant evidence shows that the state of the economy sometimes overrides the effects of other influences on voting choices, even the effects of party and ideology. Many citizens vote for or against the incumbent party on the basis of their perceptions regarding the government's economic performance. If economic growth and employment are high and inflation is low, the incumbent party will generally do well with voters, regardless of party and ideology.

A study from the 1980s concluded that, in British elections, "economic variables [exceeded] the impact of partisan identification," and those variables were generally as important as party identification in Germany.[22] Using data from presidential elections between 1956 and 1988, a prominent U.S. political scientist concluded that "each 1 percent increase in real disposable per capita income is estimated to result in a 2 percent direct increase in the incumbent's vote share, other factors held constant."[23] A recent study of British elections found that "evaluations of national economic performance are of greater importance than are personal measures," although voter perceptions of their personal economic conditions is also associated with the extent to which voters support the incumbent party.[24]

A 2006 book found that the pattern even holds in former Communist countries. Political Scientist Joshua Tucker examined voting patterns in Russia, Poland, Hungary, Slovakia, and the Czech Republic, and found that parties identified with "liberal-capitalist" reforms received more support from regions in each country in which economic conditions had improved. [25]

A general appraisal of data from several sources led to the following conclusion about economic conditions and voter choices:

> The powerful relationship between the economy and the electorate in democracies the world over comes from the economic responsiveness of the electors, the individual voters. Among the issues on the typical voter's agenda, none is more consistently present, nor generally has a stronger impact, than the economy. Citizen dissatisfaction with economic performance substantially increases the probability of a vote against the incumbent. In a sense, the volatility of short term economic performance makes this factor a particularly interesting influence on voter choices—it has its greatest effect on those with low levels of partisan attachment, and can therefore change the outcomes of elections where the parties are of relatively equal strength. Thus, in these situations, the fall of a government is more likely to come from a shift in economic evaluations than from a shift in party attachments.[26]

Given that voters in many countries appear increasingly willing to stray from their party loyalties, contemporary economic conditions will probably become even more important in future elections.

However, it is important not to overstate the importance of this factor. The relatively poor state of the U.S. economy during the months preceding the 1992 election clearly hurt George H.W. Bush, just as a strong economy obviously helped Bill Clinton in 1996. Although the U.S. economy and the stock market had started to stall during the two quarters of 2000, the economy had been quite strong for several years, and traditional indicators suggested that the incumbent party (the Democrats) would do extremely well. Vice President Al Gore did receive slightly more of the popular vote than Republican George W. Bush, but he received far less than models based on economic performance variables had predicted. The predictive models were far more accurate in 2004, suggesting a slight advantage for the incumbent Republican.[27]

In 2008, most voters felt that the U.S. economy was failing, and the voters who were most negative were far more likely to vote for Barack Obama than for John McCain. Among the few voters who judged the economy to be "excellent" or "good," McCain received 72 percent of the vote, but Obama won 54 percent of those who felt that the economy was "not so good" or "poor," according to a CNN exit poll.

A Model of Voting Choices and Opinion Formation

As the preceding sections show, the influences that shape voting choices and public opinions are diverse, complex, and changing. Figure 4.4 is a model illustrating the ways in which several influences act on voters. The idea of the model is to indicate the most important factors in general terms; in a given election in a particular country, some of those influences will be more important than in other settings. The most critical point is that research has demonstrated that voting and opinion are not random behaviors but can often be predicted and understood as the results of a complex set of known influences.

The model implies that SES normally works on opinion formation and voting choice indirectly, by determining party identification and ideological orientation. Gender, race, religion, regional identifications, and psychology, in contrast, often determine both partisan/ideological attachments and specific opinions and voting choices.

FIGURE 4.4   A MODEL OF VOTING CHOICE AND OPINION FORMATION

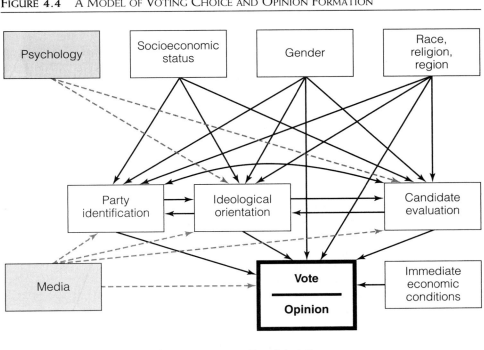

Candidate evaluation appears in the model as a factor acting independently on votes and opinions. A particularly strong candidate evaluation can also change party and ideological attachments—some citizens may change their party or even their ideology as a result of their attraction to a particular individual. (The personal popularity of Franklin Roosevelt led many Americans not only to vote for him but also to become liberal Democrats in the 1930s.) Finally, it should be noted that the media's primary potential effect is on opinions and voting choices. On the other hand, newspapers, radio, and television may have a longer-term impact, even one that changes partisan and ideological orientations, when the media are under the control of the state or a single dominant interest.

The model helps us understand why research on voting and public opinion is so important a part of political science. Simple explanations (e.g., "John Kerry lost because voters perceived him as weak on national defense," or "Nicholas Sarkozy became the new president of France because the French became skeptical about their welfare state," etc.) are almost always incomplete. Accumulated knowledge drawn from political science research makes it clear that voting outcomes and the changing distribution of public opinion are very difficult phenomena to explain and predict, but we have made great progress in terms of identifying which influences are important.

VOTER TURNOUT

Although research on public opinion and voting often focuses on the nature of the respondents' opinions or their vote preferences, it also deals with the question of **voter turnout**. The percentage of citizens who actually vote varies considerably across countries. (See Table 4.2.) The reasons for variations in turnout are many, including factors related to voters themselves (such as economic position, psychological orientation to politics, education, and access to transportation), the competitiveness of candidates and parties, and the nature of political system (legal requirements pertaining to voting, the activities of parties and other organizations to encourage turnout, and the expected closeness of elections).

Cultural norms are often important in determining voter turnout—in some countries, citizens consider voting a moral duty, and people vote for that reason even when they are unconcerned about the outcome of the election. Public opinion surveys in Venezuela and Mexico, for example, show that most voters feel that elections make little difference in determining government policy. Yet respondents in both countries stated that it was very important to vote.

A decline in partisan loyalty can also reduce turnout. People vote less often when they lose a sense of partisan loyalty, voting only when the few special issues they care about are at stake. In contrast, strong partisans would vote regularly because of their commitment to the party itself.

Legal considerations significantly affect voting turnout. Voter registration is still relatively cumbersome in many states in the U.S., often requiring a special visit to city hall; easier voter registration in some other industrial democracies thus helps to explain why U.S. turnout is lower. Other legal factors can increase or decrease turnout. In a number of Latin American countries, parents cannot register their children in school unless they have a stamped identification card proving they voted in the

---

TABLE 4.2   TURNOUT RATES FOR SELECTED DEMOCRACIES

Percent of registered voters voting in all national elections from 1945 through 2007
(number of elections held during the period is shown in parentheses)

Italy (14)	92.5
New Zealand (18)	86.2
Australia (21)	84.4
Sweden (17)	83.3
Germany (13)	80.6
Greece (17)	80.3
Israel (14)	80.0
Norway (14)	79.5
Palestinian Authority (1)	75.4
United Kingdom (15)	74.9
Ireland (16)	74.9
Uruguay (10)	70.3
Nicaragua (10)	62.0
India (12)	60.7
Honduras (12)	55.3
Switzerland (13)	49.3
United States (26)	48.3
Colombia (20)	36.2
Guatemala (15)	29.8
Mali (2)	21.7

NOTE: Turnout percentages are for national elections to the lower house of the national legislature, except for Chile, Mali, and the United States, where turnout percentages are for presidential elections.
SOURCE: Institute for Democracy and Electoral Assistance (Stockholm, Sweden) at http://www.idea.int.

---

last election (although such requirements can be overcome by paying fines or bribes). Large numbers of Italian citizens working in other parts of Europe return home to vote. Although some of these Italians may be motivated by a sense of civic duty, their behavior is also influenced by the fact that the government pays their passage home on such occasions. Moreover, many nations schedule national elections on Sunday, when people are not at their weekday jobs.

Voting is compulsory in some nations, and it is strictly enforced in Australia, Switzerland, Singapore, and Uruguay, among a few others, all of which have very high turnout rates. Part of the drop in the U.S. turnout rate since the 1960s is related to the lowering of the voting age from 21 to 18, since turnout among younger voters is usually low. Another systemic factor affecting turnout is the type of electoral system each country has: countries with **proportional representation** generally have higher turnout rates than countries with *single-member districts*. As discussed below, voters have a wider range of parties to choose from in PR systems, thus increasing the chances that each voter will have an appealing choice).

Rational Choice Theory and Voter Turnout   The rational choice approach to political analysis has had some real difficulties with the empirical fact of substantial voter turnout. Regardless of the electoral laws, other legal factors, and party loyalty and cultural norms, the purely rational individual should find it difficult to justify any expenditure of time or resources to vote. The tiny probability that a single vote will determine the election's outcome makes it, strictly speaking, irrational to vote, even when the voter cares deeply about the outcome. Nevertheless, millions of people do vote. Some rational choice scholars have attempted to reconcile their assumptions about self interest and rationality with the fact that significant voting occurs by arguing that there are some "side benefits" to voting, such as obtaining a feeling of self respect by going to the polls, or a social status benefit when others see the voter doing his or her civic duty.

Instead of trying to find out why any voting takes place at all, a recent theoretical analysis uses rational choice ideas to explore the circumstances in which voter turnout should be somewhat higher or lower. Two political scientists considered the "size effect," which suggests that voting turnout percentages should be lower when the electorate is larger (because a single vote is less likely to make a difference than it does in smaller electorates). They also studied the "competition" and "underdog" effects, which suggest that voting turnout should be higher when an election is expected to be close, and that it should be higher among those who support an unpopular candidate.[28]

The researchers found that there is support for the rational choice ideas that citizens do take the competitiveness of elections into account when they decide to vote, and that their behavior is also affected by the size of the electorate and the "underdog" effect. Thus, even though more people vote than a strictly rational calculus would suggest, factors affecting the costs and projected benefits of voting apparently do have an effect on turnout.

The Causes of Low Voter Turnout Considering the reasons for different levels of voting turnout across countries may help us understand how well, or how poorly, democracy works in practice. For example, turnout may be very low in less developed regions because of poor transportation, literacy requirements, or even intimidation. According to International IDEA (The International Institute for Democracy and Electoral Assistance, based in Sweden), literacy has a substantial influence on turnout: the 52 countries with 95 percent or better literacy rates have an average turnout of 71 percent, while the 104 less literate countries have an average turnout rate of only 61 percent. In Guatemala, where large portions of the nation's population are Indians who speak no Spanish, literacy requirements particularly suppress the vote. Violence and the threat of violence also keep citizens away from the polls.

A new study of voting turnout by International IDEA found that the gap in voting turnout between "established democracies" and newer democracies has diminished since the 1990s. (For this study, "established democracies" are democracies with a population of at least 250,000 that have been democratic for at least the last 20 years.) Figure 4.5 shows that turnout rates in both old and new democracies have declined a bit in recent years, a disturbing trend.

National voter turnout figures typically obscure great disparities in voting among different segments of society. Perhaps the most consistent research finding regarding turnout is that people of different economic conditions have different turnout rates. Before careful statistical analysis was applied to the question, many observers speculated that poorer people would probably vote more regularly than the rich because the poor were more dependent on government. This "mobilization" hypothesis

FIGURE 4.5   VOTER TURNOUT IN ESTABLISHED AND OTHER DEMOCRACIES SINCE 1945

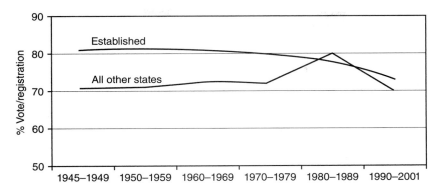

SOURCE: International IDEA.

suggested that the effect of economic distress on turnout would be to mobilize the poor to participate in politics more that the rich. Others argued for the opposite view (termed the "withdrawal" hypothesis), which is the idea that economic distress destroys a voter's sense of self-worth and hope for the future, diminishing interest in elections and leading to lower turnout among the poor.

It is well established that the mobilization hypothesis is completely wrong. Although some poor people doubtlessly respond to their economic distress by voting, a disproportionate number of them withdraw from such activities. In an often cited study from the early 1980s, Steven Rosenstone explored the extent to which this factor affects turnout in the U.S.[29] He found that people who had low incomes or who were unemployed were less likely to vote than those with high incomes and with jobs, and the negative effect on turnout increased with the severity of economic distress. More recent data confirm that not only do the poor vote less regularly than the rich but also, at least in the United States, the disparity is growing.

Census Bureau statistics reported in the August 11, 1996, *New York Times* revealed that a smaller percentage of poor U.S. citizens take advantage of the right to vote than do wealthy and middle class citizens. In 1984, only 38 percent of the poorest citizens voted, whereas 76 percent of the rich showed up at the polls. In 2000, middle-class voters (those with family incomes between $50,000 and $75,000) made up only 21.6 percent of the population, but they accounted for 25 percent of the votes cast. In contrast, those with incomes lower than $15,000 made up 9.6 percent of the population, but accounted for only 7 percent of the votes cast.[30]

A 2005 study of political inequality in 18 democracies reported that a strong association between socioeconomic status and voter turnout is not exclusively a U.S. phenomenon.[31] Table 4.3 reports the "bias" in turnout created by income and education differences for eight democracies. The table entries indicate the degree to which the turnout rate is higher among citizens in the highest income or education category, compared to the turnout rate among citizens in the lowest income or education category. (For example, the 10.8 percent "income bias" for France means that voter

TABLE 4.3 VOTER TURNOUT IS HIGHER FOR THE WEALTHY AND BETTER EDUCATED

Country	Income bias	Education bias	Year of election
Australia	5.1	4.4	2004
Britain	6.8	2.2	1997
France	10.8	7.9	2002
Germany	3.8	6.3	2002
Israel	5.9	4.4	2003
Sweden	12.3	6.8	2002
U.S.	30.0	32.9	2004

SOURCE: Data from the Comparative Study of Electoral Systems (www.cses.org), as compiled in Miki Caul Kittilson, "Rising Political Inequality in Established Democracies: Mobilization, Socio-Economic Status, and Voter Turnout, 1960s to 2000," paper presented at the 2005 Annual Meeting of the American Political Science Association.

turnout by wealthy French citizens is 10.8 percent higher than it is for poorer French citizens.)

In all these democracies, citizens with wealth and education vote at considerably higher rates than other citizens. To the extent that these citizens have different political interests or preferences than poorer, less educated citizens, the fact that they vote in greater numbers means that electoral outcomes will disproportionately favor their interests. This creates a significant challenge for virtually all modern democracies—the ballot box is not, in practice, the "voice of all the people."

Why do the poor vote less often? Wealthier citizens are more likely than the poor to be literate, to read newspapers and books, and to be members of civic associations. These activities and associations help them develop a strong interest in politics. The rich vote more because they are more involved and more informed, and because they are more likely than the poor to have developed a sense of political efficacy. Yet another problem depresses voter turnout among the poor: complicated voter registration requirements constitute obstacles to voting that are particularly difficult for the poor and uneducated. Sometimes these obstacles are intentionally designed to have this effect.

Before the Civil Rights Act of 1964, it was extremely difficult for many African Americans, particularly if they were poor, to register to vote in rural areas of the South. In many Third World countries, candidates may be so closely identified with economic elites that the poor see no purpose in voting. In Colombia and Mexico, for example, long-term declines in voting are often attributed to the perception among poor voters that the political system offers them little.

Changes in Turnout over Time

It is difficult to interpret the meaning of changes over time in voting turnout. In the United States, turnout has fallen in recent years: 62.8 percent of the voting-age population voted in the presidential election in 1960, only 52.8 percent in 1980, 53.3 percent in 1984, and only 50.3 percent in 1988. Then, after rising to 55.2 percent in 1992, turnout fell in 1996 and was only 50.3 percent in 2000. In 2004, it rose to 55.5 percent, and in 2008, well over 60 percent of eligible voters cast a ballot, the strongest turnout figure in nearly half a century.

Some are quick to suggest that declining turnout is a sign of increased alienation. Large segments of the population, say such analysts, are disgusted by scandal or hopeless about the future. Others argue that the decline in American voter turnout reflects the fact that, compared with the period before the 1960s, Americans discuss politics less often with others. Since that time, there has been a "decline in peer interaction itself, caused by a decline of the traditional family, suburbanization, and increased television watching." On the other hand, the Internet appears to have a positive impact on voting participation.[32]

Research on the causes of variations in voter turnout is an important area of political inquiry. A particularly interesting line of research has explored the impact of compulsory voting on government policy. In 2005, two researchers analyzed data on several countries, and their findings make a strong case for the importance of turnout: countries with enforced compulsory voting not only had higher turnout rates, but they also had *more equal distributions of national income.*[33] Because of the central place of voting in democratic government, understanding variations in voting across classes or across different time periods helps us to see who the "people" are in "government by the people," and it helps explain the policies governments adopt and the resulting conditions in their citizens' lives.

BELIEF SYSTEMS

Do citizens typically have well-developed, coherent approaches to making voting decisions, or are their choices haphazard reactions to chance events and personalities? In a classic study, Philip Converse explored the idea of a **belief system**, which he defined as "a configuration of ideas and attitudes in which the elements are bound together by some form of constraint."[34] A strong belief system "constrains" the voter to be consistent in selecting candidates and issue positions, and is therefore not easily swayed by superficial or extraneous information. In terms of our discussion in Chapter 2, such a person is highly *ideological;* his or her political choices are coherent and are firmly connected by some fundamental concern or orientation.

Determining the extent to which people in society can be said to have developed belief systems helps us to interpret how much real substance there is in their opinions. For example, if a large proportion of the population can be said to have recognizable belief systems, then the attractiveness of an individual candidate's personality would have less impact. Parties would offer meaningfully contrasting platforms reflecting the belief systems that shape the political views of large segments of the population. In the absence of such systems—that is, when voters' opinions are more individualized and random—parties may attempt to attract votes by emphasizing a candidate's personality, by sensation and scandal, or by other ploys.

Those who advocate democratic government thus typically hope to find some evidence of belief systems in public opinion. When citizens have coherent, systematic views of politics, a victory by one party reflects a genuine policy preference, making us confident that elections really convey demands about what people want. In contrast, if people vote mainly on the basis of personality and scandal mongering, those elected are free to make any policies they wish, knowing that reelection will have little to do with policy.

Consequently, many observers were disappointed when Converse concluded that "large portions of the electorate . . . simply do not have meaningful beliefs, even on issues that have formed the basis for intense political controversy."[35] His study built on the findings reported in *The American Voter*, one of the most famous political science books ever written. Analyzing public opinion surveys from the 1950s, the authors concluded that the typical American has a rather low "level of conceptualization" regarding political issues.[36] Even by the most generous estimate, the authors found that no more than ten percent of the population approached political issues from a well-developed ideological perspective. At best, the typical voter had only a vague idea that one of the two parties was more likely to represent his or her interests. Other research suggests that this conclusion remains accurate, both in the U.S. and in Europe.[37] Even the rapid spread of Internet technology has failed to have a substantial impact: "Our more well-educated, media-soaked public simply has not exhibited any significant increase in knowledge about public affairs . . . nor any increase in political sophistication."[38]

However, there is evidence to support the claim that voters in contemporary democracies *are* becoming somewhat more systematic in their political thinking. As the main parties in the U.S. have adopted more distinct and antagonistic issue positions, an increasing number of citizens have become more coherently ideological. In the 1950s, the Democrats and Republicans had far more similar positions on civil rights and foreign policy than they do today. In fact, a recent cross-national study lends support to the idea that the degree to which voters develop belief systems is affected by the major parties, the electoral system, and other institutions.[39] Where policy controversies and partisan conflict mobilizes citizens and generates heated political conflict, a larger number of citizens acquire "belief systems."

Research on belief systems will continue to be a major focus of study for political scientists. Although it is well established that there will always be a large segment of the population that is not politically sophisticated, the size of this segment may increase or decrease in response to the influence of parties, leaders, and events. As research continues on the content and coherence of the public's opinions, we will learn more about the ways in which the real needs and policy preferences of citizens are related to their votes.

THE ELECTORAL PROCESS AND CAMPAIGN MONEY

One of the most controversial aspects of modern elections is the impact of campaign contributions. In some countries, publicly owned broadcasting systems provide free television and radio time for candidates to present their views to voters, but candidates and their parties usually must pay for printing and dissemination of literature, for staff support, and for travel expenses. Candidates in major U.S. elections pay for most of their media time, making campaign dollars an extremely important resource.

Campaign expenditures vary widely across nations. In some nations, campaign spending is as low as $0.20 per voter, but it can be much higher than that, especially where there are no spending limits. Where most of these expenditures are covered by public funding, candidates and parties do not have to raise the funding themselves, but fund-raising becomes a vitally important task where there is less public funding.

For example, the typical Senate campaign in the United States costs the candidate over $2 million, requiring that an incumbent raise an average of nearly $7,000 *per week* during the six years he or she is in office in order to run for reelection. Since the Supreme Court, in the 1976 *Buckley v. Valeo* ruling, has said that a person can spend unlimited shares of his or her own funds in an election campaign, wealthy individuals are often able to gain a decisive advantage over their rivals who must observe strict individual contribution limits in gathering funds. For example, Senators Herbert Kohl (D.-Wisc.) and John D. Rockefeller (D.-W. Va.)—among the richest men in the Senate—spent millions of their own fortunes to win their elections.

Table 4.4 provides information on the differences among modern nations with respect to the laws governing campaign finance. There is considerable variation among the countries in this table, reflecting different cultural and political attitudes about elections and campaigns. Consider this summary statement comparing Canada and the U.S.:

> Canada pursues a more egalitarian approach, providing public financing of about two-thirds of candidate and party costs, while seeking to achieve a "level playing field" by imposing expenditure ceilings on candidate, party, and even "third party" or interest group spending. On the other hand, the United States follows more of a libertarian or free-speech approach, with more dependence upon private financing through more generous contribution limits from individual, political action committee and political party sources.[40]

TABLE 4.4   POLITICAL FINANCE LAWS IN SELECTED NATIONS

Country	Must contributions to parties be disclosed?	Is there a maximum on contributions to parties?	Is there a ban on foreign contributions to parties?	Are contributions from corporations or unions banned?		Do parties receive public funding?
				Corps.	Unions	
Australia	yes	no	no	no	no	yes
Austria	no	no	no	no	no	yes
Denmark	yes	no	no	no	no	yes
El Salvador	no	no	no	no	no	yes
France	yes	yes	yes	yes	yes	yes
Germany	yes	no	no	no	no	yes
India	yes	no	no	no	no	no
Mexico	yes	yes	yes	yes	no	yes
Nicaragua	yes	no	no	no	no	yes
Norway	yes	no	no	no	no	yes
Peru	yes	no	no	no	no	no
Poland	yes	yes	yes	yes	yes	yes
Russia	yes	yes	yes	no	no	yes
Switzerland	no	no	no	no	no	yes
Ukraine	yes	yes	yes	no	no	no
United Kingdom	yes	no	yes	no	no	yes
United States	yes	yes	yes	yes	yes	no

NOTE: For the last column, 1 = "election period *and* between elections," 2 = "election period only," and 3 = "between elections only."
SOURCE: Reginald Austin and Maja Tjernström, eds., *Funding of Political Parties and Election Campaigns*, International IDEA Handbook Series, Stockholm, Sweden: International Institute for Democracy and Electoral Assistance, 2003, pp. 181–238.

It is difficult to determine precisely the degree to which campaign spending affects electoral outcomes. In Great Britain, analysts have typically assumed that the national campaign—largely driven by publicly funded broadcasts—is the primary factor in determining the results of parliamentary elections, although a study from the 1990s suggested that local spending may have an impact in constituencies where neither party is dominant.[41]

Recent U.S. elections suggest that campaign spending can be a major factor, not only in Senate races, but also in presidential contests. Most observers believe that the very close victory of Republican Richard Nixon over Democrat Hubert Humphrey in 1968 would have been reversed if the Democratic Party had not exhausted its funds during the last weeks of the campaign. More recently, President Clinton's 1996 reelection bid was certainly made easier by the fact that his opponent, Senator Robert Dole, had to spend millions during a difficult primary contest, exhausting the spending limits that applied until after the August conventions. During the long months between April and August, the Dole campaign was relatively silent, while Clinton maintained a consistent presence on the airwaves. In 2000 and 2004, both parties had large war chests, and both elections were close.

In 2008, Democrat Barack Obama became the first presidential candidate to reject public financing in a general election since the system was created in the early 1970s. As a result, he had many millions more to spend than his opponent, Republican John McCain. There were many factors making a McCain victory very unlikely (see Box 11-3 in Chapter 11), but the fact that Obama outspent him by nearly 3 to 1 in the final weeks put McCain at a distinct disadvantage.

Because candidates and parties may be expected to make promises and commitments to groups and individuals in exchange for contributions, most countries have strict limits on such contributions, and many limit the amount that can be spent, regardless of the source of the funds. There have been troubling reports of campaign finance problems in the U.S. for decades, and the problems have involved both major parties. In 1996, the Democratic Party allegedly accepted donations funneled through a Buddhist monastery and an Indian tribe, and there were indications that the government of China had directed campaign funds to both parties in an effort to influence U.S. policy in the Far East. Similar concerns arose regarding both parties again in 2000, and a great deal of controversy surrounded campaign contributions from the failed Enron Corporation. Contributions from oil and tobacco interests to Republican candidates have been examined for many years. Concerns about these contribution patterns, coupled with the persistent efforts of Senators McCain and Feingold and others, led to the passage of the Bipartisan Campaign Reform Act of 2002, as noted above.

ELECTORAL SYSTEMS

The "people" can be said to have a real voice in any electoral system in which the right to vote is secure, the votes are counted honestly, the choices are meaningful, and the elections are regularly scheduled. Even when those conditions are met, however, the nature of the electoral system can have an important impact on electoral outcomes. In the following sections, we consider the most important kind of variation among election systems, as well as the issues of malapportionment and redistricting.

Single-Member Districts versus Proportional Representation

Electoral systems based on **single-member districts** divide the nation into a relatively large number of legislative districts with one legislative seat for each. For example, for its general elections, Britain is divided into 659 districts of roughly equal population, and each elects one Member of Parliament. Elections for the U.S. House of Representatives also follow this model. The system is sometimes called "winner take all," because the candidate who receives the most votes in a given district wins "all" the legislative power from that district. No seats are awarded to the losers, even if the election is very close. Approximately half of the democracies around the world use some form of the single-member-district system.

Proportional representation (PR)   divides the nation into a smaller number of larger electoral districts and assigns several seats to each district. (In Israel, the whole country is a single district.) Rather than vote for an individual candidate, voters normally choose among "party slates" of candidates.* When the votes are tallied, each party receives seats in the legislature in proportion to the share of the popular vote its slate received. Thus, if Party A receives 40 percent of the vote, and there are five seats in that district, two seats will go to candidates on Party A's slate. The other seats will be awarded to the other parties, in proportion to the votes they receive.† About one third of the countries around the world use a PR system. A few countries—New Zealand and Germany, for example—use some combination of the two systems. (See Box 4-2 and Table 4.5.)

Some readers may assume that the choice between these two electoral arrangements makes no difference—as long as the principles of majority rule and universal suffrage are followed, *both* systems are democratic. However, the choice of electoral system can have tremendous political effects, influencing the decisions of both parties and citizens.

In a single-member-district system, party leaders realize that they will get zero representation for their party in any given district if any opposing candidate receives one more vote than their candidate receives. Candidates and party leaders in such systems tend to take moderate positions likely to attract a winning majority or plurality of voters in many districts. Thus, all other factors being equal, systems using single-member-district electoral arrangements tend to have a small number of centrist parties, as shown in Table 4.5.

The big losers in a single-member district are smaller parties trying to establish a base of support. It can be done, as the U.S. Republican Party proved in the nineteenth century and the British Labour Party showed in the twentieth century. But doing so is quite difficult. If an up-and-coming third party succeeds in attracting 20 or 30 percent of the national vote, it will still receive virtually no seats because it will fail to come in first in many districts.

For example, as we discuss in Chapter 12, that was precisely the experience of the British Alliance and its successor, the Liberal Democrats. The Alliance (1983 and 1987) and the Liberal Democrats (1992 to the present) received 17 to 25 percent of the popular votes in the last five national elections, but they never received more than 9.6 percent of the seats in the House of Commons. Proportional representation

---

* In some countries, voters choose a party slate and indicate their top choices of individuals on the slate.

† Actual PR systems have detailed rules regarding, among other things, a "threshold" of votes that a party must receive to win any seats.

Box 4-2

NEW ZEALAND'S HYBRID ELECTORAL SYSTEM

New Zealand adopted a new system for electing its parliament in a 1993 referendum. The new system, called *mixed-member proportional* (or *MMP*), includes elements of both a single-member district and a PR system.

Under an MMP system, each citizen has *two votes:* an "electorate vote" and a "party vote." Half the 120 Members of Parliament (MPs) will be chosen by voters under the single-member-district system, using their "electorate votes" to select named candidates running for election in each electorate (or district). The other 60 winners will be "list MPs," selected from lists of candidates nominated by the political parties. Among these 60 MPs, the total number of MPs from each party will correspond to each party's share of the party votes. New Zealand's new MMP system stipulates, however, that a party must win at least 5 percent of the party votes *or* win at least one electorate seat to receive a proportional allocation of the seats for list MPs.

The sample ballot shown here is based on the one distributed to voters by the government of New Zealand for educational purposes.

The MMP system in New Zealand is an effort to secure some of the advantages of both PR and single-member-district systems. Any party that can command even 5 percent of the nation's party vote will have at least one of its members in Parliament. Such parties would never win a seat in single-member-district systems.

However the electorate votes, the system should ensure that large, established parties will continue to be dominant, since half the seats in Parliament will be awarded to candidates who have received the highest vote totals in their respective electorates. Thus, candidates receiving small percentages of the votes in each electorate will always lose. The hybrid system will produce a more diverse range of partisan voices than would a pure single-member-district system, but it will have more built-in stability than a pure PR system (since the single-member-district system for the electorate votes will ensure that large, established parties continue to dominate).

SAMPLE BALLOT—NEW ZEALAND
NATIONAL PARLIAMENTARY ELECTION

You Have Two Votes

Party Vote	Electorate Vote
(This vote decides the share of seats that each of the parties listed below will have in Parliament.)	(This vote decides the candidate who will be elected Member of Parliament of the ——— electorate.)
Vote for One Party	*Vote for One Candidate*
Carrot Party ———	Allenby, Fred ———
Peach Party ———	Barnardo, Mary ———
Squash Party ———	Dummlop, Alice ———
Banana Party ———	Edlinton, Tony ———
Broccoli Party ———	Nectar, Lizzy ———
Pear Party ———	Omega, Richard ———

would have resulted in a stronger British Alliance or Liberal Democratic presence in the House.

Party leaders are well aware of the effects of electoral systems, and sometimes parties with a majority in the legislature enact new electoral laws to benefit their own electoral chances. In a 1959 national referendum, for example, the conservative

TABLE 4.5 Electoral Systems for Selected Nations (Lower House of Parliament or General Assembly of Representatives)

	Threshold % of vote needed for seat	Effective number of parliamentary parties*
Majoritarian (Single-Member District)		
Australia	n/a	2.61
Canada	n/a	2.98
United Kingdom	n/a	2.11
United States	n/a	1.99
Combined Systems		
Germany	5	3.30
Mexico	2	2.86
Rep. of Korea	5	2.36
Russia	5	5.40
Taiwan	5	2.46
Ukraine	4	5.98
Proportional Representation		
Czech Rep.	5	4.15
Denmark	2	4.92
Israel	1.5	5.63
Netherlands	0.67	4.81
Norway	4	4.36
Peru	0	3.81
Poland	7	2.95
Romania	3	3.37
Slovenia	3	5.52
Spain	3	2.73
Sweden	4	4.29
Switzerland	0	5.08

*The *effective number of parliamentary parties* is a measure that estimates the number of political parties that have enough strength to constitute a meaningful influence in parliamentary activity.
Source: Pippa Norris, *Institutions Matter* (Cambridge, UK: Cambridge University Press, 2003).

majority in France introduced a new constitution that moved the country from proportional representation to single-member districts. A major objective was to weaken the Communist Party in the parliament. Of course, sometimes the strategy fails. In 1986, the Socialist parliamentary majority reinstituted PR in an effort to dilute the conservative opposition (they hoped PR would produce several new parties, taking voters from the conservatives). The conservatives won anyway and reinstituted single-member districts.

A comprehensive study of comparative electoral systems by Pippa Norris led her to conclude that the basic character of the political system is substantially determined by its electoral laws.[42] Single-member-district systems produce **adversarial democracy,** where the losing side is excluded from power until the next election, whereas proportional representation systems produce **consensual democracy,** because these systems require a wide range of parties (including those with relatively small shares of the nation's votes) to cooperate in forming governments. There are arguments to be made for both arrangements:

> For advocates of *adversarial* democracy, the most important considerations for electoral systems are that the votes cast in elections should decisively determine the party or parties in government. . . . At periodic intervals the electorate should be allowed to judge the government's record. . . . Minor parties in third or fourth place are discriminated against by majority elections for the sake of governability . . . [and] proportional systems are [seen as] ineffective since they can produce indecisive outcomes, unstable regimes,. . . and a lack of clear-cut accountability. . . .
>
> By contrast, proponents of *consensual* democracy argue that majoritarian systems place too much faith in the winning party. . . . For the vision of consensual democracy, the electoral system should promote a process of conciliation, consultation, and coalition-building within parliaments. [According to this view], majoritarian systems over-reward the winner, producing 'an elected dictatorship' where a government based on a plurality can steamroller its policies, and implement its programs, without the need for consultation and compromise with other parties in parliament or other groups in society.[43]

In short, proportional representation increases the electoral opportunities of new or narrow-based parties, often producing a situation in which a wider range of parties are involved in making government policy. A party able to obtain only a small share of the popular vote would still win a proportional number of seats in the legislature. Supporters of small parties would not feel that they are wasting their votes by voting for them, and potential donors would not feel that they are wasting their money by contributing. Not surprisingly, countries such as Israel and the Netherlands, which use PR electoral systems, are more likely to have multiparty systems with a number of small parties represented in the parliament.

As noted earlier, single-member-district systems usually hurt extreme leftist and rightist parties. The French experience shows how both the far-left Communist Party and the far-right National Front gained more electoral seats when the country used PR. But the single-member-district system tends to hurt *moderate* third parties as well (parties that are not in the top two). In Great Britain, the party that would gain most in a switch to PR—the Liberal Democrats (successors to the Alliance)—is more moderate than either the Labour Party or the Conservative Party. Similarly, in Germany, if PR were eliminated, the biggest loser would be the centrist Free Democrats. It is therefore more accurate to say that the single-member-district system creates an obstacle for *less established* parties, regardless of whether they are extreme or centrist.

However, the electoral system affects the political system in other ways, particularly with respect to stability, voter turnout, and the quality of representation. As we discuss in Chapter 5, the nature of the existing political divisions in society is a key factor in determining whether a country has two or three large moderate parties instead of a large number of smaller, more ideologically distinct parties, but it should be noted that most of the countries of Western Europe use some variant of PR and that most of them have maintained very moderate and stable political systems. If a country has a consensual political culture, a generally centrist electorate, and an established two-party system, as in the United States, switching to PR may have little impact. However, if a society is more conflictual and ideologically diverse, such as Israel or Italy, PR tends to produce larger numbers of parties with more polarized ideologies. Although this encourages active input from a wide range of diverse political interests, PR systems can lead to political instability, since elections will often produce a result in which no single party has enough support to govern. To minimize the problem, most PR systems have a "threshold" provision, requiring that parties receive at least a certain percentage of the vote to be represented in the parliament. (See Table 4.5.)

Instability is often a serious problem for PR systems: during the past 50 years, Italian elections have never produced governments (that is, prime ministers and cabinets) backed by stable parliamentary majorities. Italian governments have been forced to resign, on average, every 15 months.* Italy's 1993 reform created a system in which three-fourths of the legislators are elected in single-member districts. This change may increase cabinet stability in the long run. However, as noted above, PR systems generally have higher voter turnout, most likely as a consequence of the wider range of choices that citizens have. According to recent data compiled by International IDEA, countries with PR systems had an average turnout rate of nearly 70 percent, while countries with single-member-district systems had an average turnout rate of only 58 percent.

Malapportionment and District Boundaries

Whatever electoral system is chosen, **malapportionment** (having electoral districts with vastly different numbers of citizens) can also affect electoral results. In severely malapportioned systems, a rural district may be so sparsely populated that its one representative represents only 15,000 citizens. An adjacent urban district may also have only one representative for its 600,000 citizens. The political result can be easily anticipated: A legislature made up of representatives elected through such a malapportioned system would give much greater weight to rural political concerns than would be warranted on the basis of population. Put another way, each citizen in the rural district has 40 times more political power than a citizen in the urban district.

Malapportionment was held unconstitutional in the United States in the landmark decision *Baker v. Carr* (369 U.S. 186, 1962). The Court argued that severe malapportionment effectively violated the Constitution's grant of equal voting power to all citizens. Because of continuing population shifts, this decision requires that the allocation of representatives to each state be reviewed every decade and that states use **redistricting** to correct imbalances among districts. Even when the *number* of citizens in each district is roughly the same, districts can be drawn in ways that affect the ability of the electoral system to represent all voters.

As mentioned previously, when there is widespread knowledge of which parts of a metropolitan area or region support which parties, a party with a majority in the state legislature (which redraws the congressional district lines) and control of the governor's office (who must sign the redistricting) is often able to take this knowledge into account in drawing district boundaries. The requirement that electoral districts be roughly equal in population does not prevent some creative redistricting in ways

---

* As we see in our discussion of British politics (Chapter 12), under a parliamentary system, the government (the prime minister and cabinet) needs to be supported by a majority of Parliament. If the prime minister and cabinet lose that support, they must resign.

that diminish the chances of one's opponents.* The areas in which the opposing party is strong are simply divided, and the portions are then included in districts where the favored party has a clear majority.† Strategic redistricting thus creates another way to distort the vote.‡

The most controversial issue surrounding the drawing of district boundaries in the United States has to do with the issue of race. The Voting Rights Act of 1965 made it illegal to draw district lines in ways that reduce the ability of racial minorities to elect a candidate to represent them. In 1986, the Supreme Court held that districts could be found illegal if minority voting power is diluted, even if there is no specific intent on anyone's part to create such a dilution.§ The Voting Rights Act required that Southern states obtain Justice Department approval of their congressional districts, and, in many cases, boundaries were drawn that created "majority-minority" districts (in which racial minorities made up the majority of citizens). In several cases—*Shaw v.Reno* (509 U.S. 630, 1993); *Miller v. Johnson* (132 L.Ed.2d 762, 1995); and *Bush v. Vera* (135 L.Ed.2d 248, 1996)—the Supreme Court has held that districts which are drawn *primarily* on the basis of race are unconstitutional. The controversy rages on, with one side arguing that the government should not assume that members of minority groups are unrepresented unless a person of the same race is elected from their district, and the other side arguing that district boundaries drawn without regard to race will effectively preclude the election of minority representatives.

PUBLIC OPINION POLLING

Much of what we know about public opinion depends on the familiar **public opinion polls** we hear about so frequently during presidential campaigns. Candidates have their own polls, but in most industrialized democracies private organizations have been established to provide independent polling services. (In the United States, the Gallup, Harris, NBC/*Wall Street Journal*, CBS/*New York Times*, and ABC/*Washington Post* polls are the best known.) Opinion polls are essential to those running campaigns, since they help strategists identify where scarce funds should be spent and how messages should be crafted. Polls are important in other respects, too, raising questions of real significance for the health of modern democracy.

* In 1812, Governor Elbridge Gerry of Massachusetts helped engineer a particularly creative example of this practice. When it was remarked that the district drawn to his party's advantage looked like a salamander on the map, someone pointed out that it wasn't a salamander; it was a *Gerrymander*. The term has stuck as a description of partisan redistricting.

† William E. Brock, chairman of the Republican National Committee from 1977 to 1981, claimed that the Democrats used their control of state legislatures to draw district boundaries so that the Republicans routinely won far fewer congressional seats in the 1970s than their vote totals would have predicted. See John Aldrich et al., *American Government* (Boston: Houghton Mifflin, 1986), p. 238.

‡ A controversial example of strategic redistricting in the U.S. was applied in Texas in 2003. The new district lines in that state were drawn so that Republicans would gain several seats in Congress, and the strategy bore fruit in the 2004 election. The League of United Latin American Citizens in Texas went to federal court to present its claim that the redistricting plan was unconstitutional. When the Supreme Court ruled in 2006, it held that the plan did not violate the Constitution, but that it did violate the Voting Rights Act of 1965 because it effectively denied the right of Latino voters as a group to elect a favored candidate, because the plan diluted their political influence. (See *League of United Latin American Citizens v. Perry*, 548 U.S. 399, 2006).

§ See *Thornburg v. Gingles*, 478 U.S. 30 (1986).

First, the accuracy of polls is often questioned. Since it is obviously impossible to determine every citizen's views, modern opinion polling works through *sampling*. In the United States, national polls usually are based on responses from no more than two thousand people. If the sample is chosen carefully, the poll will be accurate enough to be useful.* For example, the Gallup, Harris, and CBS/*New York Times* polls were off by no more than 4 percentage points during recent elections and generally predicted the results within 1 or 2 points.[44]

The second issue raised by opinion polls has to do with their possible effects on elections. The argument is often made that undecided voters may make their final choice on the basis of which candidate is ahead in the polls. This possibility is particularly disturbing when we realize that so many news items, in both broadcast and print media, are devoted to poll results. It is not well established that polls have a predictable or significant effect along those lines, but the potential for such influences was enough to prompt the French government to adopt restrictions on poll coverage during the weeks preceding elections.

An analysis of public opinion polling by the Brookings Institution nicely captured the promise and the difficulties involved in interpreting and using the results of polls:

> "Polling results can be exceptionally powerful, largely because of their seeming legitimacy as neutral evidence. Even though many people report being skeptical of public opinion polls, these surveys do, however crudely, appear to reflect some kind of underlying reality. After all, aren't they "scientifically" conducted and accurate within a specific margin of error? Don't presidential election surveys ordinarily get the results roughly right? Besides, polling results are reported in numerical formats. If we can quantify something, that ordinarily means that we can measure it with reasonable accuracy."[45]

CONCLUSION: ELECTIONS AND PUBLIC OPINION—THE PEOPLE'S VOICE?

The study of public opinion and voting increasingly reveals the complexity of individual political choices. Because of ample data and sophisticated analytical tools, political scientists have developed a large body of knowledge regarding public opinion and voting behavior, making predictions in these areas more useful than in any other set of subjects in the discipline. Nevertheless, our knowledge tells us that useful predictions cannot be based on simple models and that results are often surprising. The most practical bit of knowledge derived from voting and opinion studies is the critical realization that opinions and votes are often influenced by organized entities, particularly political parties, the subject of our next chapter.

---

* Perhaps you have heard a national commentator report of poll results with a statement like this: "The results have a margin of error of plus or minus 3 points." This is not precisely correct. The logic of sampling means that if 44 percent of those polls support a given candidate, for example, and if we have a margin of error of plus or minus 3 points, we can be very sure (usually 95 percent sure) that the candidate's support in the whole population is between 41 and 47 percent. This level of certainty requires that the citizens polled constituted a random sample, meaning that every person in the whole population had an equal chance of being included in the sample.

 # WHERE ON THE WEB?

http://www.electionstudies.org

Home page for the American National Election Studies, an ongoing project of the Center for Political Studies at the University of Michigan. From this page, it is possible to access the National Election Studies, which provide data on responses to a wide range of survey questions gathered during national elections.

http://aceproject.org

The ACE Electoral Knowledge Network is a cooperative project of eight organizations, including three United Nations organizations and International IDEA. The site contains a great range of data and information about election laws in a number of countries.

http://www.gallup.com

Home page for the Gallup Poll, one of the most widely recognized polling organizations in the world.

http://www.fec.gov/pages/bcra/bcra_update.shtml

The U.S. Federal Election Commission's Web site for materials related to the Bipartisan Campaign Reform Act of 2002.

http://www.cfinst.org

Home page of the Campaign Finance Institute, containing a wide range of recent data on spending in U.S. elections.

http://www.publicopinionpros.com/

"Public Opinion Pros" is an "Online Magazine for the Polling Professional (and Everybody Else)." It is published several times each year at the above site.

http://www.ropercenter.uconn.edu

Home page of the Roper Center for Public Opinion Research.

http://ssdc.ucsd.edu/ssdc/pubopin.html

A guide to "Published Public Opinion Poll Statistics," from the Social Sciences Data Collection at the University of California at San Diego.

http://www.gallup-europe.be/epm/default.htm

Home page of Gallup Europe, containing data on public opinion and elections in several European countries.

http://europa.eu.int/comm/public_opinion/index_en.htm

Web site for the Public Opinion Analysis Sector of the European Commission.

http://www.ropercenter.uconn.edu/jpoll/JPOLL.html

Provides access to JPOLL, "the only comprehensive database of Japanese public opinion."

http://www.cses.org

Home page of the Comparative Study of Electoral Systems, a "collaborative program of cross-national research among election studies conducted in over fifty countries."

◆ ◆ ◆

Key Terms and Concepts _____

adversarial democracy
belief system
candidate evaluation
consensual democracy
gender gap
malapportionment
party identification

proportional representation (PR)
public opinion polls
redistricting

single-member districts
socioeconomic status (SES)
voter turnout

Discussion Questions _____

1. Compare the "mobilization" and "withdrawal" hypotheses as explanations for differences between economic classes with respect to voter turnout.
2. Why is proportional representation (PR) thought to create "consensual" democracy?
3. Why do "single-member-district" systems create "adversarial" democracy?
4. How does the rise of "postmaterialism" affect the impact of socioeconomic status (SES) on the voting preferences of upper- and lower-class voters?
5. Given that newspapers, television, and radio can influence public opinion and even vote choices, should these media outlets be restricted by the government? Why or why not?

Notes _____

1. V. O. Key, Jr., *Politics, Parties, and Pressure Groups* (New York: Crowell, 1952), Chap. 20.
2. The CBS/*New York Times* poll is available at http://www.cbsnews.com/stories/2008/04/03/opinion/polls/main3992628.shtml
3. See Paul Goren, "Character Weakness, Partisan Bias, and Presidential Evaluation," *American Journal of Political Science* 46 (July 2002): 627–641.
4. Russell J. Dalton and Martin Wattenberg, eds., *Parties Without Partisans: Political Change in Advanced Industrial Democracies* (Oxford: Oxford University Press, 2000), chap. 2.
5. Jose E. Molina, V., "The Presidential and Parliamentary Elections of the Bolivarian Revolution in Venezuela: Change and Continuity, 1998–2000," *Bulletin of Latin American Research* 21, no. 2 (2002): 219–247.
6. Morris Fiorina, "The Electorate in the Voting Booth," in *The Parties Respond*, ed. L. Sandy Maisel (Boulder, CO: Westview, 1990), p. 119. See also Fiorina's discussion in *Divided Government* (New York: Macmillan, 1992), in which he notes that party identification for many Americans has been weakened by the perception that the two major parties have become increasingly more ideological and extreme.
7. See Joe Soss and Sanford Schram, "A Public Transformed? Welfare Reform as Policy Feedback," *American Political Science Review*, Vol. 101 (February 2007): 111–127.
8. Lloyd A. Free and Hadley Cantril, *The Political Beliefs of Americans: A Study of Public Opinion* (New York: Simon & Schuster, 1968), p. 216.
9. Ronald Inglehart, *Culture Shift in Advanced Industrial Society* (Princeton, NJ: Princeton University Press, 1990).
10. See Russell J. Dalton, *Citizen Politics: Public Opinion and Political Parties in Advanced Western Democracies*, 2nd ed. (Chatham, NJ: Chatham House, 1996), pp. 167–176.
11. "Class is Not Dead—It Has Been Buried Alive: Class Voting and Cultural Voting in Postwar Western Societies (1956-1990)," *World Political Science Review* 3 (2007), available online from the Berkeley Electronic Press.
12. Ronald Inglehart and Pippa Norris, *The Rising Tide: Gender Equality and Cultural Change Around the World* (Cambridge, UK: Cambridge University Press, 2003).
13. Gabriel Almond and Sidney Verba, *The Civic Culture* (Boston: Little, Brown, 1965), p. 325.
14. Karen M. Kaufmann and John R. Petrocik, "The Changing Politics of American Men: Understanding the Sources of the Gender Gap," *American Journal of Political Science* 43 (1999): 864, 887.
15. Rasmussen Report, June 3, 2008, available at http://www.rasmussenreports.com/.
16. Data available from the Pew Research Center for the People and the Press, http://people-press.org/reports/display.php3?PageID=750.
17. Nancy J. Hirschmann explored this controversial idea in "Freedom, Recognition, and Obligation: A Feminist Approach to Political Theory," *American Political Science Review* 83 (1989): 1227–1244.

18. See Ivor Crewe and David Denver, *Electoral Change in Western Democracies* (London: Croom Helm, 1985), pp. 218–219.

19. See Herbert McClosky, "Conservatism and Personality," *American Political Science Review* 52 (1958): 27–45.

20. William Horsley, "The Press as Loyal Opposition in Japan," *Newspapers and Democracy: International Essays on a Changing Medium*, ed. Anthony Smith (Cambridge: MIT Press, 1980), p. 212.

21. Diana C. Mutz, "Effects of 'In-Your-Face' Television Discourse on Perceptions of a Legitimate Opposition," *American Political Science Review* 101 (November 2007): 521–635.

22. Michael S. Lewis-Beck, "Comparative Economic Voting: Britain, France, Germany, Italy," *American Journal of Political Science* 30 (1986): 315–346.

23. Gregory B. Markus, "The Impact of Personal and National Economic Conditions on Presidential Voting, 1956–1988," *American Journal of Political Science* 36 (August 1992): 830.

24. Sean Carey and Matthew J. Lebo, "Election Cycles and the Economic Voter," *Political Research Quarterly* 59 (2006): 543–556.

25. See Joshua A. Tucker, *Regional Economic Voting: Russia, Poland, Hungary, Slovakia, and the Czech Republic, 1990-1999.* (Cambridge, U.K.: Cambridge University Press, 2006).

26. Michael S. Lewis-Beck and Mary Stegmaier, "Economic Determinants of Electoral Outcomes," *Annual Review of Political Science* 3 (2000): 211.

27. See Robert S. Erikson, Joseph Batumi, and Brett Wilson, "Was the 2000 Presidential Election Predictable?" *PS: Political Science and Politics* 34 (2001): 815–819; and Alfred G. Cuzan and Charles M. Bundrick, "Deconstructing the 2004 Presidential Election Forecasts: The Fiscal Model and the Campbell Collection Compared," *PS: Political Science and Politics* 38 (April 2005): 255–262.

28. David K. Levine and Thomas R. Palfrey, "The Paradox of Voter Participation: A Laboratory Study," *American Political Science Review* 101 (February 2007): 143–158.

29. Steven Rosenstone, "Economic Adversity and Voter Turnout," *American Journal of Political Science* 26 (1982): 25–46.

30. U.S. Census Bureau, Current Population Survey, November 2004.

31. Miki Caul Kittilson, "Rising Political Inequality in Established Democracies: Mobilization, Socio-Economic Status, and Voter Turnout, 1960s to 2000," paper presented at the 2005 Annual Meeting of the American Political Science Association.

32. Carol A. Cassell and David B. Hill, "Explanations of Turnout Decline," *American Politics Quarterly* 9 (1981): 193. See also Caroline J. Tolbert and Ramona S. McNeal, "Unraveling the Effects of the Internet on Political Participation," *Political Research Quarterly* 56 (June 2003): 175–185.

33. Alberto Chong and Mauricio Olivera. 2005. "On Compulsory Voting and Income Inequality in a Cross Section of Countries," Inter-American Development Bank Working Paper #533, available at www.iadb.org.

34. Philip E. Converse, "The Nature of Belief Systems in Mass Publics," in *Ideology and Discontent*, ed. David E. Apter (New York: Free Press, 1964), p. 207.

35. Converse, p. 245.

36. Angus Campbell, Philip Converse, Warren Miller, and Donald Stokes, *The American Voter*. New York: Wiley, 1960.

37. See Erik R.A.N. Smith, *The Unchanging American Voter* (Berkeley, CA: University of California Press, 1989); Robert Luskin, "Explaining Political Sophistication," in *Controversies in Voting Behavior*, 3rd ed., Richard G. Niemi and Herbert Weisberg, eds. (Washington, DC: Congressional Quarterly, 1993): 114–136; and Richard S. Flickinger and Donley T. Studlar, "The Disappearing Voters? Exploring Declining Turnout in Western European Elections," *West European Politics* 15 (April 1992): 1–16.

38. See Bruce Bimber, "The Internet and Political Transformation: Populism, Community, and Accelerated Pluralism," *Polity* 31 (Fall 1998): 133–160.

39. See Geoffrey C. Layman and Thomas M. Carsey, "Party Polarization and 'Conflict Extension' in the American Electorate," *American Journal of Political Science* 46 (October 2002): 786–802; Paul Goren, "Political Sophistication and Policy Reasoning: A Reconsideration," *American Journal of Political Science* 48 (July 2004): 462–478; and Stacy B. Gordon and Gary M. Segura, "Cross-National Variation in the Political Sophistication of Individuals: Capability or Choice?" *Journal of Politics* 59 (February 1997): 126–147.

40. Herbert E. Alexander, "Comparative Analysis of Political Party and Campaign Financing in the United States and Canada," in *The Delicate Balance Between Political Equality and Freedom of Expression: Political Party and Campaign Financing in Canada and the United States*, eds. Steven Griner and Daniel Zovatto (Washington, DC: Organization of American States, 2005).

41. Charles J. Pattie, Ronald J. Johnston, and Edward A. Fieldhouse, "Winning the Local Vote: The Effectiveness of Constituency Campaign Spending in Great Britain, 1983–1992," *American Political Science Review* 89 (1995): 969–983.

42. Pippa Norris, *Institutions Matter* (Cambridge, England: Cambridge University Press, 2003).

43. Norris, *Institutions Matter*, Ch. 2.

44. See the compilation of figures in James MacGregor Burns and Jack Peltason, *Government by the People: The Dynamics of American National, State, and Local Government*, 11th ed. (Englewood Cliffs, NJ: Prentice Hall, 1989), p. 217. Also see Philip E. Converse, "The Advent of Polling and Political Representation," *PS: Political Science and Politics* 29 (December 1996): 649–657.

45. Brookings Institution. 2003. "From Hootie to Harry (and Louise): Polling and Interest Groups." Available at http://www.brookings.edu/articles/2003/summer_elections_loomis.aspx.

For Further Reading ⎯⎯⎯⎯

Adams, James. *Party Competition and Responsible Party Government*. Ann Arbor, MI: University of Michigan Press, 2001.

Alvarez, R. Michael and Thad E. Hall. *Electronic Elections: The Perils and Promises of Digital Democracy*. Princeton, N.J.: Princeton University Press, 2008.

Brams, Steven J. Mathematics and Democracy: Designing Better Voting and Fair-Division Procedures. Princeton, N.J.: Princeton University Press, 2008.

Brockington, David. "The Paradox of Proportional Representation: The Effect of Party Systems and Coalitions on Individuals' Electoral Participation. *Political Studies* 52 (2004): 469–490.

Campbell, Angus, Phillip E. Converse, Warren E. Miller, and Donald E. Stokes. *The American Voter*. New York: Wiley, 1960.

Caplan, Bryan. *The Myth of the Rational Voter: Why Democracies Choose Bad Policies*, New Edition. Princeton: Princeton University Press, 2008.

Clarke, Harold D., David Sanders, Marianne C. Stewart, and Paul Whiteley. 2008. *Performance Politics and the British Voter*. Cambridge: Cambridge University Press.

Conover, Pamela Johnston. "Feminists and the Gender Gap." *Journal of Politics* 50 (1988): 985–1010.

Dalton, Russell. 2006. *Citizen Politics: Public Opinion and Political Parties in Advanced Industrial Democracies*, 4th ed. Washington: Congressional Quarterly Press.

Dalton, Russell. *Democratic Challenges, Democratic Choices: The Erosion in Political Support in Advanced Industrial Democracies*, Oxford: Oxford University Press, 2004.

Downs, Anthony. "An Economic Theory of Political Action in a Democracy." *Journal of Political Economy* 65 (1957): 135–150.

Elazar, Daniel J. *Israel at the Polls, 1999*. New York: Routledge, 2001.

Finifter, Ada W. "Attitudes toward Individual Responsibility and Political Reform in the Former Soviet Union." *American Political Science Review* 90 (1996): 138–152.

Gschwend, Thomas and Dirk Leuffen. "Divided We Stand—Unified We Govern? Cohabitation and Regime Voting in the 2002 French Elections." *British Journal of Political Science*, 35 (2005): 691–712.

Holbrook, Thomas M. *Do Campaigns Matter?* Thousand Oaks, CA: Sage, 1996.

Holbrook, Thomas M. "A Post-Mortem Update of the Economic News and Personal Finances Forecasting Model." *P.S. Political Science and Politics* 38 (2005): 35–36.

Huber, John, Georgia Kernell, and Eduardo L. Leoni. "Institutional Context, Cognitive Resources and Party Attachments Across Democracies." *Political Analysis* 13 (2005): 365–386.

Karp, Jeffrey A., and David Brockington. "Social Desirability and Response Validity: A Comparative Analysis of Over-Reporting Turnout in Five Countries." *Journal of Politics* 67 (2005): 825–840.

Kedar, Orit. "How Diffusion of Power in Parliaments Affects Voter Choice." *Political Analysis* 13 (2005): 410–429.

King, Gary, Ori Rosen, Martin Tanner, and Alexander F. Wagner. 2008. "Ordinary Economic Voting Behavior in the Extraordinary Election of Adolf Hitler." Harvard University, Department of Government, available at http://www.gking.harvard.edu/files/naziV p.pdf.

Lewis-Beck, Michael S., William G. Jacoby, Helmut Norpoth, and Herbert F. Weisberg. *The American Voter Revisited*. Ann Arbor: University of Michigan Press, 2008.

Lijphart, Arend. "Unequal Participation: Democracy's Unresolved Dilemma," *American Political Science Review* 91 (March 1997): 1–14.

Milban, Michael J. *The Election After Reform: Money, Politics, and the Bipartisan Campaign Reform Act*. Lanham, MD.: Rowman and Littlefield Publishers, 2006.

Nicol, Mike. *The Waiting Country: A South African Witness*. London: Gollancz, 1995.

Norris, Pippa. *Electoral Engineering: Voting Rules and Political Behavior*. New York: Cambridge University Press, 2005.

Norris, Pippa. *Institutions Matter*. Cambridge, UK: Cambridge University Press, 2003.

Norris, Pippa, Montague Kern, and Marion Just, eds. *Framing Terrorism: The News Media, the Government, and the Public*. New York: Routledge, 2003.

Norris, Pippa, and Ronald Inglehart, *Sacred and Secular: Religion and Politics Worldwide*. Cambridge, UK: Cambridge University Press, 2004.

Pattie, Charles J., Ronald J. Johnston, and Edward A. Fieldhouse. "Winning the Local Vote: The Effectiveness of Constituency Campaign Spending in Great Britain, 1983–1992," *American Political Science Review* 89 (1995): 969–983.

Powell, G. Bingham. "American Voter Turnout in Comparative Perspective." *American Political Science Review* 80 (March 1986): 17–44.

Seligson, Mitchell A., and John A. Booth. *Elections and Democracy in Central America Revisited*. New and enlarged ed. Chapel Hill: University of North Carolina Press, 1995.

Wattenberg, Martin P. *Where Have All the Voters Gone?* Cambridge: Harvard University Press, 2002.

White, Stephen, Richard Rose, and Ian McAllister. *How Russia Votes*. Chatham, NJ: Chatham House, 1997.

White, Stephen, D. Stansfield, and P. Webb, eds. *Political Parties in Transitional Democracies*. Oxford: Oxford University Press, 2005.

©Jim Cole/AP Photo

5

POLITICAL PARTIES

◆ What Are Political Parties? ◆ The Functions of
Political Parties ◆ The Origins of Political Parties
◆ Party Systems ◆ Types of Political Parties
◆ Conclusion: Parties in a Changing World

> However [political parties] may now and then answer popular ends, they are
> likely, in the course of time and things, to become potent engines, by which
> cunning, ambitious, and unprincipled men will be enabled to subvert the
> power of the people, and to usurp for themselves the reins of government.
> —*George Washington's Farewell Address*

Since the time of the founders, many Americans have shared Washington's suspicion of political parties. They have regarded parties as divisive and self-serving, more interested in winning elections or representing narrow constituencies than in furthering the national good. Washington believed that government leaders should selflessly work to advance the common interest and that parties would undermine public-spirited cooperation. In recent decades, growing numbers of Americans and Europeans have viewed political parties and partisanship negatively. Indeed, since the early 1950s, growing numbers of Americans have identified themselves as "independents," loyal to no party.[1] Similarly, news analysts often accuse some congressional representatives or senators of engaging in partisan politics, just as they also praise others for "rising above party politics."

Political scientists, on the other hand, have a much more positive view of political parties as institutions, even though they may be critical of how parties currently perform in the U.S. or elsewhere. Rather than viewing parties as inherently divisive or unscrupulous (although some parties may be), they consider them indispensable vehicles for organizing the broad citizen participation that is essential to the maintenance of democracy and political stability. To best appreciate the positive impact of parties, we need only consider examples of contemporary governments that have none. For example, Saudi Arabia has no parties; the royal family and its advisers make critical political decisions. Parties have rarely existed in Afghanistan and only became significant in that nation's 2005 parliamentary elections. Under the absolute rule of Yoweri Museveni, Uganda banned political parties until 2005. Elsewhere, recent authoritarian military governments in Latin America and Africa have often banned political party activity after they seized power.

So it is obviously *possible* for governments to function without parties—but only in societies with very limited socioeconomic development and in countries ruled by monarchs or military dictatorships, where political participation is repressed. By definition, then, nonparty political systems are underdeveloped and undemocratic. But, even though democracy at the national level *requires* active political parties, the existence of parties does not *guarantee* that a country will be democratic.

Indeed, all **totalitarian** regimes and many **authoritarian** governments have a ruling political party in order to mobilize and control mass participation. Some of these parties penetrate virtually all aspects of public life. For example, the Chinese Communist Party (CCP) offers its members prestige and various material privileges. Consequently, its ranks now include not only politicians and civil servants, but millions of factory workers, doctors, teachers, farmers, and even businessmen. The Soviet Communist party had a similar structure. In all, some 70 million people currently belong to the CCP, while the Soviet Communist Party had 19 million members at its peak. Similarly, tens of thousands joined the Italian Fascist Party and Germany's Nazi Party in the 1930s, motivated either by conviction or by opportunism.

PASSING THE TORCH   South Africa's legendary president, Nelson Mandela, right, raises the hand of the new African National Congress (ANC) President Thabo Mbeki, who was elected national president soon after. As the force behind the liberation of South Africa's black majority population, the ANC has been the country's dominant political party.

In such countries, the government encourages widespread political participation, but only under the tight control of the ruling party. Similarly, in Zimbabwe and other authoritarian regimes, the ruling party promotes mass support for the government, while state security forces suppress anti-government groups. To appreciate how parties affect government and society, we must first define what distinguishes them from related political organizations and then identify their basic functions.

WHAT ARE POLITICAL PARTIES?

The enormous differences between political parties make it difficult to devise a definition that fits all of them, but they all share a few characteristics. A **political party** is an organization that unites people in an effort to place its representatives in government offices so as to influence government activities and policies. Many parties, perhaps most, explicitly or implicitly espouse an ideology or at least a set of principles and beliefs, although these vary tremendously in coherence and consistency. The British Conservative and French Socialist parties proclaim their respective ideologies in their party names. America's major political parties do not, but those who follow U.S. politics know that the Republican Party is the more conservative of the two and the Democratic Party the more liberal. In democratic political systems, parties compete to elect their leaders to public office, and voters use party labels to identify and classify candidates. Although many authoritarian and totalitarian regimes hold elections as well, their real purpose is to *legitimize* the leaders in power rather than to allow meaningful opposition.

Political parties differ from interest groups—the subject of our next chapter—in that they usually seek to control the reins of government (alone or as part of a governing coalition), whereas interest groups merely seek to influence government decisions affecting those groups' special concerns. Thus interest groups in the United States seek to influence government policy in such areas as labor legislation and minimum-wage law (unions), environmental preservation (The Wilderness Society), manufacturing regulations (the National Chamber of Commerce), and firearms regulation (the National Rifle Association).

The Functions of Political Parties

The fact that parties have become such a pervasive and central component of modern political systems suggests that they perform vital functions. An examination of those functions allows us to appreciate how parties contribute to the political process.

Recruitment of Political Leadership

Every political system must have some means of recruiting its leaders. In pre-modern systems, leaders inherited their positions as kings, feudal lords, or tribal chieftains. As the extent of mass political participation grew—first in the United States and Western Europe and then in other parts of the world—an *institutionalized* process of **leadership recruitment** through political parties became a key feature of their political systems. Conversely, governments operating without an established arrangement for selecting new leaders often face a crisis when the existing leaders die, resign, or are removed from office. In most countries, the political leadership inadequately represents segments of the population such as women or racial and ethnic minorities. In some cases, political parties have helped block recruitment of government leaders from those underrepresented groups. More often than not, however, they have served as a vehicle for broadening representation. One example of this is the efforts made by many parties—especially in Western Europe, Latin America, and Africa—to increase parliamentary representation for women (see Box 5-1). In any democracy, parties have an obvious reason for reaching out to women and minority groups—they want their votes.

By spelling out their ideologies and programs over time, political parties give the population signals about what candidates from their ranks will do if elected. Neither Britain's Tony Blair nor France's Jacques Chirac carried out all his campaign pledges, but their supporters had a general idea about where they were heading when they elected them. In contrast, voters in some developing countries have had fewer election cues since prominent political figures have created ad hoc, **"personalistic parties"** designed solely to get themselves elected president. Because such parties have no track record and have revealed few objectives other than electing their leaders, voters have little idea of what to expect if they are elected. In Peru, for example, Alberto Fujimori came out of obscurity to form his own personalistic party and then won the presidential election. While running on a very vaguely defined platform, Fujimori rejected the unpopular, but necessary, economic stabilization program proposed by his leading opponent. Once he took office, however, he

Box 5-1

PARTIES AS LADDERS (OR OBSTACLES) FOR WOMEN'S REPRESENTATION IN PARLIAMENT

Over the past decade or so, the number of women representatives in national "parliaments" throughout the world has increased from under 12 percent in 1995 to nearly 18 percent in 2008.* Western Europe, Latin America, and Sub-Saharan Africa have made the most impressive gains, while there has been slower progress in Asia, the Muslim world, and several developed democracies such as the United States, France, and Italy. To be sure, women are still greatly underrepresented in almost all national legislatures. Currently, only five countries—Rwanda, Sweden, Cuba, Finland, and Argentina—approach gender parity, with parliaments that are between 40 percent and 49 percent female.[2] As of early 2008, Northern Europe's Nordic nations (Denmark, Finland, Iceland, Norway, and Sweden) had the highest percentage of women members of parliament (MPs) of any region (41 percent), while Arab nations had the lowest, with only 10 percent. Political parties have often been the most effective vehicles for recruiting more women MPs. In some cases, however, they have shown little interest in that goal or even tried to subvert it.

There are a number of reasons why female representation has grown so rapidly since 1995 and why there continues to be so much variation between countries and regions. Changes in political cultures, the expansion of women's rights movements, and the growing number of women in the workplace have all raised the number of female elected officials at most levels. But neither the emergence of the feminist movement, nor broader cultural changes, nor greater female employment can explain why women's representation in parliaments grew only minimally from 1975 (11 percent) to 1995 (12 percent)—when these cultural and economic trends were already at work—but then increased rapidly from 1995 to 2008 (to 18 percent). Similarly, while factors such as national culture and levels of modernity explain some of today's differences between countries and regions, many others do not fall into the predicted pattern.

In some instances the level of female representation clearly reflects that nation's or region's culture and history. It is not surprising that the Nordic countries were among the first to institute procedures to increase

the percentage of women in parliament and that they currently have a substantially higher percentage of women MPs than any other region of the world. These achievements reflect their political culture's strong commitment to gender and class equality. Conversely, the relatively sheltered life of women in most Arab nations helps explain the scarcity of female MPs in those countries.[†]

But in other instances, the proportion of female political leaders is surprising given the country's or region's political cultural and history. For example, as of 2008, Latin America—known for its allegedly *macho* (male chauvinist) culture—had the second highest proportion of women MPs among all world regions (behind the Nordic countries, but ahead of the rest of Europe). Conversely, the United States—with perhaps the world's most dynamic feminist movement—has fewer women legislators than Latin America and many other developing nations. Indeed, when 186 countries are ranked according to their percentage of women MPs, we find that a number of advanced democracies—with modern cultures, a high proportions of women in the work force, high female educational levels, and a strong feminist movement—have lower than expected female representation in parliament. Thus, the United States only ranks 80th in the world. Similarly, Canada (58th), Britain (67th), France (72nd), and Italy (76th) all trail countries such as Uganda and Peru by wide margins.[3] The proportion of women in the U.S. Congress (16–17 percent in each house) is lower than the percentages in nine Latin American countries, including Cuba (43 percent), Argentina (40 percent), and Costa Rica (37 percent).

How do we account for the fact that the percent of women in a nation's parliament frequently does not seem to correlate with that country's cultural values, educational level, or degree of modernity? In her study of female representation in Western European parliaments, Miki Caul Kittilson notes that there, as in many developing nations, political parties played a critical role in increasing female representation by establishing

---

[†] Contrary to stereotype, women are not excluded in the same way from political power in non-Arab, Muslim nations. For example, Bangladesh, Indonesia, Pakistan and Turkey—all Muslim—have had women prime ministers or presidents.

* We use the generic term "parliament" here to refer to all national legislatures, including those, primarily in the Americas, that call their legislatures "Congress."

(Continued)

Box 5-1

PARTIES AS LADDERS (OR OBSTACLES) FOR WOMEN'S REPRESENTATION IN PARLIAMENT
(Continued)

gender quotas for their slate of parliamentary candidates.[4] Indeed, gender quotas are the surest and quickest way to raise the number of women MPs.

There are two major types of gender quotas:

1) **Legal quotas** are mandated by the government either in the constitution or through election laws. They are binding on all political parties and, in turn, include two subtypes. *One* reserves a certain percentage of all parliamentary seats for women (that is, only women may run for or be appointed to those seats). About 40 countries throughout the world (mostly less developed nations) have reserved some parliamentary seats for women. Some of them reserve a substantial share. For example, the African nations of Eritrea and Rwanda both reserve 30 percent of their parliamentary seats for women. In Afghanistan, a country not noted for its commitment to women's rights, the U.S. pressured the post-Taliban government to reserve 27 percent of the national assembly seats for women. At the other side of the spectrum, developing nations such as Jordan and Morocco reserve only a token number of seats for women (roughly 5 percent); not nearly enough to influence government policy. To be sure, women can also run for non-reserved parliamentary seats, but in cases such as these two, the reserved seats represent a glass ceiling since women virtually never win the non-reserved contests. Only rarely, in countries such as Rwanda, are they able to win a significant number.

The *second* subtype of legally enforced quota does not guarantee women any percentage of the seats, but instead requires each party to nominate a certain percentage of women candidates on their parliamentary tickets. Most commonly, these quotas obligate parties to nominate women for about 30 percent of the parliamentary contests, the minimum number of female MPs that appears to be needed to influence government policy on issues particularly relevant to women.[5]

2) **Voluntary quotas**, on the other hand, are not legally required but rather are introduced voluntarily by individual political parties. Such quotas were first introduced in Norway in 1975. Today, one or more parties in some 50 countries—including governing parties such as South Africa's African National Congress (ANC) and the British Labour Party—have established voluntary quotas.

Sometimes, however, quota systems do not substantially increase the number of female MPs because political parties can easily evade their intent. Even if parties are legally required to nominate women candidates for, say, 20 or 30 percent of the legislative seats, this does not guarantee that anywhere near that percentage will actually win. In countries with single-member districts (SMD, see Chapter 4)—including the United States, Britain, and France—parties may choose to nominate women mostly in districts where they have little likelihood of winning. Or, in countries using proportional representation (PR)—most of the world's democracies—political parties may place their female candidates toward the bottom of the party list, where they are unlikely to win seats (see Chapter 4).

France illustrates this point well. In 2001 parliament passed legislation that required all political parties to *nominate* women for roughly *half* the seats in future parliamentary elections. Yet following the 2002 and 2007 elections for the National Assembly, women had won only 18 percent of the seats; substantially more than the 11 percent they had held prior to the 2001 gender quota law, but well below 50 percent. What happened? Several parties failed to meet the 50 percent quota and simply paid a fine, as permitted by law. Other parties met their quota, but tended to field women candidates in districts where they had little chance of winning. For example, the neo-Gaullists (a conservative political party) nominated many women candidates in urban, blue-collar districts where they stood little chance of defeating the **leftist** candidates. Similarly, the Socialists might nominate women in upper-middle-class neighborhoods where they were unlikely to win.

Why don't political parties give women more of a chance to win? It is probably not because (mostly male) party leaders object to having more female colleagues. Rather it is because they and their male senior colleagues are not willing to give up their own seats to advance gender equality. In a country using SMD, each major party confronts an electoral map in which there are many "safe" seats (districts where their party is fairly sure to win with any candidate), many seats in which anyone they nominates has very little chance of winning, and some which are competitive and can go either way. Most of the seats that are safe for any given party are held by incumbent MPs with years of seniority (such as neo-Gaullist representatives from an affluent parts of Paris or Socialists from working-class neighborhoods in Marseille or outside Paris). Most of those "old-timers" were first elected when there were fewer women in politics, so most of them are men. Since they are unwilling to step aside and let their district nominate a woman, new women candidates end up running mostly in districts that are unwinnable for their party or that are competitive (where they will win some), but they will infrequently get to run in a safe district.*

In order to prevent evasion of the gender quotas' intent, a number of countries have imposed gender quotas that apply not only to the entire number of candidates, but also to seats for which the party is competitive. For example, most democracies in Europe and Latin America elect their parliaments through PR, with candidates on each party list usually ranked from first to last. For example, if there are 100 seats in parliament and one party receives, say, 40 percent of the national vote, candidates ranked 1st through 40th on its list (40 percent of the list) would be elected. In countries with so-called **zipper-style gender quotas,** not only must each party field women candidates for, say, 25 or 33 percent of the party list, but they are also required to place women in every third spot (for a 33 percent quota) or fourth spot (for a 25 percent quota) on the list, ranked from the top. So no matter whether that party wins only 6 parliamentary seats or sixty, one third or one fourth of the candidates taking office would end up being women. It is much harder to enforce tough gender quotas in single-member-district elections and, consequently, most of the effective quotas exist in nations with proportional representation. For example, in Argentina's three congressional elections (using PR) immediately preceding passage of a tough gender quota law in 1991, an average of only 4 percent of all congressional representatives were women. That figure jumped to 21 percent in 1993 and 40 percent today. On the other hand, countries that elect members of parliament in single-member districts—including the United States, United Kingdom, and France—tend to have lower percentages of women MPs.

Ultimately, then, political parties can either contribute to or impede greater female representation in

parliament. In South Africa, soon after the advent of majority rule (1994), the ANC, the country's dominant political party, voluntarily adopted a zipper-style quota mandating that every third candidate—ranked from the top—be a woman. As a consequence, the percentage of female MPs elected that year rose from 4 percent (141st in the world) to 25 percent (11th). Today, as other South African parties have also raised their share of women candidates, women hold 33 percent of all seats in parliament. On the other end of the spectrum, however, we have already seen how the French gender quota law fell well short of its target because too many political parties found ways around the law. The same was true in Venezuela, which passed a quota law in 1997 that badly missed its target (30 percent) in the 1998 election, when women won only 12 percent of the seats.

What causes some parties to embrace gender quotas and others to reject voluntary quotas or evade legal ones? In her study of contemporary European political parties, Kittilson identified three important factors.

First, party *ideology* plays a significant role. She placed European parties into one of several categories, including "Old Left," "New Left," centrist, conservative, religious, and ultra-right (neofascist). Old Left parties, especially Socialist parties, are parties founded in the late nineteenth or early twentieth centuries. With close links to labor unions and strong support from the working class, they have stressed bread-and-butter economic issues. By the second half of the twentieth century, Socialist parties were either the governing party or the major opposition party in most Western European nations. The Nordic Socialist parties were the first parties to voluntarily adopt gender quotas and, as a group, Old Left parties throughout Europe now have higher proportions of women MPs than their conservative rivals do. New Left parties first emerged in the 1970s and, unlike the Old Left, have focused primarily on postmaterialist concerns (see Chapter 3) such as the environment, nuclear proliferation, and women's rights, more than on class-based economic issues. The most successful of the New Left parties have been the Green parties built around environmental issues. While their share of parliamentary seats has been small (rarely won more than 6–7 percent), they have been part of several governing coalitions. New Left parties have the highest proportion of female MPs.

* In the U.S., the primary system gives a woman or any other challenger the ability to win nomination for Congress by upsetting the incumbent in their own party. Few other countries in the world—and none in Europe—have primaries. Instead, party leaders pick the candidates.

(Continued)

Box 5-1

PARTIES AS LADDERS (OR OBSTACLES) FOR WOMEN'S REPRESENTATION IN PARLIAMENT
(*Continued*)

Conservative parties are less likely to introduce voluntary gender quotas and frequently hold a more traditional view of the role of women in society. Yet as of the early 1970s they actually had a higher percentage of women MPs, on average, than the Socialists did. Since that time, however, the proportion of Socialist female MPs has grown far more rapidly, and by the 1990s they had passed the conservatives. Religious and ultra-rightist parties have had far lower proportions of women MPs than the New Left, Old Left, or the conservatives.

The second major factor influencing a party's likelihood of adopting gender quotas is its internal party organization. Parties that have adopted gender quotas and raised their share of women MPs have usually first expanded women's influence *within* the party organization.

Parties with more grassroots women's organizations and with more women in party leadership positions are subsequently more likely to nominate women for winnable parliamentary seats.

Finally, party leaders (largely men) are most likely to support effective voluntary gender quotas when they are convinced that these measures will increase the party's chances of winning. In other words, while some male party leaders back gender quotas because they believe them to be just and equitable, more of them are likely to support reform when they have been convinced that it is in their own self interest. Once party leaders see that advantage, parties that concentrate power at the top are more likely to implement reform than are those with more decentralized structures.

quickly introduced an economic program much like his opponent's, a program that he had just run against.

On the other hand, in countries where more broadly based political parties are entrenched, potential national leaders must have previously completed a de facto apprenticeship (running for lesser offices), working with the party organization, and identifying with the party's program and ideology. Indeed, in countries with modern political party systems, anyone aspiring to become president or prime minister normally must first become active in a major political party and then attain its nomination. General Dwight Eisenhower was a partial exception to this rule as he was a career military officer who had not belonged to any party and had not participated in politics prior to being drafted as the Republican presidential nominee in 1952. Previously, his party preference, if he had one, had been such a mystery that leaders of both the Republican and Democratic parties had tried to convince him to be their candidate. Yet even Eisenhower, an enormously popular World War II hero, still needed to get a major-party nomination in order to win the presidency. In 1992 and 1996, Ross Perot, a Texas billionaire, tried to break the major parties' dominance by running for the presidency as an independent. But, despite his enormous financial resources and initial popular support, at least in 1992, Perot failed to win a single state in either election or a single electoral vote.

Before the introduction of modern, electronic scoreboards, vendors at major-league baseball parks used to yell to fans entering the park that "you can't tell the players without a scorecard." So, too, parties provide voters with "scorecards" for evaluating what might otherwise be a bewildering array of individuals seeking office. By knowing the candidates' party labels, voters have important clues about their positions on major issues—whether the candidate is liberal or conservative, for example. While many independents in the U.S. base their presidential vote on the candidates' personal views and qualities (charisma, debating skills, intelligence and the like), they are less likely to know much about individual candidates for offices such as the House of Representatives or the state legislature. Using that party label as a clue, a majority of Americans still vote repeatedly, even reflexively, for the candidates of one party.

Because most major European parties are more tightly organized and, at least until recently, more ideologically unified than American parties, and because their parliamentary representatives are more likely to vote as a bloc, European voters are usually less interested than Americans in the candidate's personal characteristics and comparatively more interested in his or her party label. Knowing a candidate's party affiliation is all the information that many voters need to determine their votes. Indeed, most European countries elect their parliaments through proportional representation with closed lists (Chapter 4), an electoral system that requires voters to vote for an entire list of candidates nominated by the whole rather than for individual candidates.

Even in many nondemocratic political systems, parties play an important role in recruiting government officials. In China, for example, aspiring leaders must first rise through the ranks of the Communist Party. As they work their way up, those with more powerful political patrons, greater commitment, and greater talent are selected for party and government leadership positions. A similar process took place within Mexico's PRI during the 70 years it ran that country (Chapter 16).

As we have noted, many military regimes and monarchies in the developing world govern without parties. But military governments generally do not hold power for extended periods, falling victim to their lack of popular support, internal struggles for power, or both. Thus, General Pervez Musharraf's military government had banned opposition political party activity in Pakistan, but a national protest movement forced him to restore party participation in the 2008 parliamentary elections. Soon afterwards, he was forced to resign from office. In recent decades the number of military **no-party regimes** has declined rapidly, as democratic or semidemocratic governments have replaced them in many developing nations (see Chapter 15). Most of the remaining countries with long-lived, no-party rule are either absolute or near-absolute monarchies, including Saudi Arabia and Qatar. While the number of military governments has declined sharply, a few no-party military regimes remain in countries such as Myanmar.

Formulating Government Policies and Programs

Parties do more than merely select candidates and identify government leaders. They also help formulate government programs. All societies, particularly democratic ones, have countless interest groups trying to influence government policy. A major function of parties is **political aggregation**—that is, reducing the multitude of conflicting political demands from civil society to a manageable number of alternatives.[6]

Every four years, the Democratic and Republican national conventions devote considerable energy to the construction of a **party platform**, a long document outlining in detail the party's position on issues. Hardly any voters actually read the platforms. Indeed, shortly after the 1996 Republican convention, even the party's nominee, Bob Dole, indicated that he hadn't. Nevertheless, a platform reflects a party's efforts to turn the raw demands of citizens and pressure groups into policy proposals. Therefore, parts of the platform may become the subject of heated debate.

For example, at the 1948 Democratic convention, a number of segregationist, southern delegates ("Dixiecrats")—led by South Carolina Senator Strom Thurmond—left the party after it inserted a pro-integration plank into the platform. In the 55 years since that split, the Democrats have remained identified with civil rights for minorities. The South, once solidly Democratic, has turned Republican. More recently, the lead-up to the 1996 Republican convention featured a bitter internal conflict over the party's stance on abortion. For party nominee Bob Dole, that created a difficult dilemma. If the platform moderated the party's "pro-life" position, it would alienate some of its most important party activists within the Christian Right. If it took a hard line on the issue, it risked losing the votes of moderate, middle-class, Republican or independent, women. Ultimately, Dole's weakness among the second group of voters (referred to by the media as "soccer moms") contributed to his defeat, though it is unclear how much of a role the abortion issue actually played. In the 2000 and 2004 Republican conventions, on the other hand, George Bush more strongly committed himself to an anti-abortion position and subsequently benefited from grassroots campaigning and a strong turnout by conservative Christians.

Years ago, a leading political scientist called the Democrats and the Republicans classic examples of **catchall parties**—that is, parties that try to appeal to a wide range of social classes and groups and, hence, have had less well-defined policy programs.[7] Traditionally, American parties have articulated their ideologies less clearly than have their Western European counterparts, limited by their diverse constituencies. In recent times, however, American parties have become more ideologically homogeneous (i.e., the Democrats are more uniformly liberal and the Republicans more uniformly conservative). At the same time, many Western European parties have broadened their constituencies—for example, the British Labour Party has moved toward the center in order to attract more middle-class support. But they still tend to have more clearly defined political positions than their American counterparts. Once a Western European party has achieved a parliamentary majority, its supporters expect it to enact the programs in its platform. At the next election, voters can more easily render a verdict on the governing party's performance and hold it accountable for its record.

In Communist nations, the party has had a still more fundamental role in formulating government policy. In China, Cuba, and Vietnam, for example, it is the Communist Party leaders, rather than the national parliaments or any other government body, who make the most important policy decisions. Similarly, many of Africa's single-party systems concentrated policy making in the ruling party. During the late 1980s, Soviet President Mikhail Gorbachev shifted policy making from the Communist Party Politburo to the government, specifically the president and his cabinet. That transfer of power was one of the key factors that led party hard-liners to attempt a 1991 coup against him (Chapter 13).

Organizing Government

After national elections in democracies, either a single party or a coalition of parties commands a majority in the national legislature. In parliamentary systems, that winning party or coalition chooses the prime minister. Their party label ties governing-party MPs together and enables their leaders to present a coherent program. Even though the major American political parties have become more ideologically uniform in recent years, congressional Democrats and Republicans are still less less likely to vote as a cohesive bloc than are their European counterparts. Although Americans tend to take pride in congressional representatives and senators who do not bow to their party's line, such independence makes it harder for Congress to get programs passed.

THE ORIGINS OF POLITICAL PARTIES

Throughout the world, the growth of parties has been linked to the spread of mass political participation. As long as a small, hereditary elite ruled most nations, there was no need for broadly based political organizations. That situation began to change during Western Europe's transition from a **hierarchical**, agricultural economy to an industrial, capitalist one. Urbanization and industrialization created important new political actors—first the middle class and then the industrial working class. In the Third World, a similar process began in the twentieth century.

The first European and Latin American parties in the nineteenth century were merely competing aristocratic or upper-middle-class parliamentary factions.[8] As the right to vote was gradually extended to a larger portion of the population, however, these elite-led parties reached out to the middle class, then to workers and women (and finally, in the twentieth century, to Latin American peasants). In Great Britain, for example, the Conservative Party represented the interests of the landed aristocracy while the rising business class increasingly led the Whigs (later to become the Liberal Party). As the franchise expanded throughout the nineteenth and early twentieth centuries, however, both parties broadened their support. Similarly, in Colombia, the Conservative and Liberal parties—one headed by wealthy, rural landowners and the other by influential merchants—eventually established strong ties to the peasants through **patron–client relations**.

With the advent of universal male suffrage in Europe by the early twentieth century, new types of political parties emerged, known as **mass parties**.[9] Unlike their predecessors, which were led by elites seeking popular support, these were led by political outsiders wishing to challenge the established order. Most were Socialist parties with close ties to the labor movement, including the French Socialist Party (SFIO) and the British Labour Party. And, unlike their more conservative predecessors, they were interested in more than just winning votes.[10] They also wished to introduce their followers to socialism and thereby create a new political culture. Party members were encouraged to become party activists.[11]

During the mid-twentieth century, Western Europe's conservative and center parties also adopted aspects of mass-party structure, including grassroots organizations. Later in that century mass-party organizations and strategies became the models for many of the contemporary parties in Africa, Asia, and Latin America. Finally, yet another type of political party originated out of **social movements**. These movements are "broad mobilizations of ordinary people [seeking] a particular goal or goals."[12] Often such social movements represent political outsiders and less powerful groups in society. Examples include the civil rights movement in the United States, the human rights movement in Latin America, and the environmental movement in Western Europe. In some instances, social movements have begun as anti-system protests and eventually evolved into political parties working within the system or creating a new system. For example, in what was then called Czechoslovakia, civic protest movements eventually toppled the Communist regime and then turned into political parties.[13] Decades earlier, the nationalistic Gaullist Movement grew into France's largest political party (Box 5-2).

Box 5-2

POLITICAL PARTY LONGEVITY

Even advanced Western democracies may have considerably different political party histories. For example, the U.S. Democratic and British Conservative Parties are both more than 200 years old. The British Labour Party was born at the beginning of the twentieth century. While the British party system has experienced one important change in recent decades (the merger of the Liberal and Social Democratic parties in 1988), other major parties in both countries have enjoyed a considerable longevity.

This is not true of France. The most successful parties at the ballot box in the Fifth Republic (from 1958 to the present) have been a series of linked conservative parties commonly referred to as the Gaullist or Neo-Gaullist Party because the first was formed in 1947 in support of General Charles de Gaulle, the leader of the French resistance in World War II. Originally called the Rally of the People of France (RPF), the party's core creed was de Gaulle's opposition to the Fourth Republic's constitution (1946–58). That party was dismantled in 1955. Three years later, as the Fourth Republic fell, the Gaullists formed a new party called the Union for the New Republic (UNR), which lifted de Gaulle to the presidency of the Fifth Republic (1958–). But only four years later (1962) the UNR merged with the Democratic Union of Labor, a pro-Gaullist, labor union movement, to form the Union for the French Republic–Democratic Union of Labor. Five years after that (1967) it changed its name once again to the Union of Democrats for the Fifth Republic (UDR), but soon altered its name once again by dropping the word "Fifth" from its title. In 1976, six years after de Gaulle's death, the party was reorganized to become the electoral vehicle of Jacques Chirac, who served as France's prime minister twice and subsequently as its two-term president (1995–2007). Chirac and his supporters renamed that party the Rally for the Republic (RPR), its sixth name change in less than 30 years. Finally, during the 2002 presidential campaign, Chirac united the RPR with a majority of the centrist Union for French Democracy (UDF) and the small Liberal Democracy Party to form yet another new party, the victorious Union for a Presidential Majority (UMP) which soon changed its name again to the Union for a Popular Movement (also UMP).

The major leftist party, the French Socialist Party, traces its roots back to 1880, with the founding of the French Workers' Party. Only two years later, the party split into a Marxist faction and a more moderate faction. In 1899, several competing socialist and workers' parties consolidated into two parties: the more leftist Socialist Party of France and the more moderate French Socialist Party. Six years after that, the two parties merged to become the Unified Socialist Party. In 1920, the more left-wing portion of that party (which, despite its name, was not very unified) broke away to form the French Communist Party. The remaining, more moderate, faction of the party changed its name to the rather cumbersome official title of French Section of the Workers' International (SFIO). In 1969, future president François Mitterrand reorganized the party and changed its name back to the Socialist Party.

Are the constant name changes and reorganizations of France's two major parties (and many smaller ones as well) anything more than cosmetic? Why have the major parties in Britain and the U.S. been so much more stable (the two oldest political parties in the world are the British Conservative Party and the American Democratic Party)? The answer to the first question is that the constant party reorganizations and name changes in France *are* significant because they usually indicate the appearance of a new movement, a change in a party's programmatic emphasis, a modification of ideology, the emergence of new leadership, or some combination thereof.

Why do French parties, then, change so often in comparison to American and British parties? There is no simple answer, but two factors stand out. First, French political party leaders and voters have historically been more ideologically oriented and more concerned with fine political distinctions than their more pragmatic English-speaking counterparts. Rather than work out (or fight out) differences within their parties, as Anglo-American parties are prone to do, they are more likely to split or reorganize. This is particularly true of the French Left (Communists, Socialists, and others). Second, French parties are sometimes formed or reorganized around the political ambitions of dynamic leaders. This is particularly true of the French Right. For example, the first Gaullist party was born in the 1940s as a political vehicle for General de Gaulle and was reorganized and renamed in the 1970s to suit the political ambitions of Jacques Chirac. But the Socialists as well were reorganized and renamed in 1969 partly to serve the political aspirations of Francois Mitterrand. In the 2002 presidential elections, contesting political parties were so fragmented—especially on the Left—that 11 candidates entered the race, with none of them securing as much as 20 percent of the vote in the first round.

PARTY SYSTEMS

The term *party system* refers to the characteristics of the set of parties operating in a particular country. It indicates the number of parties that have a serious chance of winning major elections and the degree of competition between them. The number of competitive parties operating in a particular country fundamentally influences that nation's entire political system. Obviously, countries governed continuously by a single party—even if opposition parties are legal—are less than fully democratic. Conversely, countries that have multiple parties, with none able to garner a majority in the national parliament, are frequently less politically stable. Because of the great importance of the number of competitive political parties, descriptions of, for example, the Chinese, American, British, and Italian political systems typically label them, respectively, one-party, two-party, two-and-one-half-party, and multiparty systems.

Americans often think of a two-party system as "natural," since we are accustomed to it. If by that we mean that a two-party system is *preferable* to, say, a multiparty system, that claim is debatable. And if we believe that having two dominant parties is the most *common* arrangement, that belief is simply incorrect. For example, until recently, single-party systems were predominant in Africa, the Middle East, parts of Asia, and the former Communist bloc, and there are still many of them. At the same time, many European and Latin American countries have multiparty systems. In short, two-party systems are the exception, not the rule, and they predominate primarily in English-speaking democracies.

Of course, even the United States has more than two political parties. Besides the Democrats and the Republicans, American parties include, among many others, the Green Party, the Libertarian Party, and the United States Marijuana Party (founded in 2002). But although so-called "third parties" in the United States occasionally win local elections, they do not attract a large share of votes in national races. Sometimes, however, third-party candidates in the U.S. have played the role of spoilers. Had Ralph Nader not run in the 2000 presidential election as the Green Party candidate, it is likely that most of his votes (including those he won in Florida) would have gone to the Democratic nominee, Al Gore, and that Gore, rather than George Bush, would have won the presidency.

Two parties, Conservative and Labour, have dominated British politics for almost 90 years. But unlike the United States, other parties have attracted a substantial share of the vote in recent years. During the 1980s, an electoral alliance between the Liberal and Social Democratic parties attracted about one-fourth of the votes in two consecutive national elections, nearly matching Labour's share. Subsequently, the two parties merged, forming the Liberal Democratic Party, which received 22 percent of the vote in the 2005 national election. Consequently, some political scientists argue that the British currently have a **two-and-one-half-party system** (defined as a party system in which two parties predominate, but a third party presents a significant challenge).

Because they sometimes use different definitions, analysts may differ as to whether a country such as Japan or Mexico in the second-half of the twentieth century—where many parties competed but one party always won—had a single-party, or a multiparty system. Building on a classification system originally created by Jean Blondel, we offer the following party-system categories and yardsticks for identifying them.[14]

1. *No-party system:* Either political parties have never developed or an authoritarian government has banned them.
2. *Single-party system:* One party regularly receives more than 65 percent of the vote in national elections.

3. *Two-party system* (including a two-and-one-half-party system such as Britain's): Two major parties regularly divide more than 75 percent of the national vote (but no single party receives as much as 65 percent).
4. *Multiparty system:* The two largest parties have a combined total of less than 75 percent of the vote.

No-Party Systems

Although political parties are hallmarks of modern political systems, there remain a number of countries that have never formed political parties with any significant following or that have banned previously active political parties. The first group, very limited in number, consists principally of countries with pre-modern social structures and low levels of political participation. In countries such as Saudi Arabia, relatively small, elite bodies (sheikhs, princes, and tribal chiefs) have made political decisions with no need for parties.

When the armed forces take control of the government (not long ago a common occurrence in Africa and Latin America) they have often banned political-party activity. For example, for many years Chile had enjoyed one of Latin America's most vibrant party systems. But when the military, led by General Augusto Pinochet, seized power (1973–1990) it banned all political parties and party activity. With the spread of democracy in the developing world since the 1970s, military governments and their no-party systems have become far less common (Chapter 15).

Single-Party Systems

As we have noted, many authoritarian regimes, once so common in the developing world, and all totalitarian governments have single-party systems. Totalitarian parties, most notably Fascist and Marxist-Leninist parties, are mass-membership organizations that seek to exercise total control over society and to inculcate the ruling party's ideological values into the population. Following revolutions in Russia, China, Vietnam, and Cuba, each country's Communist Party launched an extensive resocialization campaign to restructure their political cultures (see Chapters 3 and 15). At least initially, many activists seemed strongly committed to the party's vision of a new social order.

Because of their capacity to penetrate and control other social institutions, totalitarian political parties were once considered nearly impossible to dislodge once they had taken power.[15] In the Soviet Union and Eastern Europe, Communist-party functionaries controlled the military, police, factories, state farms, and schools. Yet ultimately, their grip on power weakened and Communist regimes collapsed from the Soviet Union to Hungary. Currently, Communist parties retain power in only a handful of nations.

A second group of single-party states emerged—following World War II and the disintegration of Europe's colonial empires—in the newly independent nations of Africa and the Middle East. Many of these ruling parties were organized along **Leninist** lines, like Communist parties with highly centralized control. They usually espoused a nationalistic ideology and wished to resocialize the population into a new, post-colonial political culture. Many of them, however, have been too self-serving and corrupt to attract a loyal, mass following and have governed ineffectively. Consequently, ruling parties in countries such as Libya and Syria have maintained power more through intimidation than through mass mobilization.

Until the 1980s, few African or Middle Eastern countries permitted viable opposition parties. In addition, several Asian governments—in countries such as Indonesia, Malaysia, Singapore, and Taiwan—argued that developing nations needed the unifying influence and direction of a single-party system. However, with the wave of democracy that has swept across the less developed world in the past 30 years or so (see Chapter 15), many African and Asian nations have introduced relatively free and fair elections. In some cases, political parties now alternate in power.

To be sure, not all entrenched ruling parties are self-serving or incompetent. When headed by well-intentioned leaders, they sometimes have served their nations well. During the late 1930s, Mexican President Lázaro Cárdenas used the ruling party to integrate previously excluded peasants and workers into the political system. More recently, Tanzanian President Julius Nyerere's Tanganyika African National Union (TANU) channeled the demands of the country's villagers to the national government. In time, however, the absence of party competition and the passing of idealistic leaders such as Cárdenas and Nyerere have perverted even well-intentioned dominant parties. In fact, most Third World single-party systems have fallen victim to corruption and the pursuit of special interests.

Two-Party Systems

Two-party and two-and-one-half-party systems are most prevalent in Anglo-American societies, including Great Britain, the United States, Canada, New Zealand, and Australia.* However, other countries, such as Austria, Germany, Colombia, Costa Rica, and Uruguay, have had two dominant parties as well.

Why do these countries have two dominant parties while most democracies have multiparty systems? One important factor influencing the number of parties that can compete effectively is the country's electoral arrangements. We have seen (Chapter 4) that proportional representation more easily facilitates (but does not guarantee) the development of several competitive political parties, whereas single-member-district systems are more likely to produce two dominant parties.

Among advanced parliamentary democracies, two-party systems tend to be more stable than multiparty systems because one of the parties is likely to achieve a legislative majority. But in a number of Latin American countries with two-party systems, stability has been elusive. For example, Colombia has had a turbulent history of political violence. Just as they are not universally stable, neither are two-party systems always democratic. During its years of minority (White) rule, South Africa had competitive elections, pitting two leading parties against each other. But since only the white minority could vote for important posts, the two-party system was hardly democratic. Similarly, before Nicaragua's 1979 revolution, the ruling Somoza dictatorship regularly sponsored elections between its own Liberal Party and the Conservatives, a puppet opposition party. The government, however, predetermined the outcomes of those elections.

---

* Political scientists often cite Britain as an archetypal example of a two-party system. Since the 1980s, however, the two largest parties (Labour and Conservative) have often failed to receive a combined total of 75 percent of the parliamentary vote, Blondel's threshold for a two-party system. Thus, Britain technically has been moving to a multi-party system, but because of single-member districts one party still almost always wins over half the seats in parliament (Chapter 12).

Multiparty Systems

Multiparty systems predominate in Western Europe but also exist in a number of developing nations. Sometimes these parties mirror multiple societal divisions—class, religious, linguistic, racial, and ethnic—that translate into multiple political cleavages. So, it is not surprising that a country such as Switzerland—with religious divisions between Catholics and Protestants, class and ideological divisions, and several spoken languages—has a multiparty system. Yet some fairly homogeneous nations, such as Sweden and Iceland, also have multiple parties.

Indeed, social divisions are neither the only factor that determines the number of competitive parties nor even the most important one. Electoral procedures are tremendously important. We have noted that countries that elect their parliament or congress through proportional representation (PR) are more likely to have multiparty legislatures than those using single-member districts (SMD) (Chapter 4). For example, SMD elections to the U.S. House of Representatives and the British House of Commons discriminate against small parties by denying them legislative representation proportional to their voting strength (See Box 12-3). Moreover, as it becomes evident how difficult it is for third-party candidates to win in SMD elections, their initial supporters may eventually conclude that continuing to vote for them is a wasted effort.

Proponents of PR point out that it is a fairer electoral system because it makes it easier for smaller parties to win some seats in the national legislature, with their number of seats proportional to their support from the voters. At the same time, however, it makes it harder for any single party to achieve a legislative majority. Consequently, in parliamentary systems, where the government needs to command a legislative majority to stay in power, the prime minister often must secure the backing of a multiparty coalition. If there are many policy and strategic divisions among the coalition partners, the government's life is precarious because coalition members may withdraw their support at any time. For example, in Italy a succession of unstable parliamentary coalitions produced more than 50 governments during the second half of the twentieth century (although recently government coalitions have become somewhat more durable).

How unstable multiparty parliamentary systems are depends on how cooperative the political parties are. Although postwar Italy and Fourth Republic France had to live with ruling coalitions that fell apart every year or so, other countries with more cooperative political parties manage to maintain stability. These include Finland, Israel, the Netherlands, Norway, and Switzerland. Indeed, Finland and Switzerland have two of the most fractionalized party systems in the democratic world (that is, a very large number of parties hold some parliamentary seats and none predominates). Yet they are models of political stability. Clearly, they have benefited from political cultures that stress cooperation rather than conflict.

TYPES OF POLITICAL PARTIES

Let us now turn our attention from party systems to the characteristics of individual political parties. Among the many possible ways to classify these parties, we focus here on two important characteristics: internal organization and ideological message.

Party Organization

Although all major parties have similar goals—to field candidates for elected office, to win elections and, hopefully, control the government, and to implement their programs—their internal organizations differ greatly. Some are highly centralized with top-down command structures, and others are loose federations of regional or local organizations. In the United States, the combined effects of a federal structure (a division of power between the national and state governments), the separation of powers within the federal government itself, and historical and cultural preferences have created highly decentralized parties. As John Bibby has noted, "It is hard to overstate the extent to which American political parties are characterized by decentralized power structures. . . . Within the party organization, the national institutions of the party . . . rarely meddle in nominations and organizational affairs of state parties."[16]

Even at the national level, Democrats and Republicans are organizationally weaker than are most major parties in other advanced democracies. Whereas Western European and Canadian party leaders select their party's parliamentary candidates, the United States is one of the few Western democracies to select candidates through primary elections. Because American congressmen are less beholden to their party for their nomination, they are also less prone to vote cohesively as a party unit than most Western European parliamentary delegations are.

Which model is more desirable? Many Americans prefer having senators and congressional representatives who vote their own minds and do not automatically vote with their fellow Democrats or Republicans. But critics contend that the absence of party discipline (voting as a unified bloc) makes it difficult to develop coherent governmental programs or to hold either party accountable for its performance in office. In recent years, however, party discipline in Congress has increased. As the number of conservative Democrats and progressive Republicans in Congress has declined, party unity in both parties has increased.

Communist parties represent the other end of the organizational spectrum. Following the Leninist principle of democratic centralism, they concentrate policy making and candidate selection power at the top. Particularly in countries that they have governed, but even when in opposition in democratic countries, they allow their MPs little or no independence. This extreme centralization has often led to paralysis at lower party levels, whereby officials have hesitated to make even the most mundane decisions on their own. (See Box 5-3.)

Party Ideologies: Right Wing through Left Wing

A political party's ideology defines its most fundamental message and the governmental policies that it proposes. Some parties—such as the Swedish Social Democrats, the British Conservatives, and the Chinese Communists—hold well delineated ideological positions and bear names that clearly identify them. Others, such as the Mexican PRI, are more ideologically ambiguous, often housing different political factions with conflicting outlooks. Still others have no explicit ideology at all. But most parties, especially in advanced democracies, can be classified according to their ideological orientation.[19]

Box 5-3

Varieties of Party Organization

Many years ago, the legendary American humorist Will Rogers used to tell his audiences, "I am not a member of any organized political party—I am a Democrat." Although his joke specifically poked fun at the long-standing Democratic propensity for internal quarreling, it might also have referred to the organizational weaknesses of *both* American parties. In Europe and other democracies outside of the United States, candidates for parliament are selected at party meetings or conventions. In contrast, because their candidates are chosen in party primary elections, the leaders of U.S. political parties have limited control over their party's choice of nominee. Periodically, primary voters will elect fringe candidates with views that are unacceptable to the national or state party leadership. In Louisiana, for example, David Duke, a former Grand Wizard of the Ku Klux Klan won Republican nomination for a state legislative seat despite the opposition of the Chairman of the Republican National Committee, Lee Atwater, and then-President George W. Bush. To be sure, Marjorie Randon Hershey notes that both national parties, but especially the Republicans, have strengthened their national organizations since the 1980s and that their national committees now play a stronger role in supporting their parties' congressional and state campaigns.[17] Still, major American parties remain decentralized and weak compared to parties elsewhere.

It is instructive to contrast this looseness of structure with Communist Party organization in the former Soviet Union. Consider the following reaction of a local party official to the failed 1991 coup attempt by Communist hard-liners against Soviet President Mikhail Gorbachev (Chapter 13). In the Russian city of Klin, only 50 miles outside Moscow, the Communist Party held a previously scheduled lecture on the day that the coup was beginning to unravel. Asked by party members to explain what was happening, local officials waffled: "We had no instructions from Moscow," Igor Muratov, the Klin party leader, later explained. "We could not give our assessment of what was happening."[18]

Most Western European parties fall between those two organizational extremes. Those parties are far more centrally controlled and cohesive than American political parties but nowhere nearly as centralized as ruling Communist parties.

In Chapter 2 we defined the beliefs and aspirations of the major political ideologies. Here, we classify major political parties according to their ideological leanings and discuss where and when parties in each ideological camp have been successful at the ballot box. We list the party ideologies from right (ultraconservative and conservative) to left (radical).

Neofascist Parties   These ultra-**right-wing** parties generally stress militant nationalism and the preservation of alleged ethnic purity, usually mixed with explicit and implicit racism, anti-Semitism or other forms of bigotry. As such, they bear some resemblance to Hitler's Nazi Party and Italy's Fascist Party during World War II, though today's **neofascists** are generally less extreme and deny any such links. Neofascist parties have been active in both Western and Eastern Europe and have experienced a resurgence in recent decades. They have been most destructive in several multi-ethnic Central European countries—such as Serbia and Bosnia—where they have aroused hatred against minority ethnic groups and engaged in "ethnic cleansing."

In recent decades, the rising number of Third World and Eastern European immigrants to Western Europe has unleashed some racist and anti-immigrant sentiment, enlarging support for neofascist parties. The neofascists have also capitalized on public resentment against the European Union (EU) and globalization, both of which they blame for Europe's chronically high unemployment rate in recent decades. Finally, extreme-right-wing parties support tough, law-and-order policies as they seek to capitalize on public concern over rising levels of crime (though European crime rates are still far below America's). Neofascist parties have had some success in Austria, Belgium, Denmark, France, Germany, Italy, and the Netherlands. While they rarely attract more than 5–10 percent of the national vote, in a few cases they have won far more and have influenced national politics.

In France, the National Front's perennial presidential candidate, Jean-Marie Le Pen, is hostile to both Muslims and Jews. While insisting that the country's large Muslim, immigrant population should be shipped home, he has also called the Nazi Holocaust "a [minor] detail of history." After Le Pen unexpectedly edged out Socialist Prime Minister Lionel Jospin for second place in the opening round of the 2002 presidential election—thereby advancing into a two-person runoff with incumbent President Jacques Chirac—the Socialists and other leftist parties threw their support to Chirac, their erstwhile conservative opponent. With leftists joining conservatives, Chirac emerged with 82 percent of the second-round vote. But, while over 80 percent of all French voters rejected Le Pen, many Europeans were concerned that almost one in five French voters would support such an extremist.

Elsewhere in Europe, Austria's Freedom Party also ran on an anti-immigration platform while opposing the nation's membership in the EU. In 2000, it joined the governing coalition after winning 23 percent of the parliamentary vote. As a result, the EU briefly invoked economic sanctions against the Austrians. But the party has declined to about 10 percent since. Because all well-established Western European parties, from conservatives through Communists, strongly reject the extreme-right, neofascists have slim prospects of winning a national election. And, except in Austria, they have never been part of any nation's governing coalition.

Conservative Parties   Conservative parties are among the oldest parties in Western Europe and Latin America. Although their programs and styles differ from region to region and country to country, they usually share certain common beliefs (described below) regarding tradition, stability, religion, family, and country.

At the same time, however there are also important distinctions between conservative parties in different parts of the world. Latin America's conservative parties have long represented elite economic interests and, historically, opposed the full incorporation of workers and peasants into the political system. In politically polarized Latin American and Southern European nations, with strong leftist unions and political parties, many conservative parties have supported repressive measures to crush a perceived threat from the Left.[20] For example, when faced with more radical leftist challenges at the ballot box, or from labor unrest, or from guerrilla insurgencies, some conservative parties in Chile, Brazil, Uruguay, Greece, and Spain supported coups by right-wing militaries. Even France's first neo-Gaullist party, which soon became a pro-democratic, mainstream French party, had some authoritarian tendencies in its early days.[21]

In contrast, conservative parties in stable democracies with moderate left-wing parties and a relatively consensual political culture—such as the United States, New Zealand, and Germany—are firmly committed to democracy. As the perceived threat from Communist or other leftist movements has receded in Latin America and southern Europe, conservative parties in that region have also embraced democracy.

All conservative parties are strongly committed to the free enterprise system and, in varying degrees, want to limit government involvement in the economy.

Some parties—including the Republicans in the United States and, more recently, the British Conservatives—have stressed economic issues, strongly defending the free markets and other elements of capitalism. On the other hand, many European conservatives have accepted or even initiated extensive government economic planning and comprehensive welfare programs. In some cases, upper-class conservative leaders have expressed a sense of *noblesse oblige*—a responsibility of the "well born" to help those of lesser standing. Others have endorsed government welfare programs as a means of limiting working-class support for leftist parties. Consequently, Western European conservative parties such as France's neo-Gaullists and Germany's Christian Democrats have supported economic policies similar to those supported by the Democratic Party in the U.S.. But despite their economic policy differences, European and American conservatives share a commitment to traditional social principles, including family values, nationalism, patriotism, religion, social stability, and a hard line on law and order.

In the aftermath of World War II, the most prominent European conservative parties accepted and sometimes endorsed a major role for government in society. By the 1980s, however, as Europe strained to stay competitive in the world and as inflation and unemployment rose, a new generation of conservatives, led by Britain's Prime Minister Margaret Thatcher, concluded that the state had become too intrusive in the economy, taxes were too high, and benefits for workers and the poor, which far exceeded their magnitude in the U.S., had become too expensive. Thatcher and American President Ronald Reagan became symbols of a conservative resurgence. Resentful of growing budget deficits and higher inflation, the electorate began to demand a lid on taxes. As a result, almost all Western governments, even leftist ones (Socialists), have been forced to cut back on welfare measures and other spending programs.

Liberal Parties   Even more than conservatism, liberalism has meant diffirent things in diverse countries and time periods. The first liberal parties in Europe and Latin America ("classical liberals") advocated the separation of church and state, greater equality of opportunity, and the defense of personal freedom. In Europe, liberal parties generally still defend small business interests and oppose "excessive" state economic intervention. Indeed, many of Western Europe's liberal parties—including Germany's Free Democrats, Italy's Liberal Party, and the remaining wing of the French UDF—represent middle-class and small-business interests and have frequently joined conservative parties in government coalitions. Normally, European and Latin American liberal parties occupy the political center between conservatives on the right and socialists or populists on the left.

But liberalism has developed a different meaning in the United States. From the time of President Franklin Roosevelt's New Deal, the Democratic Party has supported government activism to solve social and economic problems, including the social security program and other government safety nets, student loans, food stamps, bank deposit insurance, and an assortment of social welfare programs. Because the United States, unlike Western Europe or Latin America, has no significant Socialist or **populist** parties, and since American labor unions support the Democratic Party (not the Socialists, as in Europe), the Democrats occupy the left side of the American political spectrum, although their policies would be considered middle-of-the-road in Western Europe.

But beyond these differences on economic matters, liberals in both Europe and the U.S. share a number of important social and political concerns, including their defense of civil liberties and individual rights. Similarly, liberal interest groups such as the American Civil Liberties Union use the judicial system to protect the rights of criminal defendants, minority groups, and political dissidents against government intrusion. In short, whereas conservative parties (especially in the U.S.) have been most concerned about government intrusion in the economic sphere (trying to limit taxes and government regulation), liberal parties have focused on government intrusions in areas such as civil liberties and a pregnant woman's "right to choose."

Western European liberal parties have not done well in the past half century. They have been squeezed from the left by Socialist parties and from the right by conservatives. Hence, they no longer can attract a significant portion of the vote except when they have allied with other parties as Britain's Liberal Party did when it merged with the Social Democratic Party in the 1980s. Liberal parties in Latin America have suffered a similar fate.

In the United States, the Democratic Party was usually the leading force in national politics from the 1930s (after the Great Depression) until 1980. Since then, however, far fewer American voters have identified themselves as liberals, and Democratic candidates have generally tried to escape that label. While the party has often won control of one or both houses of Congress, it lost seven of the ten presidential elections between 1968 and 2004.

Socialist Parties   As we noted in Chapter 2, the label "Socialist" is sometimes confusing, since it has been used to refer to democratic parties in Western Europe, to the Communist government of the Soviet Union, and to some of the ruling Communist parties in Eastern Europe before their fall.* We will reserve the terms "Socialist" and "Social Democratic" for parties, particularly in Western Europe, that are committed to democracy and wish to modify, but not erase, capitalism. Usually, we use the party labels **socialist** and **social democrat** interchangeably, though they sometimes denote certain ideological differences. France's Socialist Party and Germany's Social Democratic Party are both major electoral contenders that have periodically led the national government. Sweden's Social Democratic Party and Norway's Labor Party (Social Democratic) have governed their respective countries most of the time since the early 1930s. In the past 20 years, socialists or social democrats have also led governments for some period of time in many other European nations, including Austria, Britain, Denmark, Finland, France, Germany, Greece, Portugal, and Spain. In Latin America they have played major roles in Chile, Venezuela, Ecuador, and Costa Rica.

Historically, many European Socialist parties were split between more radical (Marxist) and more moderate factions. In the decades after World War II, however, most shed their Marxist factions, siding with the West against the Soviet Union in the Cold War and adopting more moderate domestic policies. Faced with a strong conservative challenge since the late 1970s, including popular disenchantment in many countries with "big government," parties such as Britain's Labour Party, the Spanish Socialists, and the German Social Democrats moved cautiously toward the political center as they reduced their commitment to government intervention and became

* The Soviet Union's official name was the Union of Soviet Socialist Republics (USSR).

more sympathetic to free markets. In Chapter 12 we will see how former British Prime Minister Tony Blair unofficially relabeled his party "New Labour" and accepted many of the free market policies of Conservative Prime Minister Margaret Thatcher. Chile's governing Socialist Party made similar modifications to its program and ideology. Hence, many Socialist parties, in Europe and elsewhere, now favor economic policies only somewhat different than their centrist and conservative opponents.[22]

That does not mean that there is no longer a significant difference between Socialists and their conservative (or centrist) competition. For one thing, Socialists are still far more likely to support welfare programs and other government safety nets. Furthermore, they differ substantially on social issues. For example, Spain's current Socialist Party government has legalized same-sex marriages, eased restrictions on abortion, and facilitated fast-track divorce in a country once known as among the most socially conservative in Europe.

Communist Parties   After the fall of the Soviet Union and its allied Communist governments in Eastern Europe, the number of nations governed by Communist parties has been reduced to a handful, mostly in Asia. China, with some 1.3 billion people and the world's second or third largest economy, is obviously the most important of these (see Chapter 14). Other single-party, Communist regimes include Cuba, Laos, North Korea, and Vietnam.

Outside of that much-reduced Communist bloc, Communist parties remain competitive at the ballot box in several European democracies, though their support has declined substantially in the past 25 years or more. At one time, Communist parties throughout the world faithfully followed policy directives from the Soviet Union. That began to change in the 1960s and 1970s, when different strains of communism emerged. For example, several Western European Communist parties, led by the Italians, followed a new path known as "Eurocommunism." They rejected Soviet-style authoritarianism and embraced (or in some cases, claimed to embrace) Western democratic values. The Italian Communists, the most democratically oriented of that group, was that country's second largest party (with up to one-third of the national parliamentary vote), and governed many of Italy's major cities. It broke openly with the Soviet Union after it condemned the Soviet invasion of Afghanistan in 1979. Since the 1990s, the party has changed its name twice. First, most of the Party abandoned communism and transformed itself into the Democratic Party of the Left, a Socialist party. It later joined with a number of other center-left parties to form the Democrats of the Left. From 1996 to 1998 and again in 2006–2008, that party joined a governing coalition behind Prime Minister Romano Prodi, an independent (non-party) economist.

Elsewhere in Western Europe, Communist parties that were once influential—most notably in France, Greece, Finland, Portugal, and Spain—have lost considerable support in recent decades. The French Communist Party regularly attracted 15 to 20 percent of the vote into the 1980s but now receives perhaps one-third of that portion. Even before the demise of Soviet communism, several demographic factors weakened Western Europe's Communist parties. Although those parties received some white-collar and middle-class support, their core constituency has always been blue-collar workers. As European workers bought homes and acquired more middle-class lifestyles during the post-war economic boom, many of them switched allegiance to more moderate political parties, abandoning the Communists and their doctrine of class conflict. In addition, as economic changes since the 1970s have reduced the proportion of blue-collar jobs in the workforce, and as the size and influence of leftist labor unions has diminished, Communist parties have lost an important part of their base.

After the collapse of Eastern European communism in 1989, most of the former ruling parties changed their names and policies, though many analysts still refer to them as "former Communist parties." Because they continue to support the welfare state and because they promise full employment, these parties have received considerable support from workers whose jobs or pensions are threatened by the transition to capitalism. Reformed Communist parties have occasionally led governments in Albania, Bulgaria, Hungary, Lithuania, Moldova, Poland, Romania, Serbia, and Slovakia. They have governed more effectively in countries such as Hungary and Poland than in nations such as Bulgaria and Moldova, whose governments were marked by corruption and incompetence.

Religious Parties   In many Catholic and Muslim countries, religiously affiliated parties have been important political players. **Christian Democratic** parties have often governed Germany, Italy, Chile, El Salvador, and a number of other European and Latin American countries. Usually, they are linked to the Catholic Church or, at least to Catholic theological doctrine. But in Germany, the party has a Protestant wing as well, and the small Christian Democratic movement emerging in Russia is associated with the Russian Orthodox Church. Religious parties are also influential in Asia and the Middle East. Violence between Moslems and Hindus in India has sometimes been stirred up by groups aligned with the BJP (Indian People's Party), a predominantly Hindu party that moderated its policies when it led governing coalitions from 1998 to 2004. In Israel, several Jewish orthodox parties have won a combined total of 10–15 percent of the parliamentary seats in recent elections. Because the parliament is highly factionalized and no single party ever comes close to winning a majority, the major parties need some support from the religious parties if they are to form a majority coalition. That gives those small religious parties leverage to push their agenda. In the Muslim world, the ties between some parties and Islamic institutions are very strong and explicit, with clerics holding key party positions. The Hezbollah, Lebanon's major political party and armed militia, is one such example. Elsewhere, links are only theological or philosophical, as with Europe and Latin America's Christian Democratic parties.

Although most religiously affiliated parties are conservative, especially on social values, others fall all along the ideological spectrum. For example, although some Christian Democratic parties in Latin America are quite conservative, others have influential leftist factions. During the early 1970s, a wing of the Chilean Christian Democrats joined the Marxist coalition government of President Salvador Allende. On the other hand, India's BJP (Hindu party) is highly conservative, and the Islamic parties of the Middle East are difficult to classify ideologically.

For the most part, the influence of religious parties in Europe has decline over the years. For example, whereas the Christian Democrats in France, and especially Italy, were once an important political force, they have since largely collapsed. The United States, with a constitutional and cultural separation of church and state, has no religious parties. But religious groups and institutions such as Evangelical Christians and the Catholic Church continue to exert a strong influence. In Muslim nations such as Iraq, Pakistan, and Iran, religious parties have grown in influence as the result of an Islamic religious resurgence. In Egypt and elsewhere, parties such as the Muslim Brotherhood would be more influential if the government did not repress them.

CONCLUSION: PARTIES IN A CHANGING WORLD

This chapter has highlighted several important trends in the current role of political parties. In Western Europe and the United States, voter preferences and the political dialogue have often swung toward the right of the ideological spectrum (though that may be changing somewhat in the U.S.). As we have noted, in these countries the public has become more skeptical of government economic intervention, be it welfare programs in the United States or government control of key productive enterprises in Western Europe.* At the same time, the relative size of the working class has diminished in these postindustrial societies, and many of the remaining blue-collar workers have acquired middle-class living standards and political attitudes.

These changes have presented substantial challenges to leftist parties in Western Europe and, to a lesser extent, to the Democrats in the United States. Changes in public opinion and the weakening of the Left's electoral base (including organized labor) have hurt them at the polls. Beyond President Clinton's two victories, the Democrats won only one presidential election from 1972 to 2004. Although Social Democratic parties remain a dominant political force in Scandinavia and currently govern Spain and Britain, they have generally been somewhat less successful in the rest of Western Europe in recent years.

In response to this challenge, many left-of-center parties now accept a more modest role for government and profess a more middle-of-the-road ideology in an effort to win back disaffected working-class voters and attract greater support from the middle class. Chastened by the Republican congressional triumph of 1994, Bill Clinton set aside his hopes for government-guaranteed health insurance and concentrated instead on such issues as safe streets, education, and welfare reform. Similarly, in the face of troubling budgetary deficits, most European Socialist and labor parties have largely abandoned their support for government ownership of strategic sectors of the economy and have accepted reductions in the welfare state. By moving the Labour Party toward the center, Britain's Tony Blair led that party to three consecutive victories in national elections after a long period in the political wilderness.

The movement of most major parties in the Western industrial democracies toward the political center has generally reduced ideological and programmatic differences between them. Thus, there are few major economic policy differences between the French Socialists and the conservative UMP or between the Labour and Conservative parties in Great Britain. Increasingly, elections in the developed world are being decided by voters' perceptions of party competence—deciding which party will be

* France illustrates the extent of government ownership that once existed in many European economies. During the early 1980s, the French government, which had already owned 12 percent of the nation's economy under the conservative governments of the previous decade, increased its share to 16 percent of GNP under the Socialists. In the 1990s, however, that proportion dropped as conservative governments re-privatized parts of the economy.

able to govern most effectively—rather than by differences in party ideology (though in the United States, differences on social issues such as the war in Iraq, abortion and same-sex marriage remain important).

The biggest losers in this move toward less ideological, centrist politics have been Western Europe's Communist parties. As we have seen, they once received an important share of the vote in countries such as France, Finland, and Italy, where they were the voices of working-class discontent and received 20–30 percent of the vote. But as Europe became more prosperous and many workers achieved middle-class lifestyles, class tensions decreased. At the same time, more centrist white-collar workers replaced once-radical, blue-collar workers in the workforce, and the strength of unions declined. All these factors diminished support for the region's Communist parties. Their authoritarian and stodgy leadership hurt them as well. Thus, even before the collapse of Soviet communism, Western European Communist parties were in decline. The notable exception had been the Italian Communist Party and its successor, the Democrats of the Left. But the party has abandoned its Communist beliefs in favor of social democracy and receives far fewer votes than the Communists once did. Like the most successful European Socialist parties, they moderated their ideology, governed efficiently, and picked up middle-class support.

Latin America has experienced a number of dramatic political and economic changes since the 1980s that have left a deep imprint on the region's political parties. First, after almost two decades of authoritarian government under military dictatorships and severe political repression in several countries, democratic civilian governments now govern almost every nation in the hemisphere. The collapse of the Soviet bloc, and the severe blow that the USSR's collapse imposed on Cuba's economy, deeply unsettled many of Latin America's leftist parties (even more than with Marxist parties elsewhere), which had subscribed to the Cuban revolutionary model. Finally, much like Western Europe and parts of Asia, Latin American governments in the last decades of the twentieth century reduced the economic role of the state—privatizing state enterprises and, in some cases, even privatizing social security systems. Faced with this new political landscape, a number of formerly radical leftist parties moderated their political and economic positions and embraced democracy.[23]

The most notable example, perhaps, was El Salvador's FMLN. Founded by leaders who had broken away from the Salvadorian Communist Party, the FMLN had waged a revolutionary war for over a decade with the Salvadorian armed forces. Faced with a stand-off, the two sides signed a peace agreement in 1992. The FMLN renounced armed struggle, moderated its positions, and transformed itself into a political party—now one of the two major parties in the country.

Many political scientists point to a broader trend in Western democratic nations—declining citizen support for political parties in general.[24] Indeed, a growing number of citizens in the U.S. and elsewhere identify themselves as independents and do not support any party. Commenting on this apparent decline of party strength, Kay Lawson and Peter Merkl had difficulty identifying a cause: "We don't know if major parties are failing because they are ideologically out of touch with their electorates, poorly organized, underfinanced, badly led, unaccountable, corrupt, overwhelmed by unethical or fanatical competition, unable to run effectively, or some combination of those factors."[25]

Russell Dalton maintains that, rather than looking for the causes of decreased *political party* support, we should look to the causes of a broader phenomenon. He points out that for decades citizens of most Western democracies have expressed declining confidence, not just in parties, but in almost all political institutions including the legal system and national legislatures.[26] In other words, declining interest in political parties is not the core problem, diminishing interest in *politics* is.

Despite these developments, however, many other political scientists insist on the continuing importance of parties in democratic societies. For example, some have argued that, if anything, parties in the United States play an increasingly important role in attracting voters to the polls and in governing the country.[27] And reports of the decline of party affiliations in the U.S. may be exaggerated. While it is true that the percentage of Americans who list themselves as independents (as opposed to Republicans or Democrats) has increased since the early 1950s (from about 22 percent in 1952 to as much as 36–39 percent in the first half of this decade), that increase took place primarily from 1952 to 1972, and support for the two major parties has remained fairly constant since that time.[28] Two other indicators suggest that the importance of independent voting in the U.S. has been exaggerated. First of all, while it is true that close to 40 percent of all Americans identify themselves as independents, more than two-thirds of them are "leaners," people who call themselves independent but lean toward one of the major parties most of the times that they vote. Second, if we divide respondents who identify themselves with a political party into two groups—strong partisans (those who are exceedingly devoted to one party) and weak partisans—we find that the percentage of people in the first group has risen significantly since 1972. So in fact, the major changes in American political identification since the 1970s are that the percentage of weak party partisans has dropped sharply and the number of independent leaners has grown sharply. But there is not a huge difference in the politics of those two groups. The number of "true" independents—people who are not influenced by party labels—has actually declined since the 1970s.[29] In short, "we should not underestimate the persistence of party ID [identification] . . . almost all Americans, if leaners are included . . . still report some degree of attachment to either the Democratic or the Republican Party."[30]

Similarly, Pippa Norris's examination of party membership over time in a large number of nations indicates that the decline in membership has been less uniform, less sharp, and indeed, less certain than many political scientists had maintained.[31]

It is even more difficult to assess or predict trends elsewhere in the world. In much of Africa, Asia, and the Middle East, parties are in their infancy or represent the narrow interests of powerful economic and political actors. Similarly, it is too early to say what kinds of party systems or party loyalties may emerge in Russia and Eastern Europe. The first free elections for the Polish parliament (in 1991) featured more than 50 competing parties, including the Polish Beer Drinkers Party. Russia had a similar multiplicity of parties, but Vladimir Putin's United Russia now totally dominates the political scene.

Although new institutions (such as neighborhood associations and social movements) have emerged in many countries to carry out functions previously reserved for political parties, and although many voters are cynical about parties, political scientists are still impressed by their enduring strength. A recent work by Juan Linz, Hans Daalder, and other leading political scientists concludes that, while support for political parties has eroded in the West (often for reasons that can't be blamed on the parties themselves), parties continue to play a critical function in democratic political systems.[32] Similarly, Thomas Carothers, a vice president of the Carnegie Endowment for International Peace, and a leading scholar on contemporary democratization, has noted that democracies cannot exist without parties and that the most productive assistance that Western nations can offer in order to buttress democratic transitions in the developing world and in former Communist nations is to help them develop and strengthen political parties.[33] Wherever national elections have been held on a continuing basis, political parties have played a fundamental role.

 ## WHERE ON THE WEB?

http://www.politics1.com/parties.htm
A guide to U.S. political parties with links to leaders of the two major parties and party organizations. Information on other American parties is included, down to the smallest and most obscure.

http://www.politicalresources.net/
A listing of political sites available on the Web, sorted by country, with links to parties and other institutions.

http://www.gksoft.com/govt/en/parties.html
Further links to political parties throughout the world, sorted by country.

http://www.psr.keele.ac.uk/parties.htm
List of political parties, interest groups, and other social movements; includes links to the home pages of hundreds of political parties around the world, organized by country.

http://www.ipu.org/english/home.htm
Inter-Parliamentary Union. An invaluable source of data on women representatives in national parliaments as well as other parliamentary information.

http://yaleglobal.yale.edu/display.article?id=6240
"Europe's Political Parties Buffeted by Globalization," an article in *Yale Global Online* dealing with the effects of anti-EU and anti-globalization movements on Europe's political parties.

http://www-sul.stanford.edu/depts/ssrg/africa/political-parties-africa.html
A comprehensive source with links to political parties throughout Africa.

Key Terms and Concepts

authoritarian
catchall parties
Christian Democrats
hierarchical
leadership recruitment
Leftist (Left-wing) political parties

personalistic party
political aggregation
political party
populist (parties)
Right-wing (Rightist) political parties
Social Democrats

Leninist (party or ideology) social movements
mass parties Socialist (parties)
neofascists parties totalitarian government (regime)
no-party regimes two-and-one-half-party system
party platform zipper-style quota
patron–client relations

Discussion Questions _____

1. What are the major functions of political parties in a democracy? What are the major arguments for and against political parties?
2. How have political parties contributed to the growth of women's representation in Western European parliaments? Discuss the reasons why some types of parties have more aggressively tried to raise their number of women MPs than have other parties. Discuss how a country's electoral system (proportional representation or single-member districts) influences its parties' ability to increase female representation in parliament.
3. Discuss the importance of religious parties today. Where are they most influential?
4. Why did left-of-center political parties in Europe, such as the British Labour Party and the Spanish and French Socialist Parties, face declining grassroots support, and how is that decline related to changes in their countries' workforces? How have those parties adjusted their programs to meet this challenge?
5. What are some factors that explain why the United States and Britain have two-party systems, whereas France, Germany, and most of Western Europe have multiparty systems?
6. Are political parties becoming less popular and less important in the United States and other Western democracies? What is the evidence on both sides of that question?

Notes _____

1. Marjorie Randon Hershey, *Party Politics in America*, 12th ed. (New York: Pearson Longman, 2007), pp. 106–107.
2. Data in this box are drawn from two sources: Inter-Parliamentary Union (IPU), "Women in National Parliaments," (Situation as of March 31, 2008), http://www.ipu.org/wmn-e/world.htm and Institute for Democratic and Electoral Assistance (IDEA), "Global Database of Quotas for Women," (2006–2008) http://www.quotaproject.org/index.cfm.
3. We initially drew these data from the Inter-Parliamentary Union, op. cit. However, the IPU incorrectly ranked countries falling behind other countries that were tied in terms of their percentage of women MPs. So, if country A has a parliament that is 48 percent female, and countries B, C and D each have parliaments that are 40 percent female (tying those three nations for second place in the rankings), and country E has 37 percent female MPs, the IPU ranks country E in 3rd place, when it should have been ranked 5th (behind A, B, C, and D). The country rankings in this box correct for the IPU ranking errors.
4. Miki Caul Kittilson, *Challenging Parties, Changing Parliaments: Women and Elected Office in Contemporary Western Europe* (Columbus: The Ohio State University Press, 2006).
5. Analysts agree that normally, in order for women MPs to change government policies on "women's issues" such as child care, elementary education, affirmative action, or divorce, they need to attain a "critical mass" of 30 percent of all parliamentary seats.
6. Gabriel Almond, *The Politics of Developing Areas*, eds. Gabriel Almond and James Coleman (Princeton, NJ: Princeton University Press, 1960), Introduction.
7. Otto Kirchheimer, "The Transformation of Western European Party Systems," in *Political Parties and Political Development*, eds. Joseph LaPalombara and Myron Weiner (Princeton, NJ: Princeton University Press, 1966).
8. Joseph LaPalombara and Myron Weiner, "The Origin and Development of Political Parties," in LaPalombara and Weiner, *Political Parties*, p. 25.
9. Leon Epstein, *Political Parties in Western Democracies* (New York: Praeger, 1967), pp. 130–166.
10. Maurice Duverger, *Political Parties* (New York: Wiley, 1954).
11. Ibid.
12. Manali Desai, "From Movement to Party to Government," in *States, Parties and Social Movements*, ed. Jack A. Goldstein, (Cambridge, England and New York: Cambridge University Press, 2003), p. 171.

13. John K. Glenn, "Parties Out of Movements: Party Emergence in Postcommunist Eastern Europe," in *States, Parties . . .*, ed. Goldstein, pp. 147–169.
14. Jean Blondel, "Types of Party Systems," in *The West European Party System*, ed. Peter Mair (New York: Oxford University Press, 1990).
15. Jeane J. Kirkpatrick, *Dictatorships and Double Standards* (New York: Simon & Schuster, 1982).
16. John Bibby, *Politics, Parties and Elections in America* (Chicago: Nelson Hall, 1987), p. 58.
17. Hershey, *Party Politics in America*, pp. 77–83.
18. *New York Times*, August 29, 1991.
19. For further discussion of the ideological classification of Western European parties, see Jurg Steiner, *European Democracies* (New York: Longman, 1991), pp. 7–64.
20. Guillermo A. O'Donnell, *Modernization and Bureaucratic-Authoritarianism: Studies in South American Politics* (Berkeley: Institute of International Studies, University of California, 1973); and David Collier, ed., *The New Authoritarianism in Latin America* (Princeton, NJ: Princeton University Press, 1979).
21. Jean Blondel, "The Government of France," in *Introduction to Comparative Government*, eds. Michael Curtis et al. (New York: Harper and Row, 1990), p. 133.
22. See, for example, Donald Share, "Dilemmas of Social Democracy in the 1980s: The Spanish Socialist Workers Party in Comparative Perspective," *Comparative Political Studies* 21 (October 1988): 429.
23. Salvador Martí I Puig and Salvador Santiuste Cué, "The Parliamentary Left," in *Politicians and Politics in Latin America*, ed. Manuel Alcántara Sáez (Boulder, CO: Lynne Rienner Publishers, 2008), pp.195–218.
24. For a study of that phenomenon in the United States, see Martin P. Wattenberg, *The Decline of American Political Parties: 1952–1988* (Cambridge, MA: Harvard University Press, 1990). For evidence that support for political parties is falling in most Western democracies, see Russell J. Dalton, *Citizen Politics*, 3rd ed. (Chatham, NJ: Chatham House, 2002).
25. Kay Lawson and Peter Merkl, "Alternative Organizations: Environmental, Supplementary, Communitarian and Authoritarian," in *When Parties Fail*, eds. Kay Lawson and Peter Merkl (Princeton, NJ: Princeton University Press, 1988), p. 3.
26. Dalton, *Citizen Politics*, pp. 240–246.
27. L. Sandy Maisel, ed., *The Parties Respond: Changes in the American Party System* (Boulder, CO: Westview, 1990); see also Paul Herrnson, *Party Campaigning in the 1980s* (Cambridge: Harvard University Press, 1988).
28. Donald Green, Bradley Palmquist, and Eric Schickler, *Partisan Hearts and Minds: Political Parties and the Social Identities of Voters* (New Haven, CT: Yale University Press, 2002), p. 15.
29. Hershey, *Party Politics in America*, pp. 106–107; Raymond E. Wolfinger "The Promising Adolescence of Campaign Surveys," in *Campaigns and Elections American Style*, eds. James A. Thurber and Candice J. Nelson (Boulder, CO.: Westview Press, 1995), pp. 184–185 made a similar observation in the 1990s; also "The ANES Guide to Public Opinion and Electoral Behavior," http://electionstudies.org/nesguide/toptable/tab2a_1.htm.
30. Hershey, Ibid, p.116.
31. Pippa Norris, *Democratic Phoenix* (New York: Cambridge University Press, 2002), pp. 218–219.
32. Richard Gunther, José Ramón Montero, and Juan Linz, ed., *Political Parties: Old Concepts and New Challenges* (New York: Oxford University Press, 2002).
33. Thomas Carothers, *Confronting the Weakest Link: Aiding Political Parties in New Democracies* (Washington, D.C.: Carnegie Endowment for International Peace, 2006).

For Further Reading _____

Alcántara Sáez, Manuel. Ed. *Politicians and Politics in Latin America*. Boulder, CO: Lynne Rienner Publishers, 2008.

Bibby, John. *Politics, Parties and Elections in America*. 4th ed. Belmont, CA: Wadsworth, 2000.

Carothers, Thomas. *Confronting the Weakest Link: Aiding Political Parties in New Democracies*. Washington, D.C.: Carnegie Endowment for International Peace, 2006.

Dalton, Russell J., and Martin P. Wattenberg. *Parties without Partisans: Political Change in Advanced Industrial Democracies*. Oxford and New York: Oxford University Press, 2000.

Eldersveld, Samuel J., and Hanes Walton, Jr. *Political Parties in American Society*, 2nd ed. Boston: Bedford/St. Martin's, 2000.

Gunther, Richard, José Ramón Montero, and Juan Linz, eds. *Political Parities: Old Concepts and New Challenges*. New York: Oxford University Press, 2002.

Hasan, Zoya, ed. *Parties and Party Politics in India*. New Delhi and New York: Oxford University Press, 2002.

Hershey, Marjorie Randon. *Party Politics in America,* 12th ed. New York: Pearson Longman, 2007.

Kittilson, Miki Caul. *Challenging Parties, Changing Parliaments: Women and Elected Office in Contemporary Western Europe.* Columbus: The Ohio State University Press, 2006.

Lawson, Kay and Peter H. Merkl, eds. *When Parties Prosper.* Boulder, CO: Lynne Rienner Publishers, 2007.

Moser, Robert G. *Unexpected Outcomes: Electoral Systems, Political Parties, and Representation in Russia.* Pittsburgh: University of Pittsburgh Press, 2001.

A Strike to Change Government Policy As a result of a strike by labor unions, French public transportation was severely disrupted in May 2008. The strike was called to protest proposed government policies to increase the number of years a French worker must work before receiving pension benefits.

6

INTEREST GROUPS

◆ Interest Groups: What They Are and How They Work
◆ The Power of Interest Groups ◆ The Growth of Interest
Groups ◆ How Interest Groups Are Formed
◆ Conclusion: Interest Groups—A Challenge
for Democracy?

Most Americans are vaguely aware that their government has had a system of farm subsidies for decades, but very few hold strong opinions about them, and even fewer citizens base their voting choices on farm subsidies. The major parties rarely mention farm subsidies in their platforms and candidates for national office have not prominently featured this issue in their stump speeches for generations. How is it that a program so costly persists without pressure from voters or parties? One of the world's leading economists, Richard Posner, offers the following explanation:

> [Farm subsidies in the U.S.] lack any economic justification and at the same time are regressive. They should offend liberals on the latter score and conservatives on the former; their firm entrenchment in American public policy illustrates the limitations of the American democratic system. A million farmers receive subsidies in a variety of forms (direct crop subsidies, R&D, crop insurance, federal loans, ethanol tariffs, export subsidies, emergency relief, the food-stamp program, and more), which will cost in the aggregate, under the pending Farm Bill, some $50 billion a year, or $50,000 per farmer on average.
>
> Farm subsidies account for about a sixth of total farm revenues. So, not surprisingly, the income of the average farmer is actually above the average of all American incomes, and anyway 74 percent of the subsidies go to the largest 10 percent of farm enterprises.
>
> There is no justification for the Farm Bill in terms of social welfare.
>
> All the subsidies should be repealed.
>
> This of course will not happen, and that is a lesson in the limitations of democracy, at least as practiced in the United States at this time, though I doubt that it is peculiarities of American democracy that explain the farm programs, for their European counterparts are far more generous.
>
> The small number of American farmers is, paradoxically, a factor that facilitates their obtaining transfer payments from taxpayers. They are so few that they can organize effectively, and being few the average benefit they derive (the $50,000 a year) creates a strong incentive to contribute time and money to securing the subsidies.[1]

Posner, along with virtually everyone else who has studied farm subsidies, attributes their existence to the power of interest groups. Each and every person living in the U.S. is a consumer of agricultural products, and nearly 99 percent are not farmers. One would think that consumers would easily prevail in a clash of political interests between consumers and producers of agricultural products. But the producers win, and the programs they demand transfer millions of dollars to them from consumers. Whatever the merits of current farm subsidy programs, it is obvious that the political power of *interest groups* is a key reason that they are very difficult to reform.

Quite simply, organized interests can be more influential than large numbers of unorganized citizens. They use a wide range of techniques to influence members of Congress and to generate votes for friendly legislators. Politicians ignore their power at their peril. If we want to understand the policy process in democracies, we must understand not only voting and parties but also the power of organized interest groups.

One of the earliest insights developed in the scientific study of politics had to do with interest groups. Toward the end of the nineteenth century, political scientists increasingly felt that they were missing something by focusing their studies entirely on laws, constitutional rights, and institutions. Although those "formal-legal" studies were (and are) vital, a growing number of political scientists came to understand that the discipline should study political *behavior*. The emphasis on behavior fundamentally changed political science. Instead of studying aspects of government contained in constitutional passages and legislative enactments, political scientists began to analyze the political behavior of citizens and to explore how that behavior affects public policy.

When they emerged from law libraries and shifted their emphasis to the observation of behavior, political scientists immediately discovered something very important: *Organized* political activity—not the outcome of elections—is often the critical factor in explaining what government does (and does not do). If we want to understand why some things are changed and others are not, we rarely find the answers by examining the words of the Constitution, or even the results of elections. At least some of the answers have to do with which interests are organized and which interests are not. The interest group thus became a basic subject of political study many decades ago.

The influence of interest groups raises some troubling questions: If some, but not all, people are represented by effectively organized groups, is a system that responds to group influence really democratic? Is such a system fair? Why do some people join groups while others do not? Does the growing power of interest groups threaten the position of political parties? Does it make voting less important? How do interest groups function in nondemocratic systems such as those in China and Egypt, or in democracies such as India's, with social systems far different from our own? These and many related questions help us see that the study of interest groups has become one of the most important, and most controversial, research problems in contemporary political science.

INTEREST GROUPS: WHAT THEY ARE AND HOW THEY WORK

An **interest group** *is an organization that attempts to influence public policy in a specific area of importance to its members.* In contrast to political parties, interest groups do not try to achieve their political objectives by electing their leaders to government office. Instead, they attempt to persuade elected leaders, administrative officials, judges, and others to make and implement laws and policies in line with their positions. They may be well organized, with strong institutional foundations and professional staffs, or they may be looser arrangements of part-time participants. People establish some organizations to be explicitly political, whereas others are created to achieve religious, economic, or other goals, only occasionally working in the political arena. The term *interest group* thus applies to a diverse array of organizations.[*]

For example, interest groups in the United States include the Tobacco Institute, the National Rifle Association, the Sierra Club, and the National Association for the Advancement of Colored People (NAACP). The British Medical Association, the Mexican Confederation of Labor, and France's National Union Federation of Agriculturalists (FNSEA) are often in the news in those countries. Although each group is unique, all seek to promote government decisions that advance their interests. (See Box 6-1.)

---

[*] Some prefer other terms, such as "factions," "organized interests," "pressure groups," and "special interests." (See the introductory chapter in Allan J. Cigler and Burdett A. Loomis, *Interest Group Politics*, 6th ed. Washington, DC: CQ Press, 2002.)

| Box 6-1 |

THE NATIONAL RIFLE ASSOCIATION IN THE UNITED STATES

The National Rifle Association is one of the most powerful and familiar interest groups currently working in the U.S. NRA members receive a publication (*American Rifleman*) and other benefits, including gun insurance and "shooter's liability insurance," but a key NRA activity is participation in electoral campaigns. According to a recent study, the NRA "participates in more than 10,000 campaigns in any given electoral cycle and raises millions of dollars for candidates committed to the goals of the organization."*

Founded in 1871 to promote the "shooting sports," marksmanship, and gun safety, the NRA has become one of the most effective and most controversial U.S. interest groups. The organization promotes gun ownership, shares information about collectible guns, and has a vigorous program regarding gun safety, but it is also prominent in its opposition to virtually any legislation limiting gun ownership. According to the NRA's "Political Victory Fund," in 2004 the organization "was involved in 265 campaigns for the U.S. House and Senate, winning in 254 of those races. These victories represent the re-election of pro-gun majorities in both the U.S. House and Senate."[2] Earlier that year, the NRA took credit for pressuring Congress to allow the 1994 ban on assault weapons

* Kelly D. Patterson and Matthew M. Singer, "The National Rifle Association in the Face of the Clinton Challenge," in *Interest Group Politics*, 6th ed., ed. Allan J. Cigler and Burdett A. Loomis (Washington, DC: CQ Press, 2002), pp. 55–78. Current membership data obtained by the authors from the National Rifle Association, Fairfax, Virginia.

to expire. In 2006, the NRA spent millions of dollars on direct mail, phone calls, bumper stickers, ads on television and radio, and over 500 billboards. Nearly 85 percent of the House and Senate candidates endorsed by the NRA were successful, and the organization claimed an 81 percent success rate in state legislative elections.[3] In 2006, the less gun-friendly Democratic Party took over the U.S. Congress, but the NRA claimed continued successes in its election efforts:

> on a day that saw an electorate expressing dissatisfaction over such things as conduct of the war, political corruption and competency to govern, Americans cast their votes for pro-gun candidates from both parties. Candidates who championed gun control in contested races were nearly non-existent.[4]

The growth of the NRA tells us a great deal about interest groups in general. For one thing, NRA membership has grown tremendously as the U.S. economy grew. More people can afford the "luxury" of contributing to an organization when they have disposable income. However, as shown in the following chart, increases in membership dues created at least a temporary decline in membership, demonstrating that people do take costs into account when they decide to join interest groups.

But the overall pattern of growth shows something else. During the 1990s, gun owners in the United States felt that the Clinton White House was a potential

Kinds of Interest Groups

Interest groups can be classified in several ways. Perhaps the most useful approach is simply to classify them descriptively, on the basis of the interests they pursue. Most fall into one of the following categories.

Labor Unions   Unions such as the Teamsters and the United Automobile Workers (UAW) in the U.S., the General Confederation of Labor (CGT) in France, and the Australian Nursing Federation are primarily collective-bargaining units that negotiate contracts for their members with employers. From time to time, however, these organizations apply their energies to the political arena, becoming interest groups by our definition.

threat to their interests. Many citizens apparently responded to that threat by joining the NRA. In fact, viewed in a longer historical perspective, the overall growth of the NRA, showing a 400-percent increase in membership since the late 1970s, corresponds well to the increased momentum in the United States for stricter gun control. Congress passed the Gun Control Act of 1968 following the assassinations of Robert Kennedy and Dr. Martin Luther King, Jr., and opinion polls have shown substantial support for stricter gun laws, especially after incidents such as the assassination attempt on President Reagan in 1981 and the Columbine High School shootings in Colorado in 1999. Although those events may temporarily dampen NRA membership (it dropped to 2.8 million following the Columbine shootings), the general perception that new gun restrictions are likely has made the NRA a larger and possibly more influential organization. In 2008, the organization had more than 4.3 million dues-paying members.

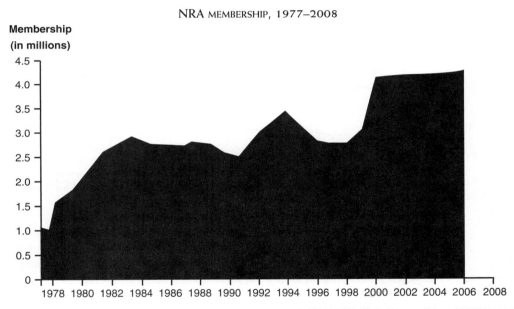

NRA MEMBERSHIP, 1977–2008

SOURCE: Figure derived from Patterson and Singer, 2002; data for 2008 membership obtained by the authors from the National Rifle Association, Fairfax, Virginia.

In Britain, the British Trades Union Congress (TUC) is directly involved in politics through its powerful role in the Labour Party. In the United States, the Teamsters, the American Federation of State, County, and Municipal Employees (AFSCME), and other unions are always an active presence in elections. In some countries, the impact of unions is less influential. For example, the governments and ruling parties of many African countries have dominated the leadership of most unions, using them as a means of controlling working-class political participation and robbing them of their status as independent interest groups.

Business Organizations   Most of the many kinds of business organizations attempt to influence government from time to time. A few business organizations pursue the interests of business itself (the National Association of Manufacturers, the Chamber

of Commerce), although most focus on the special problems of a particular economic sector (such as the Used Car Dealers Association). Business groups sometimes attempt to oppose labor-group demands and often pursue or oppose changes in tax codes or regulations that affect the profitability of their operations. In some Third World nations with powerful economic elites, business groups are linked so closely to government through family ties and friendships, that they exercise a dominant role in policy making. In El Salvador, for example, the "fourteen families," which controlled much of the country's coffee production and export, were long believed to hold veto power over government policy. In other nations, however, with Marxist-oriented regimes, business groups either do not exist or have been on the fringes of the policy process (as they were in Nicaragua during the period of Sandinista control).

Gender, Religious, Ethnic, and Age Groups   The feminist movement in the United States has led to the creation of groups such as the National Organization for Women (NOW), which seeks to influence government policies of special concern to women. Similarly, a host of civil rights groups—the NAACP, the Urban League, La Raza Unida—serve as advocates for racial and ethnic minorities. In India, religious and caste groups work closely with the political parties to advocate for their political demands. Interest groups based on age are less common, but the Gray Panthers and the American Association of Retired Persons (AARP) now forcefully advocate for the interests of the elderly in the United States. Similarly, the Children's Defense Fund promotes children's interests.

Communist governments often organize women's or youth organizations that profess to act as interest groups but more frequently are designed to mobilize support for the government. In Cuba, however, the Federation of Cuban Women purportedly helped persuade the government to implement a family code that not only called for the legal equality of the sexes but also required both spouses to share housework equally. The federation's clout was undoubtedly enhanced by the fact that its leader was Fidel Castro's sister-in-law.

Public Interest Groups   Although labor unions and business organizations would have us believe that they are selfless crusaders for the general good, they normally pursue government decisions that specifically benefit their members. A rather different type of interest group is concerned primarily with a vision of fairness and justice for some kind of general public interest. Although it is sometimes difficult to draw the line precisely between private and public interests, public interest groups are distinctive political organizations.

This kind of group is centrally featured in what is probably the most divisive public issue in contemporary U.S. politics: abortion. Organizations favoring or opposing abortion rights—each of which is very committed to strongly held principles—have become important factors in lawmaking and elections at all levels of government.

Other reform groups are formed to fight a particular social problem, such as alcohol-related traffic accidents, in the case of Mothers Against Drunk Driving (MADD). The Sierra Club works to influence government to preserve the environment by supporting such varied steps as recycling, preservation of endangered species, and restrictions on public use of wilderness areas. The Americans for Tax Reform supports a general policy of lower taxes at all levels of government. These organizations are "public interest" groups because they seek the actions and decisions that they feel are justified for the benefit of *all* citizens.

Public interest groups are most prevalent in economically developed countries, where higher levels of education and political awareness, leisure time, and disposable income facilitate their proliferation. But they also exist on a more limited basis in some Third World nations. Citizens in developing nations have begun to organize around environmental issues such as the preservation of rain forests. In Thailand, for example, a Buddhist monk organized farmers to promote environmentally sound use of the land and to work with the government for the preservation of shrinking forest preserves.

Professional Associations and Occupational Groups   Literally hundreds of professions and occupations in industrialized nations are represented by organizations. In the United States, the American Bar Association and the American Medical Association are probably the best known, but other organizations represent electrologists, plumbers, nursing home administrators, hairdressers, podiatrists, and people in many other professions. Farmers have powerful lobbies in the United States as well as in France, Japan, and Argentina. These groups are distinguished by their focus on the special interests of members of an identifiable profession or occupation.

Professional associations work actively to share information—hence the constant parade of conventions in virtually all major cities. Members attending these meetings can go to panel discussions and workshop sessions at which they learn about new techniques or materials relevant to their profession. Professional associations also attempt to influence government, however, particularly with respect to licensing laws and regulations.

These groups are concerned about licensing both because they are naturally interested in maintaining the public's confidence in their respective professions, and because they want to keep unqualified people from taking business away from them.* Since effective licensing requirements can be enforced only through governmental action, professional associations exert much of their energy by acting as interest groups.

How Interest Groups Work

Interest groups exploit a wide range of methods in their efforts to influence government. The following approaches are the main ways in which interest groups attempt to get what they want.

Lobbying Whenever interest groups communicate with governmental officials, they are **lobbying**.† Contact is sometimes informal, as when a legislator or an agency head discusses a policy issue over the phone, through correspondence, or at lunch.

Interest groups also testify before congressional committee hearings, file *amicus curiae*‡ briefs (documents arguing for or against a particular interpretation of the law) with state and federal courts, submit written reports to administrative agencies, and participate in public hearings of all kinds. All of these activities are important *access opportunities*, providing settings in which interest groups can directly contact decision makers.

Contacts between lobbyists and governmental officials in the U.S. and other established democracies are generally honest, legitimate meetings, despite popular impressions to the contrary. Interest groups lobby primarily by providing information to decision makers, not by purchasing votes. In fact, political scientists specializing in the study of the U.S. Congress often tell of the newly elected representative who, after a year in office, asked, "Where are the lobbyists? I haven't seen one yet." Of course, he had seen and heard dozens of them, but none had tried to bribe him. All the people he met with were simply giving him useful facts and introducing him to their points of view—innocent contacts that the freshman representative could not possibly interpret as lobbying.

Legislators, agency officials, and even judges listen to lobbyists because the information they have is often valuable, even though the group providing the information has an axe to grind. For example, when new legislation is considered regarding auto emission standards, one of the groups that Congress and the Environmental Protection

---

* Some analysts argue that the public would be much better off with unfettered access to these "unqualified" professionals and that, in the name of protecting us against "charlatans," professional associations merely seek to keep competition out and prices up. See Milton Friedman, *Capitalism and Freedom* (Chicago: University of Chicago Press, 1962), for the classic argument along these lines.
† This term derives from the widely observed practice among legislators of discussing major decisions with interested parties in the cloakrooms and lobbies outside the official legislative chamber. Those meeting with legislators in such settings are commonly called *lobbyists*.
‡ Literally translated, this means "friend of the court."

Agency (EPA) will turn to for data is the auto industry. Although the interest groups representing the automakers obviously have a stake in the outcome, they also have a great deal of knowledge and experience relevant to the matter at hand. Ultimately, government officials have to decide what weight or credibility they will give that information. Even when the group has a financial stake in the outcome (as with the automakers), the information may still be useful.

Interest groups can exert considerable influence by lobbying. Being in a position to provide critical information is itself a source of power. Good lobbyists are always ready to answer questions and explain the importance of their views. Decision makers often respond to lobbyists' suggestions, incorporating them in compromise solutions that take the groups' positions into account.

In countries where public agencies are not as capable of evaluating private-sector data, interest groups often exercise even more influence than in the United States. In a classic study from the 1960s, a leading expert argued that many Italian regulatory agencies relied so heavily on information from the very industrial groups they were supposed to be monitoring that they had become their virtual clients.[5] The same observation is commonly made today about interest groups in most developed and developing countries. However, in some countries, interest groups and government agencies are mutually dependent: A French study from the 1990s concluded that interest groups in that country, particularly "public" interest groups, are dependent upon the powerful central French state bureaucracy, although they are frequently able to get government elites to adopt their goals.[6]

Influencing Public Opinion   In democratic systems, it is much easier for an interest group to persuade a legislator or an agency official if public opinion is on its side. Interest groups thus often spend a great deal of time and money attempting to generate support among the public. When they succeed, legislators are less likely to introduce or support legislation opposed by the group. Interest groups in good standing with the public are more effective in influencing government officials.

Interest group efforts to influence public opinion are most common when proposals are under consideration that would hurt group interests. (They are less common when interest groups attempt to obtain something new from government; in these cases, groups prefer to work with legislative committees or with administrative agencies.) For example, you may recall seeing commercials showing people voicing opinions about what should be done to produce alternative forms of energy, followed by statements indicating that the oil company sponsoring the ads is already taking those very steps. A number of recent television advertisements from pharmaceutical companies emphasize their programs that provide free or low-priced prescription drugs to people who cannot afford them. These commercials are certainly aired in hopes of generating increased sales, but the corporations producing them also hope to persuade voters to stop pressuring Congress for even stricter environmental regulation or for price controls. To the extent that a group is successful in creating a favorable image, it reduces public demands on the government to take action against it.

Clearly, influencing public attitudes is a useful strategy used most often in developed democracies, with their high degree of political participation and awareness. It is a far less-relevant strategy in authoritarian or less-developed systems. Modern technology, such as computer-controlled telephoning, is exploited effectively by interest groups in the United States, Great Britain, and other advanced nations. Yet, even in a semi-authoritarian society, such as Mexico was before the 1990s, one could find newspaper advertisements by business or labor groups making their cases to the public.

Influencing Group Members Interest groups with large memberships can wield additional power by enlisting the active support of their members. Most interest groups publish some sort of newsletter to communicate with their members, and those publications give them a chance to promote the group's official positions and political preferences. On June 19, 2008, the American Federation of State, County, and Municipal Employees announced that it had endorsed Senator Barack Obama, after having endorsed Senator Hillary Clinton several months earlier. Through its Web site and its newsletters, AFSCME ensured that its 1.4 million members read dozens of articles making the case for Obama over McCain, and poll results revealed that the vast majority of them voted for the Democratic candidate.

An organization's efforts to persuade its members often lead to real payoffs, because individuals who are members of organizations are more likely to vote than are unaffiliated people. Government officials realize that the outcomes in close elections are frequently determined by interest group endorsements that influence the voting choices of members.

Making Campaign Contributions Usually within strict legal limits, interest groups can influence government by contributing to electoral campaigns.* Money is the most typical contribution, but interest groups often supply volunteers and in-kind services to help a candidate in an election.

There are two ways of seeing a connection between campaign contributions and legislative decisions. First, the model of *legislative influence* assumes that a quid pro quo (literally, "something for something") develops between legislators and groups: The legislator promises, explicitly or implicitly, to support or oppose certain bills in exchange for campaign contributions. Contributions can also make a difference as described in the model of *electoral influence*. In this second scenario, candidates have clearly expressed positions on important issues, and interest groups steer their contributions to the candidates whose views would advance group interests. When the campaign money produces electoral success, groups benefit because politicians supporting policies beneficial to the group are in a position to make law.[†]

---

* In the United States, the Bipartisan Campaign Reform Act of 2002, which we will discuss in Chapter 11, has significantly affected interest group contributions to campaigns. Political action committees, or PACs, continue to play a role. PACs are organizations, closely tied to their parent interest groups, set up to funnel money to campaigns. The idea of this and similar laws is to have some separation between lobbying and campaign contributions; for example, the United Auto Workers labor union does not give money to candidates for Congress, but its PAC, the "UAW Voluntary Community Action Program," contributed more than $2 million to such campaigns in 2000. The line between interest groups and their affiliated PACs was blurred considerably when court rulings in the 1970s established that the parent organization could pay for the fund-raising and administrative costs incurred by its PAC. For a good analysis of the history and behavior of PACs in the United States, see M. Margaret Conway, Joanne Connor Green, and Marian Currinder, "Interest Group Money in Elections," in *Interest Group Politics*, 6th ed., eds. Allan J. Cigler and Burdett A. Loomis (Washington, DC: CQ Press, 2002), pp. 117–140.

[†] For a helpful discussion of these two complementary models, see John R. Wright, *Interest Groups and Congress* (New York: Longman, 2003), pp. 146–148.

It is easy to see why campaign contributions from interest groups are a cause of concern in a democracy. If politicians need huge sums of money to buy television time, and if they obtain much of that money from interest groups, they obviously come to depend on interest groups. Such dependence is a source of considerable political power. In a democracy, elected officials are expected to serve their constituents, and yet they are encouraged (some would say "forced") to serve the organized interests they depend on for contributions. As discussed in Chapter 4, many democratic systems have thus made efforts to eliminate the problem by limiting how much money can be spent in campaigns, by requiring that candidates and parties disclose the sources of their funding, and by limiting the amount of money that a single person or organization can contribute.

In other political systems, there may be a much more intimate relationship among parties, candidates, and interest group campaign contributions. For example, for many years in Great Britain, unions automatically checked off a small contribution from the paychecks of their members, which went to support the Labour Party. Workers could prevent the deduction only if they told their union that they wished to "opt out," a rather uncomfortable request to make. Subsequently, a Conservative-controlled Parliament passed legislation that stipulated that contributions would be deducted only if the union member "opted in." In the Philippines and many Latin American countries, candidates or parties are sometimes so heavily financed by powerful business interests that they become virtual spokespeople for those groups.

Litigation   Court systems are normally designed to try cases involving crimes and disputes between individuals. But interest groups are sometimes able to sue a government official or agency on the grounds that they were harmed by a governmental action (or inaction).* Once in court, the interest group may be able to delay a governmental action it opposes or to obtain more forceful implementation of something it favors. In order to use the courts to influence policy, the group must somehow demonstrate that a law or constitutional provision requires that a governmental official or agency stop or start doing something. Important public policy questions are often addressed when the court hands down a decision. (See Box 6-2.)

Demonstrations and Strikes   Sometimes an interest group can advance its cause or interests by bringing attention to a problem that most people would otherwise overlook. The visual impact of demonstrations, and the fact that they can be covered in brief television news reports, make such events particularly popular in developed nations. Media events are also relatively inexpensive to organize. Virtually any demonstrating group can get exposure that would otherwise cost many thousands of dollars. In addition to getting exposure, the demonstration will often "fire up" the group's members, generating internal support that may be lagging.

---

* In the United States, Britain, and other countries using the Anglo-American system of jurisprudence, the extent to which a group can do this depends on the law of standing. The familiar phrase *standing to sue* simply means that the party wishing to litigate has a real stake in the matter, not merely an ideological position. Thus, when the Sierra Club sues the U.S. Department of the Interior, it must be able to show that at least one of its members was personally harmed by that agency (or that he or she would be harmed if the challenged agency action were allowed to go forward). The standing doctrine thus limits interest groups' access to the courts, because their concerns will not be heard if they only have an ideological position on the issue.

Box 6-2

THE "DISADVANTAGE THEORY" OF INTEREST GROUP LITIGATION

Achieving an interest group's policy goals through litigation is very different from achieving such goals by lobbying legislators or chief executives. Legislation requires that a majority of the parliament or assembly support the group's position, and both legislators and executives usually have to balance interest group demands against voter preferences and party demands. In most systems, judges enjoy some political independence, although their influence over public policy is usually limited. Still, in some circumstances an interest group may be able to convince a court that a particular governmental action must be changed or preserved, and the resulting decision of the court may produce policy changes the group wants. If a group is politically weak, it may have a greater chance of achieving its goals through litigation than through the legislative and executive branches, where they are outspent and outvoted by larger, more powerful interests.

The "disadvantage theory" of interest groups and courts is based on these observations. Initially associated with Richard Courtner, the idea holds that the interest groups that turn to litigation as a strategy for achieving their goals are those groups that "are temporarily, or even permanently, disadvantaged in terms of their abilities to attain successfully their goals in the electoral process. . . . politically 'disadvantaged' groups, [i]f they are to succeed at all in the pursuit of their goals . . . are almost compelled to resort to litigation."[7] Perhaps the best example of interest group behavior illustrating this theory involved the NAACP: During the 1940s and 1950s, this group's efforts to end public school segregation by lobbying state legislatures failed completely, but a litigation strategy eventually changed public policy dramatically, because the courts provided access denied in other quarters.

However important that example is, researchers are beginning to doubt that the "disadvantage theory" tells the whole story. Recent studies analyzing data on group wealth, goals, and strategies suggest that it is not only "politically disadvantaged" interest groups that use the courts. In fact, profit-seeking groups use litigation more than public interest groups, and groups with better staffs and more financial resources use litigation more than groups with fewer resources.[8] Any interest group with the required financial resources can use litigation to change public policy, sometimes to enforce and secure policy objectives initially won in elected institutions. In such cases, litigation strategies actually reinforce the successes that group power brings through lobbying.

Because the empirical work on interest group litigation undermines the most common understanding of the disadvantage theory, some political scientists have started to think about the problem in different ways. Cary Coglianese concludes that groups suffering a disadvantage are, in fact, the ones most likely to pursue litigation, but the disadvantage that drives them to seek their goals through the courts is *not* a lack of financial or organizational strength. Instead, the groups that file lawsuits to change policy, almost always a long-shot approach, are those groups whose goals are widely unsupported in society and who therefore face an unreceptive political system.[9]

Strikes are also sometimes used as a political statement, instead of merely a means of demanding higher wages or better working conditions. Workers in Italy, France, and Peru, for example, have often carried out one- or two-day general strikes in which transportation services, electrical power, and much of the nation's commerce grind to a halt. (See the photo at the beginning of this chapter.) In Poland, the Solidarity Movement also used strikes and demonstrations effectively in an effort that eventually brought down an entire government.

Demonstrations are most prevalent in political systems that are neither fully democratic (that is, where sectors of society do not have equal access to the political system) nor totalitarian. As long as the Communist Party controlled the mass media in the former Soviet Union and harshly repressed dissent, demonstrations were rare, and quickly (often brutally) put down. Now that Russian political

---

Box 6-3

INTEREST GROUP STRATEGIES:
EVIDENCE FROM DENMARK

In a classic of political science, *Politics, Pressure, and the Tariff*, E. E. Schattschneider classified interest groups as "insiders" or "outsiders," and this distinction has remained a familiar concept in the literature on interest groups. Direct contacts with legislators or bureaucrats are "inside" strategies; while mobilizing citizens, grassroots memberships, and using mass media are "outside" strategies. The generally accepted idea is that interest groups use one strategy or the other in their efforts to influence policy.

In a recent study, a Danish political scientist surveyed interest group representatives in that country to gather data on the strategies groups employ.

The following table lists the most important "inside" and "outside" strategies she observed.

INTEREST GROUP STRATEGIES

	Percentage of Groups Employing Each Strategy "Very" or "Fairly Often"
Inside Strategies	
Contacting Parliamentary Committees	19.5
Contacting Party Organizations	6.0
Contacting Party Spokespersons	20.6
Contacting National Public Servants	37.7
Responding to Requests for Comments	40.4
Outside Strategies	
Contacting Reporters	35.1
Arranging Debate Meetings and Conferences	42.5
Conducting Petitions	2.3
Strikes, Civil Disobedience, and Illegal Direct Action	0.7
Writing Letters to the Editor and Columns	28.0

Not surprisingly, the data show that some strategies are far more popular than others. However, the Danish study also suggests that the conventional wisdom overstates the extent to which interest groups actually choose inside or outside strategies to the exclusion of the other. Using data on all major interest groups politically active in Denmark, the researcher found that "there is no contradiction between pursuing strategies associated with insider access to decision-making and strategies where pressure is put on decision makers through media contacts and mobilization."[10] Thus, those with "privileged" access do not neglect outside strategies.

However, some groups (the author of this study terms them "cause" groups) primarily use mobilization and mass media to exert pressure. These groups may find that administrative agencies and key legislators are not inclined to meet with them, or perhaps they simply conclude that generating widespread public awareness and activism is the most fruitful approach to achieving their goals. In the U.S., we would thus expect a group like ACT-UP, a controversial gay rights organization, to use outside strategies, while the National Association of Realtors will make use of its contacts in government while also placing ads on television and radio. In practice, interest groups choose strategies that seem most promising, and this will depend on the nature of the issue at stake and the public's perception of the interest itself.

---

activity is less repressed but not yet truly democratic, demonstrations there have become commonplace.

These newer demonstrations range from the more serious and sometimes violent expressions of ethnic politics to less threatening demonstrations, such as smokers protesting the shortage of cigarettes. Of course, in Hungary, Poland, and other Eastern

European nations, demonstrations that started as a form of interest group activity by human rights organizations turned into peaceful revolutions that startled the world by toppling totalitarian regimes. In contrast, the massacre of student demonstrators in Beijing's Tiananmen Square in June 1989 revealed the limits of such demonstrations in the most repressive countries.

Demonstrations and other "confrontational" tactics are usually the choice of groups with little confidence that they will succeed through more conventional lobbying efforts. For example, in the American South, African Americans—often disenfranchised and lacking access to the local media—resorted to sit-ins and marches, particularly in the 1950s and 1960s. Similarly, blacks in the townships of South Africa used demonstrations throughout the 1980s and early 1990s to express their opposition to apartheid legislation before the political process was opened to them. Mexican slum dwellers or peasants, who have been unable to satisfy their demands otherwise, may encamp themselves in front of government agencies either to influence public opinion or to show their resolve to government policy makers. In India, where hunger strikes and sit-ins were used by the legendary leader Mohandas Gandhi to achieve national independence, farmers—as well as language, religious, and caste groups—constantly resort to such tactics. Among U.S. citizens who belong to interest groups seeking government programs to support AIDS research and treatment, those who felt most vulnerable and victimized supported confrontational tactics much more strongly than did activists who did not share such feelings.*

Although demonstrations can be a useful tool for otherwise weak or powerless groups, they also can be counterproductive. Demonstrations may become violent, producing fights and rock throwing. Even demonstrations that remain nonviolent may generate significant opposition to the group. Individuals who would otherwise be sympathetic to the group's cause may begin to see it as lawless or radical. Even though the vast majority of demonstrations are nonviolent, the distinction between demonstration and riot may be lost on much of the general public.

Corruption   We have suggested that, for the most part, the relationship between interest groups and public officials in industrial democracies is honest. In less-developed political systems, however, the roles of bribery and corruption are much more firmly entrenched.

It was widely understood that during Ferdinand Marcos's reign in the Philippines, business groups would not receive favorable government treatment without paying substantial contributions to the president. In Nigeria and the Central African Republic, bribes have been such a prerequisite for dealing with the government or influencing policy that their national leaders have become multimillionaires in societies whose populations are among the poorest in the world. In Western European democracies, corruption is generally less prevalent than in the United States.

As we have seen, interest groups can select one or more of several strategies for influencing the political process. Their choices reflect their character, the degree to which their goals are considered "mainstream," and the kind and amount of resources they command. Interest group behavior is also affected by the nature of the system

---

* See M. Kent Jennings and Ellen Ann Anderson, "Support for Confrontational Tactics among AIDS Activists: A Study of Intra-Movement Divisions," *American Journal of Political Science* 40 (May 1996): 311–334.

in which groups operate. Where political power is decentralized in both government structure and party organization (as in the United States), there are many "access points" for interest group influence. One group may find success lobbying Congress, whereas another may work for opposing policies by attempting to influence an executive department. Although the wide range of opportunities for influence makes it possible for many groups to work in the political arena, however, opposing groups can also find access.

A more centralized political system such as Great Britain's offers fewer points of access, but the groups that are fortunate enough to "get inside" can expect to have great influence. Thus, decentralized political systems tend to have more numerous and more visible interest groups, whereas centralized systems afford great power to those few interest groups that secure effective linkages.

THE POWER OF INTEREST GROUPS

Why Are Some Groups More Powerful Than Others?

Interest groups operating in the same society are usually subject to the same laws and have access to the same media for communicating with citizens and officials. But it becomes clear on a moment's reflection that some groups are much more powerful than others. Most U.S. politicians safely ignore the Women's Christian Temperance Union, for example, but few British leaders ignore the British Trades Union Congress, and no U.S. senator or representative takes the National Rifle Association or the American Association of Retired Persons lightly. Several factors determine how much power and influence a given interest group enjoys.

Size All other things being equal, groups with large memberships are more influential than groups with small memberships. A group that officially speaks for a large number of people can influence close elections, and elected officials will therefore listen to the leaders of such groups. A large membership also suggests broad public acceptance for the group's ideas, since there are usually several non-joining supporters for every supportive person who actually belongs to the group. A large size also means that the group has a huge supply of "soldiers" for its work. Letter-writing campaigns, contributions to candidates running for office, and even demonstrations are all more powerful forms of influence when the group can call on many members.

While size is an important factor, other characteristics may more than offset a given group's advantage or disadvantage with respect to size.

Unity Even large groups can lose much of their effectiveness if their members are divided. A governmental official who wants to be sympathetic to a particular cause or interest may find that a decision demanded by one segment of the group is opposed by another. The safe response is to do nothing. Hence, division within an interest group (or among organizations representing similar interests) leads to a reduction in effective influence.

Groups that can present a united front when pressing their claims are in a much better position. This point was made by a scholar of British politics in a comparison of the power of teachers and doctors. British teachers are represented by a divided array of bickering organizations, whereas doctors have the well-established, cohesive British Medical Association. Although there are more teachers than doctors, government officials regularly consult the BMA, whereas teachers' organizations are largely ignored.

Leadership   Effective leaders make a difference. Good leaders persuade the public, communicate effectively with elected officials, generate membership, and hold an organization together. Given the same resources, a group will have less success with a poor leader. This point is frequently made in discussions of the civil rights movement in the United States. During the period in which Dr. Martin Luther King, Jr. led the most important civil rights interest groups, the movement was remarkably successful; but since his death, even with more members and more money, these groups have had less success. Many suggest that without King's leadership, civil rights groups lost both their unity and some of their capacity to generate support among the general public.

Social Status   A general perception of integrity, professionalism, or prestige is helpful to an interest group. In the United States, the American Bar Association (ABA) is only moderately large (over 400,000 members in 2008) but it has a substantial reservoir of support by virtue of the prestige of the legal profession (despite all of those lawyer jokes).

Hence, when a president nominates a person to a federal judgeship or to fill a vacancy on the Supreme Court, the ABA's rating of that individual is a prominent factor in his or her evaluation by the public, and usually by senators. The ABA is also consulted on many legislative proposals, indicating that elected officials care about the group's opinions and that they are willing to let the public know it. In many Latin American nations, the government has given professional associations of architects, lawyers, and the like the authority to determine who may legally practice the profession. In contrast, the U.S. Used Car Dealers Association does not have much social status, and it has less power as a result (although it often has significant power with respect to state and local policy decisions).

Table 6.1 indicates the rather substantial differences among U.S. interest groups with respect to their reputations among the public. The first column lists the percentage of survey respondents that named that group as their "most liked" interest group, while the second column lists the percentage of survey respondents that named that group as their "least liked" interest group. The third column simply subtracts the "least-liked" percentage from the "most-liked" percentage, thus producing a net "likeability" score. As the data show, interest groups vary tremendously in "likeability," and this factor often makes a big difference in interest group influence.

Wealth   Wealth can contribute to a group's influence in several ways. An interest group with a large treasury, such as the AFL-CIO, can purchase airtime to broadcast "educational" statements and influence public opinion. Wealth can also facilitate access. A wealthy organization can purchase expensive legal services that enhance its participation in government decision making. Wealth does not always produce power for interest groups, but it helps.

TABLE 6.1   U.S. CITIZENS LIKE SOME INTEREST GROUPS MORE THAN OTHERS

	Percentage Stating that Group is Most Liked	Percentage Stating that Group is Least Liked	Net Likeability
Environmentalists	24.3	4.4	19.9
Pro-life groups	20.8	4.2	16.6
Pro-choice groups	11.0	4.0	7.0
Labor unions	13.0	6.7	6.3
Nat'l Rifle Association	13.9	14.7	−0.8
Trial lawyers	1.4	11.1	−9.7
Tobacco lobby	1.9	18.3	−16.4
Gay rights groups	1.2	23.0	−21.8

SOURCE: Taken from J. Tobin Grant and Thomas J. Rudolph, "Value Conflict, Group Affect, and the Issue of Campaign Finance," *American Journal of Political Science* 47 (July 2003): 458.

Strategic Economic Location   A business group or a labor union may also gain political influence through its control over an important economic resource or its ability to disrupt a vital economic activity. In economies heavily dependent on the export of a small number of crops or minerals, business groups that control those resources (Salvadorian coffee growers or South African diamond-mining corporations, for example) carry considerable political weight in many aspects of a nation's political life. Unions often have substantial influence when they can threaten to disrupt important segments of the economy. During the 1970s, the British coal miners' union wielded great power because of its ability to shut down a vital source of energy. In Peru, the bank workers exercised power far in excess of their numbers by demonstrating their ability to cripple the nation's economy with an extended bank strike.

Geographic Concentration   Some interest groups—such as medical and teacher associations—have members located throughout a political system, whereas others have memberships largely concentrated in a particular area or areas. Geographic dispersion often makes a significant difference with respect to political strength and influence. Groups with members in virtually all areas of the country can work effectively at the national level because they are able to make claims on representatives from virtually all legislative or parliamentary districts. Their influence may be small in any given district, but it is difficult for government to ignore an interest that can generate votes in every area of the country.

In contrast, some interests are geographically concentrated. French wine growers, for example, are primarily found in a few regions. Consumers in the United States are poorly organized compared with the strong union representing the interests of autoworkers, but consumers are obviously spread throughout the country. Thus, when a proposal to protect autoworkers' jobs by restricting imports is considered, the workers often lose. Members of Congress from a few states (including Michigan, Ohio, Wisconsin, and Tennessee) press for such proposals, but most representatives are likely to consider the damage they would do to consumers, since consumers' concerns are present in all districts.

Do Interest Groups Control the System?

One of the most widely recognized images in political science is the "iron triangle." The term is an effort to depict a close relationship among a legislative committee, an administrative agency, and an interest group in a particular policy area (e.g., agriculture, defense procurement).* According to this idea, a group, a committee, and an agency working together develop a powerful and mutually beneficial relationship. Administrators want budget increases from the legislative committees; representatives on those committees want electoral and campaign finance support from the interest groups; and the interest groups want policies favorable to them. Each part of the "triangle" has a strong interest in pleasing the others. Since virtually all important areas of public policy will have their own "iron triangles," and since each one wants to have as much independent power as possible, legislators and administrators in a given "triangle" tend to leave other "triangles" alone to make their own decisions, a favor that they expect will be repaid in kind.[11]

The "iron triangle" concept implies that *policy decisions are dominated by relatively autonomous sets of governmental officials and interest groups, leaving very little role for broader public interests in shaping what government does.* This perspective is therefore usually part of a rather negative view of the impact and role of interest groups in the policy process.

A U.S. Supreme Court decision from the 1980s provided a striking illustration of how strong, and how exclusive, the relationships in an "iron triangle" can be. In *Block v. Community Nutrition Institute* (464 U.S. 340, 1984), a group representing the interests of low-income consumers of dairy products tried to get the U.S. Agriculture Department to reconsider one of its rulings; one that would raise the cost of milk. The Court referred to the original arrangement set in place by Congress during the 1930s and denied standing to the community group. Justice Sandra Day O'Connor's statement in the majority opinion was remarkable in its frankness:

> [The intent of Congress was to] limit the classes entitled to participate in the development of [milk] market orders. The Act contemplates a cooperative venture among the Secretary, handlers, and producers the principal purposes of which are to raise the price of agricultural products. . . . Nowhere in the Act, however, is there an express provision for participation by consumers in any proceeding (at p. 346).

Advocates of the "iron triangle" concept could never hope to find a more perfect example to make their point. Agricultural policy clearly affects every citizen in one way or another, but Congress had established a "cooperative venture" among dairy producers and the Agriculture Department (overseen by congressional committees) to make decisions. Consumer interests were not only disregarded—they were authoritatively *excluded* from the process. This is the fundamental reason that "iron triangles" have long been a target of criticism.

Although the idea was a leading political science concept for many years, analysts have recently argued that the "iron triangle" is too simple or perhaps outdated in most policy areas. As discussed in the next section, there has been an explosion in

---

* Other names for "iron triangles" include "policy whirlpools," "subgovernments," and "triple alliances." Perhaps the first work to use the idea was Ernest Griffith's *Impasse of Democracy* (New York: Harrison-Hilton, 1939). Another often-cited work is J. Leiper Freeman, *The Political Process* (New York: Random House, 1965).

the growth of interest groups, especially "public interest" groups advocating broader interests. As these groups have expanded their power, they have increasingly sought to influence the government officials who previously worked only with the long-time members of the various triangles. These new groups are not always successful, of course (as in the Agriculture Department case), but they have often succeeded in breaking down the exclusive control enjoyed by some groups in earlier decades.

As a result, some political scientists began discussing "issue networks" instead of "iron triangles." The idea is that, though there still may be some relatively stable relationships among interest groups, legislative committees, and administrative agencies in some policy areas, influence is much more fluid, open, and unpredictable than is implied by the "iron triangle" concept. As new groups enter the system, it becomes difficult for any group to dominate public policy in its area of interest, and thus, the "iron triangle" image is less prominent among political scientists, as it was in the 1950s.[12] (See Figure 6.1.)

Moreover, some political scientists argue that a close relationship between interest groups and government agencies is not a negative thing at all. In 2004, two researchers studied the impact of interest group influence in 18 developed nations, focusing on the extent to which each country adopted "active labor market policies." These policies are an array of government efforts to help unemployed workers find secure jobs by providing training, subsidized jobs, and unemployment benefits. Although virtually all countries have programs to help the unemployed, there is substantial variation in their quality and effectiveness. According to this study, such policies are more comprehensive in countries in which employer interests are more coordinated in strong interest organizations, and where those organizations are closely integrated into the public policy making process.[13]

FIGURE 6.1   IRON TRIANGLES AND ISSUE NETWORKS

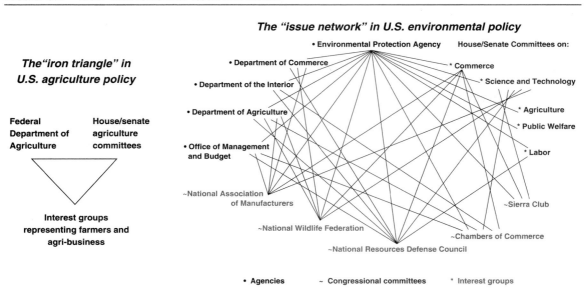

The question of interest group control of the political system is thus particularly difficult to resolve. Interest group influence sometimes produces policies opposed by a majority of a nation's citizens, but sometimes that influence is closely allied with the demands of popular movements. In some cases, interest groups form highly exclusive relationships with government bureaus and legislative committees, working to advance their interests in effective "iron triangles," while in other cases they follow an open strategy of mobilizing public opinion. Perhaps the best answer is that the extent to which interest groups control the policy process depends on many factors, including the nature of the system, the visibility of the issue at hand, and the activities of other interest groups.

THE GROWTH OF INTEREST GROUPS

Why have interest groups proliferated in industrial democracies? First, forming an effective organization with dues-paying members and political effectiveness simply takes time. The American labor movement, for example, failed to establish viable organizations for decades, finally succeeding on a grand scale many years after the worst industrial abuses had ended. So, we should expect a steady increase in the number of a nation's interest groups simply because, over time, more will overcome the barriers to organization. Second, a wealthier society can support a larger number of interest groups. When a society becomes affluent, more people have discretionary income, and some people use it to support organizations that pursue causes they care about. The organizations established to protect animal rights, for example, could only have been established in an affluent period; in poorer times, such concerns were secondary for nearly all citizens. Third, people in many countries are increasingly dissatisfied with political parties. As noted in Chapters 4 and 5, political parties seem to be losing support in several nations. As the politics of the abortion issue illustrates, millions of Americans are willing to vote for candidates of either party, as long as the candidate adopts a position on that single issue that is in line with their group's perspective. As political support and energy are directed away from political parties, interest groups become the focal point for political concerns.

The growth of interest groups has worried political scientists for generations.[14] When government decisions are increasingly influenced by organized interests, the ballot box arguably becomes less important. Moreover, as interest groups sap power away from parties, the political system is subject to more difficult demands and controversies. Whereas parties tend to aggregate and then moderate the demands of their supporters in an effort to broaden their appeal, interest groups have no such concern for moderation. In fact, taking extreme positions is often a good way to generate more members. But it is more difficult for the system to respond to an array of divisive, single-minded groups than to a few moderate parties.

Nevertheless, it is also possible to view the growth in the number of interest groups favorably. The proliferation of groups may indicate that more people find political activity and involvement useful and that they have a reasonable expectation that, if they organize properly, the system will listen to them. Without interest groups, many demands go unheard and unheeded, producing unrest that will eventually threaten political order.

HOW INTEREST GROUPS ARE FORMED

Ironically, to evaluate the ultimate effect of the proliferation of interest groups, we must take a step backward and consider how interest groups *form*. The representativeness of the interest group system is largely a matter of which groups actually become effectively organized and which ones do not, so understanding the formation of interest groups is essential if we are to appreciate the effects of interest groups in the political system.

The Pluralist View

Pluralism is one of the most widely discussed concepts in the study of modern democracies. Its core idea is simple: Pluralists believe that society has not one or two but many centers of power. In contrast to Marxism, which sees all political conflict as a struggle between capitalists and workers, pluralists argue that many interests exert influence in a political system and that public policy decisions thus incorporate most of those interests' demands and concerns. The pluralist model is also often used to distinguish industrial democracies from totalitarian societies—Nazi Germany, Maoist China, Iraq under Saddam Hussein—in which political power is highly concentrated and independent interest group or party activity is negligible. David Truman's classic, *The Governmental Process*, remains a foundational work stating the case for **pluralism**.[15]

Although pluralism is primarily a perspective on how group power is distributed, it also contains an argument regarding interest group *formation*. If political power is divided among a diverse array of interest groups, it must be true that interests naturally and easily become organized. Pluralists argue that virtually any interest can become an effective organized force. Thus, *pluralists claim that whenever a significant number of persons share an important objective, they will inevitably organize themselves*. This is the pluralists' answer to the question of how groups form.

The pluralists' straightforward and convincing perspective on interest group formation suggests an optimistic answer to many of the questions raised by the proliferation of interest groups. If virtually every interest in society is represented by effective organizations, then we can be confident that the *array of political organizations* operating in politics at any given time is reasonably representative of the *array of interests in society*. Even if organized group power influences governmental decisions, the system is still fair and balanced, because virtually all interests are effectively represented by organizations, and the largest interests produce the most powerful organizations.

The Elitist View

A very different interpretation has been offered by those who embrace **elite theory**. Instead of an open competition among a wide range of interests, elite theorists see a closed system controlled by a few. They assert that if pluralists were correct about the ability of people with shared interests to form effective organizations, the interests of the poor and racial minorities would have been more effectively advanced than they have been in virtually all developed democracies. Persistent social inequality confirms the weakness of the pluralist vision. *Real* political power is almost entirely in the hands of a **power elite** that represents the interests of only its members, leaving the rest of society and especially the poor relatively powerless.[16]

Elite theory is primarily about how political power is distributed throughout society, but, like pluralism, it derives many of its conclusions from a view of how groups form. Elite theorists accept the premise that everyone has a *legal right* to form organizations, but they insist that a relatively small range of groups actually succeed in getting a stranglehold on the primary centers of political power. In order for an interest to form an organization that will have any real impact, it must adapt itself to be compatible with the elite establishment.

Proponents of elite theory point out that leaders of the largest corporations, the most powerful political officials, and the critically important masters of military institutions all represent a narrow, elite segment of society. Most of these individuals are white males who went to the same schools, belong to the same country clubs, and associate in the same social circles. Far from representing a plurality of interests and perspectives, they are "peas in a pod," supporting essentially the same policies and programs. In short, they share political interests in governmental decisions that preserve the power of the dominant "corporate culture." Thus, instead of seeing government as steered by a plurality of diverse, competing interests, elite theorists contend that the system is dominated either by a single, all-powerful elite class or by a limited number of closely cooperating elites. Groups that exist outside the sphere of the power elite may exert influence over relatively unimportant issues, but the basic direction of social policy is firmly under the control of a narrow range of rather homogeneous interests.

Elite theory leads to a profoundly pessimistic interpretation of interest group power in society. As long as elite organizations exert power, society is not very democratic. Elite theorists claim that having the right to vote makes little difference when government action is largely determined by an unrepresentative, essentially closed set of interests. Taken to its logical conclusion, elite theory usually leads to recommendations for radical changes in the nature of society itself, usually by limiting the power of private property. (See Box 6-4.)

The Rational Choice View

Until the mid-1960s, virtually all political scientists adopted either the pluralist or the power elite perspective on interest groups. In 1965, however, a radically different idea was advanced by an economist. In *The Logic of Collective Action,* the late Mancur Olson, Jr. reached a startling conclusion: "Rational, self-interested individuals will not act to achieve their common or group interests."[19] This idea rejected *both* pluralism and elitism. It undermined the pluralist faith that people sharing a common interest would automatically form interest groups to pursue common goals, and it undermined the elitist assumption that members of the power elite would work for *their* common interests in ruling society. Olson's idea of **rational choice** infuriated everyone and seemed totally illogical. How could such a claim be made?

Olson's logic is best set out by way of a concrete example. Imagine that a person comes to your door to solicit funds for an interest group called the Citizens' Utility Board (CUB). He explains that CUB will lobby the state Public Service Commission to reduce rates for electricity and natural gas—rates that you agree are too high. He further explains that CUB is working to support a new pricing policy that, if adopted, will save all consumers $350 per year in utility bills. He asks you for a $25 contribution. What do you do?

Box 6-4

POLITICAL SCIENCE RESEARCH AND
PLURALISM AND ELITE THEORY

Logical arguments and scores of examples can be used to support *both* the pluralist and the elite interpretations of how interest groups are formed and of how power is consequently distributed in society. Elitists can point out that the poor and homeless still inhabit most large cities in developed nations and that their conditions have persisted for generations after pluralists assured us that all interests can be effectively represented by interest groups. In contrast, pluralists note that such organizations as the National Association for the Advancement of Colored People, the Sierra Club, and Mothers Against Drunk Driving are effective interest groups that certainly exist outside the power elite. Which side is right?

The research that has been done to answer this question presents a wonderful illustration of how the scholar's desire to support a conclusion can affect the research process. Robert Dahl, an important advocate of the pluralist perspective in the 1950s, analyzed the political conflicts and movements in a Connecticut city (New Haven) in an effort to determine whether the pluralist idea was valid. Dahl looked at the public policy controversies decided by city hall, considered who were the winners and losers on several decisions, and concluded that some interests win on some issues but later lose on others. This result supported pluralism, he argued, because it proved that no single power elite consistently controlled the government. A *plurality* of groups was engaged in meaningful competition, and no single segment of society had all the effective influence.[17]

In contrast, advocates of elite theory would sometimes "test" their idea by going into a city to ask knowledgeable people, "Who runs things around here?" If the answers from different people included the same names, the researchers would conclude that elite theory is correct. "This is what we expected: Virtually everyone in this town lists the same persons and organizations when asked to identify where the power is. We were right!" Both pluralists and elite theorists were criticized for letting their preconceived notions influence the ways they designed their research projects. Critics of the pluralists argued that insufficient weight was given to the power of an elite group if the researcher considered only who wins and who loses on issues debated in city hall. The *real* power of the elite could be its ability to keep the truly important questions from even reaching the decision-making arena in the first place.

Since pluralists studied only the decisions made in governmental institutions, they "saw" a world in which power shifted from one interest to another. Elite theorists contend that a positive conclusion was inevitable, given the researchers' approach. Nevertheless, if a powerful elite used its muscle to prevent important issues from reaching the agenda (for example, a major income-redistribution proposal), Dahl would not have seen evidence of that power, thus allowing him to "prove" pluralism. In short, by neglecting **nondecisions**, research proving pluralism was flawed.

Elite theorists have also been criticized. Asking people, "Who runs things around here?" implies that *someone* really is "running things." Posing such a question will certainly get answers, and we should not be surprised that many answers will contain several of the names most familiar to people in the community. Instead of "proving" elite theory, such a result may simply reflect common misperceptions or may merely reflect which personalities make the local equivalent of *People* magazine.

The debate over how interest group power is created and distributed is far from settled. It has become, if anything, more complex and uncertain in the decades since the original lines were drawn. On the one hand, in the United States and in other developed democratic nations, there are more interest groups than ever, as noted earlier, lending possible support to the pluralist way of thinking. On the other hand, social and economic equality seems as far away as ever, a point emphasized by those who claim that a power elite is firmly in control.[18]

Pluralists would predict that CUB will succeed in getting new members and contributions if many people are strongly concerned about utility bills. People will see that they have a common interest and will band together to pursue it. That is why the pluralists can be so optimistic about interest groups in general: If an interest is shared by a significant number of citizens, a political organization will pop up somewhere to pursue it. As a result, all important interests will be effectively represented, and the system is therefore healthy and fair.

Elitists would say that the CUB would fail because powerful elite forces will obstruct its formation and exclude it from effective access to the political system.

Olson claimed that both pluralists and elitists miss the fundamental point. Drawing from micro-economics, Olson began by considering what a rational, self-interested person would do when asked to join the group. The man at the door is asking for $25 to help CUB achieve an objective that, if successful, will save each consumer $350 per year. Before contributing, the economically rational individual would ask two questions. First, "Will I get the benefit of the lower utility rates that CUB is working for if you are successful, even if I refuse to help you?" The man at the door will reluctantly admit that noncontributing consumers will pay the same low rates as group supporters.

That leads the rational person to ask a second question: "What difference will *my* $25 make in the lobbying effort?" In response, the man would probably get a bit emotional and claim that "every little bit makes a difference," or words to that effect. But a moment's reflection convinces the rational decision maker that the chances are vanishingly small that a *single* $25 contribution will somehow make the critical difference between success or failure in lobbying the Public Service Commission.

The rational person will thus refuse to help CUB. If the individual makes the contribution, his or her money is certainly gone; yet, there is virtually no chance that giving the money will change utility rates. Since everyone sees the same dismal facts, the solicitor will have a very long day.

Olson emphasizes that this result will occur *even when every person contacted by the man would desperately like the group to achieve its goal.* Even when citizens want the group to succeed, it is in the *individual* interests of potential contributors to keep their money. The rational person thus becomes a **free-rider** on the efforts (if any) of others, and we reach the conclusion that groups cannot form by simply leading people to see their shared interests.[20]

Real-world examples support the rational choice idea. Consider the payment of union dues. If the pluralists were right, we would expect that unions could thrive on voluntary contributions. But unions have to force members to pay. Olson would point out that most union members strongly support the benefits, working conditions, and wages sought by the union, but each member's individual interest is in getting those advantages *while still keeping their money.* Hence, unions must arrange for forced, automatic deductions from paychecks and closed-shop laws to obtain contributions.

As a result, some 90 percent of the auto workers in this country contribute to the collective efforts of the United Auto Workers Union. In contrast, organizations such as the Sierra Club—lacking any way to force supporters of wilderness preservation to contribute funds—exist with contributions from far fewer than 1 percent of environmentally concerned American citizens. Even while acknowledging the importance of the Sierra Club's work, most people who are concerned about wilderness preservation (at least 99 percent of them) have refused to contribute to any environmental group, just as Olson would have predicted.

Olson's idea carries important implications. If interest groups do not form naturally whenever a common interest is shared, and if the size (and strength) of the groups that do exist is not proportional to the magnitude of the interests in society, we cannot reach the happy pluralist conclusion that the array of interest groups working in the system is balanced and representative. Some interests have special advantages, such as labor unions with the ability to deny a union card to anyone refusing to contribute to collective efforts. Other groups have the power to deny contracts and licenses to those who would "let George do it." Those interests form highly influential organizations, even though they may be shared by a relatively small number of citizens. However, people who only share an interest are not so easily organized. The rational choice idea thus suggests a very pessimistic conclusion: Many important interests will not be represented by effective political organizations, and those that are will unbalance the political system in their favor.*

Social Movement Theory

Largely in response to the rational choice approach, some social scientists have developed *social movement theory*, which argues that the rational choice perspective is too limited and too narrow in its view of human motivations. Instead of seeing people as soulless "maximizers of utility," advocates of social movement theory emphasize that people may decide to join a political organization because they identify with the social movement it represents. For example, a low-income citizen may be drawn to interest groups that speak for a movement to help the poor; instead of calculating the costs and benefits to himself or herself, the individual will be moved by an emotional identification with the larger movement, and that will often generate contributions. Thus, social movement theory leads to conclusions much closer to those of pluralism than to those drawn from the rational choice perspective; it contends that like-minded people will act collectively, even when a purely *individual* assessment of interests would suggest that one should be a free-rider.[21]

An important illustration of the potential power of social movements is the transnational movement to force governments and international organizations to address the problem of gender violence. One researcher has considered this movement, exploring the organizational power unleashed when people who were otherwise partly divided by race, social status, education, and other factors found themselves sharing the same perspective. When such divisions separate activists, the power of their movement declines, but when an issue emerges that highlights their shared identity, solidarity and policy influence increases.[22]

A remarkable study of collective behavior in a slum neighborhood in a Ugandan town supports the fundamental tenets of social movement theory. The researchers found that there was greater cooperative behavior to obtain public goods among people with shared ethnic identities than among people of different ethnic backgrounds. This is not particularly surprising, but the researchers determined that the greater cooperation among co-ethnics occurred "because they adhere to in-group reciprocity norms—norms that are plausibly supported by expectations that non-contribution will be sanctioned," and by the fact that the social connection among them facilitates interactions that make non-contribution uncomfortable.[23]

The study of social movements reveals that, at least in some situations, interest group activity is not entirely a matter of rational choices by self-interested individuals. Social networks and identities shape behavior in ways that cannot be explained by examining economic logic.

* Columnist David Brooks wrote an essay in 2008 interpreting contemporary U.S. politics from an Olsonian perspective. See "Talking v. Doing," *New York Times*, May 20, 2008.

A Mixed View

Many contemporary political scientists see validity in all four perspectives on the role of interest groups in industrial democracies. Jack Walker, for example, published the results of an extensive study of U.S. interest groups, concluding that there are many different paths to group formation and power. Some form as pluralists would expect, although they are often helped by wealthy benefactors who make major contributions to get groups started.[24] Most political scientists would admit, however, that traditional pluralists are overly optimistic in their expectation that virtually all interests will be represented by an effective organization. Following the elite theorists, it is widely accepted that some groups are more powerful than others and that the most powerful are typically groups pursuing the interests of the large corporations and other members of elite parts of society.[25] Social movement theorists claim that their idea is supported by the numerous and often influential political organizations that gain members by drawing on the power of identification with social movements. Finally, advocates of rational choice thinking point to the fact that groups with the ability to force members to contribute are much more powerful than are interests of the same size that lack this ability.

Each of these interpretations may apply more to some political systems and less to others. For example, a study of interest group formation in Russia concluded that citizens are more likely to act in ways that Olson would consider irrational, joining social movements when they see a specific person or institution to "blame" for their problems. Where there is no specific attribution of blame, citizens are more likely to suffer in unorganized masses.[26] Our previous discussion suggested that in developing nations (whose populations are less educated, poorly organized, and less politicized), economic wealth or political power or both are often concentrated in a small segment of society. Thus, in these countries, elite theory may be an accurate tool for describing the political power of a small array of interests that exercise a near monopoly of economic and political power. In many African nations, a small Westernized middle class often constitutes a bureaucratic elite that controls the levers of political power.

CONCLUSION: INTEREST GROUPS—A CHALLENGE FOR DEMOCRACY?

However interest groups are ultimately evaluated, it is clear that we cannot begin to understand how government works unless we appreciate their power. The growth of a modern society unleashes a wide range of competing interests, as new industries are developed and as people increasingly begin to affect the lives of others. One way or another, interest groups will form to advance many of these competing interests.

How well the society manages those interests while maintaining some degree of democracy and fairness is one measure of the health of a modern political system. For those reasons, many political scientists feel that the best way to secure a healthy democratic government in the age of interest groups is with strong political parties, as discussed in Chapter 5.

🌐 WHERE ON THE WEB?

The following World Wide Web addresses are a representative sampling of interest group home pages. Many more groups have a presence on the Web, but here are some of the more interesting Web sites.

http://www.aarp.org
The American Association of Retired Persons is a highly influential interest group advocating policies designed to "shape and enrich the experience of aging."

http://www.sec.org.sg
The Singapore Environment Council is an interest group in Singapore dedicated to global environmental concerns.

http://www.ibfan.org/
The International Baby Food Action Network is dedicated to "reducing infant and young child morbidity and mortality."

http://www.pfaw.org
"People for the American Way" describes itself as a "an energetic advocate for the values and institutions that sustain a diverse democratic society." This liberal interest group emphasizes efforts to preserve certain constitutional freedoms from what it terms the "radical right."

http://www.gipspsi.org/GIP
This French Group, GIP SPSI, or "Public Interest Group for Health and Social Protection in the International Arena," works to advance social and health policy solutions.

http://www.commoncause.org
Founded in 1970, Common Cause is a U.S. interest group focusing on ethical campaigning in the electoral system.

http://www.claremont.org
Claremont is an organization dedicated to "restoring the principles of the American Founding to their rightful, pre-eminent authority."

http://www.moveon.org/
With over 3 million members, Moveon.org claims to "bring real Americans back to the political process." It supports leftist and mostly Democratic Party campaigns and causes in the U.S.

http://progressforamerica.org/
This is the home page for "Progress for America," a conservative interest group in the U.S.

◆ ◆ ◆

Key Terms and Concepts _____

disadvantage theory	rational choice
elite theory	lobbying
free-rider	nondecisions
inside and outside strategies of influence	pluralism
	power elite
interest group	

Discussion Questions ————

1. How do political parties and interest groups compare as methods for representing and articulating citizens' interests?
2. Compare the different approaches to understanding how interest groups form. Which is the most valid, and why?
3. The most dramatic change in the politics of interest groups during the last 30 years or so has been the rise of so-called citizen groups or public interest groups. Is the emergence of these groups a good or a bad thing?
4. Compare elitism and pluralism as perspectives on the distribution of organized power. Which theory is more persuasive?

Notes ————

1. Emphasis added. See Posner's comments in full at the "Becker/Posner Blog" at http://www.becker-posner-blog.com/archives/2008/05/the_outlandish.html.
2. Information obtained from the National Rifle Association's Political Victory Fund Web site, http://www.nrapvf.org/About/Default.aspx.
3. See the information on the NRA's legislative activity Web site, http://www.nraila.org/About/ElectionActivity.
4. "Election Day 2006," NRA Political Victory Fund News Release, available at www.nrapvf.org.
5. Joseph LaPalombara, *Interest Groups in Italian Politics* (Princeton, NJ: Princeton University Press, 1964).
6. See Frank Baumgartner, "Public Interest Groups in France and the United States," *Governance* 9 (January) 1996: 1–22.
7. Richard C. Cortner, "Strategies and Tactics of Litigants in Constitutional Cases," *Journal of Public Law* 17 (1968): 287–307.
8. See Susan M. Olson, "Interest Group Litigation in Federal District Court: Beyond the Political Disadvantage Theory," *Journal of Politics* 52 (August 1990): 854–882; and Kim Scheppele and Jack L. Walker, Jr., "The Litigation Strategies of Interest Groups," in *Mobilizing Interest Groups in America: Patrons, Professions, and Social Movements*, ed. Jack L. Walker, Ann Arbor, MI: University of Michigan Press, 1991, pp. 157–183.
9. Cary Coglianese, "Legal Change at the Crossroads: Revisiting the Political Disadvantage Theory," John F. Kennedy School of Government, Harvard University, Working Paper, n.d., http://www.ksg.harvard.edu/prg/cary/legal.htm.
10. Anne Binderkrantz. "Interest Group Strategies: Navigating Between Privileged Access and Strategies of Pressure," *Political Studies* 53 (December 2005): 694–715.
11. See Jeffrey Berry and Clyde Wilcox, *The Interest Group Society*, 4th ed. (New York: Longman, 2007), chap. 9, for a good overview.
12. The first use of the term *issue networks* is attributed to Hugh Heclo, "Issue Networks and the Executive Establishment," in *The New American Political System*, ed. Anthony S. King (Washington, DC: American Enterprise Institute, 1978), pp. 87–124. Also see John P. Heinz, Edward Laumann, Robert Nelson, and Robert Salisbury, *The Hollow Core* (Cambridge: Harvard University Press, 1993).
13. Cathie Jo Martin and Duane Swank, "Does the Organization of Capital Matter? Employers and Active Labor Market Policy at the National and Firm Levels," *American Political Science Review* 98 (November 2004): 593–611.
14. For example, see E.E. Schattschneider, *The Semi-Sovereign People* (New York: Holt, Rinehart, and Winston, 1960).
15. David Truman, *The Governmental Process* (New York: Knopf, 1956).
16. The most often-cited classic statement of elite theory is C. Wright Mills, *The Power Elite* (New York: Oxford University Press, 1956).
17. See Robert A. Dahl, *Who Governs?* (New Haven: Yale University Press, 1961).
18. For a controversial discussion of this problem see John Manley, "Neo Pluralism: A Class Analysis of Pluralism I and Pluralism II," *American Political Science Review* 77 (1983): 368–383; and the responses by Robert Dahl and Charles Lindblom (384–389). The text discussion follows closely the argument by Peter Bachrach and Morton S. Baratz in "Two Faces of Power," *American Political Science Review* 56 (1962): 947–952.
19. See Mancur Olson, Jr., *The Logic of Collective Action* (Cambridge: Harvard University Press, 1965), for an accessible statement of this revolutionary idea.
20. Olson, *The Logic of Collective Action*, Chap.1.
21. For a good survey of this perspective, see Jeff Goodwin and James M. Jasper, eds., *The Social Movement Reader: Cases and Concepts* (Malden, MA: Blackwell, 2003).
22. A recent article applies the social movement concept to efforts to curb violence against women; see L. Laurel Weldon, "Inclusion, Solidarity, and Social Movements: The Global Movement Against Gender Violence," *Perspectives on Politics* 4 (2006): 55–74.

23. James Habyarimana, Macartan Humphreys, Daniel N. Posner, and Jeremy M. Weinstein. "Why Does Ethnic Diversity Undermine Public Goods Provision?," *American Political Science Review* 101 (November 2007): 709–725.
24. Jack L. Walker, Jr., "The Origins and Maintenance of Interest Groups in America," in *Mobilizing Interest Groups in America: Patrons, Professions, and Social Movements*, ed. Jack L. Walker (Ann Arbor, MI: University of Michigan Press, 1991), pp. 19–40. Walker and David C. King presented the results of a survey attempting to determine the benefits provided by different kinds of groups in "The Provision of Benefits by Interest Groups in the United States," *Journal of Politics* 54 (May 1992): 394–426. This later study helped to demonstrate that no single theory applies to all important organized interests.
25. See the remarkable and accessible empirical analysis contained a recent book by Dara Strolovitch, *Affirmative Advocacy: Race, Class, and Gender in Interest Group Politics*. Chicago: University of Chicago Press, 2007.
26. Debra Javeline, "The Role of Blame in Collective Action: Evidence from Russia," *American Political Science Review* 97 (February 2003): 107–121.

For Further Reading _____

Ainsworth, Scott H. *Analyzing Interest Groups: Group Influence on People and Policies* New York: Norton, 2002.

Balla, Steven J., and John R. Wright. "Interest Groups, Advisory Committees, and Congressional Control of the Bureaucracy." *American Journal of Political Science* 45 (October 2001): 799–812.

Baumgartner, Frank R., and Beth L. Leech. *Basic Interests*. Princeton, NJ: Princeton University Press, 1998.

Berry, Jeffrey. *The New Liberalism: The Rising Power of Citizen Groups*. Washington, DC: Brookings, 1999.

Boehmke, Frederick J. *The Indirect Effect of Direct Legislation: How Institutions Shape Interest Group Systems*. Columbus, OH: Ohio University Press, 2005.

Cigler, Allan J., and Burdett A. Loomis. *Interest Group Politics*, 6th ed. Washington, DC: CQ Press, 2002.

Finkel, Steven E., and Edward N. Muller. "Rational Choice and the Dynamics of Collective Political Action: Evaluating Alternative Models with Panel Data." *American Political Science Review* (March 1998): 37–49.

Grossman, Gene M., and Elhanan Helpman, *Special Interest Politics*. Cambridge, MA: MIT University Press, 2002.

Hall, Richard L., and Alan V. Deardorff. "Lobbying as Legislative Subsidy." *American Political Science Review* 100 (February 2006): 69–84.

Hansford, Thomas G. "Lobbying Strategies, Venue Selection, and Organized Interest Involvement at the U.S. Supreme Court." *American Politics Research* 32 (2004): 170–197.

Hansen, Wendy L., Neil J. Mitchell, and Jeffrey M. Drope. "The Logic of Private and Collective Action." *American Journal of Political Science* 49 (January 2005): 150–167.

Heaney, Michael T. "Outside the Issue Niche: The Multidimensionality of Interest Group Identity." *American Politics Research* 32 (2004): 611–651.

Heinz, John P., Edward Laumann, Robert Nelson, and Robert Salisbury. *The Hollow Core*. Cambridge: Harvard University Press, 1993.

Herrnson, Paul S., Rondald G. Shaiko, and Clyde Wilcox. *The Interest Group Connection: Electioneering, Lobbying, and Policymaking in Washington*, 2nd ed. Washington, DC: CQ Press, 2005.

Javeline, Debra. "The Role of Blame in Collective Action: Evidence from Russia." *American Political Science Review* 97 (February 2003): 107–121.

Kelly, Christine A. *Tangled Up in Red, White, and Blue: New Social Movements in America*. Lanham, MD: Rowman and Littlefield, 2001.

Kollman, Ken. *Outside Lobbying: Public Opinion and Interest Group Strategies*. Princeton, N.J.: Princeton University Press, 1998.

Lijphart, A. "The Puzzle of Indian Democracy: A Consociational Interpretation." *American Political Science Review* (June 1996): 258–268.

Lohmann, Susanne. "Representative Government and Special Interest Politics: (We Have Met the Enemy and He Is Us)." *Journal of Theoretical Politics* 15 (2003): 299–319.

Lowery, David, and Holly Brasher. *Organized Interests and American Government.* New York: McGraw-Hill, 2004.

Martin, Cathie Jo, and Duane Swank. "Does the Organization of Capital Matter? Employers and Active Labor Market Policy at the National and Firm Levels." *American Political Science Review* 98 (November 2004): 593–611.

Mills, C. Wright. *The Power Elite.* New York: Oxford University Press, 1956.

Morris, Aldon, and Carol McClurg Mueller. *Frontiers in Social Movement Theory.* New Haven: Yale University Press, 1992.

Olson, Mancur. *The Logic of Collective Action.* Cambridge: Harvard University Press, 1965.

———. *The Rise and Decline of Nations.* New Haven: Yale University Press, 1982.

Robertson, Graeme B. "Strikes and Labor Organizations in Hybrid Regimes." *American Political Science Review* 101 (November 2007): 781–798.

Rozell, Mark J., Clyde Wilcox, and David Madland. *Interest Groups in American Campaigns: The New Face of Electioneering.* Washington, DC: CQ Press, 2006.

Schattschneider, E.E. *Politics, Pressure, and the Tariff.* New York: Prentice-Hall, 1935.

———. *The Semisovereign People.* Fort Worth, TX.: Harcourt Brace, 1975.

Sheingate, Adam D. *The Rise of the Agricultural Welfare State.* Princeton, NJ: Princeton University Press, 2001.

Thomas, Clive S. (ed.) *Research Guide to U.S. and International Interest Groups.* Westport, CT.: Praeger, 2004.

Truman, David. *The Governmental Process.* New York: Knopf, 1956.

Walker, Jack L., Jr. *Mobilizing Interest Groups in America.* Ann Arbor: University of Michigan Press, 1991.

Warren, Mark. "What Does Corruption Mean in a Democracy?" *American Journal of Political Science* 48 (2004): 328–343.

Weldon, S. Laurel. "Inclusion, Solidarity, and Social Movements: The Global Movement Against Gender Violence." *Perspectives on Politics* 4 (March 2006): 55–74.

Wilson, James Q. *Political Organizations.* New York: Basic Books, 1973.

Woll, Cornelia. *Firm Interests: How Governments Shape Business Lobbying on Global Trade.* Ithaca, N.Y.: Cornell University Press, 2008.

Zhang, Daowei, and David Laband, "From Senators to the President: Solve the Lumber Problem or Else." *Public Choice* 123 (2005): 393–410.

PART III

POLITICAL
INSTITUTIONS

The primary institutions of government—parliaments, presidencies, courts—are perhaps the first things we think about when we attempt to describe or compare governments around the world. Although the design and workings of these institutions vary dramatically, virtually all political systems have some kind of legislative assembly, an executive institution, a system of courts, and an assortment of bureaucratic agencies. The chapters in Part III describe the essential functions that each of these institutions performs. Although their functions are almost universal, we explore the importance of differences in the *design* of governmental institutions: the impact of having a presidential system (like the U.S. and Chile) instead of a parliamentary system (like Great Britain or Israel); the different roles that courts play in making policy; the problems of controlling state bureaucracies; and the issue of limiting executive power. The structure of a political system's institutions has a tremendous influence on the way its government works and on its prospects for stability and democracy.

THE ITALIAN SENATE REMOVES A PRIME MINISTER   On January 24, 2008, the Italian senate
voted against a motion of confidence in the government of Prime Minister Romano Prodi,
by a close vote of 161 to 156, with one abstention. Following the vote,
Mr. Prodi resigned.

© Filippo Monteforte/AFP/Getty Images

7

LEGISLATIVE INSTITUTIONS

◆ Lawmaking ◆ Legislatures: Features, Functions, and Structure
◆ Representation ◆ Party Responsibility and
Legislative Behavior ◆ The Changing Role of
Modern Legislatures

195

This country has come to feel the same when Congress is in session as when the baby gets hold of a hammer.

—*Will Rogers*

Folks, there's going to be a leetle mite of trouble back in town. Between me and that legislature-ful of hyena-headed, feist-faced, belly-dragging sons of slackgutted she-wolves. If you know what I mean. Well, I been looking at them and their kind so long, I just figured I'd take me a little trip and see what human folks looked like in the face before I clean forgot.[1]

—*Governor Willie Stark's description of the state legislature in Robert Penn Warren's novel* All the King's Men

On May 12, 1780, when the British siege of Charleston, South Carolina, succeeded and the town surrendered, American officers were at first permitted to keep their swords. However, the swords were soon demanded by British commanders who were annoyed by the Americans' defiant shouts of "Long Live Congress!"[2]

—*George Will*

It could probably be shown by facts and figures that there is no distinctly American criminal class except Congress.

—*Mark Twain*

Citizens in most democracies have mixed and often heated opinions about their national legislatures. That is probably inevitable, given the contradictory pressures and expectations that these institutions are subject to. They are burdened with the responsibility to make collective decisions, and yet their membership mirrors divisions in society that often seem impossible to resolve. We want legislators to respond to the preferences of citizens in each district or state, but we also want them to act on the basis of all the pertinent scientific information available, even information that ordinary citizens cannot understand. We want them to help the chief executive make good public policy, but we also expect the legislature to obstruct executives who abuse their power.

Much of the study of legislative institutions is devoted to evaluating their behavior and determining the impact of various reforms and structural changes. In some legislatures, particularly the U.S. Congress, fear of excessive lawmaking power led to severe limits ("checks and balances") on the efficiency of the legislative process. Other legislatures are set up in ways that make them highly responsive to winning-party platforms. In **parliamentary** systems such as Germany's or Japan's, for example, the winning party or party coalition controls both the parliament (the legislature) and the executive branch and can more readily enact its campaign platform. Thus, the design and the operation of legislative institutions often involve basic political questions.

Are legislators supposed to make decisions in accordance with the wishes of others, or as their own judgment dictates? What is the connection between legislative and executive institutions and powers? How are legislatures organized? As we will see, the manner in which these and other issues are resolved tells us a great deal about the workings and the nature of a political system.

LAWMAKING

Societies have been subject to law for millennia, but the establishment of specialized institutions to make law is a fairly recent phenomenon. Actually, there are at least two "pre-modern" methods of creating laws. First, in many traditional societies, laws were given by a supreme being to a prophet, who then brought them to the political system where they became accepted. Second, classical philosophers identified elements of law emanating from nature itself. This notion of "natural law" is based on the assumption that "Nature endowed all beings with the faculty for preserving themselves, seeking good, and avoiding evil."[3] Thomas Jefferson's memorable opening to the American Declaration of Independence is an explicit statement of natural law: All citizens are "created equal" with "unalienable rights" that no persons or legislative institutions created or can take away. The essential element of both divine and natural law is that certain fundamental laws exist independent of *human* lawmaking (which is often termed *positive law* to distinguish it from natural law) and that these more fundamental laws prevail when laws made by people conflict with them.

A body of law that originates in "discoveries" of divine or natural law may be workable in societies that do not change very much. But even relatively underdeveloped nations are now subject to enormous forces of change created by technology, international trade, and political movements. Governments in modern nations must manage complex economic relationships, provide for the expansion and maintenance of essential infrastructure, and respond to an active array of political demands. Thus, virtually all political systems have established legislative institutions.

LEGISLATURES: FEATURES, FUNCTIONS, AND STRUCTURE

What Are Legislatures?

Although legislative institutions vary widely in size, structure, and powers, they share a few basic features. First, legislatures are *multimembered.* Individual legislators may represent provinces, districts, or even ethnic groups, but a legislature is made up of some (usually large) number of them. Second, the members are *formally equal* (although the members of one house may be more powerful than the members of another in cases where a legislature is divided into different houses). Third, legislatures make their decisions by *counting votes.*[4] The Mexican government's executive branch may sometimes resemble a legislature in that it has many officials working there to make decisions, but everyone other than the president is simply an adviser.

Legislative Functions

The primary function of legislatures is to legislate—that is, to *make laws*.* These laws create new restrictions, new rights, new programs, and new tax provisions, and they can repeal or amend existing laws.

Legislative involvement in lawmaking varies across different systems. In some countries (particularly parliamentary systems, discussed below), legislative lawmaking merely *legitimizes* policy choices made by a prime minister, a central committee, a chancellor, or some other chief executive. The U.S. Congress operates in a **presidential system**, and has more real influence over basic policy decisions than most national legislatures; the more typical parliamentary system arrangement—in Great Britain or Italy, for example—is for a legislature to affirm decisions made by the executive. That act of affirmation, even when the legislature has little realistic opportunity to affect the choice of alternatives, can be very important to the public's general acceptance of the government's laws.

A recent study of legislative influence in Germany and the Netherlands suggests that when a parliamentary system is ruled by a coalition of several parties, the legislature can play an important role in resolving tensions between the ruling parties in the coalition. Parties in the legislature form a coalition when they have agreed to some policy compromise, enabling the coalition to form a government. However, sometimes a government department minister may want to take steps that reflect his or her own preferences (or those of a faction within his or her party). In these circumstances, "the legislative process provides another important institutional device that coalition partners use to counteract the influence" of these maverick government officials. The study found that when the parties controlling the government were deeply divided, bills drafted by government ministers were more often changed by legislative decisions.[5] Although it is still common for many legislatures to simply affirm policy choices made by a prime minister, the evidence suggests that the legislative role remains an important influence.

In addition to lawmaking, most legislative institutions perform other functions. In both democratic and nondemocratic systems, legislatures *elect* or *appoint* at least some governmental officers. In most European democracies, the parliament elects the nation's executive-branch leaders, the prime minister and cabinet. In addition, legislatures often act in a *judicial capacity*, hearing charges brought against presidents, judges, and individual legislators.

Most legislatures also have the authority to *investigate* governmental operations. The information gathered may be taken into account in new lawmaking, but sometimes the investigative process itself puts pressure on government officials to change their activities, to alter the way a law has been interpreted, or simply to become more efficient. In the United States, legislative investigations have brought considerable information to the public (for example, by publishing the results of important

---

* In the United States and other countries following Anglo-American patterns of jurisprudence, laws made by a legislature are called statutes, to distinguish them from the laws made by administrative agencies, court decisions, and executive orders. Laws passed by legislatures designate the purposes for which public monies are to be expended and therefore establish the parameters of public policy. Although laws can be made by people or institutions that do not have the basic features of legislatures—as when a tyrant issues edicts or a bureaucrat promulgates rules and regulations—lawmaking is central to the behavior of most legislatures.

studies of consumer product safety). The relatively loose party control within the U.S. Congress also means that explosive legislative investigations often enable a legislator to make a name for himself or herself by exploiting the resulting media attention. This is more difficult to do in countries such as Great Britain, where party discipline is stronger and the legislative branch's opportunities for independent activity are more limited.

In many countries, legislators perform a more individualized function as well. Citizens or interest groups often feel that they can call on the legislator elected from their district, state, or province to help them with a problem or question. Legislators may find it politically profitable to respond, spending time in **constituent service**. (In especially corrupt systems, such efforts are financially profitable to the legislator.)

Consequently, legislators often act as **ombudsmen**,* helping to determine the meaning of unclear regulations, prompting agencies to process applications more quickly, and seeking changes in official decisions on behalf of affected constituents. These important activities are often vital to the legislator in generating support for reelection. Moreover, in some nations, including Great Britain and Mexico, some legislators have official links to interest groups (such as business associations or labor unions) and may act openly as their advocates in government.

Legislative Structure

Every legislature has several specific structural features designed by constitutions or shaped by age-old traditions. In this section, we discuss three basic structural issues pertinent to virtually all contemporary legislative institutions.

Legislative and Executive Power   Although a few political systems operate without a legislative institution, it is fair to say that all have some kind of executive. The executive is responsible for carrying out and managing the government's programs and laws, as discussed in Chapter 8. How the legislature and the executive work together is one of the most basic issues related to legislative structure and process.

Most political systems can be classified as either parliamentary systems or presidential systems. In parliamentary systems, the legislature chooses the "head of government"—most often known as the prime minister—and the executive must be an elected member of parliament.† To stay in office, he or she must retain the support of the party in parliament that won a majority of seats (or the support of a parliamentary majority created by a *coalition* of parties that agree to work together to support the same prime minister).

Parliamentary systems typically have a separate "head of state," a monarch or some other person with largely symbolic powers. By contrast, in presidential systems, the chief executive is both head of state *and* head of government. He or she is selected

---

* The position of ombudsman was first developed in Scandinavian countries. The person in this position investigates complaints brought by individual citizens regarding government programs, agencies, and policies.

† Strictly speaking, the prime minister in a parliamentary system may be *officially* chosen by the president or the monarch, as in Great Britain. But both political expectations and traditional observance demand that the president or monarch "select" the individual elected by the members of the majority party in the House of Commons.

FIGURE 7.1　PARLIAMENTARY AND PRESIDENTIAL SYSTEMS

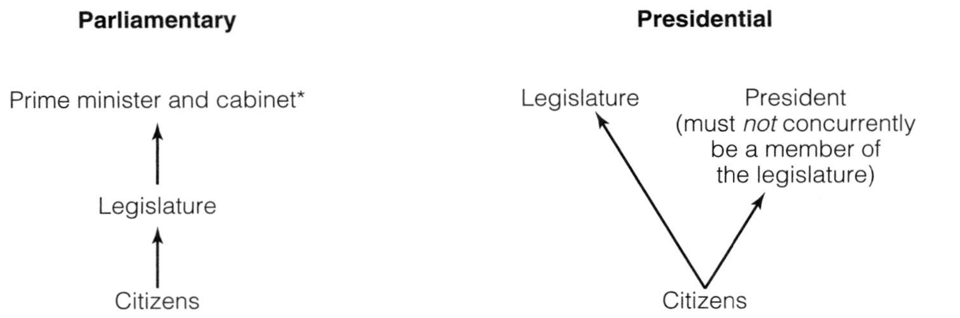

Parliamentary　　　　　　　　　　　　**Presidential**

Prime minister and cabinet*　　　Legislature　　　President
　　　　↑　　　　　　　　　　　　　　　　(must *not* concurrently
　　　　|　　　　　　　　　　　　　　　　be a member of
　　Legislature　　　　　　　　　　　　the legislature)
　　　　↑　　　　　　　　　↖　　　↗
　　　　|　　　　　　　　　　　↖　↗
　　Citizens　　　　　　　　　　Citizens

*Together, the prime minister and his or her cabinet are typically called "the Government" in a parliamentary system. In many parliamentary systems, including Great Britain, the prime minister and his or her cabinet must also be current members of Parliament.

NOTE: Arrows indicate paths of political accountability.

independently by the voters and therefore is not accountable to the legislature. (See Figure 7.1.)

It is often argued that the parliamentary system is more consistent with democratic principles. According to supporters of presidential systems, the main advantage of their systems is that they provide greater "checks" on unwise legislatures: A simple legislative majority in a parliamentary system can make any law it wants as long as support can be achieved in one assembly. Parliamentary advocates respond that this is the way it *should* be; that the only thing that should ever "check" the decisions of the parliament is the possibility that the people will vote the other party into power if members of parliament make decisions that the people oppose. That is what democracy is all about! The choice between a parliamentary and a presidential system is thus among the most basic factors in determining how a democratic political system operates. (See Box 7-1.)

Box 7-1

ISRAEL: A FAILED EXPERIMENT WITH A HYBRID SYSTEM

Underlying the two methods used to select the chief executive in almost all democracies are two distinct approaches to the allocation of power. Most nations of the Western Hemisphere intentionally separate executive and legislative powers. Hence, the president is elected directly by the electorate and, at least theoretically, enjoys a national mandate. The legislature cannot remove the executive except through a relatively rare process of impeachment and conviction—not simply as a result of disagreeing with him or her on policy matters.

On the other hand, in a parliamentary form of government—used throughout most of Europe (with the important exception of France)—the powers of the executive and legislative branches are merged rather than separated. The prime minister is elected by the parliament and technically can be removed by parliament at any time.

Israel adopted a hybrid system in 1992, with a prime minister elected directly by the voters. Supporters of this system argued that a separately elected prime minister would command broad public support and have the necessary power to lead the country during times of crisis. However, in March 2001, the Knesset amended the Basic Law to return to a more conventional parliamentary system. The factors that led Israel to abandon its hybrid system reveal a great deal about the differences between parliamentary and presidential democracy.

The rationale for the short-lived system of a directly elected prime minister had to do with what many perceived to be the inappropriately large influence of small parties. When the main parties had virtually equal shares of seats in the Knesset, small parties—often Orthodox religious parties—could determine which of the major parties could form a coalition government and appoint its leader as prime minister. Some reformers believed that a directly elected prime minister system "would 'free' the prime minister from [the]constraining or 'blackmailing' influence of smaller parties."[6]

Ironically, the main impact of the hybrid system was an *increase* in the power of small parties. In parliamentary systems, voters cannot "split" their tickets, voting for one party's candidate for the Knesset and for another party's candidate for chief executive. However, this behavior is very common where the chief executive is separately elected. Referring to the 1996 election, Gregory Mahler reported the impact of the new system on voting choices:

> Probably the single biggest surprise in the election was the significant increase in representation of the smaller parties in the Knesset, and the corresponding decrease in representation for the larger parties. The split-ballot system was in a sense "liberating" for Israeli voters. Many voters who traditionally supported Labor or Likud did so because they saw it as a way to influence the selection of the prime minister, since the leader of the party with the most seats would become prime minister.
>
> Under the new system, a voter's choice for Knesset and prime minister can be from different parties. Many voters did this in the May election:

While 50.4 percent of valid votes were cast for the Likud candidate for prime minister, only 25.1 percent of valid votes went to its Knesset list. Similarly, while 49.5 percent of the valid votes were cast for the Labor candidate, only 26.8 percent of valid votes went to its list of candidates for the Knesset.[7]

Why did voters take advantage of the opportunity to split their tickets in such large numbers? Giving voters two ballots (one to elect the prime minister and one to elect a member of the Knesset) allowed voters to select a "mainstream" candidate when voting for prime minister, and then cast a vote for a fringe candidate for the Knesset, thinking that such a vote would do little harm since a more moderate prime minister would be in place.

A British political scientist summed up the rationale for abandoning the semi-presidential system in Israel:

> Israel turned to direct election [of the prime minister] to counteract . . . fragmentation, instability, and immobilism. . . . These maladies are often associated with proportional representation (PR), particularly the low-threshold Israeli variety, which allows parties winning as little as 1.5 percent of the vote to take Knesset seats. Yet, the very effort to secure the passage of reform introduced distortions that caused it to fall short and even backfire. Much to the chagrin of reform's supporters, the 1996 and 1999 elections each led to a troubled time of coalition building. Small parties, far from being sidelined, vied to play kingmaker. And each time the result was an awkwardly patched-together coalition government with little coherence or staying power.[8]

As a result of these and other concerns, in 2001 Israel returned to a more conventional parliamentary system, used for the first time in January 2003. Voters select the members of the Knesset, and that body then selects the prime minister, who must be one of its members.

Israel's short-lived experiment with a hybrid system reflects the conflicting values inherent in the choice between parliamentary and presidential democracies. This experience also shows that the differences between the two systems depends on a great many factors, most importantly the nature of the party system.

Which system produces greater stability? There is considerable disagreement among political scientists regarding the advantages and disadvantages of each system. Some analysts contend that the parliamentary system is more directly responsive to the voters, largely because the voters determine which party has a majority, and that party then controls both the legislative and the executive branches. Such systems are not plagued by "**dual democratic legitimacy**," a situation created in presidential systems as a result of the fact that both the separately elected executives and the legislature can claim to be the true representative of the public will. The result can be gridlock and political frustration.[9]

Experience in Europe and in Latin American countries has led some observers to argue that as a result of their "dual democratic legitimacy," presidential systems have severe shortcomings. In parliamentary systems, voters may have more information about the people governing them, because department heads and other governing officials are almost always established leaders of the majority party. Newly elected presidents appoint their cabinet heads from a far less known array of individuals, drawn from their own inner circles.

But the most important argument against presidential systems is that they can produce profound instability *when a president loses popular support*. Because the chief executive in presidential systems is elected for a fixed term and will normally complete that term (unless a constitutional crisis takes place), presidential systems sometimes produce situations in which the government is led for years by a president with no real political clout and hence the inability to lead effectively. In contrast, prime ministers are forced to resign if parliamentary support substantially weakens, thereby avoiding this destabilizing condition.[10]

Supporters of presidential systems argue that since the voters directly elect the president, he or she can become a stronger leader than prime ministers in parliamentary systems can be, serving as an effective focal point to hold a nation together during times of great difficulty. Presidential systems are also less likely to have rapid and frequent changes in government as a result of abrupt changes in the balance of power among parties.

The question of which system is superior is not easily answered. The fact that the chief executive in parliamentary systems depends on legislative support more than presidents do in presidential systems presents a difficult question for political scientists. On one hand, presidential systems can enjoy greater stability during shifts in the strength of competing parties, since the president knows he or she can stay in office during a given term regardless of what happens in the legislature. The government is not likely to be replaced very often.

On the other hand, this independence from the legislature can tempt presidents to disregard growing legislative resistance to their policies. If a president overestimates his or her popular support, he or she can take actions that eventually produce disruptive or even violent opposition. In contrast, the legislature in a parliamentary system can remove a prime minister who has strayed significantly from popular demands by passing a "vote of no confidence" simply on the grounds that his or her policies have become seriously unpopular (see the opening photo and caption for this chapter). Knowing this, prime ministers are less likely to govern in ways that invite rebellious movements. Presidents, in contrast, may be removed only by impeachment, by resignation, or by a constitutional crisis of some kind, remaining in office even when they no longer enjoy political support.[11]

What about non-democratic countries—does it matter whether they have presidential or parliamentary systems? A recent study suggested that parliamentary systems may provide for a somewhat more open government in non-democratic regimes. When autocratic governments have a presidential system, elite factions work in private to manipulate the system so that the presidential candidate preferred by the elite "wins" the election. However, if the same country has a parliamentary system, "bargaining among the elites in selection of the head of state would occur *after* the elections" because "the elites would have to first secure parliamentary seats to be able to vote for the head of state. . . . [T]he balance of power among the elites in parliament would be decided by the people, giving them a voice in the process."[12]

Simply put, it is usually easier for elite factions to collude and manipulate a presidential election than it is to manipulate elections for hundreds of parliamentary seats. Once the general election is over, the Prime Minister will be chosen by bargaining among elites in non-democratic systems, but there is a somewhat greater chance that their choices will be influenced by the voters' input in selecting the members of the parliament. Under a presidential system, everything is rigged before the people vote.

In the final analysis, the nature of a country's party system largely determines which arrangement is better. The existence of a strong two-party system usually produces considerable stability in the legislature, with one party in control for extended periods of time. Such two-party systems may be ideal settings for presidential systems, since the separately elected president can learn to work with the relatively stable group controlling the legislature. However, when a country has a larger number of parties, none of which dominates the system, a separately elected president can lead to serious political problems. In that situation, the president will try to complete his or her term during a period in which the legislature is led by shifting coalitions of small parties, creating uncertainty and rapid changes in political support. Because the president is not accountable to the legislature, a deep chasm can arise between the two elected branches of government.

As one analyst put it, "Even though multi-partyism in itself is not troublesome for democratic stability, the combination of presidentialism and multi-partyism *is* problematic. In world history, only one *multiparty* presidential democracy—Chile—has survived for more than twenty-five years."[13] In short, the fact that the chief executive in a presidential system enjoys political support that is independent of the legislature creates stability and strength when there are two strong parties, but the same arrangement becomes fragile when the legislature is run by shifting coalitions of many small parties.

However, a recent study suggests that many Latin American governments have adapted, creating arrangements in which political crises are often defused before they become destabilizing. In some cases, these "presidential regimes can work like parliamentary regimes and resort to early elections or votes of no-confidence in order to defuse a crisis, or the people and social movements may have the power to force a presidential resignation . . . Latin American presidentialism is becoming more flexible and more like parliamentarism."[14] A more general theoretical essay also suggests that gridlock and instability can be encountered in either system.[15]

In which system is the legislature more powerful? On the surface, it would appear that the parliamentary arrangement gives the legislature greater influence. Since the same legislative majority that makes laws and policy also elects the executive, the parliament is hardly likely to select a prime minister who will oppose the majority's policy preferences. The parliament is formally "supreme," and the chief executive will normally be sympathetic to the legislative majority (and vice versa). When parliamentary demands must be satisfied, it is often done by executive compromises. Of course, this supportive relationship runs both ways: In most parliamentary systems it is more accurate to say that the parliament is supportive of the prime minister, who normally makes most of the policy initiatives.

Thus, both the degree of a system's stability and the relative power of the legislative and executive branches are influenced by factors other than the choice between parliamentary and presidential arrangements. The type of party system that prevails in the legislature, the constitutional powers granted each branch of government, and traditional political practices are also important. In Great Britain, where the prime minister's party regularly holds an absolute parliamentary majority and where party discipline is strong, the prime minister can be confident of getting the House of Commons to pass almost all major bills that he or she and the cabinet propose. Typically, 90 to 95 percent of the prime minister's legislation is adopted—a "batting average" that any American president would envy. Thus, by most estimates the British Parliament (whose most fundamental function is to elect a prime minister) has a much smaller role in policy initiation than does the U.S. Congress.

On the other hand, in countries where no single party holds a parliamentary majority and a coalition of parties elects the prime minister, the chief executive may be weakened by uncertain and shifting legislative support. Under the French Fourth Republic (1946–1958), for example, the legislature dominated the chief executive. Prime ministers had great difficulty getting bills passed and were regularly removed from office by the parliament. Italian prime ministers have been able to count on a surprising degree of relatively stable policy making from their very unstable legislative coalitions only by devoting a great amount of effort to building and maintaining coalitions among parties.*

Presidential systems also vary considerably. The U.S. Constitution provides for a balance of power between the executive and the legislative branches, with the president being able to veto legislation while the Congress enacts laws and sometimes overrides vetoes. In Mexico and most of Latin America, however, both constitutional design and historical practice have produced dominant presidents and very weak legislatures. Presidents can enact many programs through executive decree and generally can dominate the legislature. (For example, a recent study of Argentina found that because legislative candidates are largely selected by provincial governors and "party bosses," legislators cannot develop professional careers or specialized expertise, making the legislature very weak relative to the executive.[16]) In general, legislatures in the developing world, under both parliamentary and presidential systems, are weak and generally do the bidding of the executive.

The Constitution of the French Fifth Republic (1958–present) was designed expressly to strengthen the presidency and weaken the parliament, which had been so dominant in the Fourth Republic. The French Constitution features a dual executive, combining elements of both presidential and parliamentary systems: It has a president

---

* See Carol Mershon, "The Costs of Coalitions: Coalition Theories and Italian Governments," *American Political Science Review* 90 (September 1996): 534–554.

(directly elected by the voters) and a prime minister (selected by the president). Both officers have considerable power and dominate a relatively weak legislature.

One or Two Houses The division of legislative power into two chambers, or **bicameralism**, is the most common arrangement among the world's legislatures. However, the balance of power between the two chambers varies considerably. The U.S. Congress divides power roughly equally between its two branches. On the other hand, the French Assembly and the Japanese House of Representatives have considerably more authority than their upper houses. And in Great Britain, the House of Lords, once equal in power with the House of Commons, now can generally do little more than recommend changes to legislation passed by the Commons.*

Bicameral legislatures are popular for two main reasons. First, a second "house" makes it possible for subnational units (states, provinces) to be formally represented. Whenever seats in the legislature are apportioned on the basis of population (as in the U.S. House of Representatives), states, provinces, or other units with smaller populations will have a smaller number of representatives. The citizens of these smaller units may fear that their interests will be ignored in a legislative institution in which seats are allocated to states or provinces on the basis of population. They will be regularly outvoted on policy issues in which their citizens have preferences different from those of citizens in the more populous areas. Thus, seats in the "upper" house are often apportioned in such a way as to moderate those concerns. For example, the U.S. Senate is made up of two senators from each state, regardless of the state's population. A similar allocation of Senate seats by state prevails in Mexico. Hence, citizens in Wyoming have precisely the same voice in the Senate as do citizens in California, although their delegations to the House of Representatives are very different: California has 53, over 12 percent of the total of all Representatives in the House, and Wyoming has only one. In Germany, each state *(Land)* appoints representatives to the *Bundesrat*, the parliament's weaker chamber. Representatives from each Land vote as a bloc in accordance with instructions from their state governments.

Some political thinkers (most famously the framers of the U.S. Constitution) advocate bicameralism to make it more difficult to enact ill-considered, dangerous, or unwise legislation. James Madison and his colleagues explicitly feared "mob rule," which they felt would be encouraged by the popularly elected House of Representatives, and they saw the more patrician and politically independent Senate as an essential check needed to maintain stability and order.

Even where there is less fear of democracy itself, however, some people favor bicameralism as a kind of quality control. A genuinely bicameral arrangement means that legislation has two hurdles to clear before becoming law. Requiring passage in the additional house means that bad programs and policy decisions are more likely to be corrected or defeated. But the passage of *any* legislation (even good legislation) is more difficult in a bicameral legislature than in a unicameral arrangement. It is not at all uncommon for a bill to pass the U.S. Senate, for example, only to fail in the House.†

---

* The House of Lords can delay the passage of non-money bills (those not involving expenditures of government funds) passed by the House of Commons for one session. Lords can suggest changes to a bill involving expenditures, but Commons is free to reject it. In practice, Lords rarely rejects a bill proposed by the cabinet and never rejects a bill fundamental to the prime minister's program.

† However, in Japan and Western Europe, in the event of a split between the two chambers of the parliament, the more powerful lower house can usually override the other—sometimes with a simple majority vote.

For those reasons, many political thinkers and citizens have argued that bicameralism is an undemocratic feature: If the "people" are fairly represented in the lower house, how can a system be democratic if it permits the lower house's political choices to be overturned?

One solution is to give the lower house the power to overrule the other body (as in Italy, Japan, and Mexico). Other systems (New Zealand, the U.S. State of Nebraska) have unicameral legislatures largely in response to that concern.

Legislative Committees   The large number of members in most legislatures prevents detailed consideration of legislative proposals when the assembly meets as a whole. To work out the "fine print" of a major proposal, virtually all legislative institutions have established committees, each made up of a workable number of legislators who are usually aided by specialized staffs. Although committees were created for these obvious practical reasons, they can have a profound *political* impact.

A key consideration is whether basic policy decisions are made *before* a proposal is assigned to a committee. In the U.S. Congress, bills are usually given to committees as soon as they are introduced. Hearings, discussions, and efforts by interest groups and government agencies to exert political influence take place while the bill is in committee, helping to explain why congressional committees are often called "little legislatures."[17] If a bill fares badly in committee deliberations, its fate can be sealed by negative action or even by inaction. Normally, the whole House (or Senate) acts only on bills recommended for passage by committee vote. Parliamentary committees in Japan are also quite influential and give opposition parties additional leverage in altering legislation proposed by the government.

In contrast, committees in the British Parliament are authorized to analyze proposed legislation, but they receive bills only after the whole body has made the basic policy decisions. Consequently, British committees are comparably much weaker than their American counterparts. French committees fall somewhere in between.

The strong **committee systems** in the U.S. Congress and the Japanese Diet (Japan's bicameral legislature), among other examples, are also characterized by member *specialization*. It is possible for a particular senator or representative to spend many years on a committee that reflects a special interest or expertise or that is of special importance to his or her district or state. The specialized nature of committees makes it more likely that the whole body will accept a committee's recommendations. Where members do not develop committee specialties—again, as in the British Parliament—the committee's role as a policy-making unit is reduced correspondingly.

The political importance of legislative committees is generally greater when the legislature *decentralizes* political power. Again, the American Congress provides an extreme illustration: The majority party is often unable to enact bills that reflect its platform because committee chairs may not share the party leadership's perspectives (even though the chairs are members of the majority party). For years a majority of Democratic members of Congress favored reducing the oil-depletion allowance (a tax deduction applying to petroleum extraction), but their efforts were blocked by powerful Democratic committee chairs from Texas and Louisiana (major oil-producing states). The fact that committee power is independent of the majority party's power

Box 7-2

THE EFFECT OF THE LEGISLATURE'S SIZE ON GOVERNMENT SPENDING

In 1981, a group of noted political theorists proposed the "law of $1/n$." The idea is that legislatures made up of a large number of representatives will enact larger, more inefficient spending programs than smaller legislatures.[18] Employing the often controversial logic of rational choice theory (discussed in Chapter 1), the "law of $1/n$" is based on the idea that representatives in large legislatures have an incentive to propose projects that benefit their districts even when the total costs for the whole society drastically outweigh the project's benefits.

The incentive to be wasteful is a consequence of the fact that while the legislator's district gets all or most of the *benefits* of the project, his/her constituents only pay $1/n$ of the *cost*, where "n" is the number of legislative districts in the legislature. The larger the legislature, the smaller the share of a project's cost paid by a given representative's constituents, and thus, the greater the incentive to be wasteful. Since all legislators face the same incentives, the prediction is that countries with larger legislatures will have more wasteful government spending.

Does the "law of $1/n$" fit the facts? There is some evidence that it does. In a 2001 study, two economists found that countries with larger legislatures tend to have higher levels of government spending, although having a bicameral legislature reduces the impact of legislative size on spending levels.[19] The evidence is more mixed when comparing U.S. state governments, however. States with larger upper chambers tend to have higher levels of government spending than other states, but when the lower chamber is much larger than the upper chamber, the effect is reversed. More precisely, the "ratio of lower-to-upper chamber seats" is associated with lower spending levels.[20]

As with many theoretical concepts, the "law of $1/n$" simplifies a great deal of complexity in order to identify a factor that can influence government spending levels. Its impact, if any, may be erased by other factors, such as the nation's level of development, political culture, economic conditions, and party competition, among many others. However, the "law of $1/n$" is an interesting example of how an idea can progress from theory to hypothesis, and finally, to empirical testing. The fact that the findings partially support the theory suggests that, all other things being equal, larger legislative bodies may actually generate larger government budgets, although no one would claim that the issue is settled or that other factors may have a far more significant influence on spending levels.

---

makes it more difficult to pass legislation, and it expands the range of interests and points of view that must be accommodated.

Gender Quotas   There are fewer women than men in virtually all elected legislatures, regardless of the nature of the political system. However, substantial evidence indicates that legislatures contain a higher percentage of women where proportional representation electoral systems are used than where single-member-district systems are used. As discussed in Chapter 4, PR systems make it possible for a party receiving less than a majority or plurality of votes in a given district to place some of its candidates in the legislature. In several countries, newer and often smaller parties nominate women more often than established parties do, and thus, PR systems can increase the number of women serving in a nation's legislature. Countries with proportional representation nearly always have a higher proportion of women in their legislative assemblies.[21]

However, the international women's movement and its supporters have been successful in getting a number of countries to adopt measures designed to increase the number of female candidates elected to legislatures. As we saw in Chapter 5, nearly thirty democracies have adopted legal quotas for the inclusion of women in national legislatures. The political and policy impacts of these quotas are unclear, but, at least where they are enforced, party leaders must select at least some women to be candidates for legislative seats.

Customs and Norms   Legislatures are an intriguing mixture of conflict and cooperation. Their members normally are drawn from diverse political parties and distinctive regions, and thus the political disagreements of the country are mirrored in the legislature itself. At the same time, at least some large segments of a legislature's membership must work together to produce legislation.

Customs and norms are extremely helpful in maintaining cooperation in legislatures in which individual members have considerable independence. Where decisions are largely made by a central majority party leadership, an individual legislator's behavior is not as critical as it is where each member is given freer rein. In the latter case, the ability to get anything done requires that there be some basis for cooperation, some "rules of the game." In a landmark study of the U.S. Senate, Donald R. Matthews identified several **folkways** that, in the 1950s, firmly controlled each senator's behavior:

> *Apprenticeship*—new members are expected to be "seen and not heard"; *Legislative Work*—one must attend to the often tedious and politically unrewarding details of committee work instead of seeking publicity; *Specialization*—members should focus their attention on matters in a particular field; *Courtesy*—personal attacks are to be avoided, and members should be lavish in praise of other members, . . . ; *Reciprocity*—members should give assistance and political support to colleagues; and *Institutional Patriotism*—members should hold the Senate in high esteem, maintain loyalty to it, and seek to preserve its status.[22]

Students of the U.S. Congress are fond of recounting anecdotes that show how strong those folkways have been. One often-cited instance had to do with a freshman senator who ignored the apprenticeship norm. After several senior senators made brief speeches honoring an elderly senator on his birthday, the freshman made a similar speech. At every mention of his name, the senator being honored grumbled to a colleague, "That son-of-a-bitch, that son-of-a-bitch."[23] It was considered horribly improper for such a junior member to presume to take the floor in this manner.

In a study of norms in the U.S. Senate a quarter-century after Matthews wrote his widely read analysis, Rohde, Ornstein, and Peabody concluded that although apprenticeship and specialization have nearly disappeared (new members are now encouraged to make contributions quickly), norms that help to manage destructive conflict are still in force:

> Many of the issues with which the Senate deals are controversial. Hard policy choices must be made and there will often be disagreement. . . . While in a given instance of conflict, the proponent of one alternative might gain an advantage by a direct personal attack on the proponent of another alternative, . . . such a course of action could have a devastating effect on the general pattern of activity in the Senate. Personal attacks would encourage [retaliation]. [making] the compromises that are necessary in passing legislation difficult to achieve. While today's *opponent* may become tomorrow's ally relatively easily, it is far more difficult to make an ally of today's *enemy*.[24]

These observers found that the legislative norms that have survived are those that are of "general benefit," such as courtesy, and not those, such as apprenticeship, that primarily benefited a limited group (such as the senior leadership of the 1950s Senate).

The Senate's continuing norms act as a restraint on behavior that would otherwise threaten the effectiveness of the institution.*

Legislative customs also reflect the culture and the traditions of the society at large. (See Box 7-3.) Discussions in the British Parliament are supposedly still influenced by the style of debate (including controlled heckling of the speaker) that evolved at Oxford University hundreds of years ago. Making sense of the behavior in a particular legislature thus often requires an understanding of the unwritten rules that constitute legislative customs.

Electoral System   As discussed in Chapter 4, democracies using the proportional representation system may be very different from those employing the single-member-district system familiar to U.S. voters. Proportional representation makes it possible

---

Box 7-3

LEGISLATIVE CUSTOMS AND VIOLENCE

Anyone listening to heated debates in the U.S. Senate is struck by certain rules of etiquette that lead senators to preface a stinging attack on an opponent's position with an extremely polite opening. For example, "I believe that my distinguished friend from [New York, Mississippi] is dead wrong." If he or she opens with "my *very* distinguished colleague," it probably means that the disagreement is more intense.

In other national legislatures, the standards for debate are far less restrained, and in some nations legislative disagreement can get totally out of hand. Recently, a Conservative Canadian MP, incensed by the arguments of a New Democratic Party leader, referred to her as a "slut" (a far cry from "my distinguished colleague"). In an incident in the early 1990s in Taiwan, which has become a genuine democracy after a period of authoritarian, single-party rule, a large number of legislators demonstrated their lack of familiarity with the normal routines of parliamentary debate by breaking into a bench-clearing fist fight that would do any hockey team proud. According to the *Taiwan News*, a prominent legislator recently threatened more than a dozen of his colleagues with violence, producing at least one assault in the legislative chamber. And, a number of years ago, one Ecuadoran congressman, deeply offended by a personal

attack against him on the legislative floor, took out a pistol and started shooting. Fortunately, nobody was hurt as the representatives unceremoniously cowered under their desks. The accompanying photo shows a scene of violence outside the Indian National Assembly.

VIOLENT DEATH AND LEGISLATIVE POLITICS   A scene of violence outside the Legislative Assembly complex in Srinagar, India, in October 2001. Here, civilians are collecting pieces of bodies while paramilitary soldiers stand guard.

---

* However, there is increasing evidence that the level of civility in the U.S. Senate has deteriorated considerably. Using observations shortly after the Clinton impeachment vote, a leading political scientist concluded that partisan polarization has strained the traditional level of courtesy in the upper chamber. See Eric M. Uslaner, "Is the Senate More Civil Than the House?" presented at a conference on "Civility and Deliberation in the Senate" sponsored by the Robert J. Dole Institute through the Pew Charitable Trusts, Washington, DC, July 16, 1999.

for a party with a small base of support to get a foothold in the national legislature (since the system grants legislative seats in proportion to each party's share of the popular vote in multi-membered legislative districts). Winning a legislative seat in the single-member-district system requires that the candidate receive more votes than any other candidate. Thus, a system using proportional representation would be expected to have a greater diversity of parties than would a single-member-district electoral arrangement.

Evidence suggests that the choice between these two electoral systems affects legislatures. A study of one U.S. state (Illinois) compared the state legislature's ideological diversity before and after Illinois discarded its proportional representation system in 1970. The study is unusual because it is based on a comparison across time, rather than on a comparison of different countries. (It is difficult to draw conclusions about the effect of such factors as electoral laws when making cross-country comparisons, because cultural, economic, and other differences may be responsible for observed differences that appear to be caused by differences in the electoral systems.) The researcher concluded that the ideological diversity of the legislature diminished considerably after the introduction of the single-member-district system.*

A more recent study of the German *Bundestag* suggested that electoral-system factors have another effect on legislators. The importance of constituency service may vary with the type of electoral system under which members of parliament are elected. In Germany, some members of the *Bundestag* (the lower house) are elected through proportional representation (PR) and the others are elected in single-member districts. The study found that members elected on the basis of voters' choices among *party lists* (the PR system) received appointments to legislative committees that allow them to serve the party platform, whereas members elected under the single-member-district system gravitated to committees that allowed them to work for their geographically based constituencies.[25] Thus, when members get their seats in parliament as a result of voters choosing their *party*, they are less interested in constituent service activities, but those activities become vital for members chosen directly by the voters.

REPRESENTATION

Most of us naturally think of legislators as *representing* the citizens who elected them; most legislators are even given the title of "representative." But legislatures can make laws and perform other basic legislative functions while acting in ways that have little to do with representation. Even when legislators purport to act as representatives, they may "represent" in very different ways.

Three Models of Representation

The Delegate Model   Perhaps the simplest approach to representation is described by the **delegate model**. A legislator acting in this manner will make decisions largely on the basis of the expressed wishes of constituents, acting as their spokesperson. If a clear majority of a legislator's district favors (or opposes) a particular proposal, the

---

* See Greg D. Adams, "Legislative Effects of Single-Member vs. Multi-Member Districts," *American Journal of Political Science* 40, no. 1 (February 1996): 129–144.

legislator's decision is made. Thus, we would expect a senator from a U.S. farm state or a member of the Canadian Parliament from rural Saskatchewan to favor subsidies for farmers.

Nevertheless, it is difficult for a legislator to act as a delegate when constituents are equally divided (about abortion, for example) or when few voters have expressed views about the issue at hand. Many national issues today, such as international trade policy, are often technical or complex, and voters rarely have clear positions. Acting as a delegate is also difficult when the legislator's own views differ from those of his or her constituents.

The Trustee Model Should legislators who deeply believe that abortion or capital punishment is morally unacceptable vote against their own principles when their constituents feel differently? In these or other situations, a legislator may make decisions as his or her own judgment dictates, with little regard for the opinions of constituents. Such a legislator acts as a trustee.

Following the **trustee model**, legislators may reason that the voters selected them not only for their specific campaign promises but also for their wisdom and reasoning ability. To make decisions entirely on the basis of what the constituents say, disregarding one's own judgment would be cheating the constituents out of the best job of representing that the legislator could do. Hence, the trustee acts in accordance with his or her own views of the issues faced in legislative decisions.*

The "Politico" Model Many legislators follow a mixed approach, sometimes called the **politico model**. On some issues and at some times, these legislators will act as delegates; in other situations, they will choose the trustee approach. In both cases they are representing, by some definition, but their behavior is rather different.

Choices among Roles

A legislator's choice of exactly *how* to represent may reflect his or her philosophical position, the political culture of the society, and, of course, the legislator's judgment about the impact that adopting different roles would have on electoral success. For example, if a legislator feels that—by virtue of education, intelligence, or wisdom—he or she is better suited to make public policy choices than is the average citizen, the legislator will naturally tend toward a trustee role. Legislators who see everyone as equally qualified to make judgments will have more sympathy with the delegate model. Different views regarding the basis for government decisions also come into play. Some argue that decisions are largely a matter of scientific study and research, and others emphasize the role of different preferences. The first approach suggests a trustee role, whereas the latter is consistent with the role of delegate.

* An important contemporary political theorist has suggested that a legislative representative in a democracy has a special obligation to be honest. Mark Warren recently wrote that "the representative's role is, in part, to provide citizens with the information they need to judge when they should trust and when they should more actively participate in political decision making. The representative can fill this role only if he is worthy of ... trust in the veracity of his words and deeds. A representative who is not trustworthy in this sense also denies citizens their rightful participation in public judgments." Thus, the ideal representative is honest in revealing his or her stands on policies, and the influences that affect his or her decisions, enabling citizens to judge whether or not the representative is acting in their interests. See Mark Warren, "Democracy and Deceit: Regulating Appearances of Corruption," *American Journal of Political Science* 50 (January 2006): 160–174.

A study of members of the U.S. House of Representatives who pursued a Senate seat suggests that those who were successful in winning elections adopted more of a delegate role than those who were not. Using an innovative research strategy, Wayne Francis and Lawrence Kenny compared the ideological positions of House members' districts with the ideological positions in the whole state; they found that House members who ran successful statewide campaigns for the Senate usually changed their own ideologies to match the ideological position of the state. Those House members seeking Senate seats who maintained the ideological positions common in their home districts more often failed in the statewide election. This evidence argues that successful U.S. legislators frequently act as delegates, strategically adopting their constituents' policy positions.[26]

Party Responsibility and Legislative Behavior

Political parties are critically important in the legislatures of virtually all democracies. Each legislator is usually a member of a party, and all the members from each party form a *caucus*, or *conference*, meeting together from time to time. The relationships among legislators who are members of the same party often have a great impact on what happens in the legislature.

As we discussed in Chapter 5, political parties vary greatly according to their internal cohesion and central control. Not surprisingly, then, there are corresponding differences in the amount of power that different parties wield over their national legislators. In Germany and Great Britain, for example, members of the legislature

© PA/AP Photo

Debate in the British House of Commons　In this image made from television, Members of Parliament attend to a session in the House of Commons, in London, Friday March 11, 2005 during the latest round of debate over the government's controversial anti-terrorism powers.

are quite constrained by party discipline; that is to say, each legislator usually votes on important legislation in accordance with the wishes of his or her party's leadership. In other countries, such as the United States and Italy, party leaders have limited influence on the decisions of their members.

The German and British systems are thus said to have **responsible parties**, meaning that the voters can hold the major parties accountable for their performance because the party position is generally supported by all or most of the legislators from that party. Party discipline and responsible parties are highly valued by many political analysts who contrast that arrangement with the relatively undisciplined parties of the United States.

On first impression, the idea of individual legislators being dominated by their parties' leaders may appear unappealing. Most of us disagree with some positions taken by the parties we support, and it would seem natural and even noble for legislators to act contrary to the "party line" whenever their judgment dictates. However, it is well established among most political scientists that the *absence* of party responsibility leads to very negative consequences. Where party leaders have only limited influence over the policy choices of their members in the legislature, it becomes increasingly likely that legislators will be drawn to represent narrow special interests or will be influenced by large campaign contributions. In contrast, if voters and interest groups realize that party responsibility is strong and that therefore most legislators will vote in accordance with the party leadership's wishes, there is less incentive to try to influence individual members. They will vote the party line, regardless of the influence exerted by lobbyists and contributors.

A recent study of several Latin American countries makes a strong case for party discipline in terms of its effect on national budget management. Two political scientists examined the differences among these countries with respect to the extent to which the "personal vote" was important in determining citizens' choices of legislators. Where the party leadership has the power to control nominations, the "personal vote" is low, and it is high where the leadership is weaker. The researchers predicted that where citizens made voting choices on the basis of *candidates* instead of *parties*, the politicians elected to the legislature had less incentive to concern themselves about the national interest in budget stability, instead demanding spending policies that helped their districts even if they were wasteful in terms of the impact on national economic conditions. The findings confirmed their prediction: countries in which the "personal vote" is a major factor tended to have more severe budget deficits than those in which party responsibility was stronger.[27]

Moreover, the proponents of strong party influence contend that such distractions as a legislator's personality, appearance, or personal habits are less important when voters know that the party effectively controls each legislator's votes. Instead, voters will focus on meaningful policy differences that define the competing parties, making their voting choices on the basis of the policies they prefer. When this happens, most political scientists argue that democracy is on stronger ground, because the citizens' votes communicate what they want government to do, not simply how they feel about candidates' personalities and misadventures.

Three kinds of factors affect the extent to which party responsibility is achieved. First, the cohesion of the "party-in-the-electorate" will affect the degree of party discipline in the legislature. The American Democratic Party through most of the twentieth century is perhaps the most often cited example of a party whose divisions among its supporters often translated into divisions among its members elected to Congress. For decades, the Democrats had great electoral success in the American South (partly because of the legacy of the Republican-led Civil War) while maintaining support among most American liberals in other parts of the country. They were often severely divided as a result, and Democratic members of Congress from Southern states usually voted *against* the wishes of their party's leadership. Many French and Italian parties are also divided for similar reasons. On the other hand, voters supporting the British Labour Party or the Swedish Socialists are, relatively speaking, much less divided on issues, and the party's members in the Parliament vote with much greater unity and discipline.

Second, legislative rules and practices and national laws regarding political parties may be instituted to increase (or decrease) party control. If party leaders are to enforce discipline, they need to be able to apply sanctions that affect the political success of individual legislators. Whenever party organizations can grant or withdraw committee assignments, campaign funds, and national party support for a member's campaign, party discipline is likely to be high. British parties are able to use those and other sanctions, whereas American parties have much less leverage. Particularly since most U.S. legislators know that they must raise large sums of money *on their own* to compete in a close race, they have little reason to abide by the wishes of party leaders on policy questions. Where a legislator's political success depends more on pleasing a few important constituents or interest groups than on following the party platform, party discipline is diminished.

In the United States, the existence of *primaries* is the greatest factor detracting from party responsibility. A primary election is simply an election in which citizens vote to determine which candidate will be the nominee of their party in the *general election,* which usually takes place some months later. Before primaries were instituted (a century ago), party leaders themselves selected the nominees, and they took each potential nominee's loyalty to the party platform into account when selecting him or her as a candidate. When primaries became the main method of selecting nominees, individuals could simply label themselves "Democrats" or "Republicans" and then seek the nomination by winning in the primary. Having won the nomination through this process, the successful candidate owes little to the party leadership. (Outside the United States, this approach to selecting candidates is very rare.)

Finally, party discipline is often self-imposed, since legislators perceive the propriety of voting in accordance with their parties. The strength of tradition supporting party discipline in Great Britain leads many MPs to place great weight on party loyalty, and it affects their behavior even when the specific sanctions enforcing party discipline may not be so critical.

The Changing Role of Modern Legislatures

The role of legislative institutions changed considerably in most industrial democracies during the twentieth century. Legislatures were initially seen as the predominant power center in many democratic governments—as suggested, for example, by the fact that the framers of the U.S. Constitution devoted Article I to the Congress (not the presidency). Before the modern era, ideas for government policy often originated in legislatures themselves, and the executive role was correspondingly much less powerful.

Three related factors have diminished the prominence of legislatures in modern government. First, the growth of bureaucracies—one of the most universal developments of contemporary politics—inevitably displaces some of the influence that legislators would otherwise have in initiating policies. Proposals for new programs and changes in existing programs most often originate in the hundreds of agencies set up to administer the modern state. The size of the bureaucracy in most developed nations makes it unavoidable that **policy initiation** shifts to administrators. This tendency is most pronounced in Japan, France, and other countries in which a highly trained and knowledgeable bureaucracy dominates decisions made by the legislature and the executive. Second, modern government is often complicated by the technological nature of many public policy decisions and programs. Legislators are confronted with a dizzying level of detail and with subject matter about which they, as generalists, necessarily know very little. Legislators must allocate their scarce time and energy to matters of high visibility or high concern to their constituents, and thus most policy decisions are made without the knowledge or the direct participation of elected legislators.

Finally, the growing importance of international cooperation, the global economy, and the increasingly complicated nature of international relations in the modern world inevitably amplify the chief executive's importance in most political systems. Chief executives are necessarily the focal points of foreign policy in most countries, and the importance of international events and relationships thus makes legislatures less dominant than in earlier eras. Nevertheless, legislative institutions remain the most straightforward embodiment of democratic principles.

 WHERE ON THE WEB?

http://www.ipu.org/english/home.htm
The home page for the "Inter-Parliamentary Union," an organization maintaining a tremendous amount of information on parliaments in dozens of countries.

http://www.house.gov
The home page of the U.S. House of Representatives.

http://www.senate.gov
The home page of the U.S. Senate.

http://www.parl.gc.ca/common/index.asp?Language=E
The home page of the Canadian Parliament.

http://www.parliament.uk
The home page of the British Parliament.

http://thomas.loc.gov/home/lawsmade.toc.html
A clear synopsis of the procedural details involved in enacting a bill in the United States.

http://pdba.georgetown.edu/Legislative/legislative.html
The home page of the Legislative Branch Political Database of the Americas, providing basic information on the national legislatures of countries in North, Central, and South America.

http://www.uiowa.edu/~lsq/CLRC%20description.htm
The home page of the University of Iowa's Comparative Legislative Research Center, a research unit established in 1971 to "conduct research on legislative institutions throughout the world." The Center publishes the *Legislative Studies Quarterly*.

◆ ◆ ◆

Key Terms and Concepts ————

bicameralism	ombudsmen
committee system	parliamentary system
constituent service	policy initiation
delegate model	politico model
dual democratic legitimacy	presidential system
folkways	responsible parties
law of 1/n	trustee model

Discussion Questions ————

1. What makes legislative institutions distinctive?
2. What are the arguments for and against bicameralism?
3. Under what circumstances can a presidential system be politically less stable than a parliamentary system?
4. What is party responsibility, and why is it important in legislative behavior?
5. What are some different ways that legislators can claim to "represent" their constituents?

Notes ————

1. This monumental American political novel was written in 1946 by Robert Penn Warren (New York: Harcourt Brace Jovanovich). The quotation appears on pp. 145–146 of this edition. A film based on the book won best picture in 1950, and it was remade in 2006 starring Jude Law, Kate Winslet, and Sean Penn.
2. George Will, *Restoration: Congress, Term Limits, and the Recovery of Deliberative Democracy* (New York: Free Press, 1992), p. 1.
3. Gilman Ostrander, *The Rights of Man in America* (Columbia: University of Missouri Press, 1960), p. 88. For more recent discussions of natural law, see Mark Graham, *Joseph Fuchs on Natural Law* (Washington, DC: Georgetown University Press, 2002), and Jean Porter, *Nature as Reason: A Thomistic Theory of the Natural Law* (Grand Rapids, MI: Wm. B. Erdmans Publishing, 2005).
4. See Nelson W. Polsby, "Legislatures," in *Handbook of Political Science*, eds. Fred I. Greenstein and Nelson Polsby (Reading, MA: Addison-Wesley, 1975), pp. 257–319; and the entry for "legislatures" in *The Blackwell Encyclopedia of Legislative Institutions* (Oxford: Blackwell, 1987), pp. 329–333.
5. Lanny Martin and Georg Vanberg, "Coalition Policymaking and Legislative Review," *American Political Science Review* 99 (February 2005), 93–106.
6. Gregory Mahler, "Israel's New Electoral System: Effects on Politics and Policy," *Middle East Review of International Affairs* 1 (July 1997).
7. Ibid.
8. Emanuele Ottolenghi, "Why Direct Election Failed in Israel," *Journal of Democracy* 12 (2001): 108–109.
9. Juan J. Linz, "Presidential or Parliamentary Democracy: Does It Make a Difference?" in *The Failure of Presidential Democracy: The Case of Latin America*, eds. Juan Linz and Arturo Valenzuela (Baltimore: Johns Hopkins University Press, 1994), pp. 3–90.
10. Ibid.
11. Arturo Valenzuela, "Party Politics and the Crisis of Presidentialism in Chile: A Proposal for a Parliamentary Form of Government," in *The Failure of Presidential Democracy: The Case of Latin America*, eds. Juan Linz and Arturo Valenzuela (Baltimore: Johns Hopkins University Press, 1994), p. 141.

12. See Sherzod Abdukadirov. "The Impact of Institutional Design on Non-Democratic Regimes: A Case for Parliamentary System in Central Asia?" (Paper presented at the annual meeting of the Midwest Political Science Association, Palmer House Hotel, Chicago, IL, April 12, 2007).
13. Scott Mainwaring, "Brazil: Weak Parties, Feckless Democracy," in *Building Democratic Institutions: Party Systems in Latin America*, eds. Scott Mainwaring and Timothy R. Scully (Stanford, CA: Stanford University Press, 1994), p. 392. See also Tsebelis, G., "Decision Making in Political Systems: Veto Players in Presidentialism, Parliamentarism, Multicameralism, and Multipartyism," *British Journal of Political Science* 25 (1995): 289–325.
14. Leiv Marsteintredet and Einar Berntzen, "Latin American Presidentialism: Reducing the Perils of Presidentialism Through Presidential Interruptions." (Paper prepared for the Workshop "Parliamentary Practices in Presidential Systems: (European) Perspectives on Parliamentary Power in Latin America," European Consortium for Political Research Joint Sessions of Workshops, Nicosia, Cyprus, April 25–30, 2006.)
15. Mona Lyne. "The Voter's Dilemma and the Presidential-Parliamentary Debate: A General Electoral Theory of Legislative Conflict and Cooperation." (Paper presented at the annual meeting of the American Political Science Association, Marriott Wardman Park, Omni Shoreham, Washington Hilton, Washington, DC, September 1, 2005).
16. See Mark P. Jones, Sebastian Saiegh, Pablo T. Spiller, and Mariano Tommasi, "Amateur Legislators—Professional Politicians: The Consequences of Party-Centered Electoral Rules in a Federal System," *American Journal of Political Science* 46 (July 2002): 656–669.
17. Woodrow Wilson, *Congressional Government* (Boston: Houghton Mifflin, 1885), p. 57.
18. The idea was formalized by Weingast, Barry R., Kenneth A. Shepsle, and Christopher Johnsen, "The Political Economy of Benefits and Costs: A Neoclassical Approach to Distributive Politics," *Journal of Political Economy* 89 (August 1981): 642–664.
19. Bradbury, John C., and William M. Crain. "Legislative Organization and Government Spending: Cross-Country Evidence," *Journal of Public Economics* 82 (December 2001): 309–325.
20. Chen, Jowei and Neil Malhotra. "The Law of k/n: The Effect of Chamber Size on Government Spending in Bicameral Legislatures," *American Political Science Review* 101 (November 2007): 657–676. See David M. Primo and James M. Snyder, Jr. "Distributive Politics and the Law of 1/n." *Journal of Politics* 70 (2008): 477–486.
21. See Andrew Reynolds, "Women in the Legislatures and Executives of the World: Knocking at the Highest Glass Ceiling," *World Politics* 51(1999): 547–572; Lane Kenworthy and Melissa Malami, "Gender Inequality in Political Representation: A Worldwide Comparative Analysis," *Social Forces* 78 (1999): 235–269; and Alan Siaroff, "Women's Representation in Legislatures and Cabinets in Industrial Democracies," *International Political Science Review* 21 (2000): 197–215.
22. Donald R. Matthews, *U.S. Senators and Their World* (New York: Random House, 1960).
23. Ibid., pp. 93–94.
24. David W. Rohde, Norman J. Ornstein, and Robert L. Peabody, "Political Change and Legislative Norms in the U.S. Senate, 1957–1974," in *Studies of Congress*, ed. Glenn R. Parker (Washington, DC: CQ Press, 1985), p. 150.
25. Thomas Stratmann and Martin Baur, "Plurality Rule, Proportional Representation, and the German *Bundestag*: How Incentives to Pork-Barrel Differ Across Electoral Systems," *American Journal of Political Science* 46 (July 2002): 506–514.
26. See Wayne L. Francis and Lawrence W. Kenny, "Position Shifting in Pursuit of Higher Office," *American Journal of Political Science* 40 (August 1996): 768–786.
27. Mark Hallerberg and Patrik Marier, "Executive Authority, the Personal Vote, and Budget Discipline in Latin American and Caribbean Countries," *American Journal of Political Science* 48 (July 2004): 571–587.

For Further Reading

Bauman, Richard, and Tsvi Kahana. *The Least Examined Branch: The Role of Legislatures in the Constitutional State*. New York: Cambridge University Press, 2006.
Copeland, Gary W., and Samuel Patterson. *Parliaments in the Modern World: Changing Institutions*. Ann Arbor: University of Michigan Press, 1994.
Cotta, Maurizio and Heinrich Best. *Democratic Representation in Europe: Diversity, Change, and Convergence*. Oxford, U.K.: Oxford University Press, 2008.
Davidson, Roger H., and Walter J. Oleszek. *Congress and Its Members*, 9th ed. Washington, DC: CQ Press, 2003.
Davidson-Schmich, Louise K. *Becoming Party Politicians: East German State Legislators in the Decade Following Democratization*. South Bend, IN: Notre Dame University Press, 2006.

Dodd, Lawrence C., and Bruce I. Oppenheimer. *Congress Reconsidered*, 8th ed. Washington, DC: CQ Press, 2004.

Doring, Herbert. *Parliaments and Majority Rule in Western Europe*. New York: St. Martin's, 1995.

Duch, Raymond M., and Randolph T. Stevenson. *The Economic Vote: How Political and Economic Institutions Condition Election Results*. Cambridge, U.K.: Cambridge University Press, 2008.

Hix, Simon, Abdul G. Noury, and Gerard Roland. *Democratic Politics in the European Parliament*. Cambridge, U.K.: Cambridge University Press, 2007.

Huber, John D. *Rationalizing Parliament: Legislative Institutions and Party Politics in France*. Cambridge, U.K.: Cambridge University Press, 2008.

Jones, Mark P., Sebastian Saiegh, Pablo T. Spiller, and Mariano Tommasi. "Amateur Legislators—Professional Politicians: The Consequences of Party-Centered Electoral Rules in a Federal System." *American Journal of Political Science* 46 (July 2002): 656–669.

Leston-Bandiera, Cristina. *Southern European Parliaments in Democracy*. Oxford, UK: Routledge, 2005.

Loewenberg, Gerhard, D. Roderick Kiewiet, and Peverill Squire, eds. *Legislatures: Comparative Perspectives on Representative Assemblies*. Ann Arbor: University of Michigan Press, 2002.

Londregan, John B. *Legislative Institutions and Ideology in Chile*. New York: Cambridge University Press, 2007.

Muller, Wolfgang C., and Kaare Strom, eds. *Coalition Governments in Western Europe*. Oxford: Oxford University Press, 2000.

Oleszek, Walter J. *Congressional Procedures and Policy Processes*, 6th ed. Washington, DC: CQ Press, 2003.

Pitkin, Hannah F. *The Concept of Representation*. Berkeley and Los Angeles: University of California Press, 1972.

Remington, Thomas F. *Parliaments in Transition: The New Legislative Politics in the Former USSR and Eastern Europe*. Boulder, CO: Westview, 1994.

Schofield, Norman, and Itai Sened. *Multi-Party Democracy: Parties, Elections, and Legislative Politics*. New York: Cambridge University Press, 2006.

Troxel, Tiffany. *Parliamentary Power in Russia, 1994–2001: A New Era*. New York: Palgrave/Macmillan, 2003.

Warren, Mark. "Democracy and Deceit: Regulating Appearances of Corruption," *American Journal of Political Science* 50 (January 2006): 160–174.

Volden, Craig and Alan E. Wiseman. "Bargaining in Legislatures over Particularistic and Collective Goods," *American Political Science Review* 101 (February 2007): 79–92.

THE FRENCH PRESIDENT IN THE BRITISH PARLIAMENT   As his wife, Carla Bruni-Sarkozy, looks on, French President Nicolas Sarkozy speaks to the British parliament during a state visit on March 26, 2008.

8

EXECUTIVE INSTITUTIONS AND POLITICAL LEADERSHIP

◆ The Functions of Executive Institutions ◆ Kinds of Executive Institutions ◆ Limits on Executive Power ◆ Approaches to Executive Leadership ◆ Conclusion: The Evolving Challenges of Executive Power

In nearly all political systems, the chief executive officer is the most widely recognized and most powerful governmental figure. Although the importance of legislatures varies greatly across different kinds of governments, the chief executive is prominent in both developed and developing nations. He or she is the focus of media attention, the villain when economies and foreign relations go sour, and the hero when the country experiences success. We even name periods of time in a nation's history after chief executives (the "Thatcher years" in Britain, the "Clinton era" in the U.S.).

It is perhaps ironic, then, that a major theme found in studies of executive institutions is that executive power is limited and constrained in so many ways. Although executives have more authority than individual legislators, and although their actions usually have tremendously greater impact, a typical legislator or judge enjoys greater freedom in decision making. Particularly in modern societies, chief executives are burdened with daunting responsibilities and complicated, frustrating restraints.

This chapter's discussion of the executive is divided into two parts. First, we will examine the nature and functions of the executive *institution* in modern political systems. Second, we will discuss the important concept of *leadership*.

THE FUNCTIONS OF EXECUTIVE INSTITUTIONS

Deliberation and action are naturally contrasting processes. Legislative institutions are well designed for deliberation. They provide a setting in which opposing points of view may be expressed and debated, and they usually facilitate detailed consideration of major policy decisions through committee and staff activities. Yet the same feature that makes them ideally suited to deliberate—the sharing of power among a large number of representatives with diverse perspectives—weakens their abilities to carry out programs and policies. The nearly universal establishment of executive institutions reflects the need to place responsibility for deliberation and policy execution in different institutions. At the same time, there is often considerable tension and competition between a government's executive and legislative branches, because each tends to involve itself in functions that the other considers to be its own.

Identifying the tasks that most naturally fall to executive institutions is helpful in understanding their special nature and how they differ from legislative institutions. All these tasks have one aspect in common: *They are best accomplished under the authority of a coherent, unified institution empowered to act quickly and decisively.*

Diplomacy

It is widely recognized, even by legislators, that **diplomacy** must be primarily under executive control. Although the German *Bundestag* may hold debates on trade policy and issues raised at the United Nations, the day-to-day implementation of foreign policy is the responsibility of the German Chancellor and her advisers. For one thing, diplomacy often involves negotiation, and it is all but impossible for a multi-member legislature to negotiate with another country. The give-and-take of effective negotiation requires that the decision maker be able to respond quickly and decisively to new demands and concessions from the other side, and legislatures simply cannot work with sufficient coherence or quickness.

Secrecy is a more controversial rationale for the central executive role in diplomacy, but most observers accept it in some measure. The delicate maneuvering of former Secretary of State Colin Powell during the months following the September 11, 2001 attacks on the United States was necessarily done behind closed doors as he worked to build a multinational coalition to fight the Taliban and Al Qaeda in Afghanistan. There have been several instances in which American, French, and British executives, among others, have worked to win the release of hostages, and secrecy was critical in each case. In such situations, the other side could never be allowed to know what concessions he may or may not have been ready to make. And sometimes even the idea that negotiations are underway produces a public reaction that destroys the proceedings. Although executive control of diplomacy does not prevent all "leaks," most observers feel that diplomacy would be severely hampered if a multi-member legislature were in charge.

Even when secrecy is not an issue, diplomatic communication is simpler when only executive officials are involved. Summit meetings provide an opportunity for political leaders to explore mutual concerns, and these events often lay the foundation for more formal treaty negotiations. The flexible, personal communication that makes summits productive can take place only among executives and their staffs. Moreover, in case of an international crisis, some single official must be clearly designated as the person to contact.

Emergency Leadership

All countries need **emergency leadership** from time to time, and it is almost always the responsibility of the chief executive to coordinate and manage the governmental response. The executive can act quickly, and he or she is in a position to coordinate governmental activities.

Executives manage relief efforts when earthquakes, floods, or hurricanes occur, but they also take charge when the nation is *critically* threatened. It is during these episodes that we encounter a second justification for the executive's role in emergencies. National security sometimes requires extraordinary actions, some of which might not be acceptable or even legal under normal conditions. Most well-known, perhaps, was U.S. President Abraham Lincoln's suspension of some basic constitutional rights during the Civil War. When that kind of emergency action is necessary, only the executive has the legitimacy needed to make critical decisions. In the aftermath of September 11, actions taken to strengthen domestic security by President George W. Bush's first attorney general, John Ashcroft, were controversial as well, with many citizens claiming that constitutional protections were weakened.

In the developing world, chief executives often cite real or perceived dangers and emergencies to justify their power. Third World leaders often defend tyrannical powers by pointing to the challenges of economic development and the threat of political instability. The same holds when developing countries are involved in war (Iran and Iraq, for example) or are threatened by outside intervention (Nicaragua).

Box 8-1

The Dilemmas of Executive Branch Secrecy in Wartime: A Tragic Incident in World War II

Early in World War II, British intelligence officials successfully developed the capacity to decipher coded communications from German military sources. A Polish mathematician, Marian Rejewski, had employed advanced mathematics as early as 1932 to break code from Enigma, the name the Allies gave to the early German code machine, and he shared this information with the British in the years leading up to the war's outbreak in 1939. The British thus had access to German communications, obtaining information about where U-Boats were deployed, German invasion plans, and, eventually, Luftwaffe bombing targets.

Prime Minister Winston Churchill was keenly interested in the information obtained from the German code system. However, he was also aware that he could never permit the Germans to learn that the British had succeeded in breaking it. If German officials realized that the British had succeeded in gaining access to top secret German military communications, they would change their code, and it would then be worthless to the British. The dilemma was stark: Churchill desperately wanted continued access to the intelligence, but he could not take actions that revealed to the Germans that he had broken their codes.

The British worked out methods to conceal that they had broken the code while still acting on the secrets they had obtained. For example, when they learned where some German submarines or supply ships were headed, they were careful not to use air strikes against them unless they could do something to make the Germans believe that the British had learned about the location of the German ships through some method other than intercepting coded messages. Sometimes Churchill ordered British scout planes to fly in areas where German observers would see them, creating the impression that it was a lucky sighting by one of these planes that led to the sinking of German ships by British air strikes.

The most controversial decision that Churchill made regarding the German codes had to do with the German bombing of the town of Coventry in November 1940. Frederick Winterbotham, in a 1974 book entitled *The Ultra Secret*, reported that Churchill had knowledge of the German bombing raid on Coventry some 48 hours before the attack occurred. There was certainly time to evacuate much of the city and to take measures to avert the bombing. However, doing so would have alerted the Germans that their codes

© AP Photo

Coventry Cathedral lies in ruins November 16, 1940, after the Nazi bombing attack of November 14 on Coventry, England. The entire roof was brought down in heaps of debris, foreground, by the high explosive.

had been broken. According to Winterbotham's account, Churchill refused to alert the city. The bombings took place, killing more than 1,200 people and destroying over 4,000 homes.

Some historians (see the books by Peter Calvocoressi and Ronald Lewin, noted below) argue that the German communication that the British had intercepted was not as clear about Coventry being a target as has been often claimed. There may have been some doubt in Churchill's mind about whether Coventry was really the target, and thus it may have been this doubt that prevented him from ordering an evacuation. However, it is clear that Churchill placed a very high priority on preventing the Germans from learning that his intelligence service had broken their codes, and it is quite possible that he withheld information that could have minimized the loss of life from some attacks. On the other hand, most historians conclude that the British success in keeping Germany from learning about their success in code breaking may have shortened the war by as much as a year. But the dilemma created by the need for secrecy has rarely been as excruciating as it was in this case.

See Frederick Winterbotham, *The Ultra Secret*, New York: HarperCollins, 1974; Peter Calvocoressi, *Top Secret Ultra*, New York: Pantheon Books, 1980; and Ronald Lewin, *Ultra Goes to War*, New York: McGraw-Hill, 1978, for more about this famous example of military secrecy.

Budget Formulation

A government budget has been called a set of "goals with price tags attached."[1] In most countries **budget formulation**, or at least a budget proposal, is an executive responsibility, and for very good reasons. Legislators represent specific states, provinces, or constituencies and often develop close ties with a few groups or interests. Strictly speaking, it would not be *rational* for a legislator to consider the benefits and the costs of a spending decision from a national perspective.* When a particular expenditure is targeted for his or her state or district, that legislator's judgment will be driven by a key fact: *His or her constituents will receive virtually all of the benefit created by the expenditure while paying only a small portion of the costs* (since those are divided among the whole nation's taxpayers). Because all legislators face these same facts, it is not realistic to expect them to pursue fiscal responsibility in budget decisions.

The need for executive responsibility for the budget proposal became all too clear in the United States during the early years of the twentieth century. Before 1921, the budget of the United States was simply a patchwork quilt of unrelated acts of Congress that authorized expenditures and established tax rates. The budget process was uncoordinated and ultimately irresponsible. It was as though a family decided to let the husband buy the car, the wife buy the house, and the children buy the food and the furniture—all working with no information about what the others were spending. Even members of the U.S. Congress agreed that the central control of budget preparation was needed, and the Budget Act of 1921 was passed, creating a new executive power.[†]

Control of Military Forces

In many, but not all, countries the chief executive is the person primarily in charge of the armed forces. Chief executives are rarely empowered to direct the military on their own—the British prime minister normally must obtain the support of his or her cabinet when committing the armed forces, for example. And, after the 1973 War Powers Act was adopted, the U.S. Congress was empowered to cut off funding for military activities that extend beyond a 60-day period. Nevertheless, the chief executive has a central role in control of military forces virtually everywhere. There can be no ambiguity regarding the authority to act if a situation demands a military response, or even if the threat of a response is important.

Investing the chief executive with supreme authority over the military is important for domestic reasons as well. In less politically developed nations, military leaders have frequently seized government power through **coups d'état**. When the troops' first loyalty is to their officers, military leaders can often displace the civilian government on the grounds that national security demands it. In some cases, a chief executive's very attempt to assert control over the military leads to his or her overthrow by a military coup. (See Box 8-2.)

Chief Administrator

Most chief executives also are **chief administrators**; they have primary responsibility for managing the agencies that implement government programs and laws. Some central authority must be in charge of staffing, accounting for, planning, and coordinating

* See Box 7-2 in Chapter 7 discussing the "law of 1/*n*."

† It should be noted, however, that the U.S. president's budget proposal still must be enacted by Congress; the president simply proposes a comprehensive budget.

Box 8-2

THE MILITARY AND THE CHIEF EXECUTIVE IN HAITI

Haiti illustrates the way in which chief executives in weak political systems are often toppled by their military establishments. In 1986, President Jean-Claude Duvalier (1971–1986) was ousted from power by a popular uprising that brought to an end a corrupt and repressive dictatorship begun by Duvalier's father, FranÁois (1957–1971). In the absence of a strong political order to replace the old dictatorships, however, chief executives have been at the mercy of the military. During the four years following Duvalier's fall, the country experienced a series of military coups and an abortive election. Finally, in 1990, Father Jean-Bertrand Aristide won a landslide victory to become Haiti's first democratically elected president in an election that was widely perceived as relatively fair and open.

Yet, despite Aristide's tremendous support among the Haitian masses, the military ousted him in September 1991, less than one year after he had taken office. A major element contributing to his removal was his plan to create a Palace Guard that he would control directly, giving him independence from the military. Following his ouster, Aristide was in exile in the U.S. Thousands of Haitians were killed under the subsequent military rule, and over 40,000 Haitians attempting to leave by boat were rescued at sea by the U.S. Coast Guard. The United States and the Organization of American States placed an embargo on trade with Haiti in an attempt to bring the president back.

In September 1994, the U.S. led a multinational force to restore Haiti to a democratic government. Haiti's military leaders agreed to step down, and by October 15 Aristide had been restored to power. Following elections in 1995, Rene Preval was elected (Aristide was constitutionally barred from running for re-election), and Haiti had its first democratic transition between two elected presidents.

However, the political situation did not remain settled very long. Elections in 2000 returned Aristide

to office, although it is estimated that only some 5 percent of Haitians went to the ballot box. With severe economic deterioration taking place, political instability and violence mounted, and in 2004 a rebel group advanced on the capital. Aristide resigned and left the country, and the Chief Justice of the Haitian Supreme Court became president. Relatively peaceful elections took place in February 2006, and Rene Preval, allegedly a protégé of Aristide, won a close victory.

There was considerable optimism regarding President Preval's administration, but recent food shortages and other economic problems, coupled with his apparent efforts to change the Haitian constitution to enhance his power, have created new troubles. In June 2008, Preval had to nominate a Prime Minister to succeed Edouard Alexis, who had been removed from office by the parliament following the government's failure to address the increasingly severe food crisis. Parliament then twice rejected Preval's choices to succeed Alexis, leaving the government in turmoil and paralysis. During the same month there was a mostly peaceful demonstration in the streets of Port-Au-Prince to protest a continued wave of kidnappings. According to a Reuters report, the demonstrators shouted "Kill the kidnappers and arrest corrupt judges who release them in exchange for money," as they gathered outside the Justice Palace.[2]

Developments in the next several years will indicate whether or not Haiti has made real progress toward political stability. Its troubled and violent recent past shows, among other things, that chief executives in weak, unsettled governments can be quickly undermined by military rule. (For more information on Haiti's government and politics, see Robert I. Rotberg, *Haiti's Turmoil: Politics and Policy under Aristide and Clinton*, Cambridge, MA: World Peace Foundation, 2003; and Paul Farmer, *Uses of Haiti*, Monroe, ME: Common Courage Press, 2006.)

---

the activities of many diverse agencies. Legislatures are ill suited to those tasks for the same reasons that they cannot effectively direct diplomacy or overall budget formulation: Sound management requires a comprehensive, coherent authoritative voice that multi-member legislatures do not have.

Moreover, their managerial duties inevitably give chief executives opportunities to change policies. When appointing officials to direct agencies, a chief executive selects individuals who share his or her policy preferences and who can act on those preferences in setting agency priorities. Every new American president, for example, appoints hundreds of high-ranking federal officials. Even when the powers and duties of executive-branch agencies are established by legislation, there are usually numerous opportunities for interpretation, prioritizing, and setting new initiatives within the framework of that legislation. The executive can therefore shape policy by making key appointments to the bureaucracy.

In Great Britain and in several other European nations, the chief executive has greater control of appointment power than in the United States, where the independently elected Congress must approve many important appointments. This is, in part, because executive and legislative power typically is merged in most other democracies (the prime minister is elected or confirmed by the parliament) and the notions of separation of powers, and checks and balances are not well developed. Also, in Third World nations, with typically weak legislatures, the executive has a fairly free hand in making appointments.

Although the specific features of executive powers to manage administrative agencies vary across different systems, the main point is that those powers inevitably give the executive opportunities to shape policy. The strongest executives exploit those opportunities to the fullest, applying their powers to advance their political preferences and to secure their continued support. It is simply not possible to grant a chief executive comprehensive authority to manage without also giving him or her at least some power to affect policy itself.

Policy Initiation

Although legislative action establishes government policy in most systems, the chief executive in nearly all systems plays a prominent role in initiating policy. In Great Britain, all important policies are initiated by the prime minister and the cabinet. A similar relationship exists in other parliamentary democracies, such as Germany and Canada. In Third World countries, legislatures tend to be thoroughly dominated by the executive branch. Even the U.S. president, who often faces a Congress dominated by the opposing party, is called the *chief legislator*, since most bills that become laws begin as presidential proposals.

Symbolic Leadership

Chief executives also act as **symbolic leaders** of their countries, a role that transcends their specific powers and functions. In times of crisis, it is easier to look to a specific human being as leader than to look to a committee or an assembly.

Charles de Gaulle galvanized the French and forestalled national disintegration in 1958 when France was rocked by a constitutional crisis and unrest in Algeria, and Winston Churchill effectively motivated and unified the British during World War II, as did Franklin D. Roosevelt in the United States during the Great Depression and through all but the last months of the same war. In each instance, those countries needed strong leaders to rally the loyalty and energy of their citizens, and their chief executives led them as no other public figures could have. More recently, some Third World leaders have become symbols to their people of the struggle for democracy. Two noteworthy examples are South Africa's Nelson Mandela and Myanmar's Daw Aung San Suu Kyi (a Nobel Peace Prize winner whom the military arrested and prevented from becoming Prime Minister after her party won a parliamentary majority in 1990).

Kinds of Executive Institutions

Although each country's chief executive is unique in some respects, all can be usefully classified on the basis of two characteristics: the way in which they are selected, and their relationship to the legislature. These factors have a great bearing on how powerful the executive is and on how he or she performs executive functions.

Hereditary Monarchies

There are only some three dozen countries that currently have hereditary monarchs, and in many of those the monarchy has only a ceremonial or a symbolic role. All hereditary monarchs draw, to some degree, on **traditional authority**. Because they are selected on the basis of their parents' identities, there is usually little doubt about which person succeeds the current monarch. This is one of the benefits of the hereditary monarch system: the clear line of succession means that violent clashes over leadership can be avoided when a reigning monarch dies.

Although the hereditary monarch was the most typical chief executive in premodern times, monarchy has largely been eclipsed by more democratic types of executives. Modern political life involves widespread public involvement and participation, and—although that does not always make democracy inevitable—the chief executive must increasingly be seen as legitimate in ways that hereditary monarchs cannot be. Political history is thus filled with rejections of monarchy, including not only the American, French, and Russian revolutions but also the fall of the German Kaiser and the Shah of Iran.

Surviving hereditary monarchies are typically required to share power with legislative assemblies. Classic monarchies assumed power over all government functions, including lawmaking and even judging, but that simple arrangement has all but vanished. The monarch's powers in Great Britain, Belgium, the Netherlands, Sweden, and Norway have been lost, making them largely ceremonial. Monarchs have maintained substantial political authority in only a few countries, most notably in Morocco, Jordan, Saudi Arabia, and Kuwait.

Directly Elected Chief Executives

The presidents of Mexico, Colombia, the Philippines, the United States, and France are examples of directly elected chief executives. This method of selection creates a potentially powerful institution, because the executive is then normally the only official chosen by the entire nation's electorate. (In fact, the French president is sometimes referred to as an "elected monarch" to underscore the tremendous powers he enjoys.) No individual legislator or judge can claim the legitimacy accorded to a directly elected chief executive.

Chief Executives in Parliamentary Systems

As noted in the previous chapter, the parliamentary system is the most common form of democratic government. The chief executive in such a system is elected not by the citizens but by the members of the legislature. Since the same parliamentary majority that selects its leader as prime minister is also able (by definition) to enact legislative proposals, parliamentary chief executives may be far less constrained by

DIPLOMACY AMONG ALLIES In this photo, Israeli Prime Minister Ehud Olmert speaks with U.S. Secretary of State Condoleezza Rice prior to their meeting at the Prime Minister's residence in Jerusalem, March 4, 2008.

legislative preferences. However, as we discussed in Chapter 7, a chief executive in a parliamentary system sitting atop a shifting and uncertain multiparty coalition in the legislature can be less secure than an independently elected chief executive who has to enact policy through a separate legislative branch.*

Nondemocratic Executive Institutions

Executives tend to be strong in industrialized democracies because the executive office in such systems is at the center of a tremendous array of public programs and institutions and because these executives are highly visible in the mass media. Executive power is also dominant in developing societies, but for different reasons. Sometimes an executive is the national leader of an all-powerful ruling party, while in other cases he or she secures power by controlling the country's military forces. As we have seen, chief executives may be former heroes of wars for independence or revolution (Vietnam's Ho Chi Minh or China's Mao Zedong) or may have power and prestige by virtue of a religious position (most notably, Ayatollah Khomeini, who founded an Islamic state in Iran in 1979 and ruled there until his death ten years later). In many of these cases, the individual is more of a national leader than a true executive, perhaps performing the function of symbolic leadership but otherwise having little to do with

* Of course, other factors—such as culture, a candidate's personality, and foreign policy events—are also involved in determining how often the executive office changes hands. Israel has one of the most fractionalized party systems in the democratic world, but it has had only eight prime ministers. Israeli coalitions tend to stay together longer partly because of the perceived threat from the country's neighbors.

essential executive functions, which may be performed by other, less visible members of the executive establishment.

Moreover, legislative and judicial institutions are often less influential in nondemocratic and developing nations. They generally have less legitimacy, and many of them have been changed so often that they have not become an established part of the government. The executive, by contrast, is able to apply force and to personify the traditions and values of the dominant culture. Some twenty nations have no legislative assemblies at all, and many others have notoriously weak legislatures. The executive is thus dominant in these systems because the other institutions of government are weak and undeveloped. In the Third World, government power is primarily *executive* power.

LIMITS ON EXECUTIVE POWER

Despite the substantial authority that they hold, executives in most countries—particularly executives in democratic systems—face limits on their power. In a leading study of the U.S. presidency, Richard Neustadt concluded that, even with all the president's legal and political powers, presidential power is simply the "power to persuade."[3] President Harry Truman certainly understood this when he chuckled over the likely experiences of his successor, General Dwight Eisenhower: "He'll sit here," Truman would remark (tapping his desk for emphasis), "and he'll say, 'Do this! Do that!' *And nothing will happen.* Poor Ike—It won't be a bit like the Army. He'll find it very frustrating."[4] Chief executives in other nations have doubtless had the same experience. Having achieved the most sought-after position in their countries, they often conclude that their powers are nothing like what they imagined. In 1986, Corazón Aquino was elected president of the Philippines with the help of a peaceful popular uprising. Her courage in the wake of her husband's assassination and her commitment to democracy and nonviolence made her a hero throughout the world. Once in office, however, she was virtually powerless against the entrenched influence of the military, opposition political cliques, and business and landowning interests.

Of course, some executives are more powerful than others, but the phenomenon of limited executive power is nearly universal. Why is the power of modern executives so often a limited commodity?

Term Limits

The length and number of terms for many chief executives are restricted by constitutions or basic laws. The Twenty-Second Amendment to the U.S. Constitution (ratified on March 1, 1951) limits the president to two four-year terms. Many Latin American nations—including Mexico, Venezuela, El Salvador, Uruguay, and Chile—limit their presidents to one term. Near the end of that term limit, the incumbent often sees his or her influence diminish somewhat, since the power to reward and punish supporters is coming to an end. (This is often termed the "lame duck" period.) The French president may serve two long (seven-year) terms, making that position potentially more powerful.

Sources of Power as Limits

To maintain authority, executives are often required to make certain choices. An executive whose power is based on personal charisma, for example, finds it necessary to spend precious time and energy reinforcing the public's favorable perceptions. An executive whose authority is based primarily on citizens' respect for the law must avoid even the appearance of acting illegally, yet he or she will often find that those very laws restrict policy choices. The same point could be made about executives who draw their power from tradition or a sense of representativeness; they must continuously monitor the extent to which their actions erode the favorable perceptions that made their positions possible. Even a dictator holding power exclusively through military coercion avoids making choices that disturb the armed forces.

Examples abound of executives who lost power by exceeding these limits. While much of the world is familiar with controversies about U.S. presidents being accused of abusing their powers (Richard Nixon, Ronald Reagan, Bill Clinton, and George W. Bush can all be placed in this category), it is not only or even primarily an American phenomenon. In 2006, Thailand's Prime Minister Thaksin Shinawatra was in serious trouble despite having won a landslide election in 2005. He was accused of corruption, abuse of power, tax evasion, censoring the media, and other crimes. In the last decade, top executive officials have been in serious legal and political trouble in Kuwait, South Korea, Spain, Haiti, Italy, South Africa, and Mexico.

During the 1980s, Mikhail Gorbachev's policies of *glasnost* (openness) and *perestroika* (social and economic restructuring) in the last years of the Soviet Union ultimately undermined the authority of the Communist Party (which he also headed), leaving him virtually no basis of authority when living standards began to decline.

Thus, although most political executives have several sources of authority, maintaining power requires that they act in a prescribed manner. Their powers come with strings attached, and the most successful executives recognize that fact.

Governmental Institutions as Limits

A key characteristic of developed political systems is *institutional complexity*. Although most chief executives have formal authority over an array of institutions, the impression that one gets from looking at the "organizational chart"—that the executive's command is extensive and profound—is often misleading. Legislatures, agencies, courts, and commissions make modern, effective government possible, but they also check and constrain executive power.

For one thing, many government institutions have their own missions and often their own clientele interests. Legislators represent constituents or subnational units, and agencies are often associated with distinct groups (such as farmers, labor unions, business organizations). Executives encounter resistance when they make policy choices that undermine the interests represented by those institutions.

Even where the executive's legal authority is clear, government institutions typically have many opportunities to delay or obstruct executive wishes. Moreover, as we discuss in Chapter 10, government agencies normally develop "standard operating procedures" that become rigid over time. Executive directives that require a departure from bureaucratic routines often cause conflict and a breakdown of coordination.

In short, the wide range of institutions that a chief executive supervises constitutes only partly controllable forces that must be accommodated to make and implement policy. They are in place—with their established ways of operating and their associated interests—long before a particular executive assumes office. He or she cannot treat those institutions as "blank slates" on which new programs and policy changes can be written. Even authoritarian political leaders usually have to pay heed to powerful institutions such as the military, organized business groups, established party leaders, and the clergy.

In developing political systems, the chief executive typically deals with a smaller number of much weaker institutions. Legislatures, courts, and bureaucratic agencies usually exist, but they are normally much less influential, and citizens accord them much less respect as institutions. In a sense, chief executives in developing systems enjoy a greater latitude and freedom of decision than do their counterparts in the developed world. At the same time, the absence of effective governmental institutions limits the range and effect of what executives can accomplish. In short, when compared with their counterparts in developed nations, Third World executives are frequently stronger figures in weaker governments.

The Mass Media and Executive Power

Newspapers, radio, and television can serve as tools of executive power, and they can also severely limit it. As noted in Chapter 4, when the mass media are under the control of the government, they can be used to shape public sentiments and set the political agenda in ways helpful to those in power. Lenin, always an astute organizer and motivator of people, realized that a national newspaper could be a central tool in creating and maintaining support. The paper he established for Soviet citizens, *Pravda*, means "truth," although it was always far more concerned with ideological instruction than with accuracy. The Nazis in Germany—along with Marxist governments in China, North Korea, Cuba, and elsewhere—similarly have used the mass media as a force for strengthening the power of the political leadership.

In contrast, when the mass media are controlled by a diverse range of voices, "press reaction" can affect a chief executive's power position in a significant way. In 2003, British Prime Minister Tony Blair felt the impact of the media when a government expert on weapons, David Kelly, apparently killed himself after he was named as the source of a BBC story reporting that British analysis of weapons of mass destruction in Iraq had been intentionally distorted. The story, and the resulting suicide, considerably undermined Blair's authority.

Blair's experience with British newspapers and television coverage of his government led him to make some remarkably bitter statements. As he was leaving office in 2007, he gave a speech on the media. The following excerpts reveal a chief executive who had keenly felt the impact of journalists during his time in office:

> I am going to say something that few people in public life will say, but most know is absolutely true: a vast aspect of our jobs today—outside of the really major decisions, as big as anything else—is coping with the media, its sheer scale, weight and constant hyperactivity. At points, it literally overwhelms. Talk to senior people in virtually any walk of life today—business, military, public services, sport, even charities and voluntary organisations and they will tell you the same. People don't speak about it because, in the main, they are afraid to. But it is true, nonetheless, and those who have been around long enough, will also say it has changed significantly in the past years.
>
>   . . . the fear of missing out means today's media, more than ever before, hunts in a pack. In these modes it is like a feral beast, just tearing people and reputations to bits. But no-one dares miss out.

THE SHOT SEEN ROUND THE WORLD   Nguyen Ngoc Loan, then National Police Chief in South Vietnam, is shown executing a prisoner suspected of being a Viet Cong collaborator in 1968. The visual impact of this photo, among many others, reduced U.S. popular support for the war effort.

> I do believe this relationship between public life and media is now damaged in a manner that requires repair. The damage saps the country's confidence and self-belief; it undermines its assessment of itself, its institutions; and above all, it reduces our capacity to take the right decisions, in the right spirit for our future.[5]

The explosion of Internet technology and an army of "bloggers" in many countries make it increasingly difficult for any monopoly control of information to be secure. Chief executives cannot assume that their secrets will remain undercover when so many people have the ability to share information with millions of citizens almost instantly. As a result, media management has become a critically important skill for modern chief executives.

APPROACHES TO EXECUTIVE LEADERSHIP

The basic executive functions can be performed in widely different ways. Adolf Hitler, Franklin Roosevelt, Margaret Thatcher, Charles de Gaulle, and Saddam Hussein all performed at least many of the tasks of political executives, and all left a mark on history. Yet as leaders, they had little in common. Every chief executive is unique, of course, and each faces distinctive problems and challenges, making it difficult to generalize. Nevertheless, we can identify some important factors that affect the ways in which executives operate; understanding these factors may help us make sense of the differences among executive leadership.

The *political culture* of the country, the *personality* of the individual, and *the way in which the executive attained power* are central influences on the nature of executive leadership. The prevailing ideology also may be critical in determining how a chief executive performs. The following categories describe approaches to leadership, but it should be noted that actual executives often exhibit aspects of several approaches or change from one to another during their tenure in office.

Sociologist Max Weber (1864–1920) discussed three kinds of authority in his classic work translated and published in English in 1947.* Although he focused primarily on leadership in organizations, the first three types of authority we discuss here— charismatic, rational-legal, and traditional—are drawn from his pioneering analysis of leadership, and they fully apply to chief executives in political systems.

Charismatic Authority

Historians, sociologists, psychologists, and others have long recognized that some people are able to exert considerable influence over others by virtue of their personal magnetism. In popular parlance, we refer to such people as *charismatic*. They command respect, and even adulation, sometimes moving followers to make great sacrifices. The key point is that **charismatic authority** flows not from the legal basis of one's power but from an individual's personal "gifts."[†]

Charismatic leaders often come to power as a result of heroism in revolution, or through an ability to inspire citizens in war or during some other crisis. Some were among history's most brutal and repressive tyrants; others earned worldwide admiration for their pursuit of noble ideals; still others remain both admired and condemned. Adolf Hitler and Benito Mussolini were charismatic figures, as were Franklin D. Roosevelt, Winston Churchill, Juan Perón (Argentina), and Gamal Abdel Nasser (Egypt). Each of those leaders persuaded large numbers of downtrodden people to believe in a better future.

Charismatic leaders require more than an opportunity created by depression or war; they must also have a special personal appeal. For example, Huey Long, the infamous governor and senator from Louisiana in the 1920s and 1930s, was the object of unprecedented praise and affection on the part of many poor, uneducated residents of that state (as well as many wealthier citizens), in part because his style and personality were so appealing to them. (See Box 8-3.)

In many cases, charismatic leadership is related to *ideology*; indeed, any ideology that contains a low tolerance for political diversity (such as fascism and Leninism) provides a fertile ground for charismatic leaders. Such ideologies buttress a leader's ability to inspire the masses by focusing their energies on alleged threats to the nation (such as racial minorities, foreign powers, class enemies).

The problems of charismatic leadership stem from its foundation in the personal qualities of the leader. When one's authority derives from the personal regard in which he or she is held, and not from law or the limits of established institutions, the person's power may become dangerous. Indeed, part of the attractiveness of many charismatic leaders comes from their image as fighters—they are seen as being in combat with a selfish upper class, a hated ethnic group, or a hostile foreign power. Such leaders may even increase their personal appeal by creating new powers to wield against opposing forces.

* See Max Weber, *The Theory of Social and Economic Organization*, trans. A. M. Parsons and Talcott Parsons (New York: Free Press, 1947).

[†] The term *charisma* comes from the Greek word for "divine gift."

Box 8-3

HUEY LONG

In his biography of Huey Long, the noted historian T. Harry Williams gives us this picture of Long's ability to generate and use charisma, even though he had to gain support among both the Protestants of northern Louisiana and the Catholics of the south:

> Throughout the day in every small town Long would begin by saying: "When I was a boy, I would get up at six o'clock in the morning on Sunday, and I would hitch our old horse up to the buggy and I

would take my Catholic grandparents to mass. I would bring them home, and at ten o'clock I would hitch the old horse up again, and I would take my Baptist grandparents to church." The effect of the anecdote on the audiences was obvious, and on the way back to Baton Rouge that night the local leader said admiringly, "Why, Huey, you've been holding out on us. I didn't know you had any Catholic grandparents." "Don't be a damn fool," replied Huey. "We didn't even have a horse."[6]

Leaders whose claim to power is based primarily on their charismatic leadership often produce unstable conditions, particularly in nations with weak political institutions and little or no democratic traditions. The leader may be able to manipulate the adoration of the masses, who are often convinced that their support is justified by the executive's great wisdom or even supernatural talents. Replacing the executive in these situations is often very challenging. Term limits or constitutional restraints may be only limp impediments when a charismatic leader wants to stay in power.

Thus, the historical record of chief executives who rely primarily on charismatic leadership is mixed. As one would expect, when they are successful, charismatic leaders are extremely effective in performing the symbolic leadership function, and, in some instances, the unifying force of such leaders is precisely what a country needs. For example, Charles de Gaulle helped unify the French Resistance in World War II and brought the country together during the late 1950s when France was on the brink of civil war. And John Kennedy influenced the attitudes of many Americans toward race, laying the foundation for civil rights legislation after his assassination. Charismatic leaders are often less successful in handling other executive functions. For example, Kennedy was far less successful as chief legislator than was his decidedly *un*charismatic successor, Lyndon Johnson. Many charismatic leaders have performed poorly in financial management, in diplomacy, or in controlling the armed forces. Their failures occur because the personal quality that got them power—their ability to inspire the masses—has nothing to do with other needed leadership skills.

Traditional Leadership

In his discussion of different kinds of authority, Weber identified another distinctive kind of authority: traditional authority. People often give allegiance to leaders because the institutional positions they occupy are established in the traditions of the culture. The most common illustrations are the British monarchy and the Japanese emperorship. Great Britain's monarchy is the world's oldest continuous line of succession and is imbued with a tremendous sense of tradition. In many Third World peasant communities, councils of village elders may enjoy similar authority passed on from generation to generation.

Tradition is also a source of power for elected executives. Although the British monarch has virtually no power today, the prime minister claims authority and status by virtue of the long traditions associated with that office. A widely accepted perception that some power or prerogative is an established tradition adds to the executive's ability to lead. The force of tradition in this sense is apparent when executives attempt to wield power in nontraditional ways—they quickly find out that the executive's position is much more secure when operating within traditions than when trying to establish new ones.

For example, in the 1930s, U.S. President Franklin Roosevelt defied tradition when he proposed to "pack" the Supreme Court with justices who would be favorable to his economic wishes. Although the Constitution clearly does not specify the number of justices on the Court, the resulting public furor made it evident that *tradition* was a powerful force:

> The Court-packing plan was defeated despite the President's landslide victory at the polls only a few months earlier and despite the overwhelming popular support for New Deal legislation.... Although much of the opposition was partisan, the resistance to the Court-packing plan ran much deeper. At its source lay the American people's well-nigh religious attachment to constitutionalism and the Supreme Court, including their intuitive realization that packing the Court in order to reverse the course of its decisions would not only destroy its independence but erode the essence of constitutionalism in the United States.[7]

Nevertheless, it is fair to conclude that the importance of traditional authority diminished in the turbulent twentieth century, and most executive leaders must draw on other sources of power.

Rational-Legal Authority

Weber identified another kind of authority, which is based on the acceptance of established law. Executives make use of legal authority by making decisions and taking actions within the scope of authority granted to their positions under law. Where this kind of authority exists, people obey the executive because they accept his or her power under law.

Rational-legal authority can be a significant component of executive leadership where the people see the legal foundations of the government as legitimate and established. Leaders who come to power through a revolution or coup must rely on something else—charismatic authority, perhaps, or military force—since there is no widely recognized legal framework to lend legitimacy to their executive actions. The problem with legal authority is the opposite of the problem with charisma.

Sometimes executives must "bend" the law to maintain national security or lead the country through a crisis. If an executive's authority is based on nothing other than the people's acceptance of law, he or she may lack support when leadership requires steps of questionable legality. Thus, even in systems in which the force of law is strong, the most effective executives are able to draw on some other source of authority.

Representative Authority

The authority for some instances of executive leadership derives from the perception that the incumbent is representative of some legitimate power, usually the "people" or the "majority." This authority is distinct from the authority of a charismatic personality, tradition, or even law. In democratic systems, executives justify certain policy choices on the basis of **representative authority**, asserting that the majority elected them to make those choices. The presidents of France and the United States, for example, can make such a claim. In contrast, many analysts felt that Mikhail Gorbachev, former president of the then–Soviet Union, made a critical error when he asked the constitutional assembly, established in March 1989, to elect him president, rather than choosing to run for the post in a genuinely national election. Winning a popular election would have given Gorbachev greater legitimacy when making difficult decisions about the decaying economy.* The need to establish representative authority is even more essential in countries with strong democratic principles. In those nations, representative authority is a key ingredient in making executive actions legitimate.

Representative leadership is thus difficult to achieve if the process through which leaders are chosen is not seen as fair and open. Until the end of apartheid, the leader in South Africa could claim little or no representative authority over the majority of citizens. (For blacks, his authority was doubtless coercive.) Representative authority is rarely adequate as an exclusive basis for executive power, however, for the same reasons that legal authority is rarely enough. Executives are sometimes appointed, and sometimes even elected executives win with less than a majority of the vote. President Clinton, for example, won in 1992 and 1996 with 44 percent and 49 percent of the vote, respectively, because of the presence of a third-party candidate, Ross Perot. And George W. Bush won in 2000 even though his opponent, then-Vice President Al Gore, Jr., received more of the popular vote. Most executives occasionally face the necessity of making policy choices that are contrary to the wishes of the people who elected them (as when Franklin Roosevelt, who ran in 1940 on a peace platform, led the United States into World War II). In such cases, a chief executive would be powerless if authority rested solely on the perception that all executive power derives from the principle of representation.

Coercive Authority

The power to use force is an inescapable part of executive leadership. Effective executives generate support for their actions by staying within the law, through the attractiveness of their personalities, by embodying their countries' traditions, or by emphasizing how they are representing the people; but the possibility of force is always present. The significance of that possibility varies tremendously, of course. When charismatic leaders lose their charisma, they may use police or military force to demand the obedience that their personalities previously earned them.

In deeply divided countries, large segments of the population often reject the legal foundations and traditions that are held in high esteem by other parts of society. Both of these problems are common to the developing world. For example, General Augusto Pinochet (former president of Chile), President Hafez Assad (Syria),

---

* In fact, when Gorbachev eventually did run for the presidency in a popular election in 1996, he received only 1 percent of the vote.

and the emir of Kuwait were not elected in competitive elections and have represented only a part of the population. Executives in such countries are thus unable to lead effectively by appealing to traditional, representative, or legal authority, and even their charismatic qualities may not be recognized in many quarters. In such cases, **coercive authority** becomes essential to executive leadership. (See Box 8-4.)

In modern political life, a single foundation for executive leadership is normally too limited and too vulnerable to change to enable an executive to operate effectively. Most successful executives thus combine several kinds of authority. The actual mix will depend on the leader's personal qualities, the nature and homogeneity of the country's political culture, and the legal-institutional setting.

Box 8-4

LEADERSHIP, AUTHORITY, AND ZIMBABWE'S PRESIDENT ROBERT MUGABE

In 1965, following decades as a British colony, Rhodesia won its independence. The country's name was changed to Zimbabwe, and one of the leaders of the independence movement, Robert Mugabe (born in 1924), became the leader. His leadership style became a dangerous combination of coercive and charismatic authority, producing severe difficulties and instabilities.

©Odd Andersen/AFP/Getty Images

Robert Mugabe, President of Zimbabwe, has allegedly overseen intimidation and violence to cement his hold on power, which was extended by his "landslide victory" in a runoff election in June 2008.

CONCLUSION: THE EVOLVING CHALLENGES OF EXECUTIVE POWER

The central role of the chief executive is virtually universal among political systems. Although specific executive institutions vary considerably—and although cultural, legal, and even religious traditions create different approaches to leadership—the need to have unified control of the execution of laws, diplomacy, and emergency management has made it impossible for governments to function without executive power. The challenges of the modern world (greater use of technology, more deadly weapons of mass destruction, more immediate communication, and extensive interdependence)

Rhodesia had become a net exporter of agricultural produce and was one of the more economically successful African states during the 1950s and 1960s. It did not give equal rights to its black citizens, however, leading to considerable unrest that fueled much of the independence movement. After the nation achieved independence, the racial inequalities largely remained.

By the 1980s, Mugabe pursued violent policies that strengthened his power. Military forces massacred thousands of Ndebele civilians, brutally hacking them to death. By the late 1980s, he suppressed Zimbabwe's free press and he had several opposition party leaders imprisoned. Mugabe also allegedly rigged national elections, making it impossible to vote him out of office. He is now one of the world's longest serving chief executives.

Presumably to correct a long-standing injustice, Mugabe recently embarked on a program of confiscating farms owned by non-black descendants of the original European colonists. Some 95 percent of Zimbabwe's white-owned farms have been taken from their owners and claimed for the black majority. Most reports suggest that the lands have been given to Mugabe's supporters, thus strengthening his political position.

Although the injustices in Zimbabwe were and are real, it is also clear that President Mugabe has sought to increase his power through his policies. He appears as a savior to many poor blacks, who see him as a crusader for basic fairness, and he is able to reward influential individuals who may otherwise support someone else. But per capita Gross Domestic Product in Zimbabwe is only some $1900, and the national GDP lost 4 percent of its value in 2005. Between 1999 and 2003, the economy contracted by nearly 30 percent.

According to a *Washington Post* report, "security forces and militia groups loyal to the 84-year-old autocrat have rampaged across the countryside for the past month, targeting opposition activists and whole villages suspected of having voted against the government in the March 29 elections. In some areas, torture camps have been established where victims are taken and beaten while their homes are looted and burned."* The violence continued after a runoff election was scheduled following the report that Morgan Tsvangirai, president of the Movement for Democratic Change (MDC) party, received 47 percent of the popular vote, compared to the 43 percent that Mugabe received. The MDC party was the majority party in Zimbabwe at the time.

On June 18, 2008, Mugabe expelled a U.N. human rights officer who was in Zimbabwe to observe the runoff election between Mugabe and Tsvangirai, and he also ordered all foreign aid groups to halt their work, depriving thousands of Zimbabwe's citizens of needed relief supplies and assistance. In response to incidents of violence and intimidation, Tsvangirai boycotted the runoff, and in a one-person election, Mugabe "won" by a landslide on June 27. Tsvangirai called for a United Nations investigation in to abuses in Zimbabwe and for a declaration that the election result is void.

The case of Zimbabwe under Mugabe demonstrates how charisma and unlimited access to military coercion can produce a strong president but an unstable society. There is little basis for a hopeful outlook for Zimbabwe as long as the country's leadership is maintained through state violence.

(See Martin Meredith, *Our Votes, Our Guns: Robert Mugabe and the Tragedy of Zimbabwe* [New York: Public Affairs, 2002].)

* *Washington Post*, April 30, 2008; p. A18.

will make the executive's role even more important in the future. Understanding how executive power is wielded, and how it is limited, will remain fundamental political issues.

 ## WHERE ON THE WEB?

The best way to locate Web sites that focus on executive institutions is to search under specific country or person headings. For example, to find information about French president Sarkozy, search for links pertaining to French government. Here are some interesting sites to visit:

http://www.whitehouse.gov
The official home page of the U.S. White House offers information about White House documents, history, and tours.

http://www.number10.gov.uk
The official home page of the British Prime Minister, this site includes current news, biographical information, and a guide to current legislation.

http://www.kremlin.ru/eng
The official home page of the Russian President.

http://www.thepresidency.org
The home page for The Center for the Study of the Presidency, located in Washington, D.C.

http://www.chileangovernment.cl
This site contains updated news and an official biography of Chilean President Michelle Bachelet Jeria.

http://presidencia.gob.mx/en
The English-language version of the home page of the Mexican president.

http://www.sweden.gov.se/sb/d/577
The English-language version of the home page of Sweden's prime minister.

❖ ❖ ❖

Key Terms and Concepts _____

budget formulation   emergency leadership
charismatic authority   rational-legal authority
chief administrators   representative authority
coercive authority   symbolic leader
coups d'état   traditional authority
diplomacy

Discussion Questions _____

1. Which governmental functions are most closely associated with executive institutions? Why are they normally seen as within the executive's domain?
2. Discuss some of the limits on the power of chief executives.
3. What are the differences among charismatic, rational-legal, and traditional authority?
4. What kind of executive leadership is best suited to democracy, and why?

Notes ─────────

1. Aaron Wildavsky, *The Politics of the Budgetary Process*, 4th ed. (Boston: Little, Brown, 1984), p. 2.
2. Reuters News Service report, dated June 4, 2008.
3. Richard E. Neustadt, *Presidential Power: The Politics of Leadership from FDR to Carter* (New York: Wiley, 1980).
4. Ibid., p. 9.
5. Prime Minister Tony Blair, "Lecture on Public Life," London, June 12, 2007. Available in a June 13, 2007 report by *The Guardian*, at http://www.guardian.co.uk/politics/2007/jun/13/media.television.
6. T. Harry Williams, *Huey Long* (New York: Bantam, 1970), p. 1.
7. See Archibald Cox, *The Court and the Constitution*. (Boston: Houghton-Mifflin, 1987), pp. 149–150.

For Further Reading ─────────

Anderson, Christopher J., André Blais, Shaun Bowler, Todd Donovan, and Ola Listhaug. *Losers' Consent: Elections and Democratic Legitimacy*. Oxford: Oxford University Press, 2005.

Barber, James D. *Presidential Character: Predicting Performance in the White House*, 5th ed. Englewood Cliffs, NJ: Prentice Hall, 2008.

Beckett, Francis. *The 20 British Prime Ministers of the Twentieth Century*. London: Haus Publishing, 2006.

Canes-Wrone, Candice, and Kenneth W. Schotts. "The Conditional Nature of Presidential Responsiveness to Public Opinion." *American Journal of Political Science* 48 (October 2004): 690–706.

Chalaby, Jean K. *The DeGaulle Presidency and the Media: Statism and Public Communications*. London: Palgrave Macmillan, 2002.

Colaresi, Michael. "When Doves Cry: International Rivalry, Unreciprocated Cooperation, and Leadership Turnover." *American Journal of Political Science* 48 (July 2004): 555–570.

Dewan, Torun and David P. Myatt. "Scandal, Protection, and Recovery in the Cabinet." *American Political Science Review* 101 (February 2007): 63–78.

Fabbrini, Sergio. *Compound Democracies: Why the United States and Europe Are Becoming Similar*. New York: Oxford University Press, 2008.

Fishman, Ethan M. *The Prudential Presidency: An Aristotelian Approach to Presidential Leadership*. Westport, CT: Praeger, 2001.

Hallerberg, Mark, and Patrik Marier. "Executive Authority, the Personal Vote, and Budget Discipline in Latin American and Caribbean Countries." *American Journal of Political Science* 48 (July 2004): 571–587.

Hauss, Charles. *Politics in France*. Washington, D.C.: CQ Press, 2007.

Healy, Gene. *The Cult of the Presidency: America's Dangerous Devotion to Executive Power*. Washington, D.C.: Cato Institute, 2008.

Lewis, David L. *The Politics of Presidential Appointments: Political Control and Bureaucratic Performance*. Princeton, N.J.: Princeton University Press, 2008.

Martin, Lanny. "The Government Agenda in Parliamentary Democracies." *American Journal of Political Science* 48 (2004): 445–461.

Meredith, Martin. *Our Votes, Our Guns: Robert Mugabe and the Tragedy of Zimbabwe*. New York: Public Affairs, 2002.

Moore, Reese T. *European Leaders: A Bibliography with Indexes*. Huntington, NY: Nova Science Publishers, 2001.

Mughan, Anthony. *Media and the Presidentialization of Parliamentary Democracy*. New York: Palgrave, 2000.

Munoz, Heraldo. *The Dictator's Shadow: Life Under Augusto Pinochet*. New York: Basic Books, 2008.

Neustadt, Richard E. *Presidential Power and the Modern Presidents: The Politics of Leadership from Roosevelt to Reagan*. New York: Free Press, 1991.

Nielson, Daniel L. "Supplying Trade Reform: Political Institutions and Liberalization in Middle-Income Presidential Democracies." *American Journal of Political Science* 47 (July 2003): 470–491.

Polsby, Nelson W., David A. Hopkins, and Aaron Wildavsky. *Presidential Elections: Strategies and Structures of American Politics*, 12th ed. Lanham, MD: Rowman and Littlefield, 2007.

Rudalevige, Andrew. *Managing the President's Program: Presidential Leadership and Legislative Policy Formulation*. Princeton, NJ: Princeton University Press, 2002.

Schlesinger, Arthur M. *The Imperial Presidency.* Mariner Books Edition. New York: Houghton-Mifflin, 2004.

Seldon, Anthony. *Blair's Britain: 1997–2007.* Cambridge, U.K.: Cambridge University Press, 2007.

Skowronek, Stephen. *Presidential Leadership in Political Time: Reprise and Reappraisal.* Lawrence, KS.: University Press of Kansas, 2008.

Snow, Nancy. *Persuaders-in-Chief: The Presidents and Propaganda That Shaped Modern America.* New York: Routledge, 2008.

Williams, T. Harry. *Huey Long.* New York: Bantam, 1970.

THE LANDMARK GUN CONTROL CASE   On June 26, 2008, the U.S. Supreme Court announced its historic decision in District of Columbia v. Heller, striking down a decades-old ban on handguns in the nation's capital. In this photo, Richard Heller, the D.C. resident who first challenged the law, signs a poster outside the Supreme Court building. The Heller ruling will have important implications for gun control laws throughout the U.S.

© Jose Luis Magana/AP Photo

9

JUDICIAL INSTITUTIONS

◆ Judicial Functions ◆ Justice and the Political System
◆ Kinds of Law ◆ Judicial Institutions: Structure and
Design ◆ Judicial Decisions and Public Policy
◆ Perspectives on Judicial Policy Making

241

The judiciary is perhaps the most controversial and most confusing of the major branches of modern governments. Legislatures and executives are expected to make and enforce policies; to authorize public expenditures for roads, schools, and social programs; to enact standards for worker and consumer safety; and to maintain national security, among many other things. The judiciary's functions are fundamentally different. Its decisions are, at least to a significant degree, based on judgments regarding *justice* and the *meaning of law*, not simply conclusions about which of several alternative policies is most cost effective or most desirable.

JUDICIAL FUNCTIONS

As noted in Chapter 1, rule adjudication is a basic function of government. Narrowly speaking, it involves the application of rules to individual cases. Nevertheless, the functions of courts in modern governments go far beyond the resolution of a private conflict between individuals or the application of law to particular individuals accused of crimes. Judicial decisions have an effect on the whole society, not only on those in the courtroom.

Of course, the primary function of judicial institutions is to *resolve conflict.* In a comprehensive, cross-national study, a noted scholar found that the practice of locating a disinterested third party to broker the resolution of a conflict between two people is so basic that "we can discover almost no society that fails to employ it."[1] Sometimes courts resolve conflict between two people regarding an alleged injury or contractual obligation. Courts also resolve conflicts of a higher order, as when they interpret constitutional provisions. Where they are perceived as trusted, nonpartisan institutions, courts typically have considerable power to resolve conflicts that citizens would not resolve on their own. (See Box 9-1.)

For that reason, judicial institutions can also help to *maintain social control.* To the extent that judicial authority is well established and stable, most citizens feel an obligation to comply with judicial decisions. (See Box 9-2.) Judicial institutions thus also perform the function of *legitimizing the regime.* When a court rules that a disputed legislative or executive action is in accordance with law, or constitutional, most citizens accept the result, giving greater support to the government. For example, the court system in Germany has been particularly important in legitimizing the profound governmental transitions that occurred in the process of integrating East and West. The dramatic changes in South Africa's political system brought about by the end of apartheid and the introduction of genuine universal suffrage were also legitimized with the aid of that country's court system.

Judicial institutions also frequently perform the function of *protecting minority rights.* Particularly in democracies, where legislatures and executives are responsive to majority will, courts may have a unique ability to hear and respond to the interests of those who, by virtue of their small numbers, cannot succeed in lobbying other branches of government. Finally, judicial institutions are often involved in *making public policy*, since some judicial decisions shape policy choices made by executives and legislatures.

This list of functions emphasizes that judicial institutions often affect the functions and activities of other branches of the government, and yet judicial decisions involve a distinctive process that sets them apart. We evaluate legislative and executive

---
Box 9-1

THE COURTS, SCHOOLS, DRUGS, AND STUDENT PRIVACY

One of the most controversial aspects of the "war on drugs" in the United States is the increasingly common practice of drug testing. A number of private corporations routinely test their employees and applicants for present and past drug use, and some public school systems have initiated policies of drug testing for some students.

The issue of illegal drugs highlights a conflict between two important social goals: the elimination of damaging controlled substances, and the preservation of privacy. It was perhaps inevitable that the issue of drug testing would reach the agenda of judicial institutions in the United States. In Tecumseh, Oklahoma, the local school district adopted a policy of requiring all students engaged in extracurricular activities to take a urinalysis drug test before participating in such activities, and to submit to random drug testing thereafter. Two students, Lindsay Earls and Daniel James, were told that they must submit to the tests before they could participate in the show choir, the marching band, the Academic Team, and the National Honor Society, and they objected to the drug testing as an unconstitutional violation of their privacy.

A previous decision by the Supreme Court held that schools could insist on random drug testing for students participating in *athletic* activities, largely because rigorous physical activity could create special problems for students engaging in drug use. However, in June 2002, the Court extended that idea to *all* extracurricular activities.* Although the Constitution does not *require* drug testing in schools, the majority concluded that it does not prohibit it, and that the school can require any student electing to participate in extracurricular activities to subject himself or herself to drug testing without obtaining a warrant and without any basis for suspecting the student of drug use.

Four justices dissented, arguing that student privacy requires that there be some individualized suspicion that a student is using illegal drugs before he or she can be forced to submit to urinalysis.

* The case was Board of Education of Independent School District No. 92 v. Earls et al. 536 U.S. 822 (2002).

---

decisions by the degree to which they promote the public interest, but we evaluate judicial decisions by whether or not they are *just*. Judicial decisions involve different standards, and judges operate in distinctive institutions that have a very different claim to legitimacy. The fact that courts are so different from electoral institutions while making their own contributions to policy is the main reason that questions about the proper role of courts in the political process remain confusing and divisive.

JUSTICE AND THE POLITICAL SYSTEM

The Concept of Justice

Nearly everything we can say about **justice** is culturally bound. Cultures vary tremendously with respect to concepts of "just" punishment, for instance. As discussed in Chapter 1, there is no universally accepted list of human rights. Consequently, it is difficult to say exactly what justice means in the abstract, although there is nearly universal agreement that it includes three things.

Perhaps the most widely accepted element of justice is the notion that law must be fairly applied. If the law states that a person should lose his or her hand as punishment for stealing (as it does in Saudi Arabia and some other Islamic nations), it would be unjust for that penalty to be applied only to people from a particular region or

Box 9-2

The Courts and Social Control:
The Crisis in Colombia

The nation of Colombia has experienced severe political instability for many years. Well-armed rebel groups control parts of the country, and the influx of drug money has fueled considerable violence. According to Human Rights Watch, a Washington, D.C.–based organization focusing on violations of human rights throughout the world, there were at least 92 documented "massacres" in Colombia during the first ten months of 2001 (the office of the Public Advocate in Colombia defines a massacre as the killing of three or more people at the same place and time), and the violence has only escalated in subsequent years.

In February 2005, at least eight people, all residents of the Peace Community of San Jose de Apartadó, were brutally killed. Those who were murdered

© John Vizcaino/Reuters/Landov Media

Ingrid Betancourt, a French-Colombian who had been serving in the Colombian senate, hugs General Mario Montoya after his successful military raid in July 2008 to free her and more than a dozen other hostages held by FARC (Fuerzas Armadas Revolucionarias de Colombia) since 2002.

ethnic group. If the law states that all property will be taxed at the same rate, it would be unjust for an influential citizen to pay at a lower rate. If the law grants voting rights only to those who own land, it would be unjust for a person who owns the necessary land to be denied the right to vote because, for example, the individual is a member of a hated ethnic group. And if the law states that all young men and women must perform military service (as in Israel), it is unjust for a those with connections to escape the draft. Of course, few of us would find that simple principle of justice (equal application of the law) adequate. It describes only a part of what justice means. If justice is nothing more than consistent application of the law, what do we do about the

included four children. On the night of February 25, 2006, members of the FARC (Fuerzas Armadas Revolucionarias de Colombia, or Revolutionary Armed Forces of Colombia) stopped a bus in the state of Caquetá. They opened fire on the bus and then set it on fire with the passengers aboard. They killed nine people and injured at least that many more. Two days later, the same group shot and killed nine town council members. In March 2006, the same group killed at least 20 civilians in attacks using gas canister bombs.*

Until recently, the courts in Colombia were not very successful in maintaining social order. In May 2005, the Colombian Attorney General shut down an investigation of a general who was implicated in a 1997 massacre of 49 civilians in the town of Mapiripan, despite the fact that both military and civilian courts had ordered the Attorney General to investigate. Beginning in 2006, Colombia has become more stable. There are now fewer deaths each year in political violence, and on July 2, 2008, Colombian military forces executed a dramatic operation to free several hostages held by FARC. One of those hostages was Colombian senate member Ingrid Betancourt, whom FARC had seized in 2002 as she was campaigning for the presidency on an anti-corruption platform (see photo).

As political stability in Colombia has improved, the courts will probably have greater influence. In May 2008, the Colombian Supreme Court began an investigation of three legislators, probing their alleged ties to rebel leaders. It also investigated the government of President Alvaro Uribe, following an accusation that an official had bribed a legislator to vote in favor of a constitutional amendment that would allow Uribe to be elected to a third term as president. On June 26, 2008, the Supreme Court found that the bribery had, in fact, taken place.

As of this writing, the political situation in Colombia remains unsettled, but there are signs that the judiciary is playing a more prominent role in resolving conflicts. According to the Colombia Support Network, a Madison, Wisconsin based nonprofit organization, several allegations of abuses by military personnel are being prosecuted, and many of the accused perpetrators are behind bars.[†]

For courts to function effectively amidst significant social and political instability, it is important that judges and witnesses feel safe to do their jobs. One of the steps Colombia took in the 1990s to achieve a sense of safety was the creation of "faceless judges" and allowing secret testimony from witnesses. According to a report submitted to the United Nations in 1996, "testimony presented by a secret witness is admissible before a regional court. Only the judicial official and the agent of the Public Ministry know the identity of the witness and they are obliged to keep it anonymous until the personal security of the witness is guaranteed."

Most legal scholars have long condemned secret trials and secret testimony because such procedures often produce injustice. However, the threats against Colombian judges and witnesses are very real. In the late 1980s, Consuelo Sánchez, then the youngest judge in Colombia, signed a warrant for the arrest of Pablo Escobar, then the most notorious drug lord in Colombia. She immediately received a death threat, and the Colombian government sent her to the United States with a diplomatic post. Ms. Sánchez applied for asylum to remain in the United States.

---

* See the extended coverage of instability and judicial system weaknesses in Colombia at the Web site of Human Rights Watch, www.hrw.org.

† See the Web site for a Madison, Wisconsin-based group active in working for justice in Colombia: www.colombiasupport.net

---

possibility that the law *itself* is unjust? The example about voting and land ownership illustrates such a case. Even if judges apply that law in a just manner (that is, with consistency), most people would find it unjust to grant voting rights on the basis of land ownership. Similarly, many of us would question the justice of laws, no matter how consistently applied, that deny certain legal rights to *all* females or to *all* members of a racial minority. The problem is that cultural and historical differences across societies make it impossible to identify many universally accepted concepts of justice. Considerable agreement exists, however, about the more basic principle that—regardless of the substance of the law—*justice demands that the law be consistently applied.*

A second widely accepted principle is the idea that *the severity of punishment should correspond to the severity of the crime.* Although cultures vary radically with respect to the kinds of punishment they find acceptable, nearly all have a range of punishments that vary in severity to correspond to a range of crimes. Thus, although a number of nations deem capital punishment an appropriate penalty for murder, none finds it just to apply that penalty to traffic violations or to underage drinking.

Third, it is almost universally accepted that justice demands *an accurate application of punishment.* Whatever the law, and whatever the punishment, the innocent should not be penalized. Thus, nearly all cultures have created some kind of fact-finding process, or trial, to determine whether a person who is accused of a crime is guilty. Widely accepted judicial values preclude punishing a person for something he or she did not do.

The essential nature of justice accounts for the distinctiveness of judicial institutions in most political systems.* It takes specialized institutions to produce fair and accurate decisions about individual guilt. The legitimacy of the political system itself is enhanced when citizens perceive judicial institutions as operating in accordance with standards of justice; the regime becomes illegitimate in the eyes of most citizens when judicial institutions appear unfair, "rigged," or helpful only to a certain part of the population.

Two Systems of Justice

The actual workings of judicial institutions are significantly affected by the system of justice under which they operate. Although each country has its own special features, most have either an *adversarial* or an *inquisitorial* system. The systems vary with regard to the role of judges, the importance of lawyers, and the approach to fact-finding, although both systems are designed to evaluate evidence and apply the law fairly and accurately.

The Adversarial System   Anglo-American law operates under the **adversarial system**. The judge is supposed to be impartial, representing neither party but standing for the interests of the justice system. He or she is relatively passive as the **plaintiff** and the **defendant** present evidence, examine witnesses, and make legal arguments.

The adversarial process typically includes provision for a **grand jury** to make preliminary decisions in criminal cases, since the judge is essentially neutral. The prosecutor, who is formally distinct from the judge, first presents evidence to a grand jury in an effort to establish that a person should be formally charged (indicted) for a crime. If the grand jury issues an indictment (a formal accusation) and the case goes before the court, the judge's role is limited. Although he or she retains the power to decide which laws are applicable and how they should be understood by the jury, the judge has little power to introduce evidence or to question witnesses. The judicial decision itself thus critically depends on the positions articulated by contending prosecution and defense attorneys.

---

* Of course, we often use the terms *just* and *unjust* in a different way. We may say, for example, that it is unjust for a poor family to go without medical care or that it is unjust for wealthy people to be taxed at a higher rate than poorer ones. Such statements reflect views of what is in the public interest, rather than legal norms, and they are therefore usually discussed in the explicitly political institutions of government.

The Inquisitorial System   Among industrial democracies, France has the best-known **inquisitorial system**, the most striking feature of which is the active role played by the judge. French magistrates fully examine the evidence in a criminal case, discussing the allegations with the defendant and the witnesses. Judges can also supervise the gathering of additional information.

Thus, cases normally come to the trial stage only when the judge is convinced that the accused is guilty. The trial provides an opportunity for the accused to dispute facts publicly, but new evidence or arguments are not usually presented. The conclusion reached a quarter-century ago by a leading scholar remains accurate today: it is rare for a criminal case brought to trial in an inquisitorial system to end in anything other than conviction.[2]

The Systems Compared   No consensus exists regarding which of these two systems is superior. In democratic societies, both systems usually are acceptably fair and accurate, although serious miscarriages of justice have occurred in both systems. There are some important practical differences between the systems, however.

The adversarial system depends critically on the skill and experience of lawyers. If defendants are unable to obtain effective legal representation, their positions will not be articulated well. Since the judge assumes a largely passive role, facts and arguments that should be presented will probably not become part of the record. This problem is especially significant for poorer citizens, although most systems now provide for publicly funded legal assistance for the poor. But before 1963 in the United States, the state's experienced prosecuting attorney usually would be opposed by an unrepresented defendant. The unfairness of that situation led to the famous *Gideon v. Wainwright* decision, requiring the provision, at state expense, of a public defender so that the poor could receive legal representation.* Even so, poor criminal defendants are frequently represented today by overworked and underprepared public defenders, whereas Mafia dons, former professional athletes, or corrupt officials hire the best attorneys available.

The inquisitorial system is far less affected by differences in skill and experience among the lawyers representing defendants. Nevertheless, it requires the existence of a highly skilled and scrupulously independent judge. If French judges were widely perceived as politically motivated or ignorant of the law, the system would certainly not have the legitimacy that it has. The established tradition of selecting judges through a special training academy is thus a basic adjunct to the French inquisitorial system of justice.

KINDS OF LAW

Law is one of the most widely used terms in political analysis. Understanding the law requires first that we appreciate the different kinds of law that exist. Laws vary with respect to origin, status, and subject matter.

Natural and Positive Law

Philosophers, judges, and politicians have argued about the existence and content of natural law for millennia, and such arguments will doubtless continue as long as

---

* See *Gideon v. Wainwright*, 373 U.S. 335 (1963).

people discuss justice and government. In simple terms, **natural law** is a moral or ethical standard grounded either in nature itself (how things *should* be according to some view of a natural order) or in theology (what the Divine has dictated). Natural law exists apart from **positive law**, the body of laws devised by humans. Some legal and moral philosophers have devoted great energies to discovering principles of natural law. Among the most important are Aristotle, Cicero, Thomas Aquinas, the Stoics, Locke, and Rousseau.

Aside from the realm of philosophy, natural law emerges most often in rhetoric as people debate political movements or issues. For example, following John Locke's writings, the American revolutionaries contended that several British laws governing them were invalid because they violated *rights under natural law*. Thomas Jefferson invoked natural law in the Declaration of Independence so that the radical action the colonists were taking would not appear to be simply arbitrary or selfish. Essentially, he argued that the laws enacted by the British King and Parliament were unjust when held against the standard created by the view of natural law that he advocated.

Today, many people argue similarly that natural law demands the rejection of positive laws authorizing prison terms for political dissidents or members of particular religions. People on both sides of the abortion debate in the United States claim that natural law requires changes in positive law; some of those opposing abortion rights argue that natural law protects the right of the unborn, whereas many supporters of abortion rights assert the existence of a natural law right of privacy that prohibits legislators from enacting restrictions on abortions. The idea of natural law is enormously important in political philosophy, but its most common role is as an element in political debate.

Basic Law

The idea that some body of law is supreme exists in many political systems. **Basic law** may exist in a written constitution, in a religious document, or even in time-honored traditions. The key feature of basic law is that when other laws contradict it, basic law is assumed to be controlling. Basic law thus serves as a set of standards that limit which laws legislatures, agencies, or executives can enact.

The U.S. Constitution is perhaps the most well-known example of basic law, primarily because questions about the *constitutionality* of other laws are so often raised in disputes brought to court (see Chapter 11). Its first ten amendments itemize specific actions that Congress and the president cannot take, thereby establishing important civil rights. Although the British constitution is unwritten, the strong traditions in that system limit the kinds of laws Parliament can pass, and thus those traditions serve as a kind of basic law. (See Box 9-3.) In Iran, all legislation must conform to Islamic law as expressed in the Quran.

An inevitable problem arises when basic law appears to conflict with other laws: Someone or some institution must decide whether a conflict actually exists. For example, when a U.S. community passes an ordinance prohibiting flag burning, a sharp debate erupts between proponents of the restriction and those who feel it violates the First Amendment. Courts generally resolve the dispute, creating a potential threat to democratic accountability, as we discuss later in this chapter and in Chapter 11. But if no judicial body is capable of overriding the legislative institution that makes regular law, basic law may lose most of its importance. In such instances,

Box 9-3

DO BILLS OF RIGHTS MATTER?

The idea of a "bill of rights" is perhaps the most commonly discussed example of basic law, but it is arguable that its existence makes little difference in the actual workings of a political system. A 1996 study in the *American Political Science Review* evaluated the actual effects of bills of rights on the political process. The author, Charles Epp of the University of Kansas, noted that "nearly every new constitution or constitutional revision adopted since 1945 (almost 60 by rough count) contains a bill of rights."[3] To address the question of whether the adoption of a bill of rights has any impact, Epp studied the Canadian system, which adopted the "Canadian Charter of Rights and Freedoms" in 1982. He was therefore able to compare the system before and after the adoption of its bill of rights.

What difference are bills of rights *supposed* to make? Epp points out that supporters of such charters argue that they increase the emphasis on rights in the political culture and thus increase the tendency of courts to intervene in policy actions by the legislative and executive branches. Evidence does indicate that the Canadian Supreme Court has placed greater emphasis on civil liberties and rights cases in recent years, that it has been more likely to support rights claims, and that a greater proportion of its cases involves disputes between individuals and government. However, Epp found that most of these changes in judicial behavior have been a function of the development of a more complete "support structure" for legal mobilization, including steady growth in the size of the legal community and expanded government programs to finance rights litigation and advocacy.

The Canadian experience thus suggests that, at most, the adoption of a bill of rights is but one among many factors that can lead to greater limits on government power in the area of individual rights and freedoms.

Nevertheless, the idea of a bill of rights has considerable support in most democracies. In a May 1995 poll, over three-fourths of British citizens supported the idea of a written constitution and a bill of rights. After the signing of the European Charter of Fundamental Rights, a comprehensive bill of rights covering the European Union, they finally have one. However, a special protocol clarifies the limits of the Charter's impact on British law:

> The Charter does not extend the ability of the Court of Justice, or any court or tribunal of the United Kingdom, to find that the laws, regulations or administrative provisions, practices or action of the United Kingdom are inconsistent with the fundamental rights, freedoms and principles that it reaffirms.
>
> In particular, . . . nothing in the Charter creates justifiable rights applicable to the United Kingdom except in so far as the United Kingdom has provided for such rights in its national law.*

* From Annex II, Protocol (No. 7) "On the Application of the Charter of Fundamental Rights to Poland and to the United Kingdom," available at www.derossa.com/docs/The_Charter_of_Fundamental_Rights.pdf

---

the parliament simply passes the law it wants, along with a resolution stating that the law does not violate basic law. The impact of basic law thus varies from one political system to another.*

Statutory Law

Laws passed by the legislature or a parliament make up a nation's **statutory law**. These laws include proscriptions of criminal acts, the establishment of tax obligations, the creation of regulatory powers, and many other matters. In addition to the texts of statutes themselves, statutory law exists in **statutory interpretation**. The application of statutes, even specific ones, is often unclear. In deciding cases, courts often issue interpretations of the provisions contained in statutes, and those interpretations become

* In Canada, interpreting basic law was previously a legislative task, although since 1982 the judiciary has assumed this role under the Canadian Charter of Rights and Freedoms.

part of the law. Following the concept of *stare decisis* (Latin for "let the decision stand"), as most legal systems around the world do, the interpretations are written down and serve as guides for subsequent applications. In a very real sense, the meaning of statutes is derived *both* from their original texts *and* from judges' interpretations of them.

For example, in 2006, the U.S. Supreme Court had to interpret Congress's intentions in writing the Controlled Substances Act, a law passed in 1970. The citizens of Oregon, through a state referendum, had passed the Oregon Death with Dignity Act in 1994, which permitted licensed physicians to dispense a lethal dose of drugs on request by a terminally ill patient. The Bush Administration argued that, despite the Oregon law, physicians dispensing drugs for suicide could be prosecuted under the Federal Controlled Substances Act, because that act limited the use of controlled substances to "legitimate medical purposes." The state of Oregon argued that the Controlled Substances Act did not give the federal government power to interfere with a state's power to legalize physician-assisted suicide, because Congress never intended for the Act to apply to such practices (only to the problem of illegal sales of controlled substances).

The Court, in a 6-3 decision, interpreted the scope of the Controlled Substances Act in the way that the state of Oregon did: "we conclude the CSA's prescription requirement does not . . . bar [the] dispensing [of] controlled substances for assisted suicide in the face of a state medical regime permitting such conduct." Hence, the "law" defining the legality of physician-assisted suicide is not a matter of simply looking at the words of a statute, but must be understood by considering the statute *and* its interpretation by the Supreme Court.*

Common Law

Even with their accumulated interpretations, basic and statutory law cannot cover all situations that confront courts. **Common law** is a distinct kind of law that also guides judicial decisions. Specifically, the term derives from the evolution of the British legal system. After the time of William the Conqueror (the eleventh century), judges were appointed and authorized to rule "in the King's name." Without a comprehensive, detailed statutory code, the judges applied principles of fairness that had become established in different areas in Great Britain. They did not accept all customary practices, however, and, after generations, a set of principles that were applied uniformly throughout the land became known as common law.[4]

In the U.S. and British systems, perhaps the best illustration of common law is the law governing *torts*: "What limits a person's freedom to hurt another person? When does law say I cannot threaten someone with a blow? When can't I strike the blow? When may I not publicly insult another (libel and slander)? When may I not do careless things that injure other people (negligence)?"[5] Those and similar questions have been answered throughout much of British and American history by the precedents of common law. Traditional practices and concepts of fairness, as applied by generations of judges, delineated what constituted wrongful acts in those and many other contexts.

As a practical matter, when lawyers want to find out for their clients whether a particular activity is legal under common law, they consult the decisions in previous

---

* See *Gonzales, Attorney General, et al. v. Oregon, et al.* 546 U.S. 243 (2006).

court cases that indicate the meaning of the common law. Instead of looking at the laws made by legislatures (statutes), the lawyer must consider the "judge-made" common law to find the answer. The concept of *stare decisis* applies to matters of common law just as it applies to questions of statutory interpretation, and thus, a lawyer can argue that a previous decision involving facts similar to those faced by his client should guide the judge's ruling. The opposing lawyer will search for precedents that suggest a different conclusion, and the judge (or jury) has to decide which precedent applies.

Of course, statutory law can displace common law by specifying certain interpretations. For example, the common law on nuisance behavior is, in many U.S. states, supplemented by statutory definitions. Statutory law often incorporates principles that first appeared as precepts of common law.

Civil and Criminal Law

A distinction between civil and criminal law is found in nearly all political systems. When two individuals have a dispute, the state may or may not be concerned. If the dispute is primarily between the private parties, it is a matter for **civil law**. Examples include disputes regarding slander, the location of property lines, and liability for accident damage. One party sues another for compensation, and the court is asked to decide which party has the valid claim.

Criminal law has to do with actions that the state has defined as offenses against the state. If a person robs a bank, for example, it is not up to the bank to sue the thief. The state will prosecute the violator under criminal statutes. The rationale is that the thief not only injured the bank but also threatened the security of the society at large. In some cases, the same action can result in *both* civil and criminal litigation. In what are surely the most widely publicized trials in decades, O. J. Simpson had to defend himself in both civil and criminal courts against allegations that he murdered his wife and her friend. He was found not guilty in criminal court in 1995, but a jury in a civil trial found him liable for the victims' deaths a year later. Some people felt that it was unfair for Simpson to have to defend himself twice from the same accusation, but the state only prosecuted him once (the criminal trial). The civil action involved private parties attempting to gain compensation.

Most societies have broadened the range of conduct regulated by criminal statutes, creating the possibility of criminal convictions for actions previously settled as civil disputes under common law. This trend has great practical import, since the victim does not have to take legal action for punishment to occur when the act in question is criminal. Civil rights laws, for example, made certain acts of discrimination or harassment criminal offenses, whereas previously the injured party would have needed to institute a civil suit for relief.

JUDICIAL INSTITUTIONS: STRUCTURE AND DESIGN

We can best appreciate the distinctiveness of judicial institutions by contrasting the kinds of decisions they make with those made by legislative and executive institutions. To illustrate, consider the difference between a *legislative* question about taxation

(Should we raise the property tax rate?) and a *judicial* question about taxation (Is Jane Doe guilty of tax evasion?). The answer to the first question is a matter of our views of good public policy: the need for more revenue, the predicted impact of higher taxes on economic growth or on different income groups, and so forth. The answer to the second question has to do with individual justice: what a particular person did or did not do, when, and why.

In most systems, citizens believe that these two kinds of decisions must be made in different kinds of institutions using different procedures. For example, consider the problem of a *biased decision maker*. It is perfectly appropriate for a Canadian member of Parliament to announce that she has reached a firm decision about a national farm bill before debating the issue in the legislative chambers. Nobody expects an Irish, Italian, American, or German legislator to be impartial when he or she participates in deliberations; in fact, the legislator would not be a very good representative if he or she had *no* pre-announced positions.

However, we would find it profoundly unjust for a judge to enter the courtroom after having publicly declared his "position" about the honesty of Jane Doe's tax return. We would also consider it unfair if the judge's decision had been affected by Doe's partisan affiliation or the judge's party's attitude toward her. Pre-announced positions and external influences are fine when officials make legislative or policy decisions, but they constitute a miscarriage of justice when purely judicial decisions are at stake.

The difference between the standards applying to legislative and judicial decisions is the reason that judges and courts are given different powers and separate institutions and the reason that they are (usually) selected through a different process. Judges are even made to appear distinctive. In Western cultures, for example, judges frequently wear robes, elaborate wigs, and other striking apparel, and we often address them in ways that underscore their unique position. In African tribal societies, judges may sit on a distinctive throne when rendering decisions. Judicial decision making is a special kind of governmental action, and most political systems make great efforts to establish and preserve its legitimacy. The way judges are selected, the structure of the judiciary, and the power of the judiciary over the other parts of government are three central questions about judicial institutions that we examine here.

Selection and Tenure of Judges

Judges can be chosen by appointment or by election and can serve fixed or indefinite (life) terms. Whereas U.S. Supreme Court judges serve for life (or until voluntary retirement), members of the French Constitutional Council serve fixed nine-year terms. Judges in some countries may be removed only after a finding of illegal conduct in office; in other systems, judges may be removed as easily as cabinet officers.

Judicial behavior is significantly affected by the choices made among these alternatives. Rules governing the selection and tenure of judges usually represent a compromise between two incompatible values: *political accountability* and *judicial independence*. Democratic values require accountability to the people, but, as noted earlier, judicial decisions are usually supposed to follow standards of fairness and objectivity. Thus, democratic systems typically expect their judges to be both politically accountable *and* politically detached—responsive to public will and yet insulated from it. Systems for selecting judges are shaped by those often irreconcilable goals.

In some countries, judges are selected through a process that begins with their formal education. For example, French judges are selected only from among those who choose to enter the National Center for Judicial Studies for four years after completing their legal training. In the United States, judges may be elected (most states) or appointed (federal courts), but there are no strict guidelines regarding their education (although, in practice, a law degree is required). In contrast, Japanese judges must first pass a National Bar Examination to enter the Legal Training and Research Institute (Shihou Kenshuu Sho), and only about 1,000 of the more than 20,000 candidates who take the exam each year actually pass it. After two years of training, graduates of the institute must choose among three career options: attorney, prosecutor, or judge. There is virtually no movement between these career paths in Japan.[6] Employing yet another approach to selecting judges, those who serve on Swiss courts are elected by the two chambers of the National Assembly.[7]

Most processes for selecting judges contain features that try to minimize the extent to which either independence or accountability is compromised. Perhaps the most explicit attempt to achieve both accountability and independence in the United States is the **Missouri Plan**, an arrangement adopted by that state in 1940. Under this system, the state governor selects a judge from a set of nominees submitted by an independent nominating commission. The commission is made up of lawyers, former judges, community leaders, and citizens. Supporters contend that the Missouri Plan ensures that only qualified, competent judges will be nominated, since the nominating commission has the time and the expertise to select the best candidates. At the same time, accountability is secured because the commission is designed to be somewhat representative and because the plan usually provides for the rejection of nominees (or the recall of appointed judges) by popular referendum. Since the governor is an elected official, further accountability is introduced into the process through his or her participation.

Where judges are elected by citizens, as in 31 U.S. states, the elections are usually officially nonpartisan (that is, the candidates cannot run as members of a political party). Candidates must also satisfy certain qualifications. The election system thus is expected to establish some responsiveness to the public, but safeguards are in place to minimize explicitly partisan political influence.

However, a recent study of U.S. state judges suggests that even nonpartisan elections affect the decisions that judges make. Using data on criminal sentences from over 22,000 cases in Pennsylvania, two political scientists found that "elected judges will become more punitive" as their re-election time approaches. Voters generally are more concerned about cases in which convicted criminals receive light sentences than cases in which judges hand down overly severe sentences. Because most judges are motivated to win re-election, they apparently make sentencing decisions that reflect voters' demands. The data from this 2004 study indicate that, due to their perception that voters prefer judges that are "tough on crime," Pennsylvania judges handed down an additional 1,800 to 2,700 years of incarceration in 22,000 cases."[8] Similarly, a 2002 study found that, despite the existence of laws designed to protect judicial independence, political pressures in Argentina led judges to refrain from issuing rulings against government actions until the last months of a weakening regime. The courts there are reluctant to rule contrary to the wishes of the government while the administration is still strong. Finally, a 2001 study of Japan found that judges who support the government on "sensitive" policy questions tend to do better in their careers.[9] In short, while appointed judgeships may seem completely removed from popular control, the voters have an important indirect influence. Presidents, prime ministers, and others who appoint judges make appointments that reflect their ideological positions, and they often influence the activities of those already serving.

The independence of judges depends on the extent to which removal is possible, as well as on the manner in which they are selected. Since both prosecutors and politicians may want to influence a judge's decisions, effective judicial independence requires that judges must be protected from these improper influences. The simplest way to achieve this protection is by granting judges permanent tenure and by limiting the extent to which their salaries can be reduced (as in the case of U.S. federal judges). French prosecutors and judges are lodged in the same ministry, although the separateness of their positions is recognized. In other cases, special commissions are established to supervise judges. The purpose of all these provisions is to minimize the likelihood that judges will feel the necessity to make certain decisions to preserve their jobs or salaries. (See Box 9-4.)

Hierarchy in Judicial Institutions

Hierarchy is a nearly universal feature of judicial institutions. Virtually all political systems have multiple units of the judiciary, and some courts are explicitly subordinate to others. In the U.S. federal court system, for example, 94 district courts constitute the first level, 13 circuit courts of appeal represent the second level, and the Supreme Court stands at the top. That basic three-layer judicial system has been widely adopted, although the relative sizes of the layers vary widely across countries.*

Box 9-4

AN EXTREME CASE OF JUDICIAL INDEPENDENCE

It is possible that judicial independence can get out of hand. In most Western nations, citizens cannot sue judges or hold them personally liable for making incorrect or even illegal decisions. The rationale for that is simple: Judges are supposed to make their decisions on the basis of the facts and the law pertaining to a case, not on the basis of a concern for their own financial interests. A 1978 U.S. Supreme Court case tested that principle.

The mother of a 15-year-old girl petitioned an Indiana federal judge to have her daughter surgically sterilized. Although the girl had been making adequate progress in school, she had allegedly become sexually active. Apparently fearing the consequences, her mother told the judge that the girl was "somewhat" retarded and asked him to order her sterilization.

Without any hearing, and acting without any legal power, the judge issued a court order.

Under the order, the hospital officials told the girl that she was being taken to the hospital for an appendectomy, where the sterilization procedure was performed. When she subsequently found out why she could not bear children, she sued the judge, and her case ultimately was brought before the U.S. Supreme Court. Three justices felt that the judge's decision was so far beyond his legal authority that it should be considered outside the limits of his role and thus that he should be liable for damages. Nevertheless, the Court's majority ruled that the judge was "immune from damages liability even if his approval of the petition was in error." See *Stump v. Sparkman*, 435 U.S. 349 (1978).

---

* In France, the lower courts are the *Tribunaux de Premiere Instance*; in Germany, they are the *Landsgerichte*; and in Great Britain, the corresponding units are the county and the crown courts. The national supreme court of Germany is the *Bundesgerichtshof*; in Switzerland it is the *Swiss Federal Tribunal*; and in France it is the *Court of Cassation*.

The most important difference among levels is between the lowest court and all others. **Trial courts** are where cases are heard for the first time, and in adversarial systems they are where facts are introduced and discussed. Higher courts, known as **appellate courts**, normally do not consider new factual evidence bearing on cases but reserve their time to evaluate the application of the law in the lower court (or courts). Appellate courts attempt to determine whether the trial court applied appropriate law and whether its interpretations were correct. Appellate courts are far less numerous than trial courts, since most trials are not appealed. The hierarchy of judicial institutions has two important benefits. First, it provides for an effective check on incompetent, irresponsible, arbitrary, or corrupt judicial decisions. If a trial court improperly considers or excludes evidence, or if a judge or a prosecutor fails to follow legally required procedures, the appeals court may reverse the decision or call for a new trial. Even when errors are made in good faith, an appeal can lead to their correction. Second, a system of appellate courts creates the possibility of *uniform* interpretation of the law. Without a system of superior appellate courts, new interpretations of law would apply only in the districts in which trial courts devised them. When the highest appellate court interprets the law, the law has the same meaning throughout the system.

Judicial Review

The concept of basic law, discussed earlier, implies that ordinary or statutory law must not abridge certain basic principles. However, citizens, politicians, and scholars almost never agree about claims regarding a conflict between statutory law and basic law. Whether or not a given law (or executive action) actually violates basic law can be a matter of great controversy, and therefore some institutional power must be available to issue an authoritative judgment.

In some systems, the courts have that power. In a classic text by a leading scholar of judicial institutions, **Judicial review** was defined as "the power . . . to hold unconstitutional and hence unenforceable any law that [is deemed] . . . to be in conflict with the Basic Law."[10] Courts have the power of judicial review in the U.S., Italy, Canada, Germany, Japan, India, the Republic of Ireland, Australia, and Norway, among some two dozen other countries. In France, the nine-member Constitutional Council can overturn parliamentary legislation as well as decrees made by the prime minister or the president, but its powers are somewhat limited and sometimes subject to presidential pressures.[11]

Although one often speaks of the "Anglo-American legal system" to indicate an approach to courts and law that has been partially adopted in a number of countries, the United States and Britain follow very different approaches to judicial review. The concept of **parliamentary supremacy** is firmly established in Britain. Where there are disagreements regarding whether or not a given Act of Parliament violates basic rights or well-established practices, Parliament itself has the power to decide the issue. The British parliament is thus legally free to enact any statute it wants.

Many U.S. citizens would be uncomfortable with such a system. For example, the Bill of Rights is a set of statements prohibiting Congress from taking certain actions—if Congress itself could decide whether or not a law it wants to enact is forbidden by the Constitution, most Americans would say that the Constitution would have no real impact. Congress would do what it wants and then pass a law saying it was constitutional. On the other hand, advocates of parliamentary supremacy argue that the

U.S. system frustrates democratic government and that, even without a court system with powers to overturn Acts of Parliament, the British parliament is effectively held in check by the electoral system and competition among political parties.

Judicial review in some countries—Germany and India, for example—leads to less court involvement in public policy than in the United States but constrains the legislature more than in Britain. As one analyst put it, although courts in these systems rarely issue rulings that overturn major policy decisions, they do insist that legislative actions be "reasonable" and "nonarbitrary."[12]

Judicial Decisions and Public Policy

As we stressed at the start of this chapter, the types of decisions they make is what distinguishes judicial institutions from executive and legislative institutions. Whereas democratic values require that policy makers be influenced by citizens, vote totals, parties, and interest groups, our concept of justice requires that judges be insulated from political influence so that their actions will be free from prejudice or partisanship.

In most political systems, citizens agree on the need for an independent judiciary in cases that have no significant impact on policy, such as most criminal trials. The winds of public opinion should not influence an appellate court's decision about whether or not to uphold a murder conviction. But when judicial decisions involve policy—those affecting school integration, pollution, or abortion, for example—the question of judicial independence becomes far more controversial.

How Judicial Policy Making Occurs

Many judicial decisions involve more than a determination of the facts; they also raise questions of legal interpretation. The precise meaning of the law is often uncertain, either because circumstances arise that were not foreseen when the constitutional provision or law was written, or because policy makers deliberately avoided the politically painful process of spelling out particular applications of the law. When judges "fill in the details," they make their own interpretations, and those interpretations often include important policy choices.

Consider the following example: Before 1970, U.S. states could terminate benefits to welfare recipients as soon as the state welfare department decided that the recipient no longer satisfied the eligibility requirements. State law simply required that the agency send a letter to the recipient explaining that benefits had been terminated and that the recipient could request a hearing to dispute the agency's decision. No benefits were paid while these hearings were pending.

In accordance with applicable state law, benefits to several welfare recipients in New York were terminated. The recipients appealed to federal court, claiming that the State of New York had violated the due process clause of the U.S. Constitution. The clause, included in the Fourteenth Amendment, states that no person may be deprived of "life, liberty, or property" without due process of law. Claiming that welfare benefits are property, the plaintiffs argued that they could not be terminated unless the state gave recipients an opportunity for an oral hearing *before* the termination of benefits. Only in this way would the state be respecting the right to due process before depriving anyone of property.

The state interpreted the due process clause differently. It argued that the clause did not require the state to give the welfare recipient a hearing whenever the state concluded that he or she was no longer eligible for benefits. After all, the recipient was not being put in jail or being subjected to a fine.

The Supreme Court agreed with the welfare recipients, overturning the New York law.*

The Supreme Court's decision fundamentally altered the day-to-day administration of welfare policy throughout the country. A dissenting justice (Hugo Black) contended that the decision would require states to hire more lawyers and to devote more of the money allocated for public welfare to litigation expenses. Moreover, he suggested, the new arrangement could make welfare caseworkers reluctant to approve borderline welfare applications, since it would now be more costly and time-consuming to terminate benefits awarded in error. Whether for good or ill, the way in which welfare policy is implemented in a number of states was significantly affected by the Supreme Court's interpretation of fewer than a dozen words of the Constitution.

Judicial decisions can also change or make policy when no constitutional or basic law issues are at stake. For example, beginning in the 1930s, U.S. federal law established that employees have the right to bargain collectively with their employers, and that employers are guilty of an "unfair labor practice" when they refuse to bargain with a legally constituted union. In the 1940s, a group of "newsboys" (that rather old-fashioned term was used in the case) sought to bargain collectively with the Hearst Corporation. Hearst refused, claiming that the "newsboys" were not "employees" within the meaning of the law. At that point, federal law did not specify what the term *employee* meant; it only stated that employees had certain labor rights. In a very controversial decision, the Supreme Court held that the National Labor Relations Board could legally conclude that newsboys were "employees," and that, consequently, the Hearst Corporation was guilty of an unfair labor practice in refusing to bargain collectively with them.† The Court thereby affected the development of national labor policy by resolving this specific dispute between several dozen sellers of newspapers and one corporation.

The point here is that judicial policy making is *inevitable*. Courts cannot limit the impact of their judgments to the parties before them. The interpretation of law changes policies and programs, sometimes altering decisions previously considered to be political or even managerial matters. How we evaluate the reality of judicial policy making is a subject of continuing controversy.

PERSPECTIVES ON JUDICIAL POLICY MAKING

Judicial Restraint

The idea of **judicial restraint** is that courts should accept the decisions of legislative, executive, and administrative officials except when those decisions are *clearly* contrary to basic law or inconsistent with other legal guidelines. Challenges to the constitutional acceptability of a law should be evaluated according to the intentions

---

* The landmark case was *Goldberg v. Kelly,* 397 U.S. 254, 1970.

† See *National Labor Relations Board v. Hearst,* 322 U.S. 111 (1944).

of those who drafted the constitution or the law in question. Thus, judges should overturn a piece of legislation only if it is clearly in violation of explicit constitutional provisions.

For example, in the welfare rights case, judicial restraint would demand that courts interpret the Constitution narrowly. The drafters of the due process clause surely did not have welfare benefits in mind when they wrote it; the clause was intended to require a fair trial before a person is punished (by forfeiting life, liberty, or property) for violating the law. Advocates of judicial restraint would therefore argue that the court "made up" law when it forced New York to provide an oral hearing to welfare recipients before termination of benefits. If policy is to be changed in this way, it is legislators, not the courts, who should make the change.

An important rationale for this position is that courts lack democratic legitimacy as policy makers. In democratic systems, legislatures and elected executives are legitimate policy makers because they were supposedly selected by the voters on the basis of their announced policy positions. If they make policy choices that the people oppose, the voters will elect different legislators or executives in the next election. Judges making policy are not subject to those critical democratic safeguards.

Other reasons have been offered in support of judicial restraint. The process of judicial decision making itself arguably makes courts poor policy-making bodies. Courts can take into account only the information brought to them, and the cases that come their way may be exceptional and unrepresentative of the broader context in which the policy change will be implemented. In contrast, legislators and executives, along with administrative agencies, can gather information extensively, and they can make policy on the basis of the typical, not the extraordinary, cases.[13]

Even in European judicial systems, where judicial review is far less prominent than in the United States, judicial policy making is controversial. Politicians and judges in Italy, France, and Germany continue to disagree about the propriety of an active judicial role. Some argue that "where a gap in the [law] exists, the judge should imagine what the legislature would do. [Others] specify that the judge should imagine what he [or she] would do if he [or she] were the legislature."[14]

Judicial Activism

One of the most common responses to the judicial restraint idea is the notion that courts have a special ability to represent minority political interests, and that these interests will never obtain adequate representation from institutions that naturally respond to majorities of voters. Proponents of **judicial activism** thus argue that some minority interests are permanently excluded from effective participation. Judicial policy making may effectively represent those interests when the other parts of the political system seem closed to them.

For example, the policy of desegregating U.S. public schools was initiated by a judicial decision (*Brown v. Board of Education of Topeka*, 347 U.S. 500, 1954). Efforts to achieve desegregation had repeatedly failed in legislative action at both the state and the federal levels. In a sense, the courts provided political representation to voices left unheeded by the other policy-making institutions of the system.* If strict doctrines of

---

* The idea that courts may generally represent the interests of those who are "politically disadvantaged" in their abilities to exert influence elsewhere in the political system is discussed in Chapter 6.

judicial restraint meant that courts could not engage in policy making, courts would not be able to enhance representation in this way.

Advocates of judicial restraint quickly point out that although judicial activism sometimes produces good policies, it is, as a process, inconsistent with democracy because judges (at least on the federal level) are not elected. However, at least one political scientist has recently argued that courts should be active in policy decisions even though they are not politically accountable and even though they cannot be politically neutral. According to this view, "there is nothing wrong with a political court or with political motives in constitutional adjudication."[15] The tension between advocates of activism and restraint guarantee that this issue will remain unresolved for generations. (See Box 9-5.)

Box 9-5

THE COURTS AS POLICY MAKERS: A DEBATE

© Fareed Al-Mashat

© AP Photo

The late John Hart Ely was among the most prominent legal scholars in U.S. history. His *Democracy and Distrust—A Theory of Judicial Review* (1980) is the most frequently cited book about law published in the 20th century. He died in 2003.

A portrait by Alonzo Chappel of Chief Justice John Marshall, who headed the U.S. Supreme Court from 1801 to 1835.

Whether or not courts should be engaged in policy making continues to be a topic of heated argument among legal scholars, political theorists, and politicians.

Two well-known U.S. contemporary legal writers reflect opposite perspectives on the issue in striking terms.
(Continued)

Box 9-5

THE COURTS AS POLICY MAKERS: A DEBATE
(*Continued*)

Former President Gerald Ford, left, introduces Supreme Court Associate Justice nominee Robert Bork, Tuesday September 15, 1987, as the Senate Judiciary Committee began confirmation hearings on the nomination on Capitol Hill. Ford praised Bork as being "uniquely qualified" for the post. At right is Sen. Robert Dole, R-KS, who also made a statement on Bork.

Robert Bork, a former judge on the U.S. Court of Appeals whom the Senate refused to confirm when President Reagan nominated him for the Supreme Court in 1987, is perhaps the most famous contemporary advocate of judicial restraint. In a case involving whether the due process clause protects the right of people to engage in homosexual conduct in private, Judge Bork described the role of the court in policy making in the following way:

> [This court is] asked to protect from regulation a form of behavior never before protected and indeed traditionally condemned. If the revolution in sexual mores that the [petitioner] proclaims is to arrive, it must arrive through the moral choices of the people and their elected representatives, not through the ukase of this court. . . . The Constitution creates specific rights. A court that refuses to create a new constitutional right to protect homosexual conduct does not thereby destroy established rights that are solidly based in constitutional text and history.[16]

Bork's way of thinking—one that emphasizes that judges must be careful to follow the plain meaning of the words in the Constitution and in statutes—is often termed "strict constructionism." Perhaps the first person to use this phrase in describing how judges should interpret law was Chief Justice John Marshall, in 1824:

> What do gentlemen mean by a "strict construction"? If they contend only against that enlarged construction, which would extend words beyond their natural and obvious import, we . . . should not controvert the principle. . . . As men whose intentions require no concealment generally employ the words which most directly and aptly express the ideas they intend to convey, the enlightened patriots who framed our Constitution, and the people who adopted it, must be understood to have employed words in their natural sense, and to have intended what they have said. (*Gibbons v. Ogden*, 9 Wheat. 1, 1824).

The late John Ely, also a leading legal scholar (by one count, he is the fourth most cited legal scholar of all time), saw a broader role for judicial decision making than Marshall or Bork. Arguing that the elected institutions of government do not function perfectly to represent all of society's interests, Ely suggested that judicial policy making may fill in some important gaps:

> It is an appropriate function of the [Supreme] Court to keep the machinery of democratic government running as it should, to make sure the channels of political participation and communication are kept open. The Court should also concern itself with what majorities do to minorities, particularly [in the case of] laws "directed at" religious, national, and racial minorities and those infected by prejudice against them.[17]

Ely claimed that if courts allow themselves to infuse their own ideas into the interpretation of constitutional provisions, they can engage in judicial policy making that will be "representation enhancing." Thus, they would secure minority rights that would be demolished by the unchecked activities of other parts of the political system, and which would be unaddressed if courts simply applied the intentions of those writing

---

Box 9-5

THE COURTS AS POLICY MAKERS: A DEBATE
(*Continued*)

laws and constitutions in centuries gone by. To make the system work, claimed Ely, courts must be able to go beyond "strict constructionism," interpreting constitutional provisions not in a neutral or objective sense (which he and many others feel is impossible anyway), but by interpreting them to the advantage of groups and citizens who have little political influence in the elected branches of government.

The debate over judicial activism is a sticky problem for many political systems, but particularly for the United States, as we will see in Chapter 11.

Judicial Policy Making as a Stabilizing Force

Abrupt changes in policy can be destabilizing in any society. When legislatures create new rights or obligations, they radically affect personal, economic, and other kinds of interests. Lawmakers may attempt major transformations of policies in various areas, and although the changes may be ultimately wise, they may threaten the stability of the system. A third perspective thus approves of judicial policy making because of its potentially moderating influence on changes emerging from legislatures and executives.

In practice, judicial policy making may provide for more gradual changes in policy. Historians suggest, for example, that when the U.S. Supreme Court struck down numerous aspects of President Franklin Roosevelt's New Deal legislation in the 1930s, its decisions had the effect of making the greatly expanded federal regulation of the marketplace a more gradual development. If the Court had had no power to make policy, the country would have been subjected to radical shifts in economic policy literally overnight, with possibly severe impacts on political stability.

Hence, the judicial role in policy making is a mixed blessing, even in democratic systems. The necessity for judicial institutions, and their inevitable involvement in legal and constitutional interpretation, suggests that the role of courts in the political process will continue to be challenging and controversial as modern governments address contemporary problems.

 WHERE ON THE WEB?

http://www.conseil-constitutionnel.fr/langues/anglais/ang4.htm

The home page for the French Constitutional Council.

http://curia.eu.int/en/index.htm

The home page for the Court of Justice of the European Communities.

http://www.law.cornell.edu/supct/justices/fullcourt.html

Photos of current U.S. Supreme Court justices, along with opinions and articles written by them.

http://www.findlaw.com/casecode/supreme.html

A reference service providing links to all decisions of the U.S. Supreme Court.

http://www.stf.gov.br

The home page for the Supreme Federal Tribunal of Brazil.

http://www.supcourt.ru/EN/supreme.htm

The home page for the Supreme Court of the Russian Federation (includes English version).

http://www.law.nyu.edu/lawcourts

The home page of the "Law and Courts" section of the American Political Science Association. The site "is designed to provide a variety of services to section members and other navigators interested in law, courts, and judicial politics."

http://www.worldlawdirect.com

A commercial law site designed to provide answers to thousands of questions about law and courts around the world.

http://www.legal500.com/

The official Web site of the "Legal 500 Series," a resource for commercial lawyers worldwide.

◆ ◆ ◆

Key Terms and Concepts _____

adversarial system	judicial review
appellate courts	justice
basic law	Missouri Plan
civil law	natural law
common law	parliamentary supremacy
criminal law	plaintiff
defendant	positive law
grand jury	statutory interpretation
inquisitorial system	statutory law
judicial activism	trial courts
judicial restraint	

Discussion Questions _____

1. Why is the selection of judges often so controversial? What conflicting goals are involved?
2. What is natural law?
3. How do courts become involved in public policy making?
4. What is the difference between the inquisitorial and adversarial systems of justice?
5. Does "judicial restraint" mean that judges should never overturn legislation?

Notes _____

1. The functions of judicial institutions are discussed in detail in Martin Shapiro, *Courts: A Comparative and Political Analysis* (Chicago: University of Chicago Press, 1981). Some of the text's discussion is adapted from this source.
2. See Henry J. Abraham, *The Judicial Process*, 4th ed. (New York: Oxford University Press, 1980), pp. 105–107; and Shapiro, *Courts*, pp. 133ff.
3. Charles R. Epp. "Do Bills of Rights Matter? The Canadian Charter of Rights and Freedoms," *American Political Science Review* 90 (December 1996): p. 765.
4. Lief H. Carter, *Reason in Law* (Boston: Little, Brown, 1979), p. 110.
5. Ibid., p. 111.
6. See Sabrina Shizue McKenna, "Proposal for Judicial Reform in Japan: An Overview," *Asian- Pacific Law and Policy Journal* 2 (Spring 2001).
7. See Henry J. Abraham, *The Judicial Process*, 5th ed. (New York: Oxford University Press, 1986).
8. See Gregory A. Huber and Sanford C. Gordon, "Accountability and Coercion: Is Justice Blind When It Runs for Office?" *American Journal of Political Science* 48 (April 2004): 247–263.

9. See Gretchen Helmke, "The Logic of Strategic Defection: Court-Executive Relations in Argentina Under Dictatorship and Democracy," *American Political Science Review* 96 (June 2002): 291–303; and J. Mark Ramseyer and Eric B. Rasmusen, "Why Are Japanese Judges So Conservative in Politically Charged Cases?" *American Political Science Review* 95 (June 2001): 331–344.

10. Henry J. Abraham, *The Judicial Process* (New York: Oxford University Press, 1962), p. 251.

11. See William Safran, *The French Polity* (New York: Longman, 1991), pp. 178–182.

12. K. L. Bhatia, *Judicial Review and Judicial Activism: A Comparative Study of India and Germany from an Indian Perspective* (New Delhi: Deep and Deep Publications, 1997).

13. See David Horowitz, *The Courts and Social Policy* (Washington, DC: Brookings, 1977).

14. Shapiro, *Courts*, p. 146.

15. See Terri Jennings Peretti, *In Defense of a Political Court* (Princeton, NJ: Princeton University Press, 1999), p. 73.

16. *Dronenburg v. Zech*, 741 F. 2d 1388 (1984), pp. 1396–1397. Quoted in Archibald Cox, *The Court and the Constitution* (Boston: Houghton Mifflin, 1987), p. 331.

17. John Hart Ely, *Democracy and Distrust* (Cambridge: Harvard University Press, 1980), p. 76.

For Further Reading ⎯⎯⎯⎯⎯

Bhatia, K. L. *Judicial Review and Judicial Activism: A Comparative Study of India and Germany from an Indian Perspective.* New Delhi: Deep and Deep Publications, 1997.

Buurca, Graainne, and J. H. H. Weiler. *The European Court of Justice.* Oxford: Oxford University Press, 2002.

Cardozo, Benjamin. *The Nature of the Judicial Process.* New Haven: Yale University Press, 1921.

Carter, Lief H. *Reason in Law.* 7th ed. New York: Longman, 2004.

Dean, Meryll. *Japanese Legal System: Text, Cases, and Materials.* 2nd ed. London: Cavendish Publishing, 2003.

Dworkin, Ronald. *Sovereign Virtue: The Theory and Practice of Equality.* Cambridge, MA: Harvard University Press, 2002.

Dworkin, Ronald. *Taking Rights Seriously.* Cambridge: Harvard University Press, 1978.

Ely, John Hart. *Democracy and Distrust.* Cambridge: Harvard University Press, 1980.

Hart, H. L. A. *The Concept of Law.* 2nd ed. New York: Oxford University Press, 1997.

Helmke, Gretchen. "The Logic of Strategic Defection: Court–Executive Relations in Argentina Under Dictatorship and Democracy." *American Political Science Review* 96 (June 2002): 291–303.

Hesse, Joachim Jens, and Nevil Johnson. *Constitutional Policy and Change in Europe.* New York: Oxford University Press, 1995.

Holland, Kenneth M., ed. *Judicial Activism in Comparative Perspective.* New York: St. Martin's, 1991.

Huber, Gregory A., and Sanford C. Gordon. "Accountability and Coercion: Is Justice Blind When It Runs for Office?" *American Journal of Political Science* 48 (April 2004): 247–263.

Kritzer, Herbert. *Legal Systems of the World: A Political, Social, and Cultural Encyclopedia.* Santa Barbara, CA: ABC-CLIO, 2002.

Menski, Werner F. *Comparative Law in a Global Context: The Legal Systems of Asia and Africa,* 2nd ed. New York: Cambridge University Press, 2006.

Posner, Richard A. 2008. *How Judges Think.* Cambridge, MA.: Harvard University Press.

Ramseyer, J. Mark, and Eric B. Rasmusen. "Why Are Japanese Judges So Conservative in Politically Charged Cases?" *American Political Science Review* 95 (June 2001): 331–344.

Svensson, Marina. *Debating Human Rights in China: A Conceptual and Political History.* Lanham, MD: Rowman and Littlefield, 2002.

Trochev, Alexei. 2008. *Judging Russia: The Role of the Constitutional Court in Russian Politics 1990–2006.* Cambridge, U.K.: Cambridge University Press.

Tushnet, Mark, ed. *Arguing Marbury v. Madison,* Palo Alto, CA: Stanford University Press, 2005.

© Alan Kim/The Roanoke Times/AP Photo

10

BUREAUCRATIC
INSTITUTIONS

◆ What Is Bureaucracy? ◆ Bureaucratic Functions
◆ The Growth of Bureaucracy ◆ Bureaucracy Evaluated
◆ Bureaucracy and Democracy ◆ Can Bureaucracy
Be Improved? ◆ Bureaucracy in Political Life

On April 16, 2007, Seung Hui Cho, a senior at Virginia Tech, killed 33 people and wounded at least 28 others using two handguns and 400 rounds of ammunition. He killed two persons at 7:00 a.m. in a residence hall, then returned to his room to change clothes. Within an hour or so, he was walking around the campus like other students. Responding quickly to a 9-1-1 call received at 7:15, police officers from both the city and the campus cordoned off the initial crime scene, and they began investigating, working on the reasonable assumption that the double murder would prove to be the extent of the day's violence.

At 8:25, the "leadership team" at the university met to develop a plan to get information to students regarding the shooting. While this meeting was underway, Cho entered an engineering classroom building and quickly chained the doors from the inside to prevent those inside from escaping. He began shooting people and had killed 30 students and staff by 9:50.

In an effort to identify actions (or inactions) that may have contributed to the tragedy, analysts have emphasized two general problems. First, a confusing set of procedures and rules protecting the privacy of students may have prevented effective communication regarding Cho's worsening psychotic behavior. The Family Educational Records Privacy Act (FERPA) and the Health Insurance Portability and Accountability Act (HIPAA) both contain provisions restricting the disclosure of information about students in counseling. According to a panel of eight experts appointed by Virginia Governor Tim Kaine:

> [FERPA and HIPAA are] confusing and inconsistent. . . . [T]he records of the Cook Counseling Center at Virginia Tech come under FERPA; those of Carilion St. Albans Behavioral Health Center, where Cho was taken in December 2005 under a Temporary Detention Order because he was judged to be a danger to himself or others, come under HIPAA. But while Carilion St. Albans could and did share Cho's records with Cook under the provisions of HIPAA, it could not be assured that Cook Counseling Center would reciprocate, since FERPA is unclear about institutions' sharing records with outside entities. . . . Institutions need to break through current barriers to communication to ensure that information about potential threats is shared by everyone who needs to know.*

Moreover, there was important information about Cho's troubled high school experiences, but rules prevented Virginia Tech officials from obtaining it. No one can be sure, but some speculate that if university officials had been in possession of more information about Cho, steps could have been taken to prevent his deepening psychosis.

Second, rules governing emergency procedures at Virginia Tech created a fatal delay in notifying students that a shooting had occurred and that the perpetrator remained at large. Many institutions authorize a single official to issue emergency notifications, but Virginia Tech required that senior officials meet and decide what to include in a notification and how and when to release it. If the student body had been informed by 8:00 that two people had been shot to death by a person who might still be in their midst, the death toll could have been substantially lower.

* This account is based on a report in *Change: The Magazine of Higher Learning*, published in cooperation with the Carnegie Foundation for the Advancement of Teaching, January/February 2008, available at: http://www.changemag.org/Archives/Back%20Issues/January-February%202008/full-connecting-the-dots.html.

No serious person questions the commitment or professionalism of the Virginia Tech or Blacksburg police leadership in responding to this tragic incident. However, the rules and organizational features common to nearly all bureaucracies quite possibly had an impact on the institution's ability to prevent and minimize the bloodshed.

The problem of *bureaucracy* figures strongly in the problem of emergency management, as it does in most major governmental activities. As in this case, the nature and the behavior of bureaucratic institutions affect politics and government in all countries. We often think that government is all about policy *making*; that is why we focus so much attention on elections and on executive and legislative institutions. But policies must be *implemented*, and the workings of the **bureaucracy** often make the difference between success and failure, efficiency and waste, and even life and death.

Bureaucratic power is important in all countries. In nations with constantly shifting legislative coalitions and weak chief executives, the bureaucracy may be the primary decision-making body, largely because it is the only part of the government with experience in getting things done. Sometimes, bureaucracy dominates because leaders diminish the importance of other political institutions. During the 1960s and 1970s, military leaders seized power in several of the more economically developed countries of Latin America (Brazil, Argentina, Chile, Uruguay). The generals who took office had a bureaucratic approach to government that they had acquired in military administration, and they often blamed many of their countries' problems on political parties, elected officials, and the democratic process itself. They essentially disregarded legislatures and strengthened the hand of civilian "technocrats" (bureaucrats with economic or other technical training).[1]

Some democratic governments have delegated far greater authority to their bureaucracies than does the United States. The power of high-ranking bureaucrats in Great Britain is so widely recognized that a late 1980s television sitcom titled *Yes, Prime Minister* spoofed a fictitious prime minister who was repeatedly manipulated by senior civil servants. France's very centralized and powerful national bureaucracy predates the French Revolution and provided efficiency and stability during a period (1945–1958) when the nation's prime minister and cabinet changed on the average of once every six months. The French Fifth Republic (1958–present) brought far greater political stability. Many of the most critical policy decisions are made by the president or the prime minister in concert with high-ranking technocrats, particularly those in the planning commissions.

In short, bureaucratic power exerts great influence in virtually all political systems. In the United States, bureaucrats make more than 80 laws (in the form of administrative regulations) for each law passed by Congress.[2] Those rules establish the level of emissions that will be tolerated from coal-burning power plants, a wide range of safety requirements, and other matters that involve basic policy choices. They decide where and how roads will be built, they approve and deny requests for public welfare, and they write and evaluate environmental impact statements. Regardless of culture or form of government, bureaucracy is a fact of modern political life. In this chapter, we study what a bureaucracy is, why it tends to grow in modern societies, why it is so often criticized, and how its power challenges democratic values.

WHAT IS BUREAUCRACY?

Although we often use the term *bureaucracy* as a pejorative ("He's just a mindless bureaucrat" or "She's going to give us some bureaucratic resistance"), the term actually refers to a distinctive form of organization.

The famous German sociologist Max Weber (we discussed his classic ideas about leadership in Chapter 8) set forth the concept of the bureaucracy in 1922. His work was an attempt to describe what he believed to be the basic features of a form of organization that would eventually exist in all modern societies. In fact, Weber argued that bureaucracy was an essential part of modern life. He identified several core principles of this new form of organization:[3]

1. Bureaucratic workers operate within **fixed jurisdictions** and are responsible for specific tasks. This enables bureaucrats to develop expertise in particular areas, and it also makes bureaucracy accountable, by establishing which individuals are responsible for which concerns.

2. Bureaucrats exercise authority within a firm system of **hierarchy.** Subordinates are clearly under the control of their superiors, a fact known by subordinate and superior alike. In a well-ordered bureaucracy, this strengthens accountability, because each bureaucrat knows which person he or she is expected to obey.

3. Bureaucracy operates on the basis of *written rules.* Consistency of treatment and efficiency are improved when bureaucrats are required to keep detailed official records of their actions and when specific rules apply to specific cases. Without a system of written rules, two welfare claimants with identical circumstances would receive different treatment, for example. Written rules ensure that the workings of bureaucracy do not depend on the personality or opinions of individual bureaucrats.

4. Bureaucrats assume their positions through *expert training.* Thus, bureaucrats should not normally be appointed on the basis of political **patronage** or through nepotism.

Weber's model was an ideal that the bureaucracies of even the most modern nations fail to achieve fully. In virtually all countries, including the United States, patronage and personal connections play a role in some bureaucratic appointments. Thus, in both Chicago and Mexico City, membership or active participation in the political party in power may be necessary to hold certain bureaucratic posts.

A 2006 study of bureaucracy in Ethiopia concluded that it is particularly difficult for a political system to maintain Weber's bureaucratic neutrality when ethnic or religious conflict is severe.[4] Where there is no shared national identity or uniform political culture, it is virtually impossible for a nation's bureaucracy to embody the traditional bureaucratic values of objectivity and consistency or professionalism. In such settings, the political leadership uses the bureaucracy to its own ends, ignoring the disenfranchised and creating a spoils system that undermines bureaucratic efficiency.

Yet Weber's model is worth considering for three reasons. First, even though bureaucratic principles are not perfectly realized anywhere, they are achieved to some degree everywhere. Second, Weber's model identifies those characteristics of

This cartoon satirizes bureaucracy in the U.S., but bureaucracies in virtually all political systems could have been the target of the cartoonist.

bureaucracies that can make them effective agents of public policy. Finally, we suggest that the very characteristics that Weber enumerated may have both negative and positive consequences. Indeed, scholars, bureaucrats, and politicians alike in various countries differ about how fully governmental bureaucracies *should* match the Weberian ideal.

Who Are the Bureaucrats?

In defining which people are bureaucrats, it is necessary to distinguish between theory and practice. We usually refer to all government officials who are not elected to a legislature or to a chief executive's post, and who are not judges or soldiers, as bureaucrats. For our purposes in this text, we define the term more narrowly in accordance with Weber's usage:

> **Bureaucrats** *are public officials who acquire their positions on the basis of their qualifications and skills and who are primarily responsible for the implementation of public policy.*[5]

The degree of professionalization within actual bureaucracies varies greatly. Perhaps the most decidedly professional national bureaucracy is the French civil service. In France, most senior civil servants are recruited from the Ecole Nationale d'Administration (ENA), a highly competitive and prestigious institution of higher learning. In general, recruitment and promotion in the French civil service are closely tied to professional skills.[6] Although the U.S. bureaucracy is not as highly professionalized as the French—largely because of the absence of a national training institution dedicated to producing a corps of career bureaucrats—the use of entrance and promotional examinations ensures some level of professional skill.

British bureaucrats have a somewhat different reputation. Although they are also highly respected for their integrity and dedication, they are often criticized for elitism and lack of technical expertise. Senior civil servants often come from upper-class backgrounds and may benefit from having the proper connections in the "old boys'" network. Many have been educated at Oxford or Cambridge, but they tend to be generalists with a nontechnical education and are consequently less qualified than their French or German counterparts to deal with the economic and technical problems of a modern, complex society.

In communist political systems, government bureaucrats are often recruited and promoted on the basis of their commitment to the regime's ideology rather than on the basis of their technical expertise. Following the Cuban Revolution, for example, agricultural production suffered because managers of state farms (officials in the Ministry of Agriculture and bureaucrats in the agrarian reform agency) were often selected on the basis of their commitment to the revolution, even if they knew nothing about farming. In both the Chinese and the Mexican bureaucracies, young administrators wishing to advance up the organizational ladder must attach themselves to a more powerful patron within their ministry or agency. As that patron advances up the bureaucratic ladder, he or she will bring lower-ranking "clients" up as well.

Thus, in everyday parlance, the term *bureaucrat* applies to a rather wide variety of people in different systems. But using Weber's approach, the most "bureaucratic" bureaucrat is one who fits the ideal of being appointed on the basis of expertise and training, despite the fact that, in practice, many bureaucrats are selected on other grounds. As discussed later in the chapter, scholars and politicians have long debated whether bureaucrats should be neutral experts or people chosen for partisan reasons by an elected leader; the former may be more expert, but the latter are more likely to represent the political values of the citizenry. This tension between the values of competence and representativeness exists in virtually all bureaucracies.

BUREAUCRATIC FUNCTIONS

Although the tasks assigned to bureaucrats vary widely, even among developed democratic nations, there are certain universal bureaucratic functions. The distinguishing features of those tasks are their technical nature and the level of detail they involve.

Revenue Collection

No viable political system can govern without tax revenues, and a regular, established process for collecting taxes is a key element of effective government. A specialized agency for tax collection is typically found in all developed systems, democratic or otherwise.

National Defense

In most countries, a significant proportion of modern government spending is devoted to national defense. In addition to the members of the armed forces, this function requires a considerable "army" of bureaucrats. Civilians employed by the

U.S. Department of Defense currently number nearly 698,000, for example, and those employees are essential to the procurement of supplies and weapons systems and general management.

Service Delivery

Many services cannot be provided effectively by private means. Public health services, road construction, national park and forest management—among many other services—would not be performed as well, or would not be as widely available, if government agencies did not provide them. The magnitude of bureaucratic service delivery varies considerably, however, across systems. In Canada, New Zealand, Germany, and France, for example, bureaucracies provide a more extensive array of public services than in the United States.

Income Maintenance and Redistribution

Governments in modern industrial societies, capitalist and socialist alike, have established agencies to administer a wide variety of "safety net" programs designed to help people in financial difficulty. Bureaucrats are essential in this area because the policies require that each applicant's eligibility be determined case by case and because most programs attempt to provide follow-up help to the recipients of government assistance.

Regulation

Most societies seek to regulate individuals and businesses to ensure the safety of consumer products and the workplace, to restrict the use of public lands, to protect the environment, and to maintain the fairness of competition in the marketplace, among many other purposes. Although some people believe that regulation is excessive in modern societies, almost everyone believes that some level of regulation is needed, and regulatory agencies are established for that purpose.

Research

The market provides only things that people will buy, and basic research is not easily packaged as a consumer product. When societies want to engage in large-scale scientific work, bureaucrats often play important roles. Private universities and even corporations also make contributions to scientific knowledge, but much of the most important basic research—such as space exploration and advanced work in nuclear physics—is managed by bureaucrats.

Specialized Governmental Functions

Nearly all governments also provide a national currency and postal services, with specialized bureaucratic agencies for each.

Management of State Enterprises

In most countries, even capitalist ones, some economic activities are publicly owned. These include the Tennessee Valley Authority (TVA) and most municipal bus systems in the United States; the computer, steel, and chemical industries in France; the petroleum industry in Mexico; the railroads and electric power in most of the world's nations; and the majority of industrial and commercial enterprises in China. Administration of those enterprises is an important part of bureaucratic activity.

THE GROWTH OF BUREAUCRACY

Bureaucracies expand as modern societies develop. Legislatures generally remain at a given size (although their staffs usually constitute growing bureaucracies in their own right), and societies usually do not increase the number of their chief executives. Bureaucratic agencies multiply and expand, however, suggesting that growth itself is possibly a universal characteristic of bureaucracy.

Figure 10.1 shows the growth of bureaucracy in the United States over six decades. Federal employment has increased slowly since the 1950s, but growth has been rapid at state and local levels. Not only are there more bureaucrats today, but their activities also consume a greater proportion of the nation's gross national product (GNP), and they constitute a larger proportion of the workforce than in previous decades.

FIGURE 10.1   GROWTH OF U.S. BUREAUCRACY

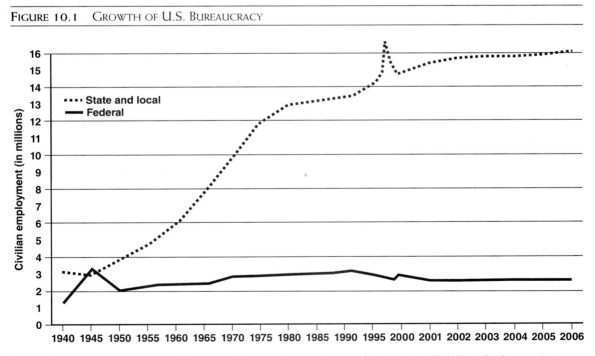

SOURCE: Department of Commerce, Bureau of the Census, *Statistical History of the U.S.* (New York: Basic Books, 1976), p. 1100; *Statistical Abstract of the U.S.* (Washington, DC: U.S. Government Printing Office, 1996), pp. 319, 346; data for 1997–2007 from the U.S. Census.

Why Does Bureaucracy Grow?

Political scientists usually give one of two basic explanations for the growth of bureaucracy. The first reflects our growing *need* for bureaucracy: We need more bureaucrats and agencies as scientific and technological advances make government activity increasingly necessary. As societies become industrialized, the tasks of monitoring and controlling pollution, regulating the safety of the workplace, and ensuring that consumer products are not harmful become more important and more difficult. Advances in science and industrial development eventually require government involvement as research expenses outstrip the resources of private organizations.

Industrial growth creates bureaucratic expansion in another way as well. When most of a society's people are concerned about their next meals, they have limited interest in broad social issues such as conservation or environmental protection. As people become more affluent, however, they often find that they care about a great range of social values. It is no coincidence that Americans and Europeans began to care deeply about protecting endangered species, ensuring the safety of workers and consumers, and wilderness preservation only after their societies became generally affluent.* Bureaucracies grow in response, as policies are made to address these concerns and agencies are established to implement them.

However, bureaucracies have also grown rapidly in developing nations, even with their lower levels of industrialization and economic modernization. For example, the devastating spread of AIDS in Eastern and Central Africa has forced governments in those regions to expand their public health bureaucracies.

Political pressures are a second reason for the growth of bureaucracies. In industrial democracies, interest groups demand regulations and services that require the creation of new agencies. In the U.S., organized labor was largely responsible for the establishment of the National Labor Relations Board and the laws it implements, and environmental interest groups successfully demanded the establishment of the Environmental Protection Agency. Indeed, in the United States almost all government agencies enjoy the support of at least a few influential interest groups.

In developing nations, bureaucracies sometimes emerge as the result of international as well as domestic political pressures. In Latin America, where farmland is generally concentrated in the hands of a small percentage of the rural population, pressures developed in the 1960s for reforms that would redistribute some land from large estates or uncultivated public property to poor farmers. In Peru, Colombia, Venezuela, Chile, and elsewhere, peasants organized federations, invaded large estates, and sometimes joined revolutionary movements to protest rural conditions. President John Kennedy, worried by the specter of the Cuban Revolution, launched a major foreign aid program for Latin America, called the Alliance for Progress. Under its terms, the United States promised economic assistance to nations that implemented land redistribution and other reforms. Anxious to maintain U.S. aid, virtually every country in the region passed reform legislation and created agrarian reform agencies. In time, only a few of those nations actually redistributed much land, but the reform bureaucracies remained, regardless of how much (or how little) change they actually administered.

---

* See the discussion of post-materialism in Chapter 3.

Box 10-1

THIRD-WORLD BUREAUCRACIES

Although bureaucracies are necessary components of any political system, they can become burdensome if they do not maintain proper professional standards. The governments of many developing countries over-staff their bureaucracies in order to reward political supporters and create employment for university and high school graduates facing a difficult job market. During the 1980s, Africa's public sector employed half the region's nonagricultural wage earners (many of whom worked in the bureaucracy). But a World Bank study of one West African country concluded that 6,000 of the 6,800 headquarters staff at two government ministries were redundant.[8]

While doing research at Ecuador's Ministry of Agriculture, one of this book's authors observed a ministry employee (whom we shall call "Mr. Sandoval") spending most of the day staring out the window or reading a book. Toward the end of the day, the office receptionist brought in a small group of peasants who wanted the ministry's help in a land dispute. When the nervous group leader had trouble getting his words out, the receptionist snapped at him, "Hurry up! Mr. Sandoval is a very busy man!" Not only do bloated bureaucracies create a drain on government expenditures, they also often justify their existence by turning out a vast array of regulations that stymie private businesses, large and small, and periodically force citizens of all kinds to spend hours on end getting unnecessary documents or permissions.

Political pressures of a different nature have also contributed to the expansion of Third World bureaucracies. (See Box 10-1.) Often, educational systems in developing nations have expanded more rapidly than employment opportunities in the modern sector of the economy. Hence, these nations are often faced with a large number of high school or university graduates who have no prospect for employment in the private sector. Left unattended, this group of skilled people might become a source of political unrest. Consequently, many governments prefer to hire them into the government bureaucracy, even if useful work cannot be found for them in the private sector. The visitor to a ministry of education or agriculture in Latin America will often see three bureaucrats doing the work of one.[7]

BUREAUCRACY EVALUATED

As noted earlier, the term *bureaucracy* often carries a negative connotation. Fortunately, real bureaucracies are not necessarily ineffective, unresponsive, or evil. Even in the United States, where bureaucracy regularly serves as a target of criticism during political campaigns, most people have fairly positive feelings about government agencies.* In a now-classic study, one researcher found that strong majorities of respondents considered government workers to be competent, efficient, and even friendly.[9] More systematic evaluations suggest a more balanced view: Bureaucracies have a great positive potential for *efficiency*, but they are almost universally plagued by *rigidity* and *resistance to innovation*.

---

* A new study of "bureaucracy bashing" in U.S. elections found that the negative comments made by politicians have actually harmed bureaucratic effectiveness by creating low morale, hampering the recruitment of talented personnel, and "fostering an environment of distrust." See R. Sam Garrett, James A. Thurber, A. Lee Fritschler, and David H. Rosenbloom, "Assessing the Impact of Bureaucracy Bashing by Electoral Campaigns," *Public Administration Review* 66 (March/April 2006): 228–241.

Positive Qualities of Bureaucracy: Efficiency and Responsibility

It may seem odd to speak of bureaucracy as efficient and responsible, but for many important functions of government, bureaucratic organization is the only way to approach acceptable levels of efficiency and responsibility. Before governments instituted bureaucracies, tasks were randomly assigned to amateurs who held positions on the basis of their friendship with a monarch or a politician. It was impossible to determine which person was responsible for which decision, and there was little specialized training. In contrast, core bureaucratic principles—clear lines of specialization and the strict application of written rules—enable the modern Internal Revenue Service, for example, to process millions of tax returns quickly and, generally, with considerable accuracy. A less "bureaucratic" arrangement would simply not work.

A Persistent Bureaucratic Problem: Rigidity and Resistance to Change

The most discussed, and probably most common, problem of bureaucracy has to do with rigidity. Bureaucracy is slow to adapt to new programs, conditions, or special concerns. It is not usually known for its encouragement of innovation. The problem of bureaucratic rigidity does *not*, however, stem from the personal characteristics of individual bureaucrats. According to Charles Goodsell's popular book on U.S. bureaucracy, "bureaucrats are no less flexible, tolerant, and creative than other people—perhaps they are a little more so."[10] If the problem is not caused by individuals, it must reflect deeper causes *inherent* in the nature of bureaucracy, and we should expect bureaucracy to resist change regardless of which people are in charge. Generations of study have identified three reasons that bureaucracies tend to resist change.

Rules and Routines   First, the same **routines**—written rules and procedures—that make possible the efficient processing of typical cases and decisions also make it difficult for bureaucracy to make adjustments or modifications when a special case arises. The mere existence of bureaucratic rules often tempts officials to try to fit unique cases into established categories when an innovative response would better serve the public. Although these rules and routines make bureaucracy more efficient *when they are appropriate*, some cases require unique solutions, and bureaucrats often try to solve them by applying established routines. (But see Box 10-2.)

Communication Problems   A second reason for bureaucratic inflexibility has to do with the fixed jurisdictions in which bureaucrats work. Communication is made difficult when each person's responsibilities are rigidly set. Bureaucrats have fixed jurisdictions and specialized responsibilities so that they can become experts in a narrow range of tasks and so that it will be clear who is responsible for which jobs, as discussed earlier. Those are important advantages to a bureaucracy. Nevertheless, some problems require discussion and cooperation among subordinates in different units. If bureaucrats feel that they can work only on problems assigned to them by their departmental supervisors, new solutions requiring joint operations with subordinates in other departments may be slow in coming.

Box 10-2

A CASE OF BUREAUCRATIC IMPROVISATION

Bureaucrats are called many things, but they are rarely considered experts at improvising. As discussed in this chapter, government organizations have strong tendencies toward rigid adherence to standard operating procedures and routines, and often that tendency is valuable in making bureaucracies predictable and dependable. However, when government encounters a situation demanding an innovative or flexible response, *sometimes* bureaucracies can rise to the task.

The state of Israel faced a tremendous and sudden challenge to its ability to provide decent housing in the 1990s. The former Soviet Union opened the doors to free Jewish emigration in 1988 after years of severe restrictions, and thousands of these citizens planned to relocate to Israel. By 1998, more than 800,000 Russian Jews had immigrated to Israel, increasing Israel's population by 15 percent.

Among the many problems that this huge influx of people caused (imagine moving all the residents of a city the size of Indianapolis suddenly into an already populated country the size of Delaware) was an impending housing shortage. Two specialists in public management who recently studied Israel's experience noted that "it was clear that [the new immigrants] would soon overwhelm the existing housing stock," and "the Ministry of Housing was thus left with the mission of providing the immigrants with a permanent roof in a very short space of time without adequate means." For a variety of reasons, the government concluded that it could not slow down the

immigrants' arrival, nor could it set up temporary tent housing.

The bureaucracy responded by improvising and cutting red tape. The Housing Ministry supported an act of the Knesset that allowed housing proposals for two hundred or more units to be approved through a streamlined process. Instead of handling everything centrally, the new arrangement gave power to six "District Housing Commissions," each of which was empowered to change existing land-use regulations, grant building contracts, and authorize building plans.

The improvising paid off. It cut construction time in half, "increased by a magnitude of four the rate of housing construction, and produced an adequate supply of housing for immigrants."* Israel's housing policy innovations show that bureaucracies can be innovative if the right conditions are in place. Specifically, bureaucracies need flexible and mentally agile personnel, and a culture that supports flexible solutions. (The authors of the study argued that the cultures in Germany, France, the Netherlands, Britain, and Australia are not very supportive of bureaucratic innovation, but that those in Italy, Spain, the United States, and Israel are.) Finally, they suggested that an "unpredictable and rapidly changing" set of problems can induce bureaucracies to depart from their standard procedures.

* See Ira Sharkansky and Yair Zalmanovitch, "Improvisation in Public Administration and Policy Making in Israel," *Public Administration Review* 60 (July–August 2000): 321–329.

© David H. Wells/CORBIS

A CRISIS FOR THE HOUSING MINISTRY Israel's Ministry of Housing faced a serious problem as hundreds of thousands of Russian Jews entered the country during the 1990s. This photograph shows the tent and drying laundry of a family of immigrants waiting for more substantial housing opportunities.

Change and Bureaucratic Power Bureaucracy also inhibits innovation because major changes in policies and operations often threaten the power position of specific managers. If a particular bureaucrat is in charge of, say, a snow-removal unit, he or she enjoys certain personal advantages (such as power, prestige, and control of a large budget). Those advantages would lead the bureaucrat to resist innovations that change his or her position. An innovative move to provide snow-removal service through contract work by private businesses may be a good idea, but it will be resisted if it leads to changes in the power positions of important bureaucrats.

Evidence from the former Soviet Union, China, and the developing world suggests that average citizens in those countries face far greater problems with bureaucratic rigidity than do citizens in other countries. One of the authors of this text

---

Box 10-3

THE FEDERAL EMERGENCY MANAGEMENT ADMINISTRATION (FEMA) AND THE NEW ORLEANS HURRICANES OF 2005

On August 29, 2005, a devastating hurricane made landfall in Louisiana, Mississippi, and Alabama. Katrina's winds, coupled with sea surges and levee failures, caused unprecedented damage, particularly to the city of New Orleans. Local, state, and federal officials were involved in evacuation and rescue efforts and agencies at all levels of government worked extensively to provide food, shelter, medical care, and transportation for thousands of evacuees.

A barrage of criticism followed the governmental response to Katrina. Thousands of people were homeless for months, shelters were overcrowded and dangerous, security for businesses was poor, and all efforts appeared uncoordinated. While some complaints were directed at New Orleans Mayor Ray Nagin, Louisiana Governor Kathleen Blanco, and President George Bush, the Federal Emergency Management Agency (FEMA) was the target of the most heated attacks.

FEMA was established in 1979 by President Jimmy Carter. It was elevated to cabinet status by President Bill Clinton in 1993 and incorporated into the Department of Homeland Security by President George W. Bush in 2003. In 1989, following another hurricane (Hugo), Senator Ernest Hollings (Democrat, South Carolina) opined that FEMA was staffed by "the sorriest bunch of bureaucratic jackasses I've ever known." Representative Norm Mineta (Democrat, California) said that "FEMA could screw up a two-car

parade." Following the Katrina disaster in 2005, Senator Trent Lott (Republican, Mississippi) specifically scolded FEMA's director Michael Browne: "If he doesn't solve a couple of problems that we've got right now, he ain't going to be able to hold the job, because what I'm going to do to him ain't going to be pretty." Senator Susan Collins (Republican, Maine) concluded that "governments at all levels failed," and expressed her concerns about the government's ability to handle a terrorist attack:

> If our system did such a poor job when there was no enemy, how would the federal, state and local governments have coped with a terrorist attack that provided no advance warning and that was intent on causing as much death and destruction as possible?[11]

Although many factors were involved in the unsatisfactory response to the Katrina disaster, there is widespread agreement that the results would have been far better if the bureaucratic institutions involved had been better organized and more efficiently managed.*

* See Sandra K. Schneider, "Administrative Breakdowns in the Governmental Response to Hurricane Katrina," *Public Administration Review* 65 (September/October 2005): 515–517. Also, see a Special Issue of the *Public Administration Review* devoted to "Administrative Failure in the Wake of Hurricane Katrina," December 2007, supplement to Vol. 67.

recalls receiving a notice in the mail, while he was living in Ecuador, telling him that a package had arrived from a family friend in the United States. Knowing that the parcel contained about $30 worth of English-language paperbacks and other items hard to come by in Quito, he headed for the post office naively believing that all he needed to do to retrieve his package was to show his slip of paper and perhaps pay a small fee. Two days later—after having passed through five government offices scattered around town, paid three minor taxes totaling $12, secured the requisite importer's license for $7, and had at least nine documents stamped— he returned to the post office to claim his package. He left feeling far more fortunate than the Ecuadoran woman in front of him on "the last line." She was solemnly informed by the postal clerk that she had underpaid one of her tax payments by 3 sucres (worth $.02 in U.S. currency) and would have to go back across town to straighten out that tax. The postal clerk was unswayed by the woman's explanation that she had merely paid what the bureaucrat at one of the tax windows had told her to pay.

BUREAUCRATIC FAILURE? Hurricane Katrina devastated New Orleans, leaving thousands homeless and destroying roads, businesses, and infrastructure. Bureaucracies at the federal, state, and local levels were severely criticized for delays and ineffectiveness in their responses.

© David J. Phillip/AP Photo

BUREAUCRACY AND DEMOCRACY

Nothing in Weber's list of bureaucratic principles mentions "government by the people." Instead, bureaucracy is "government by experts obeying their superiors." Decisions are made on the basis of training, analysis, and authority, not on the basis of opinion polls or votes. The realization that an establishment of bureaucrats makes most laws and decides most legal cases makes many people wonder whether a system with a large bureaucracy can really be democratic.

There is evidence that bureaucrats themselves are aware of the inconsistency between the guiding principles of bureaucratic activity and the ideals of democracy. According to a recent study of bureaucrats in Seoul, South Korea, many government officials regard basic elements of democracy as incompatible with bureaucracy.[12]

Why Bureaucracy Resists Democratic Control

The Bureaucrat's Information Advantage   Many administrative actions, decisions, and policies are based on scientific data, careful and elaborate studies, and highly technical issues. When a political leader questions a bureaucratic decision, he or she is usually in a poor position to evaluate whether or not the answer given by the bureaucrat is sound. The politician is a generalist; he or she knows a little about a great many issues. In contrast, the bureaucrat is usually a specialist with detailed knowledge of subject matter that may be highly technical. It is often difficult for the politician to make sense of the answers given by bureaucrats. One researcher found that there is a basic trade-off between the extent to which a bureaucracy develops useful expertise and the extent to which it remains politically dependent on elected legislators.[13] When legislators need an agency to acquire a broad range of expertise, they generally grant it a great deal of administrative independence, thus making political control more difficult.

Iron Triangles, Sloppy Hexagons, and Issue Networks   Even more important than their information advantage is the power that bureaucrats may enjoy as a result of their relationship with influential interest groups and legislative committees. The significance of this relationship is suggested by the **iron triangles** idea, as discussed in Chapter 6. Essentially, the term was coined to describe a close connection among bureaucratic agencies, interest groups, and legislative committees in specific policy areas. Interests outside the triangle are, according to the theory, typically powerless to force policy actions opposed by those inside it, and are powerless to resist what the insiders want.

Where the iron triangle concept is an accurate picture of how policy decisions are made, serious questions are raised about bureaucratic power. As discussed in Chapter 7, *reciprocity* is a common norm in democratic legislatures, suggesting that legislators often find it useful to support one member's proposals in return for that member's support on another matter. Legislative reciprocity can thus heighten the autonomy of iron triangles, since the whole legislature may be willing to permit one committee to act in accordance with its fellow triangle participants (so that the members of that committee will be tolerant in return). Taken to its logical conclusion, the iron triangle concept implies that by allying themselves carefully with influential interests,

---

Box 10-4

THE POLITICS OF BUREAUCRATIC "OPTIMISM"

Nearly all administrative agencies engage in some kind of forecasting. Bureaucrats estimate the growing (or declining) demand for the programs they implement, future cost changes, and the number of people who will need or want certain programs in the years ahead. Given that bureaucratic organization is supposed to be driven by specialized experience and expertise, we might expect that agencies would make objective forecasts relating to the programs they manage.

However, bureaucrats do not operate in the world of objective precision that Weber's famous model of bureaucracy described. The agencies they work in are part of a political system that impacts them in many ways. In 2007, two political scientists studied the accuracy of economic forecasts by the U.S. Social Security Administration and the Office of Management and Budget to determine if overly optimistic predictions could be accounted for. Their findings provide an excellent confirmation that the political system can influence bureaucratic decisions that, ideally, should reflect only careful, objective study. In other words, there is certainly a great deal of "politics" in administration.

Both the Social Security Administration and the Office of Management and Budget produce forecasts regarding inflation, unemployment, tax revenues, budget deficits, and the composition of the workforce, among other factors. Each of these factors is critical to decisions that the president and congress must make about tax reform, entitlement reform, and general spending choices. While being optimistic may be a part of a healthy human nature, governments need accurate predictions, but political considerations can apparently get in the way.

George A. Krause and J. Kevin Corder began their study by considering the incentives that bureaucrat leaders face. On one hand, they want to maintain a good relationship with the president, because he may be able to affect the agency's budget, and because he can make decisions regarding the persons appointed (and dismissed) from important administrative positions. On the other hand, bureaucrats are naturally concerned with the reputation of their agencies. Pressure from the White House may lead the agency to make rosy forecasts, but a concern for the agency's public standing will make most bureaucrats resist this influence.

Following simple rational choice assumptions, the researchers hypothesized that the OMB's predictions about economic conditions would be more optimistic than those of the SSA. Why the difference? Because there are more political appointees leading the Office of Management and Budget, the Social Security Administration is far more stable in its staffing and more independent of partisan influence. Consequently, while both agencies have to make predictions, the leadership of the OMB is not going to remain in power very long, thus giving these officials less of an incentive to safeguard the long-term reputation of their agency. The empirical findings generally confirmed the researchers' expectations. As Krause and Corder concluded: " . . . the organizational stability of executive agencies is directly linked to the ways that these public organizations balance the competing objectives of political responsiveness and neutral competence. . . ."[14]

This study will astonish few observers of bureaucracy. However, Krause and Corder have identified that the degree to which "politics" undermines the "neutral competence" of bureaucrats is, to some extent, predictable. When bureaucrats work in an agency that is closely tied to the influences of partisan strife, their objectivity is compromised more than when they are in organizations with the stability and independence to place greater weight on their long-term reputations.

---

bureaucratic agencies can insulate themselves from all but the friendliest control by the legislature.[15]

In developed countries, the explosion of interest groups during the past few decades has challenged the autonomy of the triangles. Environmental groups bring their interests to bear on, say, highway policy decisions that were previously made with the nearly exclusive involvement of a narrow range of actors. Consumer groups, feminist groups, and others similarly make demands that "invade" iron triangles. One political scientist suggested the term *big sloppy hexagons* to designate the more typical arrangement.[16] And, as we noted in Chapter 6, many analysts contend that the idea of an "issue network" more accurately describes the patterns of interaction among interest groups, bureaucrats, and legislative committees, because the term suggests the open, fluid, and diverse interactions that take place among the participants in most policy areas.[17] The situation is less predictable, with a wider range of interests involved, than when the iron triangle accurately described bureaucratic politics.

Nevertheless, the rise of issue networks and the erosion of iron triangles does *not* mean that bureaucrats are unable to use interest group power to increase their independence. The declining autonomy of the triangles simply means that bureaucrats must work harder to manage their interest group and legislative supporters, and there are few indications that they are unable to do so. Bureaucratic power continues to be an issue in contemporary democracies, and bureau and interest group alliances are still an important reason for that power.

Can Bureaucracy Be Made Compatible with Democracy?

The reality of bureaucratic power can arguably be accommodated within democratic principles in several ways. Considering them helps us appreciate the long-standing tension that has existed between bureaucracy and democracy.

The Politics/Administration Dichotomy   One approach is to deny the existence of the problem by invoking the *politics/administration dichotomy.* This is the simple idea that policies are made by politicians and that bureaucrats merely carry out, or administer, those policies. If bureaucratic power is applied only to the mundane tasks of implementing the policy choices made by political leaders, then we can be made to feel much more comfortable about the existence of bureaucratic power. Perhaps you have heard that "there is no Democratic or Republican way to pick up the garbage"; that sentiment is an expression of the politics/administration dichotomy. It suggests that bureaucrats make decisions on the basis of objective managerial considerations while steering clear of political matters. To the extent that this is true, the reality of bureaucratic power need not threaten democracy.

Nevertheless, this dichotomy cannot resolve our concerns about bureaucratic power in a democracy. As mentioned earlier, the vast majority of decisions—even many decisions involving basic policy choices—are actually made by bureaucrats. It is not enough, therefore, simply to assert the principle of the politics/administration dichotomy (see Box 10-5).

Technical Responsibility   Carl Friedrich, an important figure in political science from the first half of the twentieth century, suggested a second approach to the problem of bureaucratic power in a famous 1946 essay.[22] He began by admitting that bureaucrats make basic policy choices and, moreover, that they make so many of them, involving so much technical knowledge, that it is impossible for politicians to oversee bureaucrats effectively. Instead of concluding that democratic values are hopelessly lost, however, Friedrich suggested that bureaucrats are effectively controlled and made to act responsibly by *the force of their own standards and sense of professionalism.* He called that force **technical responsibility.**

========================= Box 10-5 =========================

THE "REPRESENTATIVE BUREAUCRACY?"

Democracies of all types claim that their legislatures, executive institutions, and possibly even their courts represent the interests, preferences, and demands of the people, but there have always been difficulties in setting up *bureaucracies* to be representative. As Ken Meier noted in his classic *American Political Science Review* essay, President Andrew Jackson was an early U.S. proponent of the **representative bureaucracy** idea, arguing that "any position in the government was so easily mastered that no training was needed," and that therefore the bureaucracy could be staffed by political allies of the party that won the most recent election.[18] The bureaucracy would then be likely to behave in ways that represent the majority of citizens, since it would be staffed by people who share the values of the politicians that won the election.

The most common complaint about politically representative bureaucracy is that it undermines the neutral competence that professionalism requires. If bureaucrats seek to please the politicians who appointed them, they cannot be expected to be fair, consistent, and professional, according to this view. On the other hand, bureaucrats who are driven *exclusively* by their sense of professional standards may become insensitive to the values of citizens. As discussed in the section on "technical responsibility," the conflict between representation and professionalism as bureaucratic principles has been a perplexing issue for generations.

Political scientists have attempted to shed light on the problem in recent years by empirical investigation. In a 1998 study, three researchers studied the staffing and behavior of the Farmers Home Administration (FmHA) to determine if an ethnically representative workforce led to policy outputs (in terms of loan approvals) that were fairer to minorities. The data confirmed the authors' hypothesis: the more representative the bureaucratic office, the greater the "likelihood that . . . officials will make loan decisions favoring minority applicants."[19] The next year, Meier and two associates analyzed some 350 local school districts over a period of six years, measuring the degree to which the staff of each district was representative of the population it served, in terms of ethnicity. They also measured the percentage of students who achieved passing grades on state-required competency exams in each district. The findings demonstrated that "both minority and non-minority students perform better in the presence of a representative bureaucracy."[20]

Finally, in 2006, Meier and Laurence J. O'Toole, Jr. reported an empirical study that compared the influence of bureaucrats and the influence of politicians, again using a school district setting. They compared the impact of bureaucratic representativeness and the impact of the representativeness of elected politicians on the educational success of ethnic minority students. They found that having a representative *bureaucracy* had more than four times the impact of having a representative *political leadership*. The clear implication is that "the influence of the bureaucracy trumps that of elected political leaders."[21]

At least in these specialized contexts, the evidence is clear that bureaucrats act differently when they are ethnically representative of the citizens they serve. In itself, this finding undermines the claim that a highly objective, neutral professionalism drives bureaucratic behavior, or that bureaucrats simply follow the directives they receive from politicians. Incorporating this realization into our understanding of democratic government remains a challenge, however. When a bureaucrat's own values lead him or her to implement and make policy in ways that work against the preferences of political leaders (and the voters who elected them), it becomes difficult to determine which interests or citizens the representative bureaucrat is representing.

==

The idea is simple. Bureaucrats normally feel the force of the standards used to evaluate performance in their respective fields. An environmental engineer considering a new pollution standard may not be effectively controlled by public opinion (since the public is not able to evaluate the decision independently), but the bureaucrat's desire to maintain his or her professional standing leads to generally sound and responsible decisions.

Friedrich's argument has merit. On a day-to-day basis, bureaucrats make more decisions on the basis of what sound professional practice demands than on the basis of public preferences. Yet, it takes little imagination to think of cases in which bureaucrats make decisions opposed by the public but nonetheless sound in technical terms. As one of Friedrich's critics pointed out, "Many a burglar has been positively hated for his technical skill."[23] Professional standards and technical responsibility may make bureaucrats skillful, but if they are doing things that the people do not want, their professionalism in doing them does not make their actions democratic.

An Expanded Role for Citizens   Other approaches emphasize changing bureaucratic procedures, especially those having to do with **citizen participation.** It is often suggested that bureaucrats will be more innovative, flexible, and responsive to public needs if they are forced to listen to the public as they make decisions. Many governments therefore require that public hearings be held before new bureaucratic rules and regulations are passed into law. The bureaucrats are not normally required to abide by the wishes expressed at those hearings, but at least they are exposed to the complaints and ideas presented. Evidence suggests that public hearings lead bureaucrats to consider problems from different perspectives as they encounter factors that had not occurred to them before such hearings, and that the hearings thereby affect actual decisions.[24]

In Cuba, elected representatives to local, regional, and even national legislative bodies (called organs of *Poder Popular,* or "popular power") meet periodically with their constituents to hear complaints about the performance of the state bureaucracy. Indeed, in a society where opposition to governmental policy is not tolerated, these sessions not only are aimed at discovering instances of bureaucratic incompetence or malfeasance but also serve as a pressure valve because they are the only real political complaint citizens may publicly lodge.

Unfortunately, most public hearings required by law in most developed or developing countries have little effect. The general public is normally not able to explore the highly technical issues involved in most bureaucratic decisions, and people's concerns are often met with such statements as: "Oh, we have considered that, and your idea cannot be adopted because of. . . . " Moreover, many ideas at public hearings are contradictory (as when hunters and animal rights advocates press for opposite changes in a compromise about hunting regulations). Thus, although it is difficult to be against the idea of citizen participation, the ability of participation to remove concerns about bureaucracy in a democracy is limited.*

Strengthened Political Supervision   This last approach has been used since bureaucracy was first established: Adopt reforms that enable elected officials to oversee bureaucracy more effectively. As mentioned earlier, the technical nature of many bureaucratic decisions, coupled with the vast number of bureaucrats and programs, normally makes it impossible for politicians to exert rigorous control. Nevertheless, steps can be taken to strengthen political supervision, thus improving the surveillance and monitoring of bureaucratic activity by both legislatures and chief executives.

---

* Internet-based surveys may be a promising approach for obtaining a fairly broad range of citizen input when bureaucrats make important decisions. See Mark D. Robbins, Bill Simonsen, and Barry Feldman, "Citizens and Resource Allocation: Improving Decision-Making with Interactive Web-Based Citizen Participation," *Public Administration Review* 68 (May/June 2008): 564–676.

Reorganizing the bureaucracy may also strengthen the hand of politicians in dealing with bureaucrats. Usually, reorganizing (that is, taking programs and officials from one agency and giving them to another or to a new agency) is advocated as an efficiency measure. Much duplication and waste are eliminated through effective reorganization. Nevertheless, reorganization can also help to disrupt the iron triangles that inevitably develop and that make bureaucrats so difficult to control. During the final years of the Soviet Union, Mikhail Gorbachev made great efforts at reorganization, largely in an attempt to counter the tremendous power of the Soviet bureaucracy. Richard Nixon initiated a failing attempt at a fundamental reorganization in the early 1970s, for much the same reason.

In conclusion, none of the methods of reconciling bureaucracy with democracy seems entirely satisfying. Even with technical responsibility, citizen participation, and strengthened political supervision, bureaucrats will inevitably have tremendous power in all modern societies. Dealing with this problem is an enduring challenge for all modern political leaders, democratic or otherwise.

CAN BUREAUCRACY BE IMPROVED?

Almost everyone agrees that governments must have bureaucracies, and yet almost everyone also feels that bureaucracies cause serious problems. Since bureaucracies cannot be eliminated, two sets of ideas have been advanced to improve them, to make them more adaptable and more easily controlled.

Make Bureaucracy Less "Bureaucratic"

Studies of business administration during the past 30 or 40 years suggest that organizations can become more adaptable if certain bureaucratic features are changed. For example, instead of maintaining the rigid lines of authority that lock people in fixed jurisdictions, many businesses have found it useful to give employees wider, more flexible job assignments. These arrangements allow workers to develop working relationships with many different people in the organization, not simply with people in the same official unit. Workers acquire a deeper interest in their tasks, since they are given a greater range of responsibility and more room for creativity. These organizations find it much easier to innovate and to adapt to changing circumstances.

The public sectors in many industrial democracies have also moved toward less "bureaucratic" bureaucracies. Although the basic bureaucratic rules are still observed to a large extent, the value of flexible organizational structure has made many public organizations more adaptable. For example, many federal agencies in the United States have adopted *flextime* scheduling, allowing workers to decide which hours during the week they will work. Workers who are given broader and more flexible jurisdictions are likely to bring more creative energy to their jobs.

Make Bureaucracy Smaller

Many people are becoming convinced that the best way to avoid the problems created by bureaucracy is to make it smaller, removing powers previously entrusted to bureaucrats and giving them to the private sector. In China, Deng Xiaoping called for sharp reductions in the bureaucracy during the 1980s. Although some of the reduction was associated with the transfer of economic activities (most notably, farming) to the private sector, bureaucratic cutbacks were an end in themselves. Clearly, Gorbachev had similar objectives in the former Soviet Union, although bureaucratic resistance stifled most of his efforts. In all communist societies, when state policy determines the prices and production of virtually all goods and services, bureaucratic shortcomings resonate throughout society. Taking some powers away from bureaucrats (and giving them to individuals making self-interested decisions in the marketplace) is one way to avoid bureaucratic problems.

Reducing the size of the vast state bureaucracies has become a high priority for many Latin American nations as well. Here, governments may be motivated as much by economic necessity as by the search for greater efficiency. Argentina, Mexico, and Brazil, for example, are saddled with huge budget deficits and vast external debts. To reduce those deficits and to secure refinancing of their debt from the International Monetary Fund (IMF) and from foreign banks, their recently elected governments have been forced to reduce the size of their bureaucracies.

In the United States, for similar reasons, some states, counties, and cities have "contracted out" for many public services previously handled by bureaucrats. When public officials decide how garbage is collected or how streets are cleaned, for example, it is argued that they have no incentive to be innovative or particularly efficient. Critics of *public* service delivery thus charge that this approach is inherently wasteful.[25] Greater efficiency would be attained if governments opened bidding among private firms for contracts to perform those services. Fewer bureaucrats would be employed, and fewer dollars would be spent.

However, the contracting approach remains controversial. Government loses some measure of control when public services are not provided directly by public servants. Some people question how diligent private contractors can be in seeing that services are provided *equitably* when they have such an incentive to maintain *efficiency*. (For example, private garbage crews working on a city contract may not serve hard-to-reach or poor sections of town as often as they serve well-to-do areas.) Attempts to privatize prisons have been particularly controversial. In any event, even if contracting out proves to be workable, it is not applicable to many bureaucratic functions.

BUREAUCRACY IN POLITICAL LIFE

What role does bureaucracy play in government and in our view of politics? Bureaucracy is obviously necessary. And if the work of government is going to be done with any measure of efficiency, consistency, and reliability, it will have to be done by organizations operating to a large degree in accordance with the principles of bureaucracy. It is worth noting that no modern system—regardless of culture, history, or ideological foundation—has been able to function effectively without a bureaucracy.*

* To some extent, China's Great Proletarian Cultural Revolution (particularly in the late 1960s) was an attempt to do without a bureaucracy. The effort failed miserably, as discussed in Chapter 14. During the first decade of the Cuban Revolution (1959–1969), Fidel Castro tried to run the country through a combination of revolutionary exhortation and personal charisma, with little bureaucratic control. Here, too, the attempt was an economic and political failure, though not nearly as disastrous as China's.

Although the necessity for bureaucracy is best understood in the context of carrying out government policy, it is also well established that bureaucrats do more than implement the decisions of others. The nature of their jobs brings bureaucrats into close contact with those they serve and regulate. That fact, coupled with their technical expertise, makes bureaucrats a powerful force contributing to public policy.

Bureaucracy, a necessary part of government, seems destined to resist control, making it a continuing source of tension in modern government. If the advantages of bureaucratic administration are to be maintained while controlling it and making it more adaptable, political leaders must approach the problem from a number of perspectives. Reforms calling for an enlarged citizen role, reorganization, strengthened political controls, and enhanced professionalism are all ways to enable political leaders to harness the power of bureaucracy without making it unable to perform its tasks. Understanding the benefits and the dangers of bureaucracy is vital for all modern political leaders.

 ## WHERE ON THE WEB?

Most Web sites pertinent to bureaucratic institutions are subject-matter specific. For example, sites are devoted to the U.S. Environmental Protection Agency, the British Department of Transport, and thousands of other agencies and bureaucracies around the world. Several universities also have sites devoted to their graduate programs in Public Administration. The following are a few illustrative sites as well as some general ones.

http://www.lafollette.wisc.edu

The home page of the Robert LaFollette Institute of Public Affairs at the University of Wisconsin, a leading graduate program providing training in public administration and policy studies.

http://www.uncc.edu/stwalker/sica

The Comparative and International Administration Section of the American Society for Public Administration.

http://www.opm.gov

The home page of the U.S. Office of Personnel Management, with information about human resource administration in the federal government.

http://www.iiasiisa.be/egpa/agacc.htm

The home page for the European Group of Public Administration, the purpose of which is "to strengthen contacts and exchanges among European specialists in Public Administration, both scholars and practitioners."

http://www.geocities.com/gov_pubad/international.html

"Cynthia's International Public Administration Page," a set of links to important information about bureaucracies in a wide range of countries and about public administration research activities.

◆ ◆ ◆

Key Terms and Concepts ————

bureaucracy	iron triangles
bureaucrat	patronage
citizen participation	representative bureaucracy
fixed jurisdictions	routines
hierarchy	technical responsibility

Discussion Questions ————

1. What are the features that make bureaucratic institutions distinctive?
2. What accounts for the tendency of bureaucracies to become rigid and resistant to innovation?
3. Why do governments need bureaucracy?
4. Can you think of an example in which a bureaucrat or agency resisted directions from an elected leader? Was the resistance proper? Why or why not?

Notes ————

1. Guillermo O'Donnell, "Reflections on the Patterns of Change in the Bureaucratic Authoritarian State," *Latin American Research Review* (Winter 1978): 3–38.
2. Quoted from a statement by U.S. Representative S. Levitas of Georgia, in John Sheridan, "Can Congress Control the Regulators?" *Industry Week* (March 29, 1976): 25–26.
3. This discussion is drawn from *Max Weber: Essays in Sociology*, ed. H. Gerth and C. Wright Mills (New York: Oxford University Press, 1946).
4. See Berhanu Mengistu and Elizabeth Vogel, "Bureaucratic Neutrality among Competing Bureaucratic Values in an Ethnic Federalism: The Case of Ethiopia," *Public Administration Review* 66 (March/April 2006): 205–217.
5. A number of political appointees are usually named to top posts in the bureaucracy when a new chief executive assumes office in most developed democracies, but this group is normally a small percentage of all bureaucrats. It should be noted, however, that in some local and state governments in the United States, a far higher proportion of positions are allocated through patronage. Nevertheless, an important Supreme Court case (*Rutan et al. v. Republican Party of Illinois*, 110 S. Ct. 2729, 1990) made it unconstitutional to require partisan affiliation as a condition for obtaining a state job.
6. Ezra N. Suleiman, *Politics, Power and Bureaucracy in France* (Princeton, NJ: Princeton University Press, 1974).
7. Similar observations were made during the Depression in the United States about the Works Progress Administration (WPA), created by the Roosevelt administration to build public works and hire the unemployed. In both cases, however, it is possible that the social or political benefits to society of reducing unemployment may have outweighed the costs of inefficiencies.
8. Richard Sandbrook, *The Politics of Africa's Economic Recovery* (New York: Cambridge University Press, 1993), p. 43.
9. Charles Goodsell. *The Case for Bureaucracy*. 4th ed. (Washington, D.C.: CQ Press, 2003).
10. Ibid.
11. The remarks by Senators Hollings and Mineta were quoted in an article by Jerry Ellig in *The Hill, The Newspaper for and about the U.S. Congress*, March 22, 2006. The quotations from Senators Lott and Collins were taken from a BBC report.
12. Sung-Don Hwang, *Bureaucracy v. Democracy in the Minds of Bureaucrats* (New York: Peter Lang, 2000).
13. Kathleen Bawn, "Political Control versus Expertise: Congressional Choices about Administrative Procedures," *American Political Science Review* 89 (March 1995): 62–73.
14. Krause, George A. and J. Kevin Corder. "Explaining Bureaucratic Optimism: Theory and Evidence from U.S. Executive Agency Macroeconomic Forecasts," *American Political Science Review* 101 (February 2007), p. 141.
15. Several classic books include discussions relevant to this problem. See J. Leiper Freeman, *The Political Process*, rev. ed. (New York: Rand McNally, 1965); and Emmette S. Redford, *Democracy in the Administrative State* (New York: Oxford University Press, 1969).
16. Charles O. Jones, "American Politics and the Organization of Energy Decision-Making," *Annual Review of Energy* 4 (1979): 99–121.
17. Hugh Heclo, quoted in Richard J. Stillman, *Public Administration: Concepts and Cases* (Boston: Houghton Mifflin, 1992), p. 426. See also Heclo's "Issue Networks and the Executive Establishment," in *The New American Political System*, ed. Anthony King (Washington, DC: American Enterprise Institute, 1978), pp. 87–124.

18. Kenneth J. Meier. "Representative Democracy: An Empirical Assessment," *American Political Science Review* 69 (1975): 526–542.
19. Sally Coleman Selden, Jeffrey L. Brudney, and J. Edward Kellough, "Bureaucracy as a Representative Institution: Toward a Reconciliation of Bureaucratic Government and Democratic Theory," *American Journal of Political Science* 42 (July 1998): 717.
20. Kenneth J. Meier, Robert D. Wrinkle, and J. L. Polinard, "Representative Bureaucracy and Distributional Equity: Addressing the Hard Question," *Journal of Politics* 61 (November 1999): 1025–1039.
21. Kenneth J. Meier and Laurence J. O'Toole, Jr. "Political Control versus Bureaucratic Values: Reframing the Debate," *Public Administration Review* 66 (March/April 2006): 187.
22. The essay was titled "Public Policy and the Nature of Administrative Responsibility." It has been reprinted many times, but it first appeared in *Public Policy* 1 (1940): 3–24.
23. See the essay written in response to Friedrich's (note 22): Herman Finer, "Administrative Responsibility in Democratic Government," *Public Administration Review* 1 (Summer 1941): 335–350.
24. See William T. Gormley, Jr., "The Representation Revolution: Reforming State Regulation through Public Representation," *Administration and Society* 18 (1986): 179–196. Other views of citizen participation are presented in D. Stephen Cupps, "Emerging Problems of Citizen Participation," *Public Administration Review* 37 (1976): 478–487; and Richard L. Cole and David A. Caputo, "The Public Hearing as an Effective Citizen Participation Mechanism," *American Political Science Review* 78 (1984): 404–416. A more recent, and rather negative, appraisal is provided by Marissa Golden, "Interest Groups in the Rule-Making Process: Who Participates? Whose Voices Get Heard?" in *Public Management Reform and Innovation: Research, Theory, and Application,* ed. H. George Frederickson and Jocelyn Johnston (Tuscaloosa: University of Alabama Press, 1999), pp. 285–311.
25. See E. S. Savas, *Privatizing the Public Sector* (Chatham, NJ: Chatham House, 1982), for the most well known statement supporting this movement. For a more recent statement see his 2005 book, *Privatization in the City* (Washington, D.C.: CQ Press).

For Further Reading ⸻

Allison, Graham, and Philip Zelikow, *Essence of Decision.* 2nd ed. New York: Longman, 1999.

du Gay, Paul. *In Praise of Bureaucracy.* London: Sage, 2000.

El-Ayouty, Yassin, Kevin J. Ford, and Mark Davies, eds. *Government Ethics and Law Enforcement: Toward Global Guidelines.* Westport, CT: Praeger, 2000.

Frederickson, H. George, and Jocelyn M. Johnston, eds. *Public Management Reform and Innovation: Research, Theory, and Application.* Tuscaloosa: University of Alabama Press, 1999.

Frederickson, H. George, and Kevin B. Smit. *Public Administration Theory Primer.* Boulder, CO: Westview Press, 2003.

Goodsell, Charles. *The Case for Bureaucracy: A Public Administration Polemic.* 4th ed. Washington, D.C.: CQ Press, 2003.

Gortner, Harold F., Carolyn Ball, and Kenneth L. Nichols. *Organization Theory: A Public and Non Profit Perspective.* Belmont, CA: Thomson-Wadsworth, 2007.

Hall, Daniel E. *Administrative Law: Bureaucracy in a Democracy.* 3rd ed. Englewood Cliffs, NJ: Prentice Hall, 2006.

Heady, Ferrel. *Public Administration: A Comparative Perspective.* 6th ed. Boca Raton, FL: CRC Publishers, 2001.

Henry, Nicholas. *Public Administration and Public Affairs.* 10th ed. Englewood Cliffs, NJ: Prentice Hall, 2007.

Huber, John D. and Charles R. Shipan. *Deliberate Discretion: The Institutional Foundations of Bureaucratic Autonomy.* New York: Cambridge University Press, 2002.

Hwang, Sung-Don. *Bureaucracy v. Democracy in the Minds of Bureaucrats.* New York: Peter Lang, 2000.

Jreisat, Jamil. *Comparative Public Administration and Policy.* Boulder, CO: Westview Press, 2002.

Klingner, Donald E., and John Nalbandian. *Public Personnel Management: Contexts and Strategies.* 5th ed. Englewood Cliffs, NJ: Prentice-Hall, 2003.

Light, Paul. *A Government Ill Executed.* Cambridge, MA: Harvard University Press, 2008.

Matheson, Craig. "In Praise of Bureaucracy? A Dissent from Australia," *Administration and Society* 39 (No. 2, 2007): 233–261.

Mayne, John, and Eduardo Zapico-Goni, eds. *Monitoring Performance in the Public Sector: Future Directions from International Experience.* London: Transaction Publishers, 1997.

Meier, Kenneth J. and Laurence J. O'Toole, Jr. *Bureaucracy in a Democratic State.* Baltimore, MD: Johns Hopkins University Press, 2006.

Mouritzen, Poul Erik, and James H. Svara. *Leadership at the Apex: Politicians and Administrators in Western Local Governments.* Pittsburgh: University of Pittsburgh Press, 2002.

Ostrom, Vincent. *The Intellectual Crisis in American Public Administration.* 2nd ed. Tuscaloosa, AL: Alabama University Press, 1989.

Peters, B. Guy. *The Politics of Bureaucracy: A Comparative Perspective.* 6th ed. London: Routledge, 2008.

Pollitt, Christopher, and Geert Bouckaert. *Public Management Reform: A Comparative Analysis.* Oxford: Oxford University Press, 2000.

Robbins, Mark D., Bill Simonsen, and Barry Feldman. "Citizens and Resource Allocation: Improving Decision-Making with Interactive Web-Based Citizen Participation," *Public Administration Review* 68 (May/June 2008): 564–676.

Rohr, John. A. *Founding Republics in France and America.* Lawrence: University Press of Kansas, 2000.

Savas, E. S. *Privatizing the Public Sector.* Chatham, NJ: Chatham House, 1982.

Savas, E. S. *Privatization in the City: Successes, Failures, Lessons.* Washington, D.C.: CQ Press, 2005.

Shafritz, Jay M., Albert C. Hyde, and Sandra J. Parkes. *Classics of Public Administration.* 5th ed. Stamford, CT: Wadsworth, 2003.

Weber, Max. "Bureaucracy," In *From Max Weber: Essays in Sociology,* translated and edited by H. H. Gerth and C. Wright Mills. New York: Oxford University Press, 1946.

PART IV

POLITICS IN SELECTED NATIONS

everal of this text's earlier chapters focus on the political system's underlying
functions or processes, such as political socialization or voting. Others examine
critical institutions, including political parties and legislatures. In Chapters 11
through 16, we will shift our attention from particular functions or institutions to a
more integrated analysis of politics in individual nations or regions. We will look at
five nations to examine how the components of their political systems interact in each
country. In addition, Chapter 15 focuses on political and socioeconomic development
in Africa, Asia, Latin America, and the Middle East. Here are some representative questions posed in this section: How has Great Britain's historical development influenced
its political culture? What factors may explain why democracy is growing in Mexico
and disappearing in Russia? How long will China be able to reconcile a free-market
economy with a Leninist political system?

The countries discussed here—the United States, Great Britain, Russia (and its
predecessor, the Soviet Union), China, and Mexico—represent a range of political
and economic systems. Their governments share certain objectives, including the
desire to protect national interests and to maintain power. But these countries also

illustrate how differently governments operate, how divergent are their policy objectives, and how greatly their effectiveness varies.

Some of those differences are best explained by analyzing the issues discussed earlier in the text. For example, we can understand a great deal about a nation's political and economic systems by knowing whether it is democratic or authoritarian, Marxist or capitalist. But each country's political practices are also products of its unique culture and history. By focusing on the interplay of historical influences, social characteristics, economic forces, political beliefs and behavior, and governmental institutions within each nation, we further our understanding of politics in a changing world.

Some Critical Approaches and Issues

In the coming chapters, we revisit some of the concerns of our earlier chapters, including the influence of political culture, voting systems, political parties, interest groups, and institutional structures. But we also examine the historical forces that have shaped each country's contemporary political values, behavior, and institutions. Although a nation's history may not predetermine its present, no country can escape its past. Great Britain's tradition of gradual and peaceful change; the birth of the United States as a "land of new settlement," free of a feudal past; China's historical struggle for stability; Russia's tradition of autocratic Czarist rule; and Mexico's distribution of wealth and income have all left their indelible marks on the contemporary political systems in those countries.

The wave of democracy that swept over Eastern Europe and parts of the Third World in the closing decades of the twentieth century has put to rest many doubts about democracy's viability in non-Western nations. To be sure, democracy remains too tenuous in many countries to inspire confidence that it will become firmly established. Still, the reality and the rhetoric of democracy clearly have been in the ascendancy in recent years. Hence, a central concern in all our case studies will be the strength of democracy or the potential for its emergence.

Finally, our case studies will focus on a critical area of contemporary government activity: economic policy. All five nations have mounted considerable debates regarding the state's proper role in the economy. In the past, Russia's and China's command economies assigned the state a dominant economic role. Great Britain and Mexico established more mixed economies, with the nature of state intervention varying considerably. Of the nations discussed here, the United States has allowed the least state economic intervention. But during the 1980s and 1990s most of the countries in our study reduced statism considerably. Time will tell how permanent a pattern that change will be and what its consequences will entail.

Great Britain and the United States: Developed Democracies

Both the United States and Great Britain are long-established industrial democracies. Both nations enjoy a high level of political freedom, a plurality of interest groups, competitive elections, and protected civil liberties. And all have advanced industrial economies guided primarily by market (capitalist) principles.

At the same time, however, important differences distinguish the two nations. Great Britain's political system has developed gradually over many centuries. Its political institutions have been emulated by other democracies and aspiring democracies throughout the world. Yet, it also maintains preindustrial traditions—a monarchy, a somewhat rigid class system—that seem inconsistent with the values of a modern democracy.

The United States, on the other hand, is still a relatively new nation whose democratic practices and public policy grew less from ancient traditions than from dramatic events such as the American Revolution, the Civil War, and the Great Depression. Its many opportunities for people of all social classes have shaped its political culture and policies. But so has its record of racial discrimination and division.

RUSSIA AND CHINA: PAST AND PRESENT COMMUNIST GIANTS

Until recently, the Soviet Union and China were the world's preeminent communist states. In both nations, Marxist-Leninist ideology established the political and economic agenda, and Communist Party leaders made critical political decisions with few external constraints. Their "command economies" featured state ownership and centralized planning.

Beginning in the late 1970s in China and a decade later in the USSR, however, both systems began to change. In the Soviet Union, Mikhail Gorbachev's reforms failed to save the established political and economic systems. Instead, they contributed to the collapse of the Soviet Union and the fall of Central/Eastern European communism. In contrast, China's leaders have decentralized and privatized the economic system well beyond Gorbachev's program of *perestroika* ("restructuring"). The country has established a dynamic capitalist economy, though one with a significant, remaining state sector and continued state regulation. The result has been phenomenal economic growth and a continuously growing private sphere. At the same time, however, China's ruling elite has resisted pressures for democratic reform.

Our case studies reveal significant similarities and important differences between the rise and decline of Marxism–Leninism in Russia and the modification of communism in China. Despite the collapse of Soviet communism in 1991, Russia first seemed to be democratizing and subsequently regressed to authoritarianism. China's economy now emphasizes a mixture of Marxist planning and (mainly) free-market activity. But despite the country's economic boom, corruption, growing inequality, environmental degradation, and political decay are contributing to growing political protest and unrest. While not yet at a level that threatens the political system, popular discontent may do just that in the coming decades.

MEXICO: A DEVELOPING NATION

Among the dozens of countries in Africa, Asia, and Latin America, none truly represents the developing world. We have focused on Mexico because it is not only a modernizing, democratizing nation, but also a neighbor of the U.S., one of this country's leading trading partners, and home to one of Latin America's most intriguing political histories. During the nineteenth century, Mexico suffered from severe economic inequalities, an exclusionary political system, political instability, and foreign domination. As a consequence, the country erupted in revolution in 1910, the first mass insurgency of the twentieth century. To address their country's political and economic problems, Mexico's revolutionary leaders created a more stable, more inclusive, and more effective political system. At the same time, however, the system was also authoritarian and corrupt. The 2000 Mexican presidential election brought full electoral democracy to Mexico as the PRI, the ruling party, was swept out of office after seventy-one years in power. Yet the country still faces major challenges from poverty, the power of drug cartels, and corruption.

HIGHWAY TRAGEDY IN MINNESOTA. Maintaining transportation infrastructure is one of the many challenges facing U.S. democracy. In 2007, a major interstate highway bridge in Minnesota collapsed, killing several people and seriously injuring dozens more. More than 180,000 people travel over the bridge each day, which was rebuilt in 2008. The Federal Transit Administration estimates that an expenditure of $131.7 billion is needed to repair "deficient" roads and bridges throughout the U.S.

© Scott Olson/Getty Images

11

U.S. GOVERNMENT: THE DILEMMAS OF DEMOCRACY

◆ The Founding Period ◆ Governmental Institutions
◆ Participation in U.S. Politics ◆ U.S. Politics: Prospects and Challenges

The study of American government inevitably confronts a basic paradox: *Americans have extensive popular control over their governmental institutions, but the fragmented power of those institutions often makes them unresponsive to majority demands.* The system reflects the ideal of democracy in its history and in its political culture, but its constitution and institutions actually weaken the immediate influence that public preferences have over governmental decisions.

Politicians, citizens, and scholars have been divided for generations over how democratic the U.S. system is and how democratic it should be. Some argue that the system's fragmentation frustrates efforts to enact needed progressive policies. The independently elected president often vetoes congressional actions, or the actions are sometimes held unconstitutional by the Supreme Court. Presidential initiatives often fail in Congress, even when the president enjoys considerable popular backing. Fragmented power thus frustrates majority rule. Others claim that fragmented power ensures the protection of minority rights; pure majority rule would threaten them. Still others point out that the extra time it takes to get the fragmented system to act allows for a careful, searching analysis of policy alternatives.

As the world looks for appropriate models of democracy to guide the formation of new governments in Europe, Latin America, and elsewhere, the U.S. arrangement appears to many as a mixed bag. Although we are well aware that democracy can be undermined by tyrants and the force of arms, the U.S. experience suggests that democracy also may be compromised by the way government institutions are designed. Despite a long tradition of open, competitive elections, U.S. voter turnout is relatively low, particularly among the poor.[1] Moreover, despite notable successes, there is a widespread perception that the U.S. system has failed to achieve social and economic equality.[2] Those and other problems arguably stem from the fragmented nature of U.S. government. Citizens and leaders cannot make long-term, coordinated policies when decisions can be blocked or checked in so many ways, and voters often feel that their choices have no meaning when victorious candidates are unable to enact their platforms. The study of U.S. government thus raises fundamental questions about the nature of democracy itself.

THE FOUNDING PERIOD

Every political system reflects both its unique historical and cultural foundations *and* the political ideas that shaped its institutions. This is particularly apparent in the case of U.S. government. Things would be different if James Madison, Thomas Jefferson, Alexander Hamilton, and a few others had never lived, but the government they crafted would have been profoundly different if they had tried to apply their ideas in some other cultural setting.

Key Cultural Features at the Founding

Many Americans living in 1787 had recently emigrated from Europe, and many others were children or grandchildren of immigrants. They had vivid memories of the European experience. People recalled that in most European nations at that time, the poor did not own their own land but worked for a landlord, and businessmen had to purchase permission from a guild or a government official before starting an enterprise. Most Europeans

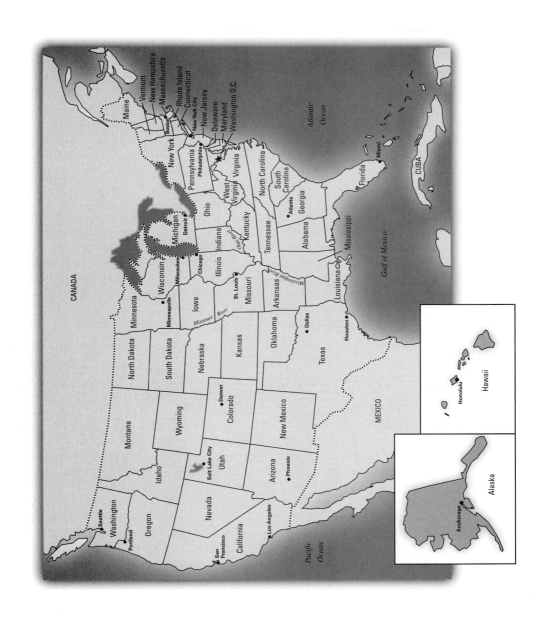

CANADA

Maine

Vermont
New Hampshire
Massachusetts
Rhode Island
Connecticut
New Jersey
Delaware
Maryland
Washington D.C.

New York
Boston
New York City
Pennsylvania
Philadelphia
West Virginia
Virginia
North Carolina
South Carolina

Ohio
Michigan
Detroit
Indiana
Kentucky
Tennessee
Georgia
Atlanta
Alabama
Mississippi

Wisconsin
Milwaukee
Chicago
Illinois
St. Louis
Missouri
Arkansas
Louisiana

Minnesota
Minneapolis
Iowa
Missouri River
Mississippi River

North Dakota
South Dakota
Nebraska
Kansas
Oklahoma
Dallas
Houston
Texas

Montana
Wyoming
Colorado
Denver
New Mexico
Phoenix
Arizona

Idaho
Utah
Salt Lake City
Nevada

Washington
Seattle
Portland
Oregon
California
San Francisco
Los Angeles

Atlantic Ocean
CUBA
Florida
Miami
Gulf of Mexico

MEXICO

Pacific Ocean

Hawaii
Honolulu

Alaska
Anchorage

lived in the same villages in which they and their parents were born.* Recurring European wars created a continuing military presence in most of the immigrants' nations.

In contrast, even many of the poorest rural Americans owned small plots of land, and there were few restrictions on those who wanted to set up shops or factories. Early Americans were accustomed to moving around to find new opportunities and jobs, and the abundance of arable land and natural resources encouraged them to do so. Physical separation from Europe isolated them from the threats that made military authority so pervasive in the lives of ordinary French, British, or German citizens.

Those factors had a great impact on the attitudes of most Americans toward politics and government. Some of them had left Europe specifically to escape restricted opportunities, and others sought religious freedom or cheap land. Of course, some people came as slaves, and women were certainly second-class citizens. Thus, the newly independent British colonies certainly did not constitute a fully free or democratic society. Nevertheless, the salient features of American society—poor farmers with claims to their own land, no requirements for "royal licenses" to start businesses, extensive geographic mobility, the absence of a large standing army—created the beginnings of a unique political culture.

In the absence of restrictive social institutions, Americans developed a sense of personal initiative, a freedom to experiment, and a faith in individualism that stood in contrast to the predominant cultural outlook in Europe.[3] When they became accustomed to the lack of arbitrary official constraints on their lives, they did not want them reinstated. They consequently did not arrange their affairs around a set of governmental or social institutions, preferring instead to confront the "challenges of the frontier."[4]

Early American Political Thought

The system's governmental institutions were designed in this cultural setting. But the culture did not create the system by itself. Two specific events shaped the political ideas of the founding period. One was the Revolutionary War and the **Declaration of Independence** in 1776, and the other was the political experiences *after* the Revolutionary War leading up to the ratification of the Constitution in 1789. Many Americans assume that the Declaration and the Constitution were simply two parts of the same movement that advanced the same political philosophy, but they were written more than a decade apart, and they embody very different ways of thinking. The first strengthened the democratic spirit, whereas the second gave impetus to the notion that government power would have to be checked and divided.

As every U.S. schoolchild learns, the Declaration of Independence proclaimed that all men were "created equal," that governmental power derives from the consent of the governed, and that people have the right to abolish government that does not answer to them. As a famous historian said nearly a century ago, "This was a complete and sweeping repudiation of the English political system, which recognized the right of monarchy and aristocracy to thwart the will of the people."[5] The successful war effort that followed vindicated those who had faith in the ability of common citizens to work together to change society. The American Revolution affirmed the value of democracy that the Declaration of Independence pronounced.

* Even as late as 1870, for example, 95 percent of the people living in Bavaria had been born there. See Karl Deutsch, Jorge Dominguez, and Hugh Heclo, *Comparative Government: Politics of Industrialized and Developing Nations* (Boston: Houghton Mifflin, 1981), p. 22.

Nevertheless, the following decade of government under the **Articles of Confederation** led many to *fear* democracy. Leading citizens expected that democratic government would permit the great mass of poor citizens to attack property rights. Their fears were heightened by **Shays's Rebellion** in Massachusetts in 1786. When farm mortgages were about to be foreclosed, Daniel Shays, a veteran of the Revolutionary War, led an assault on a Massachusetts courthouse with a mob of more than a thousand men armed with pitchforks and barrel staves. The independent states under the Articles of Confederation refused to contribute money to fund a military effort to secure order, thus requiring Massachusetts to put down the insurrection with its militia. The rebellion, along with smaller incidents in other areas, had a great impact on the framers of the Constitution:

> Shays's Rebellion, that heroic and desperate act by a handful of farmers, is surely the dominant symbol of the period and in many ways the *real source of the Constitution.* It was the frightening, triggering event that caused a particular selection of delegates to be appointed by their legislatures, induced them to spend a hot summer at an uncertain task in Philadelphia, and provided the context for their work and its later reception. . . . The need to protect property and contain democracy could hardly be made more compelling.[6]

Although the Declaration of Independence and the Revolution breathed life into the idea of democracy, the unrest during the 1780s made some of the framers anxious about it. These conflicting pressures are apparent when we compare the Declaration of Independence and the Constitution: The former document is a genuine and fervent appeal to the democratic spirit, whereas the latter is cautious and fearful of popular government.

The Politics of the U.S. Constitution

The Constitution is a collection of great compromises. It reflects democratic values in its effort to accommodate broad political participation, but it includes features designed to limit the power of majority rule. Some of the framers felt that if laws could be passed by a single legislative chamber directly representing the people—without any check applied by a separately elected upper chamber or a separately elected chief executive—perhaps the poor (the majority) would demand laws that would destroy the liberties of the wealthy (the minority). Generations of critics have claimed that the U.S. Constitution was designed to obstruct such efforts and that it is therefore profoundly undemocratic.*

Some are less severe in their interpretations. For example, George Carey argued that the framers put **checks and balances** into the Constitution not to frustrate the majority but to prevent arbitrary, lawless officials from abusing their powers. Although he admits that the framers were concerned about majority tyranny, Carey argues that they were confident that the nature of American society itself would prevent such problems. In the *Federalist Papers* (especially numbers 10 and 51), James Madison explained that the "multiplicity of interests" in the "**extended Republic**" of all thirteen states would make it practically impossible for a single, narrow interest to dominate.

> In the extended Republic of the United States, and among the great variety of interests, parties, and sects which it embraces, a coalition of a majority of the whole society could seldom take place on any other principles than those of justice and the general good.[7]

* For example, consider Robert Dahl's assessment: "Madison's nicely contrived system of constitutional checks" prevented the poor from having "anything like equal control over government policy." More recently, John Manley echoed that view: "[the framers] saw inequality, heard popular demands to change it, and acted to block these demands." See Robert Dahl, *A Preface to Democratic Theory* (Chicago: University of Chicago Press, 1956); and John Manley, "Class and Pluralism in America," in Manley and Dolbeare, *The Case against the Constitution*.

According to Carey, since Madison felt that *the great diversity of interests in the society would itself moderate majority power*, it is likely that the checks and balances in the Constitution were put there simply to restrain tyrannical officials, *not* to stifle the majority. Perhaps the framers were not so undemocratic after all.[8]

The debate over the extent to which the U.S. Constitution is, or was intended to be, democratic has raged for more than two centuries, and the controversy will continue as the world moves ever closer to democratic principles. Even if we cannot resolve the ultimate question of whether the Constitution is genuinely democratic, however, it clearly was designed to create a more deliberate, more fragmented, more cumbersome governing process. Whether that is, on balance, helpful or damaging to the political system remains a basic political science question.

GOVERNMENTAL INSTITUTIONS

Both the promise and the frustrations of democracy are reflected in the structure of U.S. institutions. Imperfectly democratic, often politically inefficient, and certainly unwieldy, these institutions have been the target of numerous reform efforts.

Congress

Although the U.S. Congress performs all the functions identified as basic to legislative institutions in Chapter 7, it remains a highly distinctive legislature.

Bicameralism   Most of the world's legislatures are **bicameral** (that is, they have two houses), but upper houses are typically rather weak. In the United States, both chambers must approve legislation in identical form if it is to become law. A bill supported by the majority of the people's representatives in the House will fail if 51 senators oppose it.

In addition to the simple fact of having two houses, the special nature of bicameralism in the U.S. Congress makes it arguably undemocratic in other ways. (See Box 11-1.) Consider the *differences* between the House and the Senate. To be eligible for election to the Senate, a person must be 30 years old; the requirement is only age 25 for the House. Citizens elect senators for six-year terms; members of the House serve two-year terms. And until the Seventeenth Amendment was ratified in 1913, *state legislatures elected each state's senators*, whereas citizens elected House members in districts of roughly equal sizes.

Those differences have great political importance. Many of the framers were concerned that the House, made up of younger citizens elected directly by the people for short terms, would adopt ill-conceived, insufficiently considered legislation, driven by the whims of public opinion and the demands of the uneducated. Senators would act as a needed restraint. With six-year terms, senators could afford to make decisions that were unpopular at the moment. They would also be older, and, most important, state legislatures would elect them, making it likely that senators would be among the most educated, most accomplished citizens in each state. For those who feared that the House would reflect the demands of the unruly mob, the Senate provided reassurance: no House decisions could become law unless they were also approved by the restrained, experienced, and judicious members of the upper house.

Box 11-1

THE FILIBUSTER AND THE "NUCLEAR OPTION"

The filibuster is among the most notorious and most colorful features that distinguish the House and the Senate. The Senate, in keeping with its image as a grand deliberative body, has had a tradition of few limits on debate. The filibuster is both a feature of that tradition and a way to protect the power of Senate minorities. Formally, it is a consequence of Rule XXII of the Senate's Standing Rules. The rule states that during a debate on a particular measure, 16 senators can demand a vote on a motion to end debate. Upon the submission of such a petition, the presiding officer must

> "submit to the Senate by a yea-and-nay vote the question: 'Is it the sense of the Senate that the debate shall be brought to a close?' And if that question shall be decided in the affirmative by three-fifths of the Senators duly chosen and sworn . . . said measure, motion, or other matter pending before the Senate, shall be the unfinished business to the exclusion of all other business until disposed of."

© AP Photo

The late Senator Strom Thurmond of South Carolina, then a Democrat, gestures while testifying before the House Judiciary Subcommittee on Capitol Hill against proposed civil rights legislation in February 1957.

What is the political impact of this obscure provision? Note that the rule states that the vote to end debate (actually to limit it for one final hour) must pass by a *three-fifths* vote. Consider what you could do if you were one of 43 senators opposing a proposed bill supported by the other 57. You know that it will certainly be enacted if a vote is taken. However, when someone makes a motion to stop debate, your group of senators votes no, and even though your group constitutes a minority, debate must continue because the motion was not supported by three-fifths of the Senate. The filibuster is broken when a few senators opposing the bill are persuaded to change their minds, perhaps in return for a favor on another bill or as a result of a change being made in the bill under consideration.

The filibuster thus gives power to a legislative minority. Lacking the votes to pass or block proposals, 41 senators can force the majority to make adjustments. Senator Strom Thurmond, then a Democrat from South Carolina, set the all-time filibuster record in 1957, speaking on the Civil Rights Act for 24 hours and 18 minutes. (The Civil Rights Act eventually passed, but not until 1964.) The filibuster also figured prominently in the defeat of President Clinton's health care plan in 1993. Like other features of the U.S. Congress, the filibuster dilutes majority rule.

However, a 2004 study found that the filibuster may be less obstructive of majority rule than is often thought. Gregory Wawro and Eric Schickler examined the filibuster and the threat of filibusters in recent Senate debates over tariff legislation and found that "narrow majorities were quite successful in legislating."*

The greatest change in the use and power of the filibuster in recent years occurred in 2005. Democrats had used filibusters to prevent the Senate from voting on motions to confirm several of President George W. Bush's nominees to the federal Courts of Appeals. Anticipating that there would be upcoming opportunities to appoint justices to the Supreme Court, the issue became increasingly heated on both sides. Democrats knew that, with 55 Republican senators, they were unlikely to be able to block any of Bush's nominees, and several Democrats therefore stated that they would support the use of a filibuster (thereby requiring 60 senators to support a motion to stop debate) whenever Bush nominated an "extremist" judge. Democrats in the Senate were under tremendous pressure from interest groups supporting them to take whatever steps were necessary to prevent the appointment of new justices that would lead to a reversal of *Roe v. Wade*, the landmark abortion case.

* Gregory Wawro and Eric Schickler, "Where's the Pivot: Obstruction and Lawmaking in the Pre-Cloture Senate," *American Journal of Political Science* 48 (October 2004): 758–774.

(Continued)

The Filibuster and the "Nuclear Option"
(*Continued*)

Filibusters have rarely been used to block judicial appointments. Republicans argued that using this method to block virtually all Bush nominees would create a precedent under which all future nominees would effectively need 60 votes in order to gain confirmation. Thus, the Republican leadership introduced the idea of the "nuclear option" (sometimes called the "constitutional option"), which would have ended the filibuster of judicial appointments.

Here's how it would have worked: Senators anticipating that they are in a minority regarding a judicial appointment would invoke Rule XXII, meaning that 60 votes would be required before the appointment could be confirmed. A senator favoring the nominee would raise a "point of order" claiming that the filibuster is not permissible in cases of judicial appointments, and the presiding officer would rule in favor of the point of order. A debate would ensue on the point of order when the minority side appealed the ruling, and the majority would move to table the appeal. The motion to table would then win, only requiring 51 votes, setting a precedent that would block filibusters of judicial appointments in the future.

The fallout from such a scenario would be difficult to predict, but it could lead to a removal of the filibuster from other Senate decisions when a new majority seeks retaliation. Because so many senators feel strongly that the filibuster is a worthy tool that promotes helpful compromise and moderation, a bipartisan group (the "gang of 14") crafted a way to stop the impasse. Democrats in this group pledged to vote in favor of closing debate (thereby allowing the confirmation votes to go forward), except in "extraordinary circumstances." In return, Republicans pledged not to support the "nuclear option."

The impasse was avoided, and the Bush nominees that had been blocked by the filibuster threat were confirmed. Later, following the death of Chief Justice William Rehnquist and the retirement of Sandra Day O'Connor, the Bush nominees for their vacancies were also confirmed (Chief Justice Roberts and Associate Justice Alito). As of this writing, it appears that the filibuster will survive.

As noted in Chapter 7, the other reason for the two-chamber structure of the U.S. Congress had to do with state power. If all legislative power were lodged in a single House of Representatives, with seats allocated on the basis of state population, small states would be dominated and possibly exploited by large states. But each state has two senators, regardless of population, giving the states equal power in that chamber. That arrangement, the **Connecticut Compromise**, was essential in obtaining the support of small states for ratification of the Constitution.

Congressional Committees   Committees perform limited functions in some legislatures, assembling information and hammering out language. British committees, for example, do not typically take it upon themselves to make basic choices about policy, and if they did, the House of Commons would not feel bound by their decisions. But much of the real deliberation that occurs in the U.S. Congress takes place in its committees. They investigate agencies, demand reports and studies, and debate major policy issues. In most instances, the whole chamber approves only bills recommended for passage by the appropriate committee.

The power of committees in the U.S. Congress reflects, in part, the relative weakness of political parties. When party discipline is strong, committee leaders are likely to be loyal to the party platform, and committees exert less independent influence. If party leaders in the U.S. system could deny a member the right to run for reelection under his or her party's label, and if party leaders could control most campaign spending (as they can in some other systems), committee chairs would naturally be inclined to support and oppose legislative proposals in accordance with the wishes of party leadership. But, to an extent unequaled elsewhere, candidates for the U.S. Congress are chosen in **primaries**, preliminary elections in which *voters* select each party's nominees. Primaries take away a basic power otherwise enjoyed by party leaders, enabling candidates to achieve political success without having to please party leaders.

Not only do U.S. party leaders lack those powers, but also the tradition of the *seniority system* in Congress actually increases the independence of committee chairs. The seniority system is the practice of electing the committee member from the majority party with the longest period of consecutive service to be the chair. When the system was firmly in place, a committee chair could act in ways that showed complete disregard for the party's expressed policy goals, knowing that his or her political position was secured through the continued respect for the seniority system. Reforms passed during the 1970s weakened the seniority system—making it easier to elect chairs who are less senior but more loyal to the majority party's platform—but it still amplifies committee independence to some degree. As a specialist on Congress concluded in the 1980s, the position of committee chair brings prestige and provides members with opportunities to secure constituent benefits.[9] The relative independence of committees enables legislative factions that would be outvoted on the floor to use committee leadership positions to affect policy choices. They can often "write their preferences into law" with little input from the membership outside the committee.[10]

Political Parties in Congress   Although a British citizen would find the absence of party discipline in the U.S. Congress striking, the parties do have considerable influence, and there are strong indications that party discipline increased considerably during the 1990s. From the mid-1950s through the mid-1980s, a majority of one party's members voted against a majority of the other party's members on less than half of the recorded floor votes, both in the House and in the Senate. On most votes, it was very common for a member to disregard his or her party's "line." As recently as 1982, "the House voted along party lines just 36 percent of the time, and the Senate just 43 percent."[11] By1995, about 70 percent of floor votes involved one party largely voting against the other. In 2007, a majority of House Democrats voted together 92 percent of the time, achieving that party's highest party unity score in over half a century. House Republicans had a party unity score of 85.[12]

Figure 11.1 shows the substantial increase in "party-line voting" that has taken place since the early 1980s. Votes identified as "party-line votes" are those on which a majority of Democrats voted one way and a majority of Republicans voted the opposite way. The figure shows that party unity has strengthened considerably since the 1970s in both the House and the Senate.

Party labels have become more meaningful and more influential in Congress for several reasons, including the recent ascendance of the Republican Party in the South. For most of the twentieth century, the states of the former Confederacy elected Democrats to Congress, even though the South was (and is) rather more conservative than the rest of the country. As discussed in Chapter 3, party identification is largely handed down from generation to generation, and the South's Democratic loyalties were forged during the Republican-led Civil War. Thus, the Democrats in the Congress were made up of liberals from the other regions of the country and conservatives from the South. These differing attitudes severely degraded party discipline, since Southern Democrats would regularly vote on many issues with Republicans. During the last 30 years or so, that pattern has changed dramatically.

FIGURE 11.1   PARTY UNITY: PERCENTAGE OF VOTES IN CONGRESS IN WHICH A MAJORITY
OF ONE PARTY OPPOSED A MAJORITY OF THE OTHER PARTY

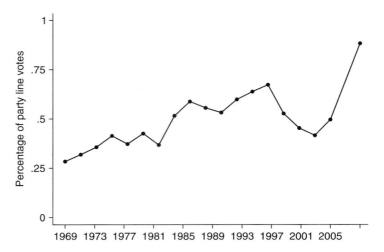

SOURCE: CQ Almanac Plus, 2001. Washington, D.C.: Congressional Quarterly, 2002, p. B-7. Copyright 2002 by Congressional Quarterly, Inc. Reprinted with permission of CQ Press, Inc.

As recently as 1952, 54 percent of the Democrats in the House of Representatives were from Southern states, while only 8 percent of the Republicans were Southerners. By 1994, 33 percent of Republicans were southerners, and in 2005 this number grew to 37.5 percent. The number of Democrats in the House who were from the South continued to drop: only 25 percent of House Democrats represented these states in 2005, and only 23 percent of House Democrats were from Southern states in the 110th Congress (2007–2009).

Those numbers indicate that a major partisan realignment has taken place in the South, and that it has persisted and deepened over time. Large numbers of Southern voters changed their party loyalties. (Contemporary Southern politicians often quip, "Whenever a good old boy's great-granny passes on, he feels it's safe to become a Republican!") But political change in the southern states is not the only factor. Members of Congress from the rest of the country are more polarized as well. Figure 11.2 shows the how the current ideological polarization of the U.S. Congress is now more extreme than at any time in the last century. The scores indicate the average liberal/conservative difference between the members of the two parties for the House and Senate, respectively. For better or worse, both parties have become more coherent and unified with regard to the platforms they advocate.

Despite the influence of parties, members of Congress still stray from their parties' platforms on occasion. Campaign contributions arguably influence their votes on pending legislation. Concerns about the effect of contributions led to the enactment of the Bipartisan Campaign Reform Act of 2002, which limited so-called "soft money" and paid issue advertisements by groups in an effort to minimize the influence of money in congressional and other federal elections. (See Box 11–2.) Reformers argue that if members of Congress were forced to adopt their parties' lines, campaign contributions from interest groups could not sway them.

FIGURE 11.2 PARTY POLARIZATION 1879–2006: IDEOLOGICAL DISTANCE BETWEEN THE PARTIES

SOURCE: From Nolan McCarty, Keith T. Poole, and Howard Rosenthal. 2006. *Polarized America: The Dance of Ideology and Unequal Riches.* Cambridge, MA: MIT Press. Copyright © 2006 Massachusetts Institute of Technology. Reprinted by permission of the MIT Press.

Box 11-2

POLITICAL ACTION COMMITTEES (PACs), THE BIPARTISAN CAMPAIGN REFORM ACT OF 2002 "527" ORGANIZATIONS, CORRUPTION, AND FREEDOM OF SPEECH

Even the appearance of corruption can create severe problems for democratic government. Citizens need to feel confident that their leaders are representing them, and that the policy process is not "rigged" by interests to whom elected leaders are obligated.[13] For years, many Americans have concluded that the way campaigns are financed creates both the reality and the appearance of corruption.

The role of **political action committees (PACs)** and the money they contribute are controversial elements in contemporary U.S. politics. Campaign contributions from corporations and unions triggered heated debate for generations, and the development of PACs actually emerged from an effort to control them.* From the early 1900s, corporations had been prohibited by law from contributing to electoral campaigns,

although labor unions could contribute freely. However, during World War II, Congress passed legislation that banned union contributions, and the ban was restated in the Taft-Hartley Act of 1947. PACs later emerged as a way for unions (and corporations) to make contributions indirectly, by setting up legally separate entities for "political education." The Federal Election Campaign Act of 1971 formalized the status of PACs and prompted dramatic growth in their numbers. The law contained an amendment that affirmed the legality of PAC operations, as long as PAC funds

* The following discussion is drawn from John R. Wright, *Interest Groups and Congress* (Boston: Allyn & Bacon, 1996), pp. 116–122.

(Continued)

Box 11-2

POLITICAL ACTION COMMITTEES (PACs), THE BIPARTISAN CAMPAIGN REFORM ACT OF 2002 "527" ORGANIZATIONS, CORRUPTION, AND FREEDOM OF SPEECH   (Continued)

were not obtained through membership dues or commercial transactions.

Union leaders did not expect that corporate interests would also take advantage of this law, but they were profoundly mistaken. By 1976, for example, 433 corporations had formed PACs; by 1992 there were 1,930 corporate PACs. According to the Federal Election Commission, a total of 4,499 PACs contributed some $604 million in the 1999–2000 election cycle. PACs can contribute only $5,000 to a single candidate in a given election, but they can give an unlimited amount to all campaigns combined. Those limits are left unchanged in the Bipartisan Campaign Reform Act (BCRA) of 2002.

However, the Act was designed to diminish the influence of money in federal elections by banning "soft money" contributions and by restricting "electioneering" ads paid for by unions, corporations, and PACs *that use the names or pictures of candidates during the weeks preceding an election.*

What is "soft" money? During the 1980s and 1990s, this term came to mean contributions to national parties or the parties' congressional and senatorial election committees, in contrast to the "hard" money contributed directly to campaigns. The term derives from the fact that "soft" money contributions were exempt from the limits applying to direct contributions to campaigns because they were to be used for "party building" instead of campaigning.

However, the advocates of the BCRA argued that, in practice, soft money contributions were used almost entirely for purchasing campaign ads that merely *claimed* to be "public education" or party-building efforts. As long as the ads did not specifically urge the viewer to vote for or against a particular candidate, and as long as the hard-money funded campaign organizations did not coordinate with soft money contributors to direct advertisements funded with soft money, no laws were broken. Given that it was difficult to prove "coordination," and that advertisements could effectively be used to sway voters without explicitly asking viewers to vote for or against a candidate, reformers argued that soft money contributions were merely a way to circumvent the limits on hard money.

If soft money contributions were really being used to advance campaigns, candidates would presumably do things in office to please the organizations that made those contributions. Reformers argued that it was therefore not adequate to limit hard money contributions and to require disclosure of those contributions. The BCRA thus prohibited parties from accepting soft money contributions after November 6, 2002.

Advocacy groups *can* accept soft money, however. The most important type of advocacy groups are the "527" organizations (named after the applicable section of the Internal Revenue Service code). As shown in Table 11.1, 527s spent a great deal of money in 2007, and the Campaign Finance Institute reported that 41 percent of the money contributed to 527s came from donors contributing $1,000,000 or more. Ostensibly, these groups may accept and spend money for party organization efforts, voter mobilization, and issue advocacy. They must file disclosure reports only if they "expressly advocate the election or defeat of a candidate" or if they engage in "electioneering communications."*

Distinguishing between issue advocacy and electioneering is not always easy, however. During the 2004 election, several groups came very close to "expressly advocating" the election or defeat of a candidate, and, in 2005 and 2006, the Federal Election Commission attempted to tighten the law. A 527 will become a "fully regulated Political Action Committee" if it is "judged to have the major purpose of 'federal campaign activity' as evidenced by organizational statements, the level of express advocacy, and contributions and other activities promoting or attacking candidates to voters."[14] For example, in 2004, three 527 groups, the Swift Boat Veterans and POWs for Truth, Moveon.org Voter Fund, and the League of Conservation Voters, received donations and spent funds to engage in what the Federal Election Commission found to be "campaign activity." Each group was forced to pay fines of $150,000 or more.[15] The Campaign Finance Institute noted that 527s became more careful after the 2004 election, simply praising or condemning "a candidate's legislative or policy positions in the midst of the campaign."

* See the discussion of 527 organizations at the Center for Responsive Politics Web site, www.opensecrets.org.

Box 11-2

POLITICAL ACTION COMMITTEES (PACs), THE BIPARTISAN CAMPAIGN REFORM ACT OF 2002 "527" ORGANIZATIONS, CORRUPTION, AND FREEDOM OF SPEECH   (*Continued*)

One of the problems with 527 groups is the fact that parties and campaigns are not always able to control their activities. Both the Democratic and Republican parties attempted to distance themselves from at least some of the most extreme messages sent by the 527s supporting them (although it is likely that both parties welcomed the support that they produced among some parts of their respective bases.) (See Table 11.1.)

Another major controversy regarding the BCRA has to do with its constitutionality. It bars unions, corporations, and nonprofit organizations (including 527s) from buying issue ads within sixty days of a general election or thirty days before a primary, *if those ads refer by name to any candidate for federal office.* This issue was addressed in *McConnell v. FEC* (540 *U.S.* 93), decided in December 2003. The court majority upheld the restrictions in the BCRA, concluding that the

TABLE 11.1   EXPENDITURES BY SELECTED FEDERAL 527S IN 2007

527s with a Democratic Party Orientation	*Expenditures*
Service Employees International Union	$13,990,434
The Fund for America	$ 2,160,149
AFSCME Special Account	$ 5,380,611
America Votes, Inc.	$ 5,437,885
EMILYS List	$ 4,697,051
Young Democrats of America	$ 1,225,968

527s with a Republican Party Orientation	*Expenditures*
American Solutions for Winning the Future	$6,830,053
The Presidential Coalition	$3,511,291
College Republican National Committee	$3,445,460
National Federation of Republican Women	$1,857,235
Club for Growth.net	$1,055,010
Stop Her Now	$ 355,042

Total contributions to all 527s that raised more than $50,000 in 2007:

Democratic 527s:	$ 54,927,025
Republican 527s:	$ 20,291,396

Sources of Contributions to Federal 527s in 2007

	Amount Contributed	Percent of Total
Labor Unions	$31,660,349	41%
Individuals	$27,392,967	36%
Business/Other	$ 1,866,284	2%
Any Source Under $5,000	$15,936,767	21%
Total	$76,856,367	100%

SOURCE: Information available through the Campaign Finance Institute (**www.cfinst.org**).

(*Continued*)

Box 11-2

Political Action Committees (PACs), The Bipartisan Campaign Reform Act of 2002 "527" Organizations, Corruption, and Freedom of Speech   (*Continued*)

government's interest in preventing "actual or apparent corruption of federal candidates and officeholders" justifies the contribution limits. Moreover, the BCRA's provisions that prohibit candidates and officeholders from raising soft money to promote and attack federal candidates is "a valid anti-circumvention provision," necessary to make sure that the overall objective of the Act is met. Justice Scalia wrote an emotional dissent:

> This is a sad day for the freedom of speech. Who could have imagined that the same Court which, within the past four years, has sternly disapproved of restrictions upon such inconsequential forms of expression as virtual child pornography, . . tobacco advertising, . . dissemination of illegally intercepted communications, . . and sexually explicit cable programming, . . would smile with favor upon a law that cuts to the heart of what the First Amendment is meant to protect: the right to criticize the government (*McConnell v. FEC*, Scalia, dissenting).

A key provision of the Act was struck down, however, in June 2008. The so-called "millionaire's amendment" increased the contribution limits for a candidate facing an opponent who spent more than $350,000 of his own funds. Thus, a candidate with the resources to devote a great deal of money to making the case for his or her election would face opponents with looser fund-raising limits than other candidates would face. The rationale for the provision had to do with an interest in leveling the playing field when one candidate is very wealthy.* Justice Samuel Alito's majority opinion concluded: "[t]he argument that a candidate's speech may be restricted

© Chip Somodevilla/Getty Images

One of the most controversial political communications in recent years was a full page ad in Section A of the New York Times in September 2007 by the liberal group Moveon.org. It included a play on the name of the Commander of the Multinational Forces in Iraq, General David Petraeus ("General Betray Us"). The ad suggested that he would present misleading testimony to Congress regarding military progress in Iraq.

in order to 'level electoral opportunities' has ominous implications because it would permit Congress to arrogate the voters' authority to evaluate the strengths of candidates competing for office" (at p. 16). The Court held the provision to be an unconstitutional violation of the First Amendment.

The challenge of regulating campaign communications while respecting Constitutional rights will ensure that this issue will be a central difficulty in U.S. politics for some time to come.

* See *Davis v. Federal Election Commission*, Supreme Court, June 2008.

Incumbency and Political Competition   One of the most hotly debated questions regarding Congress in the 1990s has to do with the power of **incumbency advantage.** In recent years, fewer than 15 percent of the seats in the House have been **marginal seats** (that is, seats won by less than 55 percent of the popular vote). Most elections have been landslides for the incumbents.[16] In 2004, 97.8 percent of House incumbents won re-election, and nearly every Senate incumbent won as well. For some observers, the decline in electoral competition is a disturbing trend. Voter turnout is low when elections are

FIGURE 11.3   DECLINE IN NUMBER OF COMPETITIVE INCUMBENT HOUSE RACES

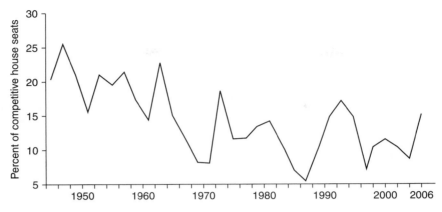

SOURCE: Data obtained from the Pew Research Center, **www.pewresearch.org**.

essentially uncontested, and voters begin to see their legislators as professional insiders, dedicated only to the advancement of their own permanent careers.

However, in 2006 there was a striking increase in competitive House races. While only 7.5 percent of House races were competitive in 2004, more than 15 percent of them were competitive in 2006. (See Figure 11.3.) Perhaps the increasing polarization of the electorate and the resulting focus on national issues diminished the incumbency advantage to some degree. Nevertheless, the vast majority of House seats remain uncompetitive.

Why do incumbents have such a large advantage? Some argue that the federal bureaucracy provides a huge array of opportunities for incumbents to help constituents (for example, by seeking funding for special projects, or obtaining exceptions to regulations). Only incumbents can profit politically from doing those things, whereas challengers have to try to get votes on the basis of their policy views.[17] The vigorous policy debates that effective challenges would produce are thus lost as incumbents gain support by effectively handling the bureaucracy, not by taking positions on the issues.

The increasingly sophisticated *gerrymandering* of district boundaries by both parties has been the major factor producing the scarcity of competitive districts in recent years. Because all states (except Iowa) have procedures for drawing district boundaries that make districts "safe" for one or the other party, it is now extremely difficult for an incumbent to be unseated. In 2005, voters in Ohio and California considered proposals to institute nonpartisan arrangements for drawing district lines, but both referenda failed.

The movement for **term limits** is largely a response to the power enjoyed by incumbents in Congress. If legislators were limited to, say, 12 years in office, they would not devote so much of their time to constituent matters, interest groups would not have such an incentive to use campaign dollars to develop relationships with legislators, and issues would become more important in elections, according to term limit advocates. Opponents of term limits argue that legislators gain essential skills only after they have had considerable legislative experience. An often-mentioned danger of term limits is that legislators facing a certain end to their congressional careers would, from their first days in office, try to curry favor with special interests so that they would have secure future positions. However the term-limit idea is resolved, the fact that it is seriously advocated reflects real concern about Congress.[18]

The Midterm Elections of 1998, 2002, and 2006: A New Pattern in U.S. Politics?
For nearly half a century, from 1954 through 1995, the House of Representatives was controlled by the Democratic Party. The Senate was also in Democratic hands during most of that period. The 1994 congressional elections produced a historic change. The Republicans won a net gain of over 50 seats in the House of Representatives, giving them a 236–199 majority, and they took over the Senate with a 53–47 edge. The 1996 elections trimmed the GOP's majority in the House a bit, but the Republicans actually won a net gain of two Senate seats. The fact that they were able to maintain control of Congress during a presidential election in which a Democrat won the White House suggested that Republican control of Congress would be secure for some time.

However, in 1998, the Democrats gained five seats in the House and four in the Senate. *That was the first time since 1934 that the party controlling the White House actually gained seats in the House of Representatives in a mid-term election.* In 2000, the Republicans won the White House, but, contrary to the normal "coattails" effect, they suffered a net loss of three seats in the House.

In the 2002 mid-term election, the 1998 result was repeated, this time to the benefit of the Republicans. The party in the White House *again* gained seats in the House of Representatives. The Republicans gained 6 seats, increasing their majority to 229–205 (with one independent who votes with the Democrats), and they also gained two seats in the Senate. There was little consensus among analysts who tried to explain the result, but most observers pointed to the effectiveness of President Bush as a campaigner, the poor campaign strategies of the Democrats, and the lingering effect of the September 11, 2001, terrorist attacks.

These recent elections challenged conclusions drawn from generations of political science research. The notion that the party winning the White House would lose seats in the House of Representatives in the "midterm" election two years later had been perhaps the most reliable prediction ever made about U.S. elections. The classic explanation is referred to as "surge and decline."

Simply put, the "surge and decline" theory holds that the higher voter turnout during presidential elections is made up of the strong party identifiers who vote in all elections, plus a large number of voters with weak party identification who usually vote only in presidential election years. For whatever reason (economic conditions, war or other crisis, scandals), the political "winds" during a given presidential election favor one party or the other, and it is the voters with *weak partisan loyalty* that are most swayed by those factors. They vote for the presidential candidate who wins with the benefit of these favorable short-term forces, and, while they are in the ballot box, they also vote for the candidate running for the House from that same party. Two years later (during the mid-term election), these weak partisan voters stay home, leaving the House election entirely in the hands of the strong party identifiers. Without the boost that the weak partisan voters produced when the presidential election was taking place, the president's party loses some close House seats, thus producing the pattern repeated in every mid-term election between 1936 and 1994.

Some political scientists now reject the "surge and decline" theory. In a recent article in the *American Political Science Review,* two analysts argue that a substantial number of voters support House candidates from the party that wins the presidency during a presidential election because they favor what that party stands for during the campaign, but that two years later, many of the same voters become disturbed by the actions of the president's party, and thus come to prefer the other party's candidates. In 1998 and 2002, the "swing" voters became more supportive of the party controlling the White House (the Democratic Party in 1998, and the Republican Party in 2002), for reasons that were perhaps unique to those elections. The Clinton impeachment controversy apparently convinced some voters that the Republicans in Congress were reckless, leading to Democratic gains in 1998, and international security threats in 2002 strengthened support for Republicans during that election.

However, in 2006 the more typical mid-term election pattern returned. The Republicans lost 31 House seats, enough to lose their majority. The Republicans also lost control of the Senate. As in any election, several unique factors were important in accounting for the outcome, and in this case the very low approval ratings for George W. Bush clearly had an impact. However, it is important to note that mid-term losses for the party controlling the White House are "normal," although factors unique to each election will affect the magnitude of the losses.[19]

Congress: An Antique Political Institution? For generations, critics of the U.S. Congress have argued that its decentralization of power impedes effective policy making. Congress is good at reflecting narrow, localized concerns, but it fails to act in response to broad policy demands made by national majorities. Yet some see value in the fact that Congress represents narrow, particularistic, local interests instead of broad, national-majority preferences. Perhaps Congress—by representing interests that are overlooked in the national view taken by the president—gives voice to interests that would otherwise go unheard. Following the majority rule principle, those interests *should* be ignored, and disregarding them would certainly make it easier to enact legislation such as meaningful deficit reduction. But Congress arguably performs a helpful role by representing the diverse interests that make up U.S. political life, even if doing so makes the institution less efficient.

Scholars studying Congress consider those and other ideas when they grapple with the realization that the U.S. Congress is typically considered to be the world's most important legislative body, while also chronically in need of fundamental reform. Congress has more political independence from the executive than other legislatures, thus giving it more prominence than the "rubber-stamp" bodies in some democracies, but its internal divisions and the absence of consistent party responsibility make it frequently unable to act on broad majority demands. This paradox of congressional strength and weakness is why the institution remains such a fascinating subject for political research.

The Presidency

John F. Kennedy described the modern presidency in the following way:

> The American Presidency is a formidable, exposed, and somewhat mysterious institution. It is formidable because it represents the point of ultimate decision in the American political system. It is exposed because decisions cannot take place in a vacuum: the Presidency

is the center of the play of pressure, interest, and idea in the nation; and the presidential office is the vortex into which all the elements of national decision are irresistibly drawn. And it is mysterious because the essence of ultimate decision remains impenetrable to the observer—often, indeed, to the decider himself.[20]

That statement captures the sense of puzzlement that strikes most observers of the presidency. The U.S. political system looks to the president for leadership, granting the office a level of attention denied to other institutions, but it also severely limits the president's power.

Presidential Powers   U.S. presidents have the basic powers generally associated with political executives: They serve as the chief diplomat, the commander of the armed forces, the nation's symbolic leader, the leader in times of emergency and crisis, and the most important source of policy proposals. Their powers are tremendous. As discussed in Chapter 8, however, chief executives in democratic systems typically have *limited* power, and the U.S. president—sometimes called the most powerful person on earth—faces particularly severe and complex limits.

A full inventory of presidential powers includes both those with origins in the Constitution and those that have evolved through history. The Constitution at least implies that the president will conduct foreign relations, and it is explicit regarding his power to command the armed forces and serve as chief of state. Other powers derive from the essential nature of the position itself and from the way incumbents have operated within it. These include the president's leadership of his party and his role as symbolic leader of the nation.

Strong presidents use their unique political position to shape the nation's agenda: Lyndon Johnson focused national attention on the plight of the poor in the 1960s, leading to dramatic legislative enactments; in the 1980s, Ronald Reagan effectively highlighted the issues of deregulation, tax reform, and renewed military preparedness. In contrast, many observers faulted George H. W. Bush for failing to emphasize any theme or purpose during his single term (1989–1993). Bill Clinton's first term (1993–1997) was marked largely by his failure to gain passage of his central policy initiative, national health reform, and his second term by scandal and impeachment. George W. Bush's presidency will be marked largely by his leadership in the nation's response to the terrorist attacks of September 11, 2001, and his controversial decision to invade Iraq in 2003.

By many historical accounts, the most important president was the only great president to serve but a single complete term, Abraham Lincoln.* The Civil War presented Lincoln with basic choices that would alter forever the nature and the stature of the presidency. If he had looked to Congress to set the direction of the war effort, and if he had been content to operate within the limits of his office, the presidency would have remained a relatively weak institution. Instead, Lincoln responded to the national emergency by crafting an expansive vision of leadership. He ignored Congress when he felt it necessary to do so, writing the Emancipation Proclamation without any observance of checks and balances. He ordered restrictions on the mail, blockades of ports, and other actions—all without congressional approval. Largely as a result of those kinds of actions, Lincoln's presidency established much of the foundation for the enormous powers of the modern institution.

---

* Lincoln had begun his second term one month before he was assassinated.

Franklin Roosevelt assumed the presidency in 1933, during a very different kind of crisis, the Great Depression. He responded by broadening the reach of government in economic and business affairs, thus initiating the modern welfare state. He also brought the presidency into closer personal contact with citizens, forging a bond that assumed almost mythical proportions. The larger governmental role that Roosevelt demanded required changes in constitutional doctrine: among other things, the Supreme Court eventually accepted the idea that Congress could delegate lawmaking power to administrative agencies.

Limits on the Presidency   U.S. presidents appear to be forced continually to assert their power, to struggle for the authority to act. The most important limit on their power is, of course, the fact that the president is elected independently of the Congress. Unlike British prime ministers, U.S. presidents cannot assume that the same popular vote that put them in office will ensure the passage of their legislative proposals. President George W. Bush's failure to gain passage of his Social Security reform proposals in 2005 illustrates how a president can be defeated, even when he has been re-elected recently and when the Congress is controlled by his party.

Of course, in the U.S. system, the president and the majority of Congress may be of different parties, a situation that occurred for all but 18 years between 1961 and 2008. This phenomenon of "divided government" is currently a subject of intense scrutiny by political scientists. The traditional view is that divided government produces near paralysis. Yet, historical research reveals that many important policy innovations have been enacted during periods of divided government. Effective presidents can work with a Congress dominated by the other party about as well as they can work with a Congress led by their own party.[21]

Bill Clinton's impeachment in 1999 suggests both the limits on presidential power and the ways in which a popular president can survive under tremendous criticism. Most observers contend that the strong economy during that period, coupled with Clinton's great popularity in certain parts of the electorate, enabled him to escape conviction in the Senate. However, by most accounts, his record of legislative successes is weak.

Besides being limited by the nature of institutions and parties, presidential power is also limited because political conflict in the United States rarely fits a clear ideological pattern. Instead of representing one dominant majority, presidents must work to balance a large array of diverse interests. When they can command a united majority of society's political energies, they have a much freer hand, even within the checks and balances that limit their authority.

The Institutional Presidency   Analysts and politicians agreed years ago that "the president needs help," and the *institutional presidency* is the term used to indicate the extensive system of supporting institutions surrounding the chief executive. Most important, the **president's cabinet**, which traditionally consists of the heads of major departments and others of similar status selected by the president to be in the group, has existed since Washington's time, and most presidents get useful advice from these individuals. But presidential cabinets rarely function as genuine policy-making bodies. Presidents typically select cabinet secretaries to please important interest groups or to repay political favors. Once in power, these officials gain independent support from important constituencies, and they usually come to identify with the goals of the departments they manage.

Box 11-3

THE 2008 PRESIDENTIAL ELECTION

Every presidential election is unique, but the 2008 election was unusual in many respects. Both parties had seriously contested primaries, and the Democratic primary was the most protracted and divisive race for that party's nomination in decades. It was the first time since 1952 without a sitting president or vice-president as one of the nominees, and the first time since John F. Kennedy was elected in 1960 that a sitting senator won the White House (a senator had won only *one* other time before that, when Warren Harding was elected in 1920). It was also, of course, the first time that a major party nominated an African-American as its presidential candidate, and the first time that the Republican Party nominated a woman as its vice-presidential candidate.

Veteran political commentator David Broder called the 2008 campaign "the best campaign I've ever covered."* Senators McCain and Obama were both long-shots a year before the election, and both picked newsworthy Vice-Presidential candidates (Obama's choice of Senator Joe Biden surprised many observers because he did *not* pick Hillary Clinton, while McCain's choice of Governor Sara Palin created controversies regarding her lack of experience and her populist appeal). Senator Obama's decision to decline public financing for the general election may have led to the end of that program, because it enabled him to out-spend his opponent by many millions of dollars. Perhaps as a result of the personal qualities of the candidates and the fact that the election took place during a time of war and economic turbulence, voter turnout was over 60%, the highest since 1960.

A few months before the election, several political scientists published their predictions.[†] Using sophisticated mathematical models that incorporated a wide range of factors, the consensus was that Senator Obama would win by a comfortable margin, but not a landslide. The predictions were based on the economy's growth for the second quarter, the approval rate for President Bush in July and August, party identification figures, economic conditions as reported in the news, and the historically low probability that a party can maintain control of the White House for a third consecutive term, among other factors.

These political science predictions were fairly accurate. Senator Obama won 52 percent of the popular vote, a decisive victory over Senator McCain, who received 46 percent. The Democratic Party added more than 25 seats to its majority in the House of Representatives, and garnered a net gain of 6 in the Senate.[‡] The 2008 election thus signaled the end of divided government, with the Democrats in control of the Congress and the White House for the first time since the first two years of Bill Clinton's first term (1993–1994). Many observers have argued that the resulting changes in public programs and fiscal policy will be as dramatic as those in the 1930s.

Along with the other usual factors, the impact of immediate economic conditions was significant. The stock market experienced its worst period since the Great Depression, and Obama's lead grew substantially in the days following the big drop in share prices. In short, the 2008 election followed conventional patterns in some respects, but it was unprecedented in many others. The history of the next few decades is yet to be written, but it is likely that historians will look back on the 2008 election as a very significant moment in American politics.

* *Washington Post*, November 2, 2008.

[†] The predictions are discussed in a special issue of *PS: Political Science and Politics*, 41 (October 2008).

[‡] As of this writing, three senate seats were still uncertain, but leaning to the Republicans. There are two independents in the senate, both of whom caucus with the Democratic Party.

This tendency toward independence on the part of cabinet officials has long been recognized, as suggested by the famous remark by Charles Dawes (Calvin Coolidge's vice president) that "the members of the Cabinet are the President's natural enemies."[22] Similarly, President Lyndon Johnson complained, "When I looked out at the heads of the departments, I realized that while all had been appointed by me, not a single one was really mine. I could never fully depend on them to put my priorities first. . . ."[23] Although hearing a diverse array of voices can be helpful to a president, the independence of many cabinet members makes the cabinet less useful than most presidents expected when they assumed office. Presidents thus usually have an informal group of close advisers, often called the "kitchen cabinet," who remain close to the president and share ideas on policies and political strategy.

The vast workings of the executive branch demand a much larger institutional establishment than the cabinet. In 1939, Franklin Roosevelt created the Executive Office of the President (EOP), an umbrella term for a group of organizations including the Office of Management and Budget, the Council of Economic Advisers, and the National Security Council. These units coordinate policy making and maintain contact between the president and dozens of administrative agencies.

The large executive establishment thus performs two somewhat contradictory functions. Some people are chosen to *secure political support* from interests who, because of the weak partisan identification and discipline in U.S. politics, would otherwise oppose the administration. The units of the EOP, in contrast, are intended to *centralize presidential control.*

Presidential Character   Social scientists are often drawn to conclusions about economic and social "forces" that can be measured and predicted. However, the U.S. presidency provides an excellent context for illustrating that individuals make a difference. Although constitutional features, economic conditions, and changes in partisan alignment, among many other things, affect presidential actions and choices, it is clear that the nature of the person in the office also has great impact. This is the basis for the study of **presidential "character."**[24]

The 44 men who have served as U.S. presidents constitute a varied lot. Some brought a strong ideological fervor to the office, acting aggressively to change the direction of government policies and programs, challenging Congress and the courts. Others were content to manage the status quo. Some enjoyed the office, relishing its challenges with enthusiasm, whereas others developed a siege mentality, focusing on perceived threats.

When James Barber explored the backgrounds and actions of several twentieth-century presidents in an effort to discover the nature of their personalities, he argued convincingly that much of U.S. history has been shaped by differences in the characters of the men who have served as president. Franklin Roosevelt's "active-positive" personality gave him strength as a leader and helped him reach for his optimistic vision in designing a new role for government. In great contrast, Barber classified Richard Nixon as an "active-negative" president, claiming that his personality led him to devote an unusual amount of energy to defeating and eluding "enemies." If presidents' personalities had been different, their presidencies would have been different.[25]

Table 11.2 lists the results of four recent efforts to assemble "ratings" of the U.S. presidents based on surveys. The first three are surveys of scholars, and the fourth is a 2007 survey of U.S. citizens. Although one would expect that the political ideology of the raters would influence their choices, it is remarkable that there is so much agreement among the scholars' rankings. Washington, Lincoln, and Franklin Roosevelt are the three most highly ranked presidents in each scholarly survey, and Buchanan, Andrew Johnson, and Harding are consistently ranked very low. There is considerable disagreement regarding recent presidents, however, with Reagan ranking in the "near great" category in two of the scholars' surveys, and first by the public opinion poll, but in the "low average" rating in Schlesinger's study. (Historians are reluctant to

TABLE 11.2   SCHOLARLY AND PUBLIC RANKINGS OF U.S. PRESIDENTS

President	RANKING BY SCHOLARS			PUBLIC OPINION	The Top Three
	Schlesinger	Federalist Society	Wall Street Journal 2005	Gallop Poll 2007***	
Lincoln	1	2	2	1	Washington
Washington	2	1	1	6	
F. D. Roosevelt	3	3	3	9	
Jefferson	4	4	4	11	
Jackson	5	6	10		
T. Roosevelt	6	5	5	9	Lincoln
Wilson	7	11	11		
Truman	8	7	7	7	
Polk	9	10	9		
Eisenhower	10	9	8	10	
J. Adams	11	13	13		F. Roosevelt
Kennedy	12	18	15	3	
Cleveland	13	12	12		
L. Johnson	14	17	18		
Monroe	15	16	16		The Worst
McKinley	16	14	14		
Madison	17	15	17		
J.Q. Adams	18	20	25		Pierce Buchanan
B. Harrison	19	27	30		
Clinton	20	24	22	4	
Van Buren	21	23	27		
Taft	22	19	20		
Hayes	23	22	24		A. Johnson Grant
G.H.W. Bush	24	21	21	14	
Reagan	25	8	6	2	
Arthur	26	26	26		
Carter	27	30	34	12	
Ford	28	28	28	13	Harding Hoover
Taylor	29	31	33		
Coolidge	30	25	23		
Fillmore	31	35	36		
Tyler	32	34	35		
Pierce	33	37T	38		Nixon
Grant	34	32	29		
Hoover	35	29	31		
Nixon	36	33	32	15	
A. Johnson	37	36	37		
Buchanan	38	39	40		
Harding	39	37T	39		
Garfield	*	*	*		
W.H. Harrison	*	*	*		
George W. Bush	**	**	**	8	

* Garfield and W.H. Harrison were omitted from the scholars' surveys because they served such short terms.

** George W. Bush was only included in the Gallup public opinion poll.

*** The Gallup poll asked the respondents the following question: "Who do you regard as the greatest United States president?" The presidents are ranked on the basis of the percentage of the sample that indicated each president as "greatest." Only 15 presidents received mentions from at least one percent of the sample; therefore the other presidents were not ranked in this poll, which was based on surveys in February 2007.

SOURCES: The Schlesinger survey was based on the responses of 32 presidential historians in the 1990s and was obtained from a feature in *The New York Times Magazine*, "The Ultimate Approval Rating," December 15, 1996, pp. 46–49. The Federalist Society survey was based on responses from 78 scholars said to represent a "politically balanced" group selected by Akhil Reed Amar (Yale), Alan Brinkley (Columbia), Steven G. Calabresi (Northwestern), James W. Ceaser (Virginia), Forrest McDonald (Alabama), and Steven Skowronek (Yale). It was obtained as published in the Wall Street Journal's "Opinion Journal," November 16, 2000. The 2005 Wall Street Journal ranking was drawn from a survey of "130 prominent professors of history, law, political science, and economics" in February and March of 2005. Finally, the Gallup poll was based on a survey of 1,006 U.S. adults taken in February 2007. The full study is available at http://www.pollingreport.com/wh-hstry.htm.

render a judgment about a president's place in history while he is still in office, and thus George W. Bush is not included in the scholars' rankings.)

Careful study of the U.S. presidency reveals much about the political system as a whole. Presidents are given great responsibilities and important powers, but the checks and balances of the system and the absence of coherent partisan or ideological divisions among citizens often deny presidents the power to implement the platform that got them elected. The great presidents are those who are able to transcend those constraints, forging support in a system not inclined to grant it.

The Judicial System

If a single institution had to be selected to illustrate the distinctiveness of government in the United States, most observers would choose the judiciary. It is both powerful and politically unaccountable, and it further fragments the policy-making power of the system.

Organization   The U.S. judiciary consists of state courts (including the various municipal courts that states create) and federal courts. Each state has a system of trial and appellate courts, although each state's arrangement is unique in some respects. State courts hear cases dealing with state law (most criminal matters are issues of state law), and federal courts deal with cases pertaining to acts of Congress, administrative rules, and constitutional provisions. Each state has at least one of the 94 federal *district courts*. Appeals from the district courts and from the agencies are heard by the 13 *U.S. Courts of Appeals*, located in geographic regions known as "circuits." The single *Supreme Court* hears appeals from the appeals courts and from state supreme courts. It decides about 140 cases per year.

The Evolution of Judicial Power   When it began operating in 1790, the Supreme Court had a rather limited and uncertain status. It received no important cases during its first few years, and it did not attempt to overturn presidential or congressional acts. However, the Court's power was greatly expanded as a result of *Marbury v. Madison,* the 1803 case regarding a minor government job that became the "rib of the Constitution."[26] President Thomas Jefferson and Secretary of State James Madison refused to grant a commission for a judgeship to William Marbury, who had been promised the job during the last days of the Adams administration. The previous secretary of state, John Marshall, had neglected to send the commission. Jefferson decided to take advantage of Marshall's oversight and give the job to a supporter of his own party. Marbury petitioned the Supreme Court to force the president to give him his commission.

Many people expected that the Court would approve Marbury's request. (After all, the chief justice was none other than John Marshall, the former secretary of state who wanted Marbury to have the commission in the first place!) But there was a legal problem: The jurisdiction of the Supreme Court as defined by the Constitution did not include the power to act in response to that kind of request; instead, an *act of Congress* (The Judiciary Act of 1789) created that power.

If Marshall had tried to force Jefferson to give Marbury the job, Jefferson might have ignored him, and a precedent would have been set establishing that the Court's pronouncements carry little weight. Instead, Marshall held that it was *unconstitutional* for Congress to alter the jurisdiction of the Court, since its jurisdiction was set forth in the Constitution, and thus the Court was powerless to act on Marbury's petition. Although Marbury *should* get the job, he argued, the Court could not hear his petition. Thus, the Court did not force Jefferson to give the job to Marbury. In accepting *Marbury v. Madison*, however, Jefferson helped to solidify the notion that the Supreme Court has the power to decide whether a law is "constitutional."*

Despite its importance, it would be wrong to assume that this case was the exclusive source of the Supreme Court's power. Americans have always been unusually reverent about the "law." (The Declaration of Independence is, after all, a rather legalistic document, particularly when compared with, say, the Communist Manifesto as a revolutionary statement.) In other countries, people are less willing to accept policy decisions by judges.[27] As a noted judge and legal scholar explained: "Struggles over power that in Europe call out regiments of troops, in America call out battalions of lawyers."[28]

U.S. voters have demonstrated their widespread acceptance of judicial independence in policy making on several occasions. During the 1930s, Franklin Roosevelt enjoyed tremendous support for his innovative policies both in Congress and among voters, but several features of his recovery plan were held unconstitutional by the Supreme Court in 1935 and 1936. Roosevelt severely criticized the "nine old men" on the Court, and then he introduced a plan to create new positions on the Court to "ease the workload" for the elderly judges—a plan that would have brought the size of the Supreme Court to 15.[29] The plan failed:

> The Court-packing plan was defeated despite the President's landslide victory at the polls only a few months earlier and despite the overwhelming popular support for New Deal legislation. Although much of the opposition was partisan, the resistance to the Court packing plan ran much deeper. At its source lay the American people's well-nigh religious attachment to constitutionalism and the Supreme Court, including their intuitive realization that packing the Court in order to reverse the course of its decisions would not only destroy its independence but erode the essence of constitutionalism. . . .[30]

In the early 1970s, judicial authority was challenged in a very different way. Richard Nixon stated that he would "ignore" an order by a federal district court to submit tapes of conversations that had taken place in his office. The judge requested the tapes because they could show evidence that Nixon directed subordinates to obstruct an investigation of a burglary committed by members of his campaign staff (the **Watergate** affair). When the matter of the tapes first came to light, public opinion was largely on the president's side—much of the evidence that he had committed a crime was uncorroborated and ambiguous.[31] Nixon's assault on the judiciary changed things dramatically, however. Not only did he ignore the order, but he also fired a special prosecutor who would not obey him. Although Nixon changed his mind within 72 hours, his support plummeted, and eventually he was forced to resign.

The Watergate affair demonstrates the peculiar importance of the independence of the judicial system in the United States. Archibald Cox noted that a Scandinavian legal scholar was astonished by this episode: "'It is unthinkable,' he said, 'that the courts of any country should issue an order to its Chief of State.'"[32] In the United States, the idea is not at all unthinkable, and voters have shown that they will not support a president who disregards judicial power.

---

* Although most analysts accept this conclusion, it should be noted that some argue along other lines. For example, see Robert L. Clinton's *Marbury v. Madison and Judicial Review* (Lawrence: University of Kansas Press, 1989).

The Court and Policy Making   As noted in Chapter 9, judicial decisions often make public policy. Adjudication involves interpreting statutes and constitutional provisions in particular contexts, and such interpretations inevitably resolve policy issues. For example, if the Constitution prohibits "cruel and unusual" punishment, and if housing a prisoner without proper space or sanitary facilities is interpreted as "cruel and unusual," then the effect of that judgment is to "make" prison management policy.

In that and many other areas, the Supreme Court has made decisions that would otherwise be made in legislative and executive institutions. Some of its policy choices simply dictate what the "political" branches of government *cannot* do (they cannot outlaw flag burning, for example), whereas others (such as the prison cases) require governments to take positive action. The status of the Constitution in U.S. society, coupled with the entrenched principle of judicial review, makes judicial involvement in policy making a fact of political life.

Nevertheless, judicial power over policy making is limited. For example, presidents and the Congress can diminish the impact of Court opinions by reducing enforcement efforts. The "power of the purse" is often manipulated to give greater or lesser weight to judicial policy making, as when Congress decided to release previously withheld federal funding from racially imbalanced school systems. Ambiguous or divided judicial opinions also leave legislators and executives uncertain about what is legal.*

Most analysts thus have a balanced view of the Court's actual impact on policy making. In a famous study from the 1950s, Robert Dahl began with the assumption that the Supreme Court *could* conceivably act against the wishes of democratic majorities whenever it wanted. He was interested in determining how often that occurred. After an extensive study of numerous cases over several decades, Dahl concluded that the Court is most likely to alter public policy when majority preferences are vague and divided and that, on most issues, judicial decisions eventually reflect public demands.[33]

A 2007 study of the Supreme Court's decisions from 1981 through 2005 found that the effect of party and ideology on its decisions is probably exaggerated. After examining dozens of opinions that struck down federal statutes during this period, the researcher noted that "more than 70% of [the Court's] decisions were issued by bipartisan coalitions, and that more than 80% invalidated statutes that had been enacted with substantial Republican legislative support." . . . Although this Court was built to rein in the liberal state, fewer than half of its decisions invalidating federal laws reached a conservative result. . . ."[34] During the period covered by the study, the Court never had more than two justices appointed by Democratic presidents, and yet, the cases did not reveal a clear partisan or ideological pattern.

Of course, it is unlikely that the Supreme Court will ever steer policy in a direction that is profoundly out of step with majority opinion, because elected presidents and elected senators select the justices. Presidents appoint justices who reflect their views (and the views of the voters electing them). Since the typical president gets to select two or three Supreme Court justices in a four-year term (along with hundreds of appointments to lower courts), the judiciary's political complexion will not remain contrary to popular demands for long periods. Nevertheless, the judiciary occasionally has tremendously important impacts on specific policy issues.[35]

* For good examples, see *Regents of the University of California v. Bakke*, 438 U.S. 265 (1978), *Bush v. Gore*, 531 U.S. 98 (2000), or *Grutter v. Bollinger* (2003).

Box 11-4

THE SUPREME COURT AND GUN CONTROL POLICY

On June 26, 2008, the Supreme Court announced one of its most anticipated decisions of the decade in *D.C. v. Heller*. The District of Columbia had the strictest gun control laws in the nation, generally banning all handguns and requiring that rifles and shotguns in private hands be disassembled or disabled with trigger locks. Dick Anthony Heller, a resident of the District, challenged the law and his case eventually reached the Supreme Court.

The Second Amendment is a single sentence: "A well regulated Militia, being necessary to the security of a Free State, the right of the people to keep and bear Arms, shall not be infringed." Some claim that this provision is simple and clear; others argue that its meaning requires a detailed examination of the words it contains and the context in which it was drafted and ratified. The *Heller* decision is an excellent illustration of the complexity of constitutional interpretation and its tremendously important policy impacts.

Writing for the five-member majority, Justice Antonin Scalia stated that the Second Amendment confers a right on individuals, not state National Guard units or other modern equivalents of the "militia" mentioned in the text. Much of the dispute over the amendment's meaning has to do with the implications

of its "prefatory" clause (the first thirteen words) for the "operative" clause. Did the Framers intend that citizens should have a right to "keep and bear" arms only when serving in a state militia? If so, the Second Amendment protects only a *collective* right, meaning that the Federal government cannot infringe the right of the states to have organized military units under their control, but that individuals do *not* have a constitutional right to own guns. The majority opinion emphasized the historical context in making the case for the claim that the amendment protects an *individual* right:

> " . . . history showed that the way tyrants had eliminated a militia consisting of all the able bodied men was not by banning the militia but simply by taking away the people's arms, enabling a select militia or standing army to suppress political opponents. This is what had occurred in England. . . . During the 1788 ratification debates, the fear that the federal government would disarm the people in order to impose rule through a standing army or select militia was pervasive. . . ." (p. 25).

The dissenting opinion by Justice Stevens took a very different view, concluding that the amendment

---

The Politics of Appointments to the Supreme Court   The Supreme Court's policymaking role makes Court appointments a very political matter. The process is quite simple: The president selects a nominee and submits the person's name to the Senate for its "advice and consent." Since 1925, nearly all nominees have testified before the Senate Judiciary Committee, answering legal questions as well as questions about their background and their positions on controversial issues. Of the 156 men and 3 women who have been nominated to serve as justices on the Supreme Court, all but 36 have been confirmed by the Senate.

The process reflects both the power and the constraints faced by presidents. Their choices have been accepted some 80 percent of the time, allowing them to shape the direction of the Court, often for a long time to come. However, the fact that appointments to the Court are effectively for life (justices serve "during good behavior") means that those appointed to the Court can develop views that are very different from the previously held positions that led to their nominations. After President Dwight Eisenhower appointed Chief Justice Earl Warren, who became one of the most liberal justices of the twentieth century, Eisenhower declared that his appointment was "one of the two biggest mistakes I made."[36] In his uniquely colorful way, Harry Truman

"protects the right to keep and bear arms for certain military purposes, but that it does not curtail the legislature's power to regulate the nonmilitary use and ownership of weapons" (dissenting opinion, p. 2).

Stevens's dissent relied heavily on a 1939 case, *United States v. Miller* (307 U.S. 174), which considered a challenge to the constitutionality of the 1934 National Firearms Act. That law prohibited the possession of sawed-off shotguns, and the Court concluded in 1939 that the Second Amendment did not prevent the government from enforcing such a restriction: "[i]n the absence of any evidence tending to show that possession or use of a 'shotgun having a barrel of less than eighteen inches in length' at this time has some reasonable relationship to the preservation or efficiency of a well regulated militia, we cannot say that the Second Amendment guarantees the right to keep and bear such an instrument" (*U.S. v. Miller*, at p. 178). Stevens used the *Miller* precedent to support his conclusion that the "right to keep and bear arms" only applies to military uses. The majority's view of the *Miller* case was narrower, concluding that this case established only that the Second Amendment does not prevent the federal government from limiting *certain types* of firearms.

Another dissenter, Justice Breyer, relied less on arguments about the original context in which the Second Amendment was drafted and ratified, and emphasized that the Court should be able to balance the national interest in crime prevention and public safety against the rights of citizens to own guns. The majority's response perfectly captures Justice Scalia's approach to constitutional interpretation:

"We are aware of the problem of handgun violence in this country, and we take seriously the concerns raised by the many *amici* who believe that prohibition of handgun ownership is a solution. The Constitution leaves the District of Columbia a variety of tools for combating that problem, including some measures regulating handguns. . . . But the enshrinement of constitutional rights necessarily takes certain policy choices off the table. These include the absolute prohibition of handguns held and used for self-defense in the home. Undoubtedly some think that the Second Amendment is outmoded in a society where our standing army is the pride of our Nation, where well-trained police forces provide personal security, and where gun violence is a serious problem. That is perhaps debatable, but what is not debatable is that it is not the role of this Court to pronounce the Second Amendment extinct" (at p. 64).

Now that the Supreme Court has weighed in on the meaning of the Second Amendment, it is very likely that the role of the judiciary in gun control policy will be as controversial as its role in the abortion debate.

---

complained about having appointed Tom C. Clark to the Supreme Court: "It isn't so much that he's a *bad* man, it's just that he's such a dumb son of a bitch. He's about the dumbest man I think I've ever run across."[37] Presidents have only an imperfect power to shape the Court's political orientation.

The Bureaucracy

As in all industrialized nations, bureaucracy has become a major feature of government in the United States. Over 16 million Americans work for administrative agencies, not counting those in the military. The U.S. bureaucracy mirrors the distinctive political traits that are apparent in the rest of the government. The same distrust of central authority that led to checks and balances within and between legislative and executive institutions has also produced a fragmented, decentralized bureaucracy.

U.S. bureaucratic institutions are deliberately arranged to maximize control by forces both inside and outside government. In countries with cultures less hostile to bureaucratic management or with strong party systems, bureaucracies are given greater latitude to make and implement policy. The majority party in such systems has the power to enact its platform, and the bureaucracy is often left free to carry it out. The U.S. bureaucracy, however, is subject to demands not only from the majority party but also from powerful individual legislators and their committees, most of which have power to affect agency funding and authority.

Ironically, the problem is magnified by the fact that the bureaucracy is often left with vague directions. Congress delegates authority to an agency to solve some problem, but when agency officials take concrete action, a legislative committee or an interest group may vigorously oppose it. The "benzene case" from the 1980s is a good example of this syndrome.* Congress had debated two very different approaches to regulating benzene (a toxic substance) in factories. One approach was to restrict exposure so that all known risks would be eliminated; the other approach was to impose only those limits deemed to be "cost-effective." Committee hearing records revealed that some members of Congress supported each approach. No bill that satisfied only one side could be passed.

What did Congress do? It delegated power to an agency to decide the issue. The Occupational Safety and Health Administration (OSHA) thus not only had the traditional duties of implementing but also had to make a basic value judgment. When the agency made up its mind (it adopted the more restrictive approach), interests opposing the decision then sued, and the agency lost. This pattern—vague mandates coupled with the need to satisfy conflicting influences—is repeated continually in the U.S. bureaucracy.

It is thus inevitable that bureaucracy in the United States is frequently the subject of severe criticism. The idea that bureaucratic agencies are "captured" by those they serve or regulate is a familiar refrain. The bureaucracy is also criticized for being wasteful, especially when policies and programs work at cross-purposes. Many complain that the bureaucracy is "out of control," noting that bureaucrats make too many basic decisions.

Some, perhaps most, criticism of the U.S. bureaucracy reflects a generalized frustration with the intractable nature of social problems. The bureaucracy may simply be a scapegoat for problems that have little to do with the efficiency or professionalism of administrative operations. The U.S. bureaucracy is expected to behave in accordance with traditional norms of efficiency and expert management and at the same time to be open to diverse and contradictory political directions. It is ordered to plan for the future from one uncertain budget to another. The fragmented power of U.S. government produces a bureaucracy that is highly open to public involvement and scrutiny but often is unable to act in a coordinated, authoritative manner.

Participation in U.S. Politics

Political Parties and Elections

Although elections and parties remain the two most dominant elements of political participation in America, studies regularly reveal a long-term decline in voter turnout

* See Industrial Union Department, AFL-CIO v. American Petroleum Institute, 448 U.S. 607 (1980).

FIGURE 11.4   VOTER TURNOUT IN U.S. ELECTIONS

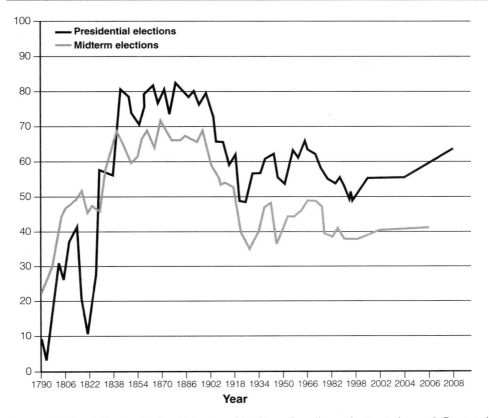

SOURCES: National Election Studies. University of Michigan (http://www.electionstudies.org/). Reprinted by permission. 2006 data from the Gallup Poll, www.gallup.com, and 2008 data from Professor Michael McDonald's "United States Election Project," available at www.elections.gmu.edu

and partisan attachment. These trends shape the character of modern politics in the United States.

Voter Turnout   Figure 11.4 is a graph of the percentage of voter turnout in presidential and midterm elections since 1790. After a dramatic increase during the 1830s, turnout declined around the end of the nineteenth century and remained at a lower level despite some fluctuations. About 62 percent of the eligible population voted in the 1952 presidential election, but only 50 percent voted in 1988, about 55 percent in 1992, 49 percent in 1996, and 55.5 percent in 2004. The 43.6 percent turnout in 2006 was the highest for a mid-term election since 1970. In 2008, turnout rose to well over 60 percent, the highest figure in more than four decades.*

* Some argue that simple turnout figures may give a distorted picture of the extent of U.S. political participation because the U.S. uses the electoral process for more offices and more kinds of decisions than do other democracies. When all of these elections are taken into account, U.S. voter turnout appears stronger.

Political scientists have identified several factors that explain the lower turnout during the period between 1970 and 2000. First, the dip in turnout between the 1968 and 1972 elections reflected the Twenty-Sixth Amendment's lowering of the voting age to eighteen, since it added a large group of citizens to the potential voting pool who do not regularly vote. Second, since the early 1960s, the proportion of voters who feel that government can effectively solve their problems has declined. The Vietnam War convinced many voters that their government could not be trusted, that it would not pursue the public interest, and that it would not always achieve its purposes. Government policies also fell short of expectations in domestic affairs. Although many citizens felt increased confidence in government as a result of experiences during the Great Depression of the 1930s, the War on Poverty initiated in the 1960s was not as successful.[38] In addition, intense media coverage of scandals made many citizens cynical about politics. Finally, declining party identification leads to lower voter turnout. One study concluded that one-fifth of the decline in turnout was caused by declining partisanship.[39]

Beginning with the tumultuous election in 2000, voter turnout has increased substantially. Several scholars have noticed an increasing polarization in the electorate, and partisan divisions are deeper.[40] More heated political conflicts should mobilize more voters. And, as noted in Chapter 4, turnout should also increase when election laws and procedures make it easier and less time consuming to vote, and the recent innovations allowing people to vote by post card and to register more easily may also have contributed to the recent increase in Americans going to the polls. When people feel a strong attachment to a party, they are more likely to vote, even if the issues and candidates in a given election may not interest them. Without strong partisan loyalty, many voters stay home.

Political Parties in the United States   The authors of a leading text about U.S. political parties described U.S. political parties in the following way:

> . . . [b]y the standards of the parties of the other democracies, . . . the American political parties cut an unimpressive figure. They lack the hierarchical control and efficiency, the unified setting of priorities and strategy, and the central responsibility we associate with large contemporary organizations and often find in parties in other nations.[41]

Remarkably, that assessment echoed a famous analysis from 1950:

> Alternatives between the parties are defined so badly that it is often difficult to determine what the election has decided even in the broadest terms.[42]

U.S. parties have long been a disappointment to political scientists and others who have looked to them as tools that would make democracy work better, *if only they were better organized and more responsible*. The two major U.S. parties still fall short of the responsible party model, but they are becoming more meaningful as symbolic labels and more effective as organizers of political energy. As discussed earlier, one of the largest obstacles to partisan coherence—the persistent division of the Democratic Party into southern conservatives and liberals from other parts of the country—is quickly being removed, enabling the parties to become more focused on a roughly consistent pair of opposing messages. Still, political parties in the United States are less disciplined and

FIGURE 11.5   PARTY IDENTIFICATION, 1952–2004

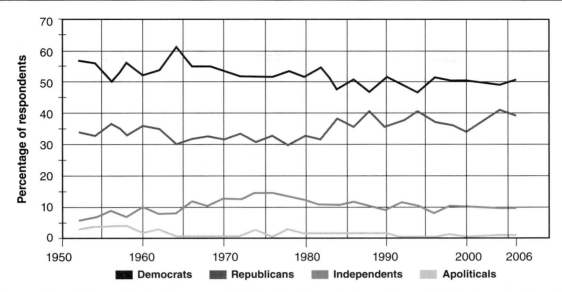

SOURCE: National Election Studies. University of Michigan (http://www.electionstudies.org/). Reprinted by permission. 2006 data from the Gallup Poll, www.gallup.com. Figures for Democratic and Republican Party identifiers includes respondents who state that they "lean" toward one of these parties.

less responsible than their counterparts in Great Britain, Israel, Germany, and many other modern democracies.

Moreover, the decline of party identification in the United States in recent years suggests that the parties' clearer distinctiveness has not produced a corresponding increase in party identification among the voters. Figure 11.5 indicates the number of U.S. voters who have claimed to identify with the two major parties since 1952. A perceptible decline in identification coincides with the increased incidence of "ticket splitting": In recent elections, more than half of all voters report voting for presidential and congressional candidates of different parties, whereas only 30 percent did so during the 1950s.

According to a 2004 study, at least some ticket-splitting by U.S. voters is driven by an explicit preference for Congress and the White House to be under the control of different parties:

> "voters who declared themselves open to different party control across electoral arenas were clearly more likely to vote one party for the presidency, another for Congress. That is, they voted to check governmental power, by dividing it between two institutions. Voters who say they want to split control tend to vote that way, and that relationship holds up under extensive testing.[43]

Voters choosing to create divided government through ticket-splitting constituted nearly one-fourth of the electorate in the 1990s, according to the authors.

The deterioration of party identification has many causes, including the dissatisfaction that many voters feel regarding public institutions in general. As discussed in Chapter 4, the advent of postmaterialism also inhibits strong partisanship. As environmental issues, abortion rights, and other noneconomic controversies dominate political life, more people are confused about which party to support. Both the wealthy suburbanite who supports the Republicans on tax issues but supports the Democrats on abortion and pollution control *and* the lower-income voter who agrees with conservative Republicans regarding prayer in the public schools but embraces Democratic positions on health policy are likely to be torn between the two major parties. Since there are many more such confused voters now than in previous decades, this pattern may contribute to declining partisanship.

The impact of the media also facilitates a decline in partisanship. When television amplifies the importance of a candidate's personal qualities (positive or negative), the party label becomes less important. Finally, interest groups increasingly provide outlets for energies that would otherwise be devoted to political parties, particularly for people who are drawn to "single-issue" politics involving, say, abortion or gun control.

It would be wrong, however, to conclude that U.S. parties are not important. Party identification remains the most important influence on voting choice, and party organizations, despite their weaknesses, still play a pivotal role in selecting candidates. Perhaps the best assessment is that the U.S. parties will continue to exert an influence but that they will share that influence with other organizations, particularly with interest groups.[44] Given the nature of the U.S. political system, we should not expect that the parties will ever become the "governing instruments" that the advocates of party responsibility envision.[45]

Interest-Group Activity   Political organizations have long been a part of U.S. politics, and, perhaps surprisingly, many political scientists had a positive view of interest groups during the first half of the last century (although many others criticized their impact). Some saw interest groups as providing ways for people to indicate the *intensity* of their preferences (compared with voting, which indicates only their *direction*). Most analysts now view interest groups in the United States more critically.

A basic reason for the growing concern about interest groups has to do with how they operate. As discussed earlier, the most distinctive political feature of U.S. institutions is the extent to which they fragment governmental authority. Interest groups exist in all modern democracies, and even in the developing world, but the fragmentation of power in U.S. government gives them great opportunities to affect public policy.

Interest groups in the United States take advantage of the arrangement of Congress by developing close connections with committees and committee staff and by providing campaign funds that central party leadership cannot command. In a sense, interest group power is both a cause and a consequence of weak partisanship; interest groups divert members of Congress from party platforms, and they provide a way for citizens who have lost faith in parties to express their demands. U.S. interest groups also exert considerable influence in courts, exploiting the policy-making opportunities that exist there. Interest groups that are effective in other political arenas compound their power by taking action in the judicial branch.[46]

Most observers are no longer confident that the interest group system is representative of the country as a whole. Whereas everyone has the right to vote, some people have the added benefit of effective political organizations acting on their behalf. Most citizens do not. If public policy depends to a significant degree on the balance of *organized* forces, then those who are not represented by effective organizations are at a disadvantage.

Beyond the problem of representation, others argue that the growing power of interest groups makes it increasingly difficult for Congress or the president to craft and implement coherent or comprehensive programs. Interest group influence is apparent in agriculture policy, education policy, transportation policy, and many other areas. U.S. interest groups will continue to create severe difficulties for government in the years to come; their existence reflects the openness of American society, but their influence may obstruct necessary policy making.

U.S. POLITICS: PROSPECTS AND CHALLENGES

The United States currently faces profound challenges that will severely test its political system. Perhaps Americans will have to construct new, less fragmented governmental institutions in order to provide for the sustained, coordinated public authority needed to solve the system's social, economic, and foreign policy problems. Or perhaps another inspirational president will emerge, who, like Lincoln or Roosevelt, will transcend narrow political divisions and mobilize support for necessary public decisions.

This will not be easy. A June 2008 Gallup poll reported that public confidence in U.S. governmental institutions had fallen to historically low levels. The numbers in the following list are the percentages of Americans who have "a great deal" or "quite a lot" of confidence in each of these institutions:

The Military	71%
Small Business	60%
Banks	33%
The Presidency	26%
Organized Labor	20%
Big Business	20%
HMOs	13%
Congress	12%

SOURCE: "Confidence in Congress—Lowest Ever for Any U.S. Institution," Gallup Poll results, June 20, 2008, available at www.gallup.com.

Each of the challenges listed below will require a sustained, committed effort from institutions already weakened by dwindling public confidence.

The Impact of International Terrorism

The attacks on the World Trade Center and the Pentagon on September 11, 2001, made U.S. citizens feel vulnerable and threatened in ways that had not been experienced in six decades. The fact that the threat was not produced directly by an enemy

---

Box 11-5

INTEREST GROUP POWER AND INEQUALITY IN THE U.S.

One of the most familiar quotations in the political science literature was supplied by E.E. Schattschneider in 1960: "The flaw in the pluralist heaven is that the heavenly chorus sings with a strong upper-class accent."[47] As discussed in Chapter 6, political scientists embracing the concept of pluralism in the 1950s typically adopted an optimistic view: unlike those embracing elite theory or Marxism, pluralists argued that there was no single center of power in U.S. society, and that the plurality of influential political organizations competing to shape policy meant that virtually all interests had an effective voice. Schattschneider was among the first of many who sounded a note of caution. Even casual observation would reveal that while there is no single center of power among the organized forces in society, most of the most active and influential interest groups tend to represent the needs and preferences of the wealthier parts of society.

A remarkable new book by Dara Strolovitch explores this problem. She begins with the observation that there are, in fact, hundreds of political organizations devoted to the interests of the poor and victims of racial, ethnic, or religious discrimination. Most of these organizations did not exist when Schattschneider wrote in 1960. It would certainly appear that the "upper class accent" of the pluralist heaven is not as pronounced as it was a half century ago. Even as long ago as 1974, James Wilson concluded that "groups once excluded are now included."

However, through an empirical study of some 286 organizations Strolovitch found that the actual work of many of these groups does not advance the interests of the poor and marginalized parts of society as much as we might expect. Realizing that some of those represented by these organizations are more "advantaged" than others, she set out to determine how much of each organization's energies is actually devoted to its neediest constituents. The results tend to confirm Schattschneider's interpretation of pluralism:

> . . . organizations employ a double standard that determines the level of energy they devote to issues affecting subgroups of their broader constituency, a double standard based on the status of the subgroup

---

state or army severely complicated the nation's response in two ways. The United States had to deal with the possibility of infiltration in not only its system of airline transportation but also its systems for mail, computer communications, power plants, and other things important in everyday life. The nature of that threat led to controversial proposals to strengthen the power of the FBI and other agencies to gather and keep information on citizens and immigrants, and to streamline judicial proceedings to prevent possibly dangerous suspects from engaging in terrorist attacks. How the nation balances its need for security with the principles of due process and individual privacy will be a major challenge for years to come.

Of course, the most controversial action taken by the U.S. government was the invasion of Iraq in 2003. Although Saddam Hussein's regime fell relatively quickly, the creation of a stable democratic government has proved difficult. The war in Iraq has had profound effects, increasing partisan discord in U.S. elections and complicating diplomatic relations with U.S. allies, particularly those in Europe. Politics and government in the U.S. will be affected for decades both by the continuing dangers of terrorism and the Iraq war.

Economic Transformation and the Global Economy

The economic transformation facing the United States at the beginning of the twenty-first century presents a serious challenge to the political system. As unskilled jobs are

affected rather than on the breadth or depth of the impact of the policy issue in question. As a consequence, the issues affecting advantaged subgroups receive disproportionately high levels of attention and resources, while issues affecting marginalized and disadvantaged subgroups, with some important exceptions, receive disproportionately low levels.[48]

Thus, Strolovitch's study suggests that the existence of political organizations devoted to advocating for the disadvantaged do so to some degree, but that they expend a disproportionate amount of their resources on the most advantaged subgroups in their respective constituencies. Her findings are, unfortunately, consistent with some other pessimistic conclusions by others who have studied U.S. interest groups. The late Mancur Olson, Jr., whose ideas about interest group formation we discussed in Chapter 6, made the following assessment regarding the impact on the disadvantaged of organized group successes in shaping government policies: "A very large part of the activities of governments, even in the developed democracies, is of no special help to the poor and many of these activities actually harm them."[49]

A 2006 study of modern democracies provides evidence for the conclusions advanced by Strolovitch, Olson, and others:

[During the last three decades] there was . . . a dramatic rise in the prevalence of democracy; yet we find little evidence that the rise of democracy contributed to the fall in infant and child mortality rates. Democracy unquestionably produces non-economic benefits for people in poverty, endowing them with political rights and liberties. But for those in the bottom quintiles, these political rights produced few if any improvements in their material well-being. This troubling finding contradicts the claims made by a generation of scholars.[50]

Representation of the poor and disadvantaged remains a challenge for the U.S. and for most other democracies. Debates regarding the power and effectiveness of organized interests have long focused on this challenge, and both political scientists and activist leaders have assumed that an array of powerful political organizations would be a key part of the solution. However, there is considerable evidence that the interest group system, at least so far, has not produced a significant change in the conditions of the most disadvantaged members of U.S. society, even those organizations ostensibly devoted to the cause. Experiences in other democracies provide little encouraging evidence.

"exported" to Mexico, Korea, and Malaysia, among many other places, the U.S. industrial base is threatened, and some jobs are lost. In recent years, General Motors, Sears, and IBM announced immediate and planned layoffs of tens of thousands of workers, devastating many communities. The aerospace industry—a leading export industry—is threatened as well.

Many analysts contend that a major coordinated public response is necessary to ease the difficulties caused by these changes. To keep the manufacturing activities that remain, U.S. industry must successfully compete with companies in Japan, Germany, and elsewhere that did not exist as competitors a generation ago. Successful competition may require investment in basic research, in urban infrastructure, and in education. A housing crisis erupted in 2007 and 2008, creating dangerous ripples throughout credit markets and the construction industry, while wiping out billions in homeowners' equity. Unlike the original movement of society from agriculture to industry, the nation's current economic changes will not be gradual or relatively self-managing.

Immigration Policy

In 2008, upwards of 12 million illegal aliens were in the U.S., the vast majority of whom came from Mexico in search of jobs and economic opportunity. Immigration policy

Box 11-6

THE CONSTITUTION, THE WAR ON TERROR, AND GUANTANAMO BAY

Detainees Processed at Guantanamo Bay. In this Department of Defense photo, U.S. Army Military Police escort a detainee to his cell in Camp X-Ray at Naval Base Guantanamo Bay, Cuba, during in-processing to the temporary detention facility on January 11, 2002.

In virtually all the wars in U.S. history, steps taken by the executive and legislative branches have raised serious questions about key provisions in the Constitution. As noted above, Abraham Lincoln undermined the most basic of our constitutional rights during the Civil War. On September 24, 1862, he proclaimed that "the Writ of *Habeas Corpus* is suspended in respect to all persons arrested, or who are now, or hereafter during the rebellion shall be, imprisoned in any fort, camp, arsenal, military prison, or other place of confinement by any military authority or by the sentence of any Court Martial or Military Commission." (A Writ of *"Habeas Corpus"* essentially demands that a person being held in custody be brought to court so that an impartial tribunal can determine whether or not the person is being lawfully imprisoned.) In 1917 and 1918, President Woodrow Wilson got Congress to pass the Espionage and Sedition Acts,

which made it a federal crime to publicly criticize the draft or the president. And, during World War II, President Franklin Roosevelt ordered the internment of thousands of Japanese Americans without due process of law. The Constitutional rights violated by these actions were firmly re-asserted when the wars ended.

During George W. Bush's two terms, the Supreme Court made four controversial decisions regarding the rights of those accused of being "enemy combatants," many of whom were held captive in Guantanamo Bay, Cuba. *Rasul v. Bush* (542 U.S. 466, 2004) had to do with three individuals captured after combat in Afghanistan. They were taken to Guantanamo Bay where they were confined, but they were not charged with wrongdoing, they were given no opportunity to consult with counsel, and they were given no access to judicial proceedings. They all claimed that they were unjustly imprisoned, and the Center for Constitutional Rights (a nonprofit foundation established in 1966 by controversial lawyer William Kunstler) brought the detainees' case to federal court.

The Bush Administration argued that the Supreme Court had no jurisdiction over the treatment of non-U.S. citizens in the custody of U.S. armed forces in foreign lands, using as precedent a 1950 case, *Johnson v. Eisentrager* (339 U.S. 763). This case had to do with German prisoners held captive by U.S. forces in Europe following World War II. When a case was brought on behalf of some of these prisoners, the Court held:

". . . in extending constitutional protections beyond the citizenry, the Court has been at pains to point out that it was the alien's presence within its territorial jurisdiction that gave the Judiciary power to act. . . . If this [Fifth] Amendment invests enemy aliens in unlawful hostile action against us with immunity from military trial, it puts them in a more protected position than our own soldiers. . . . We hold that the Constitution does not confer a right of personal security or an immunity from military trial and punishment upon an alien enemy engaged in the hostile service of a government at war with the United States."

In the *Rasul* holding, the Supreme Court did not overturn the *Eisentrager* case, but simply argued that the precedent did not apply. Specifically, the Court noted that the detainees in question are not citizens of countries who were at war with the U.S., and, unlike the German prisoners in the later 1940s, the detainees denied that they had ever been involved in acts of aggression against the U.S. Moreover, they had been "imprisoned in territory over which the United States exercises exclusive jurisdiction and control." Thus, the federal courts have jurisdiction to consider the rights of these detainees to challenge their detention.

In his dissent, Justice Scalia made the case against the holding:

"Today's opinion, and today's opinion alone, overrules *Eisentrager*; today's opinion, and today's opinion alone, extends the *habeas* statute, for the first time, to aliens held beyond the sovereign territory of the United States and beyond the territorial jurisdiction of its courts. No reasons are given for this result; no acknowledgment of its consequences made. . . . the

Court evades explaining why *stare decisis* can be disregarded, and why *Eisentrager* was wrong. Normally, we consider the interests of those who have relied on our decisions. Today, the Court springs a trap on the Executive, subjecting Guantanamo Bay to the oversight of the federal courts even though it has never before been thought to be within their jurisdiction—and thus making it a foolish place to have housed alien wartime detainees."

In 2001, a U.S. citizen named Yaser Esam Hamdi was captured on a battlefield in Afghanistan following a combat operation. He claimed that he was not fighting against U.S. forces and was in the country to help with relief efforts. Hamdi was taken to the U.S. base in Guantanamo Bay and held there until officials found out that he was a U.S. citizen. He was then kept in solitary confinement in a Navy brig in Charleston, South Carolina. Classified as an enemy combatant, Hamdi was held without a hearing or an opportunity to see a lawyer.

In June 2004, the U.S. Supreme Court announced its ruling in *Hamdi v. Rumsfeld* (542 U.S. 507). The government's position was that since Hamdi was captured in an active combat zone, he was properly classified as an enemy soldier taken on the field of battle. The Fourth Circuit Court of Appeals agreed, and concluded that "no factual inquiry or evidentiary hearing allowing Hamdi to be heard or to rebut the Government's assertions was necessary or proper."

Hamdi claimed that the Constitution guaranteed all U.S. citizens a right to due process, in particular a right to a meaningful hearing and legal representation, before they can be held in jail. If the government could avoid respecting his due process rights merely by classifying him as an enemy combatant, the government could conceivably do this whenever it wanted to deny a person a right to a hearing before incarcerating him or her indefinitely.

The case presented some tremendously difficult questions, and the Supreme Court's divided opinion reflected the tension between conflicting objectives. The court majority reached a compromise, holding that the government must give U.S. citizens incarcerated as enemy combatants a hearing, but that the normal rules of evidence would not be required (the government would be allowed to rely on "hearsay," for example, in making its case against the person being

(Continued)

Box 11-6

THE CONSTITUTION, THE WAR ON TERROR, AND GUANTANAMO BAY   (*Continued*)

imprisoned, and the burden of proof would be on the "enemy combatant," not on the government).

Two very different dissents further revealed the competing values implicated in this case. In his dissent, Justice Clarence Thomas argued that the Court was not in a position to question the judgment of the armed forces regarding the continued imprisonment of Hamdi and those taken in similar circumstances:

> The Executive Branch, acting pursuant to the powers vested in the President by the Constitution and with explicit congressional approval, has determined that Yaser Hamdi is an enemy combatant and should be detained. This detention falls squarely within the Federal Government's war powers, and we lack the expertise and capacity to second-guess that decision.

Justice Antonin Scalia, also dissenting, took the opposite approach:

> Where the Government accuses a citizen of waging war against it, our constitutional tradition has been to prosecute him in federal court for treason or some other crime. Where the exigencies of war prevent that, the Constitution's Suspension Clause, Art. I, Section 9, cl. 2, allows Congress to relax the usual protections temporarily. Absent suspension, however, the Executive's assertion of military exigency has not been thought sufficient to permit detention without charge.

Scalia and Thomas both grounded their views in Constitutional provisions, but they reached completely different conclusions. Scalia explained that the Due Process clause was designed because the authors and ratifiers of the Fifth and Fourteenth Amendments did not trust the government to incarcerate only those citizens that should be incarcerated, and therefore the government must afford citizens a right to a public trial to protest their innocence. If Hamdi is dangerous and if he fought against the U.S., argued Scalia, then the government should prosecute him for treason, and the ensuing trial will give Hamdi due process of law. Thomas argued that the Constitution's grant of power to the president as

Commander in Chief essentially authorizes him to act freely in setting policies for enemy combatants. The Court's compromise decision granted U.S. citizens taken in these circumstances a right to due process, but it made the required procedures less burdensome on the government than they would otherwise have been.

In 2006, the Court ruled on another Guantanamo Bay case, *Hamdan v. Rumsfeld* (548 U.S. 547). Hamdan, a citizen of Yemen, was charged with conspiracy "to commit crimes triable by military commission," and the commission heard his case. Hamdan claimed that the structure and procedures of the military commission violate the Uniform Code of Military Justice (an act of Congress), and the 1949 Geneva Conventions, of which the U.S. is a signatory. Specifically, the military commission hearing procedure did not afford the accused or his counsel the opportunity to see the evidence used against him.

A complicating factor in the case was that Congress had passed the Detainee Treatment Act in 2005. The DTA set up procedures for handling detainee cases, and it specifically stated that "no court, justice, or judge shall have jurisdiction to consider the habeas application of a Guantanamo Bay detainee," and the government claimed that the courts therefore could not consider the merits of Hamdan's case. The Court disagreed, stating that since his case was pending at the time the DTA was passed, the jurisdictional limits did not apply. The Court went on to find the DTA procedures inadequate.

Finally, on June 12, 2008, the Supreme Court announced its decision in *Boumediene v. Bush*. As in *Hamdan* and *Rasul*, the 2008 case dealt with a non-U.S. citizen. The detainee claimed that he had a right to challenge his detention (*habeas corpus*) under the U.S. Constitution, and that the procedures afforded him through the Detainee Detention Act did not satisfy this right. The government argued that the Constitutional provision did not apply because the detainee was not being held in territory over which the U.S. claims sovereignty.

The Court rejected the government's position and extended the Constitutional grant of *habeas corpus* to the detainees at Guantanamo. While accepting that the U.S. does not have sovereignty over the naval base, the Court nevertheless concluded that the U.S. has effective control over the territory, and that full legal sovereignty is not necessary in order for the Constitutional provision to apply.

The *Boumediene* decision was both strongly hailed and criticized. The Court's five-member majority spoke for many critics of the Bush Administration:

"Although the United States has maintained complete and uninterrupted control of Guantanamo for over 100 years, the Government's view is that the Constitution has no effect there, at least as to noncitizens, because the United States disclaimed formal sovereignty in its 1903 lease with Cuba. The Nation's basic charter cannot be contracted away like this. The Constitution grants Congress and the President the power to acquire, dispose of, and govern territory, not the power to decide when and where its terms apply."

Many of those opposing the decision argued that it will vastly extend the power of the federal judiciary over activities that are vital to the prosecution of war. If the Constitution's protections now extend not only to U.S. soil and territories over which it claims sovereignty, it may be argued that persons in parts of Iraq occupied and "effectively controlled" by U.S. forces have *habeas corpus* rights under the Constitution. Concerns over this issue prompted a vehement dissent from Chief Justice Roberts:

"Today the Court strikes down as inadequate the most generous set of procedural protections ever afforded aliens detained by this country as enemy combatants. The political branches crafted these procedures amidst an ongoing military conflict, after much careful investigation and thorough debate. The Court rejects them today out of hand, without bothering to say what due process rights the detainees possess, without explaining how the statute fails to vindicate those rights, and before a single petitioner has even attempted to avail himself of the law's operation."

Taken together, these cases provide a revealing illustration of the ways that war puts great stress on the U.S. Constitution. The issue has produced a great deal of heated commentary. Many persons

writing from the contemporary liberal perspective have praised the decisions for upholding what they see as basic Constitutional rights, while many conservatives support the dissenters' arguments that the Court has been "making up" Constitutional provisions to fit a political agenda. But there were some surprises. Justice Scalia's dissents clearly reveal his "strict constructionist" approach to Constitutional interpretation: he opposed what he saw as an expansion of judicial power in *Rasul, Hamdan, and Boumediene*, but, in *Hamdi*, he dissented because he concluded that the majority *had not gone far enough* in protecting the rights of U.S. citizens. In his view, the Constitution is quite clear in protecting a citizen's rights to due process, but the document contains no provision that would legitimize the holdings in the other cases. In this connection, it is interesting to note that the conservative and libertarian Cato Institute wrote an *amicus curiae* brief for the detainees in the *Boumediene* case. The brief states:

The Constitution . . . limits Congress's power over the writ of *habeas corpus*. The Suspension Clause [of the Constitution] limits the revocation of *habeas corpus* to times of rebellion or invasion. Congress has not invoked those exceptions. Thus, the Military Commissions Act, which purports to withdraw the jurisdiction of federal courts over the Petitioners' *habeas* claims, is unconstitutional.*

In short, it is difficult to place the controversy over the rights of Guantanamo's detainees on the conventional conservative—liberal continuum.

Presidents and Congress have often invoked national security as a justification for actions that have undercut Constitutional rights. Especially in the War on Terror, which will not end with a surrender ceremony and peace treaty, and which does not take place on a defined theater of operations, the legal and ethical concerns are particularly difficult. On the other hand, the historical record provides a bit of comfort because it shows that even the most egregious violations of Constitutional rights did not endure after the wars that led presidents to take such steps ended.

* The Cato Institute's amicus brief is available at: www.cato.org/pubs/legalbriefs/boumediene_vs_bush.pdf.

has become an extremely divisive problem, touching on a great many issues and raising difficult questions:

1. Does an unsecured border with Mexico constitute a threat to national security and an opportunity for terrorists to infiltrate the U.S.?
2. Is it appropriate, fair, or humane to condemn illegal immigrants as felons (this was proposed in a bill introduced in Congress in March 2006), when they are simply seeking employment in jobs that U.S. citizens will not take?
3. What are the costs that taxpayers must bear to provide health, educational, and other services to illegal aliens and their families?
4. Does the presence of illegal aliens in the U.S. economy drive down the wages of U.S. workers?
5. Can the U.S. economy survive without the labor of illegal aliens?

Americans are bitterly divided over immigration policy. Some favor building a wall to prevent people from entering the country illegally, and an organization of private citizens has worked in several states that border Mexico to apprehend and report illegal immigrants. Others feel that a crackdown on illegal immigrants is a kind of thinly-disguised prejudice against persons of Hispanic origin. In response to a proposal that was introduced in Congress to make it a felony to enter the country illegally, Senator Hillary Clinton expressed the outrage that many citizens felt in comments she made on March 22, 2006: "This bill would literally criminalize the Good Samaritan and probably even Jesus himself."

In 2007, eighty senators signed on as co-sponsors of the "Security Through Regularized Immigration and a Vibrant Economy Act," or STRIVE. This bill, not enacted as of this writing, includes a variety of steps intended to respond to a wide range of concerns. To enhance border security, the act provides for a "biometric" entry system, the use of the National Guard to patrol the border with Mexico, and criminal penalties for trafficking in illegal aliens and for knowingly employing them. The act would also create a "guest worker program" that would allow persons currently in the U.S. illegally to remain in the country under certain conditions, but only for a maximum of six years. After that time, guest workers could apply for permanent resident alien status if they pay a $500 application fee and agree to learn the English language and U.S. history.

However, public opinion polls suggest that any solution to the problem will be politically difficult. A CNN/Opinion Research Corporation poll in 2008 reported that 65 percent of U.S. adults would like to see the number of illegal aliens reduced. There is considerable support for taking stern measures to accomplish this goal, although many Americans oppose punitive actions. The STRIVE bill embodies both the concerns of those who emphasize the importance of border security and of those who conclude that it is impossible or inhumane to deport millions of illegal aliens in a short period of time.

The debate over immigration will be a critical challenge for the U.S. in the years to come. It involves legal, ethical, diplomatic, and economic questions, and it is profoundly divisive.

Race Relations

The status and condition of African Americans has been the most consistently difficult and controversial problem faced by U.S. government. The issue was divisive at the Constitutional Convention, when it was decided to count slaves as three-fifths of a person for the purpose of determining state population (and thus the number of seats each state would have in the House of Representatives). Slavery was, of course, the root of the Civil War. And, in the twentieth century, debates over civil rights divided Americans deeply.

As divisive and difficult as race relations were, the issues posed in the 1950s and 1960s were arguably less difficult for the system than the issues faced today. Forty-five years ago, the major civil rights controversies were about official restrictions on African American voting rights and laws that required African Americans to eat only at segregated restaurants. Although progress in those areas was difficult, it mainly required changing laws and providing security to protect those who would exercise their rights.

We can now say that African Americans enjoy the same legal rights to vote, travel, attend college, and pursue careers that other Americans have had for generations. Nevertheless, the National Urban League issued a report in 2007 that found severe remaining inequalities. The "inequality index," a measure incorporating data on housing, wealth, education, and civic engagement, was only 73 percent, indicating the average disparity between blacks and whites. Nearly a fourth of all black households still live in poverty, compared to only ten percent of white households.[51] It is clear that African Americans have not shared equally in the general prosperity of American society. Not only are income levels and wealth far below average levels, but African Americans also experience other problems more deeply. African Americans are much more likely to be victims of crime than other Americans (murder is the leading cause of death for young African American males), and in many states more male African Americans are in prison or on parole than in college.

These problems challenge the political system profoundly. The civil rights movement of a generation ago emphasized the need to *remove discriminatory practices*, whereas current problems of race relations are more controversial. In 1996, California voters ratified the California Civil Rights Initiative, which outlawed racial and gender preferences in state government and state higher education. Washington and Michigan voters adopted similar laws in 1999 and 2006, respectively, as did voters in Nebraska in 2008.

As several studies predicted, the end of racial preferences produced a significant decline in the number of African Americans at leading University of California campuses in 1997. In 2003, two important Supreme Court cases addressed the use of racial factors in admissions to institutions of higher education (*Grutter v. Bollinger*, and *Gratz v. Bollinger*), both arising from practices at the University of Michigan. In the *Grutter* ruling, five members of the Supreme Court upheld the affirmative action policy at the Law School, but in the *Gratz* case, six justices voted to hold the policy used by the undergraduate college unconstitutional.* The mixed signals coming from these cases will ensure that the legal status of racial preferences will remain unsettled for years.

The Status of Women

Although U.S. women are legally protected from most forms of discrimination, their status remains a major political issue. Interest groups such as the National Organization for Women (NOW) demand federal laws to establish national child care

---

* See *Gratz v. Bollinger*, 539 U.S. 244, and *Grutter v. Bollinger*, 539 U.S. 306, decided June 23, 2003.

facilities and insist that employers be more flexible in accommodating workers' family responsibilities.

Thus, as with African Americans, the solutions to the concerns of women in the United States go beyond the repeal of discriminatory laws. They require decisions that confront basic moral concerns (such as abortion) and others that involve elaborate government regulation of the workplace. These problems are a major challenge for the political system, and they will not be resolved easily or quickly.

Health Care

It is estimated that Americans spend nearly 20 percent of the nation's gross domestic product on health care ($2.3 trillion in 2007). Spending on health care is 4.3 times the amount spent on national defense, and the costs are rising rapidly.[52] Part of the increase reflects quality improvements, and part reflects the fact that the population has become older, but many believe that the skyrocketing costs will require some kind of governmental response. Although President Bill Clinton failed to secure passage of his health care plan in 1994, health care has remained a central issue in political campaigns, particularly in the 2008 election. Beginning in 2006, the Bush Administration's plan adding prescription drug coverage to the Medicare program went into effect, providing financial help to older Americans facing increasingly expensive pharmaceuticals. However, the cost and complexity of the program made it controversial and unpopular in many quarters, illustrating the difficulties involved in facing the larger challenge of providing health care generally.

Changes in the International System

The first half of the twentieth century saw the United States thrust into a leadership role in international relations. From an essentially isolationist posture that predominated in the 1800s, the United States became one of the two main forces in the bipolar world that emerged at the end of World War II. The United States devoted a large proportion of its productive capacity to fighting wars to contain the power of its major competitor, the Soviet Union, and to fostering nuclear deterrence. The cold war shaped foreign and even domestic policies.

The cold war ended in 1991 with the official demise of the Soviet Union. The United States responded by announcing major reductions in nuclear and conventional forces and plans for deeper reductions in the future. East–West conflict no longer defines the international system, which is increasingly marked by more complex ethnic and cultural clashes. Economic competition will almost certainly be the primary issue in foreign policy, and adversarial relations will be more complex and subtle as the world becomes more interdependent.

The problem of international terrorism thus struck at a time when the fundamental feature of the international system was no longer the "bipolar" competition that existed during the cold war years. Although that change has made many nations more flexible in their diplomacy (in that they no longer have to consider how their actions and statements affect the balance of power between two hegemonic states), it also makes diplomacy more complicated. There is greater emphasis on international law and organization than in recent years. How the United States will pursue its interests in international affairs in this changing environment will consume a great deal of the energies of our presidents.

The Future of American Democracy

The United States has faced enormous challenges throughout its history. Industrialization, the Civil War, foreign military threats, and the specter of nuclear holocaust presented the system with problems that required enormous and costly responses. For the most part, the challenges were met successfully. But the new challenges may actually be more threatening, possibly requiring fundamental changes in the system itself.

Still, democracy in the United States has been among the world's greatest successes, regardless of how success is measured. Even now, leaders in the fledgling democracies of Eastern Europe look to the United States—not to Great Britain, Germany, or Japan—as the model to emulate. Whether that success has resulted from the special features of U.S. government, or despite them, will remain an open question.

 WHERE ON THE WEB?

http://www.fec.gov/sitemap.shtml

The home page of the Federal Election Commission.

http://www.americanpresidents.org/survey/historians/

C-Span site providing "life portraits" of all American Presidents.

http://www.270towin.com/

A fascinating site allowing the viewer to enter assumptions about the states that each party's presidential candidate will win in a presidential election, showing the resulting electoral vote totals. The site also includes a map of the states won by each party in recent elections.

http://www.cfinst.org/

Home page of the Campaign Finance Institute.

http://www.pbs.org/newshour/impeachment

The Public Broadcasting System's Web site containing documents and commentary on the impeachment of President Bill Clinton.

http://www.house.gov

The home page of the U.S. House of Representatives; includes weekly updates and links to members' pages.

http://www.senate.gov

The home page of the U.S. Senate; includes weekly updates and links to members' pages.

http://www.whitehouse.gov

The home page of the White House, containing presidential speeches and other materials relevant to the presidency.

http://www.supremecourtus.gov

The home page of the Supreme Court.

http://www.fjc.gov

The Federal Judicial Center's home page. Created in 1967 as a separate organization within the Federal Judiciary System, the Federal Judicial Center is intended to "further the development and adoption of improved judicial administration."

http://www.multied.com/elections

Contains electoral vote results for all U.S. presidential elections from 1789 to the present.

http://www.democrats.org

The home page of the U.S. Democratic Party.

http://www.rnc.org

The home page of the U.S. Republican Party.

http://www.cnn.com/ALLPOLITICS

The Cable News Network's page devoted to daily and recent political news, focusing on national events.

http://clerk.house.gov/index.html

Site for the Office of the Clerk, U.S. House of Representatives, containing a wealth of historical information.

http://www.lib.umich.edu/govdocs/legishis.html

The University of Michigan's document center on the U.S. Congress.

http://thomas.loc.gov/links

A list of Web resources for Congress, designed by the Library of Congress.

http://www.campaignline.com

The online version of "Campaigns and Elections," a commercial site with information about predicting elections.

http://www.c-span.org/questions/senate.asp

A C-SPAN site set up to provide answers to frequently asked questions about congressional procedure, elections, and many other subjects.

http://www.ou.edu/special/albertctr/cachome.html

The site for the Carl Albert Center for congressional research.

http://www.apsanet.org/~lss

The Legislative Studies Section of the American Political Science Association.

http://people-press.org/dataarchive

The home page for the Pew Research Center for the People and the Press. It includes the full text of a wide range of public opinion reports.

http://www.presidentelect.org

A fascinating site showing the electoral college results for all U.S. presidential elections, along with supplementary information.

http://www.hmdc.harvard.edu/ROAD

Judged the "Best Political Science Research Website" by the American Political Science Association, the Harvard "Record of American Democracy," or ROAD, contains a tremendous amount of information.

http://www.uselectionatlas.org/RESULTS

An updated Web site with data and maps indicating the results of presidential elections from 1789 to the present.

http://www.ropercenter.uconn.edu

The home page of the Roper Center for Public Opinion Research. Includes data on Presidential approval ratings from Franklin Roosevelt to George W. Bush.

http://www.opensecrets.org

The home page of the Center for Responsive Politics. The site includes a great deal of data regarding the influence of money in U.S. elections.

◆ ◆ ◆

Key Terms and Concepts _____

Articles of Confederation
bicameral
checks and balances
Connecticut Compromise
Declaration of Independence
"extended Republic"
incumbency advantage
Marbury v. Madison

marginal seats
political action committees (PACs)
presidential "character"
president's cabinet
primaries
Shays's Rebellion
term limits
Watergate

Discussion Questions _____

1. In what respects was the Founding period ambivalent about democracy? How did that ambivalence shape the Constitution?
2. What is distinctive about the U.S. Congress, and how does it participate in policy making?
3. How is the power of the presidency limited in practice?
4. Does the Supreme Court's role in policy making make the system more or less democratic?
5. Why has voter participation been low in recent U.S. elections?

Notes _____

1. According to one observer, the American poor see government as "distant, incomprehensible, and inaccessible." See Jennifer Nedelsky, *Private Property and the Limits of American Constitutionalism* (Chicago: University of Chicago Press, 1991), p. 215.
2. See, for example, John Manley, "Neo-Pluralism: A Class Analysis of Pluralism I and Pluralism II," *American Political Science Review* 77 (1983): 368–383. Also see the symposium on Inequality and American Democracy in *PS: Political Science and Politics* 39 (January 2006).
3. Louis Hartz, *The Liberal Tradition in America* (New York: Harcourt, Brace, 1955)
4. Samuel P. Huntington, *Political Order in Changing Societies* (New Haven: Yale University Press, 1968), pp. 125–126.
5. James A. Smith, *The Spirit of American Government*, quoted in *The Case against the Constitution*, ed. John Manley and Kenneth Dolbeare (Armonk, NY: Sharpe, 1987), p. 4.
6. Kenneth M. Dolbeare and Linda Medcalf, "The Dark Side of the Constitution," in Manley and Dolbeare, *The Case against the Constitution*, p. 127.
7. James Madison, Federalist 51, in *The Federalist Papers* (New York: Modern Library, 1937), pp. 340–341. See the provocative discussion of this concept in George W. Carey, "Separation of Powers and the Madisonian Model: A Reply to the Critics," *American Political Science Review* 72 (March 1978): 151–164.
8. See also Pauline Maier, Lance Banning, *The Sacred Fire of Liberty: James Madison and the Founding of the Federal Republic* (Ithaca, NY: Cornell University Press, 1995). For a more recent and spirited attack on the democracy of the U.S. system, see Robert A. Dahl, *How Democratic is the American Constitution?* (New Haven, CT: Yale University Press, 2002).
9. David E. Price, "Congressional Committees in the Policy Process," in *Congress Reconsidered*, 3rd ed., Lawrence C. Dodd and Bruce I. Oppenheimer, eds. (Washington, DC: CQ Press, 1985), p. 167.
10. Ibid., p. 163.
11. Data from the *Congressional Quarterly Almanac* (Washington, DC: Congressional Quarterly, 1995), p. C8.
12. Data on Party Unity obtained from Congressional Quarterly, at www.cq.com.
13. See Mark Warren. "Democracy and Deceit: Regulating Appearances of Corruption," *American Journal of Political Science*, 50 (January 2006): 160–174.
14. See "Fast Start for Soft Money Groups in the 2008 Election," Campaign Finance Institute, available at www.cfinst.org.
15. See FEC press release, "FEC Collects $630,000 in Civil Penalties from three 527 Organizations," December 13, 2006, available at http://www.fec.gov/press/press2006/20061213murs.html.
16. See Robert S. Erikson and Gerald C. Wright, "Voters, Candidates, and Issues in Congressional Elections," in *Congress Reconsidered*, 6th ed., Lawrence C. Dodd and Bruce I. Oppenheimer, eds. (Washington, DC: CQ Press, 1997), pp. 143–144.
17. Morris Fiorina, *Congress: Keystone of the Washington Establishment*, 2nd ed. (New Haven: Yale University Press, 1989).
18. A former opponent of term limits, the conservative columnist George Will made a persuasive case for them. See *Restoration* (New York: Free Press, 1992). For a good statement opposing term limits, see Morris Fiorina, *Divided Government*, 2nd ed. (Boston: Allyn & Bacon, 1996).

19. For an interesting analysis of the effects of mid-term elections in the U.S., see Walter R. Mebane, Jr., and Jasjeet S. Sekhon, "Coordination and Policy Moderation at Midterm," *American Political Science Review* 96 (March 2002): 141–157.

20. John F. Kennedy, foreword to *Decision-Making in the White House*, by Theodore C. Sorensen (New York: Columbia University Press, 1963).

21. See Fiorina, *Divided Government*; and David Mayhew, *Divided We Govern* (New Haven: Yale University Press, 1991).

22. Quoted in Richard Neustadt, *Presidential Power: The Politics of Leadership from FDR to Carter* (New York: Wiley, 1980), p. 31. See also John Bibby, *Governing by Consent* (Washington, DC: CQ Press, 1992), pp. 496–500.

23. Doris Kerns, *Lyndon Johnson and the American Dream* (New York: Harper and Row, 1976), p. 253.

24. James David Barber, *The Presidential Character* (Englewood Cliffs, NJ: Prentice Hall, 1972).

25. Ibid.

26. Glendon Schubert, *Constitutional Politics* (New York: Holt, Rinehart, and Winston, 1960), p. 178.

27. Louis Hartz, *The Liberal Tradition in America* (New York: Harcourt, Brace and World, 1955).

28. Robert H. Jackson, *The Struggle for Judicial Supremacy* (New York: Vintage Books, 1941), p. xi.

29. Archibald Cox, *The Court and the Constitution* (Boston: Houghton Mifflin, 1987), p. 149.

30. Ibid., pp. 149–150.

31. Archibald Cox, *The Role of the Supreme Court in American Government* (New York: Oxford University Press, 1976), p. 8.

32. Ibid., p. 4.

33. Robert A. Dahl. "Decision Making in a Democracy: The Supreme Court as a National Policy Maker," *Journal of Public Law*, 6 (Fall 1957): 279-295.

34. Thomas Keck. "Party, Policy, or Duty: Why Does the Supreme Court Invalidate Federal Statutes?" *American Political Science Review*, 101 (May 2007): 321–338.

35. See Jonathan D. Casper, "The Supreme Court and National Policy Making," *American Political Science Review* 70 (1976): 50–63.

36. Elmo Richardson, *The Presidency of Dwight D. Eisenhower* (Lawrence, KS: Regent's Press, 1979), p. 108.

37. Merle Miller, *Plain Speaking: An Oral Biography of Harry S Truman* (New York: Berkeley, 1973), pp. 225–226, quoted in *The Challenge of Democracy*, 2nd ed. by Kenneth Janda, Jeffrey Berry, and Jerry Goldman (Boston: Houghton Mifflin, 1989), pp. 497–498.

38. Paul R. Abramson and John H. Aldrich, "The Decline of Electoral Participation in America," *American Political Science Review* 76 (September 1982): 502–521.

39. John Aldrich, David Rohde, Gary Miller, and Charles Ostrom, *American Government: People, Institutions, and Policies* (Boston: Houghton Mifflin, 1986), p. 290.

40. See Nolan McCarty, Keith T. Poole, and Howard Rosenthal. *Polarized America: The Dance of Ideology and Unequal Riches.* (Cambridge, MA.: MIT Press, 2006).

41. Paul Allen Beck and Frank J. Sorauf, *Party Politics in America*, 7th ed. (New York: Harper-Collins, 1992), p. 112.

42. Committee on Political Parties, American Political Science Association, "Toward a More Responsive Two-Party System," *American Political Science Review* 44 (1950): 2.

43. Michael S. Lewis-Beck and Richard Nadeau. "Split-Ticket Voting: The Effects of Cognitive Madisonianism," *Journal of Politics.* 66 (February 2004): 97–112.

44. Beck and Sorauf, *Party Politics in America*, p. 469.

45. Mayhew, *Divided We Govern*, p. 199.

46. See Susan Olson, "Interest Group Litigation in Federal District Court: Beyond the Political Disadvantage Theory," *Journal of Politics* 52 (1990): 854–882. Also see the discussion of the "disadvantage theory" in ch. 6.

47. E.E. Schattschneider. *The Semi-Sovereign People.* (New York: Holt, Rinehart and Winston, 1960).

48. Dara Z. Strolovitch. *Affirmative Advocacy: Race, Class, and Gender in Interest Group Politics.* (Chicago: University of Chicago Press, 2007).

49. Mancur Olson, Jr. *The Rise and Decline of Nations.* (New Haven, CT.: Yale University Press, 1982), p. 174.

50. Michael Ross. "Is Democracy Good for the Poor?" *American Journal of Political Science.* 50 (October 2006): 860–874.

51. National Urban League, *State of Black America 2007: Portrait of the Black Male*, available at www.nul.org. Data on poverty rates from the U.S. Census Bureau, at http://www.census.gov/prod/2007pubs/p60-233.pdf

52. Data available from the National Coalition on Health Care, www.nchc.org.

For Further Reading _____

Abramson, Paul R., John H. Aldrich, and David W. Rohde. *Change and Continuity in the 2000 and 2002 Elections.* Washington, DC: CQ Press, 2003.

Adler, E. Scott. *Why Congressional Elections Fail.* Chicago: University of Chicago Press, 2002.

Adler, E. Scott, and John S. Lapinski, eds. *The Macropolitics of Congress*. Princeton, NJ: Princeton University Press, 2006.

Armitage, David. *The Declaration of Independence: A Global History*. Cambridge, MA.: Harvard University Press, 2008.

Barone, Michael, and Richard E. Cohen. *The Almanac of American Politics, 2008*. Washington, D.C.: National Journal Group, 2007.

Beard, Charles A. *An Economic Interpretation of the Constitution*. New York: Macmillan, 1913.

Belsky, Martin H. *The Rehnquist Court: A Retrospective*. New York: Oxford University Press, 2002.

Bennett, Robert W. *Taming the Electoral College*. Palo Alto, CA.: Stanford University Press, 2006.

Black, Amy E. *From Inspiration to Legislation: How an Idea Becomes a Bill*. Upper Saddle River, NJ: Prentice-Hall, 2007.

Brader, Ted. *Campaigning for Hearts and Minds: How Emotional Appeals in Political Ads Work*. Chicago: University of Chicago Press, 2006.

Campbell, Colton C., and Paul S. Herrnson. *War Stories from Capitol Hill*. Upper Saddle River, NJ: Prentice-Hall, 2004.

Campbell, Tom. *Separation of Powers in Practice*. Palo Alto, CA: Stanford University Press, 2004.

Cohen, Jeffrey, Richard Fleisher, and Paul Kantor. *American Political Parties: Decline or Resurgence?* Washington, DC: CQ Press, 2001.

Conway, M. Margaret. *Political Participation in the United States*. 3rd ed. Washington, DC: CQ Press, 2000.

Cook, Timothy E. *Governing with the News*. 2nd ed. Chicago: University of Chicago Press, 2005.

Dalton, Russell J. *The Good Citizen: How a Younger Generation is Reshaping American Politics*. Washington: CQ Press, 2007.

Dunn, Charles W. *The Scarlet Thread of Scandal: Morality and the American Presidency*. Lanham, MD: Rowman and Littlefield, 2001.

Dunn, Charles W. *Seven Laws of Presidential Leadership*. Upper Saddle River, NJ: Prentice-Hall, 2007.

Epstein, Lee, Jeffrey A. Segal, Harold J. Spaeth, and Thomas G. Walker. *The Supreme Court Compendium*. 3rd ed. Washington, DC: CQ Press, 2002.

Fenno, Richard F. *Going Home: Black Representatives and Their Constituents*. Chicago: University of Chicago Press, 2003.

Finkelman, Paul, and Melvin I. Urofsky, *Landmark Decisions of the United States Supreme Court*. Washington, DC: CQ Press, 2002.

Fiorina, Morris P. *Congress: Keystone of the Washington Establishment*. 2nd ed. New Haven: Yale University Press, 1989.

Fiorina, Morris P., Samuel J. Abrams, and Jeremy C. Pope, *Culture War? The Myth of a Polarized America*. New York: Pearson Longman, 2005.

Flanigan, William H., and Nancy H. Zingale. *Political Behavior of the American Electorate*. 11th ed. Washington, DC: CQ Press, 2005.

Gelman, Andrew. *Red State, Blue State, Rich State, Poor State: Why Americans Vote the Way They Do*. Princeton, N.J.: Princeton University Press, 2008.

Geyh, Charles Gardner. *When Courts and Congress Collide: The Struggle for Control of America's Judicial System*. Ann Arbor, MI.: University of Michigan Press, 2006.

Hamilton, Alexander, John Jay, and James Madison. *The Federalist Papers*. New York: Modern Library, 1937.

Harwood, John and Gerald F. Sieb. *Pennsylvania Avenue: Profiles in Backroom Power*. New York: Random House, 2008.

Hershey, Marjorie Handon, and Paul Allen Beck. *Party Politics in America*. 11th ed. New York: Longman, 2004.

Hockin, Thomas A. *The American Nightmare: Politics and the Fragile World Trade Organization*. Lanham, MD: Lexington Books, 2003.

Holbrook, Thomas. *Do Campaigns Matter?* Thousand Oaks, CA: Sage, 1996.

Jacobson, Gary C. *The Politics of Congressional Elections.* 6th ed. New York: Longman, 2003.

Kurtz, Karl T., Bruce Cain, and Richard G. Niemi. *Institutional Change in American Politics: The Case of Term Limits.* Ann Arbor, MI.: University of Michigan Press, 2007.

Lewis, David L. *The Politics of Presidential Appointments: Political Control and Bureaucratic Performance.* Princeton, N.J.: Princeton University Press, 2008.

Lewis-Beck, Michael S., William G. Jacoby, Helmut Norpoth, and Herbert F. Weisberg. *The American Voter Revisited.* Ann Arbor: University of Michigan Press, 2008.

Manley, John F., and Kenneth M. Dolbeare, eds. *The Case against the Constitution.* Armonk, NY: Sharpe, 1987.

Manza, Jeff, Fay L. Cook, and Benjamin I. Page. *Navigating Public Opinion: Polls, Policy, and the Future of American Democracy.* New York: Oxford University Press, 2002.

Matheson, Scott M., Jr. *Presidential Constitutionalism in Perilous Times.* Cambridge, MA.: Harvard University Press, 2009.

Mayhew, David. *Divided We Govern.* New Haven: Yale University Press, 1991.

Mayhew, David. *Electoral Realignments.* New Haven: Yale University Press, 2004.

McCarty, Nolan, Keith T. Poole, and Howard Rosenthal. *Polarized America: The Dance of Ideology and Unequal Riches.* Cambridge, MA.: MIT Press, 2006.

Milban, Michael J. The Election After Reform: Money, Politics, and the Bipartisan Campaign Reform Act. Lanham, MD.: Rowman and Littlefield Publishers, 2006.

Miller, Mark C., and Jeb Barnes, eds. *Making Policy, Making Law: An Inter-branch Perspective.* Chicago: University of Chicago Press, 2004.

Posner, Richard A. *An Affair of State: The Investigation, Impeachment, and Trial of President Clinton.* Cambridge: Harvard University Press, 1999.

Rozell, Mark J., and Clyde Wilcox, eds. *The Clinton Scandal and the Future of American Government.* Chicago: University of Chicago Press, 2000.

Schier, Steven E. *You Call This an Election? America's Peculiar Democracy.* Chicago: University of Chicago Press, 2003.

Skowronek, Stephen. *The Politics Presidents Make: Leadership from John Adams to George Bush.* Cambridge: Harvard University Press, 1993.

Skowronek, Stephen. *Presidential Leadership in Political Time: Reprise and Reappraisal.* Lawrence, KS.: University Press of Kansas, 2008.

Sunstein, Cass R. *Designing Democracy: What Constitutions Do.* New York: Oxford University Press, 2000.

Sunstein, Cass R., and Richard Epstein. *The Vote: Bush, Gore, and the Supreme Court.* Chicago: University of Chicago Press, 2001.

Troy, Tevi. *Intellectuals and the American Presidency: Philosophers, Jesters, or Technicians?* Lanham, MD: Rowman and Littlefield, 2002.

Wand, Jonathan, et al. "The Butterfly Did It: The Aberrant Vote for Buchanan in Palm Beach County, Florida." *American Political Science Review* 95 (December 2001): 793–810.

Watson, Bradley C. S. *Courts and the Culture Wars.* Lanham, MD: Lexington Books, 2002.

Whitney, Gleaves. *American Presidents: Their Farewell Messages to the Nation, 1796–2001.* Lanham, MD: Lexington Books, 2002.

Zukin, Cliff, Scott Keeter, Molly Andolina, Krista Jenkins and Michael X. Delli Carpini. *A New Engagement? Political Participation, Civic Life, and the Changing American Citizen.* New York: Oxford University Press, 2006.

© Paul Ellis/AFP/Getty Images

12

GREAT BRITAIN:
A TRADITIONAL DEMOCRACY

◆ The Relevance of British Politics ◆ Contemporary British
Society and Political Culture ◆ Political Parties and Voting
◆ Interest Groups ◆ The Structure of Government
◆ Public Policy and the British Economy ◆ Conclusion:
Great Britain in the Twenty-First Century

THE RELEVANCE OF BRITISH POLITICS

Britain is intrinsically fascinating to many Americans. It is, after all, the source of many of our own cultural and political traditions. But Britain is also important to political scientists, since it has been a model of liberal democracy and political stability. Even without a written bill of rights (until 1998), it maintained considerable personal freedoms and civil liberties. British political institutions—competitive party elections, parliamentary representation, and cabinet government—have been models for democratic governments throughout the world. The country's record of gradual and relatively peaceful political change contrasts with the civil war and bitter conflict that have afflicted so many other nations, including the United States. We will suggest, however, that evolutionary change and the durability of the country's historic values have also contributed to political, economic, and social rigidities.

The Origins of British Democracy: Great Britain a Model of Stability

From the time the so-called "**Glorious Revolution**" (1688) established parliamentary supremacy over the monarch, the defining features of Britain's constitutional order have remained in place. In contrast, France has had some 20 different constitutions since 1789 and has experienced five republics, two empires, and three monarchies.[1] Indeed, during the past century alone, European countries such as Germany, Italy, and Russia have been racked by internal upheavals and dictatorships.

This is not to suggest that Britain has been free of domestic violence, even in modern times. Turbulent labor strife persisted from the nineteenth century through the 1930s, and in recent decades the conflict over Northern Ireland's fate convulsed that region. The Irish Republican Army (IRA), drawn from the minority Catholic population, fought for the North's unification with the Irish Republic, whereas Protestant unionists (including hard-line "loyalists") were determined to keep it part of the United Kingdom of Great Britain and Ireland (the country's official title).* After years of violent struggle, both sides have reached a peaceful settlement that keeps Northern Ireland in the United Kingdom while enhancing representation for the Catholic population (see below).

The Slow March to Democracy

Although the growth of parliamentary power enhanced popular sovereignty, as of the beginning of the twentieth century, the British political system was still far from democratic, and Parliament remained very unrepresentative. The House of Commons, an elected body, shared power equally with the House of Lords, whose members at that time had all inherited their seats, served for life, and, at death, passed on their seat to their male heir (women could not join Lords until 1958). Even the House of Commons was elected by a very small portion of the population (male property owners), often through corrupt electoral practices.

_____

* We use the names "Great Britain," "Britain," and "the United Kingdom" interchangeably throughout this chapter.

The landmark Reform Act of 1832 redrew electoral districts and modestly expanded the size of the electorate, from 5 percent of the adult population to 7 percent. Indeed, it was not until 1884 that **suffrage** was extended to most adult males. Women did not receive the right to vote until 1918, and even then the franchise was limited to women older than 30 whose husbands owned property. Finally, a decade later, all women over the age of 21 received the franchise with no property qualifications.

Well into the twentieth century, British electoral practices retained other elitist elements. Until 1949, for example, businesspeople that lived in one parliamentary district and owned an enterprise in another could vote for representatives in both. The same double vote existed for university graduates, who were able to cast ballots in their home district as well as for the **Member of Parliament (MP)** who represented their university.[2]

Moreover, only in 1911 did the Parliament Act give the House of Commons (the elected national legislature) legislative supremacy. Thereafter, the House of Lords could delay but not defeat some bills passed by Commons (that power was further weakened in later years). The number of bills proposed by the government (cabinet) that are rejected by the House of Lords is very limited, but varies considerably. Under Prime Minister Tony Blair (1997–2007), for example, it ranged from only two bills in 2000–2001 to 88 in 2002–2003. Constitutional reforms enacted by Blair's Labour Party government* converted Lords from a body whose members primarily inherited their seats into a largely appointed body. (See Box 12-1.) The dominance of Commons over Lords is now so strong that, although technically the words *Parliament* and *parliamentary* refer to both Houses, they are used primarily to mean the House of Commons.

Box 12-1

DEVOLUTION AND REFORMING THE HOUSE OF LORDS

Perhaps the most significant innovations that Prime Minister Tony Blair introduced involve constitutional reform, fundamental changes in the way that Britain is governed. The most important of those reforms, to date, may be **devolution**, the transfer of some power from the British central government to several regional governments. Beginning in 1997, the nation's **Parliament** transferred considerable authority over local matters to the Scottish Parliament and Welsh Assembly. Many citizens in Scotland and, to a lesser extent, Wales had felt dominated by London (and the English) for generations. The two regions felt particularly aggrieved during the most recent period of Conservative Party rule (1979–1997), and to some extent this constitutional reform was Blair's reward to two regions that had regularly produced strong

Labour pluralities and offered little support to the Conservatives. Transfer of some powers to the Scottish Parliament and the far weaker Welsh Assembly took place after each region had approved devolution in separate referendums—the Scots by a solid majority and the Welsh by a paper-thin margin.[3] And, in that same year, the people of London and other large cities could elect their own mayors directly for the first time in decades.

The second major constitutional reform, not yet complete, has involved a dramatic restructuring of the House of Lords. Of less immediate political consequence than devolution, reform of Lords still has great symbolic importance as an indication of the

(Continued)

---

* Throughout this chapter we use the British spelling for the Labour Party (rather than Labor Party) or Labour Government.

Box 12-1

DEVOLUTION AND REFORMING
THE HOUSE OF LORDS (*Continued*)

ongoing, gradual diminution of aristocratic privilege. Early in the twentieth century, the House of Lords was stripped of its ability to block any legislation involving fiscal allocations passed by the House of Commons. Since 1911, it has only been able to delay, but not sink, non-money bills. Essentially, the only real legislative function Lords now holds is to amend non-money bills passed by the House of Commons. Some of these amendments have been very constructive and were accepted by Commons. If, however, the House of Commons does not wish to accept such changes, Lords can only delay passage by one year, something it rarely does.

In the closing years of the twentieth century, Lords was composed of 759 peers who had inherited their seats and 477 "life peers," distinguished figures appointed for life through the Prime Minister's recommendation but unable at death to pass on their seats to their heirs. In addition, up to 12 Law Lords, distinguished jurists, became lifetime members of the House of Lords and served as the country's highest appeals court (in 2009 a separate Supreme Court will be created and the post of Law Lords terminated). Finally, over 20 Anglican (Church of England) archbishops and bishops automatically hold seats ("The Lords Spiritual").

Though it periodically suggests valuable amendments to legislation sent to it by Commons, the House of Lords has long been an obvious anachronism, a legislative body, however limited its powers, that was un-elected and largely hereditary. Roll-call analysis of the 2000 parliamentary session revealed that nearly 100 peers (about 1 in 12) failed to appear for a single vote.

Some of the appointed peers are distinguished figures in areas such as the arts, while many others are former politicians or statesmen who seem to have little time for their obligations at Lords. As of 2005, 192 of the appointed Lords had previously sat in the House of Commons.[4] The former Prime Minister, Lady Margaret Thatcher, who was present for only 25 percent of the votes, explained through a spokesperson that "she has lots of commitments elsewhere . . . but she tries to get to the House whenever she can." He added, "I think she works hard enough for Britain." Andrew

Lloyd-Weber, the theater composer and tycoon, voted only once out of 186 votes. Lord Attenborough, the noted film director, participated in 15 percent of the votes. Typically in the 2004–2005 session about half of the peers were present on any given day. Even some of those peers who do attend sessions—particularly elderly peers—are occasionally seen dozing through the debate.

Fearful that the Blair government might abolish all hereditary peerages, the Conservative Party leadership in Lords went behind the backs of their party's leadership in the House of Commons to work out a deal with the Labour government. A 1999 agreement allowed only 92 of the 759 hereditary peers to maintain their seats in the House of Lords. All hereditary peers were required to submit a *75-word* essay explaining their reasons for wanting to continue in Lords and their major past achievements. Based on those essays, their fellow peers chose the 92 "elected hereditary peers" (i.e., they were elected by other Lords). Lord Onslow's essay read in its entirety: "It would be as vainglorious to proclaim a personal manifesto [that is, an essay stating his reasons for wanting to stay] as it would be arrogant to list any permanent achievements." He was elected.

But this is only a temporary resolution, with a final legislation still to be hammered out regarding how members of the House of Lords are to be selected in the future. Since 1999, Parliament has voted on a series of proposals, ranging from having all House of Lords peers appointed, to having all of them elected by the public, with various combinations of election and appointment in between. So far, no proposal has passed the House of Commons and no final arrangement appears in sight. But, the combination of removing most of the inherited peers and Prime Ministerial appointment of several hundred lifetime peers has already changed the House of Lords' political orientation. In early 1999, prior to reform, 41 percent of the peers identified themselves as Conservatives and only 15 percent as Labourites. By 2007, Labour Lords (211 members) slightly outnumbered Conservatives (204), with another 279 peerages held by Liberal Democrats (77) or independents (202).[5]

The Strengths and Weaknesses of Gradual Change

In contrast to other **industrial democracies**, Britain's contemporary political institutions cannot be traced to a single event such as the French Revolution or the ratification of the U.S. Constitution. Instead, British democracy has been fashioned by gradual, **evolutionary change**, lacking the drama of major upheavals. Moreover, the British have no written constitution, but instead their "unwritten constitution" is a combination of their parliamentary legislation, statutes, legal practices, and political customs.

For many years, Britain was considered a model pluralist democracy. Its parliamentary form of government was copied in flourishing democracies such as Canada, Australia, and New Zealand and was adopted less successfully in many former British colonies in Africa and Asia. The country's history of gradual change fostered an atmosphere of political openness and tolerance. It also enshrined institutions and customs—the monarch's coronation, the changing of the guard at Buckingham Palace—that bind the population together (and also provide the pomp and circumstance that attracts millions of foreign tourists annually). That unifying cultural heritage provides an enviable foundation for democratic government.

At the same time, however, the very traditions and practices that have created national unity and stability also have frequently become barriers to progress. That is to say that although peaceful, evolutionary change has an obvious value, it also has inhibited the modernization of British institutions and beliefs. For example, the country's rather rigid class structure has, in the recent past, restricted educational opportunities and limited upward social mobility (movement up the social or class ladder) for much of the population.

Britain was the home of the Industrial Revolution in the eighteenth and early nineteenth centuries, but many of the aristocracy's cultural values subsequently contributed to the country's economic stagnation. The upper-class preference for a career in finance, law, or journalism rather than industry gave industrial entrepreneurship a diminished status. Interestingly, most of the inventors and businessmen who initiated the Industrial Revolution were from "non-establishment" religions—not Church of England—and were not "well born." From Victorian times until quite recently, industrialists were often more interested in demonstrating their social standing than in improving productivity and keeping up with foreign competition. These factors contributed to the country's decline from being the world's leading economic power in the nineteenth century to second-class status today, behind the United States, Germany, Japan, France, and others.[6] Only in the past ten to twenty years has Britain once again achieved one of Europe's fastest economic growth rates.

CONTEMPORARY BRITISH SOCIETY AND POLITICAL CULTURE

In our discussion of political culture (Chapter 3), we noted that people in different countries feel differing degrees of satisfaction or dissatisfaction with their own political institutions and their fellow citizens. Whatever their complaints and grievances, the English people and, to a lesser extent, the Scotch and Welsh are proud of Great Britain.

A number of years ago, a Gallup poll revealed that 80 percent of all Britons were proud of being British. More recent opinion surveys have indicated that national pride is higher in Britain than in many other Western European nations.[7] In part, that pride rightly reflects the strengths of British society. It is a very safe country, with homicide and overall crime rates less than one-fourth that of the United States, and a police force that normally patrols the streets unarmed. Most Britons, quite accurately, view their fellow citizens as generally trustworthy, friendly, and polite.

A part of the country's stability and political success can be attributed to its rather well developed sense of national unity. As we noted in Chapter 3, Great Britain is often considered a model consensual political culture, most of whose citizens are in substantial agreement about their political goals and practices. A political consensus is more easily fostered in a society that is not deeply divided socially. When London had to endure repeated bombings during World War II, foreign observers were impressed by the sense of national purpose that united citizens of all backgrounds. Londoners seemed to exhibit a similar sense of common purpose after the 2005 terrorist bombings. Over time, Britain has been split by fewer ethnic, racial, religious, and geographic differences than have nations such as the United States, South Africa, Russia, and Belgium. Yet important divisions do exist within British society, and some have notable political and economic consequences.

Sources of National Unity

In our discussion of political development (Chapter 15), we will suggest that nations with many religions, languages, ethnicities, or racial groups generally have had more tumultuous political systems than have countries with more **homogeneous societies** (societies that are more uniform in social composition). That may help us to understand Britain's relatively peaceful development and the sources of its political strength.

As an island nation, its people have always felt distinct from the other European nations across the English Channel on "the Continent." At times, that distinction has contributed to a false sense of superiority. Legend has it that several decades ago, when dense fog cut off all sea and air traffic across the English Channel, one British newspaper ran a headline declaring the "Continent Isolated." Compared with other Western European populations, the British people are still far less committed to merging with the rest of Western Europe and more skeptical of the **European Union (EU)**. Thus, for example, Britain is one of only three EU nations to have so far refused to adopt the Euro, the common European currency now being used in most of Western Europe. Although such insular attitudes have created problems for the British in the past—for example, their economy was hurt by their initial refusal to join the European Economic Community (now the European Union)—they did contribute to a consensus within the British Isles.

Almost 85 percent of Britons come from England, with most living in southern England, in close proximity to London. Furthermore, the population is overwhelmingly urban, with about two-thirds of the population of England and Wales found in seven metropolitan areas.[8] Not only does one person in six live in greater London, but most of the country's political, economic, and cultural elites reside in or near the capital. In many ways, then, most Britons have similar lifestyles, read the same newspapers, and relate to the same political symbols.

Sources of Internal Division

Even though the extent of homogeneity and consensus in Great Britain is impressive, important social differences also exist.

The Role of Social Class   In the absence of rural-urban conflicts or strong ethnic, racial or religious divisions, the greatest predictor of British political behavior and attitudes has been **social class**. Blue-collar workers, the poor, and those with limited educations are more prone to vote for the Labour Party. White-collar workers, professionals, businesspeople, people with more education, and the middle and upper classes in general are more likely to support the Conservative Party (also known as the **Tories**). Though there is a link in most industrial democracies between class background and party preference, historically the connection was particularly strong in Britain.[9] Since the 1970s, that correlation has weakened as more British workers vote Conservative and more middle-class voters support Labour. More generally, educational reforms, the rise of a merit-oriented leadership within the Conservative Party, and other broad cultural changes have reduced the class divide and the effects of class on everyday life. Still, social class remains the best predictor of a person's electoral preference, his or her educational achievement, occupation, and the like.

Historically, the nation's political leaders have emerged disproportionately from the upper class. Aristocratic families (those with inherited titles bestowed by the crown) dominated the political system until the late nineteenth century. The rise of the Liberal Party in the late nineteenth century and the Labour Party in the early twentieth opened greater opportunities for politicians of middle- and working-class backgrounds. Moreover, since the 1970s, most prime ministers have had middle-class origins.

It is within the Conservative Party that upper-class dominance has been most pronounced. Until the 1970s, all Tory prime ministers were drawn from the aristocracy or other segments of the upper class. Since that time, access to party leadership has opened up with Prime Ministers Heath (1970–1974) and Thatcher (1979–1990) having middle-class origins and John Major (1990–1997) coming from a working-class family. Michael Howard, a recent party leader (2003–2005) was the son of a poor Romanian immigrant. Even so, most Conservative MPs (Members of Parliament, i.e., members of the House of Commons) today still come from the upper or upper-middle classes. For example, the current leader of the party (who will become Prime Minister should the Tories win the next parliamentary election), David Cameron, is the son of a well-to-do stockbroker. He attended Eton, Britain's most exclusive boarding school, and Oxford before marrying the daughter of a British aristocrat. His shadow cabinet (those MPs who are slated to occupy cabinet posts if the Conservatives win the next election) has consisted largely of former bankers and businessmen as well as graduates of Oxford and exclusive, private secondary schools.

British class distinctions have been reinforced by distinct educational tracks for each class. At the top of the educational system are the country's most exclusive, private boarding schools, called (confusingly for Americans) **Public schools**.* The most

---

* Most British students attend secondary schools run by their local government. These have had various names, including "grammar schools," "secondary modern" and "comprehensives," but they are *never* called "public schools."

famous of these—including Eton, Harrow, Winchester, Rugby, and Westminster—are hundreds of years old. Because of these schools' high cost and elitist orientation, their students are overwhelmingly well-to-do. Although less than 5 percent of the British population attends public schools, their graduates dominate the top ranks of the Conservative Party, the civil service, and high finance. For example, currently, 60 percent of Conservative MPs went to private high schools, with roughly half of them attending exclusive "public schools"—six times the national average.[10]

While a high percentage of the nation's upper-class and upper-middle-class families send their children to private schools of some sort (either elite "public schools" or some other type), 90 percent of Britain's entire student population attend government-run schools. Within that system there were three principal types of secondary education (roughly equivalent to high schools): Secondary Grammar, Secondary Modern, and Comprehensive. Grammar schools are government schools that once admitted students based primarily on their performance on a standardized national exam (called the Eleven Plus exam) administered in the last year of primary school. Students whose Eleven Plus scores earned them admission to Grammar schools received strong academic preparation there. Consequently a high percentage of them continued on to university. Because children from more educated and well-off families generally score higher on standardized tests and have better grades than working-class kids do (a worldwide phenomenon), grammar school students have come disproportionately from the middle class. Furthermore, a comprehensive study of British secondary education found that although most Grammar schools use "fair and objective" admission standards, "a significant minority . . . [also use] criteria which appear to be designed to select certain groups of pupils [i.e., from the middle class] and exclude others [from the working class]."[11] In these schools, middle-class students not only are more likely to meet academic admission standards, but also benefit from non-academic factors such as favoring students for admission whose older siblings, parents, or grandparents attended that school.

From the mid-1940s until the late 1970s three out of four students taking the Eleven Plus exam failed to gain admission to Grammar Schools. Almost all of them continued on to Secondary Modern schools. These schools extended only to the equivalent of 10th grade and offered basic academic and technical (vocationally oriented) skills. Most students left school at the age of 16 (to take blue-collar jobs) and very few were able to continue into the last two (college preparatory) years of secondary school or to attend a university. For the reasons just discussed, their student bodies came overwhelmingly from working-class families. Thus, when compared to other Western European countries or, especially, the United States, Great Britain had a particularly class-related educational system featuring a higher percentage of early drop-outs, a relatively lower rate of university attendance, and a comparatively small percentage of working-class students at academic high schools or universities.

Since the 1970s, however, the Eleven Plus exam has gradually been phased out (ending in most districts by the late 1980s) and in 2007 the Labour government announced plans to eliminate their use entirely during the following year. At the same time, over the years the government has reduced the number of Grammar schools and totally phased out Secondary Modern schools. Thus, today most students (some 90 percent of those in the state-run system) attend "Comprehensive Schools," that is, schools that admit students regardless of academic record (as in most

American public high schools). Comprehensive school students may either take vocationally oriented courses or take academic courses that allow them to continue on to university.

These reforms have reduced, but have not eliminated, class-based distinctions in the educational system. Most upper-class students still attend public schools or other types of private institutions, with all the advantages that bestows. The remaining Grammar schools (teaching some 10 percent of all students) are still the most prestigious secondary schools in the government system and continue to be heavily middle class. The percentage of working-class students going to university remains low. And the British remain keenly aware of the class and education linkage. Thus, when current Conservative party leader David Cameron announced in 2007 that the party would oppose expansion of the grammar school system and would favor more egalitarian schools, he faced a bitter revolt by the 25% of Tory MPs who had graduated from grammar schools. In what a leading British journalist labeled a "class war" within the party, these grammar-school grads (mostly middle class) implicitly accused Cameron and other Conservative MPs, who had gone to public schools (almost all belonging to the upper class), of being elitists who wanted to place limits on grammar schools in order to attract working-class votes while leaving their own elite private schools untouched.[12]

All analysts agree that class divisions are less significant today than in the past. But almost all of them also believe that it is still an important factor in national life. For example, in early 2007 Prince William (Prince Charles and Princess Diana's son) broke up with his long-time girlfriend, Kate Middleton. According to a number of British newspapers they "broke up in part because of her mother's so-called middle class behavior" and speech, as well as her mother's former employment as an airline flight attendant.[13] In short, her mother's middle-class background was an embarrassment to the royal family.

Not surprisingly, the British are highly aware of the broader role of class in their society. Moreover, unlike Americans, they believe that there are fundamental conflicts between the interests of the upper class, middle class, and working class. In a 1996 public opinion poll, Britons were asked whether "a person's social class [at birth] affects their chances in life" a lot or a little. Sixty percent of the respondents answered "a lot." And when asked in another poll if there was "a class struggle in Britain" [presumably of a nonviolent nature], an astonishing 81 percent of all Britons answered "yes."[14] Yet, despite the country's well-known and keenly felt class divisions, Great Britain has historically been less sharply politically divided by class *antagonisms* than countries such as France and Italy, where class divisions are less obvious but more contentious. So, whereas the Communist parties in France and Italy once attracted a quarter or more of the votes (reflecting substantial working-class discontent with socioeconomic conditions and employer-labor relations), the British Communist Party has never received much support at all.

Two factors have kept British class hostilities in check. First, historically the upper class was more receptive than its counterparts elsewhere in Europe to social programs benefiting the working class and the poor. Indeed, in the late nineteenth century the Conservative Party introduced many of the country's earliest social reform programs. The Conservatives remained receptive to government welfare programs after World War II when the newly elected Labour government introduced a wide range of social programs in the "**welfare state**" (discussed later in the chapter).

Although those measures were originally introduced by the Labour Party, the Tories continued to fund and support most of them after they returned to power in the 1950s. Only since the 1970s have Conservative governments (most notably Margaret Thatcher's) criticized and pared down the welfare state.

The upper classes' more conciliatory outlook contributed to a second factor that reduced class tensions over the years: the average citizens' admiration for the **aristocracy** and widespread deference to the upper classes. Even today, despite the royal family's frequent missteps reported in great detail by the mass media, the British public retains tremendous affection for the queen (and maintains a somewhat morbid interest in royal scandals).

Regional Divisions   Regional differences are another important source of political division in Britain. Despite having belonged to the United Kingdom for hundreds of years, many Scots and Welsh remain resentful of English political and economic domination. Not long ago, for example, a number of English-owned vacation homes on Wales's north coast were burned down by angry nationalists. More peaceful alienation in Scotland peaked in the 1970s when the Scottish National Party, committed to the creation of an independent Scottish state, attained 30 percent of the region's vote. In Wales, the nationalist **Plaid Cymru** party also has attracted some support. Although the majority of Scots and Welsh wish to remain within the United Kingdom, economic and cultural tensions remain.[15] Following 1997 referendums in which both the Scots and the Welsh voted to establish their own regional parliaments, the New Labour party government established such legislatures.

A far more vexing challenge to the country's unity has come from Northern Ireland. Responding to clashes between Catholics and Protestants and to terrorist activities by the (Catholic) Irish Republican Army (IRA) and, to a lesser extent, the (Protestant) Ulster Volunteer Force (UVF) and Ulster Defense Association (UDA), the British stationed between 10,000 and 15,000 troops in the region in an attempt to keep the peace. Between 1969 and 2001, during a conflict known as "The Troubles," about 3,500 people died, and more than 25,000 were wounded. If a similar percentage of Americans had died in civil unrest, it would translate to more than 500,000 deaths.[16] The British authorities' efforts to establish order provoked numerous violations of the residents' civil liberties, particularly those of Catholics. At the same time, evidence later emerged of collusion between the British authorities and UVF terrorists. Periodically, IRA terrorism extended into England, resulting in many bombings, disruptions of public transport, and several attempts on the lives of Prime Ministers Thatcher and Major.[17]

After difficult and protracted negotiations, in 1998 both sides (along with the British and Irish governments) signed the "Good Friday" peace accord, creating a joint Catholic–Protestant government in the north. Shortly thereafter, the voters of both Ireland and Northern Ireland overwhelming endorsed the accord in referendums. While the Good Friday accord brought relative peace to the region, a final settlement was delayed for years by the refusal of both the IRA and the UVF to put their arms beyond reach. Finally, in mid-2005 the IRA announced that it was giving up the armed struggle and would disarm. Despite continued misgivings on both sides and substantial Protestant displeasure over having lost their former political dominance, home rule was finally established and peace seems to have finally come to the region. With public safety restored and religious antagonisms calmed (as evidenced by the disappearance of the once-ubiquitous, hostile graffiti that covered much of Belfast's walls), tourism and the economy more generally have boomed.

Racial Divisions   Until the 1950s, Britain's population was overwhelmingly white. Since then, however, there has been a large influx of immigrants from India, Pakistan, Bangladesh, the Caribbean, Hong Kong, and Africa. By 1989, the country had approximately 2.5 million immigrants, mostly from former British colonies. Although nonwhites still constitute only a bit more than 5 percent of the population, they tend to be concentrated in a fairly small number of urban, industrial areas. Religious differences (a majority of the immigrants are Muslim, Hindu, or Sikh), competition for jobs, and racism have contributed to ongoing social tensions, including periodic urban race riots since the 1980s, most recently in a number of northern English cities in 2001. In recent years, the National Front and the British National Party—two neofascist political parties expressing and fomenting racist backlash within the white working class—have received growing electoral support in a small number of localities, and their activists aggravated the 2001 race riots in the North. Both the NF and the BNP, however, have far less voter support than do comparable neofascist parties in France, Austria, and Germany. The rise of Islamic extremism among some Muslims (including the children of immigrants), most notably the 2005 terrorist attacks on London's buses and subways, has increased tensions and led to greater government surveillance of Islamic groups. Though quite understandable from a security perspective, this has antagonized much of Britain's large Muslim community, the vast majority of whom are law-abiding and who feel that they are under suspicion because of the sins of a small number of extremists in their midst.

POLITICAL PARTIES AND VOTING

Political party organizations dominate politics more thoroughly in Britain than in the United States for three important reasons. First, Britain has no primary elections. Hence, local party organizations (controlled by party activists), not the voters, select candidates for the House of Commons. Second, British voters get to vote for only one office in the national government: their representative in the House of Commons. The party with a parliamentary majority then selects its leader as prime minister. Thus, the executive branch and the legislative branch are controlled by the same party, and the electorate has no opportunity for ticket splitting. Finally, party delegations within Parliament usually vote as a unified bloc, with MPs usually voting as their party leaders urge them to. As a consequence, Conservatives, Labour, and Social Democrats speak to the public with a more unified and more clearly defined message than do Democrats or Republicans in the United States.

A Two-and-One-Half-Party System

Great Britain has a party system dominated by two giants, but with a third party getting a significant share of the vote. Since the decline of the Liberal Party in the 1920s, most seats in Parliament have been won either by the Conservative Party or the Labour Party. But, unlike smaller parties in the United States, Britain's "third party" attracts an important share of the popular vote and wins a number of parliamentary seats.

Two-party dominance peaked in the 1950s when the combined Conservative and Labour party votes accounted for as much as 97 percent of the total (see Table 12.1). Since the 1970s, however, that share has fallen sharply to 68 percent in 2005.

The first substantial postwar challenge to the two-party system was mounted in the 1980s, when the Liberal Party joined with the Social Democratic Party in an electoral "Alliance." Although it was able to gain about one-fourth of the popular vote in the 1983 and 1987 parliamentary elections, the Alliance ended up with less than 4 percent of the seats in Parliament (see Box 12-3 and Table 12.2). After the merger of the Alliance's two partners in 1988, the new Liberal Democratic Party won as much as 22 percent of the vote in the 2005 election, but its share of MPs still falls far short of that figure.

The prospects for British third parties are severely hampered by the country's electoral system. Because British MPs (like U.S. congressional representatives) are elected

TABLE 12.1   SELECTED NATIONAL ELECTION RESULTS, 1951–2005 (PERCENTAGE OF THE VOTE)

Year	Conservatives	Labour	Liberal/Alliance/Liberal Democratic
1951	48.0	48.8	2.6*
1983	42.4	27.6	25.4†
1987	42.2	30.8	22.5†
1992	41.9	34.4	17.8‡
1997	30.7	43.2	16.8‡
2001	31.7	40.7	18.3‡
2005	32.4	35.2	22.0‡

* Liberal Party.

† Alliance of Liberals and Social Democrats.

‡ Since 1992, the leading third party has been the Liberal Democratic Party.

SOURCE: Richard Kimber's Political Resources: British Government and Elections Since 1945, http://www.psr.keele.ac.uk/area/uk/uktable.htm.

TABLE 12.2   RESULTS OF THE 1983, 1987, 2001, AND 2005 NATIONAL ELECTIONS

	1983	1987	2001	2005
Conservatives				
Percentage of the vote received	42.4	42.3	31.7	32.4
Percentage of seats won	61.1	57.8	24.4	30.2
Labour				
Percentage of the vote received	27.6	30.8	40.7	35.2
Percentage of seats won	32.1	35.2	60.8	55.1
Alliance (1983 and 1987) or Liberal Democrats (2001 and 2005)				
Percentage of the vote received	25.4	22.6	18.3	22.0
Percentage of seats won	3.5	3.4	7.6	9.6

SOURCE: Philip Norton, *The British Polity*, 3rd ed. (New York: Longman, 1994), p. 83; The British Council, britishcouncil.org/governance-expertise-election2005.htm; The United Kingdom Parliament Web site, parliament.uk/directories/hcio/stateparties.cfm.

from several hundred single-member districts (SMDs) a political party may win a substantial proportion of the nation's vote and yet have little to show for it in Parliament if it does not win many individual districts. That proved to be the Alliance's downfall. Although it attracted approximately one-fourth of the national vote in the 1980s, it repeatedly finished second to the Conservatives in southern English districts and second to Labour in northern England, Scotland, and Wales. Consequently, although it polled almost as many votes as the Labour Party in the 1983 election (25.4 percent), it received only one-ninth as many seats (3.5 percent) in the House of Commons (Table 12.2). In the wake of the 1987 election, the Social Democrats collapsed, and the Liberal Democratic Party was formed a year later (originally with a slightly different name). The underrepresentation suffered by the Liberal Democrats in 1997 through 2005 was almost as severe. (See Box 12-3.) Another shortcoming of single-member district elections is that it is possible for a British party to win the most votes and not receive the most seats in Parliament (just as a U.S. presidential candidate can win the most votes and lose the election in the Electoral College, as Al Gore did in 2000). That has happened on two occasions in the postwar period: in 1951 and in the first of two parliamentary elections in 1974.

The Conservative Party (the Tories)

The Conservatives are Britain's oldest and most successful political party. Formally organized in the 1830s, the party began earlier as the voice of the British aristocracy and landed gentry. Over the years, however, it has become a broadly based party with electoral support from a wide range of voters.

The Conservatives continue to receive their most intense backing from upper-class and middle-class voters. Ever since universal suffrage was established in the early decades of the twentieth century, however, they have also attracted a significant segment of the working-class vote, without which they could never win at the polls. For example, Margaret Thatcher and John Major led the party to four successive electoral victories (in 1979, 1983, 1987, and 1992) by sweeping the most economically dynamic parts of the country (London and the rest of southern England) and winning over one-third of the working-class vote.

In the past, the Tories, like conservative parties elsewhere, have defended the status quo. In the tradition of Edmund Burke (Chapter 2), the party has insisted that change should be gradual so as not to undermine "the existing fabric of society." Whereas the Labour Party initiated bold new programs over the years, the Conservative position was more reactive until the 1980s.[18] Closely linked to the business community, the party favors limited taxation and lower government expenditures than Labour does, but supports a strong national defense.

At the same time, however, for many years Conservative Party leaders believed that government had an obligation to protect the less privileged members of society. Consequently, in the decades after World War II, various Conservative administrations accepted and supported an array of government welfare programs. Indeed in the decades following World War II, the economic policies of Conservative and Labour governments differed only modestly, as Tory leaders from the late 1940s until the 1970s supported "caring capitalism," which included the welfare state.[19]

That situation changed dramatically in the mid-1970s, when Margaret Thatcher assumed the party's leadership. In her years as prime minister (1979–1990), the

"Iron Lady," as she was called, launched a major assault on big government. Conservatives stridently defended free enterprise and the values of the market system.[20] In 1992, two years after Thatcher's resignation as Prime Minister, her successor, John Major, led the Conservatives to an unprecedented fourth consecutive victory.

Thus, by the start of the 1990s, the Conservatives seemed to have established themselves as the country's dominant political party. Soon, however, their strength evaporated. By 1997, the popularity of Major's government had sunk to record lows and Tony Blair had reinvigorated the Labour Party, producing a resounding Labour victory in the next two parliamentary elections (1997–2001) and a narrower win in 2005. By the early years of the twenty-first century many analysts wondered when the Conservatives would ever return to power. For almost a decade the Tories were reduced to fighting each other. A "traditionalist faction" within the party battled modernizers ("libertarians") over issues such as immigration and gay rights. The party remains divided between Euroskeptics, those who are opposed to further British integration into the European Union, and those who are more open to integration.

Meanwhile, Labour stole, at least for a decade, the reputation for efficiency and sound economic management that once carried the Conservatives to victory. With Labour repositioned as Britain's middle-of-the-road party (see Box 12-2), the Conservatives seemed out of touch and unable to appeal to the electorate. After two devastating defeats at the polls, they were finally able to reduce (but not overtake) Labour's parliamentary majority considerably in 2005 (Tables 12.1 and 12.2). But this was more a function of a decline in Tony Blair's popularity (partly attributable to public unhappiness over Britain's military involvement in Iraq) than it was to an improvement in Conservatives' standing with voters.

For much of that time, weak leadership further debilitated the Conservatives. Between 1997 and 2005, they elected a new party leader four different times. The first three were uninspiring and unable to overturn Labour's electoral dominance. Of late, however, the party's fortunes seem to be improving. This is partly the result of Labour's declining popularity. Of equal importance, however, is the fact that after enduring three unappealing leaders who could not compete with Tony Blair's charisma, the Tories selected David Cameron, a young, telegenic, and media-savvy party leader. Sobered by the Labour Party's dramatic shift to the political center-left and its resulting three consecutive electoral victories (see below, especially Box 13-2), Cameron has moved the Conservatives away from Thatcher's right-wing conservatism and back to the more moderate, center-right position it once held. Rarely mentioning Thatcher (who, until now, has been a party icon), he also speaks infrequently about the issues that most inspire the party's right-wingers: cutting taxes, opposing Britain's further integration into the European Union, and limiting immigration. Instead he has emphasized issues previously associated with Labour: saving the environment, improving health care and the school system, and caring about the lot of society's less fortunate. These positions have helped improve the Tory position in public opinion polls but have not sat well with the powerful, right ("Thatcherite") wing of the party. Hoping to replicate Tony Blair's electoral success after he moved Labour to the political center (See Box 12-2), Cameron also seems to have strengthened the Conservatives by doing the same to his party. In any event, owing to a combination of factors—the 2008 financial crisis, the public's desire for change after more than a decade of Labour governments, and the

Conservative leader's fresh political style—as of mid-2008 opinion surveys showed the Tories with a big lead. At the same time, Labour suffered several sharp defeats in parliamentary by-elections that year (special, off-year elections held due to an MP's death or resignation) including at least one seat that had long been a Labour stronghold.[21]

The Labour Party

The Labour Party was founded in 1900 from an alliance of Socialist organizations and labor unions. Within two decades, it had become the country's second-largest party, and in 1923 it headed a short-lived government. As its name implies, the party has been closely linked to the nation's trade-union movement and receives its most important electoral support from blue-collar workers. Unions have provided a large share of the party's financial resources and until recently played an important role in selecting its parliamentary leader. But even though many Labour MPs have entered politics from the union movement, the party's top leadership has come largely from the middle class, particularly teachers, university professors, and other professionals. Like all British parties, Labour draws votes across class lines.

When Labour came to power in 1945, it created an extensive state welfare system and **nationalized** important sectors of the economy, including the railroads, coal mines, and steel.* Until the mid-1990s, the Labour Party continued to favor many Socialist programs. For example, one of the most controversial sections in its charter endorsed government "ownership of the means of production" (major industries, transport, and so forth).[22]

Always controversial, government ownership of major firms had lost significant voter support by the 1970s. As the Thatcher administration reprivatized British Aerospace, Jaguar, British Petroleum, the telephone system, and other enterprises, many average citizens purchased stock in those firms. Recognizing that Labour's Socialist positions were hurting it at the polls, Tony Blair persuaded the party organization in the mid-1990s to end its support for extensive state ownership.

Labour's other important policy objective in the postwar era was creating the welfare state—an array of government programs providing health care, retirement pension, unemployment compensation, and public housing. Britain's extensive social welfare programs—including the national health system and a huge network of public housing—astounded many Americans but was fairly typical among other Western European nations. For the most part, the voters have approved of it (though they may be critical of how well it functions) and succeeding governments—Labour and Conservative alike—maintained it until it was trimmed back in the Thatcher era. Proponents of the welfare state note that it has contributed to a lower infant mortality rate, a longer life span (credited to the government-run national health program of free, universal care), and a safety net for the needy. Opponents charge that it has overtaxed the nation and stifled economic growth. Today, Labour still defends the remaining components of the welfare state, especially the National Health Service, but the party no longer wishes to expand it. In fact, although Labour has been in office since 1997, it restored few of the welfare programs that its Conservative predecessors had eliminated.

* The term *nationalization* and the verb *to nationalize* refer to the transfer of an industry or a company from private to state ownership.

Blair's first budget featured a tax cut for business and differed only marginally from John Major's. Indeed, under Blair and his successor, Gordon Brown, **"New Labour,"** as the party is now called, has abandoned most of its Socialist positions and has become a middle-of-the-road party (see Box 12-2). It has shed the image of a party of big government by promising not to raise taxes and to improve public services by making them more efficient rather than by increasing government spending. In doing so, it has taken the middle ground from the Conservatives, won considerable backing from the Middle Class, and won the last three national elections.

While accepting many of the Thatcherites' pro-business reforms, the Blair government has pursued a more pragmatic approach than either Thatcher on the right or "old Labour" on the left. Unlike Thatcherites, who were instinctively against most government programs, or the traditional Labour Party, which was instinctively for them, Blair's position (and now Brown's) has been that "what matters is what works."[23]

Although Blair's centrist policies alienated many of the old Labour Party militants (particularly leftist ideologues and trade unionists), they proved very popular with the voting public, including the middle class. Indeed, the decision to reform the party was based on the realization that the size of the working class and the political influence of the unions (Labour's traditional voting base) were shrinking, while the ranks of the middle class and white-collar workers (traditionally more likely to vote for the Tories) were growing. In order to win, Blair's team concluded, New Labour had to become more of a "catchall party" (a broadly based party) winning support from a broad array of voters. The strategy worked! In 1997, nearly one-third of all professionals and managers and nearly one-half of all skilled white-collar workers voted for New Labour, a substantial gain over prior elections and the key to New Labour's victory.[24] In all, Blair led Labour to three consecutive victories, something that the party had never previously been able to do. But the 2005 victory came with the party attracting only 35.5 percent of the vote, a record low for a winning party in modern times. Weakened by his growing reputation for being "too slick," and especially by his very unpopular alliance with the U.S. in Iraq, Blair's personal popularity began to decline in his second term. Two years after Labour's much weaker (though still victorious) performance in the 2005 parliamentary election, Blair resigned. Labour selected Blair's most powerful cabinet member and his personal rival, Gordon Brown, as the party's new leader and, hence the new prime minister.

The Liberal Democratic Party

Great Britain's leading third party, the Liberal Democratic Party, was founded in 1988. Originally called the Social and Liberal Democrats, it took its present name the following year. With a policy position to the left of the Conservatives and to the right of Labour, the Liberal Democrats originally presented themselves as a centrist alternative to the two major parties, though that distinction has weakened since the 1990s when Labour moved toward the center. Indeed, since 1997, on issues such as public health, taxes, civil liberties, and the war on Iraq, the Liberal Democrats have taken a position to the left of Labour. Thus, the party not only was the only one to strongly oppose the war in Iraq but it has been highly critical of some of Blair's anti-terrorism measures, which it views as unnecessarily violating individual civil liberties.

Box 12-2

WHAT IS "NEW LABOUR"?

From 1979 through 1992, the Conservative Party won four consecutive national elections, a record of historic proportions. While much of the credit for that feat belongs to Margaret Thatcher's strong leadership and the growing popularity of her ideology—Thatcherism—which called for less government and more latitude for free enterprise, the Labour Party's shift to the left was equally responsible. Many voters who were not pleased with Thatcher's policies found Labour's shift to the left in the 1970s (support for unilateral nuclear disarmament, major government spending programs, and the like) even less palatable. These voters either supported the Conservatives as the best of the lot, or supported the various middle-of-the-road, third-party alternatives (Liberals, then the Alliance, then the Liberal Democrats). Thus, by the mid-80s, Labour Party leaders Neil Kinnock and John Smith had recognized that their party had become too radical to win a national election and needed to shift back toward the center.

It was not until Tony Blair assumed the leadership of the party in 1994, that it was able to reclaim the center from the Tories and establish its own string of electoral victories. "Making few promises [of government activism] . . . and taming the [left wing of] the party were . . . part of a design to allow . . . Labour to escape from its past, its [socialist] ideological legacy."[25] To cement this image of a changed party in the voters' minds, Blair unofficially but constantly called his party and its program "New Labour."

In many ways, Blair's ideological reorientation was not unique. In France, Spain, Germany, and elsewhere, Socialist leaders have moved to the center in an attempt to defeat their conservative opponents at the polls. But Blair's "revolution" was particularly dramatic and involved a pitched battle with the party's more radical wing over issues such as government ownership of portions of the economy. Ultimately, Blair's faction weakened the power of the nation's trade unions in the party—heretofore a major left-wing influence—and concentrated great control in the party leader's hands.

Many party members never really reconciled themselves to New Labour's move to the political center and felt that Blair and his team had sold out the party's Socialist principles. But, as Blair led the party out of the political wilderness to three successive electoral victories, they had to admit that Labour's new face paid dividends at the voting booth, particularly

with middle-class voters. Blair, an outstanding public speaker, was able to introduce catch-phrases into the political conversation that suggested how Labour offered voters a "third way," combining the Tory's toughness with Labour's compassion. Thus, while still in opposition to John Major's Conservative government, he announced that a Labour government would be "tough on crime, tough on the causes of crime [that is, poverty, unemployment and other social ills]."

What policies did the New Labour government pursue once it came into office? To some extent, it tacitly accepted much of Thatcher's reforms. Blair not only accepted but extended privatization of many state-owned enterprises, including public services. Similarly, from the outset New Labour sought to reassure the business community and the middle class that, unlike some previous Labour governments, it was committed to limiting state spending, holding the line on taxes, and taking any necessary steps to control inflation.

Still, although it accepted and legitimized much of Thatcher's legacy, New Labour has not been a carbon copy of the Conservatives. Like Thatcher, Blair strengthened the Prime Minister's control of the ruling party and of the central government. At the same time, however, he reversed her centralization of government by restoring the popular election of London's mayor (she had undermined local government in that city) and establishing regional authorities. In the same vein, significant government authority was taken from London and devolved to Scotch, Welsh, and, eventually, Northern Irish parliaments elected by their own citizens.

Initially, at least, the New Labour government featured a stronger commitment to civil liberties than recent Tory administrations had. For example, soon after taking office Blair signed on to the European Union's "Social Chapter," which guaranteed, among other things, a minimum working age of 16, parental and maternity leaves, gender equality, minimum health care and pension rights for workers, and protection of disabled workers. When the EU replaced the European Community in 1991, Margaret Thatcher insisted that signing the Social Chapter must be optional. And for six years, under Thatcher and John Major, Britain had been the only EU member that refused to sign, as both administrations saw the

(Continued)

| Box 2-1 |

WHAT IS "NEW LABOUR"? (*Continued*)

Social Chapter as too radical (Thatcher sarcastically called it the "Socialist Chapter") and an infringement of British national sovereignty. The Blair government signed the European Convention on Human Rights as well (also a measure rejected by Thatcher and Major), thereby giving the United Kingdom the first written Bill of Rights in over 300 years. In 2005, the government passed legislation establishing for the first time a supreme court acting outside of the Law Lords. It will begin functioning in 2009. However, following the 9/11 terrorist attacks in the U.S. and the later bus and subway bombings in London, the Labour government restricted civil liberties somewhat, as the Thatcher and Major governments had done during the years of IRA terrorism.

Historically Labour has been a greater advocate than the Conservatives of minority rights, women's rights, and gay rights. Correspondingly, it has long had a higher percentage of female, Black, and Asian MPs. The parliamentary gender gap widened considerably when the party, led by Blair, established a gender quota for its 1997 parliamentary candidates. That quota, coupled with Labour's resounding victory in that year's elections, doubled the total number of women in Parliament from 60 to 120 (mostly, but not exclusively, Labourites).[26] That number has remained fairly constant and is currently 128 (that is, nearly 20 percent of all MPs; still below the Western European average).

Once enormously popular, Tony Blair's political undoing was his unrelenting support for the U.S. war on terrorism and, particularly, the war in Iraq. From the outset, Great Britain's entry into the war was opposed by most Labour MPs (though most accepted party discipline and supported their leader in parliamentary votes) and many of the party's leaders. In the months after 9/11 and the build-up for the Iraq war, Blair so articulately and forcefully presented the U.S. and British case that pundits sometimes called him "America's second Secretary of State." As the war dragged on, however, and popular support for British participation plummeted, Blair's critics derisively referred to him as "Bush's poodle."

Why did Blair's government send troops to Iraq in spite of widespread opposition among Labour MPs and activists? Why did Britain continue to fight and why did Blair continue to back U.S. strategy so steadfastly in the face of growing public opposition? Among several factors that seemingly influenced Blair, one was his determination to shed "old Labour's" image in foreign policy just as he had done with domestic policy. During the last decade of the Cold War, many voters viewed Labour as soft on national security and eager to disarm. Thus, Blair's New Labour was determined to show itself as resolute in the war on terror. Ironically, however, by the second year of his second term (2004), public opinion had turned against the war, dragging down his popularity and his party (just as U.S. public opinion eventually turned against the war and the Bush administration). In 2005 Blair did lead New Labour to a third electoral victory, but by a greatly diminished margin. Indeed, the party's share of the national vote (35.2% in a three-way race) was the smallest of any winning party since World War II. Two years later he resigned. Not surprisingly, Blair's successor, Gordon Brown, has reduced British commitment to the war and distanced himself somewhat from Bush's foreign policy. As we have noted, since he took office, Brown's popularity—and, hence, Labour's—has fallen sharply as the result of a near collapse of Northern Rock bank, a major mortgage lender, revelations about illegal contributions to the party, and Browne's lack of political skills. It appears that the British electorate may have tired of Labour government and is hoping for a change. But the Prime Minister is not required to call for a parliamentary election until 2010 and the political landscape may have changed by that time.

The foundation for this new party was laid in the 1980s through the electoral alliance between the Liberal and the Social Democratic parties. Once one of the country's two major parties (in the nineteenth and early twentieth centuries), the Liberals were passed in the 1920s by the rising Labour Party. Reduced to insignificance after World War II, the Liberals later staged a modest comeback. By the early 1970s, they were receiving almost 20 percent of the vote. The Social Democrats, on the other

A CHALLENGING ALLIANCE   Tony Blair meets with President Bush to discuss the war in Iraq. Blair's government has been the most ardent supporter of U.S. policy in the region, a position that has eroded Blair's popularity at home.

hand, were not founded until 1981, when 27 Labour MPs and 1 Conservative defected from their respective parties seeking a more moderate alternative. In the 1983 and 1987 general elections, the Liberals and the Social Democrats both endorsed a single slate of parliamentary candidates (half from each party) called the Alliance.

Following their disappointing showing in the 1987 election, the Alliance partners decided to merge into a single party soon called the Liberal Democratic Party. In recent parliamentary elections, the Liberal Democrats have attracted around 20 percent of the vote, maintaining their position as Britain's leading third party. The party's support is greatest among middle-class professionals and managers and is somewhat weaker among blue-collar workers. As we have seen (Box 12-3 and Table 12.2), the Liberal Democrats (like the Alliance and the Liberal Party before them) are unable to win a portion of parliamentary seats commensurate with their electoral strength.

INTEREST GROUPS

Interest groups play an important role in the British political process. Two have been particularly influential. The Trades Union Congress (TUC), roughly equivalent to the American AFL-CIO, represents more than eighty of the nation's largest unions and is an integral part of the Labour Party. During the 1970s, the TUC and other labor unions exercised a considerable amount of political influence. Indeed, the high level of strikes and labor strife under Conservative Prime Minister Heath (1970–1974) and Labour Prime Minister Callaghan (1976–1979) helped bring their respective governments down.

But organized labor's influence declined sharply under Margaret Thatcher. Her government passed a number of bills weakening trade unions, and, in a critical

---

Box 12-3

PARTIES AND THE ELECTORAL SYSTEM

Whereas the United States and Britain have two dominant parties, most of the world's democracies have multiparty systems. In countries such as Italy and France, for example, ten parties or more often win representation in the Parliament. Rarely in France (and never in Italy) does any single party have a majority in the legislature. Even in Germany, with fewer parties, the governing parties have often needed the support of the smaller Free Democratic Party or the Green Party to secure a legislative majority. Presently, Angela Merkel's government requires the support of both her own Christian Democratic Party and the Social Democratic Party.

Most Western European nations select their parliaments through **proportional representation (PR)**, an electoral system that enhances the prospects of candidates from smaller parties (Chapter 4). In place of many single-member districts (SMDs), members of the Parliament are elected from larger districts having multiple representatives. Voters choose between lists of candidates presented by each party. When the votes are tallied, each party attains a percentage of seats in the Parliament proportional to its share of the total vote. Had Great Britain used proportional representation, the Liberal–Social Democratic Alliance and its successor, the Liberal Democrats, would have received about 20 percent of the seats in the House of Commons in the last four elections. Instead, they had to settle for 3 to 10 percent (Table 12.2).

Although Tony Blair originally promised to hold a referendum on whether to change Britain's electoral system to proportional representation, his government failed to do so since such a change would inevitably cost Labour (and the Conservatives) seats in the House of Commons. For that very reason it is unlikely that a government headed by either major party—Conservatives or Labour—would ever allow a change in the system (just as both the Democrats and Republicans are unlikely to ever support PR in the U.S.)

A further distortion of SMD elections is that they usually (though not always) give a boost in seats to whichever party wins the highest percentage of the vote. For example, in the 1983 election, the Conservatives (led by Thatcher) finished first with 42 percent of the vote, but ended up with 61 percent of the seats in Parliament (Table 12.2). Indeed, even though they attracted a slightly *smaller* share of the vote than they had in 1979, they gained about 60 more seats. In the most recent parliamentary race (2005), Labour finished first with only 35 percent of the national vote, but won 55 percent of the seats.

---

confrontation, it defeated a bitter and prolonged strike by the powerful miners' union against the state-owned coal mines. During Thatcher's eleven years in office, union membership nationwide declined from 12 million to 10 million. The shift in the country's economy away from industry and toward the service sector has further weakened the labor movement (as it has in the United States) and by 2002, union membership was down to 7.7 million. At the same time, the number of days lost to strikes nationwide declined by almost 90 percent from 1981 to 2000.[27] Moreover, in the mid-1990s Tony Blair's organizational reform of the Labour Party reduced the unions' political influence in the party they helped found.

A second important national interest group is the "CBI, the Voice of Business." Formerly known as the Confederation of British Industry (CBI), it is the country's most influential business organization, representing three-fourths of the nation's large and medium-sized manufacturers. Unlike the TUC, the CBI is not officially linked to any party, but it has had a close relationship with the Conservatives and usually receives a sympathetic hearing from that party's leaders. And unlike the TUC (which has provided major financial support for the Labour Party), the CBI itself gives no funds to the Conservatives. But many individual members of the confederation (including most of the nation's largest corporations) contribute heavily to the Tory coffers.

From the early 1980s until 1997, the influence of all interest groups, including the Tories' allies in big business, declined appreciably as the Thatcher and Major Conservative governments relied less on their input.[28] Ironically, under New Labour, consultation between the government and the CBI has increased, as the party has sought business support. But the CBI will undoubtedly stay more sympathetic to the Conservatives.

In addition to lobbying, many interest groups are officially represented on government advisory and supervisory boards. But, although British interest groups often have been influential at the administrative and bureaucratic level, their leverage in Parliament has been more limited. Because each party's parliamentary delegation typically votes as a fairly solid bloc, interest groups do not have the opportunity to sway individual legislators as they do in the United States. Furthermore, British campaign funding is channeled through the national political party organizations. So again, unlike the United States, it is difficult for a British interest group to win an individual legislator's support through campaign contributions. Ultimately, to gain their political objectives, interest groups must win the support of the leaders of the cabinet and of the governing party.

THE STRUCTURE OF GOVERNMENT

Britain's government structure is far more centralized—and hence more simplified—than U.S. government. There is no state government, and the powers of local government are far more circumscribed than they are in the United States. In short, political power in Britain, as in most European democracies, is highly concentrated at the national level. Within the national government, authority is concentrated as well. There is no separation of powers and, hence, nothing comparable to the struggles in the United States between Congress and the president. Under a parliamentary system (which merges the legislative and executive branches), voters also have few electoral choices for national office. Whereas the U.S. voter selects a number of candidates for the national government—a member of the House of Representatives, two senators, and the president—British voters elect only one: their representative to the House of Commons (their MP).

Parliament

Following each general election, it is the task of the House of Commons to select a prime minister. In many ways, this is the most important function Parliament performs during its term in office. Normally, however, its choice is obvious, once the voters have spoken. As long as one party has won a majority of the seats in the House of Commons, its leader—and the party's spokesman during the recently concluded campaign—is assured of becoming the prime minister. And only once in the last 60 years (in 1974) has no party been able to win that majority. In that situation, the final outcome is more ambiguous, since a prospective new prime minister would have to gain the additional support of a party (or parties) other than his or her own, or would have to form a minority government.

The prime minister's government (including the cabinet) serves only as long as it can command Parliament's confidence and support. Any time that it feels the government has performed unsatisfactorily, the House of Commons may express "no confidence" in the prime minister by a simple majority vote. Following such an outcome, the prime minister must resign or have the monarch call for new elections. Unlike impeachment of a U.S. president, ousting a prime minister requires no trial by the legislative branch. Moreover, a **vote of no confidence** requires no suspicion of illegal activity and no violation of the oath of office.

On the surface, then, this process appears to place British prime ministers on extremely thin ice, subject to the whims of Parliament. In actuality, however, they can normally rest secure in the knowledge that they have a firm grip on power until the next election. As long as their party has a parliamentary majority, which it almost always has, prime ministers need only maintain the confidence of their own colleagues. Since majority MPs have no incentive to vote their own party out of power, only one prime minister in more than half a century, James Callaghan in 1979, has lost a no-confidence vote. But several times in recent decades MPs from the majority party have become so dissatisfied with the prime minister's performance that he or she has felt compelled to resign. In 1963, for example, following a sex scandal and possible breach of national security in his cabinet, Prime Minister Harold Macmillan resigned (though he himself was uninvolved in the scandal), claiming ill health. More recently, Margaret Thatcher resigned in 1990 after it became clear that she no longer had sufficient support among her Conservative MPs. Most recently, as current Prime Minister Gordon Brown's popularity has declined, there have been rumors that his fellow Labour MPs might force him to resign.

Besides serving as a watchdog over the prime minister and the cabinet, Parliament's most critical function is to consider legislation. Yet, its legislative powers are startlingly limited, compared with those of the U.S. Congress. The cabinet introduces all parliamentary bills of any national importance. Because the governing party almost always has a majority in the House of Commons, and because British parties vote largely as a bloc, rarely does a bill introduced by the cabinet meet defeat. In recent decades, **party discipline** (voting as instructed by the party leadership) has diminished somewhat, and more government bills than previously have been defeated in Parliament. The number of votes lost by the prime minister (far fewer than 10 percent), however, remains rather small compared with the legislative record of U.S. presidents who, like Bill Clinton and both Bushes, often face an opposition majority in at least one House of Congress.

Unlike Congress, then, Parliament's primary function is not so much to design legislation as to review it. Although proposed government legislation is rarely defeated, it is sometimes altered or even withdrawn if it faces sufficient parliamentary opposition. Parliament also performs a watchdog function by regularly subjecting the prime minister and the cabinet to intensive questioning. These obligatory "question sessions" are closely followed by the media and force government ministers to defend their policies before the aggressive challenge of opposition-party MPs.

The Cabinet

The cabinet is the ultimate decision-making body in British politics. Heading that body and selecting its other members is the prime minister, the "first among [ministerial] equals." The number of full ministers is normally 20 to 25. They, in turn, are

Prime Minister Gordon Brown addresses the House of Commons.

assisted by about 60 to 70 non-cabinet and junior ministers. All ministers are chosen from either the House of Commons or, far less frequently, the House of Lords. Thus, whereas the U.S. Constitution prohibits individuals from simultaneously holding posts in the executive and legislative branches, British political tradition *requires* cabinet members to sit in both.

Except for the few **coalition governments**, when more than one party joins together to form a majority (during World War II, for example), ministers are selected exclusively from the prime minister's party. They usually come from that party's most respected parliamentary members and normally represent the party's major factions. Appointment to the cabinet is the crowning achievement of an MP's political career. Ministers serve at the pleasure of the prime minister, however, and he or she can remove them at any time.

The cabinet meets regularly to discuss government policy and consider potential legislation. The country's most important political decisions are made there. The prime minister sets the agenda and sums up the discussion and policy decisions at the close of each meeting. Rarely is there a formal vote. Prime ministerial styles vary greatly. Whereas most leaders try to reach a consensus, others do not hesitate to impose their policies on the cabinet, even if theirs is a minority position. It was said of Margaret Thatcher that she summed up the conclusions of the meeting even before discussion began. John Major had a far more conciliatory style and sought cabinet consensus, while Tony Blair, though not as openly aggressive as Thatcher, dominated cabinet meetings and reduced their influence on policy.

Once the prime minister has announced a decision, all cabinet members are collectively responsible for the policy and must quiet any qualms that they have. In the past, ministers who could not abide by that decision had no recourse other than to resign. Since that would undoubtedly hurt their careers as party leaders, resignations based on open policy differences have been extremely rare, though Robin Cook, the leader of the House of Commons, former Foreign Secretary and one of Labour's most influential figures, resigned from the Cabinet after Tony Blair's decision to take the country into the war in Iraq. In recent times, extensive media coverage and the resulting news leaks often pierce the veil of secrecy over cabinet meetings, and internal policy differences are more easily known.

Although strong-willed prime ministers have overridden their cabinets and imposed their position, no prime minister can afford to oppose his or her colleagues consistently. Thus, Margaret Thatcher's frequent disregard of opposing views from other Conservative Party leaders and factions eventually contributed to her loss of leadership.

The Bureaucracy

The modern British civil service dates to 1854, when open competition replaced patronage as the basis for recruitment. Whereas new administrations in the United States appoint their supporters to thousands of high-ranking bureaucratic positions, British governments are much more constrained. All but the very top ministry positions are reserved for nonpartisan career civil servants. Since the highest-ranking civil servants (the "mandarins") normally have more experience and expertise in their fields than do the ministers and secretaries under whom they serve, they are in a position to exercise considerable influence. Indeed, in British popular culture (including a recent television sitcom), ranking mandarins are often seen as manipulating and controlling the ministers whom they serve.

In fact, the notion of an "unelected dictatorship" (of bureaucrats) is exaggerated.[29] Most informed observers admire the civil service for its dedication and fairness. For the most part, it has done an admirable job of serving both Conservative and Labour governments impartially. But critics on both the left (radical Labourites) and the right (Thatcherites) have complained that entrenched civil servants often oppose policies that seriously threaten the status quo and, consequently, may drag their heels in implementing change.

Others argue that, however well motivated they may be, senior civil servants—who are drawn primarily from the upper middle class and are often educated at elite schools—are out of touch with much of society. They observe that people of working-class origins (constituting over half the nation's population) hold only 5 percent of the three thousand senior bureaucratic positions. At the same time, not long ago a government study noted that 72 percent of those entering the civil service had attended Oxford or Cambridge universities, and 48 percent had graduated from "public schools" (the elitist private institutions that educate only 5 percent of the nation's population).[30]

The Judiciary

Although U.S. criminal and civil law are derived in large part from British law, the two judicial systems differ fundamentally concerning the courts' political role. As we saw in our discussion of U.S. politics (Chapter 11), the Supreme Court's political power derives from its capacity to overturn congressional legislation and executive actions by declaring them unconstitutional. The British court system has no comparable power since there is no written constitution. If the judicial branch rules that Parliament or the government has acted contrary to established constitutional norms (the body of legal rulings, traditions, and legislation), Parliament needs only pass a new law making its intentions explicit on the matter. Under the doctrine of parliamentary sovereignty, that new law would automatically be constitutional and not subject to reversal by the courts. But if the courts overrule an unpopular or embarrassing government practice, Parliament may be reluctant to reinstate that practice.[31]

Britain's membership in the European Union (EU)—formerly the European Community (EC)—adds another level of authority to the judicial system. The 1972 European Communities Act stated that EC law takes precedence over any member nation's domestic law. Thus, for example, the EU's Court of Justice may rule that British environmental regulations conflict with rules enacted through EU treaties. That ruling would be binding on British courts, and the British law would be struck down. In 1998 the British Parliament passed the **Human Rights Act**. The bill incorporated the European [Union's] Convention on Human Rights, giving the country its first written Bill of Rights since the late seventeenth century. At the time, civil liberties advocates hailed this as a major step forward. However, in 2005, following the terrorist attacks and attempted attacks on the London mass transit system, Blair announced new security regulations, some of which appear to contradict the European Convention and his own Human Rights Act. He declared that he would ask Parliament to amend the Act if necessary.

PUBLIC POLICY AND THE BRITISH ECONOMY

The government first began to manage the country's economy actively in the 1930s as it attempted to counter the effects of the worldwide economic depression. World War II, which brought severe shortages and extensive German bombing of London and other British cities, inflicted further suffering. At war's end, in response to the nation's prolonged period of deprivation, the newly elected Labour Government greatly enhanced the state's role in rebuilding the economy and protecting the public's welfare. Although the Conservative opposition at that time as well as Tory governments in the following decades were more cautious than Labour about state economic intervention, they still supported an activist government working for the general good. Thus, from the late 1940s until 1979, Britain's national government (like its counterparts in most of Western Europe) intervened far more intensely in the economy and enacted more welfare measures than the U.S. government did.

The Establishment of the Welfare State (1945–1951)

The postwar Labour Government introduced an array of programs revolutionizing the state's role in society. The new national health care system offered tax-funded medical care for all. To remedy the country's severe housing shortage, the state funded a vast network of **council housing**, low-income public housing, funded by the national government but administered by local government.

The government expanded unemployment compensation and retirement pensions to create a "safety net" for the needy. In all, the Labour Government created a welfare state to provide the population with "cradle to grave" security. In addition, it nationalized a number of basic industries, including coal mining, iron, and steel—believing that those industries would better serve the national interest under state ownership.

The Postwar Settlement

When the Conservatives returned to power in 1951, they reversed some aspects of Labour's economic policy but maintained many others. For example, they reprivatized (returned to private ownership) the iron and steel industries. But during the next 28 years, Conservative and Labour governments alike retained and enlarged the national health care system and other fundamental elements of the welfare state. Public housing was greatly expanded, ultimately providing shelter for *one-third* of the country's population. Still, haunted by memories of the Great Depression, Conservative and Labour administrations alike pursued full-employment policies. For example, when major private firms faced bankruptcy, the government often stepped in with loans and stock purchases, or, when necessary, it took them over to keep them running.

Political scientists maintain that during that period an unofficial and unspoken compact existed between the Conservative Party and the business community on one side, and the Labour Party and the trade unions on the other. Labour moderated its impulse for additional Socialist reform, and the Conservatives accepted existing welfare programs that provided for the working class. That compact, referred to as the **postwar settlement**, remained in place until the late 1970s.[32] For much of that period, the nation enjoyed moderate economic growth, low inflation, and unemployment levels that rarely exceeded 3 percent.[33]

The Collapse of the Postwar Settlement

Thus, in the mid-1960s, the British government could truthfully tell its people that they'd "never had it so good." The nation's standard of living was higher than it had ever been before. Beneath the surface, however, serious economic problems loomed. Britain's postwar growth and industrial productivity trailed well behind Japan, the United States, and most of Western Europe. One by one, Germany, France, the Netherlands, Norway, Sweden, Denmark, and others passed the British in per capita income (GNP per capita). Britain became less competitive in the world market. Once among the world's leading producers of automobiles, motorcycles, and ships, it lost a large portion of those industries when it could no longer compete with countries such as Japan, Germany, and the United States. Burdened by budget deficits and crippling trade deficits (exporting less than it imported), the country accumulated a large foreign debt. By the 1970s, the economy had reached a crisis.

The reasons for Britain's economic slide were complex and subject to debate. Conservative and Labour analysts offered differing explanations and conflicting solutions. As real wages (the purchasing power of people's wages) stagnated or fell, the Labour Party became more radical, and unions became more militant. At the same time, power in the Conservative Party shifted from its once-dominant centrist faction to the party's right wing. The consensus of the postwar settlement was breaking down. As inflation soared above 20 percent in the mid-1970s, labor–management conflict intensified, with both sides struggling to keep up with rising prices. During the 1970s, the country lost more days to strikes than in the preceding 25 years combined.

In the winter of 1979, six weeks of strikes cut off garbage collection, heating-oil delivery, and hospital service. That "winter of discontent," as it was called, turned public opinion against the Labour Government and helped produce a Conservative victory in the 1979 national election.

The Thatcher Revolution

When Margaret Thatcher, the newly elected Conservative prime minister, took office, she revolutionized British politics much as her friend and admirer, President Ronald Reagan, did shortly afterward in the United States. Both countries, like most industrial democracies at that time, faced stagnant economic growth, high inflation, and budget deficits.

Prime Minister Thatcher, like President Reagan, was determined to reduce the role of government in the economy and to remove what both believed were unnecessary shackles on the free-enterprise system. Thatcher's tight-fisted fiscal policies initially drove the country into a recession. Unemployment rates nearly tripled, to more than 12 percent—the highest rate since the Great Depression of the 1920s and 1930s. At the same time, however, the administration rejected a basic element of the postwar settlement. Believing that it would only lead to greater budget deficits and continued inflation, the government refused to bail out ailing industries or employ other traditional methods to combat unemployment.

Looking at the country's long-term economic slide, the administration concluded that the solution was less government rather than more. It tried to create an "enterprise culture" in which citizens would look to the free market and not government for economic solutions. At the same time, Thatcher and her successor, John Major, reprivatized a wide range of government-owned enterprises—including the telephone, electricity, natural gas, and water systems—putting their shares up for sale on the stock market. Much of the vast network of public housing was privatized as well when tenants were given the opportunity to buy their apartments or houses from the state (at favorable prices) if they wished. On the other hand, in the face of public opposition, both Thatcher and Major refrained from major assaults on state welfare plans including dismantling the national health service.

How successful was **Thatcherism**? The answer depends on whom you ask. Conservative Party and private-sector supporters insist that she cured Britain of its excessive dependence on state-sponsored economic solutions. By reducing taxes and promoting an "enterprise culture," her government encouraged the growth of thousands of new companies, particularly in the nation's south. Supporters note that by the mid-1990s, Britain had one of the fastest-growing economies in Western Europe (although there had been sharp ups and downs under both Thatcher and Major). In many cases (though not all), privatized firms have performed more efficiently than they had under state control.

Many critics of Thatcherism in the Labour Party, the unions, and even her own party conceded a number of those accomplishments but contended that too frequently they came at an unnecessarily high cost. Although unemployment rates declined from their peaks of the mid-1980s, they remained much higher than they had been before Thatcher. Much of the north—once Great Britain's industrial heartland—failed to share in the economic revival.

But no matter how history eventually judges the Conservative revolution, for now the champions of reduced government have won the day. In Britain, as in the United States and much of the world, the role of government has been significantly scaled back and is unlikely to return to its former level in the foreseeable future. Although many voters viewed the Thatcher revolution as too heartless or too extreme, most were more suspicious of the Labour Party's commitment to greater government intervention. Hence, the Conservatives won four consecutive national elections.

As we have seen, realizing this change in public attitudes, Tony Blair led the Labour Party away from Socialist or big-government solutions. "New Labour" governments led by Blair (1997–2007) and Gordon Brown (2007–) have renounced the party's previous support of government ownership of major industries, kept a lid on taxes, and left untouched most of Margaret Thatcher's major policy changes, accepting them as necessary (See Box 12-2). Much of the current Labour Party program—including improving technical and scientific education (to help private enterprise compete), lowering business taxes, and fighting crime—is quite acceptable to centrist and moderately conservative voters. Thus, the Blair and Brown governments have done as much to confirm the Conservative revolution as to challenge it.

Conclusion: Great Britain in the Twenty-First Century

Despite its impressive history of democracy and stability, Britain did not fare particularly well economically for much of the twentieth century. In recent times, the governments of Margaret Thatcher and John Major stimulated private-sector investment and opened up new opportunities for entrepreneurial talent. Progress toward improving Britain's long-sluggish economy was uneven as periods of improved growth alternated with economic downturns. But, by the 1990s the economy began to grow at an accelerated pace. For decades Britain had one of the slowest rates of economic growth in Western Europe. By the start of the twenty-first century it had one of the fastest. Faster economic growth and higher labor productivity began under John Major's administration and continued through most of the Blair Era.

Changing social attitudes and wider educational opportunities have opened up the country's confining class system somewhat. Wealthy, self-made businesspeople are more numerous and more socially accepted within the "old money" elite. The "old boys" network of aristocrats and other public school graduates no longer dominates Conservative Party leadership. The restructuring of the economy since the 1960s has diminished the size of the working class, while the middle class (particularly white-collar workers, professionals, and salaried managers) has grown. For all those reasons, there is now a weaker correlation between an individual's class origins and his or her party preference. Many workers have become homeowners, including those who bought their council housing units in the 1980s. Initially at least, many of them considered themselves more middle-class and were more likely to vote for the Conservative Party than when they were renters.

At the same time, however, since the late 1990s, as the number of public service professionals has grown substantially (including teachers, civil servants, health care professionals, and social workers), middle-class support for the Labour Party has increased.[34]

Yet, social class still divides society more sharply in Britain than in the United States, Japan, or most of Western Europe. Even with the social changes just mentioned, opportunities for upward social mobility remain more limited than in other industrial democracies. Indeed, a 1992 survey of top positions in business, the professions, and the arts by the *Economist*, a respected periodical, found that graduates of public schools and Oxford or Cambridge still dominated those posts and that there had been less change than previously believed.[35] More recent research (2002) by the University of Essex indicated that opportunities for upward social mobility were actually declining, after a period of greater fluidity, and that children of the working class faced the greatest obstacles.[36] Thus, young men and women whose parents can afford to send them to public schools still start life with tremendous advantages over the rest of society (once all male, many public schools now admit a small number of girls). And even with the weakened correlation between class origin and political preference, "class remains the single most important social factor underlying the vote."[37]

As it moves into the twenty-first century, Britain will also have to decide whether it is willing to shed its traditional insularity and become an active, economically competitive part of Western Europe. While the European Union moves, somewhat haltingly, toward greater economic unification and a single currency, Britain has dragged its heels more than any other EU member. Whereas the Labour Party once was the most suspicious of European economic unity, now it is the nationalist wing of the Conservative Party that balks at taking orders from "[foreign] EU bureaucrats in Brussels."* Tony Blair once planned to hold a referendum on whether Britain should adopt the European Union's Euro as the national currency (as almost all of the EU's members have). That change would have signified a British desire to integrate their nation more fully into the EU. That referendum was never held, nor is it likely to be, because opinion polls made it clear that it would lose.

 ## WHERE ON THE WEB?

http://politics.guardian.co.uk/
Multiple links on British politics to and through the *Guardian*, one of Britain's most respected newspapers.

http://www.keele.ac.uk/depts/por/
Keele University (UK) guide to British Politics, especially elections and parties.

http://news.bbc.co.uk/1/hi/uk_politics
Links to the British Broadcasting Company (BBC), a government-owned but scrupulously independent television and radio network.

http://classweb.gmu.edu/chauss/cponline/britain.htm
Politics in Britain: Links to a major British newspaper, government agencies, political parties.

http://www.economist.com/index.html
A leading British news analysis magazine, *The Economist*.

❖ ❖ ❖

* Brussels, Belgium is the EU's administrative home and for many Europhobic British nationals it is a symbol of the transfer of national sovereignty to the EU.

Key Terms and Concepts _____

aristocracy	Parliament
coalition government	party discipline
council housing	Plaid Cymru
devolution	postwar settlement
European Union (EU)	proportional representation
evolutionary change	public schools
Glorious Revolution	social class
homogeneous societies	suffrage
Human Rights Act	Thatcherism
industrial democracies	Tories
Member of Parliament (MP)	vote of no confidence
nationalization	welfare state
New Labour	

Discussion Questions _____

1. In what ways has British democracy served as a model for democratic government in other parts of the world?
2. Discuss the effects of class divisions on British society and British politics. What is the relationship between the British educational system and its class system? Given the historically significant role that class differences have played in Britain, why have class hostilities—as expressed in political divisions—been less sharp there than in countries such as France and Italy? Over time, what has happened to the relationship between a voter's social class and his/her choice of parties in national elections?
3. How does the British parliamentary election system discriminate against "third parties"? Specifically, how have the parties in the Alliance during the 1980s and the contemporary Liberal Democrats been weakened by Britain's single-member-district parliamentary elections? What are the relative advantages and disadvantages of single-member-district elections as compared with proportional representation?
4. Ten years ago, the Conservative Party won its fourth consecutive national election and many wondered when the Labour Party would ever regain political power. Now Labour has won three consecutive victories. What changed? Why are the Conservatives finally staging a comeback?
5. What were the major policy changes introduced by the "New Labour" governments? What was the reaction within the Labour Party to New Labour's policy positions?

Notes _____

1. Jean Blondel, "The Government of France," in *Introduction to Comparative Politics,* by Michael Curtis et al. (New York: Harper and Row, 1990), pp. 105–109.
2. Richard Rose, *Politics in England* (Boston: Little, Brown, 1974), pp. 42–43.
3. Michael O'Neill (ed.), *Devolution and British Politics* (Essex, England: Pearson-Longman, 2004).
4. The UK Parliament Web site, parliament.uk/faq/faq.cfm, August 2005.
5. *BBC News* Online (February 7, 2007), http://news.bbc.co.uk/2/hi/uk_news/politics/4828094.stm.
6. Paul V. Warwick, *Culture, Structure, or Choice? Essays in the Interpretation of the British Experience* (New York: Agathon, 1990).
7. Philip Norton, *The British Polity,* 3rd ed. (New York: Longman, 1994), p. 32.
8. R. M. Punnett, *British Government and Politics* (Prospect Heights, IL: Waveland, 1988), pp. 4–7.
9. Robert R. Alford, *Party and Society* (Chicago: Rand McNally, 1963).
10. Tania Branigan, "Cameron faces elitism claims over grammar schools," *The Guardian,* UK News and Analysis Section (June 2, 2007), p. 12.
11. Anne West and Audrey Hind, "Secondary School Admissions in England: Exploring the Extent of Overt and Covert Selection" (London: London School of Economics and Political Science, Centre for Educational Research, Department of Social Policy, 2003), p.17.
12. Nick Robinson, "Class war hots up," *BBC News* Online (May 22, 2007), http://www.bbc.co.uk/blogs/nickrobinson/2007/05/22/index.html; see also, Branigan, "Cameron faces elitist claims . . . "
13. "Why Can't the English Just Give Up That Class Folderol?" *New York Times* (April 26, 2007).
14. R. Jowell, S. Witherspoon, and L. Brook, *British Social Attitudes, the Fifth Report,* 1988–1989 ed. (London: Gower, 1988), p. 227.
15. Geoffrey Smith and Nelson Polsby, *British Government and Its Discontents* (New York: Basic Books, 1981), chap. 2.

16. BBC Web site, BBC.com.
17. For early analysis of the problems of Northern Ireland, see Kevin Boyle and Tom Hadden, "Options for Northern Ireland," in *Developments in British Politics* 2, ed. Henry Drucker et al. (London: Macmillan, 1986); Brendan O'Leary, "Northern Ireland and the Anglo-Irish Agreement," in *Developments in British Politics*, ed. Patrick Dunleavy et al. (New York: St. Martin's, 1990). A more recent account by a major player in the peace negotiations is Marjorie Mowlam, *The Struggle for Peace, Politics and the People* (London: Hodder & Stoughton, 2002).
18. Max Beloff and Gillian Peele, *The Government of the UK* (New York: Norton, 1985), p. 177.
19. Peter Dorey, *Policy Making in Britain* (London: Sage, 2005), p. 270.
20. For a discussion of Margaret Thatcher's enormous impact on contemporary British politics, see Peter Jenkins, *Mrs. Thatcher's Revolution* (Cambridge: Harvard University Press, 1988).
21. "British Tory Leader Warns Against 'Triumphalism' After By-Election Victory," *New York Times* (May 24, 2008).
22. Beloff and Peele, *Government of the UK*, p. 185.
23. Gillian Peele, *Governing the UK* (Malden, MA: Blackwell Publishing, 2004), p. 90.
24. BBC/NOP exit poll cited in Dennis Kavanagh, *British Politics: Continuities and Change*, 4th ed. (Oxford and New York: Oxford University Press, 2000), p. 128.
25. James E. Cronin, *New Labour's Pasts* (London: Pearson Longman, 2004), p. 419.
26. Bill Jones and Dennis Kavanagh, *British Politics Today*, 7th ed. (Manchester, England and New York: Manchester University Press, 2003), p. 95; Pippa Norris, "Gender and Contemporary British Politics," in *British Politics Today* (Malden, MA: Blackwell Publishers, 2002), ed. Colin Hay, pp. 38–41.
27. Peele, *Governing the UK*, pp. 349–350.
28. Neil J. Mitchell, "The Decentralization of Business in Britain," *Journal of Politics* 52, no. 2 (May 1990): 622–637.
29. Norton, *British Polity*, pp. 202–206.
30. Michael Curtis, "The Government of Great Britain," in Curtis et al., *Introduction to Comparative Politics*, p. 77.
31. Philip Norton, *The British Polity*, 2nd ed. (New York: Longman, 1991), pp. 343–345.
32. "Britain," in *European Politics in Transition*, by Mark Kesselman et al. (Lexington, MA: Heath, 1987).
33. Ian Budge, David McKay, et al., *The Changing British Political System: Into the 1990s*, 2nd ed. (New York: Longman, 1988), p. 7.
34. Ivor Crewe, "Parties and Electors," in *The Developing British Political System*, 3rd ed., ed. Ian Budge and David McKay (New York: Longman, 1993), pp. 101–104.
35. "The Ascent of British Man," *Economist* (December 19, 1992), p. 21.
36. Cited in Jones and Kavanagh, *British Politics Today*, pp. 19–20.
37. Crewe, "Parties and Electors," p. 102.

For Further Reading ────────

Bartle, John and Anthony King, eds. *Britain at the Polls, 2005.* Washington, DC: CQ Press, 2005.

Cronin, James P. *New Labour's Pasts: The Labour Party and Its Discontents.* London: Pearson, Longman, 2004.

Dorey, Peter. *Policy Making in Britain.* London: Sage, 2005.

Jones, Bill, and Dennis Kavanagh, *British Politics Today.* 7th ed. Manchester, UK, and New York: Manchester University Press, 2003.

Ludlam, Steven and Martin J. Smith, eds. *Governing as New Labour: Policy and Politics under Blair.* New York: Palgrave Macmillan, 2004.

Peele, Gillian. *Governing the UK.* Malden, MA: Blackwell Publishing, 2004.

Wring, Dominic et al. eds. *Political Communications: The General Election Campaign of 2005.* New York: Palgrave Macmillan, 2007.

13

RUSSIA: THE ELUSIVE PATH TO AND FROM DEMOCRACY

◆ The Relevance of the Russian Experience ◆ The Rise
and Fall of Soviet Communism ◆ The Birth of a New
Political System ◆ Restructuring the Economy ◆ Russia
in the Early Years of the Twenty-First Century: The Putin
Presidency and After ◆ Putin and the Creation of an
All-Powerful Presidency ◆ Conclusion: The Transition
to Democracy Derailed

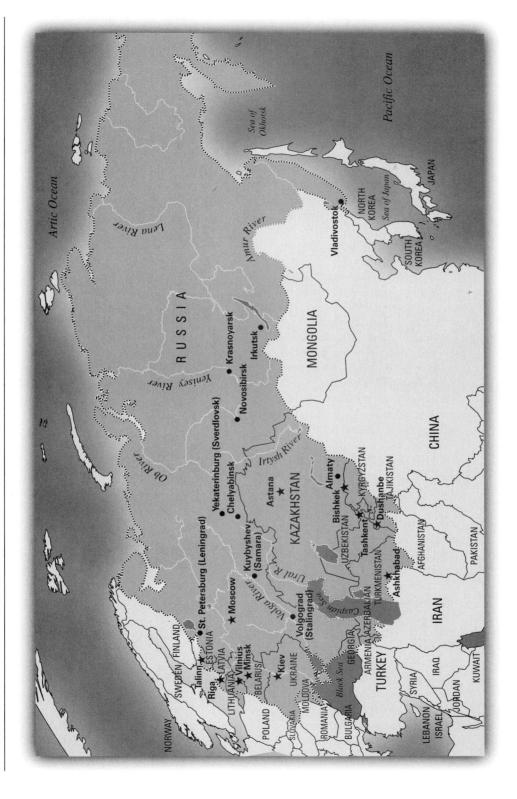

THE RELEVANCE OF THE RUSSIAN EXPERIENCE

The transition from authoritarian government to democracy is always difficult and fraught with danger, particularly in countries lacking any previous democratic experience. The conversion of a command (state-controlled) economy to a free market is no less demanding. Instead of improving living standards, Russia's early transition to capitalism brought a decade of enormous suffering. Small wonder many Russians blamed both capitalism and democracy for their predicament. Not surprisingly, many of them longed for the old days of communist economic stability. By the early part of the twenty-first century, Russia's transition to capitalism, though seriously flawed, seems secure and, after nearly twenty years of stagnation followed by collapse (1980–1999), the economy has rebounded impressively. On the other hand, despite considerable progress—however uneven—toward democracy under President Boris Yeltsin (1992–1999), the country has regressed toward authoritarianism.

The collapse of the Soviet Union's Communist dictatorship and its centrally controlled economy was years in the making. So, to understand Russia's "**dual transition**," we must first examine the political and economic systems of the USSR (Union of Soviet Socialist Republics), a country that at the close of 1991 disintegrated into 15 independent nations, including Russia (by far the largest and most influential of the 15). By exploring both Soviet communism's accomplishments and its failures we may better comprehend not only why the Soviet Union collapsed, but also why many Russians have accepted or even welcomed President (and now Prime Minister) Vladimir Putin's authoritarian measures. Although the Communist Party no longer draws a substantial portion of the vote, as it did in the 1990s, President Putin and his successor, Dmitri Medvedev, have co-opted many communist symbols and policy positions.

Few events influenced the twentieth century as intensely as the Russian Revolution of 1917, and none affected contemporary world politics more profoundly than the 1991 disintegration of the Soviet empire. The collapse of the USSR ended the Cold War, which had dominated international relations and U.S. foreign policy in the second half of the twentieth century. At the same time, it undercut the considerable influence of Marxist-Leninist ideology in much of Africa, Asia, and Latin America. The Soviet experience demonstrates that even seemingly entrenched authoritarian systems can collapse. But subsequent developments in Russia have also highlighted the difficulty of establishing a democratic regime. As that country has slid back to authoritarianism, its relations with the United States and the West have deteriorated. Although Russia no longer poses a significant military or diplomatic threat, its vast oil and natural gas holdings, as well as its permanent seat on the United Nations Security Council (and its consequent veto power in that council) gives it some international leverage.

After the fall of communism, President Yeltsin's government supported important steps toward democracy. These included greater freedom of speech, media, and religion, as well as relatively free and fair elections. But that progress was undercut by Yeltsin's successor, Vladimir Putin (2000–2008), and is likely to continue crumbling under Putin's protégé and handpicked presidential successor, Dmitri Medvedev (2008–). Today, ex-intelligence officers from the old Soviet KGB and its Russian successor, the

Federal Security Service (**FSB**), as well as a new class of corrupt multi-millionaires and an array of organized crime syndicates have deeply infiltrated the government and the economy. There is widespread corruption at all levels and political bosses wield substantial power outside the biggest cities.

If democracy fared far better in the 1990s than in the years that followed, the opposite has been true of the economy. The transition from a state-controlled economy to a free market created horrendous conditions for nearly a decade, with the Gross National Product (GNP) shrinking by some 40 percent and living standards falling correspondingly. Since 1999, however, the soaring price of petroleum—Russia's predominant export—coupled with more stable government economic policy and improved productivity has produced a dramatic economic recovery. Yet a decade of rapid economic growth has failed to erase many lingering economic and social problems. Despite some recent improvement, Russian life expectancy (particularly among men) has declined significantly as the result of a deteriorating health care system, widespread alcoholism, and exceptionally high rates of infant mortality, suicide, and homicide. In recent years infant mortality rates have fallen somewhat and life expectancy has bottomed out. But deaths continue to outnumber births and in 2006 alone the population declined by 560,000.[1] Health conditions and medical services remain seriously deficient. Similarly, although the poverty rate has also declined during the current economic boom, it remains troublingly high. And Russia's population not only continues to fall, but promises to do so for at least a few more decades.

These events demonstrate the difficulty of creating a pluralist democracy in a traditionally authoritarian society and the challenge of simultaneously introducing capitalism into a society so long dominated by communist norms.

THE RISE AND FALL OF SOVIET COMMUNISM

An Authoritarian Political Culture

Just as we can trace the origins of British democracy to the Magna Carta and other seminal historical events, so too do the roots of Russian authoritarianism lie in the country's pre-Revolutionary past. In the early thirteenth century, Mongol invaders conquered Russia. More than two centuries of Mongol rule (1236–1480) enhanced the existing tradition of royal **absolutism**. Moreover, until the reign of Czar Peter the Great (1682–1725), the country had little contact with Western Europe and remained isolated from the liberalizing cultural and political influences of the Protestant Reformation and the Renaissance.[2] Although royal despotism ended in Western Europe during the eighteenth and nineteenth centuries, the powers of Russia's czars (emperors) remained relatively unchecked.

The Fall of the Czarist Regime

The modern state in the Soviet Union, as in the United States and France, was born of revolution. During the nineteenth century, various groups challenged the repressive czarist government as a series of poorly managed military efforts, from the Crimean War (1853–1856) until World War I (1914–1918), undermined the regime's legitimacy.[3]

Finally, the suffering brought on by the world war toppled the system. In March 1917, food riots erupted in Petrograd, the nation's capital at the time (now called St. Petersburg). When mutinous troops joined the uprising, the old regime fell with hardly a fight.

The moderate, provisional government that replaced Czar Nicholas was soon challenged by the **Bolsheviks** (Communists), headed by Vladimir Lenin. As in many modern revolutions, power shifted from political moderates to the radicals.[4] On October 25, 1917, Lenin, promising to end Russian involvement in the war, sparked an uprising in Petrograd and seized control of the capital and then the nation.

Lenin and Marxist-Leninist Ideology

The Bolsheviks' victory brought them to power in an unexpected setting. As we saw in Chapter 2, Marx had expected communist revolutions to take place in more industrialized societies when the oppressed **proletariat** (working class) had developed sufficient **class consciousness** to rise up against capitalist exploitation. But Russia was among the least industrialized nations in Europe, with a comparatively small and inexperienced working class.

From Lenin's perspective, then, the Russian proletariat had yet to develop sufficient political consciousness to act in its own best interests. Consequently, he argued, the communists—who had the necessary appreciation of Marxist principles and an understanding of the mass's "true interests"—needed to organize a **vanguard party** to lead the masses (see Chapter 2). Whereas Marx had called for a transitional "dictatorship of the proletariat" followed by a "withering away" of the state, Lenin stressed an all-powerful state dominated by a vanguard Communist Party. Thus, he translated Marx's utopian vision of socialist society into an authoritarian plan. By 1921, Lenin had banned all opposition parties; placed labor unions, peasant organizations, and other interest groups under Communist Party control; and forced the press, literature, and the arts to follow the party line.

Three years later Lenin died, having only begun to create a communist state. Subsequently, he assumed mythic proportions in Soviet society. Millions of citizens, young and old, regularly visited his birthplace or viewed his body in Moscow's Red Square, and under Soviet Communism his bust graced all government buildings. Even after the fall of communism, many Russians still revere him.

Stalinism and the Totalitarian State

Following Lenin's death, power passed to the Communist Party's general secretary, Joseph Stalin, who established one of the world's most totalitarian governments. It was marked by extreme glorification of the national leader, state intervention in virtually every significant aspect of public life, and the regularized use of state terror against the population.

Stalin transformed private agriculture into state-dominated collective farms. "By forced **collectivization** of agriculture [he] put the regime in control of grain, drove millions of peasants off the land and into factories, and sent to labor camps millions of . . . kulaks [more affluent peasants]."[5] The resulting disruptions caused severe famine and millions of deaths. The all-powerful vanguard party and the state became the motors for rapid economic modernization, political repression, strident nationalism, and militarism.

Stalin concentrated all political power in his own hands, enforced by his dreaded secret police. At one time those internal security forces allegedly employed some 500,000 people, aided by millions of informers in all walks of life. Over the years, millions of ordinary citizens (an estimated 5 percent of the population) and many political leaders were sent to a network of slave-labor camps known as the **gulag**, where nearly a million of them perished.

From Totalitarian to Authoritarian Rule: Nikita Khrushchev and De-Stalinization

After Stalin's death (1953), his successor resolved to deny such absolute power and hero worship (**cult of personality**) to any future leader. Although the Party secretary remained the most potent figure in the political system, a new collective decision-making process required him to consult with the **Politburo** (the Party's elite leadership council) and, to a lesser extent, the larger **Central Committee** (the body that technically elects the Party leader). Moreover, although restraints on political dissent by Soviet citizens continued, systematic repression ceased being a fundamental tool of state policy.[6]

In 1956, Nikita Khrushchev, the first secretary of the Communist Party, shocked the Twentieth Party Congress with a historic speech denouncing Stalin's crimes. Although the speech was officially secret, its content became widely known and symbolized the process of de-Stalinization. At the same time, the government released millions of political prisoners from the gulag, and increased individual freedoms. Khrushchev's reforms were limited and his successor rolled back a number of them. Still, he ended the worst excesses of Stalinism and opened up the possibility of subsequent change. His "secret speech" inspired a college-aged generation of future leaders, including President Mikhail Gorbachev (1985–1991), later dubbed "children of the Twentieth Party Congress."[7]

Leonid Brezhnev and the Period of Stagnation

Nikita Khrushchev subsequently launched several major policies that the Party Central Committee considered irresponsible (such as placing Soviet missiles in Cuba and then being forced by President Kennedy to withdraw them). Consequently, that committee ousted him as Party leader in 1964 (making him the first Soviet leader not to die in office). Leonid Brezhnev, who led the country for the next 18 years, succeeded him. Brezhnev's administration was far less innovative and far less tolerant of dissent. The primary features of post-Stalinist politics endured: collective decision making, efforts to improve mass living standards, and increased input from scientific and technical experts. But the Brezhnev regime was obsessed with political stability and, consequently, was unwilling to risk policy innovations. As the Soviet economy began to decay in the 1970s and corruption increased, many government leaders recognized the need for change; but mindful of how Khrushchev's reform efforts had alienated his fellow Party leaders, Brezhnev refused to rock the boat. Subsequently, the Brezhnev years came to be known as "the period of stagnation." Following his death in 1982, two elderly successors as Party leader died in office relatively quickly—Yuri Andropov (1982–1984) and Konstantin Chernenko (1984–1985).

Mikhail Gorbachev and the Origins of *Perestroika*

When Mikhail Gorbachev assumed the leadership of the Soviet Communist Party in 1985, he was the nation's youngest and best-educated leader since Lenin. The country he led had changed substantially in the previous decades. For all its faults and brutality under Stalin, the communist system had modernized an erstwhile underdeveloped nation. Once populated primarily by scarcely educated peasants, the USSR had urbanized and industrialized considerably, with millions of high school and university graduates. The communist system also had provided Russians with the basic necessities of life: free (if mediocre) medical care, cheap (if inadequate) housing, and guaranteed employment.

By the late 1970s, however, that system had fallen victim to both its accomplishments and its failures. It had produced an educated population with a greatly expanded middle class. But increased contacts with the West and greater intellectual freedom led many Soviet professionals and intellectuals to chafe under the limitations of Soviet life—its poor-quality consumer goods, its inefficiencies and long lines, and its lack of political freedom. Gorbachev and his colleagues understood their discontent and recognized the necessity for change. So the new leader and his team committed themselves to greater openness and candor (***glasnost***) about the country's problems to thereby allow restructuring and modernization of society (***perestroika***).

Crisis in the Soviet Command Economy

The push for *perestroika* was motivated principally by the need to remedy the Soviet economy's increasingly poor performance. Thus, before discussing the Gorbachev era, we turn our attention to the economy he inherited, noting both its accomplishments and its failures.

Like all communist nations, the Soviet Union had a state-controlled **command economy**. The centrally planned system maximized the government's capacity to control major economic decisions. From the 1920s until the late 1980s, virtually all the USSR's productive resources—factories, farms, transport, communications, and commerce—were state-owned. Unlike free-market economies, government planners dictated production decisions, wages, and prices, not the market forces of supply and demand.

Economic Accomplishments   Despite its more obvious weaknesses, the Soviet planned economy had a number of important accomplishments, at least in the first half-century of Communist rule (1917–1970). The government turned an underdeveloped nation into a major industrial-military power in but a few decades. Western estimates of Soviet economic performance indicate that from 1928 to 1955, the GNP grew at an impressive average annual rate of roughly 5 percent.[8] "Entire industries were created, along with millions of jobs that drew peasants away from the countryside and into higher-paying jobs and higher living standards."[9] Although growth rates slowed after the 1950s, they still compared very well with those of major industrial democracies. According to the CIA, the total rate of Soviet economic growth from 1950 to the mid-1980s was 50 percent higher than in the United States.* Soviet living standards

* Of course, the Soviet economy was starting from a much lower starting point so it was easier to have a high growth rate than it was for an established large economy such as America's.

continued to improve into the early 1970s as consumers received many goods and services previously unavailable.[10]

The planned economy did not bring the country prosperity or even the amenities that Westerners take for granted. But it did provide economic security, guaranteed employment, and a high degree of equality.[11] Government subsidies gave consumers basic foods and other necessities åt very low and very stable prices. As Soviet specialist Marshall Goldman notes, the state offered the people protection from "the three evils of capitalism": unemployment, inequality, and inflation.

In the post-Stalinist era, with terror no longer the main agent of government control, those economic benefits contributed to political stability. In effect, the government struck a tacit bargain with its subjects in which the state provided economic security and improved living standards in return for which they accepted communist political control.[12]

Economic Weaknesses   By the early 1970s, however, the country's economic growth rate began to slow. Per capita income, which had grown at an average annual rate of 5.9 percent from 1966 to 1970, increased by only 2.1 percent in the five years preceding Gorbachev's administration (1980–1985).[13] Although the command economy had jump-started industrialization, it was unable to advance the country into the next stage of development. Industry and agriculture continued to use obsolete and wasteful production methods.

There were many reasons for the country's economic stagnation. In the absence of price signals, state planners could not ascertain what consumers wanted or determine how to allocate resources. Because the system rewarded factory managers primarily for meeting government production quotas, regardless of production efficiency or product quality, consumer goods usually were shoddy. Furthermore, since workers enjoyed substantial job security but had little opportunity for economic advancement, the system discouraged hard work. As a popular workers' joke noted, "They pretend to pay us and we pretend to work." As long as the Soviet people had limited educations and were only a generation removed from the wretched poverty of the countryside, they appreciated and supported a system that had given them secure employment, cheap food and housing, free medical care, and rising living standards. By the 1970s and 1980s, however, a far more educated population, including a large middle class, wanted more than the basic necessities of life. Many of them desired the improved consumer goods and the freedoms that Westerners enjoyed.

At the same time, the government faced a fiscal crisis. The arms and space races with the United States, substantial foreign aid to the developing world (also in competition with the West), and the Soviet war to restore Afghanistan's Communist government all augmented an already huge budget deficit. Moreover, the government spent far too much on consumer subsidies designed to pacify the Soviet public. One government spokesman noted, "The state pays four rubles, eighty kopecks [cents] for a kilogram of meat and sells it [to consumers] for one ruble, eighty kopecks."[14] From the 1960s until the early 1990s, bread prices never increased. Thus, by the 1980, the subsidized price of bread was so low that it was often cheaper for farmers to feed their livestock bread rather than grain. Total consumer subsidies rose from 4 percent of the state budget in 1965 to 20 percent in the late 1980s.[15] Consequently, wh[en] Gorbachev took office in 1985, the national government's budget deficit wa[s] times higher (as a percentage of GNP) than in the United States.

The Gorbachev Era: Trying to Save Communism

As we have seen, Mikhail Gorbachev's reforms had two major dimensions. *Perestroika* involved restructuring national institutions, with special emphasis on economic reform. Glasnost promised greater freedom of expression in the mass media, the arts, and general political discourse. Yet, beyond a vague commitment to change, Gorbachev failed to develop clearly conceived goals or a plan for getting there. Critics used an old Russian adage to describe *perestroika:* "If you don't know where you are going, any road will take you there."[16]

The Flowering of Political Reform　The Soviet Union's poor economic performance since the 1970 and its evident backwardness compared to the West made a compelling case for economic reform. But the reasons why the new administration also decided to open up the political system are less clear, particularly since Gorbachev remained committed to the single-party state. Ironically, he initially conceived greater political freedom—the change that earned him the most celebrity in the West—not as an end in itself, but as a vehicle for achieving economic change.

How would glasnost (political liberalization) contribute to perestroika (economic restructuring)? Jerry Hough suggested that only by offering middle-class bureaucrats, scientists, technicians, and other professionals greater freedom of expression and increased contact with the West could Gorbachev hope to win their badly needed support for economic change.[17] Furthermore, he knew that his attempts to decentralize the economy would meet stiff resistance from the **nomenklatura**, the nation's large and powerful bureaucratic elite (discussed later), who stood to lose power and privilege. By allowing the media to expose the failures of the system, he might weaken that powerful conservative opposition.

Finally, "a bit of democracy would . . . disarm the suspicions of the West, allowing him to divert resources from the Cold War and to attract foreign investment."[18] Gorbachev's top advisors had enough exposure abroad to know that Soviet economic modernization would require improved trade and communications with the capitalist world. Soviet scientists and administrators needed to be plugged more directly into the information revolution.

But whatever Gorbachev's original motivations were, the political changes during his reign were nothing short of breathtaking. The country's most acclaimed dissident, Nobel Laureate Andrei Sakharov, was released from internal exile, and subsequently elected to the national parliament. Virtually all political prisoners were freed. Television news programs and the press now discussed long-taboo subjects—from airplane crashes to nuclear accidents, from street crime to government corruption. In Moscow and Leningrad, independent newspapers and magazines criticized government policy. Religious freedom was restored. And, at least in the large cities, people lost their fear of freely expressing themselves to each other. In the words of one analyst, "Society . . . learned to talk to itself."[19] Though the USSR was still far from democracy (after all, for most of Gorbachev's tenure it still remained a single-party state), the vestiges of authoritarianism were quickly receding.

Gorbachev's foreign policy reforms were equally dramatic. He extricated the country from its bloody war in Afghanistan, the Cold War effectively ended, and Soviet military expenditures fell sharply. And when the people of Eastern Europe rose up against their communist governments in 1989, the Soviets did not intervene militarily to defend their allies. Ironically, however, as Gorbachev's popularity soared abroad, it declined at home. As the economy deteriorated (discussed below), Russians blamed him for their declining living standard and for a growing sense of chaos.

The Limits of Economic Reform   Gorbachev intended *glasnost* to support economic modernization. Instead, political change hurtled forward while economic reform proceeded at a snail's pace. The administration knew the economy needed repair but seemed to have little idea of how to do it. "Behind Gorbachev's ringing call . . . [for radical reform] stood a vague, incomplete set of generalities of little use in constructing actual reform legislation."[20]

Beyond a series of inadequate or failed measures (including a widely ridiculed campaign against Russia's severe alcoholism problem), one of Gorbachev's few successful economic reforms was the legalization of small private enterprise for the first time since the 1920s. Larger private firms soon emerged, some legal, others not. These included restaurants, nightclubs, taxis, banks, auto dealers, computer importers, construction firms, and black market merchants selling smuggled goods from the West—all of them offering services that the state had not been providing adequately. By 1991, 5.6 million people earned at least a portion of their income from the slowly growing private sector.

A Worsening Economic Crisis   It soon became apparent that, instead of curing the nation's stagnant economy, *perestroika* threw it into reverse. The GNP, which had grown sluggishly in the mid-1980s, now began to plunge. By the Soviet Union's last year (1991), the economy was in a free fall, with GNP dropping some 15 percent annually and industrial production in chaos. Consumer goods became even scarcer and inflation, never an issue in the command economy, further alienated consumers.

A fundamental problem was that the transition from a command economy to a free-market system, no matter how intelligently pursued, is inevitably terribly painful. To maintain full employment, the government had not allowed Soviet firms (all state owned) to lay off unneeded workers, and companies continued operating regardless of their profitability. As one Soviet economist had observed cynically, "Our unemployment is [really] the highest in the world. But unfortunately, all our 'unemployed' get paid."[21] Finally, as we have seen, state subsidies kept consumer prices artificially low.

When the Soviet regime collapsed in 1991, foreign economic advisors and reform-oriented Russian economists advised the new Yeltsin administration that it could only avoid bankruptcy if it phased out consumer subsidies, closed unprofitable firms, and privatized the economy. Only by laying off unneeded workers, they insisted, forcing factories to show a profit, and compelling producers to compete for customers, would production become more efficient, profitability increase, and the quality and array of consumer goods improve. Gorbachev's only chance to save the collapsing Soviet economy in the late 1980s would have been to introduce such measures. But because these reforms would have raised prices sharply (as government consumer subsidies were reduced) and created unemployment in a society unaccustomed to it, the president and his advisors were unwilling to risk the discontent and unrest that these changes would undoubtedly produce. Furthermore, the powerful government bureaucracy and most members of the ruling party, still clinging to old-line communist doctrine, slowed or blocked many of Gorbachev's limited reforms, both because it violated their orthodox ideology and because it threatened their power and material privileges.

Ethnic Unrest and the Breakdown of Control from the Center   Together with the economy, ethnic conflict was *perestroika*'s Achilles' heel. After all, Russians only constituted half of the Soviet population, while the rest came from more than 90 other ethnic groups, 22 of which had populations of 1 million or more—from Ukrainians and Estonians in the west to Muslim Uzbeks and Tajiks in the south. Most had been annexed, against their will, by Russian czars or Soviet communists.[22] The end of systematic political repression under glasnost unleashed ethnic unrest and long-suppressed calls for national independence.

The drive for secession was strongest in the Baltic States, whose populations had been independent between the two world wars. With the USSR's highest educational levels and most advanced economies, Estonia, Latvia, and Lithuania identified more strongly with Western Europe than with the other Soviet republics. There were also strong independence movements in Moldavia, Georgia, Ukraine, and Armenia. By the late 1980s, even Russia, the predominant republic in the Soviet Union, was demanding independence from the USSR. One factor that led Communist hard-liners to attempt an armed coup against Gorbachev in 1991 was their desire to prevent the disintegration of the Soviet empire. Ironically, soon after that coup failed, the Soviet Union dissolved, and all 15 of its republics became independent nations.

THE BIRTH OF A NEW POLITICAL SYSTEM

With half the Soviet Union's population, two-thirds of its area, and most of its economic and military resources, Russia dwarfed the other former republics. Now called the Russian Federation, its president and dominant political leader was Boris Yeltsin. Yeltsin had made himself a popular hero when he criticized the slow pace of Gorbachev's reform and resigned from a powerful leadership position in the Soviet Communist Party. In the 1991 election for president of the Russian republic— Russia's first free election of a leader—he easily defeated the Communist Party candidate.* Two months later, a conspiracy of hard-line generals, KGB leaders (the Soviet internal security force) and Communist Party officials attempted a military coup against Gorbachev. At considerable risk to himself, Yeltsin rallied troops and civilians to undermine that coup. Now, with a huge popular following, he held the upper hand and forced Gorbachev to agree to the dissolution of the USSR at the close of the year. For the remainder of the 1990s, he presided over Russia's difficult and often chaotic transition to capitalism and democracy. Yeltsin himself showed both authoritarian and democratic tendencies. He could be strong and decisive in times of crisis, but at other times was hobbled by indecision, poor health, and alcoholism.

---

* The presidency of Russia—the largest of the Soviet Union's republics—should not be confused with the presidency of the Soviet Union, held by Gorbachev.

The Rise and Fall of Russia's Multiparty System:
From Only One Party to Too Many to Too Few

Following Mikhail Gorbachev's legalization of opposition parties and the subsequent demise of the Soviet Union, Russia moved from one-party rule to a multiparty system. Although the last Soviet era election for the Russian Republic's legislature (1990) had permitted independent candidates to enter (winning 14 percent of the seats), it did not allow political parties other than the Communists to run candidates. By the time of Russia's first post-communist national election in 1995, however, the country had 262 legally registered parties. More than 40 of them fielded candidates for that year's parliamentary elections, of which nearly 10 had significant support.

The Russian Constitution of 1993 established a new national parliament. Initially voters cast two ballots to select the 450 Deputies in the **State Duma**, the dominant house of Parliament. One vote was for a single representative from the voter's district (1 of 225 such single-member districts nationally), and the other was for a party list of candidates. Each party list that had received at least 5 percent of the national vote received a percentage of the 225 proportional representation (PR) seats in the Duma roughly equivalent to its share of the national total. Thus, for example, if the Liberal Democratic Party's list received approximately 20 percent of the party list votes, it would receive about 45 PR seats in parliament. Some parties won several SMD seats but failed to win any through PR. Others won enough party-list votes to secure some seats, but failed to win any single-member districts. Russia's first four contested elections (from 1993 to 2003) used this two-tiered electoral system.

In 2005, however, Parliament approved President Putin's proposal to eliminate the 225 single-member districts and, instead, elect all 450 Duma members through proportional representation. In order for a party to win any seats from its list of candidates, it now needs to receive 7 percent of the vote. While such a change seems reasonable at first glance (many democracies have parliaments elected solely through proportional representation), Putin's intent was clear. In the 2003 Duma election only four parties had reached the less stringent minimum (5 percent) needed to receive seats through proportional representation. Some half dozen others were able to gain seats in the Duma only through single-member-district elections. So, the new rules—first applied in the 2007 parliamentary election—effectively eliminated small parties from the Parliament, including Putin's most outspoken democratic critics. Other legislation has made it harder for parties to register, to form electoral coalitions, and to receive government campaign funding. Fourteen political parties tried to enter the 2007 Duma elections, but the government electoral commission accepted only ten of them. Ultimately, only four parties won any Duma seats (Table 13.1).

We turn now to a discussion of Russia's transition from a single-party system (until 1990) to multiparty competition and, most recently, back to single-party dominance, with opposition parties allowed to run, but with little chance to win more than a token number of parliamentary seats.

The Soviet Union's Only Party   A fundamental requisite of democratic government is free and fair competition between at least two political parties, each capable of winning a national election at some time. Under the Soviet Union, of course, there was no such contestation. From the time of the 1917 revolution until shortly before

TABLE 13.1 RUSSIA'S PARLIAMENTARY ELECTION RESULTS: 1995–2007

Types of Parties	Percentage of the Party List Votes (Total Number of Duma Seats)			
	1995	1999	2003	2007*
Authoritarian Parties				
Communist Party	22.3% (157)	24.3% (110)	12.8% (51)	11.6% (57)
Liberal Democratic Party	11.6% (51)	6.0% (17)	11.7% (37)	8.1% (40)
Center Parties				
United Russia (Unity)	_____	23.2% (74)	38.0% (221)	64.3% (315)
Our Home Is Russia	10.1% (55)	1.2% (7)	_____	_____
Democratic Reformist Parties				
Yabloko	6.9% (45)	6.0% (22)	4.4% (4)	2.6% (0)
Union of Right Forces	_____	8.6% (29)	4.0% (3)	1.0% (0)

*In 2007 all 450 deputies were elected through proportional representation, with no single-member districts. In earlier elections, with half the Duma MPs elected from single-member districts, a party's percentage of the votes for party lists and its percent of Duma MPs often differed somewhat.

SOURCE: American Foreign Policy Council, "1999 [and 1995] Russian Duma Election Results," http://www.afpc.org/; Wikipedia, "Russian Legislative Election, 2007" [with links to 2003 election]; http://en.wikipedia.org/wiki/Russian_legislative_election,_2007.

the collapse of the USSR, the Communist Party had a monopoly of power as "the leading and guiding force of Soviet society." Not only did prominent Communist Party members hold all significant government offices, but the Party's Politburo (composed of some 14–20 of the highest ranking Party leaders), rather than the formal government leaders (the prime minister, president, cabinet, and Parliament), made all major policy decisions.

At its peak in the late 1980s, approximately 19 million people—perhaps 10 percent of the USSR's adult population—belonged to the Communist Party. In all walks of life—in every factory, collective farm, laboratory, and university faculty—there were Party members and Party units. Reasons for joining the Party included a mix of ideological commitment and opportunism. Membership frequently was a prerequisite for preferred employment and also enhanced a person's access to housing and scarce consumer goods. Surveys of Russian emigrants suggest that by the 1980s, personal advancement was a more common motive for joining than political or moral objectives.[23] Even so, its large and diverse membership allowed the Party to penetrate virtually every aspect of Soviet life.

Communist Party power was reinforced by the *nomenklatura* system. This term referred to a vast list of positions within the Soviet state bureaucracy, the military, state-owned enterprises, labor unions, the media, cultural organizations, and professional groups. Appointment to all those posts required Party consent. But "although *nomenklatura* implies only Party approval or confirmation of personnel decisions, in fact the Party often [took] the initiative in filling positions on the list."[24] In common political discourse, *nomenklatura* also referred to the thousands of bureaucrats who held those posts, constituting a tremendously powerful and privileged power elite. Indeed, even after the collapse of communism, they have continued exerting considerable influence through Russia's state bureaucracy and its remaining state-owned enterprises. Furthermore, many former *nomenklatura* members managed to become important players in the country's new private sector.

Russia: From a Fragmented Multiparty System Back to Single-Party Dominance

Although democracy requires a competitive party system, it tends to function poorly when there are *too many* parties. Under those circumstances, it is difficult for any party or even a coalition of political parties to achieve a workable majority in the national Parliament. During the 1990s, Russia suffered from an excess of political parties, many of them highly unstable—forming to advance the interests of a particular political figure or group and then dissolving before the following election. Hundreds of political parties sought legal status that decade, with almost 60 of them legally registered as of 2001.[25]

Approximately 30 political parties or coalitions fielded candidates in the 2003 parliamentary elections, with about a dozen of them winning at least one seat. As Table 13.1 indicates, in the 1995 and 1999 elections [as well as the 1993 contest, not shown] no party came close to winning a governing majority (226 seats). In 2003, however, United Russia (Putin's party) did win almost half. Furthermore, with support from a large number of other parties and deputies Putin became the first Russian president to command a secure working majority in the Parliament. Indeed he ultimately received the backing of two-thirds of all Duma deputies, giving him a "constitutional majority," enough votes to amend the constitution should he want to. Finally, United Russia, with 64.3 percent of the votes cast, secured an overwhelming 70 percent of the Duma seats in the 2007 election. Additional support from other parties gave Putin (and, since 2008, President Medvedev) the backing of nearly 90 percent of the Duma. In short, the parliamentary opposition has been reduced to insignificance. Since the last Duma election (2007), the only opposition to the president has come from the Communist Party. Indeed, it is only the Communist delegation to the Duma that now speaks out against the government's authoritarian behavior (an obvious irony given the Party's history and its continued veneration of Joseph Stalin).

Russian parties run the ideological gamut from communist to fascist. Other parties have been nationalist, liberal democratic (reformist), social democratic, centrist, religious, regional, and "single-issue" (including feminist, agrarian, military, and environmental). But most of the leading parties in the four parliamentary elections held since 1993 fall into one of three broad categories (Table 13.1): authoritarian, "parties of power" (centrist until recently), and democratic reformist. [26]

Authoritarian (Antidemocratic) Parties   For nearly a decade after the country's transition to an electoral democracy, roughly one-third of all Russian voters voted for two to three parties that reject democracy—particularly the Communist Party and the neofascist Liberal Democratic Party. What particularly distinguishes these two parties from the others—one on the far left and the other on the far right—is that they do not admit to being authoritarian, but make few attempts to appear democratic. The Communists, in particular, repeatedly clashed with Boris Yeltsin's government and, to a lesser extent, with Vladimir Putin. On the other hand, since United Russia gained control of the Duma in 2003 and Putin was overwhelmingly reelected president in 2004, the Liberal Democrats have supported most of the president's initiatives.

Although that party's strength declined in the 1999 Duma elections, it rebounded in 2003 and finished third in 2007 (still well behind United Russia).

Unlike reformed communist parties that have staged comebacks in some Eastern European countries after altering their names and ideologies, the Russian Communist Party has done neither. Since many of the Party's most capable leaders (including Yeltsin and many of Russia's current leaders) abandoned it in the late 1980s or the early 1990s, its current leaders are largely hard-liners who rejected Gorbachev's reforms but now claim to accept elements of democracy and the free market. It still advocates a strong role for the state in the economy (including the restoration of Soviet-era welfare measures) and a nationalistic foreign policy that is wary of the West.

Still, with close to one-fourth of the party-list votes in the 1995 and 1999 Duma elections, the Communist Party was the country's leading vote-getter during Russia's first decade of democracy. Only in 2003 did United Russia pass the Communists as the largest party in the Duma. Furthermore, it has finished second in the country's four presidential elections and its leader, Gennady Zyuganov, had been a serious threat to defeat President Yeltsin in 1996, nearly matching him in the first round (Table 13.2).

TABLE 13.2 Russia's Presidential Election Results: 1996–2008

1996 Presidential Elections

	First Round	Second Round
Boris Yeltsin (independent, incumbent)*	35.3%	53.8%
Gennady Zyuganov (Communist Party)	32.0%	40.3%
Alexander Lebed (independent)	14.5%	—
Grigory Yavlinsky (Yabloko)	7.3%	—
Vladimir Zhirinovsky (Liberal Democrats)	5.7%	—

2000 Presidential Election

Vladimir Putin (independent, incumbent)*	52.9%	
Gennady Zyuganov (Communist Party)	29.2%	
Grigory Yavlinsky (Yabloko)	5.8%	
Others, invalid votes, and "against all"	12.1%	

2004 Presidential Election

Vladimir Putin (United Russia, incumbent)*	71.3%	
Nikolai Kharitonov (Communist Party)	13.7%	
Others, invalid votes, and "against all"	14.3%	

2008 Presidential Election

Dmitri Medvedev (United Russia)	70.3%	
Gennady Zyuganov (Communist Party)	17.7%	
Vladimir Zhirinovsky (Liberal Democrats)	9.4%	
Others or Invalid Ballots	2.6%	

*Yeltsin and Putin officially ran as independents, but were backed by various political parties that had been formed largely for the express purpose of supporting them, most notably United Russia, now the country's dominant party and firmly under Putin's control.

Source: Wikipedia, "Russian Presidential Election, 2008" [links to the previous presidential elections], http://en.wikipedia.org/.

However, its percentage of the vote in the 2004 and 2008 presidential elections was only about half its share in the previous two elections, reflecting the Party's dwindling support.

Who are the voters who have given the Communists roughly one-eighth to one-third of the vote in either parliamentary or presidential elections? They have come disproportionately from elderly voters, less educated voters, and the poor, the groups most devastated by the 1990s' economic crisis. Senior voters saw the value of their pensions evaporate in the 1990s due to inflation and, though their situation has improved in recent years, remain in greatest need of the economic safety net once provided by the Soviet Union. Furthermore, they are least equipped to prosper in the emerging capitalist economy. Given the Party's disproportionate share of older Russians and its relative weakness among younger voters, most analysts expected its support to decline over time as increasing numbers of its supporters have died or have become too infirm to vote. The results of the most recent Duma and presidential elections suggest that this erosion has begun. At the same time, the Communists have received support from voters who wished to see the country restored to its place as a world power. In recent elections, however, many of those votes have shifted to United Russia as Putin has appealed to those same nationalistic sentiments

The other major authoritarian party over the past 16 years has been the Liberal Democrats (the LDPR). That party is largely the personal political vehicle of its leader, Vladimir Zhirinovsky. Despite its name, it is neither liberal nor democratic, but is instead authoritarian and intolerant. The LDPR came out of nowhere to win the most votes in the 1993 parliamentary elections (not shown in Table 13.1) and placed second in 1995. One of the most outrageous major political figures in contemporary Russia, Zhirinovsky at various times has advocated dropping neutron bombs on the Baltic states, waging nuclear war against Germany, and annexing former parts of the czarist and Soviet empires, including Alaska and Finland. In the past he voiced his admiration for Iraq's dictator Saddam Hussein. His speeches have often been laced with racist and anti-Semitic slurs. And recently, he was censured by the Duma after a fist fight with a fellow Deputy on the parliamentary floor.

Like other extreme nationalist groups, the party appeals to Russian patriotism and to those who regret the country's loss of superpower status. Russians have historically been distrustful of the West and many now feel that their culture is being polluted by crass commercialism, from McDonald's to the limousines of the nouveau riche. Finally, the LPDR's extreme positions on law and order also attract voters. Zhirinovsky, for example, once pledged to lower the spiraling crime rate by summarily executing 100,000 criminals.

Though its support fell in the 1999 parliamentary election, the Liberal Democratic Party rebounded in 2003 and, to a lesser degree, in 2007, finishing slightly behind the second-place Communists (but far behind United Russia). Since their surprisingly strong showing in the 1993 parliamentary election, the Party has hovered somewhere around 10 percent of the Duma vote. But Putin's aggressive foreign policy and revived nationalism stole much of Zhirinovsky's thunder and left his party little prospect for future growth.

Parties of Power Even though the so-called "parties of power" trailed the authoritarian parties in the three parliamentary elections held in the 1990s (Table 13.1; results of the 1993 election are not shown in this table), they earned that name because of their close association with Presidents Yeltsin, Putin, and Medvedev, as well as other powerful politicians. They have always had close links with the inner circles of the executive branch, which has been Russia's dominant branch of government since 1993. At the same time, however, these parties have been weak in terms of membership, organization, programs, and ideology. Instead, they are little more than a political campaign machine for an incumbent president, a presidential hopeful, or other major politicians. As such, their fortunes have risen and fallen with those of their leaders, with most of them lasting as parties for no more than five years or so.

For example, Prime Minister Viktor Chernomyrdin founded Our Home Is Russia in 1995 to support President Yeltsin's successful re-election the following year. But as Yeltsin's final term wound down and his popularity plummeted, the party collapsed (Table 13.1). Similarly, supporters of former Prime Minister Yevgeny Primakov (once considered the front-runner in the 2000 presidential election) and Moscow Mayor Yuri Luzhkov founded Fatherland All Russia in 1999 to run in that year's parliamentary election and to further Primakov's presidential aspirations. And in that same year, allies of then-Prime-Minister Vladimir Putin formed Unity to run a pro-Putin slate in the parliamentary race and to further Putin's presidential candidacy in 2000. After Unity won the parliamentary election and Putin swept the presidency the following year, Fatherland All Russia merged with Unity to form United Russia. Until that point, most of the "parties of power" were created shortly before a national election and did not last much beyond that campaign.

What distinguishes United Russia from its predecessors has been Putin's apparent success in creating a party that will likely dominate Russian politics for many years to come. In 2003, it became the first party in the post-Soviet era to win a de facto parliamentary majority (its 221 MPs were 5 short a majority, but votes from allied parties gave Putin a working majority). Four years later it won 64 percent of Duma seats and, with its allies, controlled two-thirds of that body. In 2008 (when Putin was constitutionally barred from running for a third presidential term), the party ran a virtual unknown, Dmitri Medvedev, who won 70 percent of the votes. Before ending his second term, Putin became head of United Russia and soon after Medvedev took office he named Putin as his Prime Minister.

Beyond their general, but inconsistent, support for a free market economy, the power parties' views have varied according to the preferences of their leaders. During Yeltsin's presidency, they broadly, though inconsistently, supported democracy. At that time they were called "parties of the center," meaning that they favored democracy more firmly than the authoritarian parities, but less firmly than the democratic reformist parties, described below. Under Putin's leadership, however, United Russia has become the first long-lived party of power as it also has become increasingly authoritarian.

Democratic Reformist Parties   These parties have most ardently and consistently supported democracy and a free-market economy. As Vladimir Putin (first as President, then as Prime Minister) has tightened his grip on power and curtailed the media, the democratic reformists have concentrated on defending Russia's often-threatened civil liberties. At least initially, their party leaders came from two sources: the most ardent economic reformers in the Yeltsin government (former Prime Ministers Sergei Kiriyenko and Yegor Gaidar of the Union of Right Forces) or political independents such as economist Grigory Yavlinsky of Yobloko and former world chess champion

Gary Kasparov.[27] Many have close links to the West and are well regarded by Western politicians and academics. But they have never attracted many voters. As Table 13.1 indicates, neither reformist party received as much as 10 percent of the parliamentary vote. For one thing, most Russians have feared the fast-track transition to free enterprise that ardent reformists favor. The media, generally favoring Yeltsin and Putin, degraded the 2000 presidential campaign by calling reformist candidate Yavlinsky, a "tool of foreigners, homosexuals, and Jews."

Democratic reformers have their greatest support among younger, more educated voters and residents of Moscow and St. Petersburg. By the 2003 Duma elections, however, both reform parties failed to receive the required 5 percent of the party-list vote (proportional representation) and were only able to win a few single-member seats. With the elimination of single-member districts in the 2007 Duma election and a 7 percent minimum for party list seats, the democratic reform parties lost all parliamentary representation. And, under more stringent electoral laws introduced by Putin, reform parties were unable to even get on the ballot in the 2008 presidential election. Thus, for now at least, they are irrelevant to electoral politics.

The Weakness of Russian Political Parties   Most Russian parties have weak organizations, small memberships, poorly articulated ideologies or programs, and limited life spans, all factors making effective governance more difficult. Only the Communist Party and, more recently, United Russia have had a substantial membership and grassroots structure. In the early 1990s the Communist Party claimed 500,000 members, considerably fewer than the roughly 11 million members at the time of the Soviet Union's collapse a few years earlier. For much of the decade its membership was by far the nation's largest. However, as of 2008, fewer than 200,000 people had registered with the government as Party members. Currently, United Russia claims to have nearly 2 million members. But, membership claims by all parties are notoriously unreliable and often dishonest.

As we have seen, most parties, especially the parties of power, have had limited longevity, rarely lasting beyond one or two elections. And many of them were founded just before an election. Thus, Unity (the predecessor of United Russia) was formed only months before the 1999 parliamentary elections, yet still finished first. Shortly after that election it merged with Fatherland All Russia (also established in 1999) to create United Russia. It has no fixed policies or ideology and simply supports whatever Putin favors. Only the Communist Party and the Liberal Democrats have lasted as long as 15 years. And, now with United Russia's dominance, even those two have lost any influence that they had previously exercised.

The Structure of Government: A Centralized Presidential System

The Russian constitution of 1993 created a national government with some elements of a presidential system (as in the United States) and some of a parliamentary system (such as Britain's). The president is popularly elected and if no candidate receives over 50 percent of the vote in the first round, there is a second-round contest, shortly afterwards, between the top two candidates. Presidents serve a four-year term and are limited to two consecutive terms in office. He or she, in turn, appoints a prime minister subject to the approval of the Duma.

The constitution (approved more than a year after the fall of the Soviet Union) culminated a period of intense contestations between the legislative and executive branches, and shifted political power firmly into the hands of the president. In the years since, Presidents Boris Yeltsin and Vladimir Putin often circumvented the Parliament (sometimes in defiance of constitutional procedures) whenever it failed to support them. Since 2003, however, that has no longer been necessary since United Russia has maintained a firm grip of both branches of government. In 2008, when President Medvedev succeeded Putin, and Putin became Medvedev's prime minister, power effectively transferred from the president to the prime minister, though there has been no legal change in their roles and powers. The Parliament, however, remains powerless relative to the Executive branch.

Finally, Russia maintains a federal system that, at least in theory, offers a degree of local control to its still-heterogeneous population. But, as part of a broader centralization of political power, Yeltsin and, especially, Putin transferred considerable political authority from the regional and local governments to the national government.

Parliament and President Yeltsin: The Executive and the Legislative Branches Battle for Power

Following the dissolution of the USSR, the Russian Republic's legislature at that time (as opposed to the now-defunct Soviet Parliament) was automatically transformed into the Parliament of the new Russian nation-state. Until that point, it had worked fairly smoothly with Republic President Yeltsin. That cooperation, however, derived from having a common enemy (Mikhail Gorbachev) and a common goal (removing Russia from the USSR). However, once the Soviet Union dissolved, that consensus quickly collapsed. Yeltsin and his advisors favored a broad range of reforms aimed at creating a more democratic political order and a capitalist economy. Unfortunately, the government's massive budget deficit and the spiraling inflation that the deficit helped produce posed major obstacles to economic progress. In order to reduce that deficit, economists urged the government to slash state subsidies for food and other basic necessities. Since these subsidies constituted a large percentage of the budget, cutting them sharply was clearly necessary. At the same time, however, removing price controls and subsidies would create enormous price increases for Russian consumers. Seeking to present itself as the defender of the common man, Parliament resisted these and other painful reforms. Recall that the parliamentary deputies had been elected in 1991, before the collapse of the Soviet Union, and more than 85 percent of them were Communist Party politicians who had taken office while there were no organized opposition parties. After the fall of communism, most of these MPs, motivated by some combination of conviction and desire to get reelected, opposed painful economic reforms and preferred to maintain elements of the Soviet welfare state.[28]

Conflict between the two branches of government soon intensified, centering on both institutional and programmatic issues. Like Soviet President Gorbachev before him, Yeltsin created a strong presidency, free of significant constitutional constraint by the legislature.[29] Not surprisingly, Parliament became increasingly restive. Differences over how to handle the country's worsening economic crisis (described below) added to the tension. In the new Russia's first year or more (1992–1993), conflicts between the two branches of government focused particularly on two political issues: the nature of a new national constitution and the possibility of early parliamentary and presidential elections. Faced with the prospect of government paralysis, the two sides agreed to hold a national referendum in April 1993, asking voters to express their level of confidence in Yeltsin and his policies and to determine whether there should be early elections. In that referendum, 59 percent of voters supported the president personally, while a slight majority (53 percent) also supported his economic and social programs. At the same time, two-thirds of all voters favored early parliamentary elections, while slightly over half voted *against* an early presidential election.[30] By voting their confidence in Yeltsin and his reforms—however narrowly—and by supporting early elections for parliament but not the presidency, Russian voters seemed to accept—however reluctantly—the need for painful economic restructuring.

But the referendum failed to bring peace. As conflict intensified, each side challenged the other's legitimacy. Yeltsin dismissed Vice President Alexander Rutskoi (one of his leading opponents), dissolved Parliament, and scheduled new, year-end legislative elections. In response, a parliamentary majority determined that the president had acted unconstitutionally in removing Rutskoi (independent analysts agreed) and had thereby lost his authority to govern (independent analysts disagreed). Parliamentary leaders swore in Rutskoi as the new national president and barricaded themselves in the White House, Russia's massive Parliament building. When armed supporters of this rebellion tried to seize Moscow's city hall and a nearby television station, pro-Yeltsin army troops shelled the White House and captured it at a cost of almost two hundred lives.

President Yeltsin had beaten back his communist and nationalist opponents, but it was hard to determine which side had more recklessly undermined the constitution and violated basic democratic principles. By ordering a bloody attack on the nation's Parliament, Yeltsin lost considerable moral standing. As a result, when new parliamentary elections wee held at the end of the year, the big winners were the antidemocratic parties—the Liberal Democrat, the Communists, and parties allied with the Communists. But, with the 1993 constitution greatly enhancing the president's power, Yeltsin could usually dominate or bypass the Duma for the remainder of his administration.

His power, however, was not absolute and his battles with Parliament continued, with the Duma often slowing down his reforms. On the other hand, when Putin became president, he totally dominated the legislative branch from the start of his first term. With United Russia's sweeping victories in the 2003 and 2007 Duma elections, Putin was in complete control.

RESTRUCTURING THE ECONOMY

The worst is over.
—*Boris Yeltsin: October 1992, October 1993, April 1994, July 1997*[31]

Economic Collapse under Yeltsin

Year after year, Boris Yeltsin's economic team tried to turn around the collapsing, postcommunist economy. Each time, President Yeltsin tried to reassure the public that "the worst is over" and that Russia's dizzying economic decline, which had begun in the late 1980s, would finally end. Each time, his reassurances proved false. Indeed, during the 1990s the economy shrank in every year but two (1997 and 1999), sometimes falling as much as 13 or 14 percent in a single year. Overall, from 1990 to 1998, the country's GNP declined by a total of 40 to 50 percent.

Following the collapse of the Soviet Union, many distinguished Western economists flocked to Moscow to advise the new Russian government. With the budget deficit out of control—equaling 30 percent of the country's GDP (gross domestic product)—production declining, and inflation skyrocketing, some type of economic restructuring and stabilization was clearly needed.[32] The International Monetary Fund (IMF), most foreign advisers, and Yeltsin's leading economic planners all agreed that such reforms needed to include privatizing state enterprises, freeing prices (allowing goods to be sold for their free market value), liberalizing trade (removing tariffs and other barriers to imports), and sharply reducing the budget deficit.[33]

Even though these reforms were necessary, labor unions, consumers, most members of Parliament, and some of Yeltsin's advisers opposed them. As we have noted, removing consumer subsidies would sharply increase the cost of living, at least in the short run. Privatizing state enterprises would increase unemployment as the new owners would inevitably lay off many excess workers whom the state had employed for political reasons.[34]

Shock Therapy and Continuing Economic Decline

At the start of 1992, the leading proponent of these reforms (collectively called "**shock therapy**" because of the pain they inflict), Prime Minister Yegor Gaidar, initiated the process by freeing prices on most consumer goods. With government subsidies and price controls removed, prices jumped 345 percent in the month of January alone![35] By late 1993, the government had privatized 81,000 of the country's 196,000 state enterprises, including most retail stores as well as factories that jointly employed 20 percent of the industrial workforce.[36] Millions of Russians became shareholders in the largest industrial firms through a process of government vouchers.[37] As of early 1996, some 120,000 state firms had been privatized. The private sector accounted for more than half the nation's GNP and about two-thirds of its industrial output.[38] No other former communist country has privatized so rapidly.

Still, those reforms did not end the economy's free fall. Instead, things got worse. During the first years of reform, GDP and industrial production dropped more sharply than they had in the United States during the Great Depression.[39] In 1992, the year shock therapy was introduced, *prices rose by 2,520 percent.*[40] It is estimated that 90 percent of the population saw their lifetime savings become worthless.[41] Not until 1994–1995 did the annual inflation rate drop below 300 percent. From 1990 to early 1993, the average Russian's "real wage" (the amount his or her wages could purchase) fell by more than 40 percent.[42] High inflation continued through most of the 1990s. Thus, an item that cost 100 old rubles (the Russian currency) in 1990 would cost 1,270,000 old rubles by 1998.[43] The greatest victims of rampant inflation were the elderly, reduced to poverty as their meager pensions lost half their value.[44] Between 1991 and 1998, the portion of the population living below the poverty line (unable to provide adequately for themselves or their families) rose from 12 percent to 35 percent.[45] Thus, the transition to a market economy was far more difficult than President Yeltsin and his advisers had anticipated.

Furthermore, continuing a trend begun in the Soviet era, infant mortality rose until 2002 and life expectancy declined to Third World levels. During the first half of the 1990s, life expectancy for male Russians, which had been declining slowly since the 1960s, fell astonishingly from 63.8 to 57.3 years. While recovering some ground after 1995, male life expectancy was still only 59.1 in 2007. Russian women—who have lower rates of alcoholism, smoking and violent death (murder and suicide)—can currently expect to live 14 years longer than men, the world's largest gender gap in life expectancy. Currently, Russia's overall life expectancy is only about 65 years, ranking it 119th out of 177 nations in the world, behind such underdeveloped countries as Bolivia, India, and Iraq.[46]

Vladimir Putin and an Economic Boom (1999–2008)

Since Russia's 1999 economic crisis, the country has finally reversed more than a decade of economic decline. Inflation, which had jumped to 86 percent in 1999, dropped the following year to 21 percent and to 10 percent in 2007.[47] While still high by U.S. standards, these inflationary rates were an immense improvement over the 2,500 percent inflation in 1992 or even the 86 percent rate of 1999.

Furthermore, after a decade of falling production, the Russian economy has grown for eight straight years (1999–2007), averaging 7 percent annual growth, twice the world average and surpassed by only a handful of nations.[48] During that period, the average Russian's purchasing power increased sharply, the size of the middle class has nearly doubled, and the country has been able to pay off its large foreign debt. Most importantly, the percentage of the population living in poverty fell from 41.5 percent (1999) to perhaps 16 percent today. Russia's major cities have experienced a construction boom and shopping malls are sprouting up all over.

Yet, impressive as those gains have been, many Russians have still been left behind and many glaring social and economic problems remain unresolved. For one thing, the economic boom has particularly benefited Russia's two major cities—Moscow and St. Petersburg—but has been less beneficial to other cities and of little help to small towns and rural areas. Senior citizens (especially pensioners), children under the age of 16, and unskilled workers are disproportionately poor. Indeed, the country's high level of economic inequality may have worsened during the boom. Russia's index of inequality is currently higher than in any industrial democracy and about average for an underdeveloped country. This has had a particularly negative psychological effect in a country that was once proud of its relatively high economic equality.

Furthermore, although Russia's economic surge has been extraordinary and unexpected, it may be less impressive than it first appears. The primary impetus for the boom has been a sharp rise in the price of natural gas and a major increase in the price of oil—Russia's predominant exports and the motors of its economy. The values of other important exports—timber, metals, and minerals—have also grown significantly. Russia is currently the world's second largest oil exporter (behind only Saudi Arabia), and by 2006 the value of those exports (largely held by state enterprises) reached $200 billion annually.[49] That number rose to about $300 billion the following year and will undoubtedly be much higher in 2008.

But reliance on a single commodity for economic growth has long been a slender reed. Ever since the seventeenth century, when the Dutch economy experienced an enormous boom based on tulip exports, followed by an enormous bust in prices, economists have warned that it is dangerous for a country to depend on a single export commodity for economic growth. Export booms inevitably are followed by a downturn, as high prices eventually drive down demand. Since the OPEC oil crisis of 1973, petroleum prices have reacted similarly. During those oil booms major exporters, such as Mexico and Nigeria, borrowed excessively, overestimated future prices, and were left with huge external debts that burdened their economies for years. Past surges in the price of oil have always been followed eventually by price roll backs (though usually not all the way back to the starting price) and that has already begun to happen with the most recent surge.

Another negative aspect of oil production has been that many major exporters, such as Venezuela and Nigeria, concentrate economic investment on oil—an apparently quick and easy source of wealth—neglecting other sectors such as agriculture and manufacturing. There is evidence that this has happened in Russia where productivity in the manufacturing sector has remained low. Putin has used questionable methods to reassert state control over two of the nation's most modern and efficient oil and gas firms, turning them into corrupt and inefficient state enterprises. Improvements in production have slowed substantially.[50] At the same time, Russia's richest oil fields in Siberia are beginning to run out. Oil and gas revenues currently account for one-third of the national government's budget, and declining output and productivity threaten to weaken the economy at some point down the road.

For now, though, Russia's prosperity following a decade of terrible times earned Putin astonishingly high popularity ratings. It also underlay his landslide re-election in the 2004 presidential elections, United Russia's overwhelming wins in the 2003 and 2007 parliamentary elections, and his protégé, Dmitri Medvedev's, enormous win in the 2008 presidential race.

In fact, the country's economic turnaround had little to do with Putin's leadership or policies. The recovery began shortly *before* he became Yeltsin's prime minister, caused by rising oil prices and the government's 1998 devaluation of the ruble. Putin became acting president at the end of 1999 (when Boris Yeltsin resigned because of health problems), and oil prices took off soon after. Still his administration deserved credit for ending years of weak government and vacillating policies, bringing the country political and economic stability.[51] Putin was, at 48, the youngest Russian leader since Vladimir Lenin. He was a stark contrast to Yeltsin, whose poor health and alcoholism made him an unsteady and unpopular leader during his second term. Putin, a non-drinker and non-smoker with a black belt in judo, exuded a strength and stability that reassured private investors and the public at large. His administration reinforced private property rights so that businessmen could concentrate less on quick profits and more on the long term. And, whereas rivalries between competing government factions had undermined Yeltsin's administration, Putin imposed central authority.

But the Russian economy still suffers from a number of fundamental flaws. The bureaucracy is too powerful and too corrupt. Control of the private sector remains in the hands of a small number of corrupt multimillionaires whose monopolistic holdings exempt them from the discipline of the free market. And, as we have noted, too few Russians have benefited from the economic recovery.

Enduring Obstacles to Economic Reform:
The Russian Mafia, Corruption and More

Even the most competent Russian leaders would have encountered tremendous obstacles in transforming the economy. Eastern Europe's experience has demonstrated that the transition from a command economy to the free market is very difficult anywhere. Only the Czechs and Hungarians managed the change relatively smoothly. It was particularly hard in Russia, which had experienced communist rule for a far longer period of time than its neighbors had. But the **privatization** process was also rife with corruption, with many of the old communist *nomenklatura* using their positions as industrial managers to become wealthy capitalists. In a society where anyone over the age of 25 was raised to value equality, there has been a tremendous rise in inequality. We have noted that the number of Russians living in poverty grew sharply in the 1990s. But increased inequality, not declining GNP, accounted for most of that poverty. Today the poorest 40 percent of the population earns a substantially lower share of the national income than they did in 1991. So, while a large portion of the population struggles financially, the new super-rich financiers and speculators ostentatiously flaunt their foreign luxury cars, jewelry, and expensive, high-fashion clothing.

At the same time, corruption has become pervasive in Russian life. Much of it is linked to organized crime; powerful mafias that have filled the gap left by a declining state (see Box 13-1). As one observer noted, "The market economy in Russia is lawless, like the 'Wild West,' and organized crime controls the distribution of commodities." [52] Thus, a 1994 government report claimed that three-quarters of all Russian businesses paid 10 to 20 percent of their income to the mafia as protection money. Such payments, which still continue, drive up business costs and contribute to inflation. [53] In the late 1990s Russia's Minister of Internal Affairs estimated that "40 percent of the country's private businesses and an even higher proportion of state enterprises are controlled by organized crime." [54]

As a consequence of these problems, Russia has failed to create a healthy capitalist economy. Until recent years, many Russians longed for the time when the state offered them greater economic security than they now enjoy. One opinion poll, for example, indicated that 72 percent of the population believed that the state should provide a job to anyone who needs it. Roughly 50 percent favored some state control over prices and over private business. [56] Similarly, an exit poll of more than seven thousand voters conducted during the 1996 presidential election showed that 58 percent believed that the state should own large industrial enterprises, 26 percent felt that the firms' workers should own them, and only 12 percent favored private ownership. [57]

To be sure, Russia's economic collapse began during the last years of communism (1988–1991), following a decade of economic stagnation. But that meant little to many elderly pensioners, single-parent families, farmers, and others whose living standards eroded greatly during the transition to capitalism. The country's more recent economic surge (since 1999) has reduced nostalgia for the supposed "good old days" of communist economic security, prior to Gorbachev's reforms. But rather than creating support for democracy, the economic recovery seems to have created widespread support for Putin's brand of authoritarianism.

Box 13-1

THE POWER OF THE RUSSIAN MAFIA

How did Russian organized crime become so economically and politically powerful so soon after the collapse of Soviet communism? In fact, despite a police state, criminal groups already existed during the Soviet era. Many of its members had survived Stalin's gulag (prison camps), where they had suffered unspeakable cruelties, and where gangs of inmates dominated prison life, as they frequently do around the world.

Consequently, former prisoners who subsequently joined organized crime families disdained legal norms, rejected government authority, and were prepared to use unlimited force to achieve their goals. Just like the American mafia and other U.S. criminal groups, these crime families were usually initially organized around minority ethnic groups, particularly from Georgia and other regions of the Caucasus (the southern mountain chain located where the Asian and European continents meet). These ethnic minorities had long been victims of discrimination who had limited opportunities to advance in the Soviet Union's Russian-dominated political and economic systems. So, after the fall of communism they quickly moved into new business/ criminal opportunities. Subsequently, ethnic Russians also joined them, many of them former juvenile delinquents, former athletes, or veterans of the war in Afghanistan.

Prior to the mid-1980s, most private enterprises were in criminally based activities—black marketing, prostitution, loan sharking, and the like—since "legitimate" private businesses were not allowed. Consequently, many Russians have believed that private enterprise and criminal activity tend to go hand in hand. So, when President Gorbachev finally opened the doors for limited private enterprise in the late 1980s, organized crime families—commonly referred to as mafia (but unconnected to the American or Sicilian mafias)—had the capital, know-how, and organization to move into legitimate businesses such as consumer-good imports (especially computers), auto dealerships, construction firms, and banking. Often these firms made an abnormally high profit because their owners used violence or threats of violence to drive out competitors. They also allowed criminal organizations to launder income from their continuing illegal activities (drugs, prostitution, and the like).

Following the collapse of the Soviet Union and the emergence of a weak Russian state (especially under Yeltsin), criminals became less fearful of punishment and, in fact, often allied with corrupt police officers. Law-enforcement agencies estimated that there were almost 800 criminal groups operating in Russia before the demise of the Soviet Union, but that figure exploded to some 8,000 by 1996. Of these, roughly one-third operate locally, another third are national organizations, and the final third operates internationally (including among the large Russian immigrant community in the U.S.). Estimates of the number of Russians engaged in mafia activity vary widely from 120,000 to one million. As private businesses proliferated in the new capitalist economy, criminal gangs used strong-armed tactics to eliminate competitors or to offer the emerging class of entrepreneurs protection from physical attacks by their competitors or by their own mafia "protectors." By forcing a huge number of businesses to pay as much as 20 percent of their revenues (not merely their profits), 30 percent in some cities, organized crime has, in effect, levied a tax that has cut private sector profits sharply. Sometimes, mafia protection includes contract killings of their clients' competitors. In addition, mobsters have assassinated a number of journalists and government prosecutors investigating organized crime.

As they have become richer and more powerful, many criminal groups have integrated themselves into the community in order to acquire greater legitimacy. Like their counterparts in the Colombian drug cartels and Japan's crime bosses, they have contributed to local charities and neighborhood activities such as sports leagues. At the same time, they have forged alliances with wealthy businessmen, influential politicians, and members of the Federal Security Service (FSB). The links between the Russian mafia and politicians is strongest at the local or regional level, but sometimes extends into the national government as well. A few major crime figures have been elected to regional legislatures, Moscow city government and even the national parliament. In fact, at times mafia groups have controlled the local governments of several cities, including Russia's major Pacific port, Vladivostok.[55]

© Sergey Ponomarev/AP Photo

A DIFFERENT TONY SOPRANO   Vyacheslav Ivankov and his wife head to court (2005). A Moscow jury acquitted Ivankov, an alleged Russian mafia leader, in two 1992 killings, and freed him.

RUSSIA IN THE EARLY YEARS OF THE TWENTY-FIRST CENTURY: THE PUTIN PRESIDENCY AND AFTER

In December 1999, only months before the end of his second term and the scheduled national election (to pick his successor), Boris Yeltsin resigned from office and turned the presidency over to his prime minister, Vladimir Putin. Three months later, Russians elected Putin to a full presidential term, as he defeated Gennady Zyuganov—once again the Communist Party challenger—by a margin of 53 to 29 percent (see Table 13.2). Thus, he far outperformed Yeltsin, his mentor—who had received only 35 percent of the first-round vote in the 1996 presidential election, edging Zyuganov by a mere 3 percentage points. By winning over 50 percent of the votes in the first round, Putin avoided a second-round run-off.

Putin's popularity initially stemmed from his record as a resolute prime minister, especially his hard-line military policies that eventually crushed the Chechen secessionist movement in southern Russia. Many Russians are prejudiced against the culturally distinct Muslim Chechens, and a number of bloody attacks against civilians by Chechen terrorists induced the public to support the government's brutal response. Tired of Yeltsin's alcoholism and erratic behavior, most Russians approved of Putin's strong and decisive behavior. As one voter put it, "He's someone you don't have to be ashamed of. He's the first normal person to head Russia." [58] With rare exception, Putin's public approval rating stayed at the astounding level of 70 to 80 percent throughout his two terms as president.

REVIEWING THE TROOPS IN CHECHNYA President Vladimir Putin stands with Russian soldiers following an awards ceremony near Grozny, Chechnya. First as Prime Minister and then as President, Putin won popularity at home and condemnation from human rights groups abroad for his policies aimed at crushing the secessionist rebellion in Chechnya at all costs.

Given Putin's very high approval rate and his government's domination of television (the major source of news for most Russians), there was never any doubt that he would easily be reelected in 2004. Indeed, so many of his potential opponents had dropped out of the race that his main problem was insuring sufficient opposition to give his reelection some legitimacy. According to rumors, some candidates were induced to stay in the race in return for favors by **the Kremlin**.* For example, Sergey Mironov, the speaker of the upper house of Parliament and the presidential candidate of the virtually unknown "Party of Russia's Rebirth-Party of Life," did not sound very much like an opponent when he proclaimed during the campaign, "We all want Vladimir Putin to be the next president." Indeed, the president's reelection was so assured that he made only one official campaign speech.

There is much about Putin that has disturbed Russian human rights groups and other proponents of democracy. Following his graduation from law school, he began his career in the KGB, the Soviet Union's dreaded internal security and international espionage service. In 1998, President Yeltsin appointed him chief of Russia's post-KGB domestic security agency, the FSB. As president, Putin raised concerns about his commitment to democracy because of his closed operating style, his promotion of many former KGB and FSB colleagues to prominent posts in government, and his efforts to concentrate power in the central government, particularly in the president's hands. Thus, even at the start of Putin's presidency, when he was still considered a strong ally,

* The Kremlin is a citadel in Moscow that has housed the offices of the governments of the USSR and Russia. It is also a figurative term denoting those governments themselves.

one Western analyst warned, "Now, with the political ascendancy of Vladimir Putin, [the] banality of evil has reached the summit of power in the Kremlin—a situation that should cause more concern to U.S. policymakers than it apparently does."[59]

Continuing the policies that he began as Prime Minister, President Putin pursued his iron-fisted policies toward the rebellion in Chechnya, grossly violating international human rights standards. Subsequently, the government took over Russia's independent television networks and harassed the other news media (discussed below). A number of journalists who had written exposés or criticisms of the government have been jailed or harassed. And Aleksander Nikitin, an environmentalist who helped a Japanese TV crew photograph Russian naval vessels illegally dumping nuclear fuel waste at sea, was arrested and charged with treason. Nikitin said of Putin and the president's secret-service colleagues who were behind the arrest, "There is no such thing as an ex-KGB agent, just as there is no such thing as an ex-German shepherd." Putin later introduced several measures concentrating even greater power in his hands and increasing national government control over Russia's regional governments. Together with various forms of electoral manipulation, Putin cut short Russia's experiment with democracy and has restored authoritarian rule, albeit in a far less repressive form that characterized Communist rule before Gorbachev.

Similarly, Russia's relations with the United States since 2000 have been friendlier than they were during the Cold War, but often more tense than during the Yeltsin years. Following the 9/11 attacks on New York and Washington, Putin strongly backed U.S. anti-terrorist policies (though not the invasion of Iraq), motivated in part by the presence of Islamic (Chechen) terrorists on his own soil. In his first meeting with Putin, held before 9/11, President George W. Bush said of the Russian president, "I looked the man in the eye. I was able to get a sense of his soul . . . I found him to be very straightforward and trustworthy"—words that Bush probably later regretted having said! Since that time, strains between Russia and the West (especially the United States) have increased considerably over issues such as NATO's expansion into former Soviet satellite nations in Eastern Europe, Russian interference in the internal affairs of Ukraine, Georgia and other former communist bloc nations, and the apparent murder (by Russian secret service agents) of a defecting former KGB agent living in London. Thus, while there are still areas of cooperation between Russia and the West, they are often overshadowed by tensions elsewhere.

While Russia's military no longer poses a threat to the West, its foreign policy has increasingly taken on a strongly nationalistic and sometimes hostile tone, a tone that reflects not only the Kremlin's position, but the views of most Russians who are upset with their country's loss of status as a major power. Many outside observers were shocked when, in his April 25, 2005, State of the Nation address, Putin called the collapse of the Soviet Union "the greatest political catastrophe of the last century."[60] Claiming a special interest in its Ukrainian neighbor, the Russian government openly intervened in that country's national election on behalf of the pro-Russian presidential candidate. In 2008, Russian relations with the West hit a low point when its troops invaded two break-away provinces in Georgia to protect them against the central Georgian government. At the same time, however, Putin has tried to maintain friendly ties to the West on some issues and has backed popular international efforts such as the Kyoto Accord on greenhouse emissions and global warming. But, in general, relations between Russia and the West are increasingly strained. For example, in recent months Russia—one of five permanent members of the UN Security Council enjoying veto power—has blocked tougher UN policies toward Iran's nuclear program and Sudan's genocidal policies in Darfur.

PUTIN AND THE CREATION OF AN ALL-POWERFUL PRESIDENCY

When Vladimir Putin assumed the presidency, he inherited a powerful position anchored in Boris Yeltsin's 1993 Constitution, which gave the executive branch dominance over the parliament. But Yeltsin's capacity to fully wield that power had been limited by his ill health, declining popularity (he left office with an unbelievably low 2-percent approval rating), and his frequent negotiations and compromises between different factions (clans) supporting him. Putin has none of these restraints. Consequently, he concentrated political power in his own hands in a manner unmatched since the days of the Soviet Union. As we will see, the respective powers of the president and the prime minister changed markedly in 2008, when Putin stepped down from the first job and assumed the second.

Centralizing State Power

Soon after taking office, Putin announced his plans for a system of "**vertical power**" that concentrates political control and lodges the country's destiny in the hand of its supreme leader (the president).[61] At other times, he has spoken of creating a "guided democracy" and a "managed political system." Like Boris Yeltsin, Putin frequently used the president's authority to issue laws by decree, without parliamentary approval, though that became unnecessary after his United Russia Party swept the 2003 Duma election. He also expanded presidential power in a number of new ways.

One of his goals was to transfer the authority of local and regional governments to Moscow and, ultimately, the presidency. Soon after his election to a first full term (2000), Putin pushed a tax reform bill through Parliament that shifted tax revenue from local and regional governments to the federal government. At the same time, he issued a decree dividing the country into seven federal districts, each headed by a presidential envoy who would allow Putin to manage the country's regional and special ethnic-minority republics. Subsequently, he had the Duma empower him to remove elected regional leaders if the courts (generally subservient to the president) decide that they have violated federal law. He also restructured the Federation Council—the upper house of Parliament originally created to give local officials a say in national policy—by removing regional governors from that body and making membership in the entire Council subject to presidential appointment. More importantly, the Duma passed legislation that ended popular elections of regional governors. Instead, the president, subject to the (assured) approval of Parliament, now nominates them. Legal scholars agree that the bill clearly violated the constitution, but the courts did not strike it down. With that authority, he removed the last independent force in national politics.[62]

Putin's critics were particularly troubled by his frequent appointment to key administrative posts of men drafted from the security services (including many former colleagues from the KGB) and the military, institutions not known for their democratic political culture. Indeed, the strongest of the factions vying for power in the Kremlin today is a group called the *siloviki* (meaning the "group of force" or the "group of power"), composed largely of current and former security—spying—agents (FSB and KGB). As of late 2003:

> Five of the seven heads of Russia's macrofederal districts [were] military or security officers, as [were] . . . 25 percent of the Russian political elite as a whole, representing a

six fold increase in military and security representation . . . since the late Soviet period. . . . Two-thirds of Putin's presidential staff [had] backgrounds in the security services.[63]

More recently (2007), one analyst said of the *siloviki*'s current role, "Never in Russian or Soviet history has the political and economic influence of the security organs been as widespread as it is now."[64]

Putin, the Television Media, and the Oligarchy

Another very troublesome manifestation of Putin's authoritarian tendencies was his war against independent (privately owned) television networks. Two events particularly aroused his ire over media coverage. Only months after he took office, the *Kursk*, a Russian nuclear submarine, sunk while on maneuvers, killing all 118 sailors on board. The media criticized the government's secrecy regarding the cause of the accident, its failure to ask for international help, its rather inept handling of the rescue attempt, and Putin's apparent initial detachment from the rescue. The second source of irritation was the revelation, in the surviving independent media, of military incompetence and brutality in the war to crush Chechnya's secessionist rebellion.

Soon after winning the 2000 election, Putin made it clear that he would not be as tolerant of media criticism or as respectful of press freedom as Yeltsin had been. Although Yeltsin had often manipulated the media, especially during his 1996 presidential campaign, and although his government sometimes intimidated journalists, for the most part he reluctantly allowed media criticisms. Putin, on the other hand, was far less tolerant. In his first annual address to the Russian Parliament, he declared that "sometimes [the media] turn into means of mass disinformation and tools of struggle against the state."[65]

His first major target was Media-MOST, the country's largest privately owned media conglomerate, particularly its NTV television network. Owned by billionaire **oligarch** Vladimir Gusinsky, Media-MOST had offered independent news coverage for almost a decade and was sometimes critical of the government. During the first Chechen war (1994–1996), for example, its reporters had eluded Russian troops to report on their inefficiency and frequent human rights violations. To be sure, when Boris Yeltsin faced a serious challenge from the Communist candidate Gennady Zyuganov in the 1996 presidential race, NTV, like all the oligarchically controlled news media, blatantly slanted its news coverage in the president's favor. But Gusinsky subsequently had a falling out with Yeltsin and did not support Putin in the 2000 presidential election.

Only months after his election, Putin initiated a series of police raids of Gusinsky's businesses, with employees sometimes intimidated at gunpoint. Gusinsky himself was placed under house arrest. A month later, in return for his freedom, he agreed to sell Media-MOST to Gazprom—the national natural gas monopoly that is 40 percent government owned. Shortly afterwards, he fled the country. When the staff of NTV refused to end their criticisms of the government, Gazprom security men raided the network headquarters and ousted those journalists and employees who were not willing to toe the government's line.

Boris Berezovsky is another media oligarch driven out by President Putin. During Boris Yeltsin's administration, Berezovsky had become one of the nation's most powerful men. As part of Yeltsin's inner circle, he had led a group of tycoons who financed the president's reelection campaign in 1996. He not only served in the administration, but was also Yeltsin's personal financial advisor, helping to funnel millions to the president's pocket. In addition to his private holdings—which included a major airline and much of the country's aluminum industry—he received minority ownership and operating control of ORT, the government's largest television network. Even though Berezovsky supported Putin's 2000 presidential campaign, he soon irritated the new president by criticizing his handling of the *Kursk* submarine disaster. With the prospect of criminal charges for fraud and money laundering hanging over him, he fled to England where he was granted political asylum. Soon ORT, like NTV, was faithfully following the government line. Such events have a broader chilling effect, as journalists in privately owned media (including the press) increasingly engage in self-censorship to avoid angering Putin or his advisors.[66]

Although these were the broadest assaults on media freedom, there have been other, more brutal, instances of intimidation. A number of journalists have been detained, some have found it prudent to leave the country, and others have been murdered. One study disclosed that in the year 2003 alone, 20 journalists were assassinated and there were 120 physical attacks on newspapers or their journalists.[67] These continuing attacks have made Russia one of the most dangerous countries in the world to be a journalist. The Kremlin surely has not ordered *all* of these murders. It is likely that the mafia, local government officials independent of Moscow, or even street criminals carried out many of them. But the national government has contributed to an atmosphere of media intimidation and is a likely suspect in many of the most high-profile killings. For example, Russia's most famous investigative reporter, Anna Politkovskaya, was gunned down in her apartment building in 2006. She had become famous for her articles and books on Russia's human rights violations in Chechnya and her criticisms of Putin and the security forces. Years earlier she was apparently poisoned while drinking tea on a flight to Chechnya and, on another trip to that region, she had been arrested and tortured by Russian troops. As with almost all assassinations of Russian journalists, neither the police nor the courts brought any perpetrators to justice. While the authors of Politkovskaya's murder will probably never come to light, most analysts suspect the security forces. Coincidentally (or not) she was murdered on Putin's birthday.

Although some media outlets (particularly magazines) have maintained their independence and journalistic integrity, 90 percent of Russians get their news from television, and the government controls all of the stations with a national audience. As with so many of Putin's authoritarian moves, most Russians have not appeared very concerned. In a nationwide opinion poll, some 80 percent of all Russians claimed that they considered freedom of the press to be important. Yet most of those respondents were relatively indifferent to the government's assaults on NTV and other television outlets. Perhaps because the most powerful media owners ousted by Putin were members of the widely hated capitalist oligarchy, most Russians took some pleasure in their downfall and failed to view the government takeovers as a violation of press freedom.[68]

Putin Against the Oligarchy

Vladimir Putin did not limit his attacks to the leading media barons. He also did battle with oligarchs in other economic sectors, especially targeting those who wielded substantial political power under President Yeltsin, those who tried to exercise political influence during his own presidency, and those who criticized his administration "excessively."[69] Among the most famous oligarchs—along with Berezovsky and Gusinsky—whom Putin toppled was Mikhail Khodorkovsky, then Russia's wealthiest man, whose estimated worth was some 15 billion dollars at the time. In October 2003, Khodorkovsky was arrested on charges of tax evasion, fraud, embezzlement, and theft. While he had quite likely committed a number of these infractions, those crimes were not the reason for his arrest. Nearly two years later, Khodorkovsky and his business partner were convicted and sentenced to nine-year jail terms. (See Box 13-2) Once again Putin's target had little public support, with one poll showing that only 4 percent of all Russians considered Khodorkovsky to be innocent. A number of other tycoons have since decided to flee the country.

In truth, Putin's war on the oligarchs could be justified on a number of grounds. Almost all of the country's new tycoons had acquired most of their wealth through bribery, fraud, and insider connections. They are widely despised because they amassed vast wealth during the 1990s at a time when most Russians saw their standard of living drop precipitously. Russians also resented the fact that Boris Yeltsin was so beholden to several oligarchs who had inordinate influence over government policy. Moreover, at the time that the government had great difficulty balancing the budget, oligarchs had billions of dollars in unpaid taxes. The arrest or threatened arrest of several oligarchs on charges of tax evasion under Putin produced a rapid increase in tax payments, both by oligarchically controlled firms and the private sector generally.

Box 13-2

THE OLIGARCHY: RUSSIA'S NEW CAPITALIST TYCOONS

In the early years following the collapse of the USSR, President Yeltsin and his reformist advisors, such as Prime Minister Yegor Gaidar, looked for ways to quickly privatize the predominantly state-owned economy. There did not appear to be enough wealthy Russian businessmen to purchase all the major state firms and it was politically unacceptable to sell huge chunks of the economy to multinational corporations. One solution was to distribute vouchers to workers in factories set for privatization as well as to the general population. Often, however, workers acquired only 49 percent of the stock in their company, while the former government managers received 51 percent, giving them effective control. The vouchers given to the general public could be traded for stocks in any privatized firm. Although millions of Russians did trade at least a part of their vouchers for stocks, the majority did not. Having lived their lives under communism, most had no understanding of the potential value of their vouchers and they willingly sold them to speculators for a small fraction of their face value. Armed with these vouchers, ties to the Kremlin, and healthy bribes to government officials, these budding entrepreneurs were able to purchase state firms at perhaps 10 percent of their real value, thereby emerging as a new class of super-rich tycoons widely known as the oligarchy.

Most oligarchs emerged from two groups. The first had been directors of the country's major companies during the Soviet era; that is, they were members of the Communist *nomenklatura* who quickly jumped ship in 1992 and turned themselves into so-called *nomenklatura* capitalists. The second group consisted of outsiders, ranging from university professors, to gangsters, to businessmen who had operated in the Soviet black market before the government permitted any private enterprise. Most of the businessmen had begun quite modestly. For example, one future billionaire (Alexander Smolensky) started his business career in pre-perestroika times by illegally selling bibles. Another (Vladimir Gusinsky) used his own car as a taxi. Others had unusual backgrounds, such as Boris Berezovsky, who was a Mathematics Professor in the Gorbachev era. After President Gorbachev permitted small-scale private enterprise, aspiring capitalists began legal businesses in areas such as computer imports, auto imports, and banking. When the Russian economy was largely privatized in the 1990s, these men often used funds from their own banks to acquire control of some of Russia's largest companies (at highly discounted prices), particularly in natural resources

(Continued)

Box 13-2

THE OLIGARCHY: RUSSIA'S NEW
CAPITALIST TYCOONS   (*Continued*)

such as oil, gas, and metals.[70] For example, in 1995, Mikhail Khodorkovsky and his associates bought Yukos, Russia's second-largest oil company, for $159 million, only about 5 percent of its real worth.

All told, some estimates suggest that Russia's 10 to 30 richest oligarchs controlled almost half of Russia's gross domestic product by the late 1990s. More cautious assessments in 2004 suggested that the combined wealth of the nation's 36 richest tycoons ($110 billion) equaled one quarter of the nation's GDP at that time. Shortly before the country's 1998 severe financial crisis and only two years before Putin became president, Forbes magazine included five Russians in its list of the world's billionaires. By 2007, 53 Russians made the Forbes listing, almost double the previous year's total and the third highest number for any nation in the world (even though

Russia ranked only 62nd in the world in per capita income). The number of Russian billionaires also has been growing more quickly than anywhere else on earth and, having acquired their wealth more recently, they were, on average, 20 years younger than the rest of the world's billionaires on the Forbes list. By 2008, Finans, a Russian financial journal, claimed that the number of Russian billionaires had almost doubled to 101, though that number is likely exaggerated.[71]

Some oligarchs established close links with President Yeltsin, and a number of them were largely responsible for his reelection in 1996 by bankrolling his campaign and giving him nearly exclusive campaign coverage on their television networks. They initially hoped to have a similar relationship with Vladimir Putin and supported his 2000 presidential campaign. But as we will see, he soon turned against a number of them.

But there is also good reason to suspect Putin's motives. His attacks on the oligarchy targeted only those who had criticized him or supported opposition political groups. Mikhail Khodorkovsky, for example, had funded the election campaigns of many Duma deputies who were seemingly indebted to him. Some analysts estimated that perhaps 100 of the nation's parliamentary deputies (almost one fourth of the Duma) had received significant campaign contributions from him. Seeing him and other oligarchs as potential political challengers, Putin warned them to stay out of politics. Khodorkovsky, who mistakenly believed he was untouchable, not only involved himself but funded opposition candidates while indicating that he might run for president in 2008.[72] Other tycoons, like Roman Abramovich (now living mostly in London where he is ranked as the United Kingdom's second richest man) maintained excellent ties with both Yeltsin and Putin. Another oligarch, Oleg Deripaska, is Putin's close skiing companion. Worth $29 billion at the age of 40, Deripaska was then Russia's wealthiest man and the ninth richest man in the world. The Putin government also did not crack down on another important group of multimillionaires, the mafia. Perhaps this is because many Russian mafia tycoons were once the president's colleagues in the KGB. In their case, the government continues to tolerate "shareholder abuse and corporate looting."[73]

Thus, while Putin's attacks on key oligarchs were widely applauded and bolstered his popularity, he seemed to be more interested in asserting the central government's power than in cleaning up Russian capitalism. The administration also believed that control of Russia's most important exports—oil and natural gas—should be controlled by the state rather than by private firms. In this case, then, to pay the billions of dollars in taxes that Yukos—Khodorkovsky's giant oil company—allegedly owed, the firm was turned over to Gazprom, the state-controlled natural gas company. Overall, the oligarchs continue to dominate the economy, but have lost the enormous political power they once wielded under Yeltsin. When the Russian stock market collapsed in 2008, many oligarchs saw their total worth fall by as much as 90 percent. Whereas the Yeltsin government was subservient to them, Putin reversed that power relationship.

Presidential Power After Putin's Presidency

Given his absolute control over the Duma and all sectors of Russian government, Vladimir Putin could easily have directed Parliament to change the national constitution so as to permit him to run for a third consecutive term in office. For whatever reason, he chose not to. Instead, he selected his long-time aide, Deputy Prime Minister Dmitri Medvedev to be United Russia's presidential candidate in 2008. The very next day (and before the Party had even nominated him), Medvedev showed who was in charge by announcing that, should he win the presidential election (an apparent certainty given Putin's backing), he would select Putin as his prime minister. Since Dmitri Medvedev's entire political career, culminating in his nomination for president, had depended entirely on Putin, since Medvedev was virtually unknown to the Russian public before Putin tapped him, and since he had no power base in the Kremlin, almost all analysts assumed that, at least at the start of his administration, the new president would largely be a figurehead while Putin called the shots. Indeed, before Putin finished his presidential term, Parliament passed several bills transferring a number of powers from the next president to the prime minister. Putin's control of his protégé totally reverses the president's prior dominance over the prime minister, which had marked the entire Yeltsin and Putin administrations. While it is still possible that eventually Medvedev may use his constitutional powers and newly acquired political weight to reassert the president's authority, events during his early months in office indicate that it is extremely unlikely. At some point in the future, Putin may either retire from politics or, far more likely, may again run for president (the constitution only bars three *consecutive* terms). Undoubtedly, political power would then revert to the president.

CONCLUSION: THE TRANSITION TO DEMOCRACY DERAILED

Much has changed in Russia since 1990. The country has some aspects of an electoral democracy, regularly holding somewhat free (though no longer fair) competitive elections. But after halting steps toward liberal democracy under Boris Yeltsin (democracy that guarantees basic freedoms to groups and individuals), it has moved further from that goal in recent years. The country lacks adequate safeguards for civil liberties and a free press (media), and public attitudes toward democracy are ambivalent (see Box 13-3). It has established a primarily capitalist economy, but large portions of that economy are still in government hands, belong to organized crime, or are controlled by political insiders with illegitimate government connections.

Major political and economic transitions are never easy, nor are their outcomes guaranteed. For example, the initial euphoria that followed the overthrow of dictators in Iran, Ethiopia, and Nicaragua during the 1970s and 1980s was soon dispelled by the rise of new forms of authoritarianism. Much the same seems to be happening in contemporary Russia.

As we have seen, Russians endured a tremendous deterioration in their living standards throughout the 1990s (a decline that actually began in the last decade of the

Soviet Union). Since 1999 Russians have experienced nine consecutive years of economic growth, with widespread improvements in their living standards. Yet other problems have persisted: high crime rates, rampant government corruption, and the virtual collapse of the social-welfare safety net that previously afforded citizens some protection from poverty. That there were few riots and little political turmoil (with the obvious exception of the Chechen rebellion) in the 1990s is a testament to the Russian people's forbearance. Unfortunately, however, that economic crisis made many people, perhaps most of them, far more concerned about their standards of living and personal safety than about civil liberties and democracy (See Box 13-3). Consequently, their satisfaction with the current economic boom has led them to accept a return to authoritarianism.

The Economic Challenge

The privatization of the Russian economy and the growth of the private sector have been sweeping and are likely irreversible. After a decade of calamitous decline, the economy has enjoyed robust growth since 1999. Inflation has been brought down from the astronomical levels of the early- to mid-1990s. The average standard of living

---

Box 13-3

RUSSIAN ATTITUDES TOWARD DEMOCRACY

In trying to predict the prospects for democracy in Russia, one important area of investigation is the country's political culture and political attitudes. On the one hand, political scientists generally believe that countries with little or no democratic tradition, such as Russia, are less likely to successfully complete the transition to democracy than are countries with prior democratic experience such as Chile or the Czech Republic. At the same time, however, as we saw in Chapter 3, after World War II, countries such as Germany and Japan, with little democratic tradition, re-created their political cultures through active re-socialization. Furthermore, scholars have ascertained that the more countries in the world that are democratic or in transition to democracy, the greater the likelihood of a particular country making a successful transition. So, what have Russian attitudes toward democracy been in the 17 years since the fall of communism?

A large body of public opinion surveys conducted by Russian and foreign institutions suggest a somewhat contradictory pattern. On the one hand, in a huge number of surveys over the years, most Russians have expressed their support for democracy and have been fairly optimistic that Russia has or will achieve it. On the other hand, many Russians who claim to support democracy also approve of very undemocratic behav-

ior by their government. Even in a well-established democracy, such as the United States, citizens may have very different interpretations of what democracy means. Not surprisingly we find even more variation in a country such as Russia, with no democratic tradition.

One major survey conducted early in Putin's presidency found that 64 percent of Russians supported democracy in principle, while only 18 percent were against it. They also agreed overwhelmingly (87 percent) that freedom of their own convictions, freedom of expression, and freedom to elect their own leaders were important to them. A similar number (81 percent) said that media freedom (the press, television, and radio) was also important to them.[74] By 2006, in the last quarter of Vladimir Putin's administration, support for democracy (in the abstract) had diminished. The number who now agreed that democracy was the best form of government had fallen to 57 percent (most of whom only agreed "somewhat"), while the proportion that disagreed had increased from 18 percent to 34 percent. Even so, the number of Russians who supported democracy as the best form of government was considerably higher than those who did not.[75]

But in spite of this generalized support for democracy in the abstract, Russians have given non-democratic parties the largest number of votes in each of the five

has recovered from the losses of the 1990s and reached new heights, though they are still quite low by Western standards. But serious weaknesses and concerns remain. We have noted that Russia's recent growth is precarious in nature, as it is built primarily on soaring oil prices. But, historically, oil prices have always dropped significantly (in real terms) from their high points following their upward spike. Indeed, the 2008 world economic crisis has already caused those prices to decline substantially from their peak.

Income inequality, which rose enormously in the early 1990s, has not declined since that time. As of 2002 the richest 20 percent of the population earned 40 percent of the nation's income (up from 30 percent in 1991), while the poorest 20 percent of all Russians earned only 6.4 percent. Regional differences are also wide. For example, per capita income in Moscow is more than three times the national average. Overall, Russia's distribution of income is far more unequal than that of Western Europe, and more closely resembles the profile of a developing nation.[78] We have noted that life expectancy for men has declined to shocking levels, medical care has greatly deteriorated, and the population is growing smaller. Several years ago, the World Health Organization (WHO), citing the unresponsiveness and injustices of Russia's

---

parliamentary elections since the fall of communism: the Liberal Democrats in 1993, the Communists in 1995 and 1999, and United Russia in 2003 and 2007. At the same time, the parties most clearly committed to democracy—Yabloko and the Union of Right Forces—have consistently finished toward the bottom, with each of them sinking to less than 3 percent of the vote in 2007.

Russian public opinion also overwhelmingly supported President Putin despite his implementation of measure after measure to restrict democracy. Indeed, Putin's approval rating among voters hovered around 70 percent throughout his two presidential terms, a remarkable accomplishment for any political leader. More perplexingly, while most Russians have professed support for democracy, they repeatedly endorsed Putin's authoritarian policies. Thus, for example, by a margin of 56 to 21 percent (the rest being undecided), they supported increased government control over the media. Some 43 percent supported government restriction on human rights groups, while only 32 percent opposed. When President Putin ended the direct election of regional governors and, in effect, turned governors into presidential appointees, 45 percent of all Russians had no opinion of that important authoritarian measure, 37 percent supported it, and only 18 percent opposed it.

We must conclude that, even though a majority of Russians still claim that democracy is the best form of

government, most do not supported liberal democracy as practiced in the West. For example, the 2006 survey asked which model of government "had more to offer Russia—A liberal democracy, as in the United States, or a more centrally controlled government, as in China." By a margin of 44 to 33 percent respondents favored the Chinese model.[76]

It appears that when many Russians say democracy is the best form of government, their concept of democracy is substantially different from the Western, liberal-democratic definition. Rather than encompassing civil liberties, an independent media, and an active civil society, their definition tends focus on a form of government than serves the economic and social needs of the people, one that brings stability, law and order, and greater prosperity. In view of the enormous decline in living standards during the 1990s and the sharp rise in crime, this attitude is very understandable. So, during the 2004 presidential election, when a public opinion survey asked which of Russia's current political leaders were most democratic, the two most popular choices were Putin (despite his having reduced democratic rule considerably) and Neofascist Vladimir Zhirinovsky (possibly the least democratic of Russia's leading politicians). Respondents selected both men twice as often as either Irina Khakamada or Grigory Yavlinsky, the two presidential candidates most committed to liberal democratic reform. [77]

medical-care system, ranked that system 130th out of 190 countries in the world, placing it behind less developed countries such as Yemen, Pakistan, Peru, and Bolivia.[79] Tuberculosis, a major killer, is at more than twice the rate that the WHO considers to be an epidemic. Despite the government's enormous increase in oil revenues and Putin's pledge to make health care a priority, a leading Russian physician recently estimated that over two-thirds of the country's medical equipment was "worn out" and its stock of drugs was more than 30 percent below its needs.[80]

The manner in which privatization took place has harmed the transition to capitalism. One of the strengths of the free market is that it fosters competition between business enterprises. In Russia, however, state monopolies were sold to oligarchs as private monopolies. Just as the old state monopolies had been managed inefficiently, the new private ones, not burdened with competition, are also poorly run. Small wonder that, in a 2003 survey, "77 percent of Russians believed that the results of the country's privatization process should be fully or partially revised."[81] Corruption is also rife as businessmen often have to pay off organized crime groups (the Russian mafia) as well as government officials. According to one respected survey, in 2005 Russians paid government officials $3 billion in bribes, while businesses paid as much as $316 billion—more than twice the size of the national budget. A 2005 World Bank study found that 78 percent of all Russian businesses pay bribes to government officials. That includes nearly $600 million paid to university administrators, deans, and professors by students entering university since such bribes are virtually obligatory for admission. Others report having to pay small bribes to get the results of lab tests at hospitals.[82]

Putin's crackdown on certain oligarchs for fraud and tax evasion could have contributed to greater honesty in the business world had it been fairly applied. But his government only prosecuted tycoons who antagonized him. Furthermore, when it chose to prosecute some oligarchs, the government treated them arbitrarily, with no regard for their civil liberties.

Political Decay: Turning Away from Democracy

As Russia closed out the twentieth century and the Yeltsin administration, its political system remained unsound. Surely Yeltsin had serious flaws. He seized excessive presidential powers and undermined the Parliament. He was far too closely connected to corrupt oligarchs. His 1996 presidential victory over a Communist Party opponent was not a fair contest, as the mass media (primarily owned by the oligarchs) were totally biased in his favor and gave his opponent virtually no coverage. Still, aside from that campaign, the media could and did criticize the government. Duma elections were relatively fair and honest. In fact, opposition parties outpolled Yeltsin's supporters in every parliamentary election in the 1990s. Thus, Freedom House (a highly respected research center, created to further democracy) rated Russia as "partly free." Many analysts expected further progress toward consolidated democracy, especially if the economy improved.

But, although President Putin presided over an unexpectedly strong economic recovery, he turned the country away from democracy. In its 2004 report on democracy in the world, for the first time in years, Freedom House lowered its rating of Russia from "partly free" to "not free."[83] To be sure, despite the many authoritarian aspects of Russian politics today, the political system is still far more open and less repressive than it had been under the communist regime in the Soviet Union. Nonetheless, the resumption of authoritarian practices fell into several broad categories.

Centralizing Federal Power   When Russia exited the Soviet Union it was a federation of over eighty federal units (republics, region, districts, territories, and federal cities). Indeed, the country's official name is the Russian Federation. From the outset, the central government in Moscow dominated the various federal units, but a number of institutions and practices gave those units some independence. For example, the 1993 constitution created an upper (less powerful) chamber of the national parliament, called the Federation Council, which consisted of two senators from each federal unit. They were not popularly elected, but were, instead, chosen by the local legislatures and governors (much as U.S. senators were originally elected by their state's legislature). During Yeltsin's presidency, governors and other regional political bosses exercised considerable power in their own domain and the president often needed to negotiate with them regarding his programs.

All of that changed under Vladimir Putin. First he gained control of the courts, electoral commissions, and prosecutors in those regions, allowing him to influence their selection of senators. Thus, one important component of democracy—the rule of law, including an independent judiciary—was seriously undermined. Once independent of the president, the Federal Council soon began approving all of Putin's important initiatives. To further solidify Moscow's control, in 2004 an obedient national parliament passed legislation ending the popular election of the federal units' governors. Instead, the president now appoints governors, subject to the confirmation by (compliant) regional legislatures.

State Control of the Media   During the 1990s, media freedom expanded impressively. In particular, independent newspapers, magazines, television and radio broadcasters, and book publishers offered a variety of voices, from lurid tabloids (complete with pinups and outlandish rumors) to serious analysis and independent criticisms of the government. Of courses, oligarchs owned the nation's major television networks and newspapers, and the media was not very objective. Too often these media moguls had too cozy a relationship with the Yeltsin administration. But at other times, even the oligarchical media outlets offered objective criticisms of government behavior.

Like so much else, this changed dramatically when Vladimir Putin took office. We have already discussed the government's takeover of major television networks, often forcing their previous (oligarchical) owners to flee the country. Television news now supports the administration's line almost as slavishly as it did in the Soviet era prior to *glasnost*. Opposition candidates in recent presidential and Duma elections receive very little media coverage.

There are still a number of journalists, newspapers, magazines, and book publishers that offer independent news and opinions, including criticisms of government human rights and environmental policies. Frequently, though, they are harassed or crushed by the state. In 2006, the international "Committee to Protect Journalists" found that Russia had the third most newspersons murdered among all the world's nations.[84] The government has also occasionally reintroduced a method of intimidation not used since Soviet times. Through 2007, a total of almost 20 reporters had been forcibly committed to psychiatric wards. Though the number of such victims to date is relatively small (normally fewer than five per year), it only takes a few cases to intimidate many others. In 2008 the international watchdog group, "Reporters Without Borders," rated Russia among the countries of the world with the greatest threat to press freedom. Other forms of media control have not involved violence. Several hosts of popular television talk shows have recently revealed that their networks have imposed so-called "stop lists," naming government critics who should not be invited onto their shows. Other, "softer" intimidation techniques include tax audits of journalists who are too critical of the government and police raids of independent publications for alleged fire or safety code violations.[85]

Restricting Civil Society A healthy civil society—a dense network of social organizations independent of government control—is a critical component of a democracy. In the Soviet era, civil society hardly existed as the Communist Party and the state controlled all significant organized groups: unions, professional organizations, women's groups, youth groups, and even the Russian Orthodox Church. State control largely disappeared after the fall of the Soviet Union as a range of independent organizations emerged, some quite critical of the government. Estimates of the number of functioning NGOs (non-governmental organizations) ranged from 60,000 to 350,000 (possibly even higher). Whatever the actual number, it is enormous compared to the Soviet era, but still relatively small (on a per capita basis) compared to the number of NGOs in the United States (the Boy Scouts, Shriners, NRA, NAACP, Little League, and so many more). So, most experts felt that Russian civil society remained week under Yeltsin, not because his government repressed it but because Russians had little experience with NGOs and were reluctant to join.[86]

Even so, when Putin took office his plans for a "managed democracy" called for greater control over NGOs and civil society. A number of independent groups were devoted to causes such as monitoring human rights, protecting the environment, and defending women's rights, sometimes criticizing the government or exposing government misbehavior. Some of these groups received funding from abroad or had ties to international groups such as Greenpeace and Amnesty International. This made them particularly suspect to Putin and the nationalistic *siloviki* in important government positions. A 2006 bill required NGOs to register with the government by filling out an enormous amount of paper work. The information demanded is so complicated and often vague that the process affords the authorities ample grounds for denying recognition to almost any group. NGO activists are periodically harassed, especially those with ties to international organizations.

Intimidating Opposition Group Activity Despite Putin's enormous re-election margin in 2004 and his extremely high ratings in subsequent public opinion polls, his administration still felt compelled to intimidate and subdue remaining pockets of opposition. Any group wishing to hold a public demonstration or rally needs official permission, something the authorities frequently deny to opposition groups. If groups that have been denied permits decide to hold their rallies anyway, the police often attack them. As with the press, security officials may subject opposition groups to a range of bureaucratic and legal harassment: burdensome tax audits, raids on the groups' offices in which the authorities temporarily seize their computers for some imaginary violation, such as failure to pay the import tax on those computers. Some groups have been evicted from their offices by their landlords (spurred by government pressure) and have then found that nobody will rent space to them.

Subduing Opposition Political Parties   In the first three Duma elections held after Yeltsin's constitution (1993, 1995, 1999), between 9 and 17 political parties were able to win some parliamentary seats as were a significant number of (non-party) independents. Never did parties supporting Yeltsin win anywhere close to a parliamentary majority and only in 1993 did they even win the largest number of seats (tied in that year with the Liberal Democrats).

When United Russia, Putin's party, won a working majority in the 2003 parliamentary election, the president set out to undercut many of the opposition parties. By eliminating single-member districts, changing the election of all 450 Duma members to proportional representation, increasing the number of signatures needed to get on the ballot, and raising the percentage of the vote needed to win any Duma seats at all from 5 to 7 percent, the government eliminated representation for non-party candidates and shut out a number of small parties, including those most forcefully advocating liberal democracy. In fact, in the 2007 Duma election, the number of parties that won seats fell to four. Other electoral changes made it far more difficult for parties to place candidates on the presidential ballot. Whereas the 1996 and 2000 presidential election featured 11 candidates (some with miniscule amounts of votes), by the 2008 race there were only four.

Both the 2007 Duma election and the 2008 presidential election (won by Dmitri Medvedev) showed substantial evidence of fraud at every stage. Two statistically trained bloggers examined the official figures on voter turnout and found a very improbable number of voting districts that allegedly had 100 percent turnout (everyone registered to vote did so). Not surprisingly, Medvedev and United Russia carried all of these by huge margins. In fact, in one such district (where official tabulations claimed a 100 percent voter turnout), almost half the registered voters later signed a petition saying they had not voted. Ballot boxes throughout the country were stuffed, often with absentee ballots, which were particularly easy to fabricate or forge. The number of absentee ballot requests for the 2007 Duma election (2.4 million) was four times as high as in the 2003 parliamentary race, a jump that could only be explained by electoral fraud.[87] Thus, such evidence of electoral fraud led the UN-sponsored "Electoral Observer Group" of the Organization for Security and Co-operation in Europe (OSCE) to characterize the 2007 Duma election as neither free nor fair. In the lead-up to the 2008 presidential election, the Russian government placed so many restrictions on the activities of outside election-observer groups that the OSCE Observer Group decided not to monitor the vote.

What Lies Ahead: The Mexicanization of Russian Politics?

Despite its regression to authoritarianism, Russia today remains a far cry from the Soviet system. The number of people jailed or murdered for political reasons is miniscule compared to the Stalinist era or even Brezhnev's reign. No longer do millions of secret police informants spy on their friends and relatives. Opposition political parties contest elections and sometimes win a small minority of the contests (as, for example, in the Duma). A number of independent think-tanks and democratic politicians still speak out against government excesses. And while the government controls the major broadcast media, there are still independent journals, newspapers, and books that criticize government policy. Indeed, Putin's Russia is a country with fundamentally authoritarian politics coupled with some democratic elements.

In many ways it has a political system reminiscent of another country discussed in this text, Mexico (Chapter 16). It is unlikely that Putin and his team consciously emulated the Mexican political model, but much of what they have done in the past decade is strikingly similar. In the late 1920s, after years of civil conflict, the leaders of the Mexican Revolution (1910–1920) created a governing party, later to be named the PRI. That "official" party united the victorious revolutionary factions and dominated national, state, and local politics for the remainder of the twentieth century. Opposition parties fielded candidates in regularly scheduled elections for president, congress, and state governors, but until the system began to unravel in the 1980s, they never won more than a token number of offices, much like opposition parties in today's Russia. At least for now, United Russia has become (like the PRI) the nation's "official" party. In fact, most Russians today would choose United Russia in a fair and honest election, just as most Mexicans had supported the PRI for some seventy years. But in both countries the government has given the official party unfair advantages, padded its vote total, and used fraud and intimidation when necessary. In both twentieth century Mexico and contemporary Russia, the government has been enormously corrupt and has used repressive tactics on selective (and infrequent) occasions. And, finally, both political systems concentrated enormous power in the executive branch's hands.

One of the distinctive characteristics of Mexico's authoritarian system distinguishing it from typical dictatorships was that its constitution strictly limited the president to a single, six-year term with no possibility of ever running for that office again. Unlike countries such as Cuba, Libya, North Korea, and Zimbabwe, where presidents have ruled for decades, Mexico's all-powerful presidents stepped down after each six-year term and anointed a hand-picked successor, who then became the PRI's next presidential candidate, and whose victory was assured. A decade before the PRI's domination collapsed, Mario Vargas Llosa, the famed Peruvian novelist and political activist, referred to Mexico as "the perfect dictatorship." By this he meant that the combination of supposedly competitive elections and single-term limits (imposed on all elected officials) gave the country the appearance of democracy and helped legitimize the system abroad and among its citizens.

Today, with more exacting world standards of democracy and closer international scrutiny, Putin's behavior has been more severely criticized abroad than Mexico's government was before 2000. But, within Russia itself, he has so far successfully established his own "perfect dictatorship." Russia's constitution limits the president to two consecutive four-year terms, a limitation that Putin chose to accept. As with former PRI presidents, he anointed a new candidate for the official party, a candidate whose electoral victory was assured. But Vladimir Putin's political project has differed from Mexico's twentieth-century model in several important respects. To begin with, while Mexican presidents are barred from ever seeking that office again, the Russian constitution simply limits the president to two consecutive terms. Thus, after Dmitri Medvedev has served one or two terms as president, Putin is free to run again. In fact, should Putin force Medvedev to resign before his first term ends, the constitution stipulates that the Prime Minister (currently Putin) would temporarily succeed him until a new election was scheduled (an election in which Putin would be eligible to run).

Another important distinction is that once a Mexican president completed his term, he not only could never run for that office again, but he relinquished any personal political power. Obviously this has not been the case with Putin who appears to dominate President Medvedev. Finally, one of the geniuses of Mexico's old authoritarian system was that, although the president controlled the government and the PRI during his six-year term, in the long term power resided in the party-state. That power endured for over seventy years. On the other hand, for now, United Russia is no more than a support group for Putin. For now, its power could not survive beyond him and he has yet to develop, if he ever will, a mechanism for transferring real power to a successor. On the surface President Medvedev appears to be more open to democracy and to the West than his predecessor. Unlike so many other powerful figures in Russian politics today, including Putin, he has no prior links to the security services. He has a much warmer and personable manner, is known to like the West (including Western rock bands), and has spoken out on several occasions about the need to fight government corruption and expand civil liberties. But, as we have seen, unless he is able to wrest some political power from Putin (and so far he has shown little inclination or ability to do so), these views are likely to mean little in terms of government policy. More so than any country discussed in this text, Russia's political system remains in flux.

 # WHERE ON THE WEB?

www.russiavotes.org/

University of Strathclyde (Britain) site on Russia; provides information on Russian elections, public opinion, and contemporary politics.

www.themoscowtimes.com/

The *Moscow Times* Web site is a useful English-language newspaper. Its coverage is considered balanced and objective.

http://wciom.com/

An enormous source of information on Russian public opinion compiled by the *Russian Public Opinion Research Center* (VCIOM). Survey topics are primarily related to Russian politics, but also cover a wide range of subjects including what men and women value in the other sex; and preference (in early 2008) for Clinton vs. Obama. Note that some of the articles are in Russian.

http://www.pbs.org/newshour/insider/europe/jan-june08/ russia_03–05.html

Two specialists discuss Russian politics shortly after the March 2008 presidential election on the "Online News Hour," an offshoot of PBS's widely respected "News Hour with Jim Lehrer."

◆ ◆ ◆

Key Terms and Concepts _____

absolutism	nomenklatura
Bolsheviks	oligarch (oligarchy)
Central Committee	perestroika
civil society	Politburo
collectivization	privatization
command economy	proletariat
cult of personality	shock therapy
dual transition	Siloviki
Duma (State Duma)	vanguard party
FSB	vertical power
glasnost	the Kremlin
gulag	

Discussion Questions _____

1. What is a command economy? What were the major accomplishments and failures of the Soviet Union's command economy?
2. What factors caused Mikhail Gorbachev to introduce his policies of *glasnost* and *perestroika*? What were the major accomplishments and failures of those policies?
3. Discuss the changes in Russia's party system under Gorbachev, Yeltsin, and Putin. How would you characterize Russia's current political party system?
4. What does this chapter mean when it talks of the "Mexicanization of Russian politics?" Discuss as many aspects of that process as you can.
5. Discuss the role of the president in Russian national politics. What changes have taken place in that role under Presidents Yeltsin, Putin, and Medvedev?
6. In what ways are Russian attitudes toward democracy different? What are some signs that the political culture supports democracy and what are the signs that it does not?
7. Discuss the ways Russia's oligarchs accumulated their wealth. Compare Putin's relationship with the oligarchy to Yeltsin's.

Notes _____

1. "Russia: Fight Against Diseases That Drive Population Plunge," *New York Times* (February 23, 2007).
2. D. Richard Little, *Governing the Soviet Union* (New York: Longman, 1989).
3. Frederick C. Barghoorn and Thomas F. Remington, *Politics in the USSR* (Boston: Little, Brown, 1986), chap. 1.
4. Crane Brinton, *The Anatomy of Revolution* (New York: Vintage, 1965).
5. Barghoorn and Remington, *Politics in the USSR*, p. 16.
6. Peter Hauslohner, "Politics Before Gorbachev: De-Stalinization and the Roots of Reform," in *Inside Gorbachev's Russia*, ed. Seweryn Bialer (Boulder, CO: Westview, 1989).
7. Dusko Doder and Louise Branson, *Gorbachev: Heretic in the Kremlin* (New York: Penguin, 1990), pp. 23–24.
8. Abraham Bergson, *The Real National Income of Soviet Russia Since 1928* (Cambridge: Harvard University Press, 1961), p. 261.
9. Ed A. Hewett, *Reforming the Soviet Economy: Equality versus Efficiency* (Washington, DC: Brookings, 1988), p. 38.
10. Ibid.
11. "Soviet Economic Performance: Strengths and Weaknesses," in Hewett, *Reforming the Soviet Economy*.
12. Timothy Colton, *The Dilemma of Reform in the Soviet Union* (New York: Council on Foreign Relations, 1986); "Bureaucratic Conservatism and the Post-Stalinist Settlement," in Mark Kesselman et al., *European Politics in Transition* (Lexington, MA: Heath, 1987).
13. Hewett, *Reforming the Soviet Economy*, p. 52.
14. Jerry F. Hough, *Opening Up the Soviet Economy* (Washington, DC: Brookings, 1988), p.13.
15. Byung-Yeon Kim, Causes of Repressed Inflation in the Soviet Consumer Market, 1965–1989: Retail Price Subsidies, The Siphoning Effect, and Budget Deficits, *The Economic History Review*, 55, No. 2 (February 2002), 105–127.
16. Jim Leitzel, *Russian Economic Reform* (New York: Routledge, 1995), p. 1.
17. Hough, *Opening Up the Soviet Economy*, pp. 43–44.

18. *New York Times*, February 3, 1991, p. 1.
19. Ben Eklof, *Soviet Briefing* (Boulder, CO: Westview, 1989), pp. 42–45.
20. Hewett, *Reforming the Soviet Economy*, p. 304.
21. Quoted in Hedrick Smith, *The New Russians* (New York: Random House, 1990), p. 185.
22. Barbara A. Anderson and Brian D. Silver, "Growth and Diversity of the Population of the Soviet Union," *The ANNALS of the American Academy of Political and Social Science* 510 (1), 156.
23. Donna Bahry and Brian D. Silver, "Public Perceptions and the Dilemmas of Party Reform in the USSR" (paper presented at the annual meeting of the American Political Science Association, Atlanta, September 1989), p. 13.
24. Donald Barry and Carol Barner-Barry, *Contemporary Soviet Politics* (Englewood Cliffs, NJ: Prentice Hall, 1991), p. 137.
25. *The New York Times*, February 8, 2001.
26. For a summary of the ideological spectrum of Russian political parties in the 1990s, see M. Steven Fish, "The Advent of Multipartyism in Russia, 1993–95," *Post-Soviet Affairs* 11, no. 4 (1995): 348–353.
27. For an interesting account of Kasparov's aborted 2008 presidential campaign and discussion of the obstacles facing Putin's (and Medvedev's) opponents, see David Remnick, "The Tsar's Opponent," *The New Yorker* (October 1, 2007), pp. 65–77.
28. Lilia Shevtsova, "Parliament and the Political Crisis: 1991–1993," in Jeffrey Hahn, *Democratization in Russia* (Armonk, NY: M .E. Sharpe Inc., 1996), pp. 30–31. On the percentage of Communist Party members, see David Lane and Cameron Ross, "From Soviet Government to Presidential Rule," in *Russia in Transition*, ed. David Lane (London: Longman, 1995), p. 5.
29. John P. Willerton, "Yeltsin and the Russian Presidency," in *Developments in Russian and Post-Soviet Politics* 5, ed. Stephen White, Alex Pravda, and Zvi Gitelman (London: Macmillan, 1994), pp. 25–56.
30. Lilia Shevtsova, "Russia's Post-Communist Politics: Revolution or Continuity?" in *The New Russia: Troubled Transformation*, ed. Gail W. Lapidus, (Boulder, CO: Westview, 1995), pp. 20–21; and Thomas F. Remington, "Ménage à Trois: The End of Soviet Parliamentarianism," in Hahn, *Democratization in Russia*, p. 108.
31. John Lowenhardt, *The Reincarnation of Russia: Struggling with the Legacy of Communism* (Durham, NC: Duke University Press, 1995), p. 110. We added the 1997 reference.
32. Anders Aslund, *How Russia Became a Market Economy* (Washington, DC: Brookings, 1995), p. 275. GDP is a measure similar to GNP (gross national product) but excludes earnings from abroad.
33. Alan Smith, "The Economic Challenge Facing Russia," in Smith, *Challenges for Russian Economic Reform* (Washington, DC: Brookings, 1995), pp. 1–20.
34. Josef C. Brada, "The Transformation from Communism to Capitalism: How Far? How Fast?" *Post-Soviet Affairs* 9, no. 2 (1993): 87–110; Anders Aslund, *Economic Transformation in Russia* (New York: St. Martin's, 1994); and Jeffrey D. Sachs and W. T. Woo, "Reform in China and Russia," *Economic Policy* 18 (April 1994): 101–145.
35. Abraham Shama, "Inside Russia's True Economy," *Foreign Policy* 103 (Summer 1996): 112.
36. *New York Times*, November 11, 1993.
37. Stephen White, *After Gorbachev* (Cambridge, England: Cambridge University Press, 1993), p. 277; and Michael Kaser, "Privatization in the CIS," in Smith, *Challenges for Russian Economic Reform*, p. 141. Thus, Russia now has more stockholders than does the United States.
38. Shama, "Inside Russia's True Economy," p. 112; and *The New York Times*, January 28, 1996, and June 16, 1996.
39. *The New York Times*, June 19, 1994.
40. Aslund, *How Russia Became a Market Economy*, p. 275; Goldman, *Lost Opportunity: Why Economic Reforms in Russia Have Not Worked* (New York: Norton, 1994), pp. 106–107, 109, claims a slightly lower rate of inflation.
41. Allen C. Lynch, *How Russia Is Not Ruled* (Cambridge, UK: Cambridge University Press, 2005), p. 94.
42. Peter Rutland, "The Economy: The Rocky Road from Plan to Market," in *Developments in Russian and Post-Soviet Politics* 5, p. 154.
43. Marshall Goldman, "Render Onto Caesar: Putin and the Oligarchs," *Current History* 102 (October 2003), pp. 320–326.
44. *The New York Times*, September 25, 1993.
45. Yoshiko M. Herrera, "Russian Economic Reform, 1991–1999," in *Russian Politics: Challenges of Democratization*, ed. Zoltan Barany and Robert G. Moser (Cambridge, UK, and New York: Cambridge University Press, 2001), p. 161.
46. CIA, *World Factbook* 2007. https://www.cia.gov/library/publications/the-world-factbook/index.html; UNDP, *Human Development Reports* 2007/2008 http://hdrstats.undp.org/countries/country_fact_sheets/cty_fs_rus.html; Michael Waller, *Russian Politics Today* (New York: Palgrave, 2005), p. 231.
47. WorldWide Tax and Finance Site, worldwide-tax.com/russia/rus_inflation.asp; CIA, *The World Factbook* 2007.
48. CIA, *The World Factbook* 20007; World Bank, *The World Development Report* 2007: *Development and the Next Generation*, Table 4: Economic Activity, pp. 312–313, http://www-wds.worldbank.org/.

49. Leon Aron, "After Putin, the Deluge?" *Current History*, 106 (October 2007): p. 307.
50. Ibid, p. 309.
51. William Thompson, "The Russian Economy under Vladimir Putin," in *Russian Politics Under Putin*, ed. Cameron Ross (Manchester, UK, and New York: Manchester University Press, 2004), pp. 114–132.
52. Leitzel, *Russian Economic Reform*, p. 41.
53. *The New York Times*, January 30, 1994.
54. Donald D. Barry, *Russian Politics: The Post-Soviet Phase* (New York: Peter Lang, 2002), p. 1.
55. Louise Shelly, "Organized Crime Groups: 'Uncivil Society'" in *Russian Civil Society: A Critical Assessment*, ed. Alfred Evans, Laura Henry, and Lisa McIntosh Sundstrom (Armonk, NY: M.E. Sharpe, 2006), pp. 95–109. See also, Vadim Volkov, *Violent Entrepreneurs: The Use of Force in the Making of Russian Capitalism* (Ithaca, NY: Cornell University Press, 2002).
56. *The New York Times*, April 20, 1993.
57. Poll conducted by Mitofsky Election and Polling Research in cooperation with CESSI Ltd. and quoted in *The New York Times*, June 18, 1996.
58. "Putin's Dubious Allure: 'He's Not Making Things Worse,'" *The New York Times* (March 9, 2004).
59. Amy Knight, "The Two Worlds of Vladimir Putin," *The Wilson Quarterly* (Spring 2000). At the time that Knight wrote this article, relations between the U.S. and Russia were considerably warmer than they are now and Washington was less prone to criticize human rights violations. In any event, human rights violations have become much more widespread since she wrote that piece.
60. CBC News (May 31, 2005), cbc.ca/news/background/russia/timeline.html. Perhaps, by using the words "political catastrophe," Putin was signaling that he did not mean that the collapse of the Soviet Union was a greater catastrophe than Hitler's invasion, which resulted in millions of Russian deaths.
61. Waller, *Russian Politics Today*, p. 33.
62. Allen C. Lynch, *How Russia Is Not Ruled*, pp. 160–161.
63. Ibid., p. 161; Olga Kryshtanovskaya and Stephen White, "Putin's Militocracy," *Post-Soviet Affairs* 19, no. 4 (October-December, 2003): 289–306.
64. Viktor Yasmann, "Russia: *Siloviki* Take the Reins in the Post-Oligarchy Era," *RFE/RL* [Radio Free Europe/Radio Liberty] *Newsline*, 11, No. 153 (September 17, 2007).
65. Marsha Lipman and Michael McFaul, "Putin and the Media," in *Putin's Russia: Past Imperfect, Future Uncertain*, ed. Dale R. Herspring (Lanham, MD: Rowman & Littlefield Publishers, Inc., 2003), p. 70.
66. Laura Belin "Politics and the Mass Media under Putin," in *Russian Politics Under Putin*, pp. 133–150.
67. Marsha Lipman and Michael McFaul, "Putin and the Media," in *Putin's Russia*, pp. 70–71; Waller, *Russian Politics Today*, p. 221.
68. Ibid., pp. 77–78.
69. Laszlo Csaba, "Russia's Political Economy," in *Toward an Understanding of Russia: New European Perspectives*, ed. Janusz Bugajski (New York: Council on Foreign Relations, 2002), p. 31.
70. Peter Rutland, "Putin and the Oligarchs," in *Putin's Russia*, pp. 133–152.
71. *RFE/RL Newsline*, 12, No. 35, (February 19, 2008); "The World's Billionaires," *Forbes Magazine* March 3, 2008, http://www.forbes.com/lists/2008/10/billionaires08_The-Worlds-Billionaires_Rank.html; see also, Goldman, "Render Unto Caesar"; Michael Waller, *Russian Politics Today*, p. 196; "World's richest men live in Moscow and New York," *Pravda* (Moscow) *English.Pravda* (March 13, 2006).
72. Anatoly M. Khazanov, "What Went Wrong? Post-Communist Transformations in Comparative Perspective," in *Restructuring Post-Communist Russia*, ed. Yitzhak Brundy et al. (Cambridge, England: Cambridge University Press, 2004), p. 49.
73. Marshall Goldman, "The Russian Transition to the Market: Success or Failure?" in Brundy et al. (ed.), *Restructuring Post-Communist Russia*, pp. 132–133.
74. Timothy J. Colton and Michael McFaul, "Putin and Democratization," in *Putin's Russia*, pp. 20–22.
75. World Public Opinion, "Russians Support Putin's Re-Nationalization of Oil, Control of Media, But See Democratic Future," http://www.worldpublicopinion.org/; Under the listing "By Region," click on "Europe." Last visited June 8, 2008.
76. Ibid.
77. Public Opinion Foundation (Russia), http://bd.english.fom.ru/.
78. Lynch, *How Russia Is Not Ruled*, p. 100.
79. "The World Health Organization's Rankings of World Health Systems," http://www.photius.com/rankings/healthranks.html.
80. Aron, "After Putin, the Deluge?" p. 309.
81. Waller, *Russian Politics Today*, p. 208.
82. *The New York Times*, August 13, 2005.
83. Arch Puddington and Aili Piano, "The 2004 Freedom House Survey," *Journal of Democracy* 16, no. 1 (January 2005): 103–108. Subsequent ratings of all countries appear annually in the January issues of the *Journal of Democracy*.
84. Committee to Protect Journalists, "Attacks on the Press in 2006: Europe and Central Asia," www.cpj.org//attacks_06/europe_06/eur_analysis_06.html. That ranking is based on the total number of journalists murdered, not on per capita attacks.

85. James Gambrell, "Putin Strikes Again," *The New York Review of Books*, 54, No. 12 (July 12, 2007).
86. Lisa McIntosh Sundstrom and Laura Henry, "Russian Civil Society: Tensions and Trajectories," in *Russian Civil Society: A Critical Assessment*, pp. 305–322; L. McIntosh Sundstsrom, "Women's NGOs in Russia, *Demokratizatsiya*, www.politics.ubc.ca/.
87. *RFE/RL Newsline*, 12, No. 11 (January 16, 2008).

For Further Reading ⸻

Aron, Leon. "After Putin, the Deluge?" *Current History*, 106 (October 2007): p. 305–310.

Carnaghan, Ellen. *Out of Order: Russian Political Values in an Imperfect World.* University Park: Pennsylvania State University Press, 2007.

Evans, Alfred, Laura Henry, and Lisa McIntosh Sundstrom, eds. *Russian Civil Society: A Critical Assessment.* Armonk, NY: M. E. Sharpe, 2006.

Fish, M. Steven. *Democracy Derailed in Russia: The Failure of Open Politics.* New York: Cambridge University Press, 2005.

Herspring, Dale R., ed. *Putin's Russia: Past Imperfect, Future Uncertain.* Lanham, MD: Rowman & Littlefield Publishers, 2003.

Ledeneva, Alena. *How Russia Really Works.* Ithaca, NY: Cornell University Press, 2006.

Lynch, Allen C. *How Russia Is Not Ruled.* Cambridge, UK: Cambridge University Press, 2005.

Politkovskaya, Anna. *Russian Diary: A Journalist's Final Account of Life, Corruption, and Death in Putin's Russia.* New York: Random House, 2007.

Ross, Cameron. *Russian Politics Under Putin.* Manchester, UK, and New York: Manchester University Press, 2004.

Stoner-Weiss, Kathryn. *Resisting the State: Reform and Retrenchment in Post-Soviet Russia.* New York: Cambridge University Press, 2006.

Waller, Michael. *Russian Politics Today.* Manchester, UK, and New York: Manchester University Press, 2005.

The Communist Party Secretary of the Chinese city of Mianzhu on his knees as he begs irate parents, whose children were killed in the devastating, 2008 Sichuan earthquake, to stop their protests against shoddy school construction.

© SHIHO FUKADA/The New YorkTimes/Redux Pictures

14

CHINA: SEARCHING FOR A NEW VISION

◆ The Relevance of Chinese Politics ◆ The Chinese Revolution and Its Origins ◆ The Evolution of Chinese Politics and Society ◆ Reforming the Chinese Economy ◆ China's Political System ◆ Conclusion: China's Uncertain Future

When the International Olympic Committee announced, back in 2001, that it had selected Beijing to host the 2008 summer games, the Chinese greeted the news with enormous national pride. They expected that the games would provide an excellent stage for showing the world how far China had modernized and advanced economically. At that time, nobody could have anticipated the political and natural disasters that were to overshadow the Olympics in the months leading up to the games.

Early in 2008, hundreds of Tibetan Buddhist monks led that region's largest public protest in nearly twenty years against China's political and cultural domination.* For years, Tibet's struggle for autonomy—symbolized by its widely revered spiritual leader, the Dalai Lama—has attracted widespread international support. Consequently, when the Chinese military crushed the demonstrations, it provoked worldwide condemnation. Moreover, the protests in Tibet were timed to begin only days before the start of the traditional Olympic torch relay, a months-long event in which the torch is carried from the birthplace of Olympic competition (Greece), through a number of countries, and on to the host country. But rather than being the celebrated event that it normally is, this relay provoked protests in a number of countries along its path. In addition to repression in Tibet, the Olympic-related protests also focused on China's support of highly repressive regimes in Sudan and Myanmar.

Only two months after the start of the Olympic protests, China suffered a far more devastating blow. In May, 2008 a massive earthquake hit the province of Sichuan, causing more than 70,000 deaths and leaving millions homeless. This time the international reaction was very sympathetic and the world media lauded the Chinese military's valiant rescue operations. At the same time, however, the earthquake raised troubling evidence of corruption in school construction and other instances of government neglect (see Box 14-1). One month later, natural disaster struck China once again, as floods swept across the southern tier of the country, driving millions of people from their homes, destroying millions of acres of farmland, and disrupting industrial production.

Taken together, these events reveal a lot about contemporary China's political and economic systems. They suggest a country modern enough to host the Olympic Games (with the massive infrastructure that the role requires), developed enough to mount an impressive rescue operation after the earthquake, and open enough to allow international media and the Chinese public unprecedented access to information during the rescue operation. Yet at the same time, the Olympics spotlighted how enormously polluted Beijing and many other Chinese cities have become. The protests in Tibet and the subsequent mass arrests illustrated how repressive the political system can be. And the Sichuan earthquake revealed the extent of rural poverty and the widespread corruption of local government and Communist Party officials.

---

* China, which had intervened in Tibet for centuries, conquered that country in 1950. While the Chinese government considers Tibet to be a part of China, most Tibetans deeply resent China's ongoing assault on their very distinct culture and wish for greater autonomy or even, less realistically, independence.

Box 14-1

OLYMPIC FLAMES, TIBETAN PROTEST, AND EARTHQUAKE DISASTER

In 1993, China's first attempt to host a future Summer Olympics failed narrowly when it lost its bid for the 2000 games to Sydney, Australia. It was a humiliating moment for the Chinese government, particularly since its failure was caused in part by the lingering international revulsion against the Tiananmen Square (Beijing) massacre of pro-democracy demonstrators. Consequently, years later, when Beijing was chosen to host the 2008 games, China's government and people rejoiced. By then, memories of Tiananmen had faded somewhat and individual freedoms had expanded considerably within the Chinese People's Republic. Still, many human rights advocates lamented the choice and several heads of state contemplated boycotting the opening Olympic ceremonies.

In particular, the Chinese annexation of Tibet nearly 60 years ago and its ongoing repression of Tibetan culture and religion have evoked considerable international condemnation, most recently after police shot, beat, and arrested protesting Tibetan Buddhist monks in early 2008. Most Chinese, particularly those of the predominant Han ethnicity, believe that Tibet should be part of China and that the Tibetan protests are unwarranted, especially since the Tibetan economy has improved under Chinese rule. So, they resented the international protests along the route of the Olympic torch. It is worth noting that crowds of Chinese students living in countries such as Australia, Britain, France, and South Korea (many of whom are surely critics of their own government) staged counter-demonstrations against Tibetan human rights advocates trying to disrupt the passage of the torch. For those students, nationalism overcame any concerns for Tibetan human rights.

China has also been widely criticized for its support of some of the world's most brutal regimes. For example, in pursuit of its foreign policy interests, it has established strong economic ties with the dictatorships of Sudan and Myanmar (Burma). Sudan is an international pariah because of its genocidal campaign against the residents of its Darfur region, while the Burmese military regime, with a long history of repression, may have contributed to the deaths of thousands of survivors of the nation's massive 2008 cyclone by refusing to allow most foreign assistance to enter the country. In both cases, China resisted world-wide calls for it to apply pressure on its allies.

International criticism turned to sympathy, however, when the devastating earthquake hit Sichuan province only three months before the Olympics opened. The rescue operations (spearheaded by the "People's Liberation Army," the country's armed forces) were prompt and comprehensive*. And Premier (Prime Minister) Wen Jiabao won praise at home and abroad for flying to the disaster area promptly to comfort the survivors and encourage the rescue teams. China's response evoked positive comparisons with the Burmese government's woeful management of its cyclone disaster and even with the Bush administration's handling of Hurricane Katrina in New Orleans (2005).

The Chinese regime's handling of media information was even more striking. For decades, it had a record of concealing the full extent of natural disasters and health crises such as an even more destructive earthquake in 1976 and the outbreak of Severe Acute Respiratory Syndrome (SARS), a frequently deadly, new disease which soon spread to East Asia and North America in 2002–2003. This time the government initially reverted to its old habits, offering limited news of the earthquake and ordering Chinese and foreign journalists to stay out of the disaster area for several days. When Chinese reporters violated the ban, however, the government relented and allowed full coverage of the unfolding story in both Chinese and foreign mass media. The government also welcomed foreign assistance and foreign aid workers, something it had been reluctant to do in the past. As the dimension of the disaster unfolded on television, many Chinese NGOs, some organized spontaneously, channeled civilian assistance to the earthquake zone, independently of the government. All of this represented an unprecedented level of government openness and responsiveness to public opinion.

At the same time, however, a darker side of Chinese government soon emerged. Grieving parents noted that rural school buildings had sustained disproportionate damage, resulting in a large student death toll.

---

* But, while PLA soldiers showed courage and dedication, most units lacked the equipment (helicopters, bulldozers and the like) needed to rescue victims quickly.

(Continued)

Box 14-1

OLYMPIC FLAMES, TIBETAN PROTEST, AND
EARTHQUAKE DISASTER   (*Continued*)

According to government sources, some 7,000 school-rooms collapsed and unofficial estimates are that about 10,000 students died. It appears that many small-town schools (and other government buildings) had violated the strict building codes established after China's cata-strophic 1976 earthquake. In an all too familiar pattern, construction companies had cut building costs, violated seismic construction codes, and bribed local inspectors and officials. In many cases, schools lay in rubble sur-rounded by other buildings that had remained standing. In contrast, in the large city of Chengdu, where build-ing codes were more strictly enforced, the destruction and number of deaths were much lower.[1] Since China generally enforces a one-child policy, many of the par-ents lost their only child.

In many cases the parents' grief turned to anger as they held corrupt officials and construction compa-nies responsible for many of the deaths. Often they hung up banners blaming government corruption for

their children's deaths. Elsewhere crowds of parents, many of them carrying photos of their dead or missing children, protested in front of government offices or the ruins of school buildings. In some cases, govern-ment officials actually asked forgiveness from the parents, a rarity in China. But most were not contrite. Although the government had previously allowed jour-nalists free access to the earthquake's destruction, they now clamped down on coverage of the protests. Two months later, police attacked hundreds of protesting parents in the hard-hit city of Mianzhu, arresting some of them. In a number of areas, local government offi-cials offered parents cash payments of $8,000–$14,000 along with supplemental annual pensions if they were willing to sign a contract promising to end their com-plaints.[2] Usually, the offers of payoffs were coupled with clear indications that if the parents did not stop their protests there would be retribution toward them or their relatives.

THE RELEVANCE OF CHINESE POLITICS

With 1.33 billion people, China contains about one-fifth of the human race, far ex-ceeding the combined populations of the United States, Great Britain, Russia, and Mexico. This chapter will discuss the enormous capacity of **Mao Zedong's*** totalitar-ian system (1949–1976) for implementing political and economic change. But it will also note the enormous human suffering that Maoism inflicted on the Chinese people and will trace the causes of that extreme ideology's demise. Like the Soviet Union before its collapse, China today features an authoritarian political culture, an official Marxist ideology, and an all-powerful ruling party.

The differences between these two communist giants, however, even before the decline of the USSR, were as important as their similarities. During the Maoist era, China's government and Communist Party tried to inculcate Marxist ideology in its population more ardently than the Soviet regime ever had. But, whereas Mikhail Gorbachev's attempts to reform the Soviet command economy failed miserably, China's reforms since 1978—creating a mixed communist/free-enterprise economic structure—have produced the world's fastest-growing economy.

From the 1950s through the mid-1970s, China was among the most ideologi-cally driven of all communist nations. Mao's Cultural Revolution (1966–1976), which elevated him to the level of a demigod and turned his ideology into a virtual state

* In China, as in most East Asian countries, a person's family name *precedes* his or her given name. Thus leaders such as Mao Zedong and Hu Jintao are called Chairman Mao and President Hu.

Fireworks at the Bird's Nest Stadium—2008 Beijing Olympics: China's spectacular Summer Olympic games symbolized its arrival as a major world power.

religion, caused enormous destruction and countless deaths. But the moral certainty and fanaticism that characterized Mao's rule declined soon after his death. Under the leadership of **Deng Xiaoping** (1978–1997), Jiang Zemin (1995–2002),* and Hu Jintao (2002–), China moved decisively away from Maoist orthodoxy. In the past 25 years, the government has introduced free-market economic reforms that are much more sweeping and far more successful than anything attempted by Russian President Gorbachev's *perestroika* (Chapter 13). Today, by one, widely used measure (GDP adjusted for the cost of living) China's economy is the world's second largest and is likely to surpass the United States by the year 2050.[3] Even before its recent entry into the World Trade Organization (WTO), China was one of the United States' largest trading partners, and its role in the global economy will certainly continue to grow. Consequently, not only has China been a model for market reform in the world's remaining communist countries, but its rapid growth also has been the envy of developing nations.

But those economic reforms have not been accompanied by corresponding political reforms and freedoms, as they were in the USSR during *glasnost.* In the spring of 1989, students in a number of Chinese universities staged political protests, with considerable non-student support, demanding a more honest and more responsive

---

* Although Deng remained the nation's paramount leader until his death in 1997, in his final years his advanced age and failing health forced him to share power with others, particularly Communist Party (CCP) General Secretary and national President Jiang Zemin. Hence the overlap of two years in their authority (1995–1997). Jiang served eight years (1989–1997) prior to Deng's death as CCP secretary, national president, and heir apparent, but only gained equal power with his mentor in his last two years.

government. Week after week, they organized massive rallies in Beijing's **Tiananmen Square,** the very spot where Mao had exhorted his revolutionary shock troops four decades earlier. On June 4, 1989, army tanks rolled into the square, killing several hundred student demonstrators and making Tiananmen a symbol of government repression throughout the world. China's leaders, so recently hailed in the West for their economic reforms, were reviled for their repressive politics. Since that time, political repression has eased considerably and individual freedoms "to buy what [people] want, enjoy private lives, speak more openly, and even to travel abroad. . . . " have expanded substantially.[4] But the nation still lacks guarantees of basic civil liberties and the authority of the Communist Party remains absolute.

THE CHINESE REVOLUTION AND ITS ORIGINS

The Imperial Legacy and the Battle against Foreign Domination

China, argued one leading historian, is a "nation imprisoned by her history."[5] Those traditions are particularly relevant to its modern political system. Some two hundred years before the birth of Christ, the Qin dynasty first unified the country's feudal kingdoms into an empire. Subsequent dynasties fell to military insurrections or peasant uprisings, some of which lasted up to one hundred years and caused the deaths of millions. Even today, the legacy of China's violent past—which lasted well into the twentieth century—is the widespread Chinese conviction that centralized, authoritarian rule is necessary to avert serious disorder. Like modern Maoism, traditional Confucian morality stressed social order and harmony, including "the values of the group at the expense of the individual."[6]

For centuries, Chinese leaders saw their nation as "the Middle Kingdom," the cultural center of the earth. The country's culture and technology had filled Marco Polo and other Western travelers with awe. Starting in the nineteenth century, however, China began to face increasing military and economic threats from abroad. Although never formally colonized, it suffered from Western and Japanese economic domination that also weakened its political sovereignty.[7]

Foreign control often induced internal upheavals. The Taiping Rebellion (1850–1865), a huge peasant uprising, nearly toppled the imperial regime before it was crushed at the cost of some 20 million lives. By the time Japan attacked China at the close of the nineteenth century, segments of the elite had lost faith in the government and looked, instead, to Western models of modernization. The emperors' inability to protect the country from foreign exploitation undermined their legitimacy and contributed to the demise of the two-thousand-year-old imperial order. In 1911–1912, an uprising led by dissident military officers and provincial government officials toppled the old regime.

Civil War against the War Lords (1912–1928)

For nearly two decades after the empire fell, civil war raged between nationalist reformers and the armies of regional strongmen known as **warlords.** During that time, two political parties were born that eventually dominated Chinese politics. The first, the **Nationalist Party**, or **Kuomintang (Guomindang) (KMT)**,* was led by a mix of Western-oriented intellectuals, military officers, businessmen, and rural landlords. After years of struggle, General Chiang Kai-shek's KMT army defeated the most important warlords in 1928 and established a new central government.

Meanwhile, in 1921 a small group of Marxist intellectuals had formed the Chinese Communist Party (CCP). Although the Party grew to nearly 60 thousand members in six years, its expansion was limited by its orthodox Marxist belief that only the working class could be the agent of revolution.[†] But in China, an overwhelmingly rural society at that time, industrial workers constituted less than 1 percent of the population.[8] Convinced that the country was not yet ready for a Communist revolution, the newborn CCP allied with the Kuomintang against the warlords. However, on the eve of the KMT's victory, Chiang Kai-shek turned against the Communists and decimated them. From 1927 to 1930, Chiang's launched a "White Terror," which killed thousands of Communist Party members and sympathizers, effectively destroying the Party's urban base.[9]

The Revolutionary Struggle, Japanese Occupation, and the Development of Maoist Thought (1928–1949)

Its disastrous alliance with the KMT forced the Communists to rethink their strategy. One Party faction, headed by Mao Zedong, decided to organize beyond the working class and reach out to the peasants, who made up about 85 percent of China's population. In the years that followed, Mao and his followers built a rural guerrilla army, the **People's Liberation Army (PLA)**, operating out of Communist-controlled regions.

Soon they governed some six million people in south-central China. Still no match for Chiang's more powerful army, however, the Communists retreated northward in 1934. Fewer than 10 percent of the 100,000 PLA soldiers and political activists who started that "**Long March**" north survived the arduous 6,000-mile trek, "an odyssey perhaps unequaled in modern times."[10] Despite the tremendous losses associated with it, the March itself and subsequent experience governing "liberated regions" in the northwest taught the Communist leadership important organizational lessons that later turned the tide of victory in their favor.

To win peasant support, they introduced greater economic and political equality in a society traditionally rife with inequalities of wealth, education, and gender. As the PLA eventually overcame great odds to defeat better-armed KMT armies, Mao became convinced that—properly organized and ideologically inspired—the masses (peasants and workers) could overcome any obstacles, no matter how daunting. That faith was reinforced by the PLA's impressive performance against Japanese occupation forces from 1937 to 1945, before and during World War II.

---

* Since 1979, most contemporary English-language writings on China use the pinyin system of transcribing Chinese characters into Roman letters. Thus, *Kuomintang, Mao Tse-tung*, and *Peking* (in the earlier Wade-Giles method) are now spelled *Guomindang, Mao Zedong,* and *Beijing*. Where a name is still widely written using Wade-Giles, we offer both spellings.

[†] In China and other single-party communist nations, "the Party" (capitalized) always refers to the Communist Party.

During that time the Communists expanded the area they controlled considerably. By the war's end, these "liberated zones" had a combined population of 130 million people. The Communist Party grew from 20 thousand members in 1935 to 1.2 million in 1945, and PLA troops and militias grew to 3.4 million men.

The Communist Victory (1945–1949) and Mao's Version of Marxist-Leninist Ideology

Following the end of World War II and the Japanese defeat, the civil war between the Communist and Nationalist armies resumed. But, having failed to defend China adequately or to win the peasants' loyalty, the KMT had lost its political mandate. By 1949, after a series of losses, its army and its loyalists fled the mainland to the island of Taiwan. On October 1, Mao Zedong founded the People's Republic of China. "Our nation," he declared to a cheering throng in Tiananmen Square, "will never again be an insulted nation. We have stood up." Like many other revolutionaries who achieved power after a prolonged struggle—including Lenin, Fidel Castro, and Ho Chi Minh— Mao was far more ideologically committed than his successors to believing in the power of Marxism to mobilize the masses.[11]

We have previously noted several features of Maoist thought: the central role of the peasantry, a strong egalitarian commitment, and a glorification of class struggle. But Mao also insisted that class struggle did not end with the victory of the revolutionary forces. So even after it seizes power, he argued, a Marxist regime must be ever vigilant against the families of former capitalists and landlords still residing in China, against Western imperialism, and even against corrupt Party and government officials—known as **cadres**.[12] Citing these alleged ongoing threats, Mao justified recurring mass mobilization campaigns to maintain the people's ideological commitment. While these ongoing campaigns did inspire greater mass commitment to revolutionary goals, they also disrupted people's lives, provoked great cruelties against alleged enemies of the revolution, and hurt the economy. At their worst, as in the Great Leap Forward and the Cultural Revolution, they caused millions of deaths. Not until the late 1970s were Deng Xiaoping and the new CCP leadership able to moderate the role of ideology in society.

THE EVOLUTION OF CHINESE POLITICS AND SOCIETY

Establishing the Basis of Communist Society (1949–1956)

The early years of Communist rule established the fundamental components of the new society. Acknowledging the peasants' central role in the CCP victory, the government's first priority was redistribution of farmland. Before the revolution, less than 10 percent of China's rural population owned over half the agricultural land. In just a few years, those farms were taken from the landlords and distributed to more than 300 million landless peasants.[13] In the cities, the state took over most private businesses. The end of decades of civil war and the establishment of centralized political authority facilitated an economic recovery. That growth coupled with more equitable **income distribution** improved the living standards of many poor families.

As in the USSR and other communist regimes, Communist Party authority was absolute, and perceived enemies of the revolution were brutally repressed. But for many uneducated peasants who had joined the PLA or the CCP, the new political system offered opportunities for upward mobility that were previously unimaginable. New conditions of social peace, greater equality, land reform, and improved living standards all earned the new regime considerable popular support.

The Great Leap Forward (1958–1961) and the Great Debate (1959–1965)

Although the Chinese economy grew impressively during the early years of Communist rule (1949–1956), Mao feared that the Soviet-style economic development model in place was inappropriate for China's impoverished rural society. That model emphasized capital investment and the development of heavy industry. But since China had little investment capital, Mao sought to maximize Chinese self-sufficiency and to draw on the country's primary resource—the numbers and energy of its people. As we have noted, he believed that, if properly inspired, the Chinese masses could make tremendous progress in a short period of time.[14]

Thus, for example, when the government launched the **Great Leap Forward** in 1958, it called on the people to gather scrap iron on their farms and streets for use in backyard steel furnaces. But the most radical changes took place in the countryside, where the state consolidated agricultural units into large **communes**. Peasants could no longer own private farm plots or animals, and rural life was collectivized.[15]

Although it may have promoted short-term production spurts, the longer-term effects of the Great Leap were catastrophic. In the cities, production speedups caused machinery breakdowns, production bottlenecks, and subsequent declines in output. In rural areas, the effects of Mao's radical policies were more disastrous. The communes were unpopular and far too large to manage effectively. Because of local central planners' ill-conceived decisions, much of the harvest failed to reach the market, and vast amounts of food rotted in the fields or were consumed by pests. From 1959 to 1962, those planning errors devastated production. As a result, as many as 25 million people died of hunger and malnutrition.[16]

Mao's failed radical campaigns generated sharp divisions among Party leaders regarding a proper strategy for reinvigorating economic development. The so-called "Great Debate" pitted more pragmatic Party leaders (whom China specialists have labeled the **Expert Faction**) against ultra-radicals headed by Mao (referred to as the **Red Faction**). Following the failures of the Great Leap, the Expert Faction, including the future national leader, Deng Xiaoping, forced an end to that campaign's most radical and disastrous components.

Although the Expert faction helped restore economic growth, their approach troubled Mao and his radical allies. They feared it would produce the same outcome in China as it had in other communist nations—technically trained experts would take control of the state bureaucracy from dedicated revolutionaries who were committed to egalitarianism. In fact, conflict between ideologically driven leaders and pragmatic ones became an ongoing feature of Chinese politics from that time until the 1980s.

The Cultural Revolution (1966–1976)

As the pragmatists extended their influence in the CCP, Mao turned to more radical groups for support: specifically, the military and the nation's youth. In August 1966, he launched the Great Proletarian Cultural Revolution—or, simply, the **Cultural Revolution**—seeking to root out Party and government cadres who were allegedly subverting the revolution ("capitalist roaders") and to destroy all Western and capitalist influences in China's cultural life. Toward that purpose, Mao exhorted Chinese youth to organize into militant units called **Red Guards** and attack cadres, teachers, artists, and intellectuals who were not sufficiently revolutionary.[17]

Thus, the Cultural Revolution was fought at two levels. At the elite level, Red Guards arrested, attacked, and humiliated moderate Party and government leaders. More than 70 percent of the Party's Central Committee members were purged from their posts.[18] At the mass level, Red Guards ran rampant, arresting, beating, and killing alleged reactionaries. At times, contending Red Guard and allied military units battled each other. By 1967, the nation had sunk into chaos, and Mao called in the armed forces to restore order. Within two years, the Red Guards were disbanded and the Cultural Revolution's worst excesses ended. But its thought control and intimidation continued until Mao's death in 1976.

The tragedy of the Cultural Revolution illustrates how seemingly benign objectives (keeping government officials in touch with the people and guaranteeing equality) can lead to vast human suffering when pursued fanatically in a totalitarian setting. Deng Xiaoping later claimed that nearly three million Chinese had fallen victim to political persecution during those years.[19] The number of people killed will never be known. Estimates vary wildly, from half a million to many millions, with most scholars supporting figures at the lower end of that range.[20] Intellectuals, professionals, and technicians—the Red Guards' prime targets—were traumatized for years to come. Eventually, the Red Guards themselves became the campaign's victims. By the early 1970s, Mao saw them as disruptive force, and sent many of them to the countryside for years of "reeducation."

The Death of Mao and the Struggle for Succession (1976–1981)

In 1976, a political earthquake hit China with the death of its two most important leaders: Zhou Enlai, the nation's premier (prime minister) since 1954; and Communist Party Chairman Mao Zedong, the revolution's "great helmsman" since the 1930s and Party Chair since 1943. Although Mao's revolutionary line retained much popular support, the excesses of the Great Leap Forward and the Cultural Revolution had seriously weakened the regime's legitimacy. Though still revered, by the time of his death Mao had spent much of the regime's political capital.

So, only one month after Mao died, his successor, Hua Guofeng, ordered the arrest of Mao's widow, Jiang Qing, and three other leaders of the CCP's Red faction. The "Gang of Four," as they were labeled, were accused of responsibility for the worst excesses of the Cultural Revolution and were brought to trial. With those four serving as convenient scapegoats for Mao's horrors, their arrests signaled that the Cultural Revolution was over.

Deng Xiaoping (1978–1997), Jiang Zemin (1995–2002), Hu Jintao (2002–), and the Post-Maoist Era

Hua Guofeng was soon outmaneuvered by Deng Xiaoping in the battle for national leadership. Deng, the consummate pragmatist and political survivor, had twice come back from political purgatory to outlive or outmaneuver his radical opponents. By 1981, his supporters had ousted Hua from his positions as premier and Party leader. Choosing not to hold either of the top political posts himself, Deng installed two lieutenants, Zhao Ziyang and Hu Yaobang, as chairman of the Communist Party and premier, respectively, while he retained control of the military and dominated the Party and government from behind the scenes.

A 1981 pronouncement by the Communist Party Central Committee called the Cultural Revolution "the most severe setback [to] . . . the Party, the state, and the people since the founding of the People's Republic." Leadership conflicts between left and right factions continued under Deng. But with the Maoist radicals vanquished, even CCP leftists conceded the necessity of departing from Marxist economic dogma. Consequently, the Party's leadership debates during the 1980s and early 1990s generally pitted those who favored more rapid market-oriented economic reform (or, less frequently, political liberalization) against those who wished to move more slowly.

During the 1980s, Deng Xiaoping's team instituted economic changes that were far more sweeping than those later introduced in the USSR by Mikhail Gorbachev. After Deng's death in 1997, Jiang Zemin and, then, Hu Jintao further embedded those reforms and expanded them. Unlike Gorbachev's reforms, however, China's changes have been limited to the economic arena, with far less emphasis on politics.

As we observed in Chapter 13, Gorbachev's most radical innovations were political: semi-competitive elections, the end to the Communist Party's monopoly on power, open debate in the legislature, and the opening of "political space" for public discussion. On the other hand, his economic reforms were far more limited and most were ineffective or catastrophic. China, on the other hand, has seen far more extensive and successful economic change while political reform has been slow and subject to possible reversal.

REFORMING THE CHINESE ECONOMY

What prompted the Chinese leadership to introduce a major economic transformation in the 1980s? As in the Soviet Union, the early decades of Communist rule had brought impressive economic growth. Between 1952 and 1975, even with the major setbacks of the Great Leap Forward and the Cultural Revolution, the economy grew at an impressive annual pace of 8.2 percent and industry expanded at 11.5 percent annually. Those rates far exceeded the norms in other developing nations.[21] Despite substantial population growth, per capita GNP doubled. The combination of rapid economic growth, more equitable income distribution, better health care, and increased literacy in those years greatly benefited the masses of Chinese peasants and laborers.

Despite such gains, however, China remained a very poor country, with much of the population still ill-housed and malnourished. According to the World Bank, as of 1981 over half the Chinese population still lived in extreme poverty.[22] Moreover, as in the USSR, the command economy was more effective in the earliest stages of economic growth than subsequently. By the late 1970s, the country's leaders were painfully aware that some of their capitalist neighbors were developing far more rapidly than China was and were offering their citizens much higher living standards. Once praised for outpacing India and most of Asia, China in the 1970s was criticized for lagging far behind its old adversaries Taiwan, South Korea, and Hong Kong.

In response, starting in 1978, the Chinese leadership introduced economic changes so dramatic and far-reaching that a leading scholar, Harry Harding, described them as "China's Second Revolution." Economic modernization replaced class struggle and political mobilization as the centerpiece of government policy. The People's Republic pursued economic and cultural contacts with both the West and the booming capitalist nations of East Asia that it had once scorned. Free-market mechanisms and private ownership replaced centralized state control in most sectors of the economy. We will examine the impact of those changes in three critical areas: agriculture, commerce\industry, and foreign economic relations.

The Second Revolution in Agriculture

Initially, the government's most significant reforms affected agriculture, where most of the population was employed. CCP moderates had long argued that peasants are more productive when they control their own plots of land, whereas Maoist radicals favored collectivized agriculture. During the Great Leap Forward and again during the Cultural Revolution, private farming was prohibited, and peasants were forced into less-efficient collective farms.

In 1978, however, the government announced its **responsibility system**, giving peasants control over their own family plots.[23] Within seven years, privately-run family plots had largely replaced collective farm communes. Peasants were permitted to lease land, hire farm labor, and sell a portion of their crop directly to consumers at free-market prices once they had sold their crop quota to the state. Thus, farmers had strong economic incentives, previously lacking, to boost agricultural production.

The results of "unleashing the entrepreneurial talents of China's peasants" were impressive. From 1980 to 1984, the value of agricultural output increased by approximately 40 percent. Urban consumers could now choose from a wider variety of foods. Greater output and higher crop prices produced a remarkable 12-percent annual increase in rural living standards.[24] Formerly scarce consumer items such as televisions and bicycles now dotted the countryside, particularly in areas closest to urban markets. Although the rate of agricultural growth has tapered off since the late 1980s, rural per capita income in 1999 was still *15 times higher* than it had been in 1978.[25] For all those reasons, some economists credit Deng's rural reforms with the greatest short-term improvement in human living standards ever achieved in human history.

Since the late 1980s, however, rural economic growth has lagged substantially behind urban development, and the gap between urban and rural living standards is now as wide as it ever was (as of 2007 urban incomes were over three times higher than rural ones). As peasants have become aware of that renewed inequality, as they have been burdened with high taxes, and as they have become fed up with the abuses of local Communist Party bosses, rural protests have increased substantially.

Commercial and Industrial Reforms

Seeking to reduce urban unemployment and to offer consumer services not adequately provided by the state, government reforms introduced in the 1980s permitted small private businesses to operate for the first time since the Cultural Revolution. By 1990, millions of people were employed in the urban private sector (shops, restaurants and the like). Although they still constituted only a small percentage of the population, it fostered a more consumer-oriented culture. Dress and hairstyles that were prohibited in the Cultural Revolution became commonplace in China's cities. State enterprises such as department stores, which previously enjoyed a monopoly, now faced stiff competition from private stores. During the 1990s, the country's urban housing stock was sold to its residents at low prices, creating millions of new property owners.

Even though private businesses were at first confined to small family operations, since the 1990s, the government has allowed ever-larger manufacturing enterprises in the private sector, some employing hundreds of workers or more. By 2007 private urban firms employed some 40 million people, 14 percent of the urban work force. In addition, workers in smaller state enterprises were encouraged to assume control of their factories and manage them as cooperatives. Those cooperatives (called **collectives**), together with other newly created collective industries in China's villages, accounted for over 30 percent of the nation's industrial output. Privately owned firms contribute more than 20 percent. That has left **state-owned enterprises (SOEs)**, which had produced some 90 percent of China's industrial output in the 1980s and 50 percent in 1997, with less than 30 percent in 2007. Meanwhile, the state sector's share of the urban *labor force initially* declined more gradually from 78 percent in 1977 to 61 percent in 1997. But by 2007, that proportion had dropped sharply to 23 percent.[26] In part, privatization's advance has been slowed somewhat because it has been so politically delicate. In the past, large state enterprises hired more workers than they needed in order to create jobs and keep the workers content. Typically, the SOEs also guaranteed their workers lifetime employment (barring any major infraction). With that guarantee removed, new private-sector owners usually have dismissed a portion of the previously bloated workforce. During the 1990s, most SOEs, particularly the large industrial plants, were very inefficient. About half of them lost money and needed to be subsidized by bailout loans from state banks, which often had little expectation of getting their money back. In recent years, however, state enterprises have become more profitable and in 2008 the government announced that it would be ending government bailouts at the end of the year.[27]

Although industrial reform has been enormously successful in many ways, it has also produced several undesirable consequences—higher inflation, greater unemployment, and popular discontent. For example, eliminating many government price controls unleashed higher inflation rates and prompted mounting dissatisfaction among urban consumers. Another pernicious effect of economic change has been an enormous growth in corruption. While private firms are an ever-growing force in the economy, business owners must still depend on government officials to secure vital licenses, permits, and supplies. This has opened vast new opportunities for bribery, allowing many cadres or their children (these widely despised, corrupt, adult children are disparagingly known as **princelings**—little princes) to use their political positions for personal enrichment. Corruption within the state and private sector has been a rapidly growing problem for decades and probably has done more to undermine popular support for the regime than any other factor.[28]

In 1997, the Communist Party announced that during the previous five years it had investigated more than 725,000 charges of criminal conduct within its own ranks—undoubtedly only a small portion of those who were actually guilty—and, as a consequence, had expelled 121,000 members and detained 37,000 people on criminal charges.[29] Periodically, the Party stages major show trials of corrupt government officials and businesspeople, handing down harsh punishments including occasional executions. A few years ago, the deputy mayor of Beijing committed suicide when charged with corruption. But most people view these trials as symbolic, barely hitting the tip of the iceberg, and very rarely affecting top CCP officials or their children. In fact, few cases are brought to trial at any level. In 2004, for example, the authorities caught almost 171,000 government and Party officials in corruption scandals, but fewer than 5,000 (less than 3 percent) faced criminal prosecution.[30] In many instances a complex web of corruption has developed in which businesses—such as the coal mines that violate safety regulations, firms that exploit child labor, and companies that place dangerous chemicals in nutrient-poor milk—bribe Party or government officials to overlook violations. In some cases, even journalists who have uncovered abuses have extorted bribes from guilty companies to keep their discoveries secret.[31]

A third unpopular by-product of rapid economic growth has been increasing inequality, particularly broad income gaps between the developed coast and the country's interior, and between China's urban and rural populations. To be sure, the gap between rural and urban incomes narrowed in the early years of economic reform (1978–1984), but it has widened since, especially since the early 1990s. Whereas city residents earned only a bit over 1.5 times as much as peasants did in 1984 (China's smallest urban-rural gap ever), by 2002 they were earning more than three (3.1) times as much, a higher ratio than at the start of rural reform in 1978. At the same time, income inequality *within* both the rural and urban sectors has risen steadily since the 1980s.[32] Once a country of relative equality, China's current income inequality is higher than India's. That does not mean that peasant incomes have declined in recent decades. On the contrary, they have continued to improve impressively (e.g., 9 percent real growth in 2007). But urban incomes have risen more rapidly. New gated communities, with names like Orange County, Sun City, and Manhattan Gardens, have emerged to accommodate the newly rich business class. Their huge homes, modeled after upscale suburban residences in the U.S., sold (in 2003) for anywhere between $500,000 and $1.5 million, 250 to 750 times the annual salary of a typical Chinese, blue-collar worker.

One consequence of the growing urban-rural income gap is the migration of millions of peasants to the cities in search of jobs and a better life. But migration has exceeded the urban areas' capacities to absorb additional labor, and many unskilled migrants have joined a new, often homeless, urban underclass. China's "floating population" of surplus labor (as these semi-illegal migrants are called) is estimated to be about 150 million people.[33] When the town of Shenzhen, near Hong Kong, was declared a Special Economic Region for industrial investment (see SEZs below) in 1979, it had a population of 20,000 people. Today its population has grown to over 12 million, of whom 7 million are migrant workers. Many live in wretched conditions. The growth of this new underclass throughout urban China has increased crime and other

AN ECONOMIC GIANT   As one of the world's largest and fastest growing cities, prosperous Shanghai, with its impressive skyline, has become a symbol of China's economic growth.

urban social ills. While it had been technically illegal to move to the cities without government permission, the authorities generally ignored that regulation for years and recently have removed the restriction altogether. Officials see these migrants, who drive down urban blue-collar wages, as necessary for further economic expansion. But many of these workers are exploited by their employers, who sometimes fail to pay their employees the wages due them.

China's poor farmers were the major supporters of Mao's revolution and were the major beneficiaries of Deng's early economic reforms. Yet, as the urban-rural income gap reasserts itself and farmers chafe under corruption, government regulations, and high taxes, increasing numbers of rural protests and riots suggest that the government is no longer able to count on peasant support.

Foreign Economic Ties

During the height of the Cultural Revolution, China isolated itself from the outside world and denounced Western and Soviet influences. Under Deng's **open-door policy** since the 1980s, however, cultural, trade, and investment ties to the West and to the overseas Chinese community in Asia have flourished. For example, the government opened special economic zones (SEZ) for foreign investment, primarily on China's southeast coast. It invested heavily in the infrastructure there and offered multinational companies preferred treatment to bring in advanced foreign technology and expand manufactured exports. Today, China is the world's largest exporter of manufactured goods. Deng's successor, Jiang Zemin, widened the opening to the outside world as China entered the World Trade Organization (WTO).

Between 1979 and 1991, total foreign direct investment (FDI) in China averaged $2.16 billion annually. Since that time, FDI has exploded and peaked in 2005 at $72 billion (it has dropped slightly since), making it perhaps the world's leading recipients of foreign investment.[34] That investment has brought enormous prosperity to China's coastal cities and has contributed to an expanding middle class and skilled working class. But, as we have noted, living standards in the country's interior, particularly its rural villages, have lagged far behind.

CHINA'S POLITICAL SYSTEM

The Communist Party

Turning our attention from China's economy to its political system, we will first examine the fundamental organisms of that nation's politics: the Communist Party and the government. Formal political institutions often have an ambiguous role in revolutionary societies. That was particularly true under Mao because of his inherent suspicion of the state and Party bureaucracies. The Cultural Revolution's assault on Party and state cadres was so savage that by the late 1960s, both political institutions were on the verge of collapse.

Although the constitution states that the Chinese Communist Party (CCP) is subject to state authority, in fact the Party has always been the principal policy maker. All of the country's important government, military, and societal leaders (such as union heads) are Party members and accept strict Party discipline. The Party's leader, its general secretary—previously called the Party chairman under Mao—is among the country's most powerful figures. Indeed, except for the period when Deng Xiaoping ruled from behind the scenes (1978–1997), the party secretary general (or chairman) his been the dominant force in Chinese politics.

Party Membership   As we have seen, CCP membership expanded greatly from the start of the Japanese occupation through the end of World War II, and continued to grow after the PLA's victory. At the Communist Party's Fifth Congress (1945)—the last one held before the Communists took power—national membership was 1,211,148. By the Sixth Congress (1956), it had risen to 10,734,384. As of the last Party Congress (2007) there were 73.4 million members (the world's largest political party), constituting about 7 percent of China's adult population. For many Party members coming out of the peasantry and urban poor, membership has opened previously unimaginable opportunities. However, women are still significantly underrepresented, constituting fewer than one in five Party members.

Under Mao, Party membership was a valuable asset but also a major commitment. Members were expected to participate frequently in political activities and were required to engage in "criticism–self-criticism" sessions that probed the depths of their revolutionary commitment. Today, the terms of membership are less demanding and the level of ideological scrutiny is far lower, but members are still subjected to Party scrutiny and some have been expelled for corruption or lack of adequate commitment. Indeed, the Party claims to have expelled 124,000 members for corruption between 1997 and 2002. In a few cases of extensive corruption, punishment can be extremely harsh. For example, in 2000, the vice-chairman of the National People's Congress was convicted of corruption and was executed.[35] But these prosecutions covered only a small percentage of the perpetrators.

As in the Soviet Union, people's reasons for joining the Party typically involved some mix of idealism and opportunism. Given the sharply diminished level of popular commitment to Marxism–Leninism in the last 25 years or so, the proportion of Party members who have joined primarily for personal advancement, contacts, or prestige has surely risen. At the same time, however, educational achievement is fast replacing Party membership as the key to securing better-paid, more prestigious jobs.[36]

Since Deng Xiaoping's ascendancy in the late 1970s, Party standards have changed appreciably. Income differences and other inequalities that Mao so abhorred have become acceptable and, indeed are even encouraged by government policies. Economic growth in China's coastal cities, spurred by a rising private sector, has created huge gaps between standards of living in those cities and those of the rest of the country, particularly the rural interior. With the opportunities offered by an expanding private sector and with Deng's declaration that "to get rich is glorious," a new class of wealthy business entrepreneurs and middle-class professionals has developed. Mao's exhortations to the Chinese people to sacrifice everything for the good of the whole have been forgotten as the Communist Party legitimizes itself by preaching "happiness through consumption."[37]

Although China was once among the world's most egalitarian societies, its income distribution today is not only more unequal than in much of Europe and Asia, but also worse than in the United States (one of the most unequal industrialized nations).

As one American journalist observed, "In practice there is little these days that is Communist about China, a country where laid-off workers hunt for jobs, yuppies buy stocks and houses, and since [2001], private businessmen have been recruited as Party members."[38] As a result of those changes and as a consequence of the mass disillusionment brought about by the 1989 Tiananmen Square massacre and subsequent government repression, few people in China today still believe in communist ideology. Indeed, one survey asked university-aged, Communist Party activists whether they were proud to be Party members. A surprising 43 percent said they were not.[39] In fact, independent analysts doubt that many Communist Party members of *any* age currently believe in Marxism–Leninism. Most of the more than 70 million Party members join out of opportunism—that is, for the material advantages and prestige it brings. In one survey of 800 graduating university students *who belonged to the Communist Party or Communist Youth League,* only 38 (under 5 percent) stated that they believed in Communism.[40] Even at the higher ranks of the Party and the government, China's leaders seem to espouse Communism merely for the sake of keeping themselves in power. So, as the CCP has abandoned its calls for Marxist equality and class struggle, it now seeks support as the protector of stability, prosperity, and nationalism.

Party Structure   The CCP's structure was modeled after the Soviet Communist Party and is similarly hierarchical. Party authority is exerted from the national level down through provincial and local units. The principles of "democratic centralism" demand that Party policies initially be discussed widely at all levels, but once the Party's leaders have announced their positions, they must be obeyed without challenge. In fact, the primary purpose of local Party discussions has been to legitimize leadership policies and give the rank-and-file a *feeling* of participation.

The most important components of the Party are the National Party Congress, the Secretariat, the Central Committee, the Politburo, and the Standing Committee of the Politburo. The National Party Congress met very infrequently under Mao, coming together only twice during the Communists' first 20 years in power (in 1956 and 1969). Since the early 1970s, it has met more regularly but still gathers only once every five years for a few days (meeting last in 2007). Although it is nominally the Party's supreme authority, its very brief and infrequent meetings do little more than ratify decisions made by the CCP leadership. In fact, the major function of the National Party Congress is to "elect" the Central Committee, which it also does by ratifying the choices of the Party leaders.

Between CCP congresses (i.e., most of the time), the Central Committee serves as the Party's official authority. Essentially, however, it merely endorses the choices given to its members. While its debates in recent years have been a bit livelier, it only meets once annually and, like the Party Congress, ratifies leadership decisions. Currently composed of 204 full-time members, the Central Committee represents the Party elite, including military officials and leaders of "mass organizations" representing women, youth, peasants, and workers. The number of Committee members who had graduated from college rose from 55 percent in 1982 to 98.6 percent in 2002. Over half had degrees in science, engineering, management, or finance, giving them a very technocratic orientation.[41] However, the Central Committee named at the most recent Party Congress (2007), included more members with degrees in the social sciences and the humanities than in previous years.

At the top of China's power structure sits the CCP's Politburo (with 25 members at the present time) and, particularly the Politburo Standing Committee currently a subgroup of nine members—which carries out day-to-day operations and has the Party's most powerful figures. The general secretary leads both the Politburo and the Party itself. Until the 1980s, the Politburo was an aging group whose members often traced their communist credentials to the early days of the Revolutionary War. Five of the 28 members elected in 1982 were more than 80 years old, and the entire group averaged 72 years of age. Once entrenched in power, however, Deng Xiaoping, himself then approaching 80, pushed for a younger Party leadership. By 1987, the average age of Politburo members was eight years younger than it had been in 1982. Yet, under Deng's reign, this transfer of power to a younger generation was more apparent than real. China's aged leaders, particularly Deng and a small group of Party elders (mostly over 80 years old), retained their power from behind the scenes, even after their formal retirement, and younger Party leaders still depended on them for support.

Deng's death in 1997—after years of infirmity—finally allowed the transfer of political power from Deng's "second generation" of revolutionary leadership (after Mao's) to a **third generation** composed primarily of men in their sixties or even early seventies. Jiang Zemin, who had been selected as Deng's eventual successor eight years earlier, became China's paramount leader. Today, in addition to being younger, Politburo members are more educated than their predecessors, more likely to have a technocratic background, and less likely to have come out of the military.[42] Not long after Deng's death, Jiang's supporters enforced a Party rule requiring the CCP's "core leaders" (those under consideration for appointment to the Politburo) to retire at the age of 70 and mandated that Politburo members already in their seventies retire at the next Party Congress (held that year and every five years). While Jiang violated that rule when he failed to step down in 1997, he did retire at the next Party Congress in 2002 (at age 76) and transferred his last powers (control of the military) to the new general secretary in 2004. This was the first transfer of power other than through death in Communist China's history.

When Vice President Hu Jintao succeeded Jiang as CCP general secretary at the 2002 Party Congress, he assumed the Party leadership at the relatively tender age (by Chinese standards) of 60. The premier and most of China's top Communist officials are of a similar age, with the Politburo installed at the 2002 Party Congress averaging 61 years of age. Retirement for all Politburo members is now fixed at 68 years. It is also understood that the Party general secretary will be limited to two (five-year) terms and should also retire by the age of 70 (or shortly thereafter).[43] At the 2007 Congress, Hu subtly signaled that Xi Jinping would likely succeed him as Party general secretary (hence, paramount political leader) at the Eighteenth Party Congress (in 2012), while Li Keqiang has the inside tract to become premier at that time (though apparently President Hu would have preferred that Li, rather than Xi, be his successor as Party general secretary). Both are members of the all-powerful Standing Committee of the Party Politburo and, as Hu dryly noted to the Congress, "at 54 and 52 years old [in 2007] both comrades are relatively young." Thus, China has become the first communist nation to establish effective term limits on its leader and a fairly orderly form of succession.

The Structure of Government

China's government primarily administers policies initiated by the Communist Party, but the impact of the government's vast bureaucracy on day-to-day life is enormous. The state affects vast areas of public activity, controlling a substantial (though fast declining) portion of the economy and many other functions reserved for the private sphere in pluralist democracies. Since the time of Premier Zhou Enlai, those who have filled that position (now the second highest in the government) have often provided the Party's general secretary and other leaders with technical expertise, particularly in economics.

Under Deng, the influence of China's premiers often matched that of the Party general secretary, and both figures (along with the nation's president) were beholden to Deng, who held nominally less-powerful positions. Since that time CCP Secretaries Jiang Zemin and Hu Jintao have guided the Party and the state by serving as Party general secretary and as the national president (which had surpassed the premier as the most powerful government office). Premiers have served at Jiang's and Hu's pleasure.

The National People's Congress (NPC)   The NPC is China's legislature, whose primary function is to legitimize rather than evaluate legislation proposed by the national leadership. Since the 1980s, however, NPC sessions have sometimes featured policy debates, and congress has occasionally amended government legislative proposals. For example, in 1998, 45 percent of NPC delegates would not endorse a government report on corruption (either abstaining or voting against the report). Negative votes of 20 to 30 percent on the government's draft legislation have become common. Since its members (elected every five years) include some deputies who are not Party members, the NPC offers the leaders a somewhat broader perspective on issues. In recent years a small number of its members have spoken out against government proposals and it has exercised growing influence, sometimes even convincing the leadership to amend its policies.

The State Council and the Premier　The national government's major executive body is the State Council, whose members direct the national government's ministries and commissions. Its most important concern is economic administration, but it also plays an important role in such areas as education, science, technology, and foreign affairs. In 1998, the Council was reduced in size (the number of ministers and bureaucrats was cut back), reflecting the state's diminished role in the economy. As of 2005 it had 35 members. Most ministers also sit on the CCP's Central Committee, reflecting the substantial overlap between government and Party leadership. Because of its large size, the State Council carries out most of its work in a smaller Standing Committee. Heading the State Council is the premier, who plays a pivotal role in policy making, especially economic policy. Usually, the premier is the second- or third-highest-ranking leader of the Communist Party.

Elections: The NPC and Local Officials

During the Maoist era, elections of government officials were essentially meaning-less. Popular "elections" (with no choice) took place only at the village or local level for representatives to the "basic-level" People's Congress. Those representatives then elected the legislature for the administrative level immediately above them: Basic-level delegates elected their county or city congress; they, in turn, elected their provincial representatives; and finally, the various provincial congresses elected the National People's Congress (NPC).

In 1979, the government made several very modest gestures toward greater political openness. Voters now elect township-level and county congresses directly and most can choose between two or more opposing candidates in local races. Rural villages, townships, and counties directly select their officials in competitive elections. In many villages, very likely the majority, villagers still do not have a real choice. But in other rural communities there is genuine competition. These officials make fundamental decisions on local budgets, taxes, and village development.[44] Sometimes they have challenged the authority of the local Communist Party secretaries, who officially outrank them and who are not popularly elected. National and provincial legislatures are still elected indirectly. And there are still no competitive elections for urban local officials.

The Judicial System

China's court system, be it in its many criminal cases or its far smaller number of political cases, is ultimately subject to the CCP's authority and offers defendants few legal rights. For example, the defense lawyers' role has not been to defend their clients but rather to "safeguard the interests of the state."[45] To be sure, there has been some progress since the 1980s. For example, in recent years, Chinese intellectuals, dissidents, and businesspeople have even begun to bring suit against CCP organizations and government officials for defamation of character, abuse of power, and other violations. Although these plaintiffs usually lose their case and sometimes suffer retribution, in some high-profile cases they have caused government officials to back down.[46]

Punishment in the penal system is often very harsh and international human rights groups remain very critical. Some 60 crimes—including rape, robbery of substantial sums, bribing government personnel, damaging state property, embezzlement, tax evasion, and distribution of pornography—are potentially punishable by death. Not only does China lead the world in *legal* executions, but for a number of years its *total (once estimated at 10,000–15,000 annually) has exceeded that of the rest of the world combined.* Since 2002 the number of executions has dropped in half and a judicial review process, introduced in 2006, may drop the number further. On the other hand, many international human rights groups feel that China reduced the number of executions to ward off foreign criticism in the run-up to the 2008 Olympics and that the number may begin to climb now that the games are over. Furthermore, even with the reduced rate, China still has by far the world's highest number of executions.[47]

A variety of legal reforms since the mid-1990s have expanded defendants' rights, allowed defense lawyers greater independence from the state, abolished the crime of counterrevolutionary activity, and, since 1996, established the principle that defendants are to be considered innocent until convicted. Despite those and other reforms in the criminal code, however, 99 percent of all criminal defendants are still found guilty.[48] Thus for now, any improvement in a criminal defendant's rights must come at the pretrial stage (i.e., the decision on whether or not to bring charges). Unfortunately, many abuses continue at that level. The police sometimes coerce confessions through torture, and witnesses supporting the defendant are frequently barred from testifying. One recent account details how a prisoner was tortured into admitting to have murdered a woman whom, in fact, he had never met. The judge refused to allow him to recant his confession, and he was convicted and sentenced to death. Two years later, while the defendant was on death row, a serial killer confessed to several murders, including that one, and provided information that only the killer could have known. The police tried to remove that murder from the serial killer's confession and to continue with the other defendant's execution. The man was saved only when a police official subsequently joked about the incident to a reporter.[49]

Problems of Political Reform

Discussions of transformations in the communist world often have overstated the linkages between economic reform and political reform. Some argue that a market economy cannot develop effectively without a parallel loosening of state political controls. In theory, reducing state control over the economy and over people's lives at the workplace, creating a larger and more independent private sector, and increasing the size of the middle class should eventually create strong pressures for democratic change. Yet dramatic economic changes in China so far have produced only limited political liberalization.

Since Deng introduced his first comprehensive economic reforms, contending factions in the CCP elite have debated the nature and the pace of economic and political change. During the 1980s, reformers such as Hu Yaobang (Party general secretary from 1981 to 1987) and, especially, Zhao Ziyang (premier from 1980 to 1987 and Party general secretary from 1987 to 1989) favored economic modernization and greater political freedoms, although not democracy. On the other hand, influential conservatives* remained skeptical about far-reaching economic or political reforms.

Though conceding the need to reduce centralized economic planning, conservatives have warned of the dangers they see as inherent in a transition toward the free market (including greater corruption and inflation). More important, they see no reason to link economic liberalization (reduction of state economic controls) to political reform. In earlier years, they pointed to the "economic miracles" that had taken place in Taiwan, South Korea, and Singapore under the direction of right-wing authoritarian governments.†

During the decade that followed Mao's death, political repression lessened, and the Chinese people enjoyed a more relaxed political atmosphere, particularly when compared with the terror of the Cultural Revolution. People have been spared the constant barrage of political indoctrination that had characterized the Maoist era. Dissident intellectuals such as astrophysicist Fang Lizhi spoke for a budding human rights movement. At least in the cities, average citizens have expressed themselves more freely in private conversations. And, in contrast to the all-encompassing cultural indoctrination of the Maoist era, popular culture—partly imported from Hong Kong and Taiwan—now includes rock music, independent art, and literature.[50] In general, citizens who wish to avoid politics are now relatively free to select a lifestyle of their own choosing. At the same time, however, the government has severely persecuted many members of the nation's Tibetan and Muslim minorities believed to support secessionist movements. And in recent years, it has imprisoned thousands of members of the **Falun Gong**, a spiritual sect stressing meditation and exercises, with hundreds allegedly dying while in police custody.

Thus, despite some progress, China has not achieved a degree of political openness comparable to that of the USSR under *glasnost*. Ironically, because of the great success of their economic reforms, Chinese leaders were not under the same pressures as Gorbachev was to open up the political system. Nor did Deng face the challenge from ethnic minorities that weakened the Soviet system, since 93 percent of the Chinese population is of the same ethnicity—Han (although ethnic unrest has been a factor in the more remote regions of the country including Tibet and Muslim regions in the West).

The Chinese press, despite being somewhat more open to critical discussion than previously, is not nearly as independent as the Russian media became under Gorbachev. Indeed, censorship and periodic arrests of journalists have increased since Hu Jintao assumed power in 2002. As Nicholas Kristof observed not long ago, "China now imprisons more journalists than any other country."[51] Obviously, the long prison terms to which some journalists have been sentenced have led their colleagues to practice self-censorship. In 2006, after the government had shut down Freezing Point, an

---

* The use of the terms *radical, liberal,* and *conservative* in the context of Chinese communism can be confusing to Americans. Whereas "radicals" in the Maoist era were those who supported Marxist orthodoxy, in the 1980s radical reformers (and liberals) were those who wanted to move away from mainstream Marxism. "Conservative" in today's China describe those who wish to maintain traditional Marxist ideas (just as conservatives everywhere tend to favor maintaining the status quo). In recent decades such (Marxist) conservatives have virtually disappeared from Party leadership positions.

† Ironically, just as China's hard-liners were admiring Taiwan and South Korea for having fashioned dramatic economic growth and equitable distribution under authoritarian rule, those nations started their transition toward greater democracy.

influential news journal, a group of former, high-ranking Party and press officials denounced the closure, indicating some division within the Party regarding censorship. To be sure, the mass political executions and other gross excesses that characterized the Maoist era have come to an end, but the state continues to jail and torture political prisoners selectively.

Despite a relaxation of repression since the early 1990s, there has been no real movement toward democracy. Instead, the government has permitted some **political liberalization**, a general (but not universal) loosening of authoritarian controls and repression. The Party now allows people greater freedom to choose their own lifestyles and to speak their minds in personal conversations. Indeed, as the state's economic role has receded, it has lost some of its power to control people's personal lives. The constant indoctrination campaigns of the Maoist era are long gone. Kenneth Lieberthal, a noted expert on Chinese politics, describes the present system as "fragmented authoritarianism" (indicating that some cracks in the system have opened it up somewhat), and Harry Harding calls it "consultative authoritarianism."[52]

Sources of Discontent

The Problems and Limits of Economic Reform   Although China's economic transformation since the late 1970s has been nothing short of astonishing, the Western media have often exaggerated the scope of reform and underestimated the problems that it has produced. For example, some analysts have argued that Chinese leaders were moving their nation inexorably away from centralized planning toward a market economy.

In fact, even today the state continues to own important portions of the economy and to tightly regulate other parts. The ongoing conflict between the conservative and liberal factions of the Communist Party caused government policy under Deng Xiaoping to swing back and forth from left to right, though such divisions seem to have ended since the 1990s. Although the Western media often viewed Deng as a liberal, in truth he actually tried to balance the two factions, often siding with the conservatives on political matters (cracking down on dissidents) to win their support for liberal economic measures.

Economic policy debates continued under Jiang Zemin, but policy swings were less dramatic. In part, that is because the conservatives have largely lost the battle and accepted the transition to a more market-driven economy. In part, it is because Jiang was much more cautious than Deng had been about innovating change. The current president and CCP leader, Hu Jintao, has continued the process of market reforms (indeed, his daughter is married to a rich Chinese businessman) but has frequently taken a hard line against political reform and has periodically cracked down on dissent.

The West's admiration and worry about China's economic miracle since the 1980s is quite understandable. From 1980 to 1986, the Chinese economy grew at the astonishing rate of 10.5 percent annually, the highest of any major nation in the world (only South Korea at 8.2 percent was close) and ahead of all other developing nations. After a mild slowdown in 1989 and 1990, annual GNP growth surpassed 12 percent in 1992–1994 and then averaged about 8–10 percent through 2007. In all, China's GNP quadrupled from 1978 to 2004. As we have noted, using one measuring rod of national output (PPP) it is now the world's second-largest economy.[53] The country's standard of living has increased correspondingly, though it remains low by Western European or American standards, outside the large cities.

This tremendous economic expansion, however, has produced a number of problems. Since the late 1980s, an overheated economy has periodically produced annual inflation rates of 7–15 percent. Although those rates are not high by Third World standards, they have concerned Chinese and international analysts. Perhaps the most enduring and despised negative side effect of market reform and rapid economic growth, however, has been increased government corruption. As foreign corporations and China's own private sector have rapidly expanded, private firms still depend on the state for many critical inputs. A new class of "influence peddlers" has developed, composed of people whose political influence can cut through bureaucratic red tape to secure needed licenses, credit, parts, and raw materials for the right price. As we have noted, these intermediaries are often cadres who are the children of more powerful Party and government officials.[54] Widespread official corruption and other malfeasance has undermined the government's legitimacy and battered the image of honesty that the Communist Party had created under Mao.* One opinion survey revealed that "corruption remains the most important source of public discontent with the regime," with 71 percent of respondents expressing dissatisfaction with the integrity of public officials and only 4 percent claiming they were satisfied.[55]

The Causes of the Student Democracy Movement   Discontent over several of these issues helped spawn the country's most powerful protest movement since the revolution, the student democracy movement of 1989. Ultimately, the breadth of the democracy movement and its eventual brutal repression dramatically altered China's image in the world and has influenced the course of Chinese political attitudes until today. In some ways, it is quite surprising that a major protest movement of that nature would have erupted when it did. During the preceding decade, China's standard of living had doubled, agricultural production had soared, and consumer goods had become far more available. At the same time, political regimentation had eased.

The government's open-door policy to the outside world had been designed to bring the country into the modern technological age. But as Chinese governments had discovered as far back as the early nineteenth century, it is impossible to import foreign technology and expertise without also exposing the population to new cultural and political values, some of which are threatening to the ruling elite. As thousands of young Chinese studied in Western universities; as foreign tourists and businesspeople poured into China; as foreign literature and radio broadcasts became more widely available, inevitably Chinese students, professionals, entrepreneurs, and intellectuals were influenced by new ideas. Many students were impressed by Western-style democracy, while others looked enviously at Mikhail Gorbachev's policies of *glasnost* and *perestroika* in the Soviet Union.

The initial cause of the student demonstrations was dissatisfaction over living conditions and job prospects. Upon graduation, "most [students] could look forward

---

* Not only is corruption pervasive in China, but the public's perception of the problem was originally exaggerated somewhat because many Chinese, unaccustomed to a market economy, considered some normal business practices illegitimate. For example, many Chinese felt that it is corrupt for any businessperson to make a very large profit. Such perceptions are undoubtedly declining.

to lives earning modest and largely fixed salaries in jobs not of their choosing, under less-educated supervisors who often did not appreciate their talents. . . ."[56] As their protest expanded, however, the students' goals reached far beyond their personal well-being. Though not necessarily favoring Western-style democracy, student leaders and their supporters desired a more open society—including greater freedom of speech, more independent mass media, and reduced political repression. Interviews of student activists suggested that most of them were primarily interested in reforming the system from within rather than overturning it. Some political leaders, most notably CCP General Secretary Zhao Ziyang, favored dialogue with the students.

But government hard-liners were increasingly anxious as they saw student protesters joined by large numbers of workers, government bureaucrats, and intellectuals. Protests spread to dozens of Chinese cities, and demands widened. As the base of dissent grew, marches in Beijing drew as many as one million people, many of them moved by resentment over non-ideological issues such as inflation and government corruption.

When Deng finally threw his support to the hard-liners, martial law was declared, and troops were brought to the capital to clear Tiananmen Square and break up the demonstration. On June 4, 1989, the PLA brutally ended the democracy movement, killing hundreds of young people who were encamped in the square. In the city of Chengdu, hundreds more died in clashes between protesters and police.

The Aftermath of Tiananmen Square   The crushing of the democracy movement led to a broader crackdown on political dissent and the purge of several high-ranking Party and government reformers. Zhao Ziyang was stripped of power and replaced as Party general secretary by Jiang Zemin, who later also served as the nation's president. Throughout society, political controls were tightened. Several thousand student and worker activists were arrested in the months following the massacre, many of them sentenced to long jail terms. In short, much of the progress away from totalitarian politics during the 1980s was rolled back.

But the post-Tiananmen crackdown was relatively short-lived. Pro-reform government officials at the local and provincial levels successfully resisted many conservative economic efforts and by 1992, the forces of economic reform returned in full force. The degree of political repression after Tiananmen, although substantial, was far lower than in the Maoist era. Since 1992, many freedoms have been restored and individual rights, at least outside the political arena, are now more respected than they had been before the student democracy movement. Today, young Chinese can surf the Internet (subject to government censorship), listen to Western rock or their favorite Taiwanese singers, and aspire to be rich businesspeople. At the same time, however, most of them now consciously avoid politics.

Obstacles to Democratic Change

At the height of the massive demonstrations in 1989, with hundreds of thousands of workers and students protesting and the first government troops unwilling to use force against them, some analysts speculated that the Communist regime was on the verge of collapse. In fact, it was not nearly as vulnerable as the communist governments of Eastern Europe proved to be when they fell from power later that year or when the Soviet regime itself collapsed in 1991. Today, few believe that the Chinese Communist regime will collapse in the near future. How has the Chinese government managed to maintain one of the few remaining communist states (along with Cuba, North Korea, and Vietnam)?

Some experts on democratic transitions have argued that China's political culture, like that of many other Asian nations, is not as hospitable to democracy as are Western cultures. A related historical argument contends that China has no democratic tradition to build upon and has been cut off from democratic change outside its borders.

Although cultural and historical explanations such as those no doubt have some validity, they fail to address the fact that values and traditions can change. Even if it is true that Confucian values slowed the transitions to democracy in South Korea and Taiwan (and many would dispute that), those countries *have* created a more democratic political culture and now have successfully made the transition to democratic government.

China's social structure, rather than its culture or history, may offer a more useful explanation for the regime's ability to resist democratic forces. Unlike the former USSR, Eastern Europe, South Korea, or Taiwan, China is still populated primarily by peasants. Historically, peasants throughout the world tend to be less committed to democracy than have the middle and working classes.[57] In China, the student-led democracy movement was confined to the cities and never spread to rural regions, where 75 percent of the Chinese people resided at the time. It is hard to know how the Chinese peasantry felt about the protest, but Western journalists who traveled to rural communities during the pro-democracy demonstrations found villagers generally indifferent. Few of them understood the protesters' demands, since their only information came from government radio and television. Despite China's many political mobilization campaigns, most peasants remained passive until the 1990s. Indeed, the ebbs and flows of past political campaigns and the violence and deaths often associated with them have made many peasants wary of independent political activity.

Of course, the Tiananmen protests came at the end of a decade in which the peasants had been the major beneficiaries of Deng Xiaoping's economic reforms. Rural living standards, although still very low by Western criteria, have more than tripled since resumption of private farming began in the early 1980s. Not surprisingly, then, the students' concerns about media freedom and job opportunities and the workers' anger over corruption and inflation carried less weight in China's peasant villages (although peasant resentment over corrupt local officials later became a major source of discontent).

Even today, with China's rural population still representing about 60 percent of the national total, as long as the government maintains the support of the rural population, its strength will be formidable. But, in the last two decades, peasant discontent has clearly increased. In their book *Chinese Village, Socialist State*, several noted scholars argued that, despite their economic gains in the 1980s, many Chinese peasants were unhappy about ongoing government intervention in their lives and about the state's imposition of low prices for part of their crops.[58] Since the early 1990s, rural unrest has spread as peasants have demonstrated against corrupt or repressive local government and CCP officials and have been angered by the government's one-child policy (see Box 14-2). At times, villages have seized government buildings, held officials hostage, and blocked roads. In other instances, peasants have elected non-Communist village officials who have challenged local (unelected) Party bosses. Should peasant unrest eventually become sufficiently widespread, it would pose a major threat to the regime.

Box 14-2

CHINA'S ONE-CHILD POLICY AND THE GENDER GAP

One important source of discontent in the countryside has been the government's so-called "**one-child**" policy. Despite China's huge population, during the first three decades of the Communist regime government officials insisted that population growth added to the nation's strength. By 1979, however, China's population neared one billion, almost twice what it had been in 1949. Government officials concluded that lowering population growth was imperative. They announced a new policy limiting families in cities and some rural areas to a single child. In other rural regions family size was limited to two children. Families that did not adhere to those limits would lose government benefits or might even be forced to have abortions. Government propaganda has stressed citizens' patriotic obligation to adhere to these controls, and neighborhood watch groups (consisting primarily of elderly women) have reported violators.

The policy has helped reduce fertility rates from 5.8 births per woman to 1.9 and has cut annual population growth from 2.7 percent to less than 1 percent. The greatest decline has been in the cities, where many families have embraced the one-child policy, which enables parents to concentrate their educational spending and other resources on their only child. In rural areas, however, where children are considered an important economic asset (to help farm the land and to support their parents in their old age), the policy has provoked considerable resistance. Still, even there birth rates have declined as well, though not as dramatically. Given the huge strain that China's rapid economic growth has put on its (and the world's) natural resources and on the environment, the ecological benefits of limiting population growth are very significant.

At the same time, however, the policy is not only coercive but it has had several unfortunate consequences. Because Chinese culture traditionally values sons more than daughters, especially in rural areas, a substantial number of families have made sure that their only registered child is male. This means that many expectant mothers, whose medical tests have revealed that they are pregnant with girls, have chosen to have abortions. Others have committed female infanticide or abandoned their daughters. Consequently, Chinese orphanages are largely filled with girls and female orphans have been the only orphans put up for adoption abroad. Because of the many baby girls killed shortly after birth, the ratio of boys to girls—normally 106 to 100—has reached 117 to 100. During the 1990s, the number of recorded female births was more than 6 percent below what it would normally be.[59] To be sure, not all of this can be blamed on government policy. Female infanticide was common in China long before the 1949 revolution, as families with limited resources wanted to make sure their offspring would be male. And in India, without comparable government pressures, female infanticide and selective abortions have also increased sharply because of the cultural preference for boys. Still, there is little doubt that China's compulsory program has added to the problem.

In recent years, China's leaders have become concerned about these unanticipated, negative results, particularly the bitterness that population control has caused in the countryside. Another concern focuses on the prospect of some 30 million men being unable to find partners two to three decades from now and on a rapidly growing elderly population, which will have to be supported by a diminishing urban work force. Consequently, government leaders have stressed the worth of women and female children. More importantly, the government has begun to relax its one-child policy and has made it illegal for medical providers to tell parents the sex of their expected child (though this is often unenforceable).

There are other causes of popular resentment in urban areas. The government has ended most student resistance and has contained growing, but localized, worker unrest. But it has done so at a heavy cost to its own legitimacy. The mood in the cities, particularly among young people, seems to be one of resignation. Young Chinese today are much more critical of Marxism than they were before the Tiananmen Square crackdown. While many young people in 1989 hoped to reform Communism from within, now they seem to have lost any faith in the system. Nor is cynicism limited to China's youth. A few years ago, even several high-ranking Chinese government officials (some as high up as the ministerial level) privately told a *New York Times* correspondent that they had no confidence in Communism. Disillusionment is surely even more widespread at the middle and lower levels of government and the Party.

As in the countryside, urban protests have been on the rise in recent years. Some of the largest are driven by workers' discontent over losing their jobs with state-owned enterprises (government companies). For example, in 2002, tens of thousands of laid-off workers protested in the city of Daqing when a state-owned petroleum company failed to pay them their promised severance pay. Protests by terminated workers have spread, particularly in the country's northeast, home to some of the country's most outdated industrial plants.[60] Other workers have mounted large protest about being evicted to make room for urban development projects (often promoted by government officials who had been bribed by urban developers). Still other protests have erupted in neighborhoods that had been exposed to industrial pollution. Recently, as many as 15,000 protesters in a Shanghai suburb hurled rocks at police in extended demonstrations demanding the shutdown of a pharmaceutical plant, which residents blame for polluting the atmosphere. These protesters were inspired by riots three months earlier in a city only 50 miles away, where ten thousand demonstrators had overrun police (killing several of them) and forced at least the temporary shutdown of a pesticide plant.[61] Occasionally, demonstrators may actually persuade higher-ranking government officials to curtail an unpopular local project or remove a corrupt local official. But most protests fail and the government harshly represses any movement that challenges Communist Party hegemony, such as attempts to form labor unions independent of Party control.

Consequently, almost all large protests have been aimed at specific local officials or particular complaints. There is currently little disposition to challenge Communism or the regime itself. That brings us to a final explanation for the Communist regime's longevity, the success of the country's economic reforms. Communist regimes fell in the Soviet Union and Eastern Europe after years of economic decay (see Chapter 13). Mikhail Gorbachev's halfway reform measures in the USSR only accelerated the problem. By contrast, most of China's population has enjoyed an unparalleled increase in its standard of living during the past two decades. Although that growth has not been without its problems—most notably growing inequality, pollution, corruption, and occasional inflation—the fact that most Chinese are living better than their parents could have ever imagined has made them less predisposed to challenge the political system. Indeed, an international poll taken six months before the 2008 summer Olympics, found that 86 percent of Chinese respondents said the country was headed in the right direction (up from 48 percent 2002), by far the highest percentage of the 24 countries where the survey was conducted. Australia was a distant second with 61 percent believing that their country was headed in the right direction, while in the United States the number was only 23 percent.* Similarly, the Chinese had the highest rate of satisfaction with their economy (82 percent, up from 52 percent in 2002).[62] While those results were surely influenced by the fact that the Chinese media generally report mostly good news about the country and by national pride surrounding the Olympics, it seems clear that the country's economic boom had bought substantial popular satisfaction and that the government uses that satisfaction to support its own legitimacy.

---

* Besides China, Australia and the U.S., other countries surveyed included Russia, Spain, Britain, France, and Germany

Still, while citizen protests have remained very localized and as of yet pose no threat to the government, they are becoming more frequent. In the last decade, peasants have demonstrated—sometimes violently—against corrupt and arbitrary local Communist officials, high taxes, failure to receive the government's promised price for their crops, confiscation of their land, pollution by power plants, and harsh birth-control policies. For example, many village and local Party officials have confiscated farmers' land and then sold it (for personal profit) to private developers. Farmers who resist face police intimidation. Land seizures of this sort have spawned many of the recent peasant protests. Furthermore, the sprawl of factories, housing, and shopping centers has reduced significantly the area of China's arable land, posing a threat, not only to farmers, but to the country's food supply (a particular problem since only one-fourth of China's territory is arable). Peasants are also upset that their tax rate is considerably higher than that of city dwellers although rural incomes are much lower.

According to government reports, in 1993 there were 1.5 million instances of rural protests. Most of these involved one or two people, but 830 of them included more than 500 participants and 78 involved more than 1,000 protesters. In two months of 1997 alone, various rural anti-tax riots, some of them violent, involved half a million people.[63] Thus, for example, during a single year in the early 1990s rural demonstrations caused injuries to 8,200 government officials and resulted in the deaths of 560 policemen. Since that time, rates of rural protest increased sharply. Looking only at large-scale demonstrations, another government study indicated that there had been about 10,000 protests in 1994 (urban and rural), but that figure had risen to 74,000 a decade later.[64] Sometimes local officials impose illegal taxes (bound for their own pockets), stole other tax revenues, and refuse to distribute tax refunds. Protesters sometimes succeed in removing such officials or in getting some financial satisfaction. In early 2005, responding to rural discontent, the national government promised a small reduction in rural taxes.

Occasionally, local Communist Party officials have even been put on trial for police violence committed against demonstrators. But, in general, the protesters' complaints have not been satisfied. A 2005 protest in the village of Dongzhou sought to prevent the construction of a new coal-fired electric power plant. Here, as in many other instances, farmers' land had been confiscated, with little compensation. Police opened fire on several hundred villagers, many armed with homemade bombs, killing perhaps 30 protesters. Subsequently, when news of the incident leaked, the government imposed a news blackout and bribed and threatened witnesses in the village not to reveal to outsiders what had happened.[65]

CONCLUSION: CHINA'S UNCERTAIN FUTURE

Soon after the 1989 Tiananmen massacre and the collapse of the Soviet Union, many Western journalists and Chinese democracy activists predicted that Communist rule would crumble within three or four years. Today, even the government's harshest critics concede that the Party is likely to muddle through into the foreseeable future.[66]

Of course, history is full of surprises. Nobody could have predicted in 1986 that the Communist Party would lose control of the USSR in five years, and few would have predicted in 1995 that the same would happen to PRI dominance in Mexico

(Chapters 13 and 17). China's policy lurches and internal unrest since the 1950s have exceeded those of either the Soviet Union or Mexico. But because of the combination of economic, social, and cultural factors just discussed, no credible challenge to the CCP has yet emerged. As we have observed, hardly any Chinese—not even CCP officials—believe in Marxism-Leninism anymore. And many people look upon the ruling party as a self-serving, corrupt machine. Still, there has been little disposition to challenge the nation's powerful military and internal security forces or to risk the nation's enormous economic growth.

Optimistic observers insist that there *has* been gradual movement toward a more pluralistic, open society and political system. George Gilboy and Benjamin Read, two noted China specialists, recently have argued that the country has made significant progress of late toward the development of civil society (a network of politically related organizations and institutions not linked to the government) and that the government has become more responsive to its citizens preferences. As China has modernized its economy, they maintain, a class of more educated, property-owning, media-savvy urbanites has emerged, people who are more capable of defending their rights and making demands. Environmental groups have been especially successful so far.

For example, in mid-2007, grass-root environmental groups in the city of Xiamen organized "a walk" by thousands of banner-carrying protestors in opposition to a planned, joint-venture chemical plant, which they believed carried environmental and health risks. Organizers called it "a walk" in order to evade government restrictions on protest marches. As a result, local government officials decided to build the plant elsewhere. Several months later, affluent Shanghai homeowners who opposed the extension of a magnetic levitation train line through their neighborhood, imitated the Xiamen demonstrators by organizing several "walks" and a "group shopping trip" down one of the city's major thoroughfares. The city government agreed to delay construction and to improve public review of such projects. And in 2007–2008, hundreds of homeowners in the city of Rushan (known for its scenic beauty and vacation homes) at least temporarily blocked construction of a new nuclear power plant.

The authors contend that "these walks illustrate how new social groups [and] the Communist Party continue to adapt and experiment on ways to act on new interests while avoiding or preventing direct challenges to CCP rule."[67] Protests of various kinds, they suggest, are particularly common among two types of groups on opposite ends of the socio-economic spectrum: on the one hand, there are new property owners and new professionals who are increasingly organizing peaceful protests such as these; on the other hand, there are rising numbers of protests (often violent) by "the newly needy"—poor peasants and urban migrants. At the same time, there are currently more than 360,000 registered civil society organizations (CSOs) with more than 4 million members, while there may be as many as 3 million unregistered CSOs as well. All of those numbers have increased tremendously in the past decade or so. While the government influences some of them, for the most part they have acted independently to protect the environment, defend workers' and peasants' rights, create charities, establish clubs, and much more.[68] Many civil society activities were unthinkable before the 1990s. For example, the independent Institute of Public and Environmental Affairs" operates a Web site that has "named and shamed" over 4,500 private and state-owned polluting companies. In response to public pressures, state environmental regulators turned down over $90 billion of proposed factories and other projects in 2007.

Gilboy and Read, along with other optimists about the prospects of Chinese democratization, admit that civil-society victories such as these are still the exception rather than the norm, that projects such as new damns or nuclear plants that are put on hold by environmental protestors are often later restarted (though sometimes with greater environmental safeguards), and that state and private enterprise abuses of peasants and workers remain widespread. They also concede that the government absolutely rejects and effectively represses any protests or media reports that criticize high-ranking Party or government officials or question the authority of the Communist Party. Still, they conclude that:

> Time is on the side of all . . . who wish to see greater freedom and more enlightened government [in China]. A trend toward liberalization is likely to continue gaining strength because the drivers of reform, a robust society interacting with an adaptive CCP, are likely to strengthen.[69]

Other China scholars are far more pessimistic and see the Communist Party leadership as rigid and unbending. They are not impressed with the political openings just described and do not believe that they will lead incrementally to a more democratic or even a significantly more open society. Minxin Pei, for example, argues that, in the aftermath of the 1989 Tiananmen massacre, China's economic reforms and limited political transition have actually trapped the country in an unfulfilled transition to capitalism and democracy. That is, the government has allowed only enough reform to co-opt much of the population and has repressed demands for more far-reaching change. If Gorbachev's reforms in the Soviet Union were so rapid that they undermined the whole system, Pei argues that China's changes have been so gradual as to head off comprehensive reform.[70]

In a similar vein, David Shambaugh argues that since the Tiananmen massacre the CCP has undergone a period of both atrophy—diminished control over society—and adaptation—taking corrective measures to avoid or limit further loss of authority. Following the collapse of Soviet and Central European communism, Party leaders and intellectuals carefully studied those regimes' mistakes to figure out what went wrong and how China could avoid the same fate. They have tried to co-opt potential opposition by opening up Party membership to newly emerging groups such as businesspeople, while weeding out corrupt and incompetent Party members. But, efforts by the national leadership to reduce pervasive corruption at the local level have only met with limited success.

One of the Communist leadership's most important accomplishments has been establishing unprecedented unity and stability at the top. Those China experts who expected Deng Xiaoping's death to bring about fierce internal struggles between contending leaders were mistaken, underestimating the strength of his successor, Jiang Zemin, and of the Communist regime. At the Sixteenth Party Congress in 2002, the CCP carried out its most orderly transfer of power ever (the first not brought about by the Party secretary's death), when Hu Jintao succeeded Jiang as general secretary. By the Seventeen Party Congress (2007), Hu had removed the last of the Party leaders from the so-called Shanghai Faction, a group loosely linked to Jiang, and replaced them with people loyal to him. Thus, the current Politburo and Central Committee are more united than they have been for decades. Indeed, the sharp policy and ideological splits that so often divided CCP leaders in the past are now absent. On the other hand, in trying to avoid factional splits at all levels of the

Party, the CCP has rigidly controlled its members' viewpoints, expelling some 25,000 Party cadre and sanctioning another 100,000 annually. At the same time, however, it is also trying to raise the professional skills of Party and government bureaucrats and make them more responsive to the population's needs. Given how well the Party has adapted and modernized, Shambaugh believes it may be able to hold on to power for many years.[71]

By introducing age limits and mechanisms for succession, CCP leaders hope to avoid the USSR's long period of stagnation preceding Gorbachev, when aging and tired leaders ruled that country. The new Chinese leadership, however, will have to deal with a number of underlying economic, political, and social problems that, if left unsolved, may eventually undermine the political system.

The regime's two most immediate socioeconomic challenges are maintaining the country's high rate of economic growth and combating the growing economic inequality that growth has been producing. It is extremely unlikely that China can long maintain the rapid growth that it has enjoyed for the past decade (between 7 and 15 percent annually). As any rapidly expanding economy grows from a small one into a larger one, the *rate* of growth inevitably slows down. No country has maintained annual growth rates of more than 7 percent indefinitely. In the best case, China will have to settle for steady growth at a slower rate. Moreover, there are major flaws in China's economy that will inevitably retard future growth. Andrew Nathan, a leading scholar of Chinese politics, recently wrote cynically about that country's high economic growth rate since the 1980s:

> Twelve percent growth has brought goods to the market, construction cranes to the streets. . . . The numbers are real. . . . but much of what they measure is fake. Some state enterprises consist of waste piles of spoiled goods surrounded by subsidized workers on a permanent break, but the output, jobs and cigarettes [smoked on break] increase their respective national numbers.[72]

China's state-owned enterprises (SOEs), which had generated 80 percent of the country's GDP at the start of Deng's reforms, only produced about 17 percent as of 2003. But they still employed half of the urban workforce and controlled over half of the nation's industrial assets. Most of them are very inefficient and until recently almost half of them were money-losing operations that stayed alive only through government subsidies. As of 1990, those subsidies accounted for *one-third of the national government's budget!*[73] At the same time, the government has severely damaged the banking system by forcing banks to make loans to unprofitable SOEs, loans that everyone knows are unrecoverable. Should the Chinese economy slow down, and there are signs that this is already happening, the large number of unrecoverable loans could set off a banking crisis similar to the world financial meltdown in 2008. Now that China has entered the World Trade Organization and will have to sharply reduce its tariffs and other restrictions on imports, the remaining inefficient SOEs will become even bigger money losers if they are unable to compete with imported goods. From 1995 to 2003 alone, 55 million workers were laid off in a country that had previously guaranteed them lifetime employment (know as "the iron rice bowl").[74] While many found new jobs, many others were unable to find work, especially new employment with comparable wages and benefits. Those numbers will increase as the government reduces subsidies to the remaining SOEs. As of 2000, *official* urban unemployment stood at 20 million workers.[75] In fact, the real number today may be as high as 100 million.

Even if China is able to maintain vigorous growth, it will still face the problem of increasing inequality. In most cases, income inequality intensifies in industrializing nations during their early to middle stages of development. In China, this has been a particular problem because of the government's great emphasis on equality during the Maoist era. Income gaps have been particularly wide between cities and rural areas, and between coastal China and the interior of the country. People living in villages, especially in the country's interior, have often felt left behind. In a recent poll of residents of Beijing, a city with income levels well above the national average, respondents were asked whether they felt "satisfied," "so-so," or "dissatisfied" about government performance in eight critical areas—including controlling inflation, job security, housing, and medical care. The area of government performance that drew by far the most negative evaluations was its record in "minimizing the gap between rich and poor." A total of more than 60 percent responded that they were either "very dissatisfied" (16.7 percent) or somewhat dissatisfied (44 percent).[76] Undoubtedly the level of dissatisfaction is considerably higher in the nation's poorer regions. In short, a future economic slowdown, rising industrial unemployment (caused either by privatization or by the closing of inefficient SOEs), layoffs caused by import competition through the WTO, and greater regional inequality could turn the relatively localized worker and peasant protests into a broader political movement.

Both President Hu Jintao and his premier, Wen Jiabao (who holds direct responsibility for the economy) have indicated that reducing inequality and eradicating poverty, especially in the countryside, are among their highest priorities. Both men, unlike their predecessors, had spent substantial parts of their careers in the poorer, Western provinces of the country. Consequently, the Chinese press trumpeted their commitment to reducing poverty. Rejecting the relatively secluded style of China's past leaders, Hu and Wen have often toured poorer regions of the country making populist speeches which promise reforms to help the poor, better health care for SARS (severe acute respiratory syndrome) and AIDS victims, and reduced benefits for political leaders. Sometimes they have intervened on behalf of supplicants, for example, securing back pay for individual workers who had not been paid what their employer had promised them. In 2005, the government announced new, long-term policies for agriculture designed to raise rural incomes. These included "funding for agricultural research and technology, protecting farmland against illegal confiscation, supporting irrigation and environmental projects, and directing more investment and credit toward the countryside."[77]

The following year, mindful of the spreading peasant discontent, the national government announced an expanded program of rural benefits in the areas of education, health care, and welfare. The program promises to include free education for many rural students (who must now pay school fees) and higher farm subsidies. This followed a long period in which the government had reduced rural social services. For example, the state's share of health care costs had fallen from 36 percent in the 1980s to 15 percent in 2000, leaving the burden of payment on the shoulders of poor peasants.[78] Left unresolved, at least for now, is one of the reforms most desired by villagers, giving them the right to buy or sell farmland and taking that land out of the control of village officials. Much of the recent rural unrest has come from peasants who had been forced by local Party or government officials to sell their land at modest prices to developers, who then made large profits. In October 2008 the government issued a major agrarian reform. It gave farmers the right to buy or sell farm land, making them the virtual owners.

In spite of their public pronouncements, then, and isolated interventions, to date the national government has instituted only limited changes to achieve its stated goal of greater social justice. Many of the plans are vague and long-term, and Hu has proven to be very cautious, not the bold reformer that many had hoped for. It is not clear how committed he really is to economic reform and whether he is ready to take on its entrenched opponents within China's powerful bureaucracy. A test of government intentions will be how well it carries out the rural development programs announced in 2006.

Party leaders have tried to make government agencies report more honestly on problems such as potential epidemics. Following an early official cover-up of the country's 2003 SARS outbreak (a disease that causes death in some 10 percent of those infected and which spread from China to East Asia and North America, raising fears of a worldwide epidemic), Hu purged several high-ranking health ministry officials and the government became more forthcoming about the disease's spread. But, "while both Hu and Wen had called for honest reporting about SARS and its impact, other directives were sent out to make sure the media was not able . . . to gain greater press freedom."[79] Initially, the regime was much more forthcoming about the recent outbreak of bird flu and, as we have seen, about the 2008 earthquake, though it did close down media coverage of the earthquake when evidence of government corruption (on construction codes) began to emerge.

Hu's government has also intensified efforts to control corruption among local officials, though it is not clear how effective that campaign has been.[80] The press, once prohibited from exposing corruption, has been encouraged to do so since the 1990s. But only in rare cases is it allowed to expose officials at higher levels. Contradictory government signals to the press make it difficult for journalists to determine what the boundary lines are. At the 2003 meeting of the National People's Congress, the government announced that in the previous five years it had investigated 207,103 cases of corruption. Once again, however, prosecutions rarely reached the upper levels of government.

Most analysts believe that, however sincere the government's campaigns may be, corruption continues to rise (see Box 14-1). Because Hu Jintao presented himself as a reformer when he assumed leadership of the Communist Party, many Chinese intellectuals and social scientists saw him as a possible Chinese counterpart to Mikhail Gorbachev, who might also expand civil liberties. But, while China's level of personal freedom remains far higher than it was prior to 1990, at times Hu has imposed some of the strictest limits on the press and independent political analysis in the past 15 years. For example, in a 2004 speech to the Communist Party Central Committee (not long after the pro-democracy uprisings in the former Soviet republics of Georgia and Ukraine), he warned that "hostile forces" were trying to undermine the Party by "using the banner of political reform to promote Western bourgeois parliamentary democracy, human rights, and freedom of the press." While Hu has talked about improving "intra-party democracy" (more free exchange of ideas between Communist officials), he has made it clear that, like his predecessors, he is opposed to relaxing the Communist Party's firm grip on power. Noting that openness had led to the collapse of Soviet communism, he insisted that the media not "provide a channel for incorrect ideological points of view."

Although the government has generally relaxed controls over the media, the arts, and books, it has periodically cracked down in response to perceived threats to its stability. On such occasions, dozens of journalists, authors, and writers have been arrested and sentenced to jail terms as long as 10 years. Similarly, at times the authorities have allowed domestic and foreign NGOs greater freedom, but have later restricted them when officials felt they were challenging Party-state authority.

One example of the mixed signals that the government has sent out about political reform is the issue of accountability among government officials. Under President Hu's administration, Chinese citizens have been encouraged to petition the national government regarding abuses by local or provincial (but not national) officials. Between 2003 and 2004 the number of such citizen complaints rose 46 percent in 2003 and another 100 percent in 2004. Although some officials were disciplined or even arrested, the Party leadership decided to put the brakes on this process. Consequently Hu issued new regulations that make it easier for accused local officials to punish those who lodge complaints against them. Indeed, even before that backtracking, a survey by the Chinese Academy of Social Sciences revealed that only 1 out of 5,000 people who lodged complaints felt that they had gotten any results.[81]

Historically, an emerging middle class and bourgeoisie (the business class) have been in the forefront of transitions to democracy. Most recently, the spread of advanced education and the growth of the middle class contributed to democratic pressures in Mexico and Russia (Chapters 13 and 17). In contrast, so far at least, the attacks on China's 1989 democracy movement and the years of repression that followed caused university students and young professionals to withdraw from politics and political protest. Today, young people generally seem more interested in making money than in campaigning for political reform. But that may change (Box 14-3)! As the economy modernizes and expands further, the number of educated and skilled workers and professionals available to organize and participate in a future democracy movement will expand correspondingly. Someday, they may follow in the footsteps of pro-democracy movements elsewhere.

Box 14-3

CHINA'S COMMUNICATIONS REVOLUTION

One of the greatest potential challenges facing Communist rule is likely to be China's electronic communications revolution. As of July 2008 (on the eve of the Olympics), the Ministry of Information announced that the country had 600 million cell phone users (far more than any other country in the world), a number that had grown by 8.6 million in the previous 30 *days*. At that same time, China also passed the U.S. as the world's largest Internet market, with 253 million users, an increase of 91 million (56 percent) over the previous 12 months, and up from only 17 million users in 2000. As of mid-2008 there were 12.2 million Web sites with the .cn (Chinese) domain. The government

is well aware of the potential dangers these can pose, as activists in opposition groups are able to quickly contact each other via cell phones and citizens can acquire information via the Web. The government requires search engines to accept certain limits and block "unacceptable" material. Thus, in order to operate in China, Google, Internet Explorer, and others had to agree to block search words such as "freedom" and "democracy." At the same time, the government has more than 50,000 people policing the Internet, creating what many users sarcastically call "The Great

(Continued)

Box 14-3

CHINA'S COMMUNICATIONS REVOLUTION
(*Continued*)

Firewall of China." Using some of the most sophisticated software, The Wall blocks many Web sites and other information. Most Internet users go online to play computer games or to acquire other non-political information, many of them not even knowing that the Web is censored. But millions of others resent The Wall and often disseminate software that can "leapfrog The Wall" and bypass the censors. Ultimately there is an ongoing cat and mouse game between the censors and those who try to outflank the Wall.

A few years ago, anti-Japanese demonstrations illustrated the potential danger. Students and other young people demonstrated in Shanghai to support government criticism of Japan and it's objections to Japanese permanent membership in the U.N. Security Council. Japan is still widely disliked in China for its atrocities in World War II and its refusal to apologize for them. What bothered the government was not the subject of the protests, which fully supported its policies, but rather the fact that demonstrations were expanding spontaneously and had become violent. Moreover, using text messages, instant messaging, and the Internet, grassroots organizers mobilized large

numbers of protesters and sent out banned photos of protest violence, while the government was unable to identify the movement's leaders. Ironically, the Shanghai police sent out text messages telling people to stop protesting.

At an earlier point the Falun Gong, a banned spiritual group, had used cell phones to organize their demonstrations, including one in which about 10 thousand demonstrators surrounded the Communist Party headquarters in silent protest. The government security forces have screening devices that can intercept cell phone and e-mail messages containing certain key words and then trace them back to the sender. But in the recent Shanghai demonstrations government screening was able to stop one communications medium (the Internet), but not another (cell phone text messaging). In recent years, there has been increased censorship of the Internet and closings of Web discussion groups. But the anti-Japanese and the Falun Gong protests suggest that as the communications revolution expands, the authorities will find it increasingly difficult to control would-be demonstrators.[82]

 ## WHERE ON THE WEB?

http://www.asianinfo.org/asianinfo/china/politics.htm
Brief background information and links on Chinese politics.

http://www.economist.com/countries/China/
Articles and Data on China from the British journal, *The Economist*.

http://www.wellesley.edu/Polisci/wj/ChinaLinks-New/index.html
An extensive source of links to sites on Chinese politics and other aspects of Chinese life.

http://www.hrw.org/asia/china.php
Home page for information on human rights in China and Tibet published by Human Rights Watch, a highly respected group.

http://www.washingtonpost.com/wp-dyn/content/article/2006/02/18/AR2006021801389.html
A fascinating article on independent journalism, press censorship and the influence of the Internet in contemporary China.

◆ ◆ ◆

Key Terms and Concepts ─────────

cadre	one-child policy
collectives	open-door policy
communes	People's Liberation Army (PLA)
Cultural Revolution	political liberalization
Deng Xiaoping	princelings
Expert faction	Red faction
Falun Gong	Red Guards
Great Leap Forward	responsibility system
Kuomintang (Guomindang) KMT	SOEs (state-owned enterprises)
Long March	third generation
Mao Zedong	Tiananmen Square
Nationalist Party (Kuomintang, KMT)	warlords

Discussion Questions ─────────

1. What was new and distinct about Mao Zedong's interpretation and application of Marxism-Leninism (Communism) in China? How has China's application of communist principles changed since the death of Mao?
2. What have been the major accomplishments of the economic reforms instituted under the leadership of Deng Xiaoping and his successors? What are some of the major social and political problems that arose out of those reforms?
3. China seems to be the first communist nation to produce an orderly process for changing the country's top political leaders. What changes have been introduced to guide that process?
4. Since the end of the 1970s, China has moved from a communist (command) economy to a largely free-market (capitalist) one. Describe the main features of that conversion. What are the potential political consequences of that change?
5. China stands today as the last major nation with a political system dominated by its Communist Party. What developments in recent years suggest that it has started a slow transition to democracy? What evidence suggests that there will be no such transition in the coming decades?
6. How is China's one-child policy enforced? What have been the positive and negative consequences of the policy?
7. In what ways did the devastating, recent Sichuan earthquake and its aftermath evoke both signs of greater openness and responsiveness in China's political system and evidence of continued authoritarianism?

Notes ─────────

1. BBC News, "China Anger over 'Shoddy Schools'," (May 15, 2008), http://news.bbc.co.uk/2/hi/asia-pacific/7400524.stm.
2. *New York Times*, "Protesting Parents and Police Clash in China," (July 17, 2008).
3. There are two ways of measuring a country's GDP (Gross Domestic Product is a measure similar to GNP that is used in international economic reports). The traditional method uses market exchange rates to calculate GDP, a method that ranks China's economy as the fourth largest in the world, trailing the United States, Japan, and Germany. But a more recent method of calculating national income adjusts each country's raw GDP to reflect what it can actually purchase domestically. This statistical adjustment creates a GDP based on PPP, or *Parity Purchasing Power*. With the PPP method of calculation, China's economy is larger than Japan's or Germany's. That method is widely considered to offer a more accurate picture of a nation's GDP and is now used by the United Nations, World Bank and other international organizations.
4. Orville Shell quoted in *China's Transition*, by Andrew J. Nathan (New York: Columbia University Press, 1997), p. 227.
5. John K. Fairbank, *China: The People's Middle Kingdom and the U.S.A.* (Cambridge, MA: Belknap Press of Harvard University Press, 1967), pp. 3–4.
6. Suzanne Ogden, *China's Unresolved Issues* (Englewood Cliffs, NJ: Prentice Hall, 1989), pp. 16–20.
7. James R. Townsend and Brantly Womack, *Politics in China* (Boston: Little, Brown, 1986), p. 46.
8. Maurice Meisner, *Mao's China and After* (New York: Free Press, 1987) pp. 5, 25, 28.
9. Ibid., p. 27

10. Edgar Snow, *Red Star over China* (New York: Random House, 1938), p. 177.
11. A leading work on Maoist ideology is Franz Schurmann, *Ideology and Organization in Communist China* (Berkeley and Los Angeles: University of California Press, 1968).
12. In its original usage "cadre" referred to the core members of organizations such as the military or a revolutionary movement. In China, it has developed a broader meaning, referring to a public official holding a full time, responsible position in the Communist Party or the government. China specialist, James D. Seymour, defines it even more broadly as "almost any individual with [political] authority over other adults." See Seymour, *China: The Politics of Revolutionary Reintegration* (New York: Crowell, 1998), p. 117. Thus, China has millions of Party or government cadre.
13. James Wang, *Contemporary Chinese Politics* (Englewood Cliffs, NJ: Prentice Hall, 1989), p. 13. Communist-led, peasant tribunals jailed or even ordered the execution of many local landlords.
14. Townsend and Womack, *Politics in China*, pp. 119–120.
15. For an account of the Great Leap Forward, see Roderick MacFarquhar, *The Origins of the Cultural Revolution*, vol. 2, *The Great Leap Forward (1958–60)* (New York: Columbia University Press, 1983).
16. Harry Harding, *China's Second Revolution* (Washington, DC: Brookings 1987), p. 12; Ogden, *China's Unresolved Issues*, pp. 46–50; and Nicholas Lardy, *Agriculture in China's Modern Economic Development* (Cambridge, England: Cambridge University Press, 1983).
17. There is a vast literature on the Cultural Revolution. Important works include Liang Heng and Judith Shapiro, *Son of the Revolution* (New York: Vintage Books, 1983) and K. S. Karol, *The Second Chinese Revolution* (New York: Hill and Wang, 1974).
18. Richard Baum and Louise Bennett, eds., *China in Ferment* (Englewood Cliffs, NJ: Prentice Hall, 1971), p. 2.
19. Fox Butterfield, *China: Alive in the Bitter Sea* (New York: Times Books, 1982), p. 349.
20. Harding, *China's Second Revolution*, p. 12, offers the lower estimate cited here; the higher figure comes from Liu, *How China Is Ruled*, p. 48.
21. Harding, *China's Second Revolution*, pp. 30–31. Data in this section come from Harding. For comparisons with other communist countries, see Stephen White et al., *Communist and Postcommunist Political Systems* (New York: St. Martin's, 1990), p. 322.
22. Research at the World Bank, "Fighting Poverty: Findings and Lessons from China's Success," (2005), http://econ.worldbank.org/WBSITE/EXTERNAL/EXTDEC/EXTRESEARCH/
23. Nicholas Lardy, "Agricultural Reforms in China," *Journal of International Affairs* (Winter 1986): 91–104. The responsibility system was not actually implemented until 1980.
24. Harding, *China's Second Revolution*, p. 106. Marc Blecher, "The Reorganization of the Countryside," in *Reforming the Revolution*, ed. Robert Benewick and Paul Wingrove (Chicago: Dorsey, 1988), p. 100.
25. The World Bank Group, *Transition Newsletter* (February–March 2001), pp. 13–14. http://worldbank.org/transitionnewsletter/febmarch2001/pgs13–14.htm.
26. George J. Gilboy and Benjamin L. Read, "Political and Social Reform in China: Alive and Walking," *The Washington Quarterly* 33, no. 3 (Summer 2008), p. 149; Public lecture on the Chinese Economy by Professor Rosita Chang at the University of Rhode Island (October 25, 2007); Nicholas R. Lardy, "The Challenge of Economic Reform and Social Stability," in *China under Jiang Zemin*, ed. Hung-mao Tien and Yun-han Chu (Boulder, CO: Lynne Rienner Publishers, 2000), p. 138. Data from Chang sometimes differs from those of Gilboy and Read.
27. Kang Yi, Wang Biqiang, "Special Bankruptcy Out for SOE's Coming to an End," *The Economic Observer Online* (June 13, 2008), http://www.eeo.com.cn/ens/Politics/2008/06/13/103009.html.
28. Mixin Pei, *Corruption Threatens China's Future* (Washington, DC: Carnegie Endowment for International Peace, Policy Brief 55, October 2007).
29. Richard Baum, "Jiang Takes Command: The Fifteenth National Party Congress and Beyond," in *China under Jiang Zemin*, eds. Hung-mao Tien and Yun-han Chu, p. 30, fn. 20.
30. Mixin Pei, "The Dark Side of China's Rise," in *Foreign Policy* (March/April, 2006), www.Foreignpolicy.com.
31. "Killing Puts Focus on Corruption in Chinese News Media," *New York Times* (January 31, 2007).
32. Research at the World Bank, "Fighting Poverty . . ."; The World Bank Group, *Transition Newsletter* (February–March 2001); and *China's Retreat from Equality*, ed. Carl Riskin, Zhao Renwei, and Li Shi (Armonk, NY: Sharpe, 2001), chaps. 1 and 2.
33. *The New York Times* (June 28, 2005).
34. UNCTAD Investment Brief, "Rising FDI into China: The Facts Behind the Numbers," (Nov. 2, 2007), http://www.unctad.org/en/docs/iteiiamisc20075_en.pdf.
35. *The Economist: Country Briefings* (February 9, 2004), www.economist.com/countries/China.
36. Bruce J. Dickson and Maria Rost Rublee, "Membership Has its Privileges," *Comparative Political Studies*, 33, no. 1 (2000), 87–112.
37. Jeffrey N. Wasserstrom, "China's Brave New World," *Current History* 102, no. 665 (September 2003): 267.
38. *The New York Times*, May 2, 2002.
39. Yiu-chung Wong, *From Deng Xiaoping to Jiang Zemin* (Lanham, MD: University Press of America, 2005), p. 273.

40. Peter Hays Gries, and Stanley Rosen, eds. *State and Society in Twenty-First Century China.* (New York and London: Routledge Curzon, 2004), p. 242; Stanley Rosen, "The State of Youth/Youth and the State in Early 21st-Century China," in *State and Society in 21st-Century China,* ed. Peter Hays Gries and Stanley Rosen (New York and London: Routledge Curzon, 2004), p. 242.
41. Tony Saich, *Governance and Politics of China,* 2nd ed. (New York: Palgrave, 2004), p. 99. On the 17th Party Congress (2007), see David Shambaugh, " China's 17th Party Congress: Maintaining Delicate Balances," Brookings Northeast Asia Commentary (2007), http://www.brookings.edu/opinions/2007/11_china_shambaugh.aspx.
42. Ellis Joffe, "The People's Liberation Army and Politics: After the Fifteenth Party Congress," in *China under Jiang Zemin,* pp. 88–89.
43. Yongnian Zheng, "The 16th National Congress of the Communist Party" and Gang Lin, "Leadership Transition, Intra-Party Democracy and Institution Building in China," in *Leadership in a Changing China,* ed. Weixing Chen and Yang Zhong (New York: Palgrave Macmillan, 2005), pp. 16–17 and 38–70.
44. Emerson M. S. Niou, "An Introduction to the Electoral System Used in Chinese Villages," in *Contemporary China: Approaching the 21st Century,* ed. Rebecca McGinnis (Bethesda: University of Maryland Press, 2000), p. 93; Youxing Lang, "Crafting Village Democracy in China," in *Leadership,* ed. Chen and Zhong, pp. 105–130.
45. Wang, *Contemporary Chinese Politics,* pp. 137.
46. Barrett L. McCormick, "Conclusion," in *China after Socialism,* ed. Barrett L. McCormick and Jonathan Unger (Armonk, NY: Sharpe, 1996), pp. 260–261.
47. *New York Times* (June 9, 2007), http://www.nytimes.com/2007/06/09/world/asia/09china.html?_r=1&oref=slogin.
48. Dreyer, *China's Political System,* pp. 179–184.
49. *New York Times,* "Deep Flaws, and Little Justice, in China's Court System." September 21, 2005.
50. Geremie Barmé, "Soft Porn, Packaged Dissent and Nationalism: Notes on Chinese Culture in the 1990s," *Current History* 93, no. 584 (September 1994).
51. Nicholas Kristof, "A Clampdown in China," *The New York Times* (May 17, 2005).
52. Harding, *China's Second Revolution,* p. 128.
53. See endnote 3 for a definition of PPP. *CIA Factbook* (July 28, 2005) http://www.cia.gov/cia/publications/factbook/geos/ch.html [You may want to revise this link, as I was redirected to a new URL] ; Bruce Reynolds, "The Chinese Economy in 1988," in *China Briefing, 1989,* ed. Anthony Kane (Boulder, CO: Westview, 1989), pp. 28–29; Dreyer, *China's Political System,* p. 155; and Asian Development Bank Report (April 19, 2002), http://www.adb.org/Documents/News/2002/nr2002041.asp.
54. Liang Heng and Judith Shapiro, *After the Nightmare: Inside China Today* (New York: Collier, 1986), pp. 130–148, offers an excellent personalized account of an encounter with the corrupt daughter of a government cadre.
55. Mixin Pei, "Racing against Time: Institutional Decay and Renewal in China," in *China Briefing: The Contradictions of Change,* ed. William A. Joseph (Armonk, NY: Sharpe, 1997), p. 18.
56. Martin King Whyte, "Social Sources of the Student Demonstrations," in Kane, *China Briefing, 1989,* p. 50.
57. Barrington Moore, *The Social Origins of Dictatorship and Democracy* (Boston: Beacon Press, 1967); and D. Rueschemeyer, E. Huber Stevens, and J. Stevens, *Capitalist Development and Democracy* (Chicago: University of Chicago: 1992).
58. Edward Friedman, Paul G. Pickowicz, and Mark Selden, *Chinese Village, Socialist State* (New Haven: Yale University Press, 1991).
59. Melanie Manion, "Politics in China," in *Comparative Politics Today,* ed. Gabriel Almond et al. (New York: Pearson Longman, 2006), 451–454.
60. Timothy B. Weston, "The Iron Man Weeps," in Gries and Rosen, *State and Society,* pp. 67–86.
61. "Riots in Shanghai Suburb as Pollution Protest Heats UP," *The New York Times* (July 19, 2005).
62. Pew Global Attitudes Project data reported in "Economy Helps Make Chinese the Leaders in Optimism, 24 Nation Survey Finds," *The New York Times* (July 23, 2008).
63. Joseph Fewsmith, "The Government of China," in *Introduction to Comparative Government,* 5th ed. (New York: Pearson Longman, 2006), p. 492.
64. *The New York Times* (July 19, 2005, and August 23, 2005); Patricia Thornton, "Comrades and Collectives," in Gries and Rosen, *State and Society,* pp. 87–104.
65. *The New York Times* (December 14, 2005, and December 17, 2005).
66. Willy Wo-Lap Lam, *The Era of Jiang Zemin* (Upper Saddle River, NJ: Prentice Hall, 1999), p. 289.
67. Gilboy and Read, "Political and Social . . . ," p.143.
68. *Ibid.,* p. 147.
69. *Ibid.,* p. 159; For another optimistic perspective see Bruce Gilley, *China's Democratic Future: How It Will Happen and Where It Will Lead* (Columbia University Press, 2004).
70. Mixin Pei, *China's Trapped Transition: The Limits of Developmental Autocracy* (Cambridge, MA: Harvard University Press, 2006).

71. David Shambaugh, *China's Communist Party: Atrophy and Adaptation* (Berkeley and Los Angeles: University of California Press, 2008).
72. Nathan, *China's Transition*, p. 218.
73. Dreyer, *China's Political System*, p. 149.
74. Weston, "The Iron Man Weeps," in Gries and Rosen, *State and Society*, p. 69.
75. Michael Bonnin, "Perspectives on Social Stability after the Fifteenth Congress," in *China under Jiang Zemin*, p. 155.
76. Jie Chen and Yang Zhong, "Are Chinese Still Interested in Politics?" in *Transitions Toward Post-Deng China*, ed. Xiaobo Hu and Gang Lin (Singapore: Singapore University Press, 2001), p. 158.
77. Manfred Elstrom, "The Meaning of China's New Agricultural Policy," China Elections and Governance Web site (April 2005), www. chinaelections.org. [This is a Chinese-language site.]
78. Mixin Pei, "The Dark Side of China's Rise."
79. *Ibid*. p. 89 and pp. 334–335.
80. Saich, *Governance and Politics of China*, p. 331.
81. *Washington Post* (April 24, 2005), *The New York Times* (December 31, 2004).
82. "A Hundred Cell Phones Bloom, and Chinese Take to the Streets," *The New York Times* (April 25, 2005).

For Further Reading ─────

Friedman, Edward, and Bruce Gilley, eds. *Asia's Giants: Comparing China and India*. New York: Palgrave, 2005.

Gries, Peter Hays, and Stanley Rosen, eds. *State and Society in Twenty-First Century China*. New York and London: Routledge Curzon, 2004.

Jensen, Lionel M. and Timothy B. Weston. *China's Transformations*. New York: Roman & Littlefield Publishers, 2007.

Liang Heng and Judith Shapiro. *Son of the Revolution*. New York: Vintage Books, 1983.

Lo, Chi. *Understanding China's Growth*. New York: Palgrave, 2007.

Pei, Minxin. *China's Trapped Transition: The Limits of Developmental Autocracy*. Cambridge, MA: Harvard University Press, 2006.

Saich, Tony. *Governance and Politics of China*, 2nd ed. New York: Palgrave, 2004.

Shambaugh, David. *China's Communist Party: Atrophy and Adaptation*. Berkeley and Los Angeles: University of California Press, 2008.

Pakistani lawyers led mass demonstrations against the nation's dictator, General Pervez Musharraf. Eventually, these peaceful protests restored democracy to the country.

15

THE POLITICS OF DEVELOPING NATIONS

◆ The Meaning of Underdevelopment ◆ Theories of Underdevelopment and Development ◆ Sources of Political Conflict ◆ Problems of Political Participation ◆ Women in Third World Society and Politics ◆ Third World Political Institutions ◆ Conclusion: Recent Developments and Future Trends

Even in the most modern and affluent nations, politics often evokes intense conflict as, for example, in the latest U.S. presidential election. Such conflicts are often far more intense in the world's less-developed countries—sometimes called the **Third World**—where the scarcity of government resources may provoke intense struggles between different political parties, geographical regions, religions, and ethnic groups.* In recent months, television viewers around the world watched with dismay scenes of soldiers, police, and political thugs aligned with Zimbabwe's president, Robert Mugabe, attacking, beating, and sometimes killing members of the opposition political party. In Pakistan, many of the nation's lawyers marched in the streets hoping to restore the country's independent supreme court justices to the bench and to bring down President Pervez Musharraf, the nation's military dictator. These and other demonstrations eventually restored a democratically elected parliament and limited Musharraf's power. Prior to that, however, Islamist extremists assassinated Benazir Bhutto, then the leading candidate for Prime Minister. Militias tied to Al Qaeda or the Taliban currently control large portions of the country and periodically bomb strategic targets.

THE MEANING OF UNDERDEVELOPMENT

The list of difficulties and challenges in the developing world remains immense, though there have also been significant gains. In recent decades there have been: famines in North Korea, East Timor, Ethiopia and several other African nations (most of them worsened by government policies); extended rebellions and civil wars in Indonesia, Iraq, Lebanon, Sudan, Congo, and Somalia; growing economic inequalities in Mexico and much of Latin America; warfare between Sunni and Shi'ite Muslims in Iraq; continuing political repression in Myanmar (Burma), Saudi Arabia, and many other nations. To many Westerners, these nations seem to be constantly in crisis. At the same time, however, developing nations have made important political and economic progress in a number of areas—achievements that are less likely to make headlines in the Western media but which are often more important. Democratic government has spread broadly in Latin America, Asia, and parts of Africa, while military rule has waned. The number of ethnic conflicts in Africa and Asia, though still sizeable, has actually decreased. There has been a substantial decline in the percentage of the Third World's population living in extreme poverty, while literacy rates and life expectancy have grown. Efforts by governments and private nongovernmental organizations (NGOs) promise to reduce the worldwide rate of malaria and other fatal diseases.

The more than 150 African, Asian, Latin American, and Middle Eastern nations that compose the developing world are a disparate group. An elite few, including Brunei, Singapore, and Hong Kong, have per capita incomes that currently exceed those of developed nations such as France, Germany, and Canada[1]. Others, including Trinidad-Tobago and Costa Rica, have relatively stable and effective political systems (and decent standards of living). But all of them, even the most stable and

---

* The term *Third World* refers to the politically and economically less-developed nations of Africa, Asia, Latin America, and the Middle East. It was coined to differentiate them from the world's industrial democracies (First World) and from communist countries (Second World). Although the origins of this title are now dated because of the collapse of the Second World, the term is still commonly used interchangeably with *developing world* and *less-developed countries (LDCs)*.

affluent, share *some* important elements of social, economic, or political underdevelopment, including substantial illiteracy (even in wealthier Third World nations such as Saudi Arabia), great economic vulnerability (a drop in world coffee prices, for example, can severely damage the Kenyan economy), sharp social and economic inequalities (Brazil), political corruption (the Philippines and Sudan), and authoritarian government (Singapore and Syria). In most of the **less-developed countries (LDCs)**, several factors, such as poverty, illiteracy, ethnic conflict, foreign intervention, and sharp class divisions, combine to produce political instability, government repression, or both.

What accounts for the Third World's political and economic underdevelopment? No single answer suffices. This chapter will evaluate the general phenomenon of political and socioeconomic development in Africa, Asia, the Caribbean, Latin America, and the Middle East. To begin our analysis, we define and examine two distinct, but closely related, phenomena: socioeconomic underdevelopment and political underdevelopment.

Economic and Social Underdevelopment

Upon first visiting the developing world, most outsiders are shocked by its enormous poverty: many people living in shacks, beggars in the street, inadequate infrastructure, to name a few visible signs. Table 15.1 presents basic economic indicators for two highly developed nations (the United States and Japan); one upper-income, Asian economy (South Korea); two upper-middle-income, Latin American nations (Mexico and Brazil): two lower-middle-income, Asian giants (China and India, with 40 percent of the world's population between them); one lower-middle-income Middle Eastern country (Egypt); and one low-income African country (Nigeria).*

TABLE 15.1   MEASURES OF ECONOMIC DEVELOPMENT

Country	Per Capita National Income (PPP Method)	Share of National Income Earned by Poorest 20%	Share of National Income Earned by Richest 20%	Income Ratio of Richest 20% to Poorest 20%
United States	$45,850	5.4%	45.8%	8.4
Japan	$34,600	10.6	35.7	3.4
South Korea	$24,750	7.9	37.5	4.7
Mexico	$11,500	4.3	55.1	12.8
Brazil	$ 9,370	2.8	61.1	21.8
China	$ 5,370	4.3	51.9	12.2
Egypt	$ 5,400	8.6	43.6	5.1
India	$ 2,740	8.1	45.3	5.8
Nigeria	$ 1,770	0.4	49.2	9.7

SOURCES: The World Bank, Data & Statistics, Gross National Income Per Capita (2007), http://www.worldbank.org/; United Nations Development Programme (UNDP), *Human Development Report 2007/2008: Fighting Climate Change*, Monitoring Human Development (Tables 1 and 15), http://hdr.undp.org/en/statistics/data/.

* These classifications follow the World Bank's division of the world's nations into upper, upper-middle, lower-middle, and low-income groups. That classification is determined by per capita national income based on the older (pre-PPP) Atlas calculation method. Note that India's per capita income using this classification barely exceeds the boundary between lower and lower-middle income nations.

Column 1 indicates each country's per capita income, *adjusted for purchasing power* (**PPP**). Clearly, there are broad differences among the Third World economies. South Korea—like Singapore, Hong Kong, and Taiwan—is a **newly industrialized country*** (**NIC**) whose per capita income is now comparable to that of advanced industrialized nations, but which continues to demonstrate aspects of political and social underdevelopment such as substantial political corruption. More typically, however, Third World nations have annual incomes that are somewhere between one-third (Mexico) and one-thirtieth (Nigeria) that of the U.S.

A country's per capita income gives us some measure of its standard of living, but not a full understanding. A second important factor is the way in which that income is distributed. Two countries may have the same average incomes, but if income is more heavily concentrated (in the hands of the rich) in one of them, it will have more people living in poverty. Columns 2 and 3 of Table 15.1 indicate what percentage of each country's total income is earned by the richest 20 percent of the population and by the poorest 20 percent. Thus, for example, in Brazil the richest 20 percent of the population receives 61.1 percent of the country's annual income, while the poorest 20 percent of the population earns a mere 2.8 percent. Column 4 indicates the ratio of average income within the richest 20 percent of the population to that of the poorest 20 percent. Thus, the richest 20 percent of Brazil's population earns 21.8 times as much as does the poorest 20 percent. By contrast, in Egypt the richest 20 percent of the population earns only 5.1 times as much as the poorest segment. So, although Brazil has an *average* annual income about double Egypt's, the poorest Egyptians are actually better off than their Brazilian counterparts since they earn more than three times as high a *share* of national income.

While highly developed nations generally have more equal **income distributions** than poorer countries do—the Scandinavian (or Nordic) countries, Japan, and Germany are amongst the world's most equal nations—this is not always true. For example, income is more equally distributed in Ethiopia, Pakistan and Yemen that in the United States or Britain.[†] Table 15.1 reveals considerable variation within both developed and developing countries. To be sure, Japan, a developed nation, has one of the world's most equal income distributions and Brazil, a developing economy, has one of the most unequal. At the same time, however, the United States (with one of the highest concentrations of income among developed countries) has greater income inequality than South Korea, Egypt, or India (see the last column of Table 15.1).

Although per capita income and income distribution data are important indicators of a country's economic level, they do not necessarily tell us all we need to know about the population's living standards, particularly their health conditions and education. While more affluent countries tend to have better health care and educational systems, Table 15.2 indicates that countries that make concerted efforts in those areas may achieve better social conditions for their citizens than do some richer countries that are less committed. As with our previous table, this table includes a mix of

---

[*] Hong Kong is not an independent country, but rather a semi-autonomous part of China. But its capitalist economy is separate from China's and it is treated separately in UN statistics.

[†] Economists use a measure called the Gini Index to compare different countries' income distributions. In theory, a nation's index can run from 0.0 (full equality) to 100.0 (the maximum possible inequality). In reality, current Gini Indices run from about 25.0 (Denmark, Japan, and Sweden) to 74.3 (Namibia). The U.S. index is currently 40.8. See UNDP, *Human Development Report 2008/2008*, Table 15.

Table 15.2   Indicators of Social Development

	HDI (Rank)	Life Expectancy (Years)	Adult Literacy (Percent)	Real Income Rank (PPP) Minus HDI Rank
Australia	.962 (3)	80.9	99.0	+13
United States	.951 (12)	77.9	99.0	−10
South Korea	.921 (26)	77.9	97.9	+6
Chile	.869 (38)	78.3	95.7	+15
Cuba	.809 (52)	77.7	99.8	+43
Saudi Arabia	.812 (61)	72.2	82.9	−19
Brazil	.800 (70)	71.7	88.6	−3
China	.777 (81)	72.5	90.9	+5
Egypt	.708 (112)	70.7	71.4	−1
India	.619 (128)	63.7	61.0	−11
Nigeria	.470 (158)	46.5	69.1	+4
Ethiopia	.406 (169)	51.8	35.9	−5

Source: United Nations Development Programme (UNDP), *Human Development Report 2007/2008*, Monitoring Human Development, (Table 1) http://hdr.undp.org/en/statistics/data/.

developed nations and developing countries with a range of income levels. The **Human Development Index (HDI)**, as calculated by the United Nations Development Program, is widely perceived by scholars as the best indicator of a population's well being or quality of life. The HDI is a composite index reflecting a country's per capita income, average life expectancy, literacy rate, and educational level. Statistics for all of these factors are combined into a single index, which, in theory, can range from a high of 1.000 (the best possible score) to a low of 0.000. Table 15.2 lists countries in the order of their HDI scores, from a high of .962 in Australia to a low of .406 in Ethiopia (column 1). The second number in column 1, in parentheses, indicates each country's HDI ranking among nearly 180 countries in the world. Thus, Australia has the world's third-highest HDI score (Iceland is first), the United States ranks 12th, and Ethiopia ranks 169th. Columns 2 and 3, respectively, indicate each country's average life expectancy and its adult literacy rate.

Finally, column 4 offers one of the most interesting statistics in this chapter. It compares a country's world ranking in per capita income with its HDI ranking. Since HDI scores generally correlate with per capita income (richer countries tend to have higher HDIs), we would normally expect a country with, say, the fiftieth highest per capita income in the world to rank about fiftieth on HDI and so on. In column 4, each country's HDI *ranking* is subtracted from its per capita income *ranking*. Thus, for example, the United States has the 2nd highest per capita income in the world, but only the 12th highest HDI, giving it a negative score (in column 4) of −10 (2 − 12 = −10), the negative sign indicating that its HDI ranking was lower than its per capita income ranking and that it has apparently *underachieved* in educating its population and raising its life expectancy (indicators of health care and nutrition). Conversely, Chile, ranked 53rd in the world in per capita income but 38th in HDI, giving it a score of +15 (53 − 38 = 15). That is to say, Chile *"overachieved"* by giving its population a higher quality of life (in terms of health and education) than its per capita income ranking would lead us to expect.

Not surprisingly, the table indicates that the richest countries (Australia and the United States) have the highest life expectancy and adult literacy rates and, consequently, the highest HDI scores; whereas very poor countries, such as India, Nigeria, and Ethiopia, ranked much lower on these dimensions. At the same time, however, several countries had higher HDI scores than their per capita income would have predicted, while other countries underachieved. So, even though Cuba's per capita income is less than half of Saudi Arabia's and about 25 percent below Brazil's, its life expectancy and adult literacy rates are significantly higher than theirs. Indeed, Cuba was the world's greatest "overachiever" (+43 in column 4). Its unexpectedly high HDI score reflects its government's strong emphasis on public health and educational programs. On the other hand, Saudi Arabia's poor performance (−19) indicates that its government has not used its enormous petroleum wealth as effectively to raise health and educational levels. Thus, despite having a per capita income twice as high as China's, the Saudi literacy rate is significantly lower. That educational underachievement is partially caused by Saudi Arabia's limited educational opportunities for women. Australia and Chile were overachievers, while the United States and India were underachievers.

Although economic modernization and growth in a developing nation eventually raise living standards, the early-to-middle stages of that growth frequently create new pockets of poverty and increase economic inequality. For example, as China has become an economic power, income inequality has widened considerably (Chapter 14). Since growing income gaps in society tend to generate class tensions, it is not surprising that many countries at the middle level of development, such as Brazil, Mexico, and Peru, are more prone to political unrest.[2] Early modernization in the West also produced greater income inequality but that gap narrowed in later stages of development. It is not certain whether further modernization and economic

A PICTURE OF POVERTY   Children play near their meager home in a Calcutta, India, slum.

growth in countries such as China and Brazil will eventually reduce income inequalities similarly.

Several factors underlie the high rates of inequality in many LDCs. On the one hand, per capita incomes in the more economically developed cities tend to be as much as four or five times greater than in rural areas. Within the countryside itself, particularly in much of Latin America and parts of Africa and Asia, land ownership is highly concentrated. That combination of urban-rural income inequality and disparities in rural land ownership keeps the rural poor at the bottom of the income ladder. It also helps drive the enormous migration from countryside to city that has taken place in so many developing nations. As some Third World cities have doubled their populations in little more than a decade, sprawling slum neighborhoods have developed, usually lacking adequate sanitation or water facilities. Nigeria's population was only 20 percent urban in 1970 but is now about 50 percent.[3] That creates further layers of inequality—between the urban population as a whole and the rural poor, and within the cities between the middle class and skilled working class on the one hand, and unskilled or semi-employed workers on the other. In China, the growing economic gap between the country's major cities and the countryside has induced more than 100 million peasants to migrate to the cities in the last decade or so, with another 50 million expected to do so in the coming decade.

Although initial economic growth and modernization usually produce greater inequality, the policies of *individual* governments can alter that relationship significantly. Nations such as Taiwan, South Korea, Costa Rica, and Cuba, with very different economic and political systems, have achieved more equitable income distributions through redistribution of farmland from landlords to peasants, mass education, and public welfare programs. More typically, some countries, such as Brazil and Mexico, have attained impressive economic growth coupled with poor income distribution, while others have accomplished more equitable economic distribution but only slow growth (Cuba, for example). Unfortunately, still other countries, such as Zimbabwe, Peru, and Namibia, have experienced both high inequality and low growth. Only a few, such as Indonesia, South Korea, and Taiwan, have achieved both high growth and relative income equality.

Over the past 40 years or so, much of the developing world has achieved impressive gains in health and education, but serious shortfalls remain and in some regions there has been backsliding. On the one hand, between the early 1970s and the end of the twentieth century, Third World infant mortality rates—the proportion of infants who die in the first year of life—fell by an impressive 40 percent. That decline and other health improvements lifted life expectancy from 53.4 years in 1960 to 66 years in 2007.[4] At the same time, however, since 1990 the AIDS pandemic in sub-Saharan Africa has reduced life expectancy in a dozen countries (sometimes drastically), including Botswana, South Africa, and Zimbabwe.[5] Elsewhere in the LDCs, even with lowered infant mortality, each *hour* an average of 1,200 children still die, yielding an annual mortality toll that is 36 times greater than the 300,000 people killed in the 2004 Asian tsunami. And, while the number of people living in extreme poverty (living on less than $1 per day) has fallen substantially since 1981, that group still accounts for some 17–18 percent of the world's population and at least twice that percentage in Sub-Saharan Africa and South Asia.[6]

Political Underdevelopment and Development

Of course, underdevelopment also has a political component. Defining it, however, has been elusive at times, and some leading scholars have questioned the value of the term **political underdevelopment** itself.[7] With that caveat in mind, let us consider some definitions and characteristics of political underdevelopment and development.

Fundamental Definitions   Nations suffering from low political development—most notably in Africa, Asia, and the Middle East—often have created their current government institutions—such as parliament or the bureaucracy—relatively recently compared to many Western nations that have had their major institutions for centuries. Consequently, their institutions have not been around long enough to have acquired their own traditions, while much of the population has yet to develop respect for them. If they very perform poorly or are corrupt, their **legitimacy** is weakened even further.

Second, in developed countries, most political participation takes place "within the system"—that is, within regularized and legal channels such as elections or lobbying. In contrast, political activity in many LDCs is often non-legal or even violent. For example, the conflicting needs and interests of different ethnic groups may be solved peacefully through existing political institutions or, if those institutions cannot resolve them, they may erupt into violence.[8] More politically advanced Third World countries, such as Costa Rica and the Bahamas, have made progress relatively peacefully through interest group politics, negotiation, and legislation. By contrast, where within-system solutions have failed—as in Congo, Lebanon, Zimbabwe, and Indonesia—political tensions have often provoked bloody conflict.

Finally, less-developed governments often lack the capacity to govern effectively. They may have great difficulty collecting necessary taxes, responding effectively to emergencies, or maintaining order. During the 1970s, Nigeria and Mexico, major petroleum exporters, accumulated considerable wealth from their petroleum exports and appeared on the verge of an economic takeoff. But excessive external borrowing, wasteful spending, ineffective administration, and corruption all caused their governments to squander many of their opportunities and to plunge the countries into extended economic declines.

Democracy and Development   Before the late 1980s, most political scientists stressed two goals of political development: achieving political stability and establishing effective governments. More important, many of them suggested that achieving stability was the first priority, and other goals—such as democracy, social justice, and equity—would have to follow later.[9] Some observers questioned whether democracy was yet attainable in Third World settings or even desirable at that time. In recent years, however, troubled by the numerous instances of government repression in the LDCs, a growing number of analysts have concluded that democracy and social equity must be integral parts of political development.[10]

Beyond the prima facie moral argument that *all* societies, no matter how poor, should be protected from state repression and should be free to choose their own political leaders, most experts now agree that although democracy does not guarantee political stability or efficiency, in the long run those goals may be unattainable without it. Amartya Sen, the winner of a Nobel Prize in Economics, has provided one fascinating case for democracy. He notes that among the many famines that have occurred in the Third World, none has ever taken place in a democratic country with a free press. Even when democracies such as India and Botswana have experienced natural disasters such as droughts or floods, domestic and foreign public opinion (informed by a free press) have ensured that their governments take appropriate actions to avert famine. On the other hand, dictatorships in countries such as Ethiopia and Sudan have frequently ignored or covered up famines or even enhanced them when they have killed people in "enemy" regions or ethnicities. For example, the Nigerian military government used famine as a method of subduing the Ibo break-away state of Biafra (in the 1960s), while the Sudanese regime's currently limits foreign food aid to Darfur, where several rebel groups operate. Following Myanmar's recent, devastating cyclone, the military dictatorship first delayed foreign assistance and then permitted only limited external aid. It was less concerned about saving lives than in proving it could handle the situation itself and in limiting contacts between its people and foreign relief workers.

Other Manifestations of Political Underdevelopment   Let us now turn our attention to several political conditions that do not *define* political underdevelopment but are common characteristics of LDCs. Like economic resources, political influence in the developing world tends to be unequally distributed. Power is often concentrated in the hands of particular ethnic minorities or economic and political elites. Furthermore, government policies often favor the urban upper and middle classes and, to a lesser extent, unionized blue-collar workers at the expense of the rural poor and unorganized urban workers, who together usually constitute the majority of the population (though there are various strong exceptions).

Although the number of Third World **electoral democracies** (countries with free and fair contested elections, but without extensive civil liberties) has grown substantially since the 1970s, today most developing nations still lack the fundamental standards of **liberal democracy** (substantial civil liberties as well as free and fair elections). Despite gains in recent decades, most LDCs still lack genuinely contested elections, free speech, open media, freedom of association, and other civil liberties. In the Middle East, much of Africa, and parts of Asia, military or single-party rule is still the norm. Elsewhere, in such countries as El Salvador and Guatemala, even when contested elections do take place, the military, security forces, or armed vigilantes have often intimidated certain candidates, parties, and organized groups. Few nations in Africa, Asia, or the Middle East enjoy a free press, as their governments generally control the airwaves. Prominent human rights monitoring groups, including Amnesty International and Human Rights Watch, have cited countries as diverse as Syria, Turkey, Sudan, Myanmar, North Korea, and Colombia in the recent past for their imprisonment and torture of political dissidents, and for their murder of real or imagined government opponents.

During the 1970s, as many as 30,000 young Argentineans died in prison or disappeared as a result of the military government's "dirty war" against the left. The fanatically leftist Khmer Rouge regime was responsible for the deaths of more than one million Cambodians. Since the 1980s, human rights conditions have improved dramatically in Latin America and in parts of Asia. There has also been some progress in Africa, but a considerable number of nations on that continent, in the Middle East, and in Asia are still the victims of political repression.[11]

Given the unrepresentative and repressive quality of many Third World governments, it is easy to understand why they often lack legitimacy. Citizens may view their government with apathy or hostility. In a number of LDCs, popular unrest has challenged the government, often at great risk to the protestors: student protests against government repression in Myanmar, demonstrations against government corruption and repression in Kenya, Egypt, and Zaire, and anti-corruption rallies in the Philippines. In parts of India, corruption is so pervasive that poor mothers in run-down maternity wards often have to bribe the nurse and doctor—handing over as much as one week's wages—to be permitted to see or hold their own baby.[12] The most intense forms of popular discontent have led to revolutionary movements or civil war in nations such as Sudan, Nicaragua, Angola, Afghanistan, and Pakistan.

Box 15-1

POLITICAL CORRUPTION IN DEVELOPING COUNTRIES

Political corruption can be a problem in almost any country, including the United States. To take one of many examples, in recent years, powerful California Congressman "Duke" Cunningham (a Vietnam War flying ace) pleaded guilty to taking $2.4 million in bribes (including a Rolls-Royce and other luxury items) from defense contractors. Political corruption scandals periodically emerge in other developed countries such as France, Italy, Japan, and Spain. But corruption tends to be a particularly insidious problem in developing countries, both because it tends to be more widespread and because its effects are especially harmful. In a 2004 study, the World Bank estimated that public officials worldwide collected more than $1 *trillion* in bribes every year (a figure that has almost surely grown since). While the Bank did not estimate what portion of that took place in the Third-World nations, it did indicate that officials were more likely to take bribes in less-developed countries.[13] The size of each bribe varies enormously from the $2 amount given to a Mexican policeman so that he does not ticket a driver for an imaginary traffic violation, to the hundreds of millions paid to high-ranking, Middle Eastern officials to secure a multi-billion-dollar weapons contract. In many countries, corrupt judicial systems usually either fail to investigate or acquit businesspeople who have committed fraud.

It is obviously difficult to get precise data or even very informed estimates of the extent of corruption in a country since bribes, by nature, are transacted secretly. However, the most respected information on the extent of corruption and the degree of government transparency (a measure of how openly government decisions are made) is published by a Berlin-based organization called Transparency International (TI). TI gathers information on the extent of corruption by politicians and other public officials in some 180 nations worldwide based on the perceptions of resident and foreign country experts and resident businessmen evaluating their own country. Each country is then given a Corruption Perception Index (CPI) score ranging from 0 (extremely corrupt) to 10 (extremely clean).

In 2007, the countries with the highest scores (most transparent) were Denmark, Finland, New Zealand, Singapore, and Sweden. The countries perceived to be most corrupt were Somalia (the worst), Myanmar (Burma), Iraq, Haiti, and Uzbekistan (a former Soviet republic). In short, the countries with the most political corruption were poor, developing nations, while the most honest governments were found in prosperous nations with high HDI scores. Indeed, the only Third World countries to break into the 25 highest positions were Singapore and Hong Kong, extremely prosperous economies with high education levels. Of the 20 governments judged to be most corrupt, all were low-income countries, many of them—Afghanistan, Bangladesh, Cambodia Chad, Congo, Ethiopia, Haiti, Myanmar, Somalia, and Sudan—among the poorest nations on earth.[14]

Why is corruption so much more pervasive in poor, developing countries? One partial explanation is that many of them have yet to develop a civic culture that frowns on bribes and other forms of corruption, and stresses government accountability. A second factor in the poorest nations is that their economies are so weak

(Continued)

POLITICAL CORRUPTION IN DEVELOPING COUNTRIES
(Continued)

that there are few opportunities in the private sector to become wealthy or even well-off. Moreover, foreign companies often dominate the few opportunities available. So, wielding political power becomes one of the few paths to wealth for an enterprising individual. That is, the kind of entrepreneurial spirit that might lead a young German or American to start his or her company, go to business school, or take a job with a large corporation, might lead their counterparts in Chad or Laos to become public officials.

The ramifications of widespread corruption are serious anywhere, but perhaps most particularly in a less-developed country. In Chapter 14, we noted how corruption among Chinese local officials and safety inspectors may have contributed to substandard school construction and many more student deaths in that country's recent earthquake. There have been similar charges in previous earthquakes in Pakistan

and Turkey, among others. In countries like Nigeria and Myanmar, government officials often siphon off government funds or foreign assistance designed to deliver food and health care to the very poor. A substantial amount of U.S. funding for reconstruction in Iraq has been lost to government fraud, greatly slowing the restoration of oil production, hospitals, and the like. In a broader sense, pervasive corruption causes the government to lose legitimacy and contributes to public cynicism and apathy toward politics.

Finally, it is important to recognize that not all Third World governments (and certainly not all public officials in the LDCs) are corrupt. A number of developing countries—such as Botswana, Chile, Barbados, Taiwan, Uruguay, and the United Arab Emirates, Singapore, and Hong Kong—have comparatively clean governments according to TI data.

The types of grievances that lead to violence are varied. Latin America's guerrilla struggles have been rooted in class conflict. Revolutionary movements in Cuba, Nicaragua, El Salvador, Peru, and Colombia have brought disenchanted students and intellectuals together with peasants and the urban poor. The primary sources of their discontent have been inequitable land and income distribution, poverty, rising prices, state corruption, and government repression. Violent conflict in Africa and parts of Asia, on the other hand, is more frequently tied to ethnic or regional hostilities, with class divisions playing a secondary role. Secessionist movements in Eritrea and Tigre fought for decades before gaining independence or greater autonomy from Ethiopia.

The toll from these conflicts has been staggering. From 1981 to 1991, some 75 thousand people died in El Salvador. In the Congo, over five million have perished since 1998 from the fighting itself, war-related starvation, and disease. At the start of 2008, Congolese continued to die at a rate of 500,000 annually.[15] In Nigeria, Ethiopia, Sudan, Mozambique, Guatemala, Indonesia, India, Cambodia, and Lebanon, staggering numbers of citizens—in some cases in the hundreds of thousands or even millions—have died directly and indirectly from ethnic or class conflict. Recently, attacks by pro-government militia in Sudan have caused between 200,000 and 400,000 deaths in the Darfur region.

Because governments in the developing world so frequently lack legitimacy or effective links to the people, many of them are extremely vulnerable. Often, the armed forces seize power, seeking to establish political stability, to replace an ineffective or corrupt leader, to pursue a particular development program, or, most commonly, simply to protect the military's own institutional interests. All too often, however, these military regimes have turned out to be more corrupt, more repressive, and less efficient than the civilian governments they had replaced.

Before examining manifestations of political underdevelopment in greater detail, we will consider the ways in which social scientists have tried to explain the *causes* of underdevelopment and the pathways that they have prescribed for change.

THEORIES OF UNDERDEVELOPMENT AND DEVELOPMENT

Having described the differences between developed nations and the LDCs, we must now ask why it is that some countries have developed their political and economic systems while others are still struggling. Over the years, analysts have offered two distinct explanations. The first insists that political and economic development are driven primarily by *domestic* factors (within the Third World), most notably changes in the country's cultural values. The second approach emphasizes the effects of *international* trade and investment, suggesting that *external* exploitation is the primary cause of Third World underdevelopment. These approaches are called, respectively, *modernization theory* and *dependency theory*.[16]

Modernization Theory and the Importance of Cultural Values

In the decades after World War II, as the demise of European colonialism produced a host of newly independent nations in Africa and Asia, Western social scientists formulated an understanding of development and underdevelopment known as **modernization theory**.[17] Despite the tremendous array of problems facing the Third World, modernization theorists were initially relatively optimistic about its prospects for development. They expected that most LDCs could follow a path of economic and political modernization roughly parallel to that which had earlier been traveled by Western industrial democracies. The LDCs merely needed to promote modern cultural values and to create appropriate economic and political institutions. Transforming the culture of developing nations was considered the key to modernization.

Drawing on the theories of seminal sociologists such as Max Weber and Talcott Parsons, the theory distinguished between clusters of traditional versus modern values. Modern societies, it claimed, were more prone than traditional ones to judge people by universal standards (that is, to evaluate them according to their own ability rather than their family or ethnic origins), to believe in the possibility and desirability of change, to be concerned with social and political issues beyond the scope of family, village, or neighborhood, and to believe that citizens should try to influence the political system.[18]

But how can a society with traditional values acquire modern ones? In large part, the argument ran, modern values emerge as a natural by-product of socioeconomic change, particularly urbanization and industrialization. When people leave their farms for factory jobs in the cities, they commonly become literate and are exposed to new ideas and experiences. The theory credits education and the mass media as being key agents of change.

Thus, modernization theory focused on the *diffusion* of modern ideas both from the developed world to the developing world and, within the Third World, from city to countryside. Western foreign aid, trade, and institutions such as the Peace Corps could help speed the process. At the core, then, it envisioned modernization, in part, as a process of getting developing nations to think and act "more like us." "As time goes on," Marion Levy predicted, "they and we will increasingly resemble one another. . . . The more highly modernized societies become, the more they resemble one another."[19]

Along with modern values, LDCs need to develop more specialized and more complex political and economic institutions. They need to develop trained bureaucracies, where merit determines promotions, rather than connections, and which bases decisions on universally applied standards. They also must create a modern legal system in where decisions are made fairly and in which the defendant's ethnicity and socioeconomic status do not determine the outcome. And political parties have to effectively channel popular demands and aspirations to the government.

In time, many of the early assumptions of modernization theory had to be modified. Initially, it had been too optimistic in its view of political and socioeconomic change, assuming that modernizing countries could simultaneously and relatively smoothly achieve economic growth, greater equality, democracy, stability, and greater national autonomy. As Samuel Huntington has noted, the theorists erroneously assumed that "all good things go together."[20] Eventually, a more sophisticated and pessimistic form of modernization theory emerged, asserting that change is often a painful and disruptive process involving difficult choices. Indeed, although modernity is associated with political stability, the painful transition from **traditional society** to modern society, said Huntington, is often profoundly destabilizing.[21] In countries such as South Korea and Brazil, social and economic modernizations were initially spurred by authoritarian governments rather than by democracy.

Dependency Theory

Beginning in the 1950s, a number of social scientists, primarily in Latin America and the United States, raised more fundamental objections to modernization theory. Under the banner of **dependency theory**, they challenged most of its fundamental assumptions.

To begin with, they rejected the notion that LDCs could follow the same path to development as Western nations had. When Great Britain became the world's first industrial power, they noted, it had faced no external competition. In today's world, nations trying to industrialize have to compete against well-established industrial giants. In addition, argued Theotonio Dos Santos, LDCs have to borrow capital and must purchase advanced technology from the developed world, thereby making them dependent on external economic forces and ultimately weakening their growth.[22]

Whereas modernization theorists generally saw Western influence in the Third World as beneficial, so-called *dependencistas* insisted that it was Western colonialism that had turned Africa and Asia into poorly paid sources of cheap food and raw materials for the colonial powers. And long after Third World nations had achieved political independence, they remained economically and politically dependent on the developed world. Production and export of manufactured goods—the most profitable economic activities—were allegedly confined to the highly industrialized democracies, called "**the core.**" Third World nations ("the periphery") were largely relegated to the production and export of food and raw materials, condemned to trade for industrial imports on unfavorable terms.[23]

In the political realm, dependency theorists insisted that Third World economic elites, backed by the economic and military power of the "core nations," maintained a political system that benefited the few at the expense of the majority. Dependency theory was obviously an attractive model for Third World scholars, suggesting that underdevelopment was not the LDCs' fault, but, rather, the result of foreign exploitation. But in U.S. universities, as well, dependency theory challenged and sometimes displaced modernization theory as the major scholarly explanation of underdevelopment.

But just as early modernization theory had been overly optimistic about the prospects for simultaneous economic and political development, early dependency theory proved to be excessively pessimistic. When *dependencistas* proposed solutions to the Third World's problems, they were often very vague.

Despite that bleak prognosis, however, nations such as Brazil and Mexico began to enjoy substantial industrial growth. In his more sophisticated version of dependency theory, Fernando Henrique Cardoso rejected the contention that all Third World countries were condemned to underdevelopment. Drawing heavily from the experience of his native Brazil, Cardoso contended that the active intervention of the state and the linking of domestic firms with multinational corporations could allow some LDCs to industrialize and enjoy considerable economic growth. He referred to this process as "associated-dependent development."

Cardoso noted that countries such as Brazil, Colombia, and Mexico could industrialize while remaining dependent on multinationals in the "core" for investment, credit, and technology. Nevertheless, he and other critics viewed that kind of development as undesirable in several ways. The engines of such growth, they charged, were frequently mechanized companies that did not hire sufficient local labor and produced more profitable—hence more expensive—goods that benefited middle- and upper-class consumers but were beyond the reach of the masses.[24] Indeed, instead of reducing poverty, dependent development had allegedly contributed to a growing income gap between the poor and the more affluent classes. At the same time, an alliance of many Third World economic, political, and military elites with multinational corporations helped keep unrepresentative regimes in power.

Modernization Theory and Dependency Theory Compared

Dependency theory offered a useful correction to modernization theory in various ways. It highlighted an important influence on Third World societies that previously had been largely neglected—the role of international trade, finance, and investment. Eventually, modernization theorists came to recognize that development required more than adopting new values or changing domestic political structures. Thus, dependency theory shifted the focus of research on the Third World from overwhelmingly internal factors to greater recognition of international influences.

Dependency theorists also helped redefine the concept of economic development. Whereas earlier research had stressed the importance of economic growth, *dependencistas* emphasized the significance of economic distribution. When rapid economic growth produces increased concentration of wealth and income, as has frequently happened, the poor may even end up worse off. Influenced by dependency theory and similar critiques, even establishment groups such as the World Bank reoriented their goals toward "redistribution with growth."[25]

But just as modernization theorists tended to overemphasize the internal causes of underdevelopment, early *dependencistas* erroneously attributed virtually all Third World problems to external economic forces. LDCs were often portrayed as virtually helpless pawns with little hope for development. Cardoso refined the theory by insisting that developing nations had options within the broad limits of dependency. With the proper government policies and the appropriate relationships between social classes, Third World nations could achieve associated-dependent development.

But even Cardoso's refinement fails to explain East Asia's spectacular development record since the 1960s. Those economies have been tremendously dependent—that is, very closely tied to the developed world (the core) through trade, credits, investment, and technology transfer. Indeed, they are far more globalized (integrated into the world economy) than any other part of the developing world. But contrary to what Cardoso and other dependency theorists had predicted, highly globalized economies in East and Southeast Asia have been the economic stars of the Third World, coupling astonishing economic growth with comparatively equitable economic distribution. Similarly, rather than support entrenched dictatorships in that region, greater economic dependency in countries such as South Korea, Taiwan, and Indonesia opened the way to democratic transitions. Although the East Asian experience does not prove that greater economic interdependence would have similar success in Africa, Latin America, or the Middle East, it does indicate that one must look for factors beyond economic dependency to explain underdevelopment.

At the same time, however, more recent economic events in East Asia demonstrate that extensive economic linkages to the world economy and to the core also carry certain risks. To attract foreign investment, Thailand and other countries in the region kept the value of their national currencies stable and artificially linked to the dollar. In 1997, when the Thai government was no longer able to maintain the exchange rate for its overvalued currency, the *baht*, its worth plunged. The value of Malaysia's, Indonesia's, and South Korea's currencies soon fell sharply as well. Foreign investors, seeing the dollar values of their holdings plummet, withdrew their investments whenever possible. At the same time, local firms that had borrowed dollars from U.S. banks saw the cost of those debts in their local currencies skyrocket, forcing many companies to shut down. As many of those borrowers defaulted on their loans, international banks cut off new credit to the region, further depressing their economies. As one observer noted, "Along the way, billions of dollars in production and hundreds of millions of jobs [were] lost."[26] Recovery took several years.

Thus, the evidence regarding foreign economic penetration is somewhat mixed. Today, many political scientists agree that a full understanding of development must draw on the strengths of both modernization and dependency theories while recognizing the limits of each. In the sections that follow, we turn from general development theories to an examination of specific challenges and obstacles to development facing Third World nations today. (See Box 15-2.)

Box 15-2

ARGENTINA: THE VOYAGE FROM DEVELOPMENT TO UNDERDEVELOPMENT

Whereas the concerns of political analysts studying the Third World have largely focused on the question of how an underdeveloped nation can develope, Argentina poses a disturbingly contrasting question: How did it change from having been one of the world's wealthiest nations to being underdeveloped? Indeed, Argentina may be the only country in the world that changed from being economically developed to underdeveloped.

Blessed with abundant and rich agricultural and ranching lands and low population density, the country attracted huge numbers of Italian, Spanish, and other European immigrants during the late nineteenth and early twentieth centuries. Possessing a level of human capital (education, skills) rarely found in the Third World, those immigrants joined other relatively educated and skilled Argentineans in creating an industrial base that supplemented Argentina's dynamic grain and meat exports. As of the early 1930s, the country had the fifth highest per capita income in the world. Ranking behind only the United States, Canada, Australia, and Switzerland, it was far wealthier than Italy or Japan.

Today, Argentina still has one of the highest educational levels and standards of living in Latin America. But its per capita income currently ranks only 66th in the world, roughly half that of Hong Kong, Singapore, or South Korea. Beginning in the 1930s, Argentina's economic stagnation contributed to political stalemate. Bitter labor–management conflicts produced frequent unrest, the military often intervened in politics, and in the 1960s and 1970s revolutionary guerrilla groups helped provoke a brutal military dictatorship. Since the early 1980s, the military has exited from politics. But the financial crisis of January 2002 gave the country five civilian presidents in a period of just two weeks.

How did Argentina decline so precipitously? Supporters of dependency theory argue that, over time, Argentina had to pay developed nations increasingly higher prices for imported manufactured goods while the value of its agricultural exports did not rise correspondingly.

But believers in modernization theory point out that other countries that depend heavily on the same exports, including Australia and New Zealand, have fared very well economically and politically. They note that ever since Argentina's charismatic strongman, Juan Perón, rose to power in the 1940s, successive governments have spent beyond their means to win popular support. Meanwhile rich agricultural exporters failed to modernize their production techniques to stay internationally competitive. No matter which side is correct, Argentina serves as a somber reminder that achieving economic development does not guarantee keeping it.

SOURCES OF POLITICAL CONFLICT

Viewers of the evening news might understandably believe that the Third World is in a constant state of upheaval. News stories stress revolutions, civil wars, riots, and **military coups** in such countries as Afghanistan, Colombia, Iraq, Liberia, and Zimbabwe. While, in fact, large portions of the developing world are peaceful, sharp internal divisions do plague many nations. Two particularly vexing sources of tension have been class conflict and ethnic conflict.

Class Conflict

In all nations, modern and developing alike, some people are much wealthier than others. Invariably, that inequality causes some degree of political division. In more harmonious societies, class differences merely influence the voters' electoral preferences. For example, blue-collar workers tend to vote for the Labour Party in Great Britain and the Democratic Party in the United States, whereas well-to-do businesspeople tend to support, respectively, Conservative and Republican Party candidates. Because wealth and income in the developing world are often more unequally distributed, and because the political battle for scarce economic resources is frequently more heated, class conflict in the LDCs is frequently more intense or even violent.

As we have noted, the initial stages of economic modernization often heighten class tensions as income gaps between the poor and the social classes above them tend to widen. In the cities, industrialization frequently expands the size of the middle class and creates a "labor elite" of skilled, unionized factory workers, while many unskilled, underemployed workers are left behind in the slums. In the countryside, as large commercial farms expand their operations to take advantage of new export opportunities, they often evict neighboring peasant cultivators from their small, family plots.

Early economic modernization not only tends to sharpen class tensions but also increases the political capacity of previously powerless groups. For example, as the gap between rural and urban living standards widens, increased rural migration to the cities raises the literacy rate of these former peasants and exposes them to more political information from the mass media. Consequently, the newly arrived, urban poor tend to be better informed and more politically active than they had been in the countryside. In time, some of these urban migrants may return to the countryside and mobilize their fellow villagers. Peasants being forced off their land by the expansion of large, commercial farms also may be radicalized. Industrialization also generates labor unions, giving workers an important vehicle for political mobilization. The growing middle class—particularly university students, professionals, and intellectuals—provides leadership for anti-establishment political parties, labor unions, or even revolutionary groups in some nations.[27]

For all those reasons, the earlier periods of economic development—when a country moves out of socioeconomic backwardness toward greater modernity—often witness heightened class tensions. That conflict may express itself peacefully at the ballot box and through union activity. In Chile, for example, organized labor formed the backbone of Popular Unity (the UP), a Marxist coalition that elected Salvador Allende to the presidency in 1970. Eventually, however, political tensions pitting the UP government and its labor and peasant supporters against opposition parties, business groups, and parts of the middle class precipitated a brutal military coup against Allende in 1973. More recently, disgruntled peasants and the urban poor have helped elect leftist presidents such as Hugo Chávez in Venezuela and Evo Morales in Bolivia.

The most intense class conflict in the developing world has often pitted the rural poor against local landlords and the national government. At the bottom of the political and economic hierarchy and often unable to assert their demands within the political system, peasants sometimes turn to violence. Vietnam and China, for example, had peasant-based, communist revolutions. Peasants also played important roles in the Mexican, Cuban, and Nicaraguan revolutions. Recently, they have formed the backbone of guerrilla insurrections in Colombia and Nepal, and not long ago were the core of revolutionary movements in El Salvador and Vietnam.[28] Thus, although Karl Marx, the father of modern revolutionary theory, had expected class conflict to manifest itself in the tensions between urban capitalists and blue-collar workers, twentieth- and twenty-first-century revolutionary struggles in the LDCs have far more frequently been waged in the countryside. No matter how appalling living conditions for many Third World industrial workers may be, those workers are generally better off economically and politically than peasants and, hence, are less prone to join armed insurrections. Although urban labor unions may be quite militant and often support radical political parties, most still work within the framework of legal and peaceful political action.

However, with the fall of the Soviet communist bloc and China's embrace of capitalist economic policies leading to greater inequality, class conflict seems to be declining as a source of political polarization in the developing world, only to be replaced by increased ethnic conflict.

Ethnic Conflict

No type of political division has brought developing nations more protracted and bitter conflict than **ethnicity** has. Throughout the Third World, people have been drawn into opposing camps based on language, culture, religion, and race with an intensity that frequently exceeds the influence of socioeconomic class.[29]

Of course, ethnic conflict is not limited to the Third World. It has flared up fairly recently in such disparate places as Serbia, Northern Ireland, the former Soviet Union, and Canada. But it is frequently particularly bitter in the LDCs because of the intense competition for scarce economic resources. So, although American urban politics has sometimes featured competition between Anglo-Saxons, Irish, Italians, Jews, Hispanics, and African Americans, the stakes of ethnic competition have never been as high as in Indonesia, Lebanon, and India. In those countries, contending ethnic groups frequently feel that their very survival depends on how the state distributes public-sector jobs, schools, and development projects.

Ethnic tensions have been most intense in Africa and parts of Asia, where colonial powers frequently drew national boundaries that threw conflicting ethnic groups into a single country. In India, the struggle for independence highlighted deep divisions between Muslims and the Hindu majority. Ultimately, it resulted in the establishment of Pakistan, a separate Muslim state carved out of India. In the months leading up to and following independence, communal violence between Hindus and Muslims led to some two million deaths and uprooted twelve million refugees.[30] Today, periodic, religiously based strife continues in the Indian state of Kashmir, where Islamic rebels seek independence or unification with Pakistan, and in Punjab, where the Indian military and Sikh separatists also have waged a bloody conflict (though that has abated somewhat).

In Africa, tribal-based civil wars have plagued the continent for decades, producing widespread destruction and vast numbers of fatalities in countries such as Nigeria, Sudan, Ethiopia, Congo, Mozambique, and Angola. Interethnic violence has also torn apart Sri Lanka, Indonesia, Lebanon, India, and other Asian and Middle Eastern nations. Ethnicity and race relations are not as volatile in Latin America, but in the recent past rural guerrilla movements in Guatemala and Peru drew support based on indigenous (native Indian) resentments against white domination. Currently, tensions between Bolivian Indians supporting President Morales and his White opponents have occasionally burst into violence.

Not all ethnic divisions have led to violent conflict, however. Although nearly all African nations have multi-tribal populations, many have reached accommodations between ethnic groups. Elsewhere, in countries such as Malaysia and possibly Lebanon past interethnic violence may have been brought under control. Worldwide, after 50 years of steadily rising conflict, the level of ethnic protests and rebellion within nations began falling somewhat in the early 1990s.[31] Still, ethnic conflict is likely to remain among the Third World's greatest challenges for years to come. These tensions not only can endure for generations but also may resurface after a long period of apparent calm. One need only look to the enduring strains between blacks and whites in the United States, between Catholics and Protestants in Northern Ireland, and between Christians (especially Serbs) and Bosnian Muslims in Yugoslavia.

PROBLEMS OF POLITICAL PARTICIPATION

The intense political and economic tensions that divide many LDCs present them with a difficult dilemma. In many ethnically divided nations, large portions of the population are denied full political participation. In Iraq, for example, Saddam Hussein and his ruling elite were drawn primarily from the country's Sunni Muslim minority, and both the Shiite majority and the Kurds were denied representation. Today, following the toppling of Saddam's regime, it is the Sunnis who fear being excluded from political power. Similarly, Guatemala's large Indian population has often been denied political rights.

In other LDCs, some divided by class or ethnic tensions, military or single-party governments deny the entire population participation in meaningful elections. Even in the growing number of nations with contested elections, the peasantry and the urban poor often lack the resources, political skills, or connections to receive a fair hearing from government policy makers. The denial of political representation to so many citizens means that governments are not being held accountable for their actions, corruption flourishes, and inadequately represented groups, such as the poor, do not get their fair share of government resources. For all those reasons, political development must create additional channels for mass political participation.

On the other hand, there is also a danger that political participation may expand faster than the nation's political institutions can accommodate. Years ago, Samuel Huntington warned that developing countries may experience an explosion of demands on the political system as formerly non-politicized people move to urban areas, attain higher educational levels, and otherwise increase their political awareness.[32] Unless more sophisticated political institutions can be created to channel those rising demands, he argued, political disorder and decay lie in waiting.

Huntington's thesis was controversial because it suggested to many readers that LDCs frequently are not ready for democracy and that some degree of authoritarianism may be necessary during the early stages of economic and political modernization in order to maintain stability. But he also looked to longer-term solutions through the creation of political institutions that could channel citizens' demands in an effective and orderly manner. Developing strong and effective political parties, he argued, is the key to orderly political participation, bringing together diverse groups in society and translating a wide array of conflicting demands into workable political alternatives. Other institutions also need improvement in the process of political development. Government bureaucracies, for example, must become more competent and honest so that they can better implement state policies and satisfy popular needs.

Ultimately, then, there is a delicate balance between the need for increased political participation and the dangers of an excessively rapid escalation in participation. It is probably unreasonable to expect all developing nations—many of them torn by class or ethnic divisions—to conform fully to Western standards of democracy. However, since the 1970s there has been an explosion of democratic government throughout the world, including the former communist world and the LDCs. The change has been most dramatic in Latin America, a region previously governed almost exclusively by authoritarian regimes and now composed almost entirely of democracies.

Mexico completed that transformation in 2000 when the PRI was ousted from office after 71 years as the ruling party (see Chapter 16). Although democracy has advanced far more haltingly in Africa, the number of electoral democracies on that continent has grown impressively. And in Asia, authoritarian governments have given way to democratic ones in Thailand, South Korea, Taiwan, Indonesia, the Philippines, and elsewhere. Only in the Middle East has democracy made little headway.

Although the developing world's new democratic governments have not always performed well (many are corrupt, incompetent, and even occasionally repressive), on the whole they have opened up new avenues of participation to their citizens without the resulting unrest that Huntington feared. What has caused this flurry of democratic transitions in what has been the most extensive democratic revolution in world history?

There are many reasons, but we will highlight two. The first factor involves contagion—the tendency of certain political trends or forces to spread from one country to another. From the late 1940s to the 1960s, as the former European colonies in Africa, Asia, and the Middle East gained independence, many new national leaders were attracted to Marxism because it seemed to offer them a path to rapid economic development and reduced dependency on their former colonial rulers. In countries such as Ghana, Egypt, and Indonesia, authoritarian governments (usually left-wing) offered a host of arguments (many of them self-serving) claiming to demonstrate that meaningful electoral competition would be too divisive in ethnically and economically divided countries such as theirs. In Latin America, on the other hand, right-wing military dictatorships seized power in countries such as Argentina, Brazil, and Chile, allegedly to avert a communist threat. By the 1970s, however, as the weaknesses of military and single-party rule became increasingly apparent, democracy began to acquire new legitimacy. By the start of the 1990s, as communism collapsed in the Soviet Union and Eastern Europe, authoritarian government of any sort fell "out of style" and democracy became more fashionable. Democracy also became contagious. For example, when South Korean students—watching the local news or CNN— witnessed their counterparts in the Philippines overthrow the Ferdinand Marcos dictatorship, they began to think more seriously of toppling their own authoritarian government (and, subsequently, they succeeded).

The second important factor is that, in time, socioeconomic modernization in many developing nations has produced a more hospitable environment for democratic government. Despite serious setbacks in certain cases, LDCs as a whole have significantly raised their educational levels in the past three or four decades and often have improved their per capita incomes. Those two developments have important political implications, since there is substantial evidence that nations enjoying higher income and literacy levels are more likely to sustain democracy. For example, at least until recently, few countries with literacy rates of less than 50 percent have been able to sustain democratic government (though there are notable exceptions, such as India), whereas countries above that point are likely to be democracies.[33] At the same time, countries that are better off economically are much more capable of sustaining democratic government. In a study of how well democracy endured in 135 countries over a 40-year period (1950–1990), the authors found that it is most fragile in poor countries (with per capita incomes of less than $1,000) and becomes more sustainable as national income rises. "Above $6,000 [per-capita income]," they note, "democracies are impregnable and can be expected to live forever; no democratic system has ever fallen in a country where per capita income exceeds $6,055 [Argentina's level in 1976]."[34]

Women in Third World Society and Politics

In most of the developing world, women have found it difficult to attain full political and economic participation. More fundamentally, they are often the victims of social and economic deprivation and exploitation. For example, in parts of Asia and Africa, millions of young girls—often as young as nine or ten—have been sold by their impoverished parents into arranged marriages, while thousands of others live in virtual slavery. In **fundamentalist** Islamic states such as Iran and Saudi Arabia, laws restrict the types of jobs that women may hold and the kinds of apparel they may wear.

Women's Economic and Social Status

Today, in much of the developing world women continue to have fewer educational opportunities than males, shorter life expectancy, and fewer occupational opportunities in both government and the private sector (see Table 15.3). To be sure, the educational gender gap has narrowed in most LDCs. In 1995, for every 100 boys enrolled in secondary school in the developing world, there were only 84 girls (with obvious variations between individual countries). By the early years of the twenty-first century, there were 91 girls for every 100 boys.[35] Yet, as Table 15.3 makes clear, there are still important gaps.

The first column in the table indicates how the female adult literacy rate in each country compares to the male rate. Thus, the literacy rate of women in Egypt is slightly more than two-thirds that of men (71 percent as high), while in Chile and Brazil, women and men have the same literacy rate. This offers us an indication of the educational opportunity gap (if any) between women and men. There are a very small number of countries, such as Botswana, where women actually have a higher rate of literacy than men do (see Table 15.3). In Jamaica, the adult female literacy is

TABLE 15.3   GENDER INEQUALITY IN THE DEVELOPING WORLD

	Ratio of Female Adult Literacy to Male Rate	Gender-Related Development Index GDI and (Rank)	Gender Empowerment Measure GEM and (Rank)
Norway	1.00*	.957 (3)	.910 (1)
United States	1.00*	.937 (16)	.762 (15)
South Korea	1.00*	.910 (26)	.510 (64)
Chile	1.00	.859 (40)	.519 (60)
Brazil	1.00	.798 (60)	.490 (70)
China	.91	.776 (73)	.534 (57)
Thailand	.95	.779 (71)	.472 (73)
Iran	.87	.750 (84)	.347 (87)
Egypt	.71	nd	.263 (91)
Botswana	1.02	.639 (109)	.518 (61)
Tanzania	.80	.464 (138)	.597 (44)

* The UNDP does not provide data for more-developed countries such as Norway, the U.S., and South Korea. However, since the combined adult literacy rates are 99 percent or higher, we can be sure that literacy ratios for males and females in all three of these nations are approximately 1.00.

nd = no data available.

SOURCE: United Nations Development Programme (UNDP), *Human Development Report 2007/2008: (Tables 28–30)*, http://hdr.undp.org/en/statistics/data/.

16 percent higher than the man's, and in the African nation of Lesotho female rates are 23 percent higher (neither country appears in this table). More typically, Third World women have lower literacy rates than men, as illustrated in Table 15.3 by Egypt, Tanzania, China, Iran, and Thailand. In other countries not shown in the table, such as Chad (.31) and Niger (.35), the female literacy rate is only about one third of the men's. Note that column 1 does not tell us a nation's actual literacy rate (such data appear in Table 15.2). *It only compares the two sexes.* If, for example, only 30 percent of males and 30 percent of females were literate in country X, the score for column 1 would be 1.00, since the women's rate is equal to the men's. Country Y might have a much higher adult literacy for both sexes (say, 80 percent for men and 60 percent for women), but its score in column 1 would only by .75 because the female rate is only three-fourths (75%) of the male's.

Column 2 presents each country's ranking on the **Gender-Related Development Index (GDI)**. Basically, this begins by comparing the Human Development Index (HDI),* of females with those of males. The better women do relative to men, the higher the country's GDI. Again, the countries are ranked (in parenthesis) according to their GDIs. Thus, Norway has the third highest GDI score in the world (again, Iceland is first), meaning that it has the third smallest gender gap on HDI measures. The United States ranks 16th. Two developing nations—Botswana (109th in the world) and Tanzania (138th)—have the lowest GDI rankings in Table 15.3. More generally, when we consider all the countries not on the list as well, we

* A combined measure of life expectancy, literacy, educational attainment, and income.

find that GDI scores generally correlate with income. That is, the poorest nations generally have low overall HDI scores and also tend to have a wider gap between men and women.

Finally, the last column compares each country's GEM and ranks them from first to last on this dimension. The **Gender Empowerment Measure (GEM)** is a composite index of how women compare to men on four dimensions: the degree of economic participation and decision-making, the degree of political participation and decision-making, the proportion of academic and technical positions, and estimated income. Thus, the GEM number and ranking are indications of women's power in the economic and political system. Unfortunately, GEMs have been calculated for less than half countries in the world (93 of some 200 nations) and generally are not available for the world's poorest countries. This means, hypothetically, if a country's HDI or per capita income ranked 90th, it would fall almost exactly in the middle of the 180–200 nations for which HDI and per capita income data exist. If, however, that same country's GEM also ranked 90th, that would place it nearly last out of the 93 countries for which GEM scores are available.

If we examine Table 15.3 and consider the other 82 countries with GEM scores that are not in the table, we would find once again that more economically developed countries (i.e., those with higher per capita incomes and HDIs) tend to have higher GEM scores. Once again the five Nordic countries, headed by Norway, had the highest GEMs. That means that, for example Norwegian, Swedish, and Finnish women have more political and economic power relative to men than anywhere else on earth. At the other end of the spectrum, the most impoverished countries, such as Tanzania, Nepal, and Cambodia, had some of the world's lowest GEMs.

But economic development is not the only critical determinant. More so than with the gender-related indices discussed until now, GEM rankings are often influenced by the nation's religion, political culture, and ideology. For example, the socialist tradition of egalitarianism in the Nordic countries helps explain why four of those five nations had higher GEM scores than more affluent countries such as Luxemburg, Switzerland, and the United States. Conversely, several wealthy East Asian nations—including Japan and South Korea—had much lower GEM scores than their per capita income or HDI scores would predict. Their traditionally male-dominated culture seems to have prevented women from attaining a share of important political and economic positions commensurate with their educations or income levels. So, although Japan's and South Korea's per capita incomes place them within the richest 16 percent of all world nations, they both have GEM rankings in the bottom half of all countries with available data.

However, the countries with the lowest GEM rankings relative to their income levels are the Muslim countries. For example, Saudi Arabia's per capita income placed it in the top third of all countries, but its GEM was nearly dead last (92nd out of 93 countries with GEM data). Turkey's per capita income ranks in the highest 40 percent of all countries, but its GEM rank is in the bottom 5 percent. And, while Malaysia's per capita income is in the top third of all countries, its GEM places it in the bottom third. Indeed, of the 93 countries with GEM rankings, the seven nations with the lowest scores and 10 of the lowest 13 are Muslim. Thus, it appears that Muslim cultural values are barriers to female economic and political empowerment.

Women as Political Leaders

If we turn our focus from the socioeconomic and political status of Third World women generally to women's opportunities for high-level political leadership, we find a mixed picture. A surprising number of women have risen to the pinnacle of their political system, serving as prime ministers or presidents. Thus, for example, while the United States has never had a woman president, the Muslim countries of Turkey, Bangladesh, and Pakistan have all been governed by women prime ministers. So too have India and Sri Lanka, while the Philippines has had two women presidents. On the other hand, as we will see, those women have almost all made it to those positions as heirs to political dynasties begun by male relatives. Looking at political leadership positions below the very top, we find that the percentage of women in parliament (or congress) has risen in recent years, but still trails well behind men, as it does in most advanced industrial democracies as well.

The list of current and past women government leaders includes Indian Prime Minister Indira Gandhi, Argentine Presidents Isabel Perón and Cristina Fernández, Nicaraguan President Violeta Chamorro, Filipino Presidents Corazon Aquino and Gloria Macapagal Arroyo, Pakistani Prime Minister Benazir Bhutto, Bangladeshi Prime Ministers Begum Khaleda Zia and Sheik Hasina Wazed, Sri Lankan Prime Minister Sirimavo Bandaranaike and President Chandrika Kumaratunga, Panamanian President Mireya Elisa Moscoso Rodríguez, Indonesian President Megawati Sukurnoputri, and about a dozen lesser-known leaders. Two important breakthroughs took place in 2005–2006. Ellen Johnson-Sirleaf—a Harvard-trained banker—was elected president of Liberia and became Africa's first elected female head of state. At about the same time, Michelle Bachelet—a doctor, former defense minister, and former political prisoner under the rule of General Augusto Pinochet—was elected as Chile's first woman president.

A BREAKTHROUGH FOR WOMEN Chilean President Michelle Bachelet addresses the Congress and the nation. She had won a decisive electoral victory, the first for a woman in a country known for its conservative social values.

© AP Photo

While this list is impressive, it may give an exaggerated picture of the opportunities open to women. Almost all of the women just named assumed the leadership of their country as the widow or daughter of a former prime minister, president, or opposition leader, many of them national heroes. For example, Indira Gandhi was the daughter of India's revered first prime minister, Jawaharlal Nehru. Bangladesh's two most recent prime ministers have been, respectively, the widow and daughter of assassinated presidents. The Philippines' Corazon Aquino and Nicaragua's Violeta Chamorro were elected president following the assassination of their husbands, who had been opposition leaders against their country's dictator. Former Prime Minister Benazir Bhutto was the daughter of a prime minister who had been executed by the military. Argentina's Isabel Perón was the widow of legendary President Juan Perón, while that country's current President Cristina Fernández de Kirchner succeeded her husband. Indonesia's former President Megawati was the daughter of Sukarno, the first president of the country. Some of these women proved to be very qualified. Others were not. But what brought them to the top of the political ladder was primarily their lineage. Chile's Bachelet and Liberia's Johnson-Sirleaf, however, were elected entirely on their own merits and may presage a new model.

All of them, including Johnson-Sirleaf and Bachelet, have had family ties and elite social status that make them very unrepresentative of other women in their country. For example, former Prime Minister Bhutto (assassinated in 2007) was born to a wealthy land-owning family and was educated at Harvard and Oxford. Similarly, Burmese opposition leader Aung San Suu Kyi, the winner of the 1991 Nobel Peace Prize, is the daughter of the country's most revered founding father and received academic degrees from Oxford and Harvard. For women who are not born to the nation's elite and, more significantly, are not the daughters or widows of prominent national leaders, opportunities for political leadership remain limited (see Box 15-3). Nor does the election of a female president or prime minister necessarily lead to improvements in the lives of the average woman in their country. Nations such as Bangladesh, India, Indonesia, Sri Lanka, and Turkey, all of which have had female government leaders, still have relatively low GEMs and GDIs. For example, while Bangladesh has been led most of the time since 1991 by two different women prime ministers, it currently ranks 81st among the 93 countries that report GEM scores.

Third World Political Institutions

Often the weaknesses of Third World political institutions, especially political parties, compound the problems of inadequate political participation and ineffective government representation. For example, political parties are most productive when they reach out to a large segment of the population, incorporate their supporters into the political system, socialize them into the prevailing political culture, build coalitions, and forge compromises among contending groups in society.

In the LDCs, however, political parties often fail to provide badly needed representation to newly mobilized urban migrants, peasants, oppressed minorities, and women. All too frequently, they represent the particular interests of economic elites or those of a single ethnic group, religion, or region. Consider the example of Iraq, where the major political parties are either Shi'a, Sunni, or Kurdish and politicians have been unable to bridge the gap between those three antagonists. Sometimes

Box 15-3

WOMEN'S REPRESENTATION IN PARLIAMENT OR CONGRESS

Since women make up slightly over half the adult population of most countries, full gender equality in political representation would produce parliaments (a term used broadly here to include congresses) that were roughly half women. In fact, only a few countries in the world come close to that mark (women constitute about 40 percent of the members of the single house of parliament in the five Nordic nations— Denmark, Finland, Iceland, Norway, and Sweden). In many developing nations, female representation is somewhat lower than in the West due partly to their lower educational and occupational opportunities and/ or cultural prejudices. As of 2008, Latin America and the Caribbean had the Third World 's highest female legislative representation (over 21 percent). Asia and sub-Saharan Africa were a bit lower with 18 percent female representation, and Arab states were well behind with only 9 percent (see Table 15.4, last column). While women in the developing world are clearly underrepresented, aside from the Arab nations their average parliamentary representation is about the same as Western Europe's outside of the Nordic nations. At the national level, the Inter-Parliamentary Union provides data for only the usually more powerful

chamber, the lower house of parliament or congress. Some of the countries with the world's highest percentage of women in the major parliamentary chamber are developing countries: Rwanda (49 percent women; highest in the world), Cuba (43 percent; third highest), Argentina (40 percent; 5th highest), Costa Rica (37 percent), and Mozambique (35 percent), for example. These levels far surpass female representation in developed nations such as Canada (21 percent), France (18 percent), the United States (17 percent), and Japan (9 percent). Most developing countries with one-fourth (25%) or more female representation reached that proportion through the use of gender quotas, reserved seats or other electoral methods designed to afford women more equal representation (See Chapter 5, Box 5-1).[36]

From 1996 to 2008, the number of women members of parliament worldwide rose from 10.1–18.4 percent. Analysts have determined that women need to reach a level of 33-percent representation before they can have a significant influence on the parliamentary agenda and can help pass "women-friendly" legislation in such areas as education, health care, child care, maternity leave, and abortion.

TABLE 15.4   THE PROPORTION OF WOMEN IN NATIONAL PARLIAMENTS (REGIONAL AVERAGES AS OF MAY, 2008)

Region	Single House or Lower House	Upper House	Both Houses Combined
Nordic countries*	41.4%	—	—
Americas	21.6%	20.0%	21.4%
Europe—OSCE (excluding Nordic countries)	19.3%	18.8%	19.2%
Sub-Saharan Africa	17.2%	20.8%	17.6%
Asia	18.4%	16.6%	18.2%
Arab States	9.7%	7.0%	9.1%

* Parliaments in the Nordic Countries are unicameral (one house)

SOURCE: Inter-Parliamentary Union, Women in National Parliaments (May 31, 2004), http://www.ipu.org/ wmn-e/world.htm Comments: Data only used - Fair use

political parties are built around a single charismatic leader without a well-defined political program. Once in power, such parties often cannot govern effectively. The **wave of democracy** since the 1970s has restored or given birth to more effective political parties in a substantial number of countries. But, for the most part, parties—as well as other key political institutions—remain relatively weak.

Although civilian governments in the Third World generally have structures that resemble our own, those institutions tend to operate quite differently. Congresses and parliaments are frequently subservient to the executive branch. Their legal powers are often limited, and many regularly rubber-stamp the chief executive's policies. The judicial branch is usually weaker still, rarely challenging the executive's authority.

Political power, then, tends to be concentrated in the hands of the executive branch and its large government bureaucracy. Even when civilian governments are overthrown by the armed forces, change is largely confined to the top, with the civilian president being replaced by a single military officer or military council and the bureaucracy headed by other military officers or by civilians loyal to the military regime.

Military Intervention

One of the most persistent and most troublesome characteristics of Third World politics, at least until recently, has been the frequent intervention of the military in national politics. Between the 1930s and 1960s, more than half of the developing nations had suffered at least one military coup attempt during the previous 40 years, some of them experiencing four or more during that period. During the 1970s and early 1980s, the number of military takeovers and the frequency of extended military rule peaked with most of Latin America and about half of Africa governed by the armed forces. Countries experiencing military takeovers during that time included Argentina, Brazil, Chile, Nigeria, Pakistan, Syria, Thailand, and Turkey. But the tide began to turn toward the end of that period. Since 1980, there have been relatively few new coups and a growing number of military regimes have returned power to elected civilian governments.

Of course, coups are but the most comprehensive form of military intervention. El Salvador's armed forces controlled the political system for decades under the cover of carefully controlled elections. Until recently, even elected civilian governments in nations such as Brazil, Guatemala, Nigeria, and Thailand have been subject to the military's veto power in certain policy areas. Some still are. For example, the armed forces are often able to veto civilian government policies affecting national security and foreign affairs.

What accounts for the frequency of armed intervention? The answer lies less in the nature of Third World militaries than in the weakness of civilian governments and their political institutions. The military is more likely to seize power when civilian governments are inept and corrupt, when elected officials have little legitimacy or popular support, when there is internal disorder or economic chaos, or when there is a real or perceived likelihood of revolution. Studies of Africa, for example, show that military coups are far more likely to succeed against authoritarian regimes than against democratic governments. That does not mean that military coups under those circumstances are justified or that they are likely to improve internal conditions. And many coups are motivated solely by self-interest. For the most part, however, the more legitimate a civilian government is, the more a strong political party backs it; and the more effectively it governs, the lower the likelihood of a coup.

The goals of military governments are as varied as the circumstances that produce them. In the most underdeveloped political systems, military officers tend to have little professional training. Consequently, the armed forces in such countries generally have no developmental goals and seize power simply to further their own financial interests. These types of coups often revolve around the personal ambitions of a single leader seeking power and wealth. So-called **personal coups** (led by a dominant, charismatic figure) were once common in Central America and other parts of Latin America but have largely passed from that political scene as those nations and their military training have modernized. In recent decades, Africa has experienced a number of personal coups by ambitious officers, including Uganda's Idi Amin, Liberia's Sergeant Samuel Doe, and the Congo's General Mobutu Sese Seko. Most of those regimes governed disastrously. The Central African Republic's General Jean Bokassa, for example, killed and tortured thousands of his people (including schoolchildren). Declaring himself emperor, Bokassa spent millions of dollars on his coronation as emperor while his subjects suffered some of the world's worst poverty. Idi Amin's government in Uganda killed up to half a million people.

In the more-developed Third World nations, where the officers' corps normally has greater professional training, military governments generally represent the military as an institution, rather than a single officer, and they tend to have broader objectives. For example, in 1973 the armed forces of Latin America's two most long-standing democracies, Chile and Uruguay, seized power for the purpose of reordering their nations' political and economic systems. Each coup sought to crush strong leftist movements or topple a leftist government, destroy the labor movement, and create a healthy environment for business investment.

Institutional coups elsewhere also have frequently been designed to confront radical mass movements; however, their strategies have varied. For example, military regimes in Argentina, Chile, and Indonesia had a distinctly conservative cast and often imprisoned, tortured, or killed leftist union and radical political party activists. In contrast, the Peruvian military government tried to outflank revolutionary movements by implementing its own radical reforms—instituting one of Latin America's most sweeping land reforms, organizing the poor into government-directed unions, and introducing limited worker ownership of urban businesses. On the whole, however military dictatorships in Latin America and East Asia have been conservative, whereas in Africa and the Middle East (e.g. Ethiopia, Libya, and Sudan) they have often been leftist.

Whether left-wing or right-wing, whether seeking selfish goals or perceived national objectives, most military regimes have had poor human rights records. In the most appalling cases, they have killed many thousands (Argentina, Uganda). Elsewhere (Panama, Ecuador) they have been relatively benign but still have harassed political opponents and the press. Ultimately, all of them, no matter how well intentioned, inhibit the spread of political participation and the development of badly needed political institutions. Although some military regimes have succeeded in specific areas—agrarian reform in Peru and Ecuador, industrialization in Brazil, rapid economic growth in Indonesia and South Korea—military rule elsewhere has generally been marked by incompetence, corruption, and repression. For example, in Nigeria, a low-income nation, the former military ruler, General Sani Abacha, stole over $3 billion while in power (1993–1998) and previously as a power behind the throne.

As democracy has spread across Latin America and parts of Africa and Asia, the number of military governments has fallen substantially and the likelihood of future military takeovers has fallen sharply. In countries such as Argentina, Brazil, Chile, Indonesia, Nigeria, and South Korea, where the military was once politically domi-nant, the armed forces seem committed to removing themselves from the front lines of politics. But there continue to be a significant number of attempted coups in Africa. And since the start of the twenty-first century, the armed forces have toppled govern-ments in over ten developing nations including Ecuador, Haiti, and Thailand.

Strong States, Weak States

One of the most disturbing government failure in many LDCs has been the state's inability to control its national territory, maintain law and order, defend national sovereignty, or provide essential public services to its citizens (including education and public health programs). In some cases, the state has collapsed. Journalists, aca-demics, and diplomats often refer to such countries as "failed states." Since 2005, The Fund for Peace (a research center) and the journal *Foreign Policy* have produced a *Failed States Index*, which ranks the strength or weakness of all United Nations member-states based on 12 criteria, including economic stability and growth, human rights, number of fleeing refugees, and provision of public services. Failed states are those that perform most poorly on these dimensions. According to their 2008 index, the world's most badly failed states are (in rank order) Somalia, Sudan, Zimbabwe, Chad, and Iraq. Beyond Iraq, the next five "biggest failures" include two other coun-tries of critical strategic interest to the United States—Afghanistan and Pakistan. Most of the "top" 20 on the list are extremely poor countries such as Bangladesh, Cambodia, Myanmar, the Central African Republic, Ethiopia, Somalia, and Haiti. Perhaps, half of those 20 have been torn apart by ethnically related or religious conflicts.[37]

Of course, most Third World states have not failed, but they have often taken on responsibilities that exceed their capabilities. Either because the private sector ap-peared incapable of dealing with important economic objectives or because of the government's political ideology, Third World nations frequently turned to the state (governmental authority) for solutions. For example, because it is not sufficiently prof-itable for private developers to build housing for the urban poor, many LDCs have created public housing agencies to address shortages in that area.

In the past, many Latin American governments, backed by populist political co-alitions representing the middle and working classes, used government resources to promote industrial growth and expand education. Following World War II, the gov-ernments of newly independent countries in Africa and Asia were particularly inclined to intervene in the economy. Some of their founding fathers shared a socialist vision acquired during their studies in Europe. They believed that a powerful state could promote economic development in countries with inadequate private capital. Gov-ernment, they argued, could also achieve greater economic and social equality and could provide better education and health care for their impoverished populations.

But leftists were not the only ones who favored a powerful state. During the 1960s and 1970s, several right-wing military regimes in South America increased state power in order to control radical labor unions and to stimulate industrialization. Even in the Far East, where conservative political leaders have revered the free-enterprise sys-tem, the governments of Taiwan, South Korea, and Singapore helped plan and direct industrial growth.

Thus, throughout much of the Third World, the size and the formal power of the state expanded substantially from the 1940s to the 1980s. Large government bureaucracies were created to promote education, health care, and economic development. State enterprises often dominated banking, transportation, communications, electrical power, mining, and the marketing of agricultural products. On both the left and the right, proponents of broad government intervention felt that a powerful state was the solution to a range of socioeconomic and political problems. More recently, however, critics have blamed excessive state intervention for many of the developing world's political and economic ills.

At the same time, despite the enormous expansion of state activities and the proliferation of government agencies, most Third World governments are actually weaker than they seem.[38] That is to say, states that have appeared to be strong are often actually weak. As Lynne Hammergren has noted, "constitutions and legislation often accord enormous powers of control to central governments, but . . . the limited success of . . . governments in enforcing their own legislation suggests that the extent of this control is not great."[39] Extensive governmental programs that look impressive on paper often are far more limited in their application.

The reasons for that gap vary. In some countries, powerful, vested-interest groups such as agribusiness or bankers are able to block governmental initiatives that threaten their interests. Elsewhere, governments lack the financial or technical resources to satisfactorily implement proposed programs in areas such as public health, education, and transportation. And, in other instances, government agencies simply lack the trained personnel needed to implement approved legislation.

In general, governments seem to be least successful when they manage large firms such as railroads, telephone companies, and steel mills. Frequently, such enterprises face no competition, leaving them little incentive to be efficient. All too often, the size of their payroll spirals out of control as they hire loyal supporters of the government or the ruling party for patronage jobs. Finally, many of these companies lose money by design because their products are sold at a subsidized price determined by political pressures rather than by the market. Not surprisingly, consumers soon view benefits such as cheap utility and transportation prices as their right. Consequently, few governments were prepared to alienate voters by ending those subsidies.

As government spending for subsidies and other programs spiraled without commensurate tax revenues, central governments often covered their deficits by borrowing abroad. By the 1980s, many LDCs found themselves deeply in debt to foreign banks and had alarming government budget deficits and high rates of inflation. As a consequence, there has been a strong trend in recent decades toward reducing state economic involvement. Many governments—from India and Pakistan to Argentina and Mexico (see Chapter 16)—have reduced state economic regulation and embarked on **privatization** programs (the sale of state enterprises to the private sector). Although some state enterprises had been successful, others had clearly been inefficient. As large government deficits and spiraling foreign debt forced many developing nations to reduce state economic intervention, they usually borrowed conservative economic models (labeled in the literature as "neoliberal reforms") from the West. The aggressively conservative economic policies of Great Britain's Prime Minister Thatcher (Chapter 12) and American President Reagan influenced many Third World governments. Finally, the collapse of the communist Soviet bloc further discredited state-centered economies.

It is probably too early to evaluate fully the effects of privatization and government downsizing. Plagued by budgetary deficits and rampant inflation, many governments had no choice but to reduce state subsidies for basic consumer items. Undoubtedly, many privatized enterprises are now run more efficiently and make healthier profits. Yet there are also social costs to these changes. Since government subsidies were removed, already-malnourished urban families have been forced to pay higher (sometimes far higher) prices for necessities such as bread, milk, and rice. Newly privatized companies have fired thousands of workers in nations already burdened with high unemployment.

In countries such as Mexico and Pakistan, high-ranking government officials have used their inside information and influence to make fortunes in the sale of state firms. Thus, policy makers must balance the uncertain promise of longer-term economic gains with the more immediate economic and political costs of transforming their economies.

Although most analysts agree that the size of Third World governments had gotten out of hand, some worry that the pendulum has swung too far in the other direction. They argue that the state can have a positive economic influence if it channels its activities prudently. For example, working closely with the private sector, East Asian state planners have played an important role in promoting the area's economic boom. Similarly, Taiwan and South Korea achieved relatively low levels of income inequality through government intervention in the form of agrarian reform and education policy. Conversely, unfettered private enterprise may intensify the existing sharp economic inequalities in many LDCs. It remains to be seen how well governments will be able to balance the need for economic efficiency with demands for social justice and greater economic equality.

CONCLUSION: RECENT DEVELOPMENTS AND FUTURE TRENDS

The road to development has been more difficult to travel than many Third World leaders or outside analysts had originally imagined. Africa remains the most impoverished region in the developing world—devastated by civil war, dictatorship, and corruption. Famine, the result of war and government policy, as well as of natural disasters, continues to plague parts of countries such as Somalia, Malawi, and Sudan. Since the 1990s there have been some signs of improvement in both economic and political development. South Africa has created a vibrant multiracial democracy, which, whatever its limitations and current problems, has impressively reduced racial antagonisms. Between 1988 and 1994 alone, the number of electoral democracies on the African continent rose from 5 to 21.[40] In its most recent rankings, Freedom House rated 11 sub-Saharan African nations as "Free," 23 as "Partly Free," and 15 as "Not Free."[41] At the same time, with some notable exceptions, African economies have experienced one of their longest periods of sustained growth. The continent's annual economic growth rate, which averaged 2.7 percent in the 1990s, has jumped to over 4 percent since 2000.[42] Still, with populations growing at annual rates of 3 percent or more in countries such as Madagascar, Congo, Uganda, and Liberia, economic growth rates are still struggling to keep up. Moreover, most African economies remain heavily dependent on a few commodity exports (such as petroleum, coffee, cocoa, copper, and sugar).

Commodity prices have generally boomed in recent years, contributing heavily to the region's economic surge. But these prices have always been cyclical in the past and may very well come down in the future.

The 1980s debt crisis brought Latin America the most intense economic decline since the world depression of the 1930s. Per capita GNP diminished, unemployment rose sharply, and high rates of inflation badly eroded consumers' purchasing power.[43] Since that time, the severe inflation that had afflicted countries such as Argentina, Brazil, Mexico, Peru, and Nicaragua has been brought under control and much of the region has experienced economic growth. But that growth has been rather erratic, and some countries have suffered sharp reverses. Thus, although Argentina was growing at a very rapid clip in the early 1990s, it experienced a severe economic crisis at the start of the new century that sent living standards plunging. After 2002 the economy resumed growth, but the rate of poverty has only fallen slowly from its record highs. And even in countries that have enjoyed more sustained economic growth, that growth often has not translated into greater employment or improved living standards for the poor. The current world economic crisis will undoubtedly negatively affect both Latin America and Africa.

Ironically, at the very time Latin America's economy was at its worst, the region was making impressive progress toward more democratic and responsible government. In the mid-1970s, most of Latin America was ruled by military dictatorships, some benign and others quite ruthless. By the start of the 1990s, however, democratically or semi-democratically elected governments had been installed in nearly every country in the region. Human rights and personal liberties have improved considerably in such countries as Argentina, Brazil, Chile, El Salvador, and Uruguay, though other governments such as Colombia's and Haiti's still frequently violate their citizens' fundamental rights.

The Far East and parts of Southeast Asia have enjoyed the Third World's greatest economic success in recent decades. The economies of South Korea, Taiwan, Singapore, Hong Kong, China, Thailand, Malaysia, and Indonesia all grew at annual rates of 7–10 percent or more from the 1980s into the late 1990s and resumed that rate in the twenty-first century. As we noted earlier (Chapter 14), China, the world's faster growing economy, now has the second largest economy in the world (using the PPP measure of GDP). Moreover, countries such as South Korea, Taiwan, Singapore, and Indonesia have achieved extraordinary growth rates while maintaining relatively equitable distributions of income. The impressive success of the Far Eastern economic model suggests the importance of industrial exports, balanced development strategies, and a cooperative relationship between government planners and private enterprise. To be sure, East Asia's 1997–1999 financial crisis threw millions of people out of work in Thailand, Malaysia, Indonesia, South Korea, and Singapore, indicating that the region's heavy dependence on the international economy has some risks. But those economies have since recovered.

Politically, however, the region has made slower progress toward democracy and the protection of human rights than Latin America has. Until relatively recently, NICs such as Taiwan and South Korea retained nondemocratic governments long past the thresholds of economic growth and literacy that enabled other countries to turn to democracy, though they have now made that democratic transition. Singapore and Malaysia, two of the most economically developed LDCs, have yet to achieve even electoral democracy. Indonesia now has enjoyed a fair and honest national election but still suffers from continuing human rights abuses, especially in its treatment of rebellious ethnic minorities. And nations such as Bangladesh, Myanmar, and Vietnam have made little progress toward any kind of democracy.

All of that suggests the enormous difficulty of trying to achieve economic growth, equitable income distribution, political stability, democratic government, and national autonomy simultaneously. Although many of the world's LDCs hope to become "another Hong Kong" or "another Taiwan," it is unclear how many will have the internal capabilities or external possibilities that will permit them to do so. Prospects for democracy are also clouded. Since the nineteenth century, there have been three important worldwide waves of democratization (1828–1926, 1943–1962, and 1974–present). The first two advances were followed by more limited reverse waves back to authoritarianism. So, although worldwide pressure is growing for Third World governments to democratize and honor human rights (that is, to join the "Third Wave" of democratization that has changed so many Eastern European and developing nations), it remains uncertain how effective or how permanent those pressures will be. In regions such as sub-Saharan Africa, the movement toward democracy has already weakened.[44] The paths of political and economic development are challenging, complex, and sometimes difficult to predict. So far, there has been no reverse wave in the developing world. But opportunities for further democratization are limited.

 WHERE ON THE WEB?

**http://astro.temple.edu/~bstavis/courses/
nature-of-underdevelopment.htm**

Common characteristics of underdevelopment: The site includes links to subjects such as corruption and armed conflict.

http://www.globalissues.org

Information on a number of major issues, many related to LDCs, including international trade, Third World debt, and the War on Terror.

http://www.freedomhouse.org

Home page for Freedom House, a widely used and respected rating of democracy and civil liberties throughout the world.

http://www.worldbank.org/poverty/wdrpoverty/report/

World Bank report on attacking poverty.

http://www.ipu.org/english/home.htm

Inter-Parliamentary Union: Up-to-date data on the percentage of women in parliaments throughout the world.

http://web.worldbank.org/data/

World Bank data on economic and social statistics.

http://web.sipri.org/contents/webmaster/databases

A reliable source of data on military spending, arms transfers, etc., for developing (and developed) countries.

◆ ◆ ◆

Key Terms and Concepts _____

(the) core
coup (or coup d'etat)
dependency theory
electoral democracy
ethnicity
fundamentalism/fundamentalist
Gender Empowerment Measure (GEM)
Gender-Related Development Index (GDI)
Human Development Index (HDI)
institutional coups
legitimacy
less-developed countries (LDCs)

liberal democracy
military coup
modernization theory
newly industrialized country (NIC)
personal coups
political underdevelopment
PPP (Parity Purchasing Power)
privatization
Third World
traditional society
wave of democracy

Discussion Questions _____

1. Discuss the main characteristics of economic and political underdevelopment. Be sure to include as many features of each as you can. What is the relationship between political and economic underdevelopment?
2. Compare the explanations for underdevelopment offered by modernization theory with those offered by dependency theory. What are the strengths and the weaknesses of each theory?
3. What are the major economic and political problems that particularly confront women in the developing world? How well represented are women in important political offices? How have some women managed to make it to the top of the political system in a number of Asian countries?
4. What factors account for the wave of democratic change that has swept over much of the developing world since the mid-1970s?
5. What accounted for the traditionally high number of military takeovers in the politics of Third World nations? Why has military intervention been declining recently?
6. What are the major causes of government corruption in developing nations? What are some of corruption's most important negative effects? To what extent is or isn't government corruption a particularly Third World problem?

Notes _____

1. World Bank, "GNIC Per Capita, 2007" http://siteresources.worldbank.org/DATASTATISTICS/Resources/GNIPC.pdf" The rankings in the text are based on PPP calculation of per capita income (see Glossary).
2. Samuel P. Huntington, *Political Order in Changing Societies* (New Haven: Yale University Press, 1968). Huntington focuses on other causes of unrest in this book, but elsewhere he has noted the close linkage between rural inequality and peasant unrest.
3. UN Population Division estimates cited in Globalis, http://globalis.gvu.unu.edu/.
4. United Nations Development Programme (UNDP), *Human Development Report*, 1997 (New York: Oxford University Press, 1997), pp. 24–26; Population Reference Bureau, 2007 *World Population Data Sheet*, http://www.prb.org/pdf07/07WPDS_Eng.pdf.
5. UNDP, *Human Development Report*, 1997 (New York: Oxford University Press, 1997), pp. 24–26; *Human Development Report*, 2007 (New York: Oxford University Press, 2007).
6. The World Bank Group, *World Development Indicators* (2005); http://devdata.worldbank.org/wdi2005/Section1_1_1.htm.
7. Samuel P. Huntington, "The Goals of Development," in *Understanding Political Development*, ed. Myron Weiner and Samuel Huntington (Boston: Little, Brown, 1986), p. 3.
8. Howard Handelman, *The Challenge of Third World Development*, 5th ed. (Upper Saddle River, NJ: Prentice Hall, 2008), Chapter 4.
9. Huntington, *Political Order in Changing Societies*.
10. Guillermo O'Donnell and Philippe Schmitter, *Transitions from Authoritarian Rule: Tentative Conclusions about Uncertain Democracies* (Baltimore: Johns Hopkins University Press, 1986); and Abraham Lowenthal, ed., *Exporting Democracy* (Baltimore: Johns Hopkins University Press, 1991).
11. See data by Freedom House published each year in the January issue of the *Journal of Democracy*.

12. *The New York Times*, "Where a Cuddle With Your Baby Requires a Bribe," August 30, 2005.

13. Ben Heineman and Fritz Heimann, "The Long War Against Corruption," *Foreign Affairs* (May/June, 2006). As of 2005, one Russian think tank estimated that that country's public officials receive $300 billion in bribes annually.

14. Transparency International, "Corruption Perception Index 2007," http://www.transparency.org/policy_research/surveys_indices/cpi/2007.

15. International Rescue Commission, *Special Report: Congo, Forgotten Crisis* (March 2008), http://www.theirc.org/special-report/congo-forgotten-crisis.html.

16. For a useful summary of major theories of development, see Alvin Y. So, *Social Change and Development* (Newbury Park, CA: Sage, 1990). For more challenging discussions, see Weiner and Huntington, *Understanding Political Development*; and Vicky Randall and Robin Theobald, *Political Change and Underdevelopment* (London: Macmillan, 1985).

17. The body of modernization literature is enormous. The most important works include Huntington, *Political Order in Changing Societies*; Gabriel Almond and James Coleman, eds., *The Politics of Developing Areas* (Princeton, NJ: Princeton University Press, 1960); Lucian Pye and Sidney Verba, eds., *Political Culture and Political Development* (Princeton, NJ: Princeton University Press, 1965).

18. For examples of such arguments, see Talcott Parsons, *The Social System* (Glencoe, IL: Free Press, 1951); Gabriel Almond and Sidney Verba, *The Civic Culture* (Princeton, NJ: Princeton University Press, 1963); Alex Inkeles and David Horton Smith, *Becoming Modern: Individual Change in Six Developing Countries* (Cambridge: Harvard University Press, 1974); Daniel Lerner, *The Passing of Traditional Society* (Glencoe, IL: Free Press, 1958); and David McClelland, *The Achieving Society* (Princeton, NJ: Van Nostrand, 1961).

19. Marion Levy, Jr., "Social Patterns (Structures) and Problems of Modernization," in *Readings on Social Change*, ed. Wilbert Moore and Robert Cooke (Englewood Cliffs, NJ: Prentice Hall, 1967), p. 207.

20. Huntington, "The Goals of Development."

21. Huntington, *Political Order in Changing Societies*.

22. Theotonio Dos Santos, "The Structure of Dependence," *American Economic Review* (May 1970).

23. Werner Baer, "The Economics of Prebisch and ECLA," in *Latin America: Problems in Economic Development*, ed. C. T. Nisbet (New York: Free Press, 1969). Major early dependency studies include Andre Gunder Frank, *Capitalism and Underdevelopment in Latin America* (New York: Monthly Review Press, 1967); see also Paul Baran, *The Political Economy of Growth* (New York: Monthly Review Press, 1957).

24. The most influential work in this more sophisticated version of dependency theory is Fernando Henrique Cardoso and Enzo Faletto, *Dependency and Development in Latin America* (Berkeley and Los Angeles: University of California Press, 1979). A far more readable work with that perspective is Peter Evans, *Dependent Development: The Alliance of Multinational, State and Local Capital* (Princeton, NJ: Princeton University Press, 1979).

25. Hollis Chenery et al., *Redistribution with Growth* (London: Oxford University Press with the World Bank and the University of Sussex, 1974).

26. Jeffrey A. Winters, "Asia and the 'Magic' of the Marketplace," *Current History* 97 (December 1998): 419. This is one of the clearest analyses of the 1997–1998 financial crisis. See also Joseph Stiglitz, "Bad Private-Sector Decisions," *Wall Street Journal* (February 4, 1998).

27. The many works on revolution include Jeffrey Page, *Agrarian Revolution* (New York: Free Press, 1975); Theda Skocpol, *States and Revolutions: A Comparative Analysis of France, Russia and China* (Cambridge, UK: Cambridge University Press, 1979); John Walton, *Reluctant Rebels: Comparative Studies in Revolution and Underdevelopment* (New York: Columbia University Press, 1984); and Barry Schultz and Robert Slater, eds., *Revolution and Political Change in the Third World* (Boulder, CO: Lynne Rienner Publishers, 1990), chaps. 1–3.

28. Eric Wolf, *Peasant Wars in the Twentieth Century* (New York: Harper and Row, 1969); John Booth, *The End and the Beginning: The Nicaraguan Revolution* (Boulder, CO: Westview, 1985); Scott Palmer, *Peru's Shining Path* (New York: St. Martin's, 1992).

29. Crawford Young, *The Politics of Cultural Pluralism* (Madison: University of Wisconsin Press, 1976); and Cynthia Enloe, *Ethnic Conflict and Political Development* (Boston: Little, Brown, 1973).

30. Young, *Politics of Cultural Pluralism*, p. 301.

31. Ted Robert Gurr, preface and "Long War, Short Peace: The Rise and Decline of Ethnopolitical Conflict at the End of the Cold War," in *Peoples Versus States: Minorities at Risk in the New Century*, ed. T. Gurr (Washington, DC: United States Institute of Peace Press, 2000), pp. xiii, 27–56; and David Carment and Frank Harvey, *Using Force to Prevent Ethnic Violence* (Westport, CT: Praeger, 2001), p. 5.

32. Huntington, *Political Order*; and Samuel P. Huntington and Joan Nelson, *No Easy Choices* (Cambridge: Harvard University Press, 1976).

33. Mitchell A. Seligson, "Democratization in Latin America: The Current Cycle," in *Authoritarians and Democrats: Regime Transition in Latin America*, ed. James M. Malloy and Mitchell A. Seligson (Pittsburgh: University of Pittsburgh Press, 1987), pp. 7–9.

34. Adam Przeworski et al., "What Makes Democracies Endure," in *Consolidating Third Wave Democracies*, ed. Larry Diamond et al. (Baltimore: Johns Hopkins University Press, 1997), p. 297. The dollar amounts quoted here are in constant dollars—that is, the effect of inflation over the years is statistically factored out—so that a per capita national income of $6,000 in 1996 would have the same purchasing power as that dollar income for 1962.
35. Population Reference Bureau, "Taking Stock of Women's Progress," www.prb.org.
36. Inter-Parliamentary Union (IPU), *Women in National Parliaments*, http://www.ipu.org/wmn-e/world.htm. The data was updated as of May 31, 2008.
37. "The Failed State Index, 2008," *Foreign Policy* (July/August, 2008), pp. 64–72.
38. Joel Migdal, *Strong Societies and Weak States* (Princeton, NJ: Princeton University Press, 1988).
39. Linn A. Hammergren, "Corporatism in Latin American Politics: A Reexamination of the 'Unique' Tradition," *Comparative Politics* (July 1977): 449; Stephan Haggard, *Pathways from the Periphery* (Ithaca: Cornell University Press, 1990).
40. Michael Bratton and Nicolas van de Walle, *Democratic Experiments in Africa: Regime Transitions in Comparative Perspective* (New York: Cambridge University Press, 1997), p. 120. Using slightly different definitions, Larry Diamond claimed the number of democracies had jumped from 3 to 18. See Diamond, *Prospects for Democratic Development in Africa* (Stanford, CA: Hoover Institute Press, 1997), appendix.
41. Freedom House data for 2007 cited in African Elections Database, "Freedom in Africa" (2007), http://africanelections.tripod.com/fh2007.html.
42. Frans Cronje, "SAIRR Today: African Growth—20th June 2008," http://www.sairr.org.za/sairr-today/sairr-today-african-growth-20-june-2008.html/
43. Howard Handelman and Werner Baer, eds., *Paying the Costs of Austerity in Latin America* (Boulder, CO: Westview, 1989), p. 2.
44. Julius Ihonvbere, "Where Is the Third Wave? A Critical Evaluation of Africa's Non-Transition to Democracy," *Africa Today* 43, no. 4 (October–December 1996): 343–368.

For Further Reading ⸺⸺⸺

Burnell, Peter and Vicky Randall, eds. *Politics in the Developing World*. New York: Oxford University Press, 2005.

Datta, Rekha, and Judith F. Kornberg. *Women in Developing Countries: Assessing Strategies for Empowerment*. Boulder, CO: Lynne Rienner Publishers, 2002.

Diamond, Larry, ed. *The Global Divergence of Democracy*. Baltimore: Johns Hopkins University Press, 2001.

⸺⸺. *Assessing the Quality of Democracy*. Baltimore: Johns Hopkins University Press, 2005.

Handelman, Howard. *The Challenge of Third World Development*. 5th ed. Upper Saddle River, NJ: Prentice Hall, 2009.

Haynes, Jeff. *Politics in the Developing World: A Concise Introduction*. Malden, MA: Blackwell Publishers, 2002.

Huntington, Samuel. *The Third Wave*. Norman: University of Oklahoma Press, 1991.

Payne, Richard J. and Jamal R. Nassar. *Politics and Culture in the Developing World*. New York: Longman, 2008.

Sachs, Jeffrey. *The End of Poverty*. New York: Viking Penguin, 2005.

Smith, Peter H. *Democracy in Latin America*. New York: Oxford University Press, 2005.

As the power (and firepower) of the Mexican Drug Cartels has grown to new Heights, President Felipe Calderón has turned to the armed forces, shown here, to supplement or replace often-corrupt police antidrug units.

© Tomas Bravo/Reuters/Landov Media

16

MEXICO: THE BIRTH OF DEMOCRACY

◆ The Relevance of Mexican Politics ◆ Mexico's Formative Years and the Legacy of the Mexican Revolution (1910–1920) ◆ The Postrevolutionary Order ◆ The Making of a Modern Economy ◆ The Struggle for Political Development ◆ Conclusion: A Developing Democracy

The 1991 collapse of Communist Party rule in Russia briefly left Mexico's **Institutional Revolutionary Party (PRI)*** as the world's longest continuously ruling political party. But less than a decade later, the wave of democratic change that had transformed the Soviet Union, Eastern Europe, Latin America, and parts of Africa and Asia finally swept the PRI from power after 71 years of continuous rule. On July 2, 2000, Vicente Fox—candidate of the **National Action Party (PAN)**—was elected as Mexico's first president of the twenty-first century and the first fully democratically elected president in the nation's history. It was an outcome that few Mexicans would have predicted and that many, including the winners, initially found hard to believe.

For most of the twentieth century, Mexican political and economic development was structured by the country's 1910 revolution and by the "official party" that emerged from that struggle. The revolution unleashed a period of chaos and devastation, but ultimately it also laid the foundation for the nation's political and economic modernization. It spawned a ruling party that governed Mexico from 1929 to 2000, establishing political stability, improved political representation, and 50 years of rapid economic growth. At the same time, however, the revolution and the PRI also introduced or maintained authoritarian rule, rampant corruption, and severe economic inequality. Because of its accomplishments and its willingness to win at any cost, the PRI won all elections of any importance until the 1980s and continued to hold Mexico's all-powerful presidency until 2000.[†]

The country continues to face serious political, social, and economic problems. But since 2000 it has taken the first giant steps toward creating a more democratic and responsive political system.[1]

THE RELEVANCE OF MEXICAN POLITICS

As America's neighbor, one of its largest trading partners, the third largest source of its imported petroleum, and the point of origin for substantial legal and illegal immigration, Mexico's importance to the U.S. is profound. Its impressive record of growth and industrialization until the early 1980s seemed to offer valuable lessons for other developing nations. During the late 1980s and the 1990s, the country reversed its long-standing, state-centered, protectionist economic model and became a leader in "neoliberal" reform (the process of opening up the country to greater foreign trade and investment, while reducing government's role in the economy). And before the recent worldwide wave of democratization, some observers cited Mexico's modified one-party political system—featuring both political stability and regular transitions from one civilian president to another—as a political model for other Latin America nations.

More recently, however, the flaws in Mexico's economic and political development models have become more apparent. The economic crises of 1982 and 1995 highlighted both the continuing poverty that afflicts about half the Mexican population and the inefficiencies of the country's economy. Although there has been

---

* Mexico's three leading political parties—the Institutional Revolutionary Party, the National Action Party, and the Party of the Democratic Revolution—are known, respectively by their Spanish acronyms (PRI, PAN, PRD).

† The party had two other names before changing its name in 1946 to the PRI. To simplify matters, we will call it the PRI even when referring to events that occurred before it took that name.

MEXICO

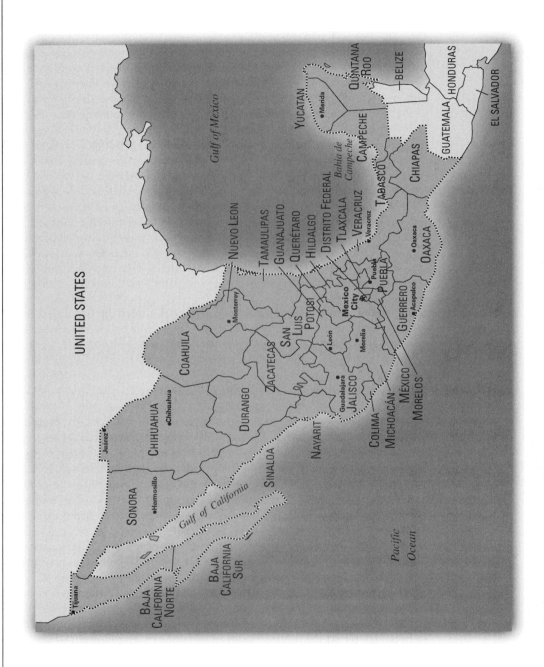

slow economic growth since 1996, it has barely exceeded population growth. And although the neoliberal reforms of the 1990s were surely necessary, they also caused great suffering among the nation's poor.

At the same time, the combination of extensive political corruption, periodic government repression, and growing political opposition revealed that Mexico was not "a peculiar democracy" (as it had once been labeled) but rather an authoritarian system in need of reform. The slow but steady erosion of PRI dominance since the 1980s and the emergence of two major opposition parties reflected mounting discontent with the old political order. That progress culminated with Vicente Fox's 2000 presidential victory. In 2006 the PAN once again won the presidential election, with the PRI candidate finishing a distant third. But although Mexico has achieved the primary prerequisite of democratic government—fair and competitive elections—it still retains some of its old authoritarian characteristics.

Before looking at Mexico's current political system, however, we must first examine Mexico's past. Its colonial heritage of sharp class divisions (reinforcing racial distinctions), its weak political system in the nineteenth century, and its twentieth-century efforts—starting with the Mexican revolution—to create a strong nation-state and a more equitable society have all left indelible marks on the contemporary political scene.

MEXICO'S FORMATIVE YEARS AND THE LEGACY OF THE MEXICAN REVOLUTION

Like many developing nations, Mexico achieved independence (in 1821) with few of the prerequisites for a successful nation-state. During much of the nineteenth century, the central government was unable to control the country's regional military-political bosses. Thus, during Mexico's first 40 years of independence, some 50 presidents (including some repeats) governed the country. Internal strife and government instability left the country vulnerable to foreign intervention. Consequently, Texas's secession and the subsequent war with the United States (1848) stripped the nation of nearly half its territory.[2]

In addition, Mexican society was sharply divided along ethnic and class lines. The Spanish colonial conquest had imposed European culture and religion on a large Native American population, with power concentrated in the hands of the Spanish authorities and a small upper class of whites born in the New World (*criollos*). At the same time, the largest segment of the population consisted of poor Indian or *mestizo* peasants*, who were often forced into virtual serfdom on white-owned agricultural and ranching estates. Independence failed to temper those racial and class cleavages. And even when subsequent modernization reduced racial divisions, class-based barriers to social mobility remained strong.

In 1876, General Porfirio Díaz established himself as the country's supreme military strongman. He was the first Mexican national leader to exercise firm control over the regional **caciques** (political bosses), and ruled with an iron fist until 1911. Attracted by Mexico's newfound stability, its favorable climate for investment, and its

---

* In Latin America, the term *Mestizo* generally refers to Indians who have been integrated, either forcefully or voluntarily, into the dominant European culture. It may also include people who are of mixed racial backgrounds (Indian and White), but that is less common.

restrictive labor laws, foreign investors built Mexico's railroad, electrical power, and telephone networks, while further developing manufacturing, mining, agriculture, and ranching. Although those investments contributed to economic growth, they also provoked a nationalist backlash. Díaz himself allegedly exclaimed, "Poor Mexico, so far from God and so close to the United States!"

The economic modernization that Díaz fostered carried within it the seeds of his regime's destruction. The expansion of plantation agriculture in the south and ranching in the north further encroached on the small farms of the beleaguered peasantry. The development of mining, petroleum, railroads, and limited manufacturing created an incipient working class that lacked the fundamental right to unionize or strike. In the cities, economic growth produced a small but influential middle class. With political and economic power in the hands of foreign corporations and the tiny Mexican elite, this emerging group of professionals and small businesspeople had few opportunities for upward mobility and, consequently, had their own grievances.

In 1910, Francisco Madero, a wealthy political reformer who had just lost to Díaz in a fraudulent presidential election, appealed to the Mexican population, particularly the middle class, to overthrow the government. Although Madero's goals were largely modest political reforms, his call for revolt provoked the twentieth century's first mass-based revolution. In the cities, workers mobilized to fight for trade-union rights. In various parts of the countryside, peasants and cowboys organized to regain their lands under the leadership of men such as Emiliano Zapata and Pancho Villa. For the next decade, the revolutionary struggle convulsed the nation.

© Hulton Archive/Staff/Getty Images

ZAPATA AND HIS MEN   Despite his limited education and political experience, Emiliano Zapata was one of the most important regional military leaders of the Mexican Revolution. He is shown here seated in the center of the photo, flanked by his officers and men. A man of great personal integrity, he remains today perhaps the most revered revolutionary hero. The Zapatista rebel movement that shook Mexico in the 1990s was, of course, named after him.

Before the fighting ended, it killed more than one million people (out of a total population of 14.5 million) and wiped some eight thousand villages off the map.[3] Unlike many other twentieth-century revolutions, however, the Mexican insurrection lacked a unifying political party, ideology, or charismatic leader. Peasants, workers, land owners, the middle class, and military leaders all fought for different political and socioeconomic goals. Counterrevolutionary forces soon assassinated Madero. Eventually, many other revolutionary leaders—Zapata, Villa, Carranza—lost their lives in the struggle.

Although numerically superior, the peasants and workers lacked the leadership, the funds, and the organization to carry the revolution's radical wing to victory. It was the centrist forces, led by middle-class (or upper-class) military men that emerged triumphant. Although the constitution of 1917 called for limits on foreign investment, pledged land to the peasants, and offered union rights to the workers, it would be almost two decades before Mexico's government seriously addressed most of those more radical promises.

THE POSTREVOLUTIONARY ORDER

Political Consolidation (1920–1946)

Political turmoil and bloodshed carried into the next decade. In 1929, seeking to end the perpetual conflict between regional strongmen and to stabilize the political system, Mexico's political leaders created the National Revolutionary Party (PNR), a coalition of the winning factions in the revolutionary upheaval. The party brought together various regional parties, military and civilian strongmen, and organized sectors of the civilian population. "From the beginning the PNR was envisioned as a dominant, governing party."[4] Its function was to represent and control significant sectors of the population: the peasantry, labor, the middle class, and the military. Other parties ran candidates, but for more than half a century they hardly ever won at any level. In the late 1930s, the party strengthened its labor and peasant wings, and soon afterward ended party representation of the military. In 1946, its name was changed (for the second time) to the Institutional Revolutionary Party, or PRI. From its inception until the 1988 national election, the party never lost a race for governor, lost only one election for senator, and never received less than 68 percent of the presidential vote.

The Cárdenas Era of Social and Economic Reform (1934–1940)

Having established political stability, Mexico's leaders turned their attention to the revolution's still unfulfilled social and economic promises. President **Lázaro Cárdenas's** election in 1934 was a victory for the more progressive wing of the ruling (official) party. Cárdenas initiated Latin America's most far-reaching land reform, distributing some 29 million acres to the nation's peasantry.* He also expanded the country's

---

* In fact, he distributed more land to the peasantry than the combined total of all previous presidents since the 1910 Revolution. The agrarian reform reduced peasant unrest and rural poverty somewhat.

labor movement substantially and incorporated previously excluded radical unions into the PRI. Finally, Cárdenas implemented many of the revolution's nationalist objectives. Recall that widespread resentment of foreign economic dominance was a major cause of the revolutionary struggle. But the post-revolutionary regime did little to address that issue until Cárdenas's administration nationalized Mexico's petroleum industry and railroads. In the following decades, the government also took control of the electrical power, telephone-telegraph, and banking sectors, and established substantial footholds in steel and in agricultural marketing. Although most of the economy remained in private hands, the state became the country's largest economic player by controlling most of the country's infrastructure (transportation, telecommunications, energy—most notably petroleum and electric power) and many of its largest corporations in a mixture of state-controlled and market economies known as **state capitalism.**

Government economic activity expanded further in the 1970s and early 1980s. But by the late 1980s and 1990s, a large portion of the once-substantial public sector was **privatized** (sold to the private sector) as part of a package of neoliberal (free-market) reforms.

THE MAKING OF A MODERN ECONOMY

The Mexican "Economic Miracle"

Cárdenas's radical reforms (particularly those designed to redistribute resources to the poor) proved to be a short-lived deviation from the otherwise centrist path of the revolution. From the 1940s onward, state economic policy was designed to stimulate growth, with little concern for how that affected the distribution of income and resources. Agricultural credits and state irrigation projects that Cárdenas had directed toward the peasant communities were instead channeled toward agribusiness. From the 1940s until the 1980s, Mexico's government, like its counterparts in most of Latin America, supported private-sector industrialization through government subsidies, tax credits, and restrictions on competing imports. At the same time, government control over the nation's labor unions restricted labor unrest and kept wages down in order to attract greater business investment.

Those policies led to what many scholars have called the "**Mexican economic miracle.**" The country's gross domestic product (GDP) grew at an average annual rate of more than 6 percent (Table 16.1) from the 1940s to the 1980s, a more prolonged period

TABLE 16.1   MEXICO'S AVERAGE ANNUAL GROWTH, 1940–1980
(AVERAGE PERCENTAGE GROWTH PER YEAR)

	1940–1950	1950–1960	1960–1970	1970–1980
Population	2.8	3.1	3.8	3.6
GDP	6.9	5.6	7.0	5.5
Agriculture	5.1	4.6	3.7	2.4
Industry	8.1	6.5	8.8	6.7
Service	7.0	5.6	6.8	5.2

SOURCE: Robert Looney, *Economic Policymaking in Mexico* (Durham, NC: Duke University Press, 1985), p. 7 (tab. 1.2).

of high growth than either the United States or Japan had enjoyed during their primary economic expansions.[5] As a consequence, within several decades Mexico changed from a predominantly rural, agricultural country to a largely urban nation with a workforce primarily employed in the service and manufacturing sectors.[*] Education expanded apace. Whereas only 10 percent of the population had been literate at the time of the revolution, nearly 90 percent of all Mexicans were literate by the end of the century.

The Other Side of the Miracle

Despite the country's dramatic record of modernization and growth, critics insisted that the economic miracle left too many people behind. Peasants and workers had fought and died in the revolution hoping to improve their living conditions. Champions of economic redistribution, such as Emiliano Zapata, became national folk heroes. Yet, it has clearly been the poor, especially the peasantry, who have gained least from the revolution and its aftermath.

The economic boom that began during World War II expanded the size of the urban middle class and created a significant number of better-paid industrial jobs for skilled workers. But government policies placed a higher priority on economic growth than on equitable **income distribution**. Table 16.2 indicates that during Mexico's extended economic expansion (1940 to 1982), the richest 20 percent of the population earned between 54 and 64 percent of the nation's income, an extremely high concentration of wealth in the hands of a few.[6] Although income concentration diminished somewhat in the 1970s, the gaps have widened again since the 1980s, enabling the country to regain its dubious distinction of being one of the Latin America's more unequal nations (Table 16.2).[7] In 2001, *Forbes* magazine's annual listing of the world's richest people indicated that Mexico, with a per capita income about one-fourth that of the United States and

TABLE 16.2   INCOME DISTRIBUTION IN MEXICO, 1950–2000

| Year | Percentage of National Income | | |
	Poorest 50 Percent	Middle 30 Percent	Richest 20 Percent
1950	17.4	23.7	58.9
1969	15.0	21.0	64.0
1992	18.4	27.4	54.1
2000	15.6*	26.2*	58.2*

* The 2000 data are extrapolated from the World Bank, *World Development Report, 2000/2001,* which breaks down the population slightly differently for the 40th to 50th percentiles of the population.
SOURCE: Daniel Levy and Gabriel Székely, *Mexico: Paradoxes of Stability and Change* (Boulder, CO: Westview, 1983), p. 144; Daniel C. Levy and Kathleen Bruhn, "Mexico: Sustained Civilian Rule without Democracy," in *Politics in Developing Countries: Comparing Experiences with Democracy,* ed. Larry Diamond, Juan J. Linz, and Seymour Martin Lipset (Boulder, CO: Lynne Rienner Publishers, 1995), p. 195; and World Bank, *World Development Report, 2000/2001: Attacking Poverty* (New York: Oxford University Press, 2001), pp. 282–283.

* In 1940, some 65 percent of Mexico's economically active population worked in agriculture. Consequently, agrarian reform was a major issue. By 2000, however, only about 5 percent of the country's GDP (though perhaps two to three times that proportion of the workforce) came from agriculture, 69 percent came from the service sector, and 27 percent came from industry (see the Economist Intelligence Unit, April 19, 2001).

less than half its population, had 24 billionaires, the fourth highest number in the world (behind the United States, Japan, and Germany) and more than Great Britain and France combined (the number and rank of Mexico's super-rich has since declined).

In the decades following World War II, the government's preferential treatment toward large-scale, mechanized farming undermined peasant producers and contributed to rural poverty. Many peasants who could not compete with larger farms instead had to work as poorly paid agricultural laborers or migrate to the cities. Today, Mexico's rural poor are still more likely to be malnourished than their urban counterparts, less well-paid, less educated, and less likely to enjoy amenities such as electricity or clean drinking water.[8]

As a consequence of that gap, Mexico, like many developing nations, has experienced substantial rural-to-urban migration. Between 1940 and 1981, despite higher birth rates in the countryside, urban centers grew from 22 percent of the nation's population to 55 percent.[9] But because industrial development has been capital-intensive rather than labor-intensive, the cities have failed to produce sufficient employment to meet the needs of their burgeoning workforce. Consequently, even at the height of Mexico's economic boom, some 35 percent of the economically active population lacked full-time employment.[10] As a consequence of the economic crises in the 1980s and 1990s, and slow growth this decade, that figure has increased.

Excessive migration to cities has produced other problems as well. Mexico City's metropolitan area currently houses some 20 million people, making it one of the world's largest urban centers. Moreover, each year an additional 500,000 people migrate to the capital. Because resources have not matched that enormous growth, it has become one of the world's most polluted and most traffic-congested cities.* Millions of inhabitants live in shantytowns and slums, where they suffer from unsanitary conditions, crime, and inadequate social services. For many others who feel that neither the countryside nor the cities offer sufficient opportunities, the United States has always beckoned. Although illegal immigration obviously creates problems for U.S. policy makers, it does provide Mexico with an important pressure valve for its social and political tensions.

A number of government programs since the 1970s, under PRI and PAN presidents alike, have sought to improve living conditions and incomes for the poor. At various times, these plans have included irrigation projects for poor farmers, potable water and sewage services for low-income urban neighborhoods, construction of schools and medical clinics, employment programs, and, most recently, a program granting subsidies to poor families whose children stay in school. But the benefits from these programs have failed to compensate for declining living standards caused by the country's economic crises since 1982. Nor, as we have seen, have they reduced Mexico's great income inequality.

Since the 1980s: From Boom to Bust to Slow Recovery

During the 1970s, Mexican economic growth, as in most of Latin America, was fueled by a large infusion of loans from international banks and lending agencies. When President Luis Echeverría took office in 1970, support for the regime was at a low point in the wake of a government massacre of as many as three hundred student

---

* In recent decades the government has reduced air pollution in the capital by restricting auto traffic, introducing taxis and buses with lower emissions, and moving industry out of the city. Still, pollution remains a problem, as do poor sewage and other environmental health hazards.

protestors shortly before Mexico City hosted the 1968 Summer Olympics. He tried to rebuild the government's support by introducing a number of welfare programs and business subsidies. As spending increased and revenues failed to rise correspondingly, the government turned to external borrowing.

Fiscal deficits and eternal borrowing increased further under Echeverría's successor, José López Portillo (1976–1982). Unfortunately, the state petroleum corporation's discovery of vast new oilfields in the mid-1970s gave the government an exaggerated sense of the country's projected oil-export revenues in the coming years. As a consequence, it accelerated its spending far faster than its short-term revenues grew in order to satisfy the population's increasing demands for services and benefits. Mexico's private sector shared the government's optimism about future economic growth as corporations also accelerated their borrowing from abroad. Both the Mexican government and foreign lenders (U.S., Japanese, and European banks) believed that the sharp rise in oil prices in the early 1970s would continue into the foreseeable future, guaranteeing Mexico sufficient funds to repay its debt. From 1970 to 1981, the government's foreign debt grew from $4.3 billion to $53 billion and private-sector external debt jumped from $1.8 billion to $20.3 billion. Other Latin American countries, including those without oil, became similarly indebted, but Mexico and Brazil led the way. When the price of oil dropped sharply in 1981, Mexico's economic boom unraveled.

President José López Portillo's August 1982 announcement that Mexico was no longer able to make payments on its debt put a brake on further loans to all of Latin America and precipitated the region's **debt crisis**, which lasted throughout the decade. For one thing, it became more difficult to receive international loans. To deal with the crisis, the Mexican government was forced to introduce **economic austerity**—belt-tightening measures including cutbacks on government spending, ongoing devaluation of the nation's currency, and policies that prevented wages from keeping pace with inflation.

From 1982 to 1988, the country experienced almost no economic growth (the GNP actually declined in three of those years), whereas the population increased by approximately 15 percent. Inflation rose sharply, peaking at an annual rate of 160 percent in 1987, but wages failed to keep pace. As a consequence, the average worker's real income (actual purchasing power) declined by 40 to 50 percent in the 1980s, wiping out many of the gains achieved during the oil boom. A United Nations study in the late 1980s revealed that over half the population was at least somewhat malnourished.

By the end of the decade, the government had brought inflation under control, but living standards had not recovered.[11] Not surprisingly, support for the PRI and the government—which had been bolstered by the earlier economic boom—eroded. Finally, soon after the country resumed modest economic growth in the early 1990s, a renewed fiscal crisis in 1995 sent it into another severe depression. GDP fell by 6.9 percent that year, the worst decline since the Mexican Revolution, and unemployment increased by two million as many companies became bankrupt.[12] Although economic growth resumed after 1996 and per capita income has returned to 1994 levels, this growth has been quite slow, especially since 2000, and many of the nation's poor have yet to benefit from the recent recovery.* Because Mexico's state petroleum monopoly (Pemex) is now so inefficient and so badly strapped for investment funds, oil production and exports (in volume) have stagnated in recent years. So, the country

---

* According to World Bank data, Latin America had the slowest rate of economic growth of any world region from 2000 to 2005 (2.3%, about half of Africa's rate and a bit over one-fourth of East Asia's). And, Mexico's average annual growth rate of 1.9% during that period was among the lowest in Latin America.

has not benefited nearly as much as it should have from the recent period of soaring oil prices. The current world-wide economic crisis, particularly the U.S. recession is sure to reduce Mexican exports and damage the country's economy in the next few years.

THE STRUGGLE FOR POLITICAL DEVELOPMENT

Creating a Powerful State

As we have seen, the years from the end of its Revolution (1920) until the early 1980s, Mexico experience substantial growth in state power over the economy and society. By the 1970s, as the task of managing the economy became more complex, a growing number of key government decisions were made by a new elite of highly trained government bureaucrats—often with graduate degrees in economics, public administration, or planning from leading American universities—rather than by elected politicians.[13] Since Mexican political institutions are often less than they seem—the Congress, for example, exercised very little independent power until the late 1990s—the discussion of Mexican politics that follows focuses less on political institutions and more on the role of the state in mediating conflicts in society over income distribution, economic growth, political rights and freedoms, and other issues fundamental to developing nations. We will also be examining the proper role and size of the state itself. And finally, we will look at Mexico's recent transition to democratic government and will discuss future prospects for Mexican democracy.

Nominally, Mexico is a federal republic modeled after the United States. Like the U.S., it features a division of federal powers between the president, Congress, and the courts. In practice, however, Mexican politics has featured a tremendous concentration of power. State governments depend on the federal government for revenues, and until recently presidents could remove state governors from office when dissatisfied with their performance (although formally it was Congress that declared the post vacant). Within the national government itself, the president exercised extraordinary power, though that has begun to change since 1997 when Ernesto Zedillo (1994–2000), became the first Mexican president in some 70 years to lack a Congressional majority. His successors, Vicente Fox (2000–2006) and Felipe Calderón (2006–2012), also lacked majority support in Congress. Furthermore, Zedillo and Fox voluntarily restricted some of their presidential authority and transferred some power from the central government to state and local authorities.

The Executive Branch and the Bureaucracy

Before the revolution, Mexico alternated between rule by *caudillos* (military strongmen) such as Porfirio Díaz, and periods of great instability. The chaos of the revolution and the spate of political assassinations that continued through the 1920s convinced the revolutionary elite that the country had to invest great power in the presidency. The president, no matter who held the office, dominated the political system until quite recently. Before the 1980s, even opposition newspapers and political parties hesitated to criticize the chief executive directly, focusing instead on his advisers or his policies. But, at the same time, to prevent the return of an extended dictatorship like Díaz's, the 1917 Constitution limited the president (as well as all other elected officials) to a single term in office. Subsequently, the length of that term was fixed at six years. Until 1997, "congress . . . [was] a rubber stamp, passing nearly all laws proposed by the president without effecting major modifications; the judicial branch of government . . . exhibited only a slightly greater degree of autonomy."[14]

But even before the recent transition to democracy, one person could not rule a nation as large and complex as Mexico. Hence, a vast bureaucratic network developed within the executive branch, whose members constituted a new ruling class of administrators. At the pinnacle of that administrative elite has been the cabinet. The president has given cabinet ministers—particularly those holding such posts as finance minister and interior minister—extensive powers (subject, of course, to his approval). Under PRI governments, the cabinet also served as a stepping-stone to the presidency.

Until the election of Vicente Fox (a former governor with extensive prior experience as a business executive), presidents in recent decades had emerged from that bureaucratic elite. Typically, modern PRI presidents started their careers by attaching themselves to a patron in a powerful ministry, following him up the rungs of the administrative ladder. When their own patron eventually reached the presidency, he named them to his cabinet and in the last months of his presidency, he picked one of them as the PRI candidate.

For most presidents from the 1970s through the 1990s, their presidential campaign had been their first race for elected office. That pattern of political advancement through a bureaucratic, patron-client network (called a *camarilla*) has now seemingly come to an end. In the 2000 presidential election, the PRI presidential candidate was elected in a party primary, a far cry from the past practice of the outgoing president handpicking his own successor. Fox, the candidate of a party (PAN) that had never previously won a presidential election, took a different route to that office. He first established himself as a rancher and a Coca-Cola executive in Mexico and was then elected governor of his home state of Guanajuato. Indeed, in a reversal of recent patterns, all three major presidential candidates in both the 2000 and 2006 elections had previously served as state governors (or, in one case, as "governor" of Mexico City).

Presidentialism (presidential political supremacy), although undemocratic, fulfilled several important functions. Symbolically, the head of state was the bearer of the revolutionary tradition and a source of unity for a geographically and socioeconomically diverse nation.[15] Ironically, when President Zedillo tried to promote greater democracy by limiting the "imperial presidency"—including renouncing his own right to handpick the next PRI presidential candidate—much of the Mexican public dismissed him as weak, so widely accepted had the idea of an all-powerful presidency become. Vicente Fox faced some of the same criticisms.

Congress

Mexico's Congress is composed of two branches, the Senate and the Chamber of Deputies, with the former holding more power over foreign policy and the latter in charge of fiscal appropriations and the budget. Between 1929 and the late 1980s, only one senator was ever elected who did not belong to the PRI. In response to public pressure for greater representation of other parties, the size of the Senate has been enlarged and the method for electing senators has been changed several times since 1993. Currently, 128 senators are elected from the 31 states and the Federal District

(Mexico City) through a complicated mix of single-member districts, proportional representation, and allocation of a seat to second-place finishers.

Elections for the Chamber of Deputies have also become more complex. Historically, deputies were elected from single-member districts. Beginning in the 1960s, however, a small number of seats in the chamber were allocated to the opposition through proportional representation (PR). The number of PR seats has been raised several times over the years in response to demands for greater democratization. Currently, 300 deputies are elected from single-member districts. Until 1988, opposition parties had never won more than a handful of those races. Consequently, to give added representation to the opposition, 200 additional deputies are now elected through proportional representation.

Given the PRI's dominance of Congress until the late 1990s and the president's domination of the PRI, it is not surprising that the national legislature rather routinely passed the president's proposed legislation. Thus, for example, between 1934 and the mid-1990s, the Chamber of Deputies approved at least 95 percent of executive-sponsored bills and in some years that figure reached 100 percent. Almost all of those bills passed the Congress without amendment.[16] In 1997, in what proved to be a precursor of Fox's electoral upset three years later, the PRI lost its absolute majority in the Chamber of Deputies for the first time since its founding, though it remained the largest party in the chamber.

Therefore, during the second half of his presidency, Ernesto Zedillo (PRI) could no longer demand the congressional subservience to presidential desires that all his predecessors had enjoyed, nor did he use his powers as party leader to pressure PRI deputies to the extent that his predecessors had. Consequently, the success rate of executive-sponsored bills dropped from 97 percent to *"only"* 90 percent.

Congress has become even more independent of presidential control since 2000. During the 2000–2003 congressional sessions, President Vicente Fox's party, the PAN, held 41 percent of the seats in the Chamber of Deputies, but was unable to form a majority coalition with other parties on many key votes. Consequently, in that period Congress passed 86 percent of his proposed legislation, significantly lower than his predecessors' success rate. While 86 percent may still seem like a high success rate, "nearly every single bill [proposed by the executive branch] that could [legally] be amended was modified."[17] In the 2003 congressional elections PAN's representation in the Chamber of Deputies declined further and while it reemerged as the largest congressional bloc in the 2006 elections, it still is short of a majority.

Another way of measuring the extent to which presidential control over the Congress has declined during the past decade is to look at the origin of bills that *are* passed. During the 56th congressional session (1994–1997) three-fourths (74 percent) of all bills passed by Congress were originally proposed by the executive branch. But in the first two years of the 59th Congress (2003–2005), under Fox, only one-eighth (12 percent) of the approved legislation had been introduced by the executive branch, while 62 percent originated with the deputies themselves.[18] And, although the percentage of the president's proposed legislation that passed may seem high, most of them were routine and uncontroversial. On the other hand Congress rejected many of the president's key legislative proposals or modified them substantially, sometimes to the point of gutting them.

For example, when President Fox took office, one of his key priorities was settling a long-term stand-off between the government and the **Zapatista** rebels—officially called the Zapatista Army of National Liberation (the EZLN)—in the impoverished southern state of Chiapas. The rebels—consisting of 600–1,000 lightly armed peasants led by their charismatic spokesperson, Subcomandante [Subcommander] Marcos (a former university professor from the country's north)—had gained enormous national and international attention during their brief armed seizure of four towns in 1994 on behalf of the state's oppressed Indian population. Initially, at least, the Zapatistas attracted considerable support among Mexican intellectuals and professionals. Most compellingly, unlike previous Marxist rebels, Marcos coupled his demands for social justice with a call for more liberal democracy, including honest elections. During the next six years, EZLN leaders—always appearing in ski masks so as to hide their identities—articulated the grievances of the Chiapas Indians and, more generally, the nation's rural poor.[19]

In time, the government and the Zapatistas called a truce and they sporadically pursued negotiations aimed at a peace treaty for years, though direct negotiations have been stalled since 1996. Soon after taking office, Vicente Fox agreed to terms of a settlement with the rebels that had eluded his predecessors. He proposed a number of constitutional amendments to improve indigenous (Indian) human rights, proposals that the Zapatistas found acceptable. To give Marcos and other rebel leaders an opportunity to explain their position to their supporters, President Fox offered safe passage to hundreds of EZLN militants so that they could stage a "march" (actually a bus caravan) from Chiapas to Mexico City, with rallies in a number of towns and cities along the way. But when the Congress stripped key provisions from Fox's proposed settlement, the Zapatistas rejected the package as inadequate. In this case, as with a number of his other reform proposals, the president was unable to count on the support of all of his own party's congressmen.

Some analysts argued that, given his lack of a congressional majority, Fox initially did reasonably well. Among the important presidential initiatives passed by Congress were: a federal Law for Transparency and Access to Public Government Information (to expose more government policy making to public scrutiny); a Science and Technology law (designed to increase the transparency of government decisions to award grants in scientific research); a federal law prohibiting discrimination based on race, ethnicity, sex, age, sexual preference, or marital status; reforms of the Federal Tax Code; and amendments to the Federal Criminal Code designed to protect child victims of sexual exploitation. Various other reforms have made government more accountable to its citizens. At the same time, the administration released previously secret government documents on political repression under the PRI.

However, by the middle of his term, following serious PAN losses in the 2003 congressional elections, Vicente Fox became an ineffective lame duck (Table 16.3). So when he left office in 2006, although he still enjoyed substantial personal approval, he was widely considered a failure who was rarely able to deliver on his reform proposals. Even though his successor, Felipe Calderón (PAN), started his term under very adverse conditions (discussed below), he has been more successful in his dealings with the Congress and in advancing his programs.

Of course, Congress's newfound ability to say no to the president and to reject his legislative proposals promotes the separation of powers and greater democracy (since Congress is no longer the president's lapdog). On the other hand, particularly under Fox, opposition congressmen have often used their votes to stymie presidential initiatives for purely partisan motives, sometimes blocking needed reforms. Critics

Table 16.3   Results of Chamber of Deputies Elections: Percentage of Seats Won

Year	PRI	PAN	PRD
1976	80.1	8.5	—
1988	50.4	18.0	10.5[a]
1997	39.1	26.6	25.7
2000	42.0	41.4	10.4
2003	44.8	30.6	17.6[c]
2006	24.2[b]	41.2	32.0[c]

[a] These votes were won by the Democratic National Front (FDN), an electoral coalition of small parties, most of whom later merged into the PRD.

[b] PRI was the dominant member of a coalition slate called Alliance for Mexico.

[c] PRD was the dominant member of coalition slate called Alliance for Mexico (unrelated to the subsequent PRI coalition of the same name) and in 2006 it was the dominant member of the Coalition for the Good of All.

Source: Mexican Federal Electoral Institute (IFE); Howard Handelman, *Mexican Politics* (New York: St. Martin's, 1997), p. 75; David Shirk, *Mexico's New Politics* (Boulder, CO: Lynne Rienner Publishers, 2005), p. 217.

faulted President Fox for putting too much energy into promoting legislation that Congress was unlikely to pass and for not introducing some of those reforms through executive-branch actions where that was possible and legal.[20] He also made important concessions to the PRI initially in the mistaken belief that he could get that party's support for some of his major legislation. Given the three-party system that has emerged, future presidents will likely lack a congressional majority for some time to come and will have to confront that reality. Even current President Felipe Calderón, whose party holds a strong plurality in both houses of Congress (something it never accomplished under Fox), still needs some PRI (or, less likely, PRD) votes to pass his proposed legislation.

Fox's experience did not bode well for cooperation between parties and between branches of government. It suggested that unless a president's party had a congressional majority (an unlikely development in the near term), the national government will often be bogged down in stalemate. Since 2006, however, President Calderón has worked far more harmoniously with Congress and had managed to gain approval of a number of important bills. For example, after extended debate and negotiation, Congress agreed on a tax reform bill (amended somewhat from Calderón's original proposal) that closed a number of major loopholes for businesses. Even by Latin American standards, Mexico has a low rate of tax collection and it has been overly dependent on oil revenues to support the federal budget. The intent of this bill is to reduce that dependency while producing new revenues for schools and for road construction. Though the legislation is generally popular, some of the very business groups that had supported Calderón's candidacy opposed it.

Another administration initiative, a constitutional amendment on electoral campaigns, attracted multi-party support. It limits the amount of outside spending for campaign advertising and also restricts negative advertisement. Ironically, it passed as a reaction to a major mudslinging campaign against the PRD presidential candidate, Andrés Manuel López Obrador, in the 2006 presidential race, which had been funded by pro-Calderón business groups. Finally, Congress overwhelmingly passed the president's overhaul of the justice system. On the one hand, the bill gave criminal suspects the presumption of innocence for the first time, and hopefully will reduce the common police practice of holding suspects in jail for long periods without any evidence against them. At the same time, however, the law gave the police broad investigative powers that trouble civil libertarians (Congress did remove a provision that would have allowed police to search homes without warrants in special circumstances).

Given how acrimonious the battle was between the PAN and PRD over the outcome of the 2006 election, this improved cooperation between the president and the Congress has been a surprise (though much of the cooperation has been between the PRI and PAN delegations). There appear to be several reasons for this change. First, Calderón seems to be a more capable negotiator than his predecessor. While Fox had been a businessman most of his life and had limited political experience prior to becoming president (he remained something of an outsider in his own party), Calderón, the son of one of the PAN's founders, has been a political insider since his twenties when he was elected president of the party's youth wing and has served in a variety of political posts since then, including the presidency of PAN (he was the youngest party president ever), Congressional Deputy, and presidential cabinet member. All that experience gave him political skills that Fox lacked.

Second, after 71 years of single-party dominance, Mexico's parties, especially the PRI, have finally begun to learn the "game" of multi-party politics and presidential/congressional divides. After their loss of the presidency in 2000, PRI's congressional delegation, which still held a slim plurality at that time (Table 16.3), may not have been ready to play the role of loyal opposition. Some of them believed that 2000 had been just a temporary setback. Then, when it greatly widened its congressional lead in the 2003 congressional election, the PRI could easily conclude that its intransigent opposition to the Fox administration seemed to be paying dividends. But, following the party's resounding defeat in the 2006 elections—finishing a distant third in both the presidential and congressional races—it appeared that the best way for the PRI to remain politically relevant was to strategically cooperate with the new president on certain issues while gaining some concessions from him at the same time. Currently, with no single party holding a majority of congressional seats, the PRI holds the balance of power on votes that pit the conservative PAN against the left-center PRD.

The Judiciary

As in the United States, the Mexican judiciary has local, state, and federal components. Unfortunately, the level of professionalism is generally low in local and state courts, many of which are riddled with corruption. Moreover, that problem has worsened in the past decade or two as narcotics dealers have exercised growing influence over the courts. Until the 1990s, the Mexican judiciary exercised little political influence and was normally subservient to the executive branch. Judges who showed independence could face severe retribution. In 1995, for example, the government's wish to prosecute several union leaders was stymied when Superior Court Judge Abraham Polo ruled that there was insufficient evidence to issue an arrest warrant against them. Subsequently, the judge publicly charged that the chief justice of his own court had pressured him to change his decision. Polo, though a longtime PRI activist, refused to back down. Several months later an unknown assailant gunned him down.[21]

The courts occasionally showed some independence and on rare occasion, even handed down decisions unfavorable to the executive branch.[22] To be sure, the Supreme Court has had the constitutional power to address the complaints of individuals claiming that the government has violated their rights. If the court finds in favor of that complaint, it may issue writs that command the government to cease a particular act or undertake a remedy. But, traditionally the courts used these writs exclusively for nonpolitical cases and refrained from challenging the political power of the presidency as the U.S. Supreme Court has periodically.[23] But while the Mexican Supreme Court could remedy a particular government action, it could not rule on the constitutionality of government behavior. "In other words, the decision would only affect the appealing party, not any other citizen."[24]

Presidents Zedillo and Fox committed themselves to judicial reform as an important component of democratization. The Fox administration attacked corruption in law enforcement and had limited success in trying to clean up anti-narcotics units. But it failed to pass significant court reforms. At the same time, however, the Supreme Court itself assumed a more activist role following the end of PRI dominance. For example, during the *six* years of the Zedillo administration (the last PRI government) the Court ruled on issues of constitutionality 27 times. But during the first *three* years of the Fox government alone, it ruled on such cases 44 times.[25] Furthermore, the high court gave circuit courts the power to rule on the constitutionality of local laws. Zedillo introduced constitutional initiatives designed to increase the independence and the integrity of the judicial system. Perhaps the most important of these empowered the Supreme Court to declare laws unconstitutional under stipulated circumstances.

In short, since the end of PRI dominance, higher-level courts have been more assertive and independent. Thus, for example, the Supreme Court, which had never previously ruled against a President, has done so several times since 2000.[26] But, while there has been progress toward establishing a more independent and trustworthy judiciary, there is considerable distance to go. As in most of Latin America, judicial reform has progressed quite slowly, and establishing the rule of law has been one of the greatest challenges of the transition to democracy. Although important reforms have taken place at the top of the judicial system, law enforcement by the local courts and police remains enormously corrupt. This, in turn, promotes gang violence, particularly by groups involved in the narcotics trade. As a result Mexicans still have little confidence in the police or the legal system.

Political Parties

Until the late 1980s, most political scientists described Mexico as a "modified one-party authoritarian state."[27] To be sure, other parties beyond the PRI existed, but they served a purely symbolic role. As a leading observer of Mexican politics during that period noted, "Without formal opposition, elections would be meaningless. And without elections the system would lose its mask of democratic legitimacy."[28] But PRI electoral dominance began to diminish in the late 1970s and especially during the economic depression of the 1980s. Once able to attract more than 90 percent of the seats in the Chamber of Deputies, PRI dropped below 50 percent for the first time in 1997, and in 2000 they were surpassed as the leading congressional party by the PAN-led Alliance for Change (Table 16.3). After a comeback in the 2003 congressional elections, the PRI finished a distant third in 2006 (with less than one-fourth of the seats), an unimaginable outcome just 10 years earlier. And, most significantly, Vicente Fox's presidential victory ended the PRI's 71-year choke hold on political power. Thus, Mexico has become a truly competitive multiparty system, currently dominated by three major political parties.

The Institutional Revolutionary Party (PRI)   Mexico's ruling party (later to be called the PRI) was created in 1929 and was designed both to be the ruling party and to give official representation to the groups that had been part of the victorious revolutionary coalition. Beginning in the 1940s, the core of the party organization was its three occupationally based sectors: a labor sector to which most of the nation's blue-collar unions belonged (the Mexican Labor Confederation, or CTM); a peasant sector called the National Peasant Confederation (CNC) representing villages throughout the country; and a catchall, largely middle-class sector, including professional associations (representing such groups as lawyers, doctors, and accountants), small-business associations (taxi owners and street vendors, for example), and most importantly, powerful unions of white-collar, public employees, including teachers and many government bureaucrats.

Drawing heavily on peasant, blue-collar, and white-collar votes, the PRI and its predecessors were able to win every presidential election, every gubernatorial race, and all but one Senate seat until the late 1980s. PRI candidates were able to illegally draw on government funding and government programs to outflank the opposition. The party could also count on biased television news coverage in favor of PRI candidates. Until 2000, the PRI presidential candidate received three or four times as much air time as their opponents. Meanwhile, poor peasants and slum dwellers understood that producing a strong PRI vote in their village or neighborhood was the surest way to secure government aid (irrigation projects, potable water, electricity, or the like). In the rare event that PRI candidates, despite all their advantages, were not certain of a victory, the party resorted to vote fraud. Compliant unions endorsed government economic policies, even when they damaged workers. Ironically, the PRI's most dependable source of votes used to be poor peasants who were the most impoverished, least educated group in Mexican society and, thus, the group that had benefited least from PRI rule. Yet, because they were so weak and marginal, they were especially dependent on government assistance and, hence, were more likely than any other group to vote for the PRI so they could hope to receive state aid.

By the 1980s, however, as the government reduced its role in the economy, the party-state (the government and the PRI) could not deliver as many economic rewards to its constituents. Consequently, the party shifted its focus from the corporatist representation just described (representation of occupational groups through their unions and associations) to mobilizing individual party members.

Unlike many other ruling parties, including the Chinese and Cuban Communists, the PRI never offered a clearly articulated ideology, nor was it responsible for formulating policy. Instead, the official party was the national president's instrument and its primary purpose was to co-opt important interest groups and to mobilize support for the government and PRI candidates. In the 1990s President Zedillo struggled against his party's old-style bosses, seeking to democratize the PRI. In perhaps his most dramatic reform, he ended the long-standing practice of the outgoing PRI president personally picking the party's next presidential candidate, which until 2000 was tantamount to naming his own successor. Instead, the last two PRI nominees were chosen in a party primaries.

The party's historic defeat in the 2000 presidential election has forced it to compete for the first time in a democratic setting without the benefit of government financial support. While many political analysts predicted that, stripped of government patronage and financial resources, the PRI would wither away, so far it has been more resilient than they expected. In 2000 the party elected the largest delegation to the Chamber of Deputies and it enlarged its plurality in 2003. Moreover, from 2001 to 2005 it won 50 percent of the governors' races and 57 percent of the mayoral elections, matching or exceeding the combined total of its two party rivals.[29] As of 2007 it held over half of Mexico's governorships (17 of 32). Still, as noted previously, it performed disastrously in the 2006 national election, finishing a distant third in both the congressional and presidential races. Incredibly, the PRI's percentage of all congressional votes fell to almost half its 2003 level (see Tables 16.3 and 16.4). It is perhaps too early to know whether this decline is a portend of things to come or whether it will soon be reversed. The PRI's strongest electoral support continues to come from poorer, less-educated, and older voters.

Party leaders tend to fall into two contending groups: younger modernizers and old guard political bosses (known as "the dinosaurs"). Modernizers favor increased democracy within the party and hope to the transform the PRI, which has never had a well-defined ideology, into a social democratic party similar to Britain's Labour Party. On the other hand, the dinosaurs distrust internal party democracy, favor a greater role for the state in the economy (but not social democracy), and believe in using government programs to reward PRI supporters. Finally, a smaller **technocratic** faction (technologically skilled bureaucrats) remains from the 1980s and 1990s, when it dominated PRI leadership. This group also favors party democracy, but unlike the modernizers, it supports neoliberal, free-market-based economic policies.

The National Action Party (PAN)   The National Action Party (PAN) originated in 1939 as the voice of conservative Catholics who opposed growing government intervention in the economy and the ruling party's anti-clericism (opposition to the Church hierarchy) at that time. For nearly four decades, the party offered the only significant electoral opposition to the PRI. As relations between church and state have improved over the years, the party has ceased stressing religious positions. At the same time, however, it continues to draw disproportionate support from observant Catholics and, not coincidentally, the current President, Felipe Calderón of the PAN, is a devout Catholic who opposes abortion, gay marriage, and euthanasia. The party has considerable support within the business community (particularly smaller businesses) and within the middle-class more generally.

Since the 1980s, it has stressed the principles of free enterprise and reduced government intervention in the economy. But it has also received support outside the ranks of economic conservatives by branding itself as the party of "good (honest) government." During the closing decades of the twentieth century, it staked its claim to office by opposing one-party dominance and official corruption. That reformist image was enhanced by the comparative efficiency and honesty of PAN mayors and governors elected in the 1980s and 1990s when the political system began to open up (though there certainly were cases of corrupt *panista* mayors). The PAN receives its greatest electoral support in urban areas and in Mexico's more prosperous, northern states such as Coahuila and Chihuahua. At the same time, however, it has broadened its support in recent years and won several gubernatorial races in states outside the North. Similarly, although its core support remains the urban middle class and the business community, of late it has also picked up many urban working-class votes.

Ironically, the PAN began mounting its successful challenge to PRI dominance in the 1990s, not long after the PRI government enacted neoliberal economic reforms that mirrored the PAN's position. When the party did finally win the presidency, Vicente Fox's image highlighted his commitment to honest government and human rights more than his conservative economic polices (though he still favored those policies). The administration's commitment to honest government, protecting civil liberties, and exposing past government repression of left-wing activists from the 1960s to the 1980s, initially earned it praise from many moderate leftists. At the same time, Fox's independence from his own party's party structure, his eclectic ideology, and his appointment of several moderate leftists as cabinet ministers and key advisers alienated many PAN leaders.

In the 2000 national elections, the PAN won the presidency, some 41 percent of the seats in the Chamber of Deputies, and 36 percent of the Senate (Table 16.3). Three years later, however, the party suffered substantial losses in the Chamber of Deputies (losing seats to both the PRI and the PRD), in part because of Fox's failure to deliver on so many of his overly optimistic promises. Of course, that defeat made it even more difficult for Fox to get his legislative initiatives passed. Yet, PAN rebounded strongly in the 2006 election, winning the presidency once again (though barely) and, for the first time ever, winning the largest number of seats in each house of Congress (Tables 16.3 and 16.4). On the other hand, it has not performed as well in local and state elections. For example, as of 2007 it held only eight governorships, a great improvement over its position a decade earlier, but still fewer than half the PRI's total. To this point, President Calderón's programs have emphasized conservative (anti-statist) economic policies and a hard line on law and order, particularly in the war on drugs. Needless to say, after a very bitterly contested 2006 presidential contest and charges of fraud by the center-left (see below) Calderón has not had the contacts with center-left academics and intellectuals that Fox enjoyed.

The Party of the Democratic Revolution (PRD)   For many years prior to the 1980s, an array of small parties, each with its own ideological slant, challenged the PRI from the left. Whereas the PAN at that time attacked PRI governments for excessive state intervention in the economy (prior to the PRI's conversion to neoliberal economics in the '80s), the independent Marxist parties criticized it for failing to fulfill its revolutionary promises of reduced poverty and greater economic independence from the United States. In other words, whereas the PAN disagreed with the PRI's revolutionary ideology, the independent left chided the official party for failing to live up to its revolutionary rhetoric.

But, although many Mexican intellectuals and student activists have been attracted to Marxism, leftist candidates never mounted a serious electoral challenge. In fact, the combined vote of the half-dozen leftist parties never exceeded 10 percent. In the late 1980s, however, the major left-of-center parties finally overcame their internal conflicts and united behind the candidacy of Cuauhtémoc Cárdenas, the son of modern Mexico's most revered president, Lázaro Cárdenas. The younger Cárdenas had been elected governor of Michoacán on the PRI ticket. In 1987, he and several other leaders of the PRI's progressive wing were expelled from the party in the wake of their unsuccessful campaign for internal (party) democratic reforms. Cárdenas's 1988 presidential candidacy won the support of the dissidents (such as himself) who had left the PRI and several small Marxist parties, forming a coalition called the National Democratic Front (FDN).

The left's unification behind the son of the PRI's legendary leader could not have come at a worse time for the then-ruling party. The economic crisis of the 1980s—bringing higher unemployment and declining living standards—had weakened PRI control over the peasantry and the urban working class. Cárdenas's campaign called for greater democratization and a rollback of President Miguel de la Madrid's harsh economic austerity policies (1982–1988), which had lowered Mexican living standards. Whereas the PAN's demand for less government appealed to many middle-class voters and the more prosperous regions of the north, Cárdenas's call for public works programs and a suspension of international debt payments won him considerable support among the nation's poor. The official 1988 presidential vote count showed Cárdenas surging past the PAN to take 32 percent of the vote, while the PAN candidate received only 17 percent. Carlos Salinas, the PRI candidate, finished first but barely achieved 50 percent in the official tally and reached that level only through substantial vote fraud.

Not long after the 1988 elections, the FDN dissolved and portions of that coalition formed the **Party of the Democratic Revolution (PRD)**. In the 1994 and 2000 presidential races, the party faded somewhat and Cárdenas finished a weak third both times (Table 16.4). Although the disgrace of outgoing president Salinas in 1994 (he and his brother were exposed for engaging in massive corruption) and an extremely severe economic crisis in 1994–1996 opened new opportunities for opposition parties, the PRD was weakened by internal squabbles and political ineptitude. Instead, the PAN reemerged as the primary challenger to the PRI in the 1994 presidential contest and went on to win the 2000 and 2006 elections, thereby decisively ending the PRI's dominance.

TABLE 16.4   RESULTS OF RECENT PRESIDENTIAL ELECTIONS

Party	1976	1988	1994	2000	2006
PRI*	92.3	50.7	53.4	36.1	22.3
PAN**	—	16.8	28.6	42.5	35.9
PRD†	—	32.5	18.0	18.9	35.3
Other	7.6	15.8	—	3.7	6.53

*In 2006, the PRI was the dominant party in an electoral coalition called the Alliance for Mexico. Six years earlier (2000), the PRD had headed a party coalition with the same name.

** The PAN boycotted the 1976 presidential election. In 2000, the PAN was the major party in the Alliance for Change coalition, which backed Vicente Fox's presidential candidacy.

† In 1988 Cuauhtémoc Cárdenas was the candidate of the Democratic National Front (FDN) coalition, many of whose members later formed the PRD. By 1994, the Party of the Democratic Revolution (PRD) had replaced the FDN. In 2000, the PRD was the dominant member of the Alliance for Mexico coalition, which backed Cárdenas's presidential candidacy (and was unrelated to the PRI-led coalition of the same name in 2006). In 2006 the PRD headed the "Coalition for the Good of All."

SOURCE: CFE and IFE; Pablo González Casanova, *El estado y los partidos políticos en México*, 3rd ed. (México, D.F.: Ediciones Era, 1986), pp. 132–134; and María Amparo Casar, *The 1994 Mexican Presidential Elections* (London: Institute of Latin American Studies, 1995), pp. 14.

The PRD's foremost stronghold is in Mexico City, DF (Federal District), the country's vast capital, inhabited by nearly 9 million people (nearly 9 percent of the nation's population), with many millions more in the greater metropolitan area. From the first time that the citizens of Mexico City first received the right to elect their own governor (mayor) in 1997, the PRD has always held that post, considered the second-most-powerful elected position in the country*. Beyond its base in Mexico City (the most wealthy "state" in the country), the party's greatest support has come from the South, particularly the country's poorest states, such as Chiapas and Oaxaca.[30] At the individual level, PRD is strongest among lower-income voters. In the 2000 national election, the PRD lost over half of its seats in the Chamber of Deputies, but it bounced back in 2003 and especially 2006, when it gained more seats than the PRI (Table 16.3). As of 2007, it held the governorship of six states.[†]

When the PRI was still in power, the PRD often sided with the PAN on issues of political reform and human rights, while sometimes siding with the PRI on economic policies. After Vicente Fox's 2000 victory, the PRD leadership had to decide whether to support the new president, a fiscal conservative with close ties to business, or join forces in the Congress with its enemy, the PRI, against Fox. After having suffered a sharp loss of support in the 2000 congressional election, the PRD increased its share of seats in the Chamber of Deputies from 10.4 percent in 2000 to 17.6 percent in 2003, as the PAN suffered sharp losses (see Table 16.3). At the same time, however, the PRD had lost ground in the previous two presidential elections (1994 and 2000) relative to Cárdenas's strong run in 1988. Through most of 2005 and the early months of 2006, most public opinion polls indicated that the party's candidate, Andrés Manuel López Obrador—the popular, charismatic, and very controversial former governor of Mexico City—led the race. In the last months of the campaign, however, the PAN candidate, Felipe Calderón—aided by a major, business-funded media smear campaign that depicted López Obrador as an authoritarian, left-wing extremist—erased that lead. Calderón officially won the July 2 election by a razor-thin margin (0.56%). López Obrador and his supporters insisted that he had been denied victory by fraud (see Box 16-2).

From its inception, the PRD (formed out of a coalition of parties) has suffered from factional and leadership divisions. As of 2008, in the aftermath of its severe setbacks in the latest presidential election (a race it thought it had won), the party was deeply divided between left-leaning and centrist factions. If it is eventually to win the presidency, it will need to solve these internal disputes and the many other ones that have plagued it over the years.

A Changing Political Culture

Even though Mexico remained an authoritarian political system after the 1910 revolution, opportunities for political participation expanded greatly.[31] As a rule, an individual or group's degree of political participation is closely related to its educational level. Since the Mexican population was overwhelmingly illiterate at the time of the revolution—and since alternative sources of political information, such as radio, did not yet exist—the country's level of political involvement was predictably low.

---

* Before 1997 the nation's president appointed the mayor.

† One state's governor (Yucatán) is backed by an unusual coalition of the conservative PAN and leftist PRD.

Through the first decades of the twentieth century, many Mexicans belonged to what political scientists call a "parochial political culture" (see Chapter 3).[32] That is, they generally lacked sufficient political knowledge to fully appreciate the impact of government policies on their lives and, consequently, tended to abstain from active political participation even when they could*. But, during the course of the twentieth century, as the country's literacy rate climbed past 90 percent, political involvement grew. The spread of radio and television along with urbanization also increased political awareness.

At the same time, however, even today many Mexicans have received fewer than six years of formal education and do not actively follow politics. When compared to the United States, Mexicans are still more skeptical of their political institutions—political parties, the Congress, the police, and the judiciary.[33] But, as the urban middle class has expanded and more people have graduated from high school and university over the years, more and more Mexicans have become involved with politics and seek to influence the political system. The spread of education has affected other aspects of society, including the role of women. But traditional "macho" attitudes remain a problem (Box 16-1).

Box 16-1

The Place of Women in a Macho Culture

As elsewhere in the developing world, Mexico's socioeconomic modernization (higher educational and literacy levels, along with increased urbanization), has advanced the status of women. Signs of progress include a rising proportion of women in the workforce (now about 35 percent of the total) and the decisions of the PRI and PRD (both of whom have recently elected female party presidents) to set a 30 percent quota for women on their list of candidates for the Chamber of Deputies. Still, most of the female candidates have been designated as "alternates" who only serve in Congress if a regular deputy is unable to serve. And the country's traditional **macho** (male-dominated) culture has limited progress, as many Mexicans continue to believe in male dominance.

Two of the areas where women have faced the greatest challenges are in the police and judicial systems. For example, a woman named Claudia Rodríguez was arrested after she fought off and injured a rapist who subsequently died when medical help failed to arrive for several hours. She served a year in jail for manslaughter before protests by women activists forced her release.[34] Since 1993 more than 400 women have been murdered in the border city of Ciudad Juárez, perhaps half of them having been tortured and/or sexually violated. Many were mutilated before or after death. Another 400 women are missing and are presumably dead.

Few of the murders have been solved, and human rights groups such as Amnesty International and WOLA charge that the police and local PAN officials "have done little to investigate or prosecute those responsible" and that "women can be killed with complete impunity."[35] Various government officials, including former President, Vicente Fox, have claimed that the number of murders in the Ciudad Juárez area has been exaggerated and that the police have effectively investigated a substantial portion of the cases. At the same time, the police have tortured several innocent men into giving coerced confessions. Almost certainly this many murders must be the work of more than one individual or group. Thus, it is widely believed that both policemen and drug cartels are involved in at least some of the killings.[36]

---

* Of course, at that time opportunities for political participation were limited, particularly in the case of the rural poor.

Voting and the Changing Electoral System

Although but a few generations ago voting was extremely restricted, Mexican citizens have come to view it as an important right, which they have exercised in substantial numbers even when the PRI candidates faced no serious opposition. In the presidential election of 1917, only 5 percent of the *total* population voted, but by the 1970s that figure approached 30 percent of the population (but a much higher percentage of adults or registered voters).[37] The PRI's electoral dominance until 1988 meant that presidential elections in Mexico served a different purpose from their role in more democratic nations. They were vehicles for introducing the PRI presidential candidate (who usually had never run for public office before) to the population and a means of legitimizing his authority. In the 1982 race, for example, the PRI's Miguel de la Madrid made more than 1,800 campaign speeches, although he faced little serious opposition. The new, competitive electoral scene since 2000 has added far greater urgency to the major parties' campaigns.

Clearly, the lack of a viable electoral opposition to the PRI for much of twentieth century limited both the election's impact on government policy and the population's incentive to vote. Increased voter cynicism caused abstention rates (registered voters who do not actually vote) to rise from about 30 or 35 percent in the 1960s to nearly 50 percent in the 1985 congressional election.

At the same time, after the 1970s, the government (and the PRI) responded to growing pressures from the increasingly educated population by introducing electoral reforms that made it easier for small parties to run candidates and for opposition parties to gain office. It added additional seats to the Chamber of Deputies (the more influential house of Congress) that were exclusively set aside for opposition parties and it subsequently increased the number of seats allocated to them several times. As a consequence of these reforms and a changing electorate, the PRI's share of seats in the Chamber declined from more than 80 percent in 1972 to 39 percent in 1987 and 24 percent in 2006. Thus, the once-dominant "official party" has now lost the presidency, its majority in the Chamber of Deputies, and a significant number of state and local governments.

Interest Groups

Recognized Interest Groups   Between elections, Mexican citizens engage in a range of interest group activities. Indeed, for a less-developed country, Mexico is a relatively highly organized society. But, until 2000 the government and the PRI controlled most significant interest groups. As the ruling party developed, it organized itself on a corporatist model. **Corporatism** involves the organization of the population into government-sanctioned interest groups based on occupation or other socioeconomic characteristics. These organizations have a direct communication channel to the government and in some countries may be the only legally sanctioned representatives of that sector of society.[38] Thus, as we have seen, most Mexican labor unions, the giant peasant confederation (CNC), and a large array of professional and small-business associations have been represented in the three sectors of the ruling PRI. That relationship gave these unions, peasant organizations, and professional associations a voice within the government that their counterparts elsewhere in Latin America often lacked. At the same time, however, corporatism gave the government and the PRI leadership a high degree of control over those groups.

Most of Mexico's blue-collar labor unions belong to the Congress of Labor (CT). Within the CT, the most powerful force is the Mexican Confederation of Labor (CTM), once representing some six million workers. Because of its links to the PRI, the CTM used to exercise considerable political influence, but that influence has declined considerably since the 1980s. Most powerful unions have been led by corrupt labor bosses who use strong-arm tactics to stay in power and are more interested in amassing wealth and power than in effectively representing their rank and file. Moreover, Mexican unions tend to organize only the more skilled and more highly paid workers, employed in modern industries such as petroleum, steel, automobiles, and electric power. Thus, as in the U.S., most of Mexico's urban workforce is not organized into unions, especially the poorest, unskilled workers, who are in most need of help.

Big labor had close ties to the government during the years of PRI political dominance, offering unwavering support in return for government favors. However, the 1980s economic crisis and the sale of many major state enterprises to the private sector (privatization) since that time diminished the state's (hence the PRI's) ability to reward unions. As the PRI's strength has declined since the 1990s, the party's corporatist links with labor unions and peasant organizations have weakened, and the number of independent (non-CTM) unions has risen. The independent National Workers Union (UNT)—consisting of unions that had broken with the CTM and the PRI—was born in 1997 and within five years claimed to include more than 100 unions with some two million members. Another influential union federation committed to union democracy is the Authentic Workers' Front (FAT). The old CTM labor bosses suffered a further blow in 2001 when the Mexican Supreme Court overturned portions of the Federal Labor Law that had favored the PRI's corporatist unions over independent challengers. At the same time, the Court ruled that employer could no longer fire workers for leaving a union that has a collective bargaining contract with the company. This reduced a company's opportunities to sign a sweetheart contract with an undemocratic union and reduced the corrupt labor bosses' ability to intimidate their rank-and-file.

These changes are likely to have both positive and negative consequences for organized labor. On the one hand, the emerging independent unions are generally more democratic and more responsive to their members' desires. On the other hand, they have less influence on government policy than PRI-affiliated CTM unions once had.[39]

While the PAN had not enjoyed good relations with either the CTM or independent unions in the past, President Fox's election did not bring the open break between government and organized labor that many expected. Opportunistic as always, CTM leaders tried to work with the Fox administration (2000–2006) and accepted or even endorsed parts of his program. As we have noted, as the state's power over the economy and its ability to offer its supporters economic rewards have eroded, corporatism lost much of its importance in the closing decades of the twentieth century. Following the PRI's loss of the last two presidential elections, and the PAN's and PRD's substantial gains at the state and local level, the role of state corporatism has declined sharply. Even if the PRI should win the presidency in the years to come, those structures will be difficult to revive.

Under the PRI regime, businesses above a certain size were legally required to belong to one of two government-sanctioned business federations; the Chamber of Industry or the national Chamber of Commerce. Mexican law "grant[ed] semiofficial status to the chambers . . . and allow[ed] the state to intervene in various facets of the chambers' operation," although state interference in business groups [was] usually low.[40] So, like labor unions, businesses were incorporated into a corporatist structure (in which government only dealt with the sanctioned chambers), but in this case the structure lay *outside* the PRI. Rather than serve as a hindrance, the exclusion of business organizations from the PRI allowed them a greater degree of independence than peasant and labor groups enjoyed. A 1996 Supreme Court decision eroded the corporatist relationship by ending mandatory membership in the chambers, thereby opening the door to independent business groups. Some private-sector interest groups have traditionally maintained close ties to the government, particularly those representing economic activities originally established with government support. Others had more conflictual relationships with the government under the PRI but now have close ties to the PAN administration. Mexico's richest and most powerful businessmen have long maintained informal contact with the president and his advisors. Sometimes a group of them will meet with him as a semi-secret big-business council. Business contacts have become more frequent and more important since the PAN took office.

Prior to the privatizations of the 1980s, Mexico's huge state economic sector— growing out of the earlier nationalization of petroleum, railroads, electricity, telephone, and telegraph—led some observers to erroneously characterize the economy as socialist. In fact, most of the nation's productive resources always remained in private hands. Moreover, for the most part the government nationalizations (mostly in the late 1930s) only affected foreign corporations and mostly affected infrastructure. Subsequently those government takeovers served Mexican business well as state-owned firms provided them with subsidized power, transport, and communications. Through much of Mexico's "economic miracle," powerful business interest groups (represented informally by major conglomerates, known as *grupos*) maintained close links to the government and the PRI.

During the early 1970s, business groups became more hostile to the government, as President Luis Echeverría and, to a lesser extent, his successor, President López Portillo (1976–1982), antagonized them through their expansion of the state sector. For the first time, some powerful *grupos*, particularly those located in the industrial capital of Monterrey, allied themselves with the PAN. In the following years, however, neoliberal reforms by President de la Madrid (1982–1988) and, especially, President Salinas (1988–1994) won back much of the business community's support. A number of the country's richest businessmen contributed large sums to Salinas, which sometimes gave them insider access to purchasing state enterprises that his administration privatized. But never have the bonds between big business and the government been so strong as they were under President Fox, who, after all, was a wealthy former businessman whose party (PAN) has long been linked to business. Indeed, during the years of PRI dominance, business leaders kept a low profile in politics and relied on behind-the-scene contacts with the government to lodge any grievances or requests. Since the 1990s, however, many business organizations have openly supported and contributed to the PAN. That business-community support has continued during the Calderón administration.

"Outsider" Interest Groups: The Politics of Protest   For those representing the nation's poor—non-unionized and unskilled workers, peasants, and other "outsiders" who lack the political clout or resources to participate in the normal interplay of Mexican interest-group politics—the political system increasingly has permitted an alternative form of pressure-group activity—political protest. Like the U.S. civil rights movement in the 1960s, Mexican students, peasants, and urban poor organize sit-ins, protest marches, and the like. To succeed, protests by political outsiders must attract media attention and some level of sympathy or support from within the middle class.

Protestors must walk a fine line, however. To be effective, they need to demonstrate their capacity to disrupt daily life or to arouse popular support. Yet, they must be wary not to threaten the stability of the political system or to question its fundamental legitimacy. In 1968, when huge student protests threatened to disrupt the Summer Olympics (hosted by Mexico) and embarrass the government, the authorities brutally suppressed them. By contrast, Mexico's most-noted recent rebel group—Chiapas's Zapatista guerrillas, while initially appearing as a threatening, armed, revolutionary movement, has, in fact, evolved into a political group working peacefully within the system. Under presidents Fox and Calderón the federal government has given protestors far more room to operate. But local or state governments still occasionally repress these activities.

After the EZLN's initial, violent uprising in January 1994, the group attracted considerable public support, halted their armed struggle, committed themselves to democratic change, and entered into negotiations with the authorities. The government, in turn, ceased its military activities against them and negotiated with them for

---

Box 16-2

A HOTLY DISPUTED ELECTION

As we have noted, for most of its 70 years in power, the PRI frequently stuffed ballot boxes and otherwise manipulated the vote count in order to inflate their margin of electoral victories (only rarely did they need fraud to prevent an opposition-party victory). Understandably, most Mexicans were skeptical about the integrity of the electoral process. In the 1988 presidential election, supporters of left-center candidate, Cuauhtémoc Cárdenas, were convinced that he had been defrauded of his rightful victory.* While election procedures undoubtedly became more transparent and honest in the 1990s, once again, following the 2006 presidential election, the left-center PRD candidate, Andrés Manuel López Obrador (widely known by his initials AMLO), and his supporters felt that he had been robbed.

When the Federal Election Institute finally issued its official election results, four days after the July 2 election, it declared that conservative PAN candidate, Felipe Calderón, had defeated López Obrador by less than 1 percent (with the PRI candidate a relatively distant third). Claiming he had been victimized by ballot stuffing in the (pro-PAN) North and by arithmetical errors in over half of the nation's 130,000 polling stations, AMLO refused to accept the results and demanded a recount of *all* ballots cast. Subsequently

the Federal Election Tribunal ruled that such a complete recount was unfeasible and unwarranted. Instead it ordered a partial recount covering those polling stations where it believed there might be legitimate grounds for a challenge (about 9 percent of all locations). Following that recount, it ruled that while there had been some irregularities, the partial recount had reduced Calderón's margin of victory by only a miniscule amount (from 0.58% to 0.56%), and so the PAN candidate remained the winner. That decision, by law, was final and could not be appealed.

López Obrador and his supporters refused to accept those results and insisted that he was the legitimate president-elect. Public opinion polls indicated that 35–40 percent of all Mexicans (and about 60 percent of Mexico City residents) believed that the results were fraudulent. Hundreds of thousands of his supporters camped out in tents (provided by the PRD and the Mexico City Government) in the heart

* For Cárdenas's supporters, including many American academics, it is an article of faith that their candidate was cheated out of a victory. But one respected exit poll suggested that, while fraudulent tactics had almost certainly widened Salinas's margin of victory and raised his vote total to the symbolically important 50-percent level, he probably would have still won, though more narrowly, in an honest count.

years (without resolution).[41] The Fox administration was more receptive to protest demonstrations than PRI administrations had been. For example, when thousands of peasants protested (sometimes violently) against construction of a new international airport on their farmland outside Mexico City, Fox, despite the objections of law-and-order advocates, announced that the airport would be built at a different location. It seems likely that the government will continue to be more tolerant of protests and possibly, like Fox, more responsive to their legitimate demands.

CONCLUSION: A DEVELOPING DEMOCRACY

As a consequence of Vicente Fox's 2000 electoral victory, Mexican politics will almost surely never be the same. Now that the Mexican people have seen that they can vote out the old ruling party, without negative consequences, single-party domination is very unlikely to return. As we have seen, the PRI not only lost again in the 2006 presidential and congressional elections, but they dropped to third place. Elections for president, Congress, state governors, and mayors are now competitive in most parts of the country. An official network of citizen electoral monitors instituted in the 1990s,

---

of the city, blocking streets leading to the Zócalo, the central square since pre-Colonial times. In the words of one American journalist, "The blockade looks more like a fair than a protest. City workers and party members have erected enormous circus-like tents the length of the avenue. There are stages where musicians entertain the protesters. . ."[42] The sit-in lasted for weeks punctuated by huge demonstrations and speeches by AMLO to as many as one or two million people. Other protestors briefly occupied government buildings and seized a several tollbooths on roads leading into the city (allowing motorists to pass through free of charge for a period of time).

Subsequently, about a week before the end of Fox's term in office, López Obrador was unofficially "sworn in" as president of Mexico in a symbolic ceremony held before 100,000 supporters. Finally, in a bizarre twist, the PRD congressional delegation announced that it would not allow Calderón's official inauguration to take place and would block the halls of Congress, where that ceremony is held. In a preemptive move, PAN congressmen seized the Congress's main floor three days before the scheduled inauguration. This was followed by several days of verbal taunts and fist fighting between PAN and PRD deputies. Finally, in a surprising and unprecedented move, outgoing President Fox appeared with Calderón on national television shortly before midnight on the eve of inauguration day (December 1) and turned over presidential power to him. The next morning, accompanied by the Presidential Guard, Calderón was sworn in on the floor of Congress, punctuated by shouts of support from PAN congressmen and cat calls from the PRD. The new president stayed for less than five minutes and then left.

Ultimately, while the demonstrations reinforced the militancy of many PRD supporters, it weakened López Obrador's national standing. Even though most Mexico City voters had supported him for mayor and a strong plurality voted for him for president, many of them were put off by the continued demonstrations. They felt that, while PRD supporters had legitimate grievances, that did not justify a month-long occupation of the city center, causing great inconvenience for many and financial hardships for businessmen and street vendors in the Zócalo area. Others felt that the continued demonstrations, the seizure of buildings, and the fist fights on the floor of Congress indicated that AMLO and the PRD lacked respect for legal procedures. A number of notable leftist intellectuals, who had supported his candidacy, and even some PRD leaders, criticized his post-election tactics. At the same time, however, the election count and the demonstrations reinforced the distrust many Mexicans feel toward their electoral process.

Several hundred thousand protestors fill the Zócalo (Mexico City's central square) insisting that election fraud had robbed PRD presidential candidate, Andrés Manuel López Obrador, of his victory.

and other related reforms now promise an honest vote count, although we have seen that the PRD claimed fraud in the 2006 presidential election. State and local elections in the economically developed North now frequently feature competition between the PAN and PRI candidates. Currently, the PRD dominates electoral politics in Mexico City contests, with some competition from the PRI. And elections in the poor southern states generally pit the PRI against the PRD. In some areas, there is intense competition among all three major parties. In only a few states does a single party dominate. In short, the phenomenon of competitive elections, which began slowly in the 1980s, is now firmly established. To succeed politically, candidates and elected officials from all three parties will need to be responsive to the needs of individual voters and organized interest groups.

Unlike many Third World leaders who have been elected after pledging democratic change, but subsequently dropped that promise once they took office, President Fox delivered on many of his promised political reforms. He appointed a respected independent human rights advocate to head national security; his government revealed long-suppressed documents about the 1968 government massacre of political protestors; it allowed charges to be brought against former-president Luis Echeverría for his role (as a cabinet minister) in that massacre (ending a tradition of full immunity for all ex-presidents); his administration opened long-secret documents on the disappearance of some 500 people killed by government security forces in the 1970s; he passed laws prohibiting the use of torture against criminal suspects (though it is still widely practiced); and he ended the government practice (under the PRI) of bribing journalists to elicit favorable media coverage.

At the same time, the Fox government seemed more even-handed than prior administrations in dealing with "outsiders" political protests. For example, he softened the government's negotiating stand with the Zapatista rebels in Chiapas and offered a peace settlement that the EZLN accepted until Congress altered it. And, as we have noted, he refused to use force to crush peasant demonstrators protesting the construction of Mexico City's new international airport. Thus, in a variety of ways—from the ballot box to protest demonstrations—the appeals and demands of a growing number of Mexican citizens are being heard. For the most part, Calderón has respected democratic practices as well.

But the struggle for full democracy is far from over. While the judicial system tends to operate more honestly and fairly today, it is still plagued by considerable corruption and injustice. Many government bureaucrats and politicians continue to demand bribes for their services. According to one estimate, during the last years leading up to Fox's victory, Mexicans paid $2.5 billion in bribes to government functionaries annually, averaging $100 per family.[43] That "corruption tax" may have eased since then, but it is still considerable.

Political corruption and misbehavior continue to pose a fundamental challenge to Mexico's new democracy. Misconduct has crossed party lines. In the 2004 mayoral election in Tijuana, the PRI used intimidation, vote-buying, and patronage to secure victory for its candidate, Jorge Hank Rhon. Hank, the son of a notorious party boss, had previously been convicted of smuggling. He is widely believed to have links to Tijuana's drug cartel, and two of his bodyguards have been jailed on charges of assassinating an investigative journalist. But the PRI had no monopoly on corruption. A senator from the Green (ecology) Party, formerly allied with Fox, was videotaped taking a bribe from a businessman who wanted to build a hotel in an ecological preserve. Within the PRD, several high-ranking Mexico City officials have been taped taking bribes and the city's director of public finance was caught gambling in Las Vegas with public funds. And, within the current PAN administration, Calderón's Interior Minister, one of the party's rising stars, has recently been implicated in an influence-peddling scandal.[44]

Compared to Vicente Fox, President Calderón's record on human rights and civil liberties has so far been mixed. Critics charge that in his first two years in office, dozens of leftists, including members of a guerrilla group, have been kidnapped by government forces, and have subsequently disappeared. Because the drug cartels have corrupted so many police officers, President Calderón has sent the military and special police units into a number of their strongholds where the local or state police appear incapable of containing them. The tactic has achieved some success against the drug lords and against street crime (it is not clear how much success), contributing to the rise in Calderón's approval rating. But it has also been associated with many human rights violations, some involving innocent civilians. According to Amnesty International, Mexican law enforcement agents continue to use torture against many criminal suspects.[45] Calderón's overhaul of the justice system extended some civil liberties to police suspects (including the presumption of innocence), but also offered police some questionable new powers.

Meanwhile, the country's drug bosses have lashed back against the military's offensive, creating a virtual street war in several cities between cartel gunmen and government forces (as well as between corrupt and honest police). In Calderón's first 16 months in office, over 4,000 people (members of drug gangs, police, military, and innocent bystanders) died in the conflict, with the death rate rising sharply in 2008. The toll included more than 170 local police (some of whom were working for the drug lords), a number of federal agents, several police commanders, and several "top security officials who were once thought untouchable." Many of the assassinated anti-drug officers were killed with the help of corrupt police.[46]

Another important political challenge for Mexico's new democratic order is the relationship between branches of government. Although Congress's new independence from presidential dominance is an important step forward, all too frequently the legislature has replaced blind obedience (before 1997) with indiscriminate opposition (at least under Fox). Although Calderón has worked more effectively with Congress, whenever any president lacks a congressional majority (likely to be the norm), there is a danger of gridlock between the branches of government.[47] Hopefully all three parties will learn to master the art of political compromise. And while the judiciary is far more independent of the executive branch than it used to be, there needs to be further progress in that area.

In the economic sphere, Mexico's major challenge—achieving greater economic justice and equity—remains even more elusive. Presidents Fox and Calderón have proposed a number of targeted programs designed to help Mexico's poor, but the basic structural obstacles to greater equality remain in place and in some respects have grown stronger. The two PAN Presidents have been even more committed to neoliberal reforms than the previous PRI governments. Those policies—which focus on increased competition between firms, reduced government subsidies for producers, lower government regulations of business, and the consolidation of farmland into larger commercial units—are all designed to make the Mexican economy more efficient and competitive. When applied in various developing nations, these reforms have frequently stimulated economic growth (still modest in Mexico), lowered inflation rates, and reduced government budget deficits. But typically, they have also widened economic inequalities, at least initially, and removed government safety nets for the poor. On the other hand, the needs of Mexico's poor are now sufficiently evident and well-articulated that even a conservative president such as Felipe Calderón finds it politically necessary to propose poverty-alleviation programs.

Despite Mexico's modest economic growth in recent years (it has the highest per capita income in Latin America), almost half the population remains below the poverty line, making less than $2 per day. Most poor Mexicans, particularly those from rural areas, still lack an adequate diet, satisfactory health care, and an education for their children that will enable them to compete in the twenty-first century. Income inequality remains among the highest in Latin America. These are great challenges that the nation will continue to face for decades.

And despite substantial democratic gains in recent years, many Mexicans remain suspicious of government institutions. In polls taken after the 2006 presidential election, over one-third of all Mexicans indicated that they believed the election had been stolen from López Obrador. A year later, despite Calderón's high approval ratings in national polls (generally ranging from 50% to over 60%), the proportion of the population believing that he had been elected illegitimately remained the same.

 ## Where on the Web?

http://lanic.utexas.edu/la/mexico/

The Mexico page at the University of Texas's extensive Web site on all of Latin America; the best source of information and links related to Mexico (including politics). Many of these links are in Spanish.

http://dir.yahoo.com/Regional/Countries/Mexico/Government/Politics/

Yahoo links to Mexican government and politics.

http://directory.google.com/Top/Regional/North_America/Mexico/
Google links to resources on Mexican society, culture, and politics.

http://www.sonoma.edu/users/w/warmotha/awmexico.html
An extended essay on Mexican politics, culture, and economics by a Mexican scholar. Useful for background on Mexican politics and the North American Free Trade Agreement (NAFTA), but much has changed since this was written.

◆ ◆ ◆

Key Terms and Concepts ————

caciques	National Action Party (PAN)
corporatism	Party of the Democratic Revolution (PRD)
debt crisis	Presidentialism
economic austerity	privatization
Institutional Revolutionary Party (PRI)	state capitalism
Lázaro Cárdenas	technocrats
macho (machista) culture	Zapatista
Mexican economic miracle	

Discussion Questions ————

1. The Mexican Revolution of 1910 dramatically changed that country's political and socioeconomic systems for the remainder of the twentieth century. Discuss the major positive and negative political and socioeconomic effects of that revolution.
2. After decades of rapid economic growth, Mexico has suffered several severe economic setbacks since the early 1980s. What caused that economic decline, and to what extent did government policy errors contribute to the economic crises of the 1980s and 1990s?
3. Discuss the relationship between Congress and the president under the PRI presidencies. Who had the upper hand and why? How has that relationship changed since the late 1990s, particularly since the election of Vicente Fox?
4. Why has Mexico's balance of strength among the major political parties created obstacles for effective government, and why is it likely to do so in the near future?
5. What factors led to the gradual decline of PRI political dominance since the late 1970s, and what factors accelerated that decline since, ultimately leading to the 2000 presidential victory of PAN candidate Vicente Fox?
6. What were the major successes and failures of the Fox administration?

Notes ————

1. See Vikram K. Chand, *Mexico's Political Awakening* (Notre Dame, IN: University of Notre Dame Press, 2001).
2. See Michael C. Meyer, William L. Sherman, and Susan Deeds, *The Course of Mexican History*, 7th ed. (New York: Oxford University Press, 2003).
3. See Anita Brenner, *The Wind That Swept Mexico* (New York: Harper and Bros., 1947); and Judith Adler Hellman, *Mexico in Crisis*, 2nd ed., with new "Afterward" (New York: Holmes and Meier, 1988).
4. Dale Story, *The Mexican Ruling Party* (New York: Praeger, 1986), p. 21.
5. Martin Needler, *Mexican Politics: The Containment of Conflict* (New York: Praeger, 1982), p. 108; see also Miguel Ramírez, "The Social and Economic Consequences of the National Austerity Program in Mexico," in *Paying the Costs of Austerity in Latin America*, ed. Howard Handelman and Werner Baer (Boulder, CO: Westview, 1989).
6. R. M. Sundrum, *Income Distribution in Less Developed Countries* (New York: Routledge, 1990), p. 77; René Villarreal, "Import-Substituting Industrialization," in *Authoritarianism in Mexico*, ed. José Luis Reyna and Richard Weinert (Philadelphia: ISHI, 1977), p. 80; and United Nations Development Program, *Human Development Report 2000* (New York and Oxford: Oxford University Press, 2002), p. 195.

7. Manuel Pastor and Carol Wise, "The Fox Administration and the Politics of Economic Transition," in *Mexico's Democracy at Work*, ed. Russell Crandall, Guadalupe Paz, and Riordan Roett (Boulder, CO: Lynne Rienner Publishers, 2005), pp. 98–99.

8. Hellman, *Mexico in Crisis*, pp. 82–89; and Rosa Elena Montes de Oca, "The State and the Peasants," in Reyna and Weinert, *Authoritarianism in Mexico*.

9. Peter Ward, *Welfare Politics in Mexico* (Boston: Allen and Unwin, 1986) p. 17.

10. Daniel Levy and Gabriel Székely, *Mexico: Paradoxes of Stability and Change* (Boulder, CO: Westview, 1987), p. 147.

11. Nora Lustig, *Mexico: The Remaking of an Economy* (Washington, DC: Brookings, 1992).

12. Sidney Weintraub, "Detour on the Way to the Promised Land," *Hemisfile* 7, no. 3 (May–June 1996): 6–7.

13. Miguel Angel Centeno, *Democracy Within Reason: The Technocratic Revolution in Mexico*, 2nd ed. (University Park: Pennsylvania State University Press, 1997).

14. Centeno, *Democracy Within Reason*, p. 49.

15. See Carlos Monsiváis, "'En virtud de las facultades que me han sido otorgadas, . . .' Notas sobre el presidencialismo a partir de 1968," in *La transición interrumpida: México 1968–1988* (México: Nueva Imagen, 1993), pp. 113–125.

16. Jeffrey A. Weldon, "Changing Patterns of Executive-Legislative Relations in Mexico," p. 137, and Kevin J. Middlebrook, "Mexico's Democratic Transitions," in *Dilemmas of Political Change in Mexico*, ed. Kevin J. Middlebrook (London, England: Institute of Latin American Studies of the University of London, 2004), p. 24.

17. Weldon, Ibid, p. 165.

18. Wayne Cornelius and Jeffrey Weldon, "Politics in Mexico," in *Comparative Politics Today* (New York: Pearson Longman, 2006), ed. Gabriel Almond et al., p. 486.

19. The Mexican journal *Proceso* is the best Spanish-language source on the Zapatista movement. Among the many books on the Zapatistas are Philip L. Russell, *The Chiapas Rebellion* (Austin, TX: Mexico Resource Center, 1995); and Neil Harvey, *The Chiapas Rebellion: The Struggle for Land and Democracy*. (Durham, NC: Duke University Press, 1998).

20. Middlebrook, "Democratic Transitions" in *Dilemmas of Political Change*, p. 25; Edna Jaime, "Fox's Economic Agenda." in *Mexico Under Fox*, ed. Luis Rubio and Susan Kaufman Purcell (Boulder, CO: Lynne Rienner Publishers, 2004), p. 58.

21. *The New York Times*, June 7, 1995.

22. Needler, *Mexican Politics*, p. 90.

23. Ibid.

24. Roderic Ai Camp, *Politics in Mexico* (New York: Oxford University Press, 2007), p. 190.

25. Ibid., p. 191.

26. Julia Preston and Samuel Dillon, *Opening Mexico: The Making of a Democracy* (New York: Farrar, Straus and Giroux, 2004), p. 514.

27. Samuel P. Huntington, "Social and Institutional Dynamics of One-Party Systems," in *Authoritarian Politics in Modern Society: The Dynamics of One-Party Systems*, ed. S. Huntington and C. Moore (New York: Basic Books, 1970), p. 5.

28. Alan Riding, *Distant Neighbors* (New York: Vintage, 1986), p. 135.

29. Daniel C. Levy and Kathleen Bruhn (with Emilio Zebadúa), *Mexico: The Struggle for Democratic Development* (Berkeley and Los Angeles: University of California Press, 2006), p. 94.

30. Andrew Gelman and Geronimo Cortina, "Income and Voter Choice in the 2000 [and 2006] Presidential Election[s]" (July 13, 2006), pp. 4 and 9. Available at SSRN: http://ssrn.com/abstract=1010104.

31. Excellent survey data on the period leading up to the 2000 election can be found in Jorge Domínguez and Alejandro Poiré, eds., *Toward Mexico's Democratization: Parties, Campaigns, Elections, and Public Opinion* (New York and London: Routledge, 1999).

32. For a discussion of political culture and types of subcultures, see Chapter 3 of this text and G. Almond and G. B. Powell, *Comparative Politics: A Developmental Approach* (Boston: Little, Brown, 1966), pp. 27–30; and Gabriel Almond, "The Intellectual History of the Civic Culture Concept," in *The Civic Culture Revisited*, ed. G. Almond and S. Verba (Boston: Little, Brown, 1980).

33. Camp, *Politics in Mexico*, 4th ed. (2003), pp. 54–74.

34. Marta Lamas, "The Role of Women in the New Mexico," in *Mexico's Politics and Society in Transition*, ed. Joseph Tulchin and Andrew Selee (Boulder, CO: Lynne Rienner Publishers, 2003), p. 136.

35. Washington Office on Latin America (WOLA), "Violence Against Women in Ciudad Juárez" (November 2, 2004), http://www.wola.org/Mexico/hr/ciudad_juarez/juarez.htm.

36. *The New York Times*, "In Mexico's Murders, Fury Is Aimed at the Police," (September 26, 2005).

37. Needler, *Mexican Politics*, p. 5. Increased voting over time resulted from higher educational levels, extending the vote to women and lowered the voting age from 21 to 18.

38. While corporatism is often associated with European fascism, governments throughout Latin America and even many Western democracies have corporatist features. See Howard Wiarda, *Corporatism and National Development in Latin America* (Boulder, CO: Westview, 1981).

39. Katrina Burgess, "Mexican Labor at the Crossroads," in *Mexican Politics and Society*, ed. Tulchin and Selee, (Boulder, CO: Lynne Rienner Publishers, 2003) p. 100.

40. Dale Story, *Industry, the State and Public Policy* (Austin: University of Texas Press, 1986), p. 82.

41. Howard Handelman, *Mexican Politics: The Dynamics of Change* (New York: St. Martin's, 1997), pp. 82–90.

42. "Leftist's Blockade Divides City and His Supporters," *New York Times* (August 6, 2006).

43. Martin Needler, "The Government of Mexico," in *Introduction to Comparative Government* (New York: Pearson Longman, 2006), p. 617.

44. Denise Dresser, "Fox's Mexico: Democracy Paralyzed," *Current History* 104, no. 679 (February 2005): 64–68.

45. Open letter from Amnesty International to Mexican President Felipe Calderón (February 7, 2008), http://www.amnestyusa.org/countries/mexico/coxtocalderonenglish.pdf.

46. "Mexico's War on Drugs Kills Its Police," *New York Times* (May 26, 2008).

47. Chappell Lawson, "Fox's Mexico at Midterm," *Journal of Democracy*, 15.1 (2004), 139–153.

For Further Reading ⸻

Camp, Roderic Ai. *Politics in Mexico: The Decline of Authoritarianism.* 5th ed. New York: Oxford University Press, 2007.

Grayson, George W. *Mexican Messiah: Andrés Manuel López Obrador.* University Park: The Pennsylvania State University Press, 2007.

Levy, Daniel C., and Kathleen Bruhn (with Emilio Zebadúa). *Mexico: The Struggle for Democratic Development*, 2nd ed. Berkeley and Los Angeles: University of California Press, 2006.

Middlebrook, Kevin J., ed. *Dilemmas of Political Change in Mexico.* London, England: Institute of Latin American Studies of the University of London, 2004.

Preston, Julia, and Samuel Dillon. *Opening Mexico: The Making of a Democracy.* New York: Farrar, Straus, and Giroux, 2004.

Schlefer, Jonathan. *Palace Politics: How the Ruling Party Brought Crisis to Mexico.* Austin: University of Texas Press, 2008.

Speed, Shannon. *Rights in Rebellion: Indigenous Struggle and Human Rights in Chiapas.* Stanford, CA: Stanford University Press, 2008.

PART V

INTERNATIONAL RELATIONS

U p to this point, this text has focused primarily on the domestic aspects of politics—how political behavior, institutions, and ideologies function within the boundaries of the nation-state. In Part V, we turn our attention to another important field within political science, the international relations between nation-states. In truth, domestic politics and international relations are frequently intertwined. A country's decision to go to war may be motivated by domestic politics. A nation's environmental policy may affect the purity of the air or water in neighboring states. But, in the absence of some form of regional or world government, the rules and norms of political and economic relations between sovereign states are distinct from those of domestic politics.

Chapter 17 deals with approaches to the study of the causes of war, nuclear weapons, foreign policy decision making, international political economy, international organization, and international law. Chapter 18 examines important contemporary issues in international relations such as world trade, human rights, and international terrorism.

JOINT COMBAT OPERATIONS   In this photo, soldiers from the U.S. 12th Cavalry and the Iraqi Army raid a site suspected of containing enemy weapons. The picture was taken in April 2007.

© Ashley Gilbertson/Aurora Photos

17

APPROACHES TO INTERNATIONAL RELATIONS

◆ International Relations versus Domestic Politics ◆ Idealists and Realists ◆ War and International Relations ◆ The Politics of Nuclear Weapons ◆ Foreign Policy Decision Making ◆ International Political Economy ◆ International Law and Organization ◆ Ethics and International Relations ◆ Conclusion: War, Trade, Foreign Policy, and the Stakes of Politics

Despite the transforming effect of the terrorist attacks on September 11, 2001, and the 2003 invasion of Iraq and its troubling aftermath, domestic affairs continue to dominate the political concerns of most U.S. citizens, as they do for citizens of the United Kingdom, Japan, France, and other modern democracies. Because their access to international news is so limited, citizens in most developing countries discuss international affairs only rarely. Nevertheless, and especially in recent years, it is clear that international relations affect people everywhere in profound ways.

Many citizens immediately think of the possibility of armed conflict when they consider international relations, and indeed, wars are among the most important events in human history. Even the preparation for war transforms the allocation of economic resources and influences how nations treat their citizens. But international relations are also important when wars are not raging. Economic relations among countries dramatically change domestic conditions everywhere. Modern advances in transportation, communications, and weapons systems have created a world of complex interdependence among nations in which economic progress and national security increasingly require attention to conditions and policies in other countries.

Although international relations is basic to the study of politics and government, approaches to this field are fundamentally different from those encountered in the study of domestic politics. For example, we cannot apply the concepts of political participation through voting, interest group membership, and party identification in explaining international relations in the same ways that we employ these concepts in analyzing domestic politics. In this chapter, we discuss the most important approaches to studying international relations, and we devote Chapter 18 to a discussion of contemporary issues.

INTERNATIONAL RELATIONS VERSUS DOMESTIC POLITICS

When we think of international politics, the first topic that occurs to many of us is war or the threat of war. We study not only how wars are fought but also their causes, the complex issue of deterrence, the effects of shifts in the balance of power, strategy and tactics, the political impact of nuclear weapons, and even the ethical questions suggested by the idea of a "just war." We are sometimes tempted to assume that international relations is distinguished from domestic politics purely by its emphasis on violence.

Yet the problem of conflict, even violent conflict, is a part of both domestic and international politics. The difference is not in the *existence* of conflict but in *how conflict is managed*. Kenneth Waltz, a leading theorist, explains the point in this way:

> The threat of violence and the recurrent use of force are said to distinguish international from national affairs. But in the history of the world surely most rulers have had to bear in mind that their subjects might use force to resist or overthrow them. If the absence of government is associated with the threat of violence, so also is its presence. . . . To discover . . . differences between internal and external affairs one must look for a criterion other than the occurrence of violence. . . . *The difference between national and international politics lies not in the use of force but in the different modes of organization for doing something about it.*[1]

Domestic politics usually takes place within a context of a generally settled order, whereas international politics takes place in a state of relative anarchy. In domestic affairs, the state assumes a "monopoly on the *legitimate* use of force, [meaning] that public agents are organized to prevent and to counter the private use of force."[2] Because such a monopoly on the use of legitimate force does not exist in international relations, Waltz describes the international arena as one in which nations engage in **self-help**; each nation must look to its own security because there is no higher authority that can consistently and effectively perform that function. Of course, forces of stability and order do exist in the international system, such as shared cultures and ideologies, and international law and organization—and they prevent some violent conflict. The difference between domestic and international politics lies in the extent to which a given actor is on its own with respect to protecting its security. Although both citizens and individual nations can be threatened with adversaries, and although both may work to defend themselves, the *primary* approach to security in domestic politics is reliance on a higher authority (for example, the police), whereas the *primary* approach to security in international politics is self-help. This difference is at the heart of contending approaches to the field.

IDEALISTS AND REALISTS

Historians and philosophers have been analyzing international relations since the time of ancient Greece. Among the earliest works in the field was *The Peloponnesian War*, written in the fifth century BCE by the Greek historian Thucydides.[3] Other ancient studies include Sun Tzu's *The Art of War* and Kautilya's *Arthasastra*.[4] Those works continue to suggest insights to modern scholars. The unprecedented destruction and complex origins of World War I, however, led to rapid growth in academic study of the field, producing two sharply opposing perspectives: idealism and realism.

Idealism*

Idealists assume that war and international tensions can be prevented by establishing international law, by creating effective international organizations, by asserting rights and obligations in international affairs, and by educating citizens and leaders regarding the wastefulness of war. **Idealism** thus advocates a set of normative principles—it tells us what we *should* do. Yet, idealism also contains implicit explanations of national behavior, thus approaching the status of an empirical theory.

Idealists suggest that the causes of war can be found in ill-conceived ideologies, in excesses of nationalism, and in the underdevelopment of law. If we want to know why a given war was started, we should look to those factors. On a positive note, idealism reflects the belief that effective political management can help prevent wars that

---

* Some analysts prefer the term "liberalism" or "liberal idealism" in this context. For example, a text by Charles W. Kegley, Jr., and Eugene R. Wittkopf, *World Politics, Trend and Transformation* (New York: St. Martin's, 1997), uses "liberal idealism," which they define as the assumption that "people are not by nature sinful or wicked but that harmful behavior was the result of structural arrangements motivating individuals to act in their own self-interest" (p. 19). Joseph S. Nye, Jr., in *Understanding International Conflicts: An Introduction to Theory and History*, 3rd ed. (New York: Longman, 2000), pp. 39–45, discusses "liberalism" in a broad sense, including several different meanings. We prefer to use the term *idealism* here to avoid confusion with the rather separate set of ideas associated with the term *liberalism* in social and economic domestic policy (as discussed in Chapter 2), and because "liberalism" is synonymous with advocacy of free trade in the subfield of international political economy, as we discuss later in this chapter.

otherwise appear unavoidable: People can be brought to understand the wrongfulness of belligerent ideologies or aggressive forms of national pride, and they can be persuaded to accept a workable code of international law. Wars need not be fought.

U.S. President Woodrow Wilson (1913–1921) was a key proponent of idealism. Following World War I, his support for the creation of the ill-fated League of Nations (an international organization intended to maintain international security) was a moral mission, one that reflected a sincere belief that war could become obsolete if nations had a forum in which they could solve their differences without recourse to armed conflict. Wilson believed that war is something that humankind can "grow out of," much as adults can emerge from a rocky adolescence to become cooperative, productive citizens.

Realism

Although many people share the goals of idealism, few analysts of international relations fully accept its assumptions about the underlying forces governing international affairs. **Realism** holds that the actual motivations for national behavior are often quite different from what is implied in the public rhetoric of leaders: A national leader may *claim* to act in accordance with moral, religious, or even legal principles, but his or her real purpose is almost always the pursuit of security and power. Realists claim that because idealism is flawed as a way to explain the origins of war, it cannot serve as a blueprint for preventing war. It is necessary to identify the forces that lead to war, and then leaders can make policies that make war less likely.

Hans J. Morgenthau, an important twentieth-century realist, described realism as the assumption that "politics . . . is governed by objective laws" and that "the main signpost that helps political realism to find its way through the landscape of international politics is the concept of interest defined in terms of power."[5] If we want to understand the behavior of nations in international affairs, according to realist thinking, we must begin with the assumption that everything of importance that nations do is driven by their interests in maximizing their power and security.

By emphasizing *power* and *security*, realists minimize the place of ideals as a motivating force in international relations. Proponents of realist theory have probably produced the most influential research in the field of international relations. Beginning with the assumption that "states, . . . at a minimum, seek their own preservation and, at a maximum, drive for universal domination," realism is the foundation for a wide range of useful predictions about international behavior.[6] (see Box 17-1).

For example, whereas idealists would see the outbreak of World War II as caused by the fanatical ideology of fascism, realists feel that Hitler's or Mussolini's totalitarian ideologies were less instrumental in producing the war than was the imbalance of power that developed between the two world wars. Since nations will *always* seek power and domination (regardless of the ideologies that may be in fashion at a given moment as expressed in stump speeches), realists contend that the more basic "cause" of the war was the military weakness of Great Britain, France, and the United States, which presented Germany (and perhaps Japan) with the opportunity to pursue expansionist plans.

According to this way of thinking, realists often criticize British Prime Minister Neville Chamberlain (the chief executive who preceded Winston Churchill) for his actions during the months preceding World War II. Chamberlain sought to appease

Box 17-1

IDEALISM, REALISM, AND THE INVASION OF IRAQ

In September 2004, more than a year after the invasion of Iraq, President George W. Bush spoke to the United Nations General Assembly. He referred to terrorist attacks that had taken place after the invasion and overthrow of Saddam Hussein, including an attack on September 1, 2004 in the Russian town of Beslan that killed nearly 200 children and adults. Bush's speech strongly embodies the idealist perspective, using rhetoric that echoed that of Woodrow Wilson nearly a century earlier:

> In this young century, our world needs a new definition of security. Our security is not merely found in spheres of influence, or some balance of power. The security of our world is found in the advancing rights of mankind.
>
> These rights are advancing across the world—and across the world, the enemies of human rights are responding with violence. Terrorists and their allies believe the Universal Declaration of Human Rights and the American Bill of Rights, and every charter of liberty ever written, are lies, to be burned . . . and forgotten. They believe that dictators should control every mind and tongue in the Middle East and beyond. They believe that suicide and torture and murder are fully justified to serve any goal they declare.
>
> And they act on their beliefs.
>
> In the last year alone, terrorists have attacked police stations, and banks, and commuter trains, and synagogues—and a school filled with children. This month in Beslan we saw, once again, how the terrorists measure their success—in the death of the innocent, and in the pain of grieving families. Svetlana Dzebisov was held hostage, along with her son and her nephew—her nephew did not survive. She recently visited the cemetery, and saw what she called the "little graves." She said, "I understand that there is evil in the world. But what have these little creatures done?"
>
> The Russian children did nothing to deserve such awful suffering, and fright, and death. The people of Madrid and Jerusalem and Istanbul and Baghdad have done nothing to deserve sudden and random murder. These acts violate the standards of justice in all cultures, and the principles of all religions. All civilized nations are in this struggle together, and all must fight the murderers.

> We're determined to destroy terror networks wherever they operate, and the United States is grateful to every nation that is helping to seize terrorist assets, track down their operatives, and disrupt their plans. . . . [M]y nation is grateful to the soldiers of many nations who have helped to deliver the Iraqi people from an outlaw dictator.*

Several commentators classify President Bush and many of his supporters as "neo-conservatives," a term often applied to those who believe in activist government programs and aggressive foreign policies to achieve conservative goals. Traditional conservatives tend to be more skeptical about governmental efforts to improve societies or to spread democracy throughout the world. Thus, conservatives like columnist George Will criticized the Bush Administration's attempt to create democracy in Iraq, arguing that the effort was driven by the "Jeffersonian poetry of democratic universalism." Brent Scowcroft, a key adviser to President George H.W. Bush and a key advocate of the 1991 war to remove Iraq's forces from Kuwait, similarly criticized the 2003 invasion. His remarks were rooted in the realist school of thought, contrasting starkly with Bush's idealism.

Scowcroft, in a *New Yorker* interview in 2005, discussed an argument over Iraq he had had two years earlier with Condoleezza Rice, who was then national security adviser. "She says we're going to democratize Iraq, and I said, 'Condi, you're not going to democratize Iraq,' and she said, 'You know, you're just stuck in the old days,' and she comes back to this thing that we've tolerated an autocratic Middle East for fifty years and so on and so forth," he said. The interviewer noted that Scowcroft, with a "barely perceptible note of satisfaction in his voice", added: *"But we've had fifty years of peace."* Scowcroft's retort embodied the realist idea that peace is more secure when nations pursue *realist* principles than when they act to achieve *idealist* goals.

It is certainly possible to construct a realist argument to explain the invasion of Iraq and the extended U.S. presence there. Despite the public speeches that embody idealism, the real reason for the invasion,

---

* The full text of the president's speech may be found at http://www.globalsecurity.org/military/library/news/2004/09/mil-040921-whitehouse01.htm.

(Continued)

Box 17-1

IDEALISM, REALISM, AND THE INVASION OF IRAQ
(Continued)

according to realists who supported it, was to remove a threat to stability in the region and to assert U.S. power in order to inhibit aggression by other regimes. Those taking this view point to the fact that Libya publicly announced its decision to abandon a nuclear weapons program shortly after the invasion, a decision that Libya's leader admitted was driven by his concern that he would suffer the same fate as Saddam Hussein.

It is also arguable that realist thinking led to the Bush administration's different policies toward Iraq and North Korea in late 2002. The president had used idealist rhetoric when he stated that no part of the "axis of evil" (a term he used for Iraq, Iran, and North Korea) should be allowed to have nuclear weapons. When North Korea admitted that it too had violated the Non-Proliferation Treaty and was working to obtain nuclear weapons, some citizens and observers felt that the president's policy would lead to invasions of both North Korea and Iraq. After all, both countries had violated treaties, both had nuclear bombs, and both were aggressive.

However, the difference in U.S. policy toward Iraq and North Korea suggests that the idealism of

the Bush Administration was tempered by a strong element of realism. Some have argued that despite its possession of nuclear weapons, North Korea is surrounded by much stronger neighbors and that it is economically weak. Thus, economic and diplomatic pressure could be brought to bear on North Korea, possibly resulting in progress toward disarmament without war. Iraq, in contrast, is surrounded by vulnerable neighbors and had shown itself to be essentially immune to economic pressures. Moreover, North Korea does not control any strategically important resources.

Realism and idealism in U.S. foreign policy will both figure in the nation's response to problems in Iran, as discussed in the next chapter. It is often difficult to separate considerations of morality and international law from concerns for stability and power, and whatever U.S. policy turns out to be, statements and speeches justifying it will certainly contain realist and idealist notions. Which of these approaches generates the best foreign policy decisions remains the subject of a never-ending debate.

DELICATE DIPLOMACY   U.S. Secretary of State Condoleezza Rice, left, gestures while speaking with EU foreign policy chief Javier Solana during a round table meeting at an Iraqi International conference in Brussels, Wednesday June 22, 2005.

Hitler as Germany moved its armies into Austria and Czechoslovakia. He refused to accelerate British defense spending in the face of the rising German military threat because he thought that Hitler would see this as provocative. Hitler exploited the opening created by British weakness, and World War II began. Realists employ this example to support their contention that preventing wars requires a consistent recognition that all nations seek power and security, and that military weakness in critical areas will present opportunities that aggressors will exploit. The positive element in realism is the idea that the behavior of most states is predictable.

Criticisms of Both Approaches

Critics of idealism argue that an approach based on national interest and the assumption that nations will always pursue security and power provides a better foundation for explaining conflict and war. Skillful politicians may engage in florid rhetoric to persuade their citizens to sacrifice for a "moral" cause, but the objectives they most often pursue are their more concrete concerns for power, security, and self-interest.

On the other hand, critics of realism contend that realists narrowly read history as being determined exclusively by a small set of influences. Edward Hallett Carr, whose analysis of idealism and realism remains an influential statement, pointed out that realist thinking is excessively cynical. Although overt moral positions do sometimes serve simply as a cover for the pursuit of self-interest, it does not follow that the behavior of nations is as simple or predictable as realists claim.[7] Moreover, the concept of a nation having "a" national interest is more applicable to nations that are governed by a single monarch or ruling elite (whose precise and explicit interests can be identified and acted on) than to democratic nations, whose citizens and groups have multiple and usually conflicting interests. Realism is thus an over-simplification of the motivations involved in foreign policy.

The U.S. and European intervention in Bosnia, the U.S. military action in Somalia in 1992–1993, and U.S. aid to central African refugees are policy choices that cannot be easily explained by realist assumptions. The United States has no strategic interests in those areas. The relief efforts placed some U.S. military personnel in real danger and cost billions of dollars. Although it is fair to say that the United States did not jeopardize its security by taking those actions, no significant U.S. interests in security and power interests lay behind them. Similarly, some claim that the policies former British Prime Minister Tony Blair adopted in 2002 and 2003 supporting the U.S.-led invasions of Afghanistan and Iraq cannot be explained through realism. Arguably, British security from terrorist attacks would have been enhanced if he had taken a more neutral position during this period.

In fact, the idea that nations pursue foreign policies *entirely* on the basis of a simple concern for self-interest is becoming increasingly difficult to defend. A recent study by a leading analyst concluded that the existence of a "security community," defined as "a group of countries among which war is unthinkable," can influence policy. He claims that a security community has developed among the United States, Western Europe, and Japan. The shared conviction among these countries—that war would be absurdly costly, whereas peace produces real gains—exerts real force over their policy choices.[8] Although realists would claim that the idea of a "security community" is consistent with their view (because the "security community" concept does not imply that nations disregard or act against their national interests), it certainly suggests that foreign policy choices are not a simple matter of nations acting exclusively on the basis of their independent concerns. Something larger than a nation's individual interests may shape foreign policy, and idealists would point to that observation as support for the idea that peace may be maintained or strengthened by building on these larger, collective influences.

Debates over the usefulness of realism and idealism in international relations will not be resolved soon. Realists have always noted that the political rhetoric used to justify states' foreign policy choices usually makes it *appear* that idealistic motivations are involved; the *actual* motivations are power and security even when domestic politics requires speeches implying a higher purpose. Empirical research is unlikely to yield definitive answers to this debate partly because of the difficulty of ascertaining the motives of national leaders.

WAR AND INTERNATIONAL RELATIONS

The possibility of armed conflict often influences behavior even when other issues dominate relations among nations. A country's ability to attack its enemies or to defend itself in war represents a critical factor in its interactions with other nations. Thus, a great deal of scholarly attention is rightly devoted to the study of war. In this section, we consider the most widely known approaches to understanding war, and then we focus on two special issues: the balance-of-power concept and the problem of nuclear weapons.

The Causes of War: Waltz's "Images"

The fact that war is both horribly wasteful and a seemingly inescapable part of life has led philosophers and politicians to devote a great deal of attention to discovering its ultimate causes. Kenneth Waltz's classic book, *Man, the State, and War,* synthesized much of the prevailing scholarly thinking about the subject into a three-way classification of "images."[9] (In terms of the discussion in the previous section, Waltz would say that the third image is most closely associated with realism and that the first image is most closely tied to idealism.)

The First Image: Human Nature and the Causes of War The most common approach to understanding the causes of war is to look to human nature. Waltz described this "first image" of international relations as follows: "The locus of the important causes of war is found in the nature and behavior of man. Wars result from selfishness, from misdirected aggressive impulses, from stupidity."[10] To find out why World War II occurred, for example, we study Adolf Hitler's personality, his foolish ideology, and his tragic power to inspire millions of followers. Quoting Confucius, Waltz summed up the first image: "There is deceit and cunning and from these wars arise."

There are both optimistic and pessimistic versions of this first image. If the cause of war is found in human nature, then war can be ended if education and experience can correct human failings. Perhaps people can be brought to see war as wrong and avoidable. Others, who believe that war is an inherent part of human nature, imply that wars can never be fully prevented. The "laws" of human nature, they argue, are no more malleable than are the laws of physics.

Although the importance of human nature cannot be easily dismissed, it becomes quickly limited as a basis for generally understanding international conflict. Other factors must be involved. If human nature were all that mattered in the origin of wars, *then we have no way of understanding why there are periods of peace.* Since nations are not always at war (or peace), human nature cannot be the exclusive source of war. "The causes that in fact explain differences in behavior must be sought somewhere other than in human nature itself."[11]

The Second Image: The Nature of States and the Causes of War   An alternative explanation of the cause of war focuses on the nature of states. Even if people could control their aggressive impulses, the nature of the states that govern them may create conditions leading to war. The second image implies that we can explain war by looking at the ways in which different *kinds* of states increase or diminish the likelihood of war.

There are two excellent illustrations of the Second Image approach: the concept of the Democratic Peace, and Marxist-Leninist views on international conflict. Proponents of the former argue that it is largely non-democratic governments that are prone to war (see Box 17-2). Such states need to repress dissent, and it is easier to do so if the citizens are unified and loyal. The leader of a non-democratic government thus may start a war in order to make citizens focus on a common external threat. By some interpretations, there has never been a major war between two genuinely democratic nations—an idea that seems to confirm this connection between the nature of a state's political system and its tendencies toward war. The conventional Marxist-Leninist interpretation of international affairs also accounts for conflict by focusing on the nature of states. As discussed in Chapter 2, one of Lenin's contributions to Marxist thinking was the idea that capitalist states engage in aggression because their economic systems force them to do so. States with socialist systems (or very primitive states) do not go to war because they are not forced to do so by the consequences of capitalist economics.

The limitation of the second image is its assumption that the warlike (or peaceful) nature of states is entirely determined by domestic factors. Waltz points out that just as individual behavior cannot be understood apart from the societies in which individuals live, the behavior of individual *states* cannot be understood apart from the world in which they operate. Many actions taken by states reflect the nature of the international system as much as they reflect their own internal structure and domestic political needs.

The Third Image: The International System   Waltz's third image emphasizes that understanding international relations requires an appreciation of the nature of the system in which states operate. The key feature of that system is *anarchy*, as noted earlier. For Waltz, the fact that the system is anarchical creates a situation in which each state is potentially threatened, and most of the important actions of states are driven by the pervasiveness of those threats. As Waltz points out, the third image has been around a long time: "Thucydides implied an appreciation of this idea when he wrote that it was 'the growth of the Athenian power which terrified the Lacedaemonians and

Box 17–2

THE "DEMOCRATIC PEACE"?

The **democratic peace** concept has gathered momentum among specialists in international relations during the last few decades. In simple terms, its proponents argue that the more democratic a nation is, the less likely it is to be involved in a war with another democracy. There is considerable empirical support for this proposition, although it is less well established that democracies are *generally* less involved in wars—the key finding is that they rarely fight other democracies.[12]

Why should this be so? Although the matter is far from settled among political scientists and diplomats, a few themes consistently appear in discussions of the "democratic peace" phenomenon. Perhaps the root of the idea can be traced to a 1795 essay by philosopher Immanuel Kant, entitled "Perpetual Peace: A Philosophical Sketch," in which he concluded that governments that act in "responsible" ways would be reluctant to go to war. The most obvious explanation is that, in democratic systems, the people will force their leaders to avoid war because they know that they will bear its terrible costs. Dictators, not being similarly constrained by public opinion, will initiate wars much more often.

While this makes intuitive sense, it only tells part of the story. One recent study found that, when faced with war, leaders in democratic systems are more likely to allocate a greater share of national resources to military efforts than leaders in authoritarian regimes. Voters in democratic systems dislike military defeats even more than they dislike war. Consequently, nations of all kinds are less likely to attack democratic systems, thus bringing them into war less often. Moreover, democratic leaders try to avoid defeat by being very selective about the countries they would make war upon. Because they are less reckless about engaging in war, and because would-be aggressors fear the all-out effort that democracies would

make in response, the historical record indicates that democracies are less likely than non-democracies to be involved in war.[13]

A newer refinement to the "democratic peace" theory is a distinction between established democracies and newer democracies. In a 2005 book by Edward D. Mansfield and Jack Snyder, entitled *Electing to Fight: Why Emerging Democracies Go to War*, the authors found that it is only *mature* democracies that are less likely to be involved in war.

Why would the *maturity* of a democracy matter? A country that has taken the first steps toward democracy, holding free elections, probably has not yet established institutions that create real accountability (such as a civilian-controlled military, a genuinely free press, and a strongly independent judiciary). In such countries, political leaders may actually be particularly motivated to take their countries to war. They realize that engaging in aggression can generate domestic support, because they can "sell" the resulting war to their citizens as a response to a past injustice at the hands of the invaded country, for example. Not being restrained by well-institutionalized legislative or judicial bodies, or by a competitive party system, leaders in emerging democracies may actually be more belligerent than dictatorships.[14]

One of the most troubling questions raised by Mansfield and Snyder's research has to do with the future of Iraq. Will Iraq be torn by an intractable civil war? Will it return to a dictatorship just as horrific as Saddam Hussein's? Mansfield and Snyder suggest that, even if Iraq continues on its path toward democracy, it will be just as likely to go to war against its neighbors as it was when it had a fascist dictatorship. The Iraqi case raises important questions about the "democratic peace" idea, even if the historical record generally supports it.

---

forced them into war.'"[15] Wars are not the consequence of human nature, or even of the nature of political systems, but of the way in which the anarchy of international relations creates insecurity.

As alternative approaches to understanding the causes of war, all three images can be coherent and persuasive. Biologists and psychologists may convince us that human nature is innately aggressive, but we see that some states prevent such alleged tendencies from leading to war. Switzerland, for example, has managed to avoid direct involvement in armed conflicts for centuries. And although the anarchical nature of the international system may create widespread insecurity, nations are sometimes able to conduct themselves in ways that avoid turning insecurity into armed conflict.

Along with most mainstream experts in the field, Waltz places the greatest importance on the third image, but the complexity of the origins of war makes it likely that all three approaches will continue to find able advocates.

The Balance of Power

At its core, the concept of the **balance of power** says that the *relative* power levels among competing states is the main determinant of stability in international relations and that "the behavior of individual states is explained in terms of the state of the whole system."[16] Where power is balanced, some wars will be prevented; imbalanced power invites aggression by the superior power or prompts the formation of alliances among weaker states to restore balance.

Most analysts agree that the balance-of-power concept applied most convincingly to the European "multipolar system" as it existed between 1648 and 1945. One of the clearest statements about the balance-of-power idea was made by Winston Churchill, who stated that "for four hundred years the foreign policy of England has been to oppose the strongest, most aggressive, most dominating power on the Continent." At least until World War II, the shifting balance of power in Europe prevented any one nation from dominating the world.[17]

As Waltz explains, nations that do not preserve their own security "will fail to prosper [and] will lay themselves open to danger, [and thus] . . . fear of such unwanted consequences stimulates states to behave in ways that tend toward the creation of balances of power."[18] If one state begins to threaten another state (as Germany threatened the Soviet Union and Great Britain in the 1930s), the threatened state will normally attempt to augment its power, perhaps by forming alliances (as did those two nations during that period). The aggressor's threatening posture will prompt others to make similar alliances.

The balance-of-power concept is a third-image approach because it focuses on what states do in response to the essential character of the international system. It can also be taken as a special application of realist principles because it explains war and the avoidance of war without reference to the idealist notions that wars occur because of misguided ideologies and that they can be prevented by nurturing the love of peace. Nevertheless, a major source of confusion regarding the balance of power is that the idea is sometimes presented as an *empirical* statement (states *do* act in ways that preserve or restore a balance of power) and sometimes as a *normative* statement (states *should* act in such ways). In any event, in one form or another, the idea is one of the oldest concepts in political science. Writing in 1742, David Hume argued that "the maxim of preserving the balance of power is founded so much on common sense and obvious reasoning, that it is impossible it could altogether have escaped antiquity. . . ."[19]

A fundamental but common misunderstanding of the balance-of-power concept is the idea that balanced power and efforts to maintain balanced power always *prevent war*. As stated by Edward Vose Gulick in 1955, "The basic aim of the balance of power was to insure the survival of independent states. This . . . should be distinguished from those goals, such as 'peace' and (to a lesser degree) the 'status quo,' which were incidental to it."[20] To maintain their security, states will seek to keep power between states balanced. Sometimes power can be brought back into balance by engaging in war (perhaps to weaken an enemy); on other occasions, balancing power may require that established alliances be dismantled. The ultimate effect of the balance of power is to preserve state survival, not to secure peace.

While still useful, the balance of power is less useful in the modern world than it was a few centuries ago. The concept assumes that leaders are free to respond, quickly and with subtle precision, to a continuously changing power calculus. If an alliance with an evil tyrant or with a former enemy would improve the balance of power, such an alliance will and should be made. But modern states often find that their policy choices are constrained by economic forces, by culture, or by domestic politics. Whereas Germany's Bismarck or France's Napoleon could craft foreign policy decisions with considerable secrecy and latitude, their modern descendants are forced to carry out diplomacy in a more constrained, more public, and more complex environment. The balance-of-power idea cannot produce useful predictions of state behavior when that behavior is subject to the political demands inherent in today's democracies.

The Politics of Nuclear Weapons

Many analysts believe that the development of nuclear weapons has fundamentally changed the nature of international relations. Before the nuclear age, the military force available to major nations was a small fraction of what it is now. The largest bombs dropped in World War II before the atomic bombs that leveled Hiroshima and Nagasaki were capable of destroying no more than a city block. By contrast, a 10-megaton nuclear device, yielding the destructive power of 10 million tons of TNT, is incredibly more devastating. Such a bomb would collapse all but the strongest buildings within a radius of more than 12 miles; it would inflict immediate second-degree burns on anyone within 24 miles of the blast; it would engulf a whole city in a raging firestorm; and, under "ideal" conditions, it would produce severely destructive radioactive fallout over an area of some 100,000 square miles (roughly the size of New York, New Jersey, and Pennsylvania combined).

The availability of this kind of power not only has made war more appalling but it has changed the way nations conduct their foreign policies. In earlier eras, war was an instrument of policy through which one nation dissuaded another from doing something it opposed. Nuclear weapons have reduced the extent to which the threat of war can serve as a policy tool. A state holds nuclear missiles and bombs so that a potential aggressor will be convinced that aggression will be unacceptably costly. For that reason, it is often pointed out that—in a statement attributed to former U.S. Defense Secretary Robert McNamara—nuclear weapons are not weapons at all; they are only deterrents. The certainty of large-scale retaliation undercuts the credibility of most threats to start a nuclear war. Moreover, since the possibility exists that a nuclear power will use its nuclear weapons to retaliate for even a conventional (non-nuclear) attack, these weapons may serve as a deterrent to *any* direct aggression.

The idea of *mutual assured destruction* (MAD) thus suggests that the overwhelming destructiveness of nuclear war prevents armed conflict among nuclear powers, as long as a balance of *nuclear* power is maintained. The logic is simple, as described here in a hypothetical statement from the leader of one nuclear power to another:

> We both know that the outcome of a nuclear exchange is incalculable in advance, because if such an exchange occurs, we shall probably prove incapable of limiting the damage, whether we consider ourselves under those circumstances to be rational or irrational. For

on one side or the other or both there will be "rationalists" who will say that to stop now is to accept defeat. They will be joined by the irrationalists who are primarily driven by the desire for excitement, revenge, or suicide, or something else. Thus we both face the danger of escalation to mutual extinction, simply because we shall exercise all the advantages of war once we are in it.[21]

Both sides thus choose alternatives to war. In Winston Churchill's memorable words, "Peace is the sturdy child of **nuclear terror**."[22] That logic, according to many analysts, accounts for the fact that the major powers of the world have not fought each other in more than half a century. There has never been a longer period of peace among the most powerful nations on earth in all of recorded history. In fact, it may be argued not only that wars have been avoided but also that "reckless" behavior among the superpowers has been reduced. If we count the 1962 Cuban missile crisis as the last time there was a superpower conflict that brought the world to the brink of nuclear war (see Box 17-3), it has been more than 40 years since anyone came close to pushing the "button."[23]

Box 17-3

THE CUBAN MISSILE CRISIS

In October 1962, the United States and the Soviet Union had a dangerous confrontation over the existence of offensive nuclear weapons in Cuba. When U.S. intelligence discovered the missile-launching facilities under construction, President Kennedy was deeply concerned. If he did nothing, he would leave the country vulnerable, but he did not want to provoke the Soviets into a military response.

After negotiations proved fruitless, Kennedy considered several options. One was an immediate military strike to destroy the weapons. Some advisers were concerned that delay would allow the Soviets to make the weapons operational, at which point no military response would be possible without the risk that they would be launched. A second option was to set up a naval blockade to prevent any additional Soviet ships from reaching Cuba.

Kennedy chose the second option while continuing to pursue negotiations. It was an extremely tense moment, because a naval blockade is an act of war and neither Cuba nor the Soviet Union had attacked the United States. To make the blockade less provocative, Kennedy called it a "quarantine," and he instructed the navy not to try to board any Soviet ship approaching the blockade (as is normal procedure in a blockade). The Soviets backed down, promised to remove the missiles, and the crisis passed. Some believe that they withdrew the missiles because the U.S. nuclear arsenal was so much larger than theirs at that time, making the Soviets unwilling to risk a nuclear exchange. Another possibility is that the proximity of Cuba to the United States made it possible for the United States to assemble a much stronger conventional armed force than the Soviets could assemble in a short period of time, making it likely that they would lose a conventional battle in Cuba.

We now know that the United States and the Soviet Union were far closer to nuclear war in 1962 than had previously been realized. In 1992, a conference was held in Cuba regarding the missile crisis. Top Soviet, U.S., and Cuban officials involved in that historic event spoke with amazing frankness about their thinking and strategies at the time. The most dramatic revelation was that, unknown to President Kennedy and U.S. defense and foreign policy officials, not only did Soviet troops in Cuba have tactical nuclear weapons at that time, *but also the military commander in the field had authorization to use them without having to obtain approval from Moscow!* Moreover, Castro had urged the local Soviet military commander to use his nuclear weapons if the United States launched an attack on Cuba (a definite possibility). When Robert McNamara—secretary of defense at the time of the missile crisis and a participant in the 1992 conference—learned all this, he was visibly shaken, noting that the world had come far closer to nuclear war than he had realized.

The idea that nuclear weapons reduce the usefulness of war and the threat of war as tools of foreign policy rests on basic calculations of costs and benefits. According to Robert Jervis, fighting is rational if a country expects to be better off after the fighting than before *or* if it would be better off by fighting than by granting the concessions needed to avoid war.[24] He notes that engaging in war was rational in that sense for some countries in World War II: "Although Britain and France did not improve their positions by fighting, they were better off than they would have been had the Nazis succeeded. Thus it made sense for them to fight even though, as they feared at the outset, they would not profit from the conflict."[25] But no country would improve its position by fighting in a nuclear war.

However, the assumption that nuclear weapons will continue to make war less likely has at least two major problems. First, it assumes that the nuclear weapons of the world are controlled by a small number of major powers, each having a sufficiently developed society so that large-scale retaliation would be costly. Although 189 countries have signed the Non-Proliferation Treaty, committing them to refrain from producing or transferring nuclear weapons, most observers now know or suspect that several unstable or potentially aggressive nations possess nuclear weapons. North Korea announced in October 2002 that it had a weapons program, and it withdrew from the Non-Proliferation Treaty in 2003. Iraq had a substantial program in the past, and Iran is almost certainly working on one now. Some other states, including Israel, India, and Pakistan, never signed the treaty and have demonstrated tests of nuclear weapons. Moreover, the possibility that a "stray" nuclear device could come into the hands of a fanatic sect or group essentially outside the control of any responsible leader is obviously destabilizing. In those kinds of situations, a nuclear war could break out, despite the influence of mutual assured destruction on the behavior of the major powers.

Second, some analysts fully reject the idea that nuclear weapons have ever been an influence for peace. John Mueller argues that the absence of a major war since 1945 is the result of several factors that have nothing to do with nuclear weapons. The **superpowers** that emerged from World War II—the United States and the Soviet Union—were relatively content with their clear dominance in world affairs, in great contrast to the unsettled situation persisting after World War I. The Soviet Union's ideology, moreover, stressed revolution rather than armed conquest. Finally, World War II demonstrated that armed conflict can escalate far beyond initial expectations, making leaders arguably more cautious about starting wars. In short, the major players in international relations may have simply become either satisfied with their situations or ideologically driven to alternatives to war, while sharing a realization that war is too costly. Mueller argues that those factors, *not the distinctiveness of nuclear weapons*, prevented war.[26]

Waltz also contends that the effect of nuclear weapons on international politics is often overstated. For example, some analysts expected that nuclear weapons would essentially equalize state power (since any one of many nations could conceivably start a war that would bring doomsday). According to Waltz, nuclear weapons did not accomplish that:

> Gunpowder did not blur the distinction between the great powers and the others, however, nor have nuclear weapons done so. Nuclear weapons are not the great equalizers they were sometimes thought to be. The world was bipolar in the late 1940s, when the

United States had few atomic bombs and the Soviet Union had none. Nuclear weapons did not cause the condition of bipolarity; other states by acquiring them cannot change the condition.[27]

Contemporary international relations seem to confirm Waltz's idea regarding the primacy of economic power. Although many factors are certainly important, the far superior economic base of the United States relative to that of the former Soviet Union was one reason for the latter state's inability to "keep up" in the arms race. The demise of the Soviet Union adds support for the view that the economic bases of a nation's power, if fundamentally weak, cannot be offset by the possession of nuclear weapons. Conversely, even without nuclear weapons, Japan and Germany have emerged as two of the most powerful players in the post-Cold-War era.

FOREIGN POLICY DECISION MAKING

In recent decades, the *process* of making foreign policy has become an increasingly important area of inquiry. Politics and government in the modern era make the decision-making process itself more complex and less predictable than in earlier times. Analysts once spoke of "France" taking some step or of "Washington" or "Tokyo" preferring some alternative. Such statements implied that a single actor decided foreign policy or, at least, that a highly unified governing elite framed and implemented policies to further a single vision of the national interest. Drawing on insights derived from studies of organizations, psychology, and even economics, contemporary international relations analysts now stress that foreign policy decision making involves a wide range of often conflicting interests and actors, making it more difficult to predict and more important to understand.

Rationality and Foreign Policy Making

When we want to understand why someone made a particular choice, we generally begin by assuming that the decision maker was *rational.* We assume his or her actions were driven by an effort to achieve the objective furthered by those actions. In foreign policy, the rationality assumption means that, for example, when a nation increases or decreases defense spending, abrogates a treaty, or invades a neighbor, we consider what purpose may have been behind the actions taken. We then infer what the nation was trying to accomplish.

This assumption of rationality is often valid and useful. Many foreign policy actions do reflect a clear policy goal. But much of the work on foreign policy decision making has been devoted to discovering the ways in which foreign policy decisions are *not* "rational." For several reasons, actual foreign policy decisions may be shaped by something other than a straightforward effort to attain a clearly defined goal.

First, foreign policy decisions may be constrained or influenced by the force of *organizational routines* in the institutions involved in a nation's foreign policy system. Whereas rationality assumes that a single decision maker is free to shape his or her choices purely on the basis of a clear policy objective, the actual decision-making process requires the cooperation of an array of institutions (for example, the Ministry of Defense, the State Department, congressional committees). Even when those institutions share the same overall goals, their established routines or traditional ways of operating may affect their contributions to the decision-making process, leading to a result that deviates from the ultimate objective.

Graham Allison's study of the 1962 Cuban missile crisis demonstrated how a decision regarding the positioning of U.S. naval forces in a blockade of Cuba reflected, in part, the organizational routines (standard operating procedures, or SOPs) of the navy (see Box 17-3). The force of those routines was a factor that could have influenced policy actions. When the Navy was instructed to carry out President Kennedy's decision, high naval officials wanted to use the Navy's "standard operating procedures" to implement the president's plan. According to the navy's standard procedures, the U.S. ships were supposed to be many miles from Cuba (which would have reduced the amount of time that would elapse before the arriving Soviet ships encountered them), and the U.S. forces would insist on boarding any ships approaching the blockade. If the navy's insistence on its routines had not been overcome, the a naval confrontation would have taken place sooner, and US sailors would have tried to board the Soviet vessels. Seeing these actions, the Soviets would conclude that the *apparent* policy of the United States would have been much more threatening than President Kennedy intended. A Soviet analysis would have concluded that *Kennedy wanted to provoke war.* Although the Navy was forced to depart from its standard procedures in that case, the influence of those procedures was a real factor that had to be overcome.[28]

Second, foreign policy decisions may not amount to a rational plan to achieve a leader's clear objectives because of conflicting political influences that affect those policies. Especially in modern democracies, the actual foreign policies of nations often deviate from the policies that pure rationality would predict, because the process involves interest groups and other participants with conflicting goals. The ideal condition for rational decision making is a single leader acting in isolation, free from demands by interest groups, parties, and campaign contributors. Yet such influences exert significant power over foreign policy choices, particularly in democratic systems.

For example, some argue that the United States sends more military aid to Israel than the rational pursuit of the U.S. national interests requires; the amount of the aid is influenced, in part, by a significant lobbying effort supporting increases in such aid. To the extent that foreign policy decisions reflect an effort to accommodate diverse political demands, the decision will not be a straightforward application of "rationality."

Finally, limits on information and on time for careful deliberation can produce "irrational" decisions. A leader may fail to choose the best option because he or she did not know about it or because there was not time to consider all options. Intelligence failures have influenced policy choices in many cases, including the U.S. failure to take action to prevent the Pearl Harbor attack in 1941. In such instances, it would be inaccurate to assume that policy actions were fully informed, coherent choices in pursuit of clear objectives.

Public Opinion, Mass Media, and the Foreign Policy Process

Chief executives generally have a much freer hand in making foreign policy than in making domestic policy, in part because the public is less informed about foreign policy than about domestic affairs. Popular influences on foreign policy can be significant, however, particularly in democracies.

The idea that the public's "mood" affects decisions is a well-known axiom in the study of foreign policy.[29] The public's "mood" is a rather general matter, taking the form of, for example, greater or lesser support for "an active role" in world affairs. In the U.S., the public mood has changed significantly, strongly supporting an activist foreign policy during the years following World War II and then becoming more isolationist in the 1990s. After the attacks of September 11, 2001, many U.S. citizens became increasingly aggressive in their support of military activities. And, after years of daily reports of U.S. military deaths in sectarian violence in Iraq, the public's "mood" began to turn against the idea of an indefinite presence for U.S. troops there. The prevailing mood affects the range of choices that a leader can consider.

Of course, typical citizens in most countries have little information regarding foreign affairs. A 1994 survey reported in *Time* magazine asked citizens in Germany, Italy, France, Great Britain, Canada, Spain, the United States, and Mexico a series of four questions (what group Israel was trying to achieve peace with, the name of the president of Russia, the name of the Secretary General of the United Nations, and who was fighting at that time in Bosnia). The average U.S. citizen got a score of 38 percent, the average German was right 68 percent of the time, Mexican citizens averaged a score of less than 20 percent, and the average across all the nations was less than 45 percent.[30]

Clearly, foreign policy leaders in the United States (and in most other countries) do not follow the public's opinions very closely on many matters. However, leaders in modern democracies cannot ignore public sentiments, and with the influence of the contemporary mass media, public attitudes are becoming increasingly important. Before the 1950s, newspapers and radio had minimal impact, since they primarily reported information received from official military sources. Today, modern technology has enabled journalists to get information quickly and independently and to communicate with citizens almost instantly. (Camera crews were actually on the beaches in Somalia *before* the marines landed in the U.S. relief action in late 1992!) Television coverage of civilian casualties is a powerful force, and some leaders actually choose tactics that will lead to particularly disturbing pictures to influence public opinion.

Some critics contend that, beyond the impact of violent images, the U.S. press was actively biased in its coverage of the Vietnam War, undermining public support for U.S. military involvement. In a famous broadcast in early 1968, Walter Cronkite (then the CBS News television anchor) indicated that, despite heavy losses, no real progress was being made in the war effort. His announcement reportedly had a great impact on President Lyndon Johnson, who halted some bombing operations shortly thereafter.[31] Cronkite made his pessimistic statement during the Tet Offensive, a large-scale Viet Cong military effort in January 1968 (named after the Vietnamese lunar New Year). According to most historians, the Tet Offensive was a significant military setback for the Viet Cong and North Vietnamese; they suffered heavy casualties and took no new territory. Nevertheless, U.S. media coverage created the widespread perception that the enemy was about to overrun U.S. and South Vietnamese forces.[32] Although historians disagree about the ultimate significance of media coverage in influencing policy choices, the influence of newspaper and television on U.S. public opinion during the Vietnam War was certainly a factor considered in the decision-making process.

The media can also be a useful *tool* of foreign policy, in addition to being an influence on it. According to K. J. Holsti, most Poles learned about the Solidarity Movement in the 1980s from British radio broadcasts and from broadcasts on Radio Free Europe and the Voice of America, two pro-U.S. radio networks. North Korea broadcasts "commentaries" intended for an audience in South Korea; the content of those broadcasts depicts South Korea as a fascist state propped up by U.S. imperialists.[33] Radio is a cheap and generally effective way of reaching a target domestic population, even in areas where illiteracy limits the effectiveness of print media.

In short, leaders usually are forced to take public views into account as they make foreign policy decisions, and the mass media are playing an increasingly important role in developing a supportive or an opposing public. Whether that is a positive development remains an open question. On the one hand, an independent, inquisitive press and an informed public may act as a restraining force, preventing leaders from taking their countries into disastrous military involvements. Perhaps the greatest impact of the heightened importance of the media and public opinion in foreign policy (especially in democracies) is that it makes leaders emphasize quick, low-casualty military options when military responses are necessary. If costly military steps are necessary to maintain national security, and if the pressure of the media and public opinion inhibits appropriate action, the country may suffer. On the other hand, political leaders may be actually tempted to take certain military steps in order to produce the "rally 'round the flag" support that the inevitable media coverage often generates.

If the foreign policy decision-making process could be more insulated from the influences of organizational routines, interest groups, and public opinion, leaders would be free to act "rationally" to achieve their goals. But if the policy in question is particularly important to a specific, organized interest, national leaders will be especially likely to respond to the pressure. The issue of time is also critical. When a policy problem can be handled quickly, public opinion will be less important because there will not be time for it to take form. Foreign policy issues that remain in the public's attention for a long period are more likely to be subject to public influence.[34]

Foreign policy decision making is not a simple process of a unified, well-informed leadership choosing the optimum alternatives to achieve a definite objective. If the process was ever that simple, it is certainly more complex now. In the modern world, the foreign policy process involves a wide range of organizational and political influences and requires access to accurate information about a staggering array of factors. Understanding the influences affecting that process, and how the process can be improved or degraded, is thus a central problem in the study of foreign policy.

INTERNATIONAL POLITICAL ECONOMY

The nature of economic relations among states has been an important subject of study for hundreds of years. In fact, until the terrorist attacks of September 11, 2001, economics had surpassed security concerns in foreign policy debates. Modern advances in communications and transportation make multinational corporations a common form of business organization, and their activities significantly affect prices, wages, and even economic security in many nations. The strategic value of petroleum, coupled with the geographic concentration of oil fields in a few areas, creates a volatile situation. The persistent economic underdevelopment of much of the world challenges the industrialized states that rely on them for labor and raw materials. Growing interdependence makes international political economy an increasingly important issue.

As with military affairs, in economic matters states can relate to one another in antagonistic or cooperative ways. The character of those relations depends on many things, including the nature of each country's domestic economy, its ideology and culture, and its other (noneconomic) foreign policy objectives. Although a great range of factors affects international economic relations, specialists have outlined three general approaches designed to explain them.[35]

Liberalism (or Economic Internationalism)

Employing the term *liberal* differently from its usage in common parlance, Robert Gilpin identified **liberalism** (sometimes termed **economic internationalism**) in this context as the international counterpart to free-market economics. Derived from the ideas of Adam Smith (1723–1790), the architect of classical economics, "liberal" political economy suggests that states should naturally become cooperative in economic affairs. The concept of **comparative advantage** is basic to the approach. If one state is able to produce a particular good or service cheaply and efficiently, it is said to have a comparative advantage in that area. The principles of liberal political economy imply that as long as governments do not interfere with economic affairs, nations will ultimately produce goods or services for which they have (for whatever reason) a comparative advantage.

Liberal political economy assumes that most, if not all, states enjoy a comparative advantage with respect to *some* goods or services. If governments do not get in the way, the production of all goods and services worldwide will naturally gravitate to the state or states that can produce them with the highest quality and the lowest costs. A state that tries to produce something for which it has no comparative advantage will quickly find that it cannot produce it at competitive prices, and, because the countries that *do* have comparative advantages with respect to this good or service will capture the world market, the state will eventually devote its resources to producing other things. Thus, goods and services will end up being produced where they can be made most efficiently. However, if a government restricts imports into its country so that a comparatively *inefficient* domestic industry is protected from competition, the good or service will be produced domestically, consuming more of the world's resources to produce them than would be consumed if countries with a comparative advantage produced them.

Liberal political economy thus implies that the *total productivity of the world economy* will increase as goods and services are produced where comparative advantages exist. The world would suffer a net loss in output if, for example, a country that is unable to produce steel very efficiently still allocates significant resources to steel production (motivated perhaps by the prestige of producing steel). The resources of such a country could produce a more valuable output in a different usage.

Since the world economy grows indefinitely as goods and services are produced in accordance with comparative advantage, liberal political economy assumes that economic relations will normally be cooperative. Every state will be better off if all states act in accordance with the principle of comparative advantage.

In regard to policy, liberal political economy advocates free trade (eliminating import restrictions and tariffs). Of course, governments are often under severe domestic pressure to restrict imports. For example, textile and clothing manufacturers in Thailand, Korea, Taiwan, Sri Lanka, and Malaysia have recently developed a comparative advantage over U.S. producers. Although U.S. consumers benefit from the importation of cheaper clothing, U.S. textile workers and many U.S. companies have demanded protective tariffs to restrict Asian imports. As you will recall from our discussion of interest groups in Chapter 6, it is likely that the domestic producers will be more influential politically than domestic consumers, and thus governments often enact import restrictions. In the light of those political realities, liberal political economy remains more a *prescription* for good policy than a *description* of how nations actually behave in economic terms.

Still, as we will see in Chapter 18, the ratification by the U.S. Congress of the North American Free Trade Agreement (NAFTA), and the Central American Free Trade Agreement (CAFTA), in 1993 and 2004, respectively, were major steps toward free trade in the Western Hemisphere. Such treaties are controversial because at least in the short run, they may jeopardize some jobs and lead to the production of goods and services in areas with the lowest costs, which may be a result of lax environmental or safety standards.

Economic Structuralism

Unlike those who advocate the "liberal" approach, some analysts and many Third World leaders argue that international political competition does not take place on a level playing field. Generally speaking, this perspective focuses on the fact that Japan, North America, and Europe have advanced industrial states, whereas most of Africa and Latin America are, on average, less advanced, and that this difference in development makes free trade unavoidably unfair.

In regard to international political economy, **economic structuralism** (closely identified with Marxist-Leninist thinking) sees states' economic relations as simply one component of the capitalist oppression that dominates all political life. Whereas liberalism claims that advancing productivity and cooperation are at least possible, economic structuralism implies that increasing conflict and exploitation will characterize international relations.*

The North–South conflict in international political economy is often interpreted from this perspective. (The term comes from the observation that, generally, the Northern Hemisphere contains countries that are wealthier than those in the Southern Hemisphere.) Those who reject liberalism because of the persistent disparities in North–South development generally oppose free-trade agreements. According to their way of thinking, such agreements make it impossible for the poorer countries to gain a foothold in the international economy, since they will always be undersold by the more advanced nations in anything they produce.

Economic structuralists thus argue for strict state controls on imports and exports, or state ownership of all industry. In accordance with Marxist principles, they contend that public control of commerce will end exploitation of the poor, both at home and abroad, creating a system of fair compensation for workers, environmental protection, and general world prosperity.

---

* See the discussion of *dependency theory* in Chapter 15.

Economic Nationalism (Mercantilism)

Ironically, both liberal (free-market) and Marxist-Leninist ideas about international political economy assume that economic relations are the primary force behind politics. For liberals, economics determines where comparative advantage exists, and economic structuralists claim that economics explains the inevitability of capitalist exploitation. In contrast, **economic nationalism**, sometimes termed **mercantilism**, sees *politics* as the primary force in international economic relations. It emphasizes the importance of state interests in national security, power, and industrial development, and it claims that states naturally pursue economic policies that promote those foreign policy goals.

For example, mercantilists argue that governments have a clear national interest in protecting their domestic industries from foreign competition, and that this interest may outweigh the purely economic advantages associated with free trade. Even if such restrictions mean that consumers have to pay higher prices for less efficiently produced local goods and services, the state may have a legitimate reason to act contrary to the principles of liberal political economy.

Some analysts argue that a policy of free trade for the steel industry may endanger a country's ability to maintain a steel production capacity, something that is essential for national defense. If other countries can make steel more cheaply, domestic plants will eventually shut down, and they cannot be reconstructed quickly. That was one of the arguments used to justify President Bush's decision to sign a bill establishing tariffs of up to 30 percent for imported steel in 2002. These tariffs perfectly illustrated the "economic nationalism" approach. However, advocates of liberal political economy

"Yep, first the gold run out, then the microchip manufacturing went overseas."

HARD TIMES   Economic changes created by free trade often lead to demands for government intervention.

point out that there was a price to be paid for the tariffs, and that price is paid by consumers. It was estimated that, for example, automobiles sold in the United States cost between $100 and $300 more as a result of the new steel import policy than they would have cost without it. Perhaps as a result of these costs, President Bush ended the tariffs in December 2003.

As we discuss in Chapter 18, the growth of international trade during the second half of the last century has had many important consequences. Those favoring economic nationalism argue that one of those consequences is a reduction in the autonomy and power of nation-states. Whether for good or for ill, many analysts agree that the globalization of finance has "undermined the capacity of states to determine their own future."[36] The advancing global economy thus brings political and economic concerns into conflict in several ways, ensuring that this will be a challenge for governments for decades to come.

Each of the three main approaches to international political economy provides persuasive explanations for certain patterns or events in international affairs. The concept of comparative advantage describes an arrangement that produces an efficient allocation of productive resources, but sometimes other objectives naturally dominate a nation's foreign policy. Some analysts find Marxist-Leninist ideas helpful in explaining the economic underdevelopment of much of the Third World. Economic nationalism helps explain the motivation for seemingly inefficient economic policies based on national security needs. As economic relations become increasingly critical in international relations, the connections among domestic politics, foreign policy, and economic productivity will command increasing attention from analysts and policy makers.

INTERNATIONAL LAW AND ORGANIZATION

Although anarchy is the essential characteristic of the international system, the presence of international law and international organization suggests that the anarchy of the international system is not absolute. International law and organization can be seen as attempts to create order and stability in international relations.

International Law

International law   consists primarily of traditionally recognized treaties and rights and duties. Treaties can be *bilateral* (between two countries) or *general* (ratified by a large number of countries). Some treaties are highly specific, such as a treaty in which the United States and Canada cooperate with respect to usage of the Great Lakes; some treaties apply to a broad range of related matters, such as the General Agreement on Tariffs and Trade (GATT). Other "laws" are simply traditions, such as long-accepted ideas regarding self-defense and the size of the area that each country claims as national waters.

Law is an attempt to constrain behavior. For law to be effective, there must be some way to interpret when a given action runs afoul of the law and to enforce the requirements of the law. In those respects, international law is much weaker than domestic law (in well-established political systems). The International Court of Justice (ICJ, or World Court), established as part of the United Nations, has broad jurisdiction to hear disputes about international law, but it has been ignored in many cases, thus reducing its status and influence. For example, in 1979, Iranian students took over the U.S. embassy in Tehran, holding more than a hundred U.S. citizens hostage. The Iranian government essentially supported the students' effort and refused to recognize the jurisdiction of the ICJ to adjudicate the dispute leading to the hostage-taking. In the 1980s, the United States engaged in military activities against Nicaragua (mining harbors and funding an insurgent movement) when the country was governed by the Sandinistas, a Marxist party. When the ICJ concluded that it had jurisdiction to hear a Nicaraguan complaint that the United States had violated international law with those actions, the United States refused to participate in the judicial process. When the court eventually found that the United States was in violation, the court's influence was severely weakened by U.S. disregard for it in this matter.

Box 17-4

THE LAW OF WAR AND THE INTERNATIONAL CRIMINAL COURT

Most citizens consistently comply with established laws in developed democracies. As noted above, however, the realm of international relations is distinguished from domestic politics by the absence of a settled order and the resulting inability to rely on institutional enforcement of law as a method for managing conflict. Nevertheless, international law exists, and most specialists in international relations agree that it has important effects.

Researchers and theorists generally can be classified as "realists," "liberals," or "constructivists" on the issue of how international treaties affect the behavior of states. As discussed earlier in this chapter, realists assume that leaders make foreign policy on the basis of what is good for the national interest (defined in terms of power and security), and thus they will only comply with treaties and international law when they would have acted the same way in the absence of the treaties or laws. Liberals argue that treaties and international law can create some stability and order in the international system and that leaders take their value into account when making decisions. Clearly, leaders occasionally violate treaties, but violations are less frequent when they are enforced by a principle of reciprocity. Finally, "constructivists" contend that treaties and international laws create "shared understandings of proper conduct" and that these understandings actually structure the conduct of foreign affairs.

In a remarkable study of compliance with the laws of war from the Boxer Rebellion (1899–1901) through the Gulf War (1990–1991), political scientist James D. Morrow looked for patterns of compliance and non-compliance among the dozens of nations and wars contained in the data.[37] He found that several factors help to explain when compliance with the laws of war are more likely:

- Compliance is more probable when both sides have a "legal obligation through joint ratification."
- The degree of legal clarity in the law in question increases the probability of compliance, but clarity has no real effect when both sides have ratified it.
- Democracies comply more often and more completely than non-democracies, if they have ratified the treaty or law in question.
- Democracies commit more violations than non-democracies if they have *not* ratified the treaty or law in question.
- Joint ratification (i.e., both countries involved signed the treaty in question) produces higher rates of compliance.
- The issue addressed by the treaty or law in question affects the degree of compliance.
- Chemical and biological weapons treaties have the strongest record of compliance, followed by armistice/cease fire agreements, treaties relating to conduct on the high seas, and those regulating aerial bombardment. Laws relating to the treatment of civilians have the worst record of compliance.

(Continued)

Box 17-4

THE LAW OF WAR AND THE INTERNATIONAL
CRIMINAL COURT   (*Continued*)

The data provide some support for the realist perspective in that *reciprocity* is a key factor in explaining compliance—the fact that leaders take the likely behavior of other states into account when deciding whether or not to comply is an indication that state actors are following their national interests and not the existence of the law itself in making decisions. The data lend some support for the constructivist view by revealing the increased effect that ratification has on democracies. If realism provided a complete explanation, it is arguable that the ratification status of a law would have no significant impact on behavior. Finally, the "liberal view emphasizes how law can reinforce the successful operation of reciprocity."[38]

Morrow's research sheds some light on recent controversies regarding the treatment of detainees captured by U.S. and coalition forces in Afghanistan and Iraq. "Faced with non-state opponents who do not recognize the laws of war and adopt atrocity as their central strategy, the willingness of the Bush administration to stretch and perhaps break the standards of humane treatment to which the U.S. is legally committed is not surprising in light of the results reported here."[39] The absence of reciprocity may affect compliance, even by democracies.

In another article in the same issue of the *American Political Science Review*, political scientist Judith Kelley assembled and analyzed data on the decisions of states regarding a U.S. request that they refuse to surrender Americans to the International Criminal Court.[40] The U.S. government claimed that its soldiers and others would not receive fair treatment from the ICC, and thus asked other states to sign bilateral agreements not to surrender Americans to the Court. Some countries signed these agreements and others did not; Kelley wanted to know the factors that accounted for the differences in behavior.

One of her key conclusions is that "some states refused [to sign] nonsurrender agreements because they valued the ICC highly, defending it on moral and normative grounds. . . . Some states prize adherence to commitment for its own sake."[41] Kelley's findings provide strong support for the idea that international commitments are not irrelevant or that they only serve as "cover" for actions taken for other reasons. A realist would probably argue that a nation's refusal to sign one of these bilateral agreements only means that the decision had no significant national interest implications for that nation. However, the findings make it difficult to reject the idea that a the value nations place on their treaty commitments have no effect on the behavior of states in foreign affairs.

The International Criminal Court was established through a treaty (the "Rome Statute"), which became effective on July 1, 2002.* Over 100 nations have joined in supporting the ICC, although the U.S., Russia, China, Israel, and several other countries have not. In the case of the U.S., refusal to sign the agreement was based on concerns that the ICC would engage in "politically motivated" investigations and prosecutions of military personnel.

Even if international law is often unenforceable, however, it may still serve as a basis for communication. "To present one's claims in legal terms means to signal to one's partner or opponent which [norms] one considers relevant or essential, and to indicate which procedures one intends to follow and would like the other side to follow."[42] Law can also be a source of *prestige*, since nations that can claim to abide by legal requirements enjoy greater legitimacy both in domestic politics and in foreign capitals.[43] In some circumstances, international law can be used as a *tool of policy*, strengthening a position and mobilizing domestic and allied support.

* The Home page of the International Criminal Court contains the Rome Statute and other information, including a complete, updated list of the countries that have ratified the ICC. http://www.icc-cpi.int/about.html.

Still, international law has its liabilities. Once a state uses a provision of international law to legitimize an action, it may experience a loss of flexibility in future policy choices. Although leaders are often "selective" in observing international law, repeatedly using it as a legitimizing tool may make it difficult or costly to disregard international law when the national interest requires it.[44]

If democracy becomes more widespread, international law may become increasingly influential. With the end of the cold war and the growing international dominance of the United States, Western Europe, and Japan, such "outlaw" states as North Korea and Iran may find it increasingly difficult to violate international law. Since superpower conflict is no longer the dominant fact in international affairs, a state that openly violates international law cannot depend on prestigious support from a superpower sponsor, who previously would have advocated the position of its client state and protected it from sanctions. The fact that the most powerful states are less divided by profound ideological conflicts increases the potential that international law will be a significant force.

International Organization

Although the individual nation-state remains the most important kind of actor in international relations, the fastest-growing force in international affairs is the **international organization** (often termed an *intergovernmental organization*, or IGO). These bodies include general-purpose organizations such as the United Nations and, with narrower memberships, the Organization of American States or the Organization of African Unity. Other IGOs are "functional" units with a more specific purpose, such as the Central American Common Market or the Association of South East Asian Nations. Whereas the number of states has more than doubled since 1950 (primarily as a result of colonies gaining independence), the number of IGOs has nearly quadrupled.

As a force in world affairs, international organization is often discussed in regard to its limitations. Many analysts felt that the failure of the League of Nations to prevent World War II demonstrated that nations will not sacrifice much of their sovereignty to an international organization. Similarly, critics note that the United Nations has been allowed to survive only because five major powers have been able to veto any significant proposed action. In other words, the UN's existence has depended on the fact that those nations did not have to sacrifice any real sovereignty in order to join it. Moreover, the United Nations has not prevented numerous "small" wars (in Vietnam and in the Persian Gulf region).

Nevertheless, the United Nations remains an important feature of the international system, and its prominence is likely to increase. Since 1945, nearly one-fourth of the international and civil conflicts that have erupted have been submitted either to the UN or to regional organizations. According to Holsti, those organizations have handled 291 cases during that time, many of which were "high-intensity" conflicts. Until 1985, only one-fourth of the submitted cases were handled successfully, but between 1985 and 1990 the success rate increased to more than one in three.[45]

As with international law, the United Nations provides a context for communication, and its approval and disapproval can provide nonviolent support for foreign policy choices. Moreover, there are signs that in the 1990s the United Nations may approach the ability to "maintain or restore international peace and security," as called for in its charter. Bruce Russett and James Sutterlin point out that the United Nations has traditionally used force often for "peacekeeping": standing between hostile forces, maintaining stability in an unsettled region, and even monitoring elections.[46]

Although it did not prevent the war, the United Nations arguably functioned to enforce "the will of the council on a state that has broken the peace" in the 1991 Gulf War. Russett and Sutterlin point out that "the Gulf action became possible because the permanent members of the Security Council cooperated on a matter of peace and security in the way originally foreseen when the UN was founded."[47] The UN has handled scores of smaller conflicts, and the demise of East–West conflict as the centerpiece of international affairs will probably make the organization even more important in the future.[48] Recently, with varying degrees of success, the United Nations has involved itself in peacekeeping operations in El Salvador, Cambodia, the states of the former Yugoslavia, Somalia, and Afghanistan (see Figure 17.1).

FIGURE 17.1   UNITED NATIONS PEACEKEEPING OPERATIONS SINCE 1948

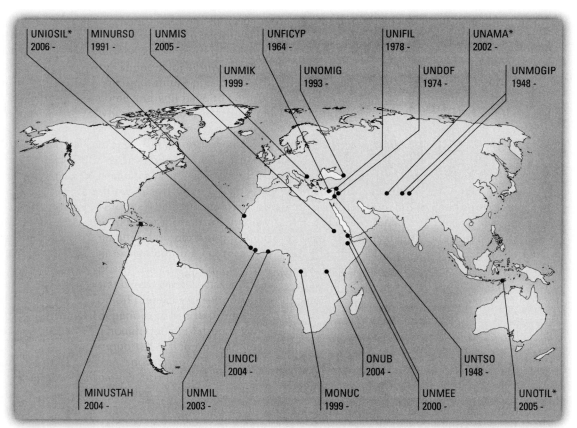

Map No. 4259 (E) R01   UNITED NATIONS
March 2006

FIGURE 17.1   UNITED NATIONS PEACEKEEPING OPERATIONS SINCE 1948   (CONTINUED)

PERSONNEL

Uniformed personnel serving in peacekeeping operations	72,778
Countries contributing military and police personnel	107
International Civilian personnel	10,010
UN Volunteers	1,607
Total number of personnel serving in peacekeeping operations	89,682
Total number of fatalities in peace operations since 1948	2,242

KEY TO ABBREVIATIONS AND PERSONNEL COMMITMENTS:

UNTSO: United Nations Truce Supervision Organization
            Military observers 153; international civilians 164; local civilians 139
            Fatalities: 44

UNMOGIP: United Nations Military Observer Group in India and Pakistan
            Military observers 43; international civilians 38; local civilians 56
            Fatalities: 11

UNFICYP: United Nations Peacekeeping Force in Cyprus
            Troops 859; police 67; international civilians 60; local civilians 117
            Fatalities: 176

UNDOF: United Nations Disengagement Observer Force
            Trrops 1,152; international civilians 48; local civilians 111
            Fatalities: 42

UNIFIL: United Nations Interim Force in Lebanon
            Troops 1,985; international civilians 190; local civilians 319
            Fatalities: 257

MINURSO: United Nations Mission for the Referendum in Western Sahara
            Troops 28; military observers 190; police 8; international civilians 121; local civilians 113
            Fatalities: 14

UNOMIG: United Nations Observer Mission in Georgia
            Military observers 121; police 12, international civilians 107; local civilians 186
            Fatalities: 10

UNMIK: United Nations Interim Administration Mission in Kosovo
            Military observers 38; Police 2,221; international civilians 797; local civilians 2,277
            Fatalities: 43

MONUC: United Nations Organization Mission in the Democratic Republic of the Congo
            Troops 15,044; military observers 712; police 1,087, international civilians 861; local civilians 1,656
            Fatalities: 85

UNMEE: United Nations Mission in Ethiopia and Eritrea
            Troops 3,149; military observers 208; international civilians 179; local civilians 217
            Fatalities: 13

UNMIL: United Nations Mission in Liberia
            Troops 14,867; military observers 203; police 1,028, international civilians 788; local civilians 1,363
            Fatalities: 70

UNOCI: United Nations Operation in Cote d l'voire (Ivory Coast)
            Troops 6,704; military observers 191; police 698; international civilians 362; local civilians 431
            Fatalities: 16

MINUSTAH: United Nations Military Stabilization Mission in Haiti
            Toops 7,472; police 1,761; international civilians 632; local civilians 1,329
            Fatalities: 17

ONUB: United Nations Operation in Burundi
            Troops 4,396; military observers 173; police 87; international civilians 318; local civilians 467
            Fatalities: 21

UNMIS: United Nations Mission in the Sudan
            Troops 10,000; police 715; international civilians (proposed) 1,053; local civilians 1,229
            Fatalities: 2

SOURCE: United Nations Peacekeeping Operations, Background Note, February 28, 2006, http://www.un.org/Depts/dpko/dpko/bnote.htm Comments: Note on UN website says " UN Dept. of Public Information". - BK 12/20/06

The growth in number and significance of other IGOs similarly reflects the more complex interdependence of the modern world. Environmental and economic issues increasingly transcend national borders, making international cooperation essential to the policy process. The heightened impact of domestic politics in democratic and newly democratic systems makes it politically useful for leaders to gain legitimacy for their actions by appealing to international organizations for approval. Even if the "national interest" is still the driving force behind most foreign policy decisions, IGOs will undoubtedly play an ever more significant role in international affairs in the future.

Ethics and International Relations

Most discussions of international affairs deal with explanations of state *behavior*, just as the study of domestic politics normally focuses on explaining the observable behavior of citizens, parties, and institutions. Nevertheless, the ethical dimensions of international relations have long been a subject of inquiry by politicians, philosophers, and others.

The oldest ethical perspective relevant to international affairs is pacifism. Pacifists contend that war is simply and inherently *wrong* and that any alternative (including submitting to domination by a foreign power) is morally superior to fighting. Although there have always been many individuals and religious movements that support pacifist principles, most leaders and citizens reject pacifism as an absolute guide for policy.

A much more widely accepted ethical concept is the idea of the **just war.** Richard Miller explains that the just war tradition shares with the pacifist tradition a conclusion that war is evil and should be avoided; but whereas pacifists claim that war should *always* be avoided, advocates of the just war concept feel that war can be justified under certain special circumstances.[49]

Just war theory has two components, the first pertaining to *when war is justified* and the second addressing *how wars are conducted.* War is justified when necessary to defend against outside threats, when innocent lives would otherwise be lost, when basic human rights are severely deprived, or when the future of the world community is at stake. The idea of the just war requires that war be a last resort, that only competent authorities make war (no "private" wars are just), that no "futile" fighting in defense of a cause be undertaken, and that there be no intentional attacks on civilians.[50]

The ethical issues related to war offer moral philosophers fertile ground for discussion. If the basic concepts of the just war become widely accepted, those ideas may assume some moral force, thus limiting the incidence of war. Just-war principles are obviously subject to varying interpretations, however: What appears to be a just war to one side is naked aggression to the other. However, ethical concerns have widespread impact in other foreign policy issues, notably in matters involving human rights and humanitarian assistance.

Conclusion: War, Trade, Foreign Policy, and the Stakes of International Politics

The same interests and motivations that characterize domestic politics—economics, moral disputes, ethnic and racial divisions, and political power—are also basic to the relations among states. Nevertheless, the virtual absence of central authority in international relations creates a different kind of political system from that which prevails in domestic affairs. The approaches discussed in this chapter represent different and useful ways of interpreting and predicting the behavior of states.

As we noted with respect to domestic politics, international relations is currently undergoing fundamental change. The demise of communism in most of the world, increasing economic interdependence, and contemporary concerns about nuclear proliferation and the global environment are but a few of the issues that will make international relations more complex and more critical. International organizations and law exert more force now than in previous eras in which national sovereignty was unchallenged. Chapter 18 addresses the most important of these issues in an effort to identify and evaluate the central problems in modern international relations.

 WHERE ON THE WEB?

http://www.ceip.org

The home page of the Carnegie Endowment for International Peace. Established in 1910, the endowment conducts research and publishes the journal *Foreign Policy*.

http://www.iiss.org

The home page of the International Institute for Strategic Studies. "The IISS is the primary source of accurate, objective information on international strategic issues for politicians and diplomats, foreign affairs analysts, international business, economists, the military, defense commentators, journalists, academics and the informed public." Members of the institute are drawn from 13 countries in Europe, North America, and Asia.

http://www.justwartheory.com

A Web site created and maintained by Mark Rigstad, an Assistant Professor of Philosophy at Oakland University. It contains a great deal of information about just war theory, including classic texts.

http://www.csis.org

The Center for Strategic and International Studies, a U.S. think tank with over 190 researchers focusing on national and international security, specific problems in particular geographic regions, and "new methods of governance for the global age." Many recent studies are available at no charge at the Web site.

http://www.isanet.org

The home page for the International Studies Association, the leading professional association of researchers specializing in international relations.

◆ ◆ ◆

Key Terms and Concepts ───────

balance of power	international organization
comparative advantage	just war
democratic peace	liberalism

economic nationalism   mercantilism
economic structuralism   nuclear terror
idealism   realism
International Criminal Court self-help
international law   superpowers

Discussion Questions _____

1. How is the existence of violence different in domestic and international relations?
2. Compare the three "images" regarding the causes of war. Which do you find most persuasive in explaining the cause of the War on Terror?
3. What factors can lead a nation to adopt foreign policies that do not amount to a rational effort to pursue a clear objective?
4. What is a "just war"?
5. Explain how wars can be prevented by international law and international organization.

Notes _____

1. Kenneth Waltz, *Theory of International Politics* (New York: McGraw-Hill, 1979), pp. 102–103; italics added.
2. Ibid., p. 104.
3. Thucydides, *The Peloponnesian War*, trans. Crawley (New York: Modern Library, 1951).
4. Sun Tzu (sixth century BCE), *The Art of War*, trans. Samuel B. Griffith (Oxford: Clarendon Press, 1963); and Kautilya, *Arthasastra*, trans. R. Shamasastry (Mysore, India: Mysore Printing and Publishing, 1967).
5. Hans J. Morganthau, *Politics among Nations*, 5th ed. (New York: Knopf, 1973), pp. 4–5.
6. Waltz, *Theory of International Politics*, p. 118.
7. Edward Hallett Carr, *The Twenty Years' Crisis, 1919–1939: An Introduction to the Study of International Relations* (London: Macmillan, 1939).
8. Robert Jervis, "Theories of War in an Era of Leading-Power Peace," *American Political Science Review* 96 (March 2002): 1–14.
9. Kenneth Waltz, *Man, the State, and War* (New York: Columbia University Press, 1959).
10. Ibid., p. 16.
11. Ibid., p. 33.
12. Some of the most important writings on the "democratic peace" are Erich Weede, "Democracy and War Involvement," *Journal of Conflict Resolution* 28 (December 1984): 649–664; T. Clifton Morgan and Sally Howard Campbell, "Domestic Structure, Decisional Constraints, and War," *Journal of Conflict Resolution* 35 (June 1991): 187–211; Alex Mintz and Nehemia Geva, "Why Don't Democracies Fight Each Other?, *Journal of Conflict Resolution* 37 (September 1993): 484–503, Michael E. Brown, Sean E. Lynn-Jones, and Steven E. Miller, *Debating the Democratic Peace* (Cambridge, MA: MIT University Press, 1996), and David Leblang and Steve Chan, "Explaining Wars Fought by Established Democracies: Do Institutional Constraints Matter?" *Political Research Quarterly* 56 (December 2003): 385–400. Also see Paul D. Senese, "Territory, Contiguity, and International Conflict: Assessing a New Joint Explanation," *American Journal of Political Science* 49 (October 2005): 769–779.
13. See Bruce Bueno De Mesquita, James D. Morrow, Randolf M. Siverson, and Alastair Smith, "An Institutional Explanation of the Democratic Peace," *American Political Science Review* 93 (December 1999): 791–807.
14. See Edward D. Mansfield and Jack Snyder, *Electing to Fight: Why Emerging Democracies Go to War*. Cambridge, MA: MIT Press, 2005.
15. Ibid., p. 159.
16. Holsti, K.J., *International Politics*, 7th ed. Englewood Cliffs, NJ: Prentice Hall, 1995, p. 17.
17. John T. Rourke, *International Politics on the World Stage*, 9th ed. (Guilford, CT: Dushkin, 2002), p. 34.
18. Waltz, *Theory of International Politics*, p. 118.
19. David Hume, *Essays and Treatises on Several Subjects*, vol. 1 (Edinburgh, Scotland: Bell and Bradfute, and W. Blackwood, 1825), pp. 331–339, quoted in *Contending Theories of International Relations* by James E. Dougherty and Robert L. Pfaltzgraff Jr. (Philadelphia: Lippincott, 1971), p. 30; Edward D. Mansfield and Jack Snyder, *Electing to Fight: Why Emerging Democracies Go to War* (Cambridge, MA: MIT Press, 2005).
20. Edward Vose Gulick, *Europe's Classical Balance of Power*, (New York: Norton, 1955), p. 30.
21. Dougherty and Pfaltzgraff, *Contending Theories*, p. 265.
22. Quoted in John Mueller, "The Obsolescence of War in the Modern Industrialized World," in *International Politics*, 3rd ed., ed. Robert J. Art and Robert Jervis (New York: HarperCollins, 1992), p. 188.

23. Robert Jervis, "The Utility of Nuclear Deterrence," in Art and Jervis, *International Politics*, p. 202.
24. Ibid., p. 204.
25. Ibid.
26. Mueller, "Obsolescence of War," pp. 188–189.
27. Waltz, *Man, the State, and War*, pp. 180–181.
28. Graham Allison, "Conceptual Models and the Cuban Missile Crisis," *American Political Science Review* 63 (1969): 689–718. Also see Allison and Philip Zelikow, *Essence of Decision: Explaining the Cuban Missile Crisis*, 2nd Edition. (New York: Addison-Wesley, 1999).
29. See Jack E. Holmes, *The Mood/Interest Theory of American Foreign Policy* (Lexington: University Press of Kentucky, 1985).
30. *Time*, March 28, 1994, p. 22.
31. As a *New York Times* reporter noted, "It was the first time in history that a war had been declared over by an anchorman." See David Halberstam, *The Powers That Be* (New York: Knopf, 1979), p. 514; See also Austin Ranney, *Channels of Power: The Impact of Television on American Politics* (New York: Basic Books, 1983).
32. See Peter Braestrup, *Big Story* (New York: Anchor Books, 1978). For a different view, see Daniel Hallin, *The "Uncensored War": The Media and Vietnam* (New York: Oxford University Press, 1986).
33. Holsti, *International Politics* p. 160.
34. Bruce Russett and Harvey Starr, *World Politics: The Menu for Choice*, 3rd ed. (New York: Freeman, 1989), p. 241.
35. Much of the text discussion is drawn from Robert Gilpin, "The Nature of Political Economy," in Art and Jervis, *International Politics*, pp. 237–253.
36. Charles W. Kegley, Jr., and Eugene R. Wittkopf, *World Politics: Trend and Transformation*, (New York: St. Martin's, 1997), p. 257.
37. James D. Morrow. "When Do States Follow the Laws of War?" *American Political Science Review* 101 (August 2007): 559–572.
38. Ibid., p. 568.
39. Ibid., p. 571.
40. Judith Kelley. "Who Keeps International Commitments and Why? The International Criminal Court and Bilateral Surrender Agreements," *American Political Science Review* 101 (August 2007): 573–589.
41. Ibid, p. 573.
42. Stanley Hoffmann, "The Uses and Limits of International Law," in Art and Jervis, *International Politics*, pp. 90–91.
43. Holsti, *International Politics*, p. 301.
44. Ibid., p. 92.
45. Ibid., p. 354.
46. Bruce Russett and James Sutterlin, "The U.N. in a New World Order," in Art and Jervis, *International Politics*, pp. 102–103.
47. Ibid., p. 106.
48. Ernst B. Haas, "Collective Conflict Management: Evidence for a New World Order?" in *Collective Security in a Changing World*, ed. Thomas G. Weiss (Boulder, CO: Lynne Rienner Publishers, 1993), pp. 63–120.
49. Richard B. Miller, *Interpretations of Conflict: Ethics, Pacifism, and the Just-War Tradition* (Chicago: University of Chicago Press, 1991), p. 106.
50. Ibid., pp. 13–14.

For Further Reading _____

Art, Robert J., and Robert Jervis, eds. *International Politics: Enduring Concepts and Contemporary Issues.* 8th ed. New York: Longman, 2007.

Axelrod, Alan. *American Treaties and Alliances.* Washington, DC: CQ Press, 2000.

Bardhan, Pranab, Samuel Bowles, and Michael Wallerstein, eds. *Globalization and Egalitarian Redistribution.* Princeton, NJ: Princeton University Press, 2006.

Baylis, John, James Wirtz, Eliot Cohen, and Colin Gray, eds. *Strategy in the Contemporary World.* New York: Oxford University Press, 2002.

Clark, Ian. *The Post-Cold-War Order.* New York: Oxford University Press, 2001.

Christopher, Paul. *The Ethics of War and Peace: An Introduction to Legal and Moral Issues.* 3rd ed. Upper Saddle River, NJ: Prentice Hall, 2004.

D'Amato, Anthony A. *International Law and Political Reality.* Boston: Kluwer Academic Publishers, 1995.

Dolan, Chris J. *In War We Trust: The Bush Doctrine and the Pursuit of Just War.* Burlington, VT: Ashgate, 2005.

Elshtain, Jean Bethke. *Just War Against Terror: The Burden of American Power in a Violent World*. New York, Basic Books, 2003.

Fordham, Benjamin O., and Timothy J. McKeown, "Selection and Influence: Interest Groups and Congressional Voting on Trade Policy." *International Organization* 57 (2003): 519–549.

Friedman, Thomas L. *The World Is Flat: A Brief History of the 21st Century*. New York: Farrar, Straus, and Giroux, 2002.

Goldstein, Lyle J. *Preventive Attack and Weapons of Mass Destruction: A Comparative Historical Analysis*. Palo Alto, CA: Stanford University Press, 2006.

Gibson, Martha L. *Conflict and Consensus in American Trade Policy*. Washington, DC: Georgetown University Press, 2000.

Hess, Gary R. *Presidential Decisions for War: Korea, Vietnam, and the Persian Gulf*. Baltimore: Johns Hopkins University Press, 2001.

Holsti, K. J. *Taming the Sovereigns: Institutional Change in International Politics*. Cambridge, UK: Cambridge University Press, 2004.

_____ *The State, War, and the State of War*. Cambridge, UK: Cambridge University Press, 1996.

Hoogvelt, Ankie. *Globalization and the Post-Colonial World: The New Political Economy of Development*, Baltimore: Johns Hopkins University Press, 2001.

Keohane, Robert O. *International Institutions and State Power*. Boulder, CO: Westview, 1989.

Miller, Richard B. *Interpretations of Conflict: Ethics, Pacifism, and the Just-War Tradition*. Chicago: University of Chicago Press, 1991.

Morgenthau, Hans J. *Politics among Nations*. 5th ed. New York: Knopf, 1973.

Paul, T.V., James J. Wirtz, and Michael Fortman. *Balance of Power: Theory and Practice in the 21st Century*. Palo Alto, CA: Stanford University Press, 2004.

Rousseau, David L. *Democracy and War: Institutions, Norms, and the Evolution of International Conflict*. Palo Alto, CA.: Stanford University Press, 2005.

Runciman, David. *The Politics of Good Intentions: History, Fear, and Hypocrisy in the New World Order*. Princeton, NJ: Princeton University Press, 2005.

Stern, Sheldon M. *The Week the World Stood Still: Inside the Secret Cuban Missile Crisis*. Palo Alto, CA: Stanford University Press, 2005.

Thomas, Kenneth P. *Competing for Capital: Europe and North America in a Global Era*. Washington, DC: Georgetown University Press, 2000.

Thucydides. *The Peloponnesian War*, translated by Crawley. New York: Modern Library, 1951.

Viotti, Paul R., and Mark V. Kauppi. *International Relations Theory: Realism, Pluralism, Globalism*. 3rd ed. Upper Saddle River, NJ: Prentice Hall, 1999.

Wagner, R. Harrison. *War and the State: A Theory of International Politics*. Ann Arbor, MI.: University of Michigan Press, 2007.

Waltz, Kenneth N. *Man, the State, and War*. New York: Columbia University Press, 1959.

Walzer, Michael. *Arguing about War*. New Haven, CT: Yale University Press, 2004.

18

A CHANGING WORLD ORDER

From the End of the Cold War to the Beginnings of an Uncertain Future ◆ Policing Trouble Spots: A New World Order or a World without Order? ◆ The Changing Nature of the International Arms Race ◆ Current Trends in World Trade: Economic Unification and Beyond ◆ North–South Relations ◆ Protecting the Environment ◆ Human Rights ◆ Women's Rights ◆ International Terrorism ◆ Conclusion: The Changing Face of International Relations

As each new year approaches, many mass media outlets list the major international news events of the preceding year. It seems that every year brings major challenges, unforeseen developments, new threats to regional or world peace, and in some years, reason for hope. But international developments during the past two to three decades have been particularly dramatic, featuring: the fall of Soviet and Eastern European communist regimes; the spread of democracy to those countries and much of the developing world; China's rise as an economic superpower; and the emergence of international terrorism as a major threat to world security. The title of this text, *Politics in a Changing World*, reflects the authors' keen awareness that in an era of mounting environmental concerns, rapid technological breakthroughs, widening political participation, and constantly redefined ideologies, political behavior and beliefs in the twenty-first century are being played out against a background of constant change. Nowhere has that been more apparent than in the realm of international relations—the interaction between nation-states, multinational alliances (economic, military, and political), **non-governmental organizations (NGOs)**, multinational corporations, armed nongovernmental militias, and armies (especially terrorists and cross-national rebels). In many ways, economic development, technological innovation, intensified human migration, and changing lifestyles have increased international interdependence. Problems such as the growing pressures on the world's natural resources (including oil, arable land, and water), illegal immigration, Third World debt, trade competition and its effect on employment, environmental decay, and drug trafficking cannot be resolved exclusively at the national level.

FROM THE END OF THE COLD WAR TO THE BEGINNINGS OF AN UNCERTAIN FUTURE

From the end of World War II (1945) to the late 1980s, the "**Cold War**" was the defining element of the international system: a protracted confrontation pitting the United States and its allies in the **North Atlantic Treaty Organization (NATO)** against the Soviet Union and other nations of the Warsaw Pact (the Eastern European military alliance). Tensions between the two superpowers rose and fell periodically, but for each, the underlying factor shaping its foreign policy was fear of the other one.[1] Throughout the Cold War, each side maintained a negative "mirror image" of its opponent.[2] Even when President Mikhail Gorbachev was about to reform the USSR, a 1985 article in the Soviet journal *International Affairs* insisted that "many facts show that modern militarism and . . . the arms race [are] the product of the . . . system of imperialism, primarily its most developed and most reactionary component—American imperialism."[3]

The United States and the USSR had been allies in World War II. But relations became hostile in the war's aftermath as the Soviet army overran Eastern Europe. The Truman Doctrine (1947) established the U.S. policy of "containment": The United States, President Harry Truman declared, would resist Soviet armed aggression and the spread of communist insurgencies.[4] At the same time, the Russians felt threatened by Western "capitalist imperialism." As most of the former European colonies in Africa, Asia, and the Middle East gained independence in the decades after World War II, both superpowers perceived the problems of the developing world through the lens of East–West conflict. Each side extended foreign aid to developing nations primarily to counter the influence of its rival, rather than to serve the recipients' needs. For example, American aid to Pakistan rose sharply when the U.S. needed to funnel arms to anti-Soviet guerrillas in neighboring Afghanistan, and then subsequently surged again after 9/11 to pursue the War on Terror in both of those countries. In neither period was the boost in U.S. assistance caused by a rise in Pakistan's internal needs.

As recently as 1988, Europe was divided between Western democracies (mostly allied with the U.S.) and the communist, Central and Eastern European bloc of countries tied politically, militarily, and economically to the Soviet Union. Only in the late 1980s was the so-called balance of terror—the "mutually assured destruction" (MAD) awaiting both sides if they went to war—replaced with greater mutual understanding and negotiations for arms reduction.

By the start of the twenty-first century, so much had changed. The fall of communism in Eastern Europe (symbolized so dramatically by the collapse of the Berlin Wall), the subsequent disintegration of Soviet communism and the decline of Russian military might, the growth of the **European Union (EU)** as a major economic and political actor, and the continued spread of democracy into developing nations all seemed to promise a more tranquil and peaceful world. The United States had become the world's dominant economic, military, and diplomatic force, with no other superpower to challenge it. To be sure, Russia retains a formidable arsenal of nuclear weapons, and its renewed nationalism and suspicion of the West have worsened its relationship with the United States. But with its reduced economy and a greatly weakened military, that country is no longer in a position to challenge the West as forcefully as the USSR had.[5]

That is not to say that the world felt trouble free. Far from it! The problems of poverty, financial crises, overpopulation, environmental degradation, ethnic warfare, and political repression, just to name a few, remained enormous concerns. As the expanding economic reach of vast **transnational corporations (TNCs)** created far-flung industrial and financial empires that showed little concern for national boundaries, and as a globalized economy promised (or threatened) to weaken the importance of the nation-state, many observers worried about such a concentration of economic power and saw it as a challenge to national sovereignty. Debt and other monetary crises have not only undermined the economies of nations such as Brazil, Indonesia, Mexico, and Thailand in recent years, but they currently pose a grave to the entire world economy. Still, as the new millennium began, much of the world felt safer than at any point since the start of the nuclear arms race.

All of that changed, of course, with the terrorist attacks of September 11, 2001. Suddenly, the War on Terror became the centerpiece of American foreign policy and a central concern of governments from Europe to the Philippines. Fear of even worse assaults heightened public anxieties—visions of nerve-gas attacks, biological terrorism, or a nuclear attack delivered not by missiles but in a backpack. At the same time, the War on Terror has had important implications for domestic policy as well. As the U.S. and other nations search for the right balance between counter-terrorist surveillance and the protection of civil liberties, many voices have weighed in on different sides of the issue, including politicians, intelligence agencies, journalists, and scholars. The Bush administration often held that the U.S. was effectively in a state of war and that the dangers of another 9/11-type, terrorist attack meant that certain strong counter-terrorism measures were necessary tools in the War on Terror—including warrant-less wiretaps of U.S. citizens, indefinite imprisonment of suspected terrorists without trial, and the use of "enhanced coercive interrogation techniques" (torture) on prisoners suspected of terrorism. Civil libertarians argued that these methods were unconstitutional, and often ineffective. They further maintained that it was wrong (and illegal) to give the government powers that were not needed to fight terrorism and posed a threat to individual freedoms.

While the end of the Cold War removed the dangers of a full-scale nuclear war between the world's superpowers, a new nuclear security concern has taken center stage—the proliferation of nuclear weapons to nations such as Israel, India, and Pakistan, and, possibly, to so-called "rogue states" such as North Korea and Iran.* When the Soviet Union was still a world power it had been a major source of military and economic assistance to those states. Not wishing to be drawn into a war with the West by these sometimes irrational allies, the Soviets restrained them from developing their own nuclear weapons. Now, with the Soviet Union's demise, ironically, that constraint has ended. Moreover, Russia itself is now awash with nuclear weapons that lack adequate security and are managed by underpaid military and civilian personnel, who could be tempted to sell them to rogue states or terrorist organizations. To be sure, the danger of an all-out nuclear war—an event that would dwarf the worst terrorist attack—has all but disappeared, at least for now. Still, great challenges remain, with terrorism being the most newsworthy, but possibly not the most immediately dangerous. If these are to be successfully resolved, it will require a greater degree of international cooperation and purpose than we have seen to date. This chapter examines several critical issues that will hold center stage in the twenty-first century. The topics discussed are obviously not exhaustive, but they do illustrate the opportunities and the problems facing our ever-shrinking world.

POLICING TROUBLE SPOTS: A NEW WORLD ORDER OR A WORLD WITHOUT ORDER?

In the aftermath of the 1991 Gulf War, President George H. W. Bush envisioned a **new world order (NWO)**. The NWO would entail close cooperation among all the world's major powers to deter future aggression and maintain international stability. It "would be founded on the rule of law and on the principle of collective security."[6] In addition to stability, the new world order would include a commitment to defending and spreading democracy and free-market economies throughout the world.

Clearly, international politics has not proceeded as smoothly as the elder Bush had envisioned. Subsequent wars in Yugoslavia, Afghanistan, Lebanon, and Iraq have demonstrated how elusive world peace still is. Indeed, in some respects we may be facing a more unstable world today, since the old East–West "balance of terror" no longer inhibits regional conflicts. For example, analyst John Gaddis argued that had the Cold War still been raging, the USSR would have prevented its ally, Iraq, from invading Kuwait, lest it draw the Soviet Union into a war with the United States.[7] The rise of international terrorism also presents a particular problem. With no defined

---

* The term *rogue state* refers to regimes that violate their citizens' human rights, breach international law, may support terrorism, and have or seek weapons of mass destruction. It has been used primarily in the U.S. and is not widely accepted elsewhere. Former President Bush also used the term "axis of evil."

home territory and an ideology that enshrines martyrdom, terrorist organizations such as al Qaeda cannot be contained by the prospect of nuclear or conventional retaliation.

The collapse of the Soviet bloc unleashed old ethnic hostilities in Bosnia, Macedonia, Armenia, Tajikistan, and elsewhere. Observing those events in the early 1990s, former Secretary of Defense and CIA chief, James Schlesinger, warned, quite prophetically, that "although the world after the Cold War is likely to be a far less dangerous place because of reduced risks of a cataclysmic clash, it is likely to be more unstable rather than less."[8] In fact, some observers point to events since the end of the Cold War—including internal wars in Yugoslavia, Russia, Africa, and Asia, continued Middle East conflict, the September 11 assaults, and the rising menace of terrorist organizations—as evidence of a "new world disorder." While the major Western democracies, among others, are very concerned about containing or removing these threats to peace, they sometimes disagree as to what diplomatic or military actions are appropriate for particular situations. Thus, for example, while Britain joined the U.S. invasion of Iraq, the French and Germans refused to do so because they opposed the U.S. policy.

During the 1990s, some Washington foreign-policy planners favored working with United Nations peacekeeping operations in selected world trouble spots. That was the framework for the 1991 Gulf War intervention that freed Kuwait from an Iraqi invasion.[9] But poorly conceived UN interventions in Somalia and Bosnia raised doubts about how well that body functions as a peacekeeper in difficult situations. Repeated UN condemnations of the massacre of tribesmen in the Sudanese region of Darfur have lacked teeth, as member states are not willing to commit substantial military forces to that region. At the same time, many in the U.S. Congress, particularly conservatives, feel that the United States should stay clear of UN-sponsored peacekeeping missions because the United Nations should never be in a position to dictate or even influence U.S. foreign policy. Initially, foreign policy planners in the George W. Bush administration were divided between those (mostly in the State Department) who wanted the war against Iraq to be part of a broader United Nations operation and those (mostly in the Defense Department) who were more willing to go it alone.

In the coming years, ethnic hostilities will likely precipitate civil or international wars in Africa, Asia, and, perhaps, Eastern Europe. In fact, most of the world's trouble spots in the post-Cold-War era have included some level of ethnic hostility: Somalia, Liberia, Sudan, India (Kashmir), Afghanistan, and Yugoslavia come to mind. In addition, a further upsurge in Islamic Fundamentalism could provoke civil conflict in the Middle East and North Africa. When these conflicts occur with a single nation-state, they raise difficult new challenges for the international community and its most powerful member, the United States. Should the United Nations, NATO, the African Union (AU), or the United States send peacekeeping forces to contain civil wars in countries such as Bosnia, Liberia, or Sudan? The U.S. and other Western powers generally have been reluctant to intervene in ethnic or other internal conflicts, even when hundreds of thousands (Rwanda, Sudan, Indonesia) or even millions (Zaire) of people have been slaughtered. While there may seem to be a moral imperative to intervene, they argue, the international community should not violate a nation's sovereignty by interceding militarily. China and Russia have been even more insistent that neither the United Nations or individual members should violate national sovereignty no matter what. For example, both have used their veto powers in the United Nations Security Council to limit the role of UN peacekeeping troops in Sudan's Darfur region. African leaders, many of whom face ethnic tensions in their own countries, have generally been reluctant to criticize governments that allow or encourage ethnic massacres.

In Washington, "realist" critics of intervention insist that these ethnic conflicts rarely pose a threat to U.S. national security. Absent that threat, the United States was unwilling to put American ground troops in harm's way in Bosnia and limited its defense of Kosovo's Albanian population (against the Serbian government) to the use of air power. European nations have been equally reluctant to send their troops into potentially dangerous trouble spots, particularly if the United States does not take the lead. Thus, for example, the United States, France, Belgium, and the United Nations stood by while Rwanda's Hutu population massacre perhaps 500,000–800,000 Tutsis.

To be sure, the United States *has* been willing to involve itself militarily when the President and his advisors believe its national interests are at stake—as in Afghanistan and Iraq. But many of the internal wars and ethnic conflicts in the Third World and Eastern Europe do not particularly affect the national interests of the United States or other major powers. Consequently, neither the U.S. nor NATO nor other powerful actors have been willing to send peacekeeping forces to end horrendous civil wars or other forms of brutality in Rwanda, Liberia, Mozambique, Congo, and the Sudan even though those conflicts have collectively killed millions of people.

Proponents of international peacekeeping missions and other intervention to halt or contain ethnic conflicts argue that many internal ethnic quarrels spill across national borders and may create international conflicts that could threaten American national interests and international stability. For example, when Hutu forces fled Rwanda into Congo, troops from Rwanda and Uganda crossed the border—along with smaller forces from four other African nations—and joined the Congo's own civil war into what has been called "Africa's First World War." As that war dragged on for years (despite multiple peace treaties), more than 5 million Congolese (primarily civilians) died from war, starvation, and disease.[10] Elsewhere, proponents of international intervention maintain that had the Serbian offensive against the Kosovo's secessionist forces (it was then a province of Serbia) continued unchecked, it could have spilled over into Albania, Macedonia, and Greece. A second argument for peacekeeping interventions is that if the United States is to maintain its status as a world leader, it cannot succumb to isolationism and must take some responsibility as the "world's policeman." Proponents of that position note that the U.S. lost status in Western Europe when it initially failed to assume leadership during the Bosnian crisis. Finally, some who favor international intervention into internal ethnic conflicts and massacres raise a moral challenge. When the international community sits back and allows mass starvation in Somalia, tribal genocide in Rwanda and Burundi, or death camps in Bosnia, they argue, it is as morally bankrupt as those who did nothing to help the Jews escape Hitler's genocide.

Despite such moral arguments, however, foreign governments are understandably reluctant to risk the lives of their nations' soldiers to save the lives of civilians in far-off nations. Nor is it realistic to expect external intervention every time there is a human rights crisis. Therefore, the question of where and when to intervene will continue to be a major issue facing the United Nations, NATO, and the United States, among others.

The Changing Nature of the International Arms Race

East–West Disarmament

President Mikhail Gorbachev's political-economic reforms (Glasnost and Perestroika) in the Soviet Union and the USSR's collapse both contributed to a series of agreements between the world's two greatest military powers, reducing their nuclear arsenals and, in turn, the likelihood of nuclear war. In 1988, the two nations signed the Intermediate-Range Nuclear Force (INF) Treaty calling for the destruction of more than 2,500 missiles between them. That treaty constituted "the first formal agreement that actually reduced the number of nuclear weapons in existence rather than just slowing down the rate of increase. . . ."[11]

Three years later, following the demise of the Soviet Union, Russia and the United States signed START I (the Strategic Arms Reduction Treaty) committing each of them to reducing the number of deployed strategic nuclear warheads to 6,000 on a total of 1,600 ICBMs (Intercontinental Ballistic Missiles), bombers, and submarine ballistic missiles. On December 1, 2001, both Russia and the United States announced that they were in compliance with those terms. Soon afterwards, Russian President Boris Yeltsin declared that Russia would no longer target its missiles to hit U.S. cities. START II, signed in 1993 (but not ratified by the U.S. Senate until 1996 nor by the Russian Duma until 2000) mandated further cutbacks of strategic nuclear weapons to 3,000–3,500 for each country and banned multiple-warhead (MIRVed) ICBMs.

Finally, in a rather unexpected move, Presidents George W. Bush and Vladimir Putin announced in May 2002 that their countries would reduce the number of their strategic nuclear warheads to 1,700–2,200 by the close of 2012 (the Strategic Offensive Reductions Treaty, SORT). Critics of that agreement note that the decommissioned warheads were to be placed in storage but not destroyed, and warn that there are no provisions for verifying compliance. Indeed, there are potential flaws in several of these bilateral agreements. One of the limitations is that either county has the right to opt out of these or previous accords. So, for example, in June 2002 the United States withdrew from the 1967 Anti-Ballistic Missile Treaty. That treaty had limited its signatories' ability to build antimissile defense systems, which presumably would reduce the chances that either side would launch an offensive attack. Deteriorating relations between Russia and the U.S. since the early years of the Putin and Bush administrations offer cause for concern. Still, there can be no question that both superpowers have appreciably reduced their nuclear arsenals and the likelihood of massive nuclear war has declined substantially.

The Dangers of Nuclear Proliferation

Ironically, at the very time that prospects for global nuclear war have receded, actual and potential **nuclear proliferation** to the Third World has intensified, as has the possibility of regional nuclear conflicts. In fact, the very collapse of the Soviet Union created another possible source of proliferation. Because Russian professionals, including nuclear scientists and technicians, now draw very low salaries, some may be hired by Third World nations seeking to develop their weapons programs. There is also concern that nuclear weapons or components will be sold abroad by Russian military officers wishing to enrich themselves. While those fears now have receded, other developments have been troublesome. Currently, two Asian rivals—India and Pakistan—have tested nuclear weapons. Israel undoubtedly has them as well. And in 2006 North Korea announced it had tested its first nuclear device.

Several factors make Third World proliferation particularly worrisome. First, two potential nuclear powers—Iran and North Korea (Libya, formerly in that category, has terminated its nuclear program)—are considered rogue states with records of belligerence that do not inspire confidence (see Box 18-1). Others—India, Pakistan, and Israel—with nuclear capabilities are embroiled in bitter regional conflicts with each other or with non-nuclear nations. Finally, even if all new nuclear powers were to try to act responsibly, the chances of war by miscalculation increase greatly as the world's nuclear club grows.

The Nuclear Non-Proliferation Treaty (NPT) came into effect in 1970 and currently has 189 national signatories. The treaty's purpose was to prevent the spread of nuclear weapons beyond the hands of the five countries (the U.S., the Soviet Union, Britain, France, and China) that possessed them at that time. The treaty prohibited countries with nuclear weapons from giving or selling them to non-nuclear countries and from sharing weapons technology with them (though China and France did not become signatories until 1992). One difficulty with the treaty is that it allows countries without nuclear weapons to develop nuclear energy for peaceful purposes even though such uranium enrichment programs can be converted to weapons production. Enforcement depends on inspections by the International Atomic Energy Agency (IAEA), an arm of the United Nations.

So far, the NPT has been fairly effective but not totally so. For one thing, some countries—including India, Israel, and Pakistan—never signed the treaty. India and Pakistan have announced that they have nuclear weapons, and Israel probably has 100 to 300 warheads (though it officially refuses to confirm that it has any). Some nations (such as North Korea) have withdrawn from the NPT, while still others have evaded inspection. South Africa secretly developed some nuclear weapons in the 1980s but dismantled its program and its weapons in 1990 and signed the NPT the following year.[12] Iraq apparently had a nuclear weapons program for a number of years, but seems to have abandoned it in the early 1990s, years in advance of the U.S. invasion. As new countries have developed nuclear weapons, the risk of further proliferation increases. Israel is believed to have assisted the South African program. Pakistan has admitted that the father of its nuclear weapons program, Abdul Qadeer Khan, sold Libya and North Korea technology and equipment for building nuclear weapons (Libya has since abandoned its program and agreed to IAEA inspection).

The post-Cold-War world will be hard-pressed to contain the Third World nuclear arms race and possible regional nuclear wars. As nuclear expertise spreads and as it becomes easier to deliver nuclear weapons in small packages, the possibility that a group such as al Qaeda may acquire nuclear capability, though currently unlikely, remains chilling. This is one of the reasons that the West is so concerned about Iran developing nuclear weapons, given its ties to Islamist terrorist groups (though not al Qaeda).⁎

⁎ Shi'a clergy govern Iran, while al Qaeda is Sunni. As the civil strife in Iraq has demonstrated, those two branches of Islam are usually hostile toward each other.

Box 18-1

NUCLEAR WEAPONS PROLIFERATION AND "ROGUE STATES"

Currently, the two most worrisome examples or potential examples of nuclear proliferation are North Korea and Iran, the former because of its unpredictable and belligerent behavior, the latter because of its association with Islamic extremism and terrorism. The North Korean weapons program dates back to the 1960s or 1970s. Generally reclusive and paranoiac, its communist regime felt particularly threatened by American deployment of nuclear weapons in South Korea in 1958 (weapons that were removed by 1991). Despite later signing the Nuclear Non-Proliferation Treaty and an additional pact with the United States promising to dismantle its plutonium program, North Korea continued its clandestine weapons program. In early 2003 it became the first nation to ever withdraw from the Nuclear Non-Proliferation Treaty. Later that year it reactivated a reactor at its main nuclear complex and announced a joint program with Iran to develop long-range ballistic missiles with nuclear warheads. In 2005, the North Koreans claimed to have produced nuclear weapons, one of which they declared they tested in 2006. Equally ominously, they have been testing missiles capable of delivering such weapons.

Six-Party Talks (involving both North and South Korea, the United States, China, Russia, and Japan) designed to dismantle North Korea's program have crawled on since 2003, with the first substantial signs of progress only emerging in the summer of 2008. At that point the North Koreans began to dismantle their Yongbyon nuclear reactor, which has been used to produce plutonium. They also handed over details of their nuclear program, though outside inspectors have yet to verify those documents. As a reward, President Bush removed North Korea from the State Department's list of states sponsoring terrorism. As of this writing, however, the Koreans have yet to agree on details of external inspection. Furthermore, they have not provided information on whether North Korea is trying to produce nuclear weapons in a uranium-enrichment program, whether it has actually produced weapons (and, if so, where they are stored), and whether it had helped Syria develop a nuclear weapons program (subsequently destroyed by Israeli bombers).[13] If North Korea provides that information and allows outside inspectors to verify all the details, the six nations will enter the final stage of the negotiations leading to North Korea handing over all its nuclear material and permanently disabling its nuclear facilities (all of which will be subject to outside inspection). Among the benefits the Koreans would get as the process unfolds are substantial fuel deliveries and other economic aid from the other five negotiating nations.[14] Since North Korea has stalled and withheld information for the past five years of negotiation, there is no certainty that the negotiations will reach a successful ending, though there are some clear benefits for the Koreans if they do.

Iran's nuclear energy program dates to the late 1960s when Shah Mohammad Reza Pahlavi, a close ally of the West, governed it. Hence its (non-weapons) program received assistance during the following decade from the United States and West Germany. Its purpose was to produce energy for internal consumption, allowing Iran to export more of the petroleum it produced. As a signatory to the NPT, Iran allowed inspection by the IAEA. Following the 1979 Islamic Revolution overthrowing the Shah, the program was frozen and during the Iran-Iraq War of 1980–1988 the entire nuclear program was suspended. Iran resumed nuclear energy development in the 1990s, and in 2002 the United States accused it of seeking to develop nuclear weapons at secret plants. However a few months later, the IAEA stated that its inspectors had found no evidence to support the American charge.

Still, in 2004, that Agency's Director General, Mohamed ElBaradei, accused Iran of not fully cooperating with inspectors. As with the North Korean case, the U.S. has taken a harder line on this issue than its allies. For example, a leaked, confidential IAEA report in 2004 again asserted that, contrary to U.S. claims, there was no evidence of an Iranian nuclear weapons program. Britain, France, and Germany have held periodic talks with Iran in which the European nations have offered to give Iran assistance for its nuclear energy program if it would agree to stop uranium enrichment. In response, Iran did voluntarily suspend uranium enrichment in 2004, but resumed activity in late 2005.

Experts agree that Iran is moving toward the capability to produce nuclear weapons, but they disagree about how long that might take and what, if anything,

(Continued)

Box 18-1

NUCLEAR WEAPONS PROLIFERATION AND "ROGUE STATES"   (Continued)

it would take to stop them or persuade them to stop. Recalling the United States' mistaken belief that Saddam Hussein's Iraq had weapons of mass destruction, some analysts suggest that Iran may not even intend to build a bomb. In fact, the November 2007 U.S. National Intelligence Estimate* concluded that Iran had, in fact, halted its nuclear weapons program in 2003, but it was "keeping open the option to develop nuclear weapons."[15] Since 2005, the European Union has been engaged in slow and halting negotiations with Iran with the intention of giving that country assurances and assistance in return for international inspection that could verify its claim that its nuclear program is solely designed for peaceful purposes. Like North Korea's behavior in the Six-Nation Talks, Iran has used repeated stalling techniques. The Bush administration, which had taken a tougher stance toward Iran, somewhat changed course in 2008 and joined the negotiations. Liberal critics of administration policy

argue that the U.S. has been too unbending and not sufficiently committed to negotiations. Conservative critics, such as former UN Ambassador John Bolton, faulted the Bush administration with entering into negotiations that are doomed to failure.

Whatever the uncertainty over where Iran's program now stands and where it is headed, the prospects are worrisome. Not only does that nation have links with Middle Eastern terrorist groups, but it has very hostile relations with Israel. At the same time, the Iranians have announced that they have successfully tested nuclear-capable missiles able to reach Israel (and other potential enemies). In fact, Israel has hinted that if it becomes convinced that Iran is close to developing a nuclear weapon, it could launch a preemptive air attack on Iranian nuclear facilities just as it had done to an Iraqi reactor in 1981 and to a suspected Syrian nuclear facility in 2007. However, the Iranian facilities present a far greater challenge. They have built a very widely dispersed system of centrifuges, many (or most) of them hard to locate. Thus, many military experts feel that it may be impossible for Israel (or the United States) to destroy the program.

* The Intelligence Estimates are published by the United States Intelligence Community and expressed the coordinated evaluations of all 16 U.S. intelligence agencies, including the CIA.

Not only might some rogue state give a terrorist group nuclear technology, but an individual high-level scientist might do it independently, as illustrated by the case of Abdul Qadeer Khan, the former director of Pakistan's program, who passed nuclear secrets to Libya and Iran.

CURRENT TRENDS IN WORLD TRADE: ECONOMIC UNIFICATION AND BEYOND

Globalization (economic, cultural, and political) is a very different type of international concern. Unlike other issues discussed in this chapter, globalization presents both benefits and disadvantages. As a trip to any American shopping mall quickly reveals, the world is becoming more interconnected. Labels on clothing indicate that they were made in an array of developing countries such as Honduras, Guatemala, Turkey, Sri Lanka, and Indonesia. An enormous range of household items—from toys to dishware and home tools—are manufactured in China. Electronic goods such as clock-radios often come from Malaysia and Thailand, while computer keyboards and computers come from Mexico, Brazil, South Korea, and Taiwan. In the

IRAN: A NUCLEAR THREAT?   An Iranian security official, dressed in protective clothing, walks inside that country's Uranium Conversion Facility. Iran's 2005 decision to restart uranium conversion and exclude international inspectors raised Western fears that the country was planning to build nuclear weapons.

shopping malls of Los Angeles, Chicago, Boston, and Miami, many of the good for sale, as well as many of the customers and sales staff, were born in dozens of foreign nations.

Perhaps the most widely discussed and analyzed economic and political phenomenon of the early twenty-first century, **globalization** involves the rapid spread of economic activity, political interactions, migration, culture, and ideas across national borders, often in de facto defiance of national sovereignty. Through the World Wide Web, e-mail, cell phones, films, and the mass media, the quantity of international communications and cross-cultural contacts are growing enormously. For example, "Hollywood" movies are now among the primary exports of the United States. And more than one billion people worldwide have access to CNN news broadcasts.[16] Some view globalization as a positive development, promising economic growth, greater cross-cultural understanding and cooperation, and even the spread of democracy. For others in the United States and Europe, it is a suspect force that frequently causes plant closings, the loss of jobs to countries with cheap labor, and a flood of undocumented immigrants. Finally, many Third World political activists and analysts believe that globalization spreads American imperial dominance, exploits factory workers in the LDCs, and destroys cultural diversity. Thus, Benjamin Barber warns that globalization could force "nations into one homogeneous global theme park, one McWorld, tied together by communications, information, entertainment, and commerce."[17]

Perhaps, nowhere has the growth of international economic links been more impressive and important than in the realm of world trade. As Figure 18.1 indicates, on the eve of World War I (1913) the total value of world trade was a mere $20 billion annually. During the next 50 years, it grew gradually to an annual rate of $154 billion in 1963. At that point, international trade began to spiral rapidly upward, increasing by about 700 percent from 1973 to 1993, and then nearly doubling again in the following eight years (1993–2001). That unprecedented growth was stimulated by a number of factors, including improved transportation technology; the dramatic growth of the world economy from the late 1940s to the 1990s; the creation of multinational economic unions and free-trade agreements such as the North American Free Trade Agreement (NAFTA), the European Union (EU), APEX (Asian-Pacific Economic Cooperation), and MERCOSUR (an agreement of four South American nations); worldwide free-trade agreements and enforcement mechanisms through the General Agreement on Tariffs and Trade (GATT) and its successor, the World Trade Organization (WTO); a sharp drop in the rates of tariffs on imports; and the explosion of exports by **newly industrialized countries (NICs)**, particularly from East Asia.* For example, today about 40 percent of Taiwan's, South Korea's, Singapore's, and Hong Kong's respective GNPs are devoted to exports. The volume of trade varies according

FIGURE 18.1 GROWTH IN THE WORLD TRADE, 1913–2001

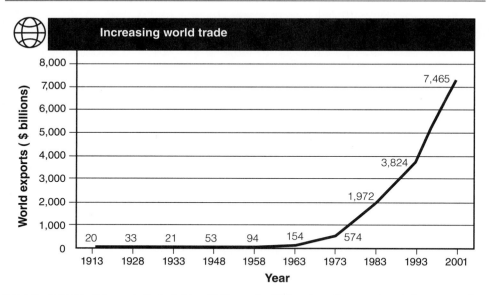

SOURCE: IMF, *World Economic Outlook*, May 2002, on the Web at http://www.imf.org/. As presented in John T. Rourke, *International Politics on the World Stage*, 9th ed. (Guilford, CT: McGraw-Hill—Dushkin, 2003), p. 410.

* The term NICs refers to countries (and the city of Hong Kong) in East Asia (especially South Korea, Taiwan, Singapore, and Hong Kong) and in Latin America (especially Argentina, Brazil, and Mexico) that have recently developed substantial industrial manufacturing and export capacities. More recently, countries such as Thailand and Malaysia have joined that club and China obviously should be included.

to the rate of global economic growth, picking up during high growth periods such as the 1980s to 1990s and slowing during periods of slow growth such as 2004–2008.[18] But, the size of international trade has grown at a far greater pace than the world's economy has. For example, from 1990 to 2005, the volume of world trade grew at twice the rate of the world's GDP.

While experts differ as to exactly when economic globalization took off, many trace its origins to the early years after World War II. In 1947, seeking to rebuild the world economy after the devastations of the war, the United States and 22 other nations signed the GATT, designed to remove barriers to international trade.[19] By mid-2008, the WTO, the successor to the GATT, had 153 member nations (with more than 20 other countries, including Russia, negotiating for admission). Between them, they conduct more than 90 percent of world trade.[20] With the recent addition of China to its membership rolls, the WTO is continuing the process of opening up most of the world's markets to **free trade** (international trade that is relatively unrestrained by quotas, tariffs, or other government-imposed barriers).

The newly emerging economic order has several important features that will influence interstate relations and economic conditions worldwide in the 21st century. First, the international division of industrial production has shifted. During the 1960s and 1970s, the first East Asian NICs—South Korea, Taiwan, Hong Kong, and Singapore—enormously expanded their exports of low-cost, labor-intensive consumer goods, such as garments, footwear, textiles, and inexpensive consumer electronics.

Taking advantage of their low wages, they were able to undersell Western producers. In the 1980s and 1990s, these "East Asian tigers" emerged from underdevelopment and, as their wage scales rose substantially, they shifted to production of more expensive, technology-intensive products, such as computers, computer software, automobiles, and steel, whose prices are less connected to labor costs.[21] In Latin America, more industrially developed countries, particularly Brazil and Mexico, and, to a lesser extent, Argentina, have also increased exports of sophisticated industrial products. At the same time, production of components, lower-end industrial exports, and apparel has moved to in East Asian countries with lower labor costs (including China, Malaysia, and Thailand) and to Latin America's more recent export manufacturers, such as Honduras and Costa Rica.

Overall, a significant share of the world's industrial production and exports (especially labor-intensive manufacturing) has shifted from the developed to the developing world. The NICs can no longer be ignored as trade competitors. Not only have many former textile- and shoe-manufacturing towns in the American South and New England seen their plants and jobs shift to East Asia and Latin America, but steel companies in Germany, France, and the United States have been unable to compete with modern mills in Brazil, Mexico, and South Korea.

Developing nations are now not only major exporters of parts to American industries and of manufactured goods and food to American consumers, but they are also major importers of American products—both trading partners and competitors. In 2000, China replaced Japan as the nation with whom the United States has the largest trade deficit. Table 18.1 indicates how critical the U.S. market is to Third World exporters. At the same time, however, Third World NICs and other developing economies are also major importers of U.S. products. Currently, some 40 percent of U.S. exports are destined for the Third World.

TABLE 18.1   TOTAL EXPORTS (MANUFACTURED AND NON-MANUFACTURED) OF SELECTED
DEVELOPING NATIONS (FIRST HALF OF 2001)

	Total Exports (billions)	Exports to U.S. (billions)	Percentage to U.S.
Mexico	$68.89	58.05	84.3
Brazil	26.31	5.59	21.2
Chile	9.14	1.57	17.2
China	144.63	41.20	28.5
South Korea	75.52	16.68	22.1
Hong Kong	80.87	14.91	18.4
Thailand	33.29	6.86	20.6
Indonesia	30.85	4.64	15.0

SOURCE: *The New York Times*, July 1, 2001.

A second important trend in world trade is the growing importance of services as an exportable commodity, particularly from the United States. As a portion of the world's industrial production has moved to Asia and Latin America in recent years, the service sector (banking, insurance, computer services, social services, education, health care, and the like) has accounted for a growing portion of America's GNP and exports. Currently, over one-third of the value of world trade is in services, with the United States playing a major role.

Finally, a third major development has been the emergence of regional trading blocs and investment zones. We have already referred to the most important of those, the EU and NAFTA. Starting with the European Coal and Steel Community (1952) and the creation of the European Economic Community (1958), Western Europe has moved steadily toward a fully integrated economy. Today, a tourist or a businesswoman traveling to any significant Western European nation except Switzerland, Norway, and Great Britain—or a U.S. firm investing in the region—only needs to work with a single currency, the Euro, which has replaced the French franc, the German deutschmark, and other national currencies. The single currency capped a half-century of steadily growing economic integration resulting in virtually a single economy for most of Western and Southern Europe. New, Eastern European members of the EU—most notably Hungary, the Czech Republic, and Poland—hope to convert their currencies to the Euro relatively soon. The combined Gross National Product of all EU members had already exceeded that of the United States prior to the Union's expansion into Eastern and Central Europe.

Unlike other regional trading blocs, the EU has gone beyond trade and fiscal unification, moving toward growing political unity as well. For example, the European Court of Justice has the authority to overturn decisions made by the national courts of EU member states, thereby limiting national sovereignty somewhat.[22] The popularly elected European Parliament passes legislation in a number of policy areas that is binding on all members. Moreover, pan-European linkages may override national identification as a determinant of parliamentary behavior. For example, rather than organizing themselves into national voting blocs, European MPs organize according to their political orientations: Conservatives, Christian Democrats, Social Democrats, Greens (environmentalist parties), and the like. Very slowly (sometimes haltingly), the EU had been moving toward a loose political union, a process recently slowed by nationalistic backlashes in countries such as France and the Netherlands.

In East Asia, less-formal economic zones have developed based on trade and investment. As China has opened its doors to foreign investment, Hong Kong and Taiwanese businessmen have moved in to forge strong economic ties. Since June 1997, China has administered Hong Kong (a former British colony), producing even closer economic bonds between the two. At the same time, Japan has established important trade and investment links with Thailand, Malaysia, and Indonesia. Those ties, however, are bilateral (between two countries), rather than the multinational arrangements found within the EU.

Finally, in North America, the United States, Mexico, and Canada have created NAFTA, which, at the time it took effect (1994), became the world's largest free-trade zone. Initially subject to bitter opposition in the United States from many labor unions and from independent presidential candidates Ross Perot and Ralph Nader, NAFTA for the most part merely cemented the already growing economic ties among the three nations.[23] Today, the United States is Mexico's largest trading partner, while Canada and Mexico are currently America's first and third largest trading partners (China is second). Subsequently, the Clinton and [George W.] Bush administrations called for the eventual incorporation of the U.S. and most Latin American nations into a proposed Free Trade Area of the Americas (FTAA). There is little prospect of that happening soon (if ever), but in the meantime Latin American countries have been expanding existing free-trade agreements with each other, forging new ones, and opening their doors to investment and trade from both within and outside the region.

These changes mark a dramatic shift away from the economic nationalism that had previously characterized Latin American trade policy. Supporters of free trade argue that it will force the region's formerly protected companies to become more competitive and will allow Latin America to emulate East Asia's rapid, export-based, economic growth. But critics of the new, "outward looking" development model worry that, at least in the short run, the relatively unrestricted entry of American, East Asian, and European goods will drive less competitive local firms and farmers out of business and create substantial unemployment. Both sides of the debate, however, recognize that, one way or another, Latin America must inevitably join North America, Europe, and Asia in an increasingly interdependent world economy.

Issues such as these often pit the interests of many developed nations against those of the less-developed countries. (See North–South Conflicts, below). Thus, in July of 2008, seven years of negotiation between WTO members (the so-called Doha Round) collapsed when the United States and the EU were unable to come to terms with India and other developing nations over trade tariffs and export subsidies on agricultural and manufactured goods.

NORTH–SOUTH RELATIONS

One type of international economic-political relationship that has been particularly sensitive over the years is the one between the world's advanced, industrialized nations (referred to as "the North") and the less developed, Third World countries ("the South"). The demise of Western colonialism (beginning in the late 1940s and largely completed by the 1960s) produced a steadily growing number of sovereign Third World nations. The United Nations General Assembly became a forum in which developing nations expressed their views and aired their grievances. Many of them, subscribing to theories of dependency and Western imperialism (see Chapter 15), blamed the capitalist nations of North America and Europe for their region's economic difficulties. Others held the United States and the Soviet Union equally culpable for spending billions on the arms race while ignoring the needs of the world's poor. Unhappy with international trade patterns and desiring more foreign assistance, they demanded that the major economic and military powers pay more attention to **North–South relations** (particularly to issues pitting developed nations against underdeveloped countries) and less to the East–West conflict (between the West and the Soviet bloc).

Yet ironically, the end of the Soviet–U.S. conflict has had several negative consequences for less-developed countries. Whereas the Soviet Union once provided significant economic and military aid to countries such as Cuba, India, Syria, and Iraq, contemporary Russia, particularly during its economic crisis of the 1990s, has no longer been in a position to provide significant foreign aid to the Third World. At the same time, developing nations have far less leverage over the United States, which, during the Cold War, often gave them foreign assistance to keep them from falling into the Soviet sphere of influence. Similarly, Third World governments (including a number of corrupt and repressive ones) could count on American assistance if they were threatened by a communist insurgency. However, since the end of the Cold War in the early 1990s, foreign aid has represented a dwindling percentage of the U.S. federal budget. In fact, the share of the U.S. federal budget devoted to foreign aid was four times higher in 1965 than in 2003. In recent years, the amount of American development assistance per capita ($58 in 2002–2003) has ranked it only sixteenth among major donors: Norway, which gave over six times as much as the U.S. per capita in 2003 ($381), Netherlands ($203) and France ($96) ranked first through third.[24]

Still, as a consequence of growing economic interdependence, increased trade, and the United States' standing as the world's only military and diplomatic superpower, developing nations have fallen more deeply into the American sphere of influence. In years past, many Third World leaders complained that the Western industrial powers had victimized Africa, Asia, Latin America, and the Middle East, first through colonialism and then through unjust postcolonial economic relations. Consequently, they once argued, the West had a moral obligation to aid Third World development. But, following the demise of the Soviet bloc and the failure of their alternative development strategies, most LDCs had no alternative other than seeking closer economic ties to the U.S. and other First World industrial powers. They now look to foreign aid and, particularly, improved trade relations with the North to help them escape poverty.

Trade and Investment

Although most developing nations now see increased North–South trade as both inevitable and desirable, the *terms* of that trade remain controversial. As we saw in Chapter 15, Third World analysts have maintained that, over time, international "terms of trade" have deteriorated for developing countries that depended on the export of commodities.

In other words, they argued that, in the long run, the prices of the commodities that they export—including bauxite, copper, cotton, coffee, fruits and sugar—have increased more slowly than have the prices of their manufactured imports such as tractors, autos, or refrigerators. Consequently, over the years, they contended, countries such as Costa Rica and Guatemala have needed to export more and more bananas and coffee to pay for the same number of imported televisions and trucks. Years ago, economists at the United Nations Economic Commission for Latin America (ECLA) produced extensive statistics on Latin American trade that supported that assertion. More recent economic data, however, show no consistent pattern in the comparative prices of Third World commodity exports and their manufactured imports. Commodity prices, it seems, can rise or fall sharply in a rather short period of time. Therefore, Third World commodity exporters are at a disadvantage in some years and benefit in others. Of course, petroleum exporters such as Saudi Arabia, Mexico, Venezuela, and Nigeria have reaped huge comparative price advantages in recent years. But even oil has oscillated greatly since the first price spikes of the early 1970s, and economies that have relied excessively on oil income (such as Mexico, Ecuador, and Nigeria) have stagnated. Most recently, the world price of crude oil per barrel, controlled for inflation, soared from $30 in September 2003 to $147 in July 2008. But between July and October of that year the price plunged to below $65.

This suggests a different kind of obstacle to economic development. Commodity prices tend to fluctuate wildly over time, making it difficult for LDCs to anticipate their future export revenues. How, for example, can countries such as Ghana make long-term development investments absent some idea of their anticipated income from cacao (plants producing chocolate), one of its major exports, over the next ten to twenty years? In an attempt to remedy that problem, from the 1970s into the 1990s many commodity exporters tried to create international cartels of banana-, coffee-, or cacao-growing nations, which, when the price of a crop or mineral export dropped too low, could limit the supply and thereby restore prices to an acceptable level.

Industrialized nations have viewed commodity cartels as an unreasonable restraint on free trade. Ultimately, with the obvious exception of OPEC (the Organization of Petroleum Exporting Countries), most cartels have been short-lived and have failed to protect their members from declines in world prices. Their effectiveness depends on the cartel members' willingness to limit their exports of, say bananas, when the price drops too low (in an effort to drive up the price). But that is precisely the time when banana-producing nations are most desperate for export revenues and therefore are most tempted to break ranks and export more bananas.

In recent decades, the principles of free trade have become widely accepted internationally. Indeed, when the World Bank, IMF, or the United States extends economic assistance to developing nations, they often insist that the recipient remove its barriers to trade. Moreover, as increasing numbers of Asian and Latin American countries have diversified their exports, adding manufactured goods to their traditional exports of crops and minerals, they too have often benefited from free trade. Whereas Brazil may have once favored a coffee cartel to control that crop's volatile price, today it is more concerned with reducing trade barriers to its exports of airplanes, weapons, and shoes. In fact, aircraft have recently replaced coffee as Brazil's leading export.

Yet, while the world's industrialized nations have pressed developing nations to accept free trade, they have violated its principles. The U.S., EU, and Japan provide their own agricultural producers some $300 billion annually in subsidies. That gives, say, American, French, or Japanese farmers an unfair competitive advantage over Third World farmers. In 2003, the G20 alliance of "Southern" nations (later expanded to 22), led by Brazil, China, and India, challenged the industrialized nations in WTO negotiations over a new treaty, demanding that the North end its agricultural subsidies. The following year, in the so-called Doha (Qatar) round of negotiations (named after the city where the talks started), a general agreement was reached calling for the North to reduce its agricultural subsidies and the South to lower tariff barriers to manufactured goods. But participants were unable to reach final agreement on a new WTO treaty and the Doha round ended in failure in 2008.

Foreign investment has also generated North–South friction. Lacking sufficient investment capital and technological expertise, developing nations have long solicited foreign investment. But often they did so warily. For one thing, some transnational corporations (TNCs) have meddled in the domestic politics of their host countries, bribing local officials or even trying to topple unfriendly governments. For example, International Telephone and Telegraph encouraged the CIA to destabilize Salvador Allende's democratically elected, leftist government in Chile. Even when TNCs act responsibly, many LDCs were uncomfortable having their leading exports controlled by foreign corporations, as the United Fruit Company did in Guatemala and in other banana-exporting countries. More recently, however, as free-market ideals have triumphed in the international community, attitudes toward foreign investment have changed. Countries that were once wary now yearn for more investment. For example, China, once the most forceful voice against "capitalist imperialism," is now the Third World's largest recipient of foreign direct investment. Fernando Henrique Cardoso, once the most articulate, academic exponent of dependency theory (and its suspicion of foreign investment), later vigorously courted transnational corporations' investments during his two terms as Brazil's president. His successor, leftist president Luiz Inácio Lula da Silva, has established good relations with both the U.S. government and Wall Street.

The Debt Crisis

A final issue dividing North and South concerns the Third World's foreign debt. Starting in the 1970s, many developing nations, particularly in Latin America, incurred substantial external debts in order to invest in economic development projects, compensate for international trade deficits, or cover budget deficits. Western and Japanese commercial banks extended credit to LDCs whom they felt were reasonable risks. When OPEC raised petroleum prices sharply in the 1970s, American, Japanese, and European banks accumulated billions of "petrodollars" (money deposited by oil-exporting nations), much of which they, in turn, lent to countries such as Argentina, Brazil, Mexico, South Korea, Indonesia, and Nigeria.

By the early 1980s, the developing world (excluding the Middle East's petroleum-exporting nations) had accumulated a total foreign debt exceeding $700 billion.[25] By the end of the twentieth century, Third World debt had climbed to $2.06 trillion ($2,060 billion) and then to $3.35 trillion in 2007.[26] Some of those loans were invested wisely in roads, schools, or factories, helping to stimulate economic growth. But some went to less productive uses: covering short-term budget deficits, making payments for imported consumer goods, or purchasing armaments. Too often, a substantial amount of money was wasted because of corruption and poorly designed economic policies. Latin American nations, by far the largest Third World debtors, borrowed most of their money at variable interest rates, as did many countries in Africa (Asian debtors generally locked into fixed rates). As interest rates shot up at the end of the late 1970s, those countries were often unable to keep up with their payments. Thus, by the end of that decade many LDCs were burdened with debts that were taking up large, and growing, portions of their export earnings and their Gross Domestic Product (GDP).

In 1982 when Mexico—the developing world's second-largest debtor—announced that it was unable to pay the interest on its external obligations, the international banking system faced a serious crisis. Loans to Latin America constituted up to two-thirds of the net corporate assets of some international banks. Unwilling to expose themselves any further in the wake of Mexico's partial default, they curtailed additional loans to the developing world. The consequences for Latin American and African economies were disastrous, since they had depended on a steady inflow of new credit to maintain any economic growth. Therefore, both regions suffered a steep economic decline that lasted until the 1990s.

Ultimately, most debtors received additional funding, often then used to roll over their old debts. To secure that additional credit, however, countries such as Argentina, Brazil, Mexico, and Nigeria had to agree to stringent economic austerity programs, often designed by the International Monetary Fund (IMF). These programs required debtor nations to slash government spending, privatize state-owned enterprises, and devalue their currencies in order to reduce their budgetary and trade deficits. While these measures were necessary to restore their financial health (though some analysts feel that these austerity programs could have been designed in a more gradual and humane manner), their immediate effects were devastating. In order to cut huge budget deficits, debtor nations needed to cut back on social services such as health care and education, reduce consumer food subsidies (which sharply increased the price of basic foods), and lay off government employees. Privatization allowed governments to sell major firms (telephone companies, steel mills etc.) whose bloated payrolls and inefficiencies kept them permanently in red ink. But when private sector firms purchased them, the new owners slashed payrolls by firing many workers. Finally, currency devaluations improved a country's balance of trade by stimulating its exports and reducing imports. However, since so many consumer items and factory inputs had been imported, this further drove up the cost of living. Throughout Africa and Latin America, economies plummeted and living standards dropped as much as 40 percent.

As their economies staggered under the weight of these measures, many LDCs complained that they would never recover unless they were granted some form of debt relief. Although initially unsympathetic to such requests, the U.S. government ultimately responded modestly. By the mid-1990s, the worst of the **debt crisis** seemed to have passed, except in Africa. After a decade of stagnation, a number of countries have resumed economic growth. Still, despite the considerable debt relief or forgiveness extended in recent years to the LDCs by the World Bank and the world's most developed nations, debt payments remain a tremendous burden. Total debt services (the amount paid annually in interest and principal) accounted for 2.8 percent of GDP in 1980, grew during the debt crisis to 6.9 percent in 1999, before declining to 5.2 percent in 2006 (as a result of stronger economic in the Third World and debt relief). Still, even with that improvement in recent years, this means that for every 20 dollars these economies produce annually, they still pay over one dollar to servicing their debt. In fact, the LDCs' annual debt service far exceeds the amount of foreign assistance they received from the developed world. So in Africa, the most impoverished region of the developing world, debt payments often soak up funds badly needed to improve the economy and to fight malnutrition and diseases such as AIDS. These problems have led to a worldwide movement of concerned citizens seeking to persuade their governments to forgive the debts of the most poverty-stricken nations (see Box 18-2). The 2008 world economic crisis is likely to reduce demand for African exports, though perhaps less so than for other developing areas.

Box 18-2

ROCKING THE DEBT: BONO MAKES AFRICA'S EXTERNAL DEBT A HOT ISSUE

At first glance, few topics seem drier and less hip than Third World debt. Not surprisingly, the issues of foreign exchange rates, balance of trade, commodity prices, and variable interest rates do not normally attract the interest of rock stars. But the huge external debt that so many Third World nations accrued during the 1960s and 1970s took a terrible toll, the effects of which are still being felt, especially in sub-Saharan Africa.

At the close of the twentieth century, Africa was home to 16 of the 17 poorest nations in the world (as measured by per capita income).[27] Although the total size of that continent's debt is actually much smaller than Latin America's, it constitutes a much higher percentage of its foreign export revenues and GDP. Currently, in some African nations, annual debt repayments account for as much as 60 percent of the country's export earnings.[28] That means that LDCs must allocate most of the income that they receive for coffee or copper exports to interest payments rather than to roads, factories, or electric power plants. And because most of the debt is owed by the region's governments (rather than the private sector), debt payments consume a major portion of the national budget, taking away funds that would otherwise be used to fulfill critical needs in education and health care. To take one extreme example, between 1972 and 1986 allocations for education in Zaire (now called Congo), one of Africa's largest countries, fell from 15.2 percent of the national budget to 0.8 percent.[29] And for most of Africa, the debt burden continues to take its toll. In a number of countries, including those ravaged by AIDS, the cost of debt payments dwarfs government expenditures on health care.

In the past decade, a number of grassroots NGOs have tried to put a human face on the suffering that lies beneath the dry statistics on the foreign debt. One such group, Jubilee 2000, has pressured the world's wealthiest nations to forgive the debts of Africa's poorest nations. Although nobody doubts that corrupt and ineffective African governments bear much of the responsibility for their own countries' debt crises, various NGOs argue that it is unfair to make starving villagers and AIDS victims pay the costs.

Africa's debt has become a trendier topic in recent years since the rock star Bono, of the famed Irish group U2, became Jubilee's most prominent spokesman. Like other famous music and film stars who have campaigned for political or social causes—including Sting, Angelina Jolie, and George Clooney—he has given much wider visibility to what might otherwise have been an obscure issue. But unlike many celebrity advocates, Bono is also extremely knowledgeable about the nuances of the African debt issues and has been quite persuasive in his conversations with powerful political leaders who formulate Western debt policy toward the LDCs. Columbia University's Jeffrey Sacks, perhaps the most influential American economist analyzing debt issues, has joined with Bono in a series of visits to the finance ministers of the world's eight largest economic powers, arguing for debt relief. And, indeed, at their 1999 summit in Cologne, Germany, the Group of Seven (G7)—the group of leaders from the world's major economies—promised to cancel up to $100 billion of Africa's $300 billion debt. Although the amount of subsequent assistance fell well short of that total, Cologne still provided helpful relief. It is true that many other actors and factors beyond Bono and Jubilee 2000 influenced that decision, but we should not discount the importance of star power in these changes.

ROCKING THE DEBT   Irish Rock Star Bono has become perhaps the leading spokesperson for a campaign to convince Western governments to cancel the foreign debt of Africa's most impoverished nations. Here he is joined by Irish singer Bob Geldof and Italian singer Jovanotti at a news conference in Italy.

Responding to calls for debt relief, in 1996 the World Bank initiated a program called the Heavily Indebted Poor Countries initiative (HIPC), which enabled a number of very poor nations to reduce their loan payments to the Bank if they agreed to channel those savings into education, health care, and other vital social services. Critics have argued that any financial "bailout,"—be it for African nations or for U.S. financial institutions currently threatened by the crisis in the housing market—creates a "moral hazard," i.e., it may encourage borrowers (or lenders) to make questionable loans in the future, expecting that they will be bailed out if the loan can't be repaid. The Bush administration was initially skeptical of debt cancellation, but came to support the idea of some relief. Interestingly, the United States' overthrow of the Saddam Hussein regime in Iraq played some role. Following its occupation of that country, the United States cancelled its share of Iraqi debt and pressured other nations to do the same, arguing, in part, that the Iraqi people should not have to pay the debt accrued by a corrupt dictator. Debt relief advocates argued that countries such as Congo (formerly Zaire) and Nigeria—also indebted by corrupt dictators—should get the same consideration. While some conservative analysts remain concerned about the "moral hazard," many supporters of debt relief argue that the world's richest nations have not done enough. They note that developed nations give their own farmers $300 billion yearly in subsidies, a contradiction in free trade principles. These subsidies give U.S. and European farmers a tremendous advantage when competing with Third World growers in the international market.[30]

Protecting the Environment

Worldwide concern for the environment has grown steadily since the birth of the ecology movement in the 1960s. In the United States, it has expressed itself through celebrations of Earth Day and other consciousness-raising events; the growth of environmental groups such as Greenpeace and the Sierra Club; and a spate of congressional legislation designed to clean the air, water, and soil. In many Western European nations, environmentalists have become an electoral force. **Green Party** candidates, for example, have won seats in the European (EU) Parliament and in the national parliaments of several member states.

The ecology movement originally focused on domestic remedies such as the American "Clean Air Act." But environmentalists soon realized that many important ecological problems cross national borders and are only amenable to international solutions. For example, pollutants from American power plants create acid rain*, some of which falls on Canada, killing, fish and vegetation. Industrial pollution on the Rhine River flows across the borders of Switzerland, France, Germany, and the Netherlands. The smoke and ash from fires intentionally set to clear jungle in Indonesia pose a health threat to neighboring Malaysia and Singapore. And the deforestation of the Amazon basin reduces the world's oxygen supply. Preserving the ozone layer, slowing global warming, and protecting endangered sea life are but a few of the environmental concerns that can be addressed only through international agreements.

Frequently, however, these issues pit environmental needs against national sovereignty. For example, European and North American environmentalists are extremely concerned about the rapid decimation of the Third World's tropical rain forests. Possible consequences include reduction of the world's oxygen supply, intensification of global warming, destruction of endangered species, and loss of potential medical cures from jungle plants. But nations such as Brazil, Indonesia, and Malaysia view their forests as a valuable source of exportable timber, potential locations for commercial plantations and cattle ranches, and areas for resettling poor, land-hungry peasants.

Because they badly need foreign exchange—particularly when carrying huge external debts—these countries frequently are reluctant to accept environmental regulations that would reduce their export capacities. With some justification, they complain that the industrialized nations now pointing an accusatory finger at the Third World have already depleted their own forests at an earlier stage of development and continue to be the major sources of air and water pollution as well as the depletion of other resources (see Box 18-3). For example, as of 1990, industrialized countries—with only 25 percent of the world's population—consumed 75 percent of its energy and 85 percent of its forest products. They were also responsible for 75 percent of global warming.[31] Since that time, the developed nations' contribution to global warming has fallen to about 57 percent of the world's total, largely because emissions from industrializing Asian countries, most notably China and India, have grown so dramatically.[32] So in many ways industrialized nations cause more ecological damage than developing countries do.

In recent decades, as the world has recognized the magnitude of worldwide ecological damage—particularly global warming—there have been a growing number of

---

* Acid rain describes acid-based pollutants (containing sulfur and nitrogen oxides), mostly from power plants, that may be carried in rain, fog, or snow and then fall to earth elsewhere.

Box 18-3

ECONOMIC DEVELOPMENT AND ECOLOGICAL CONCERNS

Like the industrialized nations, Third World countries face difficult trade-offs between economic needs and ecological considerations. Often, the poor recognize the dangers of industrial waste and other environmental hazards but must accept them to survive. One extreme example of such a calculation occurred in an impoverished village outside Bahia de Salvador, Brazil. Villagers there catch and eat fish containing dangerously high levels of mercury emitted from nearby industrial plants. Well aware that the mercury will eventually kill or paralyze many of them, they continue to fish. "What is better," asked one poor villager, "to die of starvation now or to die from the mercury later?" Like many U.S. politicians, Third World political leaders and bureaucrats often give the immediate needs of economic development precedence over long-term ecological concerns. When one of this text's authors questioned the environmental consequences of a Jamaican development project he was visiting, he received a frosty reply from a government economist: "You Americans raped your environment in order to become a wealthy industrialized nation," he said. "We Jamaicans insist on the right to do the same." Still, environmental movements have begun expanding in many Third World nations. In the long term, environmentally harmful development may actually be counter-productive for the economy. But companies and governments often fail to think in the long term.

international treaties and agreements aimed at preserving the environment. In 1997, during negotiation of the Kyoto Climate Change Protocol (an international agreement aimed at reducing global warming), the United States resisted European pressures for stronger emissions restrictions. Eventually, a treaty emerged requiring signatories to reduce their emissions of carbon dioxide and other greenhouse gases (gases believed to contribute to global warming) back to 1990 levels by the year 2010.

But in 2001, shortly after enough nations had satisfied the Kyoto agreement to put it into effect, the Bush administration surprised and upset its Western European allies by announcing that the United States would not abide by the treaty because it would limit American economic growth, and because some scientists rejected a number of the treaty's assumptions. Some analysts feel that by that point (2001) it already would not have been feasible to meet the Kyoto standards for 2010. They argue that meeting that deadline would have only been possible if President Clinton had secured Senate approval of the treaty when it was signed in 1997 (and it is not certain that the Senate would have approved). By not presenting the treaty to the Senate for three years (possibly trying to secure the necessary votes) and by letting greenhouse emissions continue to climb, the Clinton administration left office with the U.S. no longer able to meet the treaty's demands.[33] Of course, even if the U.S. could not have reached the 2010 target, had it signed the Kyoto Protocol it would still have reduced greenhouse emissions considerably. The United States also has resisted clean-air regulations designed to reduce acid rain, despite strong pressure from Canada. In all of those cases, the United States has placed economic growth ahead of environmental safeguards, even when that decision has antagonized many of our allies. But other countries have resisted particular international environmental pressures as well. Norway and Japan, nations with important fishing industries, have rejected international treaties designed to protect whales.

Political scientists note that problems such as protecting natural resources and cleaning up the environment face two related decision-making problems: how to protect "collective goods" and "the tragedy of the commons." A collective good is a product or service to which members of a particular community (e.g., the world-wide community of nations) has free access, such as ocean fishing waters beyond national boundaries. The tragedy of the commons describes a "situation in which [actors] have an incentive to increase their consumption of a collective good even though their consumption will [eventually] significantly reduce either the quality or the supply of that good."[34] Thus, every country bordering on the ocean has access to international fishing waters (the collective good). For each vessel and each nation's fleet, its immediate interests (making money) lie in catching as many fish as it can. Of course in the long term, if all the boats maximize their catch, they will deplete the supply of valued fish (such as salmon and cod). But absent some enforceable international agreement, no boat or country will reduce its catch while its competitors do not. Similarly, although it is obviously in the collective interest of all nations to protect the world's ozone layer, each nation seeks to maximize economic growth (even at the expense of the collective good) while hoping that the other nations make the necessary sacrifices.

The challenge, then, is to reconcile a country's economic interests and its environmental concerns. On the one hand, as we have seen, many LDCs were hard-pressed to repay their large debts to Western banks. So debtors, like Indonesia, that were home to large jungle or forest regions found it hard to resist payments from lumber or agro-business companies (in this case, mostly Japanese) planning to exploit those resources. On the other hand, international environmental groups such as the World Wildlife Federation, hoping to avert such transactions, have arranged a number of "debt for nature swaps" in which they have purchased external debt notes of countries such as Ecuador and Bolivia at highly discounted prices.* They then have canceled those debts in return for a commitment from the debtor government to protect an agreed-upon area of forest from exploitation. In countries such as Costa Rica, the rain forest and other environmentally threatened resources have been preserved and transformed into an economic resource through "eco-tourism." In most cases, however, international environmental efforts will have to weigh difficult trade-offs. First, as we have seen, each country (including developed ones) will have to weigh environmental protection against pressures for economic growth; second, international regulations will have to balance the sovereignty of independent nations with the need for international cooperation.

HUMAN RIGHTS

Even more than environmental issues, human rights concerns frequently confront fundamental conflicts between the emerging values of the global community and the sovereignty of individual states. Recent world history is replete with massive human rights violations. Not long ago, the world recoiled in horror when the Khmer Rouge government murdered one million Cambodians and when Hutus in Rwanda

---

* Since the banks were pessimistic about recouping anywhere near the full value of their loans, many of them sold their debt notes—for as little as 10 percent of their face value—to purchasers who were willing to assume the risk. Consequently, an environmental protection organization such as the World Wildlife Fund could purchase (and retire) $100 million of the Bolivian debt notes for as little as $10 million.

massacred an estimated 500,000 to 800,000 people, most of them ethnic Tutsis. More typically, governments in Myanmar, Syria, Iran, China, Sudan, and Colombia, among others, at times have imprisoned, tortured, or killed real or falsely suspected political opponents.

International NGOs devoted to protecting human rights, such as Amnesty International and Human Rights Watch, have raised public consciousness about political repression. The media have brought some of these horrors into our living rooms, and celebrities such as Sting and George Clooney have involved themselves in global campaigns for human rights. Although particular governments, international agencies, and NGOs often employ different standards, there is a growing consensus that three fundamental types of human rights violations are unacceptable: the execution, imprisonment, or torture of individuals because of their political beliefs; repression based on race, religion, ethnicity, or gender; and the use of cruel and unusual punishment such as torture or excessive punishment for nonviolent crimes. For example, in China criminals convicted of such nonviolent crimes as tax evasion, embezzlement, pornography, and accepting bribes are sometimes (legally) executed.

Human rights concerns have played a particularly important role in the foreign policies of countries such as Sweden, Norway, Canada, and the Netherlands. As a world superpower with a complex network of alliances, the United States has found it harder to take a consistent position on this issue. On the one hand, as a leader of the "free world," Washington has spoken forcefully against political repression and discrimination. At the same time, however, administrations of both political parties have violated those norms for strategic purposes. During the Cold War, for example, the United States provided aid and support for a number of regimes that flagrantly abused human rights, but were considered needed allies in containing communism. These included the military government of El Salvador (in the 1980s), the Brazilian military dictatorship (1960s to 1980s), the Shah's government in Iran (overthrown by the 1979 Islamic Revolution), and the Saudi Arabian monarchy. Supporters of American policy argued that this double standard was necessitated by the requirements of realpolitik.* Human rights activists countered that it was not only immoral to ally with repressive governments, but that it often proved counterproductive. They point to countries such as Cuba, Iran, and Nicaragua, where American-backed dictators were toppled, only to be replaced by leftist or radical, Islamic regimes that remained resentful over U.S. support for the unpopular governments that they had topple.

The end of the Cold War largely freed the U.S. foreign policy of this dilemma, at least temporarily. Congress and the State Department turned critical of governments such as the Pinochet dictatorship in Chile, which Washington supported during the Cold War. But the War on Terror following the 9/11 attacks once again raised a human rights dilemma. The issue was, "What tactics are necessary or acceptable in order to keep the U.S. and Western Europe safe from terrorist attacks?" Because terrorist networks are secret and have no territorial base, many Bush administration policy makers (particularly those allied with then Vice President Richard Cheney) and intelligence officials felt it was necessary to extract information from captured operatives, regardless of the methods used. As a consequence the U.S. used a program of

---

* Realpolitik means political policies that are based on realism and power, rather than on ideology or idealism. The term is frequently applied to particular foreign policy decisions.

"extreme rendition" in which suspected terrorists or sympathizers from countries such as Egypt, Afghanistan, and Pakistan were secretly sent back to their home countries, so that they could be tortured for information in manner that would not have been permitted in the U.S. Other terrorist suspects were sent to the U.S. military base in Guantanamo Bay, Cuba where, for a period of time, they were subjected to tortures such as "waterboarding." Proponents of these techniques argued that they were justified if they could save innocent civilians from dying at the hands of terrorist bombers. Critics of torture techniques, including Republican presidential candidate, John McCain, argued that torture is illegal and immoral, that it puts American soldiers at risk to suffer similar treatment if they become prisoners of war, that it is not an effective means of securing reliable information, and that it has often unknowingly been used on innocent suspects.

Today torture is widely condemned and virtually no country admits using it (the U.S. claimed for a period of time that waterboarding was not torture). Ethnic massacres (such as in Darfur) and other mass human rights violations are also widely condemned. But, no matter what their moral concerns or outrage, countries have rarely intervened individually or collectively in the internal affairs of even the worst human rights violators. There are several reasons for that reluctance. Sometimes they feel that intervention would have little effect. For example, many experts felt that Western democracies could do little in the short run to reduce Chinese political repression in the wake of the 1989 Tiananmen Square massacre, and argued that foreign pressure would actually be counterproductive. Human rights groups have generally disagreed. In other instances, as we have noted, geopolitical considerations have led world powers to overlook human rights violations by their own allies.

Ultimately, however, the main reason that the international community rarely intervenes to avert or stop human rights' abuses is that such intervention breaches a basic tenet of international law, national sovereignty. The principle of nonintervention is "the most important embodiment of the modern idea that states should be treated as autonomous entities."[35] The primary function of international organizations such as the United Nations and the Organization of American States (OAS) has been to deter international aggression, not domestic repression. Even in the 1990s, when the United Nations determined that human rights violators in Bosnia should be brought to trial before the International Court of Justice in The Hague (the Netherlands), American and European peacekeeping troops were reluctant to arrest well-known Serbian war criminals for fear of upsetting Bosnia's fragile peace.

As the international community's focus on human rights has intensified, some actors have overstepped the traditional limits on intervention imposed by norms of national sovereignty. In 1998, when former Chilean dictator General Augusto Pinochet was in London for medical treatment, the Spanish government asked Britain to extradite him to Spain so that he could be tried for the murder of Spanish citizens residing in Chile. Two factors made this request significant. First, it challenged the international norm of "head-of-state immunity," which holds that a head-of-state (or a former head) cannot be prosecuted for behavior committed while he or she was in office.*

---

* There are some exceptions to that rule. For example, UN conventions state that the head of state (or former head) has no immunity from prosecution for the crime of genocide.

Second, the Spanish court asked for extradition for a crime that had not occurred on Spanish soil and had not been committed by a Spanish citizen. After extended legal proceedings, the British courts ruled that Pinochet could legally be extradited to Spain to face the charge of torture. Ultimately, however, the British government decided (perhaps for diplomatic reasons) not to extradite him because at his advanced age he suffered from diminished capacity and allegedly would not be able to understand the charges against him. He returned to Chile, where he subsequently spent time under house arrest and charges of human rights violations in Chilean courts. No matter the particulars of the case, the British courts' decision that former President Pinochet could be extradited and tried by a non-Chilean court on charges of torture set an important precedent in international law. In other important cases, the former President of Serbia, Slobodan Milosevic, the former Bosnian Serb President, Radovan Karadzic, and former Liberian President, Charles Taylor, all were apprehended and brought before UN war crimes tribunals.[36]

In 1993, Belgium issued a more far-reaching challenge to the principle of sovereignty when it passed a War Crimes Law, giving Belgian courts "universal jurisdiction" over persons suspected of "crimes against humanity." That is, Belgium gave itself the right to try anyone accused of committing war crimes regardless of their nationality or that of their victim, and no matter where the crime was committed. In 2001, a Belgian court convicted four Rwandans (including 2 Catholic nuns and a university professor) of war crimes for their participation in the 1994 massacre of Hutus in their homeland. Several international human rights groups hailed the law and the convictions as positive contributions to international law.

But while various Belgian prosecutors filed charges against an array of alleged war criminals—many of them famous, others little-known—the Rwandan convictions turned out to be the only ones secured under that country's War Crimes Law. The law faced two serious problems—one practical and the other legal. The practical problem was that suspected war criminals could only be brought to trial if they were extradited to Belgium (something no countries were willing to do) or if they set foot in Belgium. The four convicted Rwandans had taken refuge in Belgium and were recognized by Hutus from their town. The second, more important, problem was that the law enabled prosecutors to file charges against a huge array of political leaders, including Israeli Prime Minister Ariel Sharon, Cuba's Fidel Castro, Palestinian leader Yasser Arafat, President George Bush, and British Prime Minister Tony Blair.* These charges were clearly unenforceable and generally considered legally questionable. Ultimately, the Belgian government and courts throughout many of the indictments and many of the law's provisions until it was finally scrapped and replaced with much narrower legislation.

At times, individual nations and international organizations have reacted against human rights violators by means short of direct intervention. For example, the United States, the British Commonwealth, the EU, and much of the Third World invoked trade and cultural-exchange sanctions against South Africa when its minority-controlled (White) government pursued apartheid policies of racial segregation and repression. In the 1980s, the United States suspended military assistance to Uruguay, Chile, and Guatemala because of their human rights violations. Today, most Western countries have suspended aid to Myanmar for the same reason.

---

* Bush, Blair, and a number of American officials were charged with committing war crimes in the Iraq war.

Although many scholars and diplomats laud the growing world concern for human rights, the question of international enforcement remains controversial. For example, many Third World nations fear that human rights issues could be used as a wedge for Western (or UN) intervention in their internal affairs. There is also a problem of consistency. If international sanctions are invoked to protect democratic rights in Myanmar or Sudan, shouldn't they also have been used to protect Catholics in Northern Ireland or Native Americans in South Dakota? The international system has yet to settle on universal standards for answering such questions. But, in spite of these obstacles, a growing number of Western nations and international organizations seem inclined to incorporate human rights concerns in formulating their foreign policies.

WOMEN'S RIGHTS

Both socioeconomic statistics and case studies make it clear that in many parts of the world women have fewer economic opportunities than men, suffer disproportionately from poverty, exercise less political power, and are more often the victims of exploitation. As with other concerns discussed in the chapter, we find that governments, NGOs, and scholars disagree over which of these women's issues are the proper subject of international action. For example, in some countries religious custom may mandate the veiling of women or offer them fewer rights of inheritance than men. Elsewhere, local custom may permit or encourage practices such as arranged marriages, child brides, or educational limitations for girls. Unfair as such practices may seem, they are generally protected by the rules of national sovereignty. There is no international compact, for example, that would force Saudi Arabia to let women vote and drive, or that would end bridal dowries in India. But international concern has grown in recent decades over acts of violence and brutality routinely inflicted on women in some nations.

For years human rights groups focused primarily on assisting "prisoners of conscience," people who had been imprisoned, tortured, or executed because of their political or religious beliefs. In time, rights activists turned their attention to genocide and other abuses perpetrated by some governments against particular ethnic groups or religions. With the rise of the women's rights movement, the world has paid greater attention to systematic violations of women's rights, such as compulsory female circumcision, forced marriages, and enslavement in the international sex trade. In all, these violations and a host of others probably make women the largest group of victims of rights abuses.

International attention on women's rights issues intensified in the 1970s, prompted by the growth of the feminist movement in many Western industrialized nations. Declaring 1975 International Women's Year, the United Nations staged its first conference on the status of women, with 133 member states attending. After that, the UN held three additional World Conferences on Women at five-year intervals, designed to develop strategies for improving women's status worldwide. At the same time, a wide range of NGOs has emerged, dedicated to address issues such as violence against women and female poverty.

Forced labor generates over $30 billion annually, half of that produced in the United States and Europe. Much of that total comes from the sexual exploitation of women (forced prostitution). A substantial portion of the women involved come from Eastern Europe and the developing world. By one recent estimate, two million women and children are sold into the sex trade annually, either within their own country or across national borders. In India alone, perhaps as many as 200,000 girls from neighboring Nepal, many under the age of 14, work as sex slaves.[37] Since 1996, the European Union has promoted greater international cooperation in combating human trafficking. And in 2000, the U.S. Congress passed the Victims of Trafficking and Violence Protection Act, which enhanced a victims' ability to bring suit or testify against international traffickers. It allowed them to stay in the U.S. for a longer period of time and offered them legal assistance. But such efforts have failed to make a serious dent in this trade, as many LDCs have not been responsive to the problem and Western industrialized nations have not always given the issue the priority it deserves.

Other abuses of women grow out of traditional, Third World customs and values. In some countries (mostly, but not exclusively, Muslim) women are sometimes victims of "crimes of honor." **Honor killings** are defined as punitive murders of women whose families feel they have shamed them by acting "immorally." The victims usually are women who have allegedly committed one of the following offenses: adultery, refusing to participate in a marriage arranged by their parents, or acting immodestly. Typically they are murdered by their brother(s), father, or uncle. Even if a woman is merely *accused* of having premarital or extramarital sex they are considered to have brought dishonor on their family. In some instances, they are banished. But in other cases they are murdered. In Pakistani, which appears to have the world's largest number of honor killings, most of them are committed by Pashtun tribal communities, some 40 million people living on both sides of the Pakistani-Afghan border (and who contribute the majority of Taliban troops in both countries). In both countries, civil and religious courts treat these crimes very differently than other homicides. Perpetrators generally receive a much lighter sentence or, more commonly, go unpunished. Indeed, of the thousand or more honor killings committed in Pakistan every year, only about 10 percent ever go to trial. At the same time, hundreds of Indian and Pakistani woman are set on fire and then reported as the victims of accidental kitchen fires.

Many women are murdered by their families for rejecting an arranged marriage or for seeking a divorce. Even more shockingly, husbands, fathers, or brothers sometimes punish, even execute, a woman who has been raped, because she (the victim) has brought dishonor on her family. In other cases, relatives have killed women merely because they are suspected of having an unacceptable relationship with a man. In one documented case in a Pakistani village, two brothers killed a man who had disobeyed their orders not to walk past their house to talk with their sister. Then they murdered the sister. As one human rights worker told Amnesty International, "the distinction between a woman being guilty and a woman being *alleged* to be guilty of illicit sex is irrelevant. What impacts on the man's honor is the public perception, the belief in her infidelity. It is this which blackens honor and for which she is killed . . . It is not the truth that honor . . . is about, but [rather] public perception of honor."[38] According to some estimates there are approximately 7,000 honor killings annually throughout the world. But, honor killings rarely receive media attention at home, much less abroad. They are not an issue easily addressed by international actors. Still, local and international NGOs have often helped victims and focused attention on the most grievous examples. In some cases international pressure has forced some changes, as when Pakistan shifted jurisdiction for honor killings from religious to civil courts. But substantial improvement will only come when traditional values begin to change.

INTERNATIONAL TERRORISM

The use of terrorism as a political tactic is not new. During the nineteenth century, for example, anarchist revolutionaries in Russia, Italy, Spain, and other parts of Europe perpetrated bombings and assassinations designed to destroy organized government and capitalism. But the September 11, 2001 attacks on the World Trade Center and the Pentagon brought death and destruction to the heart of American society on a scale never previously experienced. Suddenly, in spite of its vast military and economic power, the United States seemed vulnerable.

Although 9/11 was the most horrendous attack of its kind, it was not the first terrorist action against the United States or the West undertaken by Islamic fundamentalist groups. Al-Qaeda terrorists or allied groups had previously bombed U.S. military housing in Saudi Arabia (1996), American embassies in Kenya and Tanzania (1998), and the navy ship *USS Cole* off the coast of Aden (2000). Since the September 11 assault on the World Trade Center and the Pentagon, some of the bloodiest terrorist attacks have included: a bombing that killed 202 people (mostly foreign tourists) in a Bali (Indonesia) night club (2002); a series of bombs on several Madrid commuter trains, which killed nearly 200 commuters and wounded over 1,700 people (2004); bombs on three London underground trains and a transit bus, which killed over 50 passengers and wounded some 700 more (2005). More recently, terrorist attacks have killed thousands of Iraqi civilians since the fall of Saddam Hussein and a growing number of Afghans.[39] But Islamic extremists (Islamists) have no monopoly on terrorism. As we have seen, terrorist activity in Europe (as well as Asia and Latin America) predates today's Islamists. And even in recent decades there have been many deadly, non-Islamic terrorist groups, including the Irish Republican Army (IRA) in Northern Ireland and England, Tamil extremists in Sri Lanka, and paramilitary armies in Colombia.

Yet despite its frequency, there is still no broad consensus on what constitutes terrorist activity. Some analysts have questioned why only violence perpetrated by nongovernmental actors is considered terrorism. Why, they ask, are Palestinian suicide bombings and the Bali assault called terrorist acts, whereas Russia's purposeful bombing of Chechen civilians, Israel's retaliations against Palestinian civilians, and the Guatemalan army's massacre of more than 100,000 Indian villagers are not similarly labeled? Another debate pits those who support the causes of alleged terrorists against those who oppose them. As more than one observer has noted, "Your terrorist is my freedom fighter." Many Catholic Irish Americans took that position when they contributed substantial funds to the IRA, whose gunmen were seen as heroes by some and terrorists by others.

The U.S. Department of Defense defines terrorism as: "The calculated use of violence or the threat of violence to inculcate fear; intended to coerce or to intimidate governments or societies in the pursuit of goals that are generally political, religious, or ideological."[40] For our purposes, we will further define a terrorist act as an act of violence carried out by nongovernmental actors against civilians or against soldiers who are not engaged in war*. This does not mean that intentional slaughters of civilians by the military (as in Chechnya, Guatemala, and Darfur) are any less immoral or reprehensible than bombings by terrorists. It is simply that those atrocities fall in a separate category, sometimes labeled "state terrorism." Ironically, economic and cultural globalization in recent decades has unwittingly contributed to the surge in international terrorism. The spread of capitalism, Western values, and Western culture—including democracy, McDonald's, and R-rated Hollywood movies, among many other things—has led many in the Third World, most notably Islamic fundamentalists, to believe that they are being engulfed and spiritually polluted by westernization. Living in societies that have little military power and limited international influence, some of them see terrorism as their only means of defending themselves and preserving their religious and ideological values.

So, precisely at a time when wars between nations have become less common and war between major military powers is almost unimaginable, terror has become perhaps the leading cause of anxiety in international relations. Because terrorist groups such as al-Qaeda operate in the shadows and cannot be targeted as easily as a nation-state, and because their behavior is so hard to predict, terrorist groups evoke intense fear.

Another feature of terrorist organizations is their capacity to create carnage and chaos with very limited resources. The only weapons held by the men who killed some three thousand people on September 11, 2001 were box cutters. And although the Bush administration revived plans for building a "Star Wars" missile defense system, many experts believe that the greatest threat of nuclear attack comes not from missiles but from terrorists that sneak the weapons into their target countries. It is a threat that is not likely to go away for many years to come.

CONCLUSION: THE CHANGING FACE OF INTERNATIONAL RELATIONS

Political trends are hard to predict, perhaps especially in the area of international relations, where so many uncontrolled forces are at play. Few analysts or policy makers anticipated the end of the Cold War only five or six years before it happened. Only a year or two before the September 11 terrorist attacks few could have predicted their magnitude or how they would change the nature of domestic and international politics. Today, as U.S. and allied forces face an uncertain future in Iraq and Afghanistan, as scientists still warn of possible worldwide pandemics killing millions of people, and others debate the dangers of global warming, we do not know what other major developments will unfold in the next five to ten years.

However, some developments seem likely to continue. While there may be little likelihood of a new arms race between world powers, nuclear proliferation will remain an ongoing danger in Iran, North Korea, and elsewhere. Should most of the democratic gains made since the 1970s in the developing world and central Europe consolidate, it would bode well for the prospects of world peace. Until now, at least, democratic nations have never waged war against one another (or virtually never, depending on how each scholar defines democracies).[41]

* Other definitions do not include *any* attack on military men and women as terrorist acts.

Small wars will continue to rage in the Third World. Some conflicts—such as Middle East hostilities and ethnic violence in Africa—seem more intractable than even pessimists had imagined. The Russian conflict with Georgia indicates that some East-West tensions remain and are likely to flare up periodically. But competition among the world's major powers seems likely to be primarily economic, rather than military or ideological. That conflict will pit the United States against Japan, China, and the EU, with rapidly industrialized countries such as India, South Korea, Taiwan, and Brazil likely to play important secondary roles. Third World poverty, protecting the environment, ethnic conflict, and human rights are likely to demand increasing attention. Solving these problems will be extremely difficult and may require new levels of international cooperation.

 WHERE ON THE WEB?

http://www.terrorismanswers.com/havens/afghanistan.html
Council on Foreign Relations: information on terrorist history in Afghanistan.

http://www.academicinfo.net/terrorism.html
Links to a wide variety of scholarly articles, papers, and other online resources on terrorism.

http://www1.worldbank.org/economicpolicy/globalization/
The World Bank presents an optimistic picture of the benefits of globalization.

http://www.ifg.org/
Web site for the International Forum on Globalization, a research institute critical of the negative effects of globalization.

http://www.hri.ca/
Human Rights Internet—A human rights gateway.

http://www.nautilus.org/archives/cap/orgs/ngos.html
Links to NGOs involved in Environmental and Human Rights Issues.

http://www.hrweb.org/
History of the human rights movement and links to leading human rights groups.

http://europa.eu.int/
The European Union (EU) online.

◆ ◆ ◆

Key Terms and Concepts _____

Cold War	new world order (NWO)
debt crisis	nongovernmental organizations (NGOs)
European Union (EU)	North Atlantic Treaty Organization (NATO)
free trade	North–South relations
globalization	nuclear proliferation
Green Party	transnational corporations (TNCs)
honor killings	

Discussion Questions ⸻

1. Since the end of the Cold War, how has the prospect of nuclear war decreased in some respects and how has that prospect increased in other ways?
2. In what ways has protection of the environment become an international issue? Why must solutions to some environmental problems transcend national boundaries?
3. What are the principal arguments in favor of substantial external debt cancellations for the poorest developing nations? What are the major arguments against cancellation?
4. Discuss how international efforts to protect human rights (including prosecution of leaders who violate those rights) may come into conflict with the doctrine of national sovereignty. In what ways has the international community begun to change the balance between human rights principles and principles of national sovereignty?
5. In what ways are Third World women particularly victimized by human rights abuses and, therefore, in need of special protection?
6. What progress, if any, has there been in talks with Iran and North Korea aimed at getting them to halt their apparent nuclear weapons programs? Why are their programs of particular concern?

Notes ⸻

1. For a picture of how each nation saw the world during the Cold War, see Walter S. Jones, *The Logic of International Relations* (New York: Harper Collins, 1991).
2. Urie Bronfenbrenner, "The Mirror Image in Soviet-American Relations," in *Analyzing International Relations*, ed. William Coplin and Charles Kegley, Jr. (New York: Praeger, 1975), pp. 161–166.
3. Y. Katasonov, "Socio-Economic Factors of the Arms Race," *International Affairs* (January 1985): 47.
4. The concept of containment was first developed by diplomat George Kennan, writing under a pseudonym. See "X," "The Sources of Soviet Conduct," *Foreign Affairs* (July 1947): 566–582. Later, Kennan charged that foreign policy makers had misinterpreted his arguments.
5. See *Transition to Democracy in Eastern Europe and Russia: The Impact on Politics, the Economy and Culture*, ed. Barbara Wejnert (Westport, CT: Praeger, 2002).
6. Bruce Russett and James Sutterlin, "The UN in a New World Order," *Foreign Affairs* (Spring 1991): 69.
7. John Lewis Gaddis, "Toward the Post-Cold War World," *Foreign Affairs* (Spring 1991): 111.
8. James Schlesinger, "New Instabilities, New Priorities," *Foreign Policy* (Winter 1991–1992): 4.
9. Gaddis, "Toward the Post-Cold War World."
10. Tom Porteus, "Resolving African Conflicts, in *Crimes of War Project: War in Africa*, http://www.crimesofwar.org/africa-mag/afr_04_collier.html.
11. James Lee Ray, *Global Politics* (Boston: Houghton Mifflin, 1990), p. 375; see also Marshall Shulman, "The Superpowers: Dance of the Dinosaurs," *Foreign Affairs* (Winter 1987–1988).
12. Wikipedia, "Nuclear Non-Proliferation Treaty," retrieved on August 39, 2005, http://en.wikipedia.org/wiki/Nuclear_Non-South Africa is the only country to have produced a nuclear weapon and then destroy it and close its program.
13. Robert Norris and Hans Kristensen, "North Korea's Nuclear Program, 2005," *Bulletin of the Atomic Scientists* (May/June 2005): 64–67; "Accord in North Korean Talks," Washington Post (July 13, 2008).
14. "Rice holds N. Korea nuclear talks," *BBC News* (July 24, 2008), http://news.bbc.co.uk/2/hi/7519159.stm.
15. Quoted in Greg Bruno, "Backgrounder: Iran's Nuclear Program," *Council on Foreign Relations* Web site (July 17, 2008), http://www.cfr.org/bios/13554/greg_bruno.html?groupby=0&hide=1&id=13554&filter=397.
16. John T. Rourke, *International Politics on the World Stage* (New York: McGraw-Hill-Dushkin, 2002), p. 42. Rourke cites a figure of one billion and the numbers have obviously grown since 2002.
17. James Barber, *Jihad vs. McWorld: How Globalism and Tribalism are Reshaping the World* (New York: Ballantine, 1996), p. 4.
18. United Economic and Social Council, "World Economic Growth Has Slowed Considerably Since 2004," (July 2, 2006), http://www.un.org/News/Press/docs/2006/ecosoc6189.doc.htm.
19. Jack Finlayson and Mark Zacher, "The GATT and the Regulation of Trade Barriers: Regime Dynamics and Functions," *International Organization* (Autumn 1981): 561–602.
20. World Trade Organization Web page; available at http://www.wto.org; Uri Dadush and Julia Nielson, "Governing Global Trade," *Finance and Development (IMF)*, 44, no. 4 (December 2007), http://www.imf.org/external/pubs/ft/fandd/2007/12/dadush.htm.
21. Gary Gereffi, "Rethinking Development Theory: Insights from East Asia and Latin America," *Sociological Forum* (Fall 1989).
22. Geoffrey Garrett, R. Daniel Kelemen, and Heiner Schultz, "The European Court of Justice, National Governments, and Legal Integration in the European Union," *International Organization* 52 (1998): 149–176.
23. Robert Pastor, *Integration with Mexico* (New York: Twentieth Century Fund Press, 1993), pp. 14–15, 42–50.

24. Steven Radelet, "Think Again: U.S. Foreign Aid," *Foreign Policy* (February 2005), http://www.foreignpolicy. com/story/cms.php?story_id=2773&page=0.
25. For a summary of the debt crisis and its consequences see Howard Handelman, "Consequences of Economic Austerity: Latin America and the Less Developed World," *Britannica Book of the Year: 1990* (Chicago: Encyclopaedia Britannica, 1990), pp. 192–193.
26. World Bank data; World Bank, *Global Development Finance: Volume 2,* Summary Debt Data, http://www. undp.org/publications/annualreport2008/downloads.shtml.
27. United Nations Development Program, *Human Development Report* 1999 (New York: UNDP and Oxford University Press, 1999), pp. 136–137.
28. Nikoi Kote-Nikoi, *Beyond the New Orthodoxy* (Brookfield, VT: Avebury, 1996), p. 15.
29. Bill Turnbull, "The African Debt Situation"; available at http://www.thewhitefathers.org.uk/302dt.html.
30. "Can Africa Get Out of Debt?," *Time Europe* Web site (October 3, 2004), http://www.time.com/time/ magazine/article/0,9171,708965,00.html. "Debt Forgiveness Gathers Steam," *Christian Science Monitor* (September 30, 2004).
31. Women, Population and the Environment," in *Great Decisions: 1991* (New York: Foreign Policy Associa- tion, 1991), p. 65.
32. International Energy Agency, *World Energy Outlook* 2002. http://www.iea.org/textbase/nppdf/free/2000/ weo2002.pdf.
33. Thomas C. Schelling, "What Makes Greenhouse Sense," in *International Politics,* ed. Robert J. Art and Robert Jervis (New York: Pearson Longman, 2005), p. 542.
34. Alan Lamborn and Joseph Lepgold, *World Politics in the Twentieth Century* (Upper Saddle River, NJ: Prentice Hall, 2003), p. 418.
35. Charles Beitz, *Political Theory and International Relations* (Princeton, NJ: Princeton University Press, 1979), p. 71; quoted in Ray, *Global Politics,* p. 497.
36 Bruce Broomhall, *International Justice and the International Criminal Court Between Sovereignty and the Rule of Law* (New York: Oxford University Press, 2004).
37. "Sex trade's reliance on forced labour," BBC News (May 12, 2005), http://news.bbc.co.uk/2/hi/ business/4532617.stm : Jan Jindy Pettman, "Gender Issues," in *The Globalization of World Politics,* 3rd ed., ed. Jon Baylis and Steve Smith (New York: Oxford University Press, 2005), p. 678; "Sex Slavery: The Growing Trade," CNN archive Web site (March 8, 2001). http://archives.cnn.com/2001/WORLD/ europe/03/08/women.trafficking/index.html.
38. "Pakistan: Cost of a Lie," in *Le Monde Diplomatique,* English version (May 2001), http://mondediplo. com/2001/05/13pakistan.
39. However, more Iraqis currently die from sectarian violence (Shi'a versus Sunni) than from terrorist bombings.
40. Available at http://terrorism.about.com/od/whatisterroris1/ss/DefineTerrorism_4.htm.
41. Jack S. Levy, "Domestic Politics and War," *Journal of Interdisciplinary History* 18, no. 4 (Spring 1988): 653–673. Some scholars challenge these findings.

For Further Reading _____

Art, Robert J., and Robert Jervis, eds. *International Politics: Enduring Concepts and Contemporary Issues.* 9th ed. New York: Longman Pearson, 2009.

Baylis, John, and Steve Smith, eds. *The Globalization of World Politics: An Introduction to International Relations,* 3rd ed. New York: Oxford University Press, 2005.

Hebron, Lui, and John F. Stack, Jr. *Globalization: Debunking the Myths.* Upper Saddle River, NJ: Prentice Hall, 2009.

Kelleher, Ann, and Laura Klein. *Global Perspectives: A Handbook for Understanding Global Issues.* 3rd ed. Upper Saddle River, NJ: Prentice Hall, 2009.

Nacos, Brigitte L. *Terrorism and Counterterrorism: Understanding Threats and Responses in the Post-9/11 World.* New York: Penguin Academics, 2006.

Nye, Joseph S. *The Paradox of American Power: Why the World's Only Superpower Can't Go It Alone.* New York: Oxford University Press, 2002.

_____. *Understanding International Conflicts: An Introduction to Theory and History,* 7th ed. New York: Longman, 2009.

Welch, Claude E., Jr., ed. *NGOs and Human Rights: Promise and Performance.* Philadelphia: Univer- sity of Pennsylvania Press, 2001.

World Bank. *Globalization, Growth, and Poverty: Building an Inclusive World Economy.* New York: Oxford University Press, 2002.

PART VI

EPILOGUE

SEEKING A BETTER LIFE   One of 67 would-be African immigrants takes his turn bailing out water as their boat lands in the Canary Islands (Spain). On that weekend alone (in 2006) a record 1,000 "boat-people" were intercepted trying to make their way from African to the Canary Islands.

19

FUTURE CHALLENGES AND DEVELOPMENTS

◆ Climate Change and Public Policy Responses
◆ Resource Conservation ◆ Serving the Elderly: Health Care and Retirement Pensions ◆ Immigration Policy in Developed Nations ◆ Russia and the West: A New Cold War? ◆ The Asian Century? ◆ Conclusion

As the title of this book indicates, change is, paradoxically, a constant in both American and world politics. Consider the following partial list of dramatic and unexpected political, economic, and social changes in recent years: the Soviet Union and communist regimes throughout Eastern and Central Europe collapsed, bringing an end to the Cold War; China, only recently an impoverished nation, has built one of the largest and most dynamic economies in the world; India, though still a relatively underdeveloped nation, has created nuclear weapons, has sent men into space, and is an increasingly important economic power; South Africa, long a symbol of the most pernicious form of racism, has developed a democratic, multiracial political system led by a predominantly Black political party; radical Islamic terrorism has emerged as the greatest threat to world peace; global warming and other environmental challenges have moved to the forefront of international concerns; and, the 2008 presidential race featured the first major woman presidential candidate and the first African-American president in U.S. history.

Throughout the text, we have examined a number of recent political and economic trends and challenges. In this epilogue we will briefly discuss a number of these, some highlighted in previous chapters and some not, which may serve as guideposts to changes and challenges in the coming years. Although some of the issues discussed here are essentially economic or social, they all have significant political implications and will require political solutions. We offer this list with the full knowledge that others will undoubtedly emerge that we, and perhaps everyone, failed to anticipate.

CLIMATE CHANGE AND PUBLIC POLICY RESPONSES

Many environmentalists (including members of the scientific community) and policy makers are very concerned about apparently ominous changes in the world's climate. In various parts of the world, droughts, hurricanes, and floods are occurring more frequently and more intensely. At the same time, there is now substantial evidence that Earth's temperature is slowly warming. And there is a growing consensus within the scientific community that this global warming poses a major environmental threat that may include: the deterioration of the polar icepack, resulting in rising sea levels; endangerment of plant and animal life such as polar bears; potentially severe declines in world food production; and flooding of island and coastal population centers.

To be sure, there has been debate over the origins, extent, and potential dangers of global warming. For a number of years, some scientists and some governments (most notably the Bush administration in the U.S.) argued that there was still insufficient evidence to determine how much danger global warming represented and how to deal with it. Though there is now general agreement that global warming is a threat (including a warning by the U.S. National Academy of Sciences), there is still disagreement about how rapidly it is taking place and what to do about it.[1] The United States government has supported voluntary targets on carbon emissions (mainly from industry, power plants, and cars), whereas approximately 90 percent of the world's nations (181 in all) have signed the 1997 Kyoto Protocol *mandating* reductions in emissions of

When researchers began work on Adelie penguins on Litchfield Island, Antarctica 30 years ago, there were 1000 breeding pairs on the island. As global warming has reduced nearby sea ice, which supports the krill—the penguins' diet—the population has been reduced to 20 pairs.

greenhouse gases by industrialized nations.* Emerging economic giants such China (which has recently passed the U.S. as the world's largest contributor of greenhouse gases), India, and Mexico agree that it is important to cut greenhouse emissions, but maintain that it is the early industrialized nations (Japan and the West) who should be making the major reductions.†

Many environmentalists and policy makers believe that only strong government environmental regulations (such as setting limits on auto and factory emissions) and significant government investments or tax breaks for non-polluting technologies (such as wind and solar power) can deal adequately with major environmental threats. But others believe that market mechanism can more efficiently and less arbitrarily reduce pollution. Thus, for example, one program with considerable support from industry and from many environmental groups has governments issuing tradable emissions permits to electrical power plants, setting their target for carbon dioxide emissions. The sum total of those permits sets the industry's emission ceiling. However, if a particular company emits less than its target it is allowed to sell (trade) its remaining pollution allowance to other companies that were unable to meet their targets. This would

* A greenhouse gas is any gas (most notably carbon dioxide and methane) that traps heat in the earth's atmosphere. A certain amount of greenhouse gas is necessary to keep the earth from becoming too cold. But currently, massive burning of fossil fuels is producing a very excessive amount of carbon dioxide.

† China points out that, although it now has passed the United States as the world's leading producer of greenhouse gases, its population is about four times as large as the U.S. Hence, its emissions per capita are far lower than the American rate.

not only set an overall ceiling on emissions, but would provide companies with an economic incentive to lower their own emissions.

In dealing with global warming and other important environmental threats, voters in democratic societies and policy makers in all nations will have to decide how much government intervention is helpful and what form that intervention should take.

RESOURCE CONSERVATION

As the price of gasoline climbed well over $4 per gallon in mid-2008, Americans began to change their driving habits. Taking stay-at-home summer vacations or switching to four-day work weeks (at ten hours per day), many people cut down on their driving. Thus in April 2008 the U.S. Department of Transportation calculated that Americans drove 20 billion fewer miles than they had in April of 2007. At the same time, SUV sales were nearly 40 percent below the number sold in the same month a year earlier.[2] In Western Europe, which taxes gasoline very heavily, motorists are probably slightly bemused by the dismay of American drivers, since Europeans have been paying more than $4 per gallon since about 2002. As of July 2008, most Europeans were paying over $9 per gallon, with the price in the Netherlands reaching $10.64.[3]

But while petroleum is surely the most important natural resource commodity—because its price affects the cost of any other product that must be transported—it is only one of many commodities whose price and supply may become important political issues in coming years. There may be escalating demand and supply shortages for other natural commodities found in finite quantities, such as water, arable land, and forests. There are many reasons for the rapidly growing demand for these commodities, including: the enormous economic growth of a few new industrial giants (China, India, and Brazil) and several smaller, newly industrialized nations (including Taiwan, South Korea, Chile, and Thailand); rapid population growth in Africa and the Middle East; and the emergence of a substantial middle class (with higher levels of consumption) in expanding Third World economies.

Conservationists warn that we will need to take strong preemptive measures to head off shortages of critical commodities. For example, the World Energy Council predicts that demand for energy will double by 2050, but production will peak around 2023. Similarly, the Organization for Economic Cooperation and Development (OECD) predicts that by 2030 nearly half the world's population will be living in areas with severe water distress.[4] Critics of these dire warnings point out that a number of similar predictions in the past (some dating back to the 1960s) that the world would run out of petroleum or other crucial commodities turned out to be excessively alarmist. In some instances, innovative exploration and extraction techniques have uncovered enormous deposits of petroleum, iron, and other commodities. In other cases alternative technologies have reduced demand as, for example, the development of hybrid and fully battery-powered automobiles.

Analysts and politicians who are alarmed about the dangers of shortages of oil, clean water, or arable land tend to support government-imposed restrictions on consumption and government support for new technologies. Other experts feel less urgency and believe that market mechanisms can solve the problem. Both sides of this debate agree that some apparent solutions (involving either government or private sector activities) have had unintended negative consequences. For example, in several countries, government tax incentives and private initiatives helped develop ethanol (alcohol derived primarily from corn or sugar), which can be used for automobile fuel, either alone or mixed with gasoline. The major advantage of ethanol or ethanol blends is reducing dependency on imported oil. Unfortunately, however, the spread of ethanol production has diverted substantial farmland from food production to more profitable crops used to create fuel. This has contributed to a worldwide food shortage and rising prices, causing particular hardship to the world's poor.

SERVING THE ELDERLY: HEALTH CARE AND RETIREMENT PENSIONS

In his best-selling 1968 book, *The Population Bomb*, renowned biologist Paul R. Ehrlich warned of massive starvation and other catastrophic outcomes unless the world curtailed its rate of population growth. Whereas most anxieties over population growth have focused on the developing nations, Ehrlich was particularly concerned about population increases in highly developed countries because those nations consume the world's resources at a far greater rate per capita than poorer countries do. Though some of Ehrlich's predictions were excessively ominous and some of them have so far failed to come true, numerous demographers still shared his apprehension about population growth in economically advanced countries. Still, it is important to remember that his warnings came after a period of exceptionally high population growth in North America and Western Europe known as "the baby boom" (1946 to the mid-1960s).

Although high rates of natural population growth remain worrisome in many developing nations, especially in much of Africa and the Middle East, growth rates have fallen significantly in most Third World countries, including Mexico, Brazil, China, Vietnam, and India. But the most dramatic declines in birth rates (and population growth) have occurred in the world's most economically advanced countries, so much so that many demographers now worry that these nations will have too few people. In order for a country to maintain its present population (without immigration)—known as "the population replacement level" it must have a fertility rate of 2.1 children per woman (i.e., adult women need to give birth to an average of 2.1 children). In fact, however, only two highly developed countries—the United States and Iceland—currently reach that level and both have fertility rates of exactly 2.1 (replacement level). In all, Western Europe's fertility rate is only 1.6 and Eastern Europe's is even lower at 1.3. Furthermore, the most economically developed East Asian countries now have equally low fertility rates: including China (1.6), Japan (1.3), and South Korea (1.1). Because some of these countries have a large backlog of women of child-bearing age, who were born before the relatively recent sharp drop in fertility rates, their populations will continue to grow for a period of time, though at a decelerating rate. Eventually, however, if current trends persist, their populations will start to decline. Some developed and semi-developed countries have reached zero *natural* population growth (i.e., not counting any growth caused by immigration) including Japan, Italy, Greece, Poland, and Portugal. Before long, their populations will begin to fall. Other countries—Germany, Russia, Ukraine, Hungary—are already experiencing population declines.[5] In fact, demographers expect Europe's total population (currently 733 million) to decline to 669 million by 2050 (with the largest drops coming in Eastern Europe).

Similarly, they project that Japan's current population of 128 million will fall to 95 million by 2050.*

For those, like Paul Ehrlich, who had been troubled by the developed world's massive consumption of natural resources, these developments are welcome news. Low fertility rates will not only reduce resource consumption and pollution, but also allow industrialized nations to spend less in areas such as education and child care. But population declines raise serious worries as well. Countries such as Japan are already experiencing significant labor shortages and many European nations will face the same problem in the coming decades.

Moreover, a combination of lower birth rates and longer life expectancy means that in China, Japan, Europe, and even the United States, the percentage of the population over 65 years of age—people drawing on social security and retirement pensions and incurring far higher medical expenditures—will rise sharply relative to the percentage of the population in the work force (ages 18–65). As of 2007, some 16 percent of the population of industrialized nations were 65 years or older. By 2050 that percentage is expected to grow to 26 percent.[6] As that percentage rises, it will be increasingly difficult for the active work force to fund programs for the elderly. The U.S., for example, faces a looming crisis in its Medicare system. Advocacy groups and policy makers disagree over how to address this problem, but any solution will involve hard choices. Governments will either have to cut health care and pension benefits, or they will need to raise the qualifying age for retirement benefits to compensate for the population's greater longevity, or wage earners will have to pay substantially more into retirement and health care programs (or some combination of these choices). To date, most political leaders have preferred to put off these difficult decisions, presumably hoping that the looming fiscal crisis will not happen until they have left office. Unfortunately, the longer political leaders put off their decisions, the worse that predicament will be.

Immigration Policy in Developed Nations

Mass migration across national borders is not a new phenomenon. For example, during the nineteenth century millions of Europeans (Germans, Greeks, Irish, Italians, Russians, Spaniards, and many more) migrated to "countries of new settlement" in North and South America or Australia. But in recent times, mass communications offer people in developing nations a greater glimpse of life in wealthier countries, increasing the lure of migration. At the same time, transportation networks have expanded and become more affordable. These factors have helped stimulate a particularly massive migration from Africa, Asia, and Latin America to Europe and North America. From 1960 to 2005 the number of people in the world who had migrated from their country of origin to other countries increased from 75 million to 191 million annually, totaling about 3 percent of the world's population. Many of those people migrated from one developing country to another. For example, during Afghanistan's long guerrilla war against occupying Russian troops (1978–1989), hundreds of thousand of refugees fled

---

* On the other hand, the United States—with a replacement level fertility rate and substantial immigration—will grow from 302 million (2006) to 420 million in 2050. In Africa and the Middle East, populations will continue to grow and challenge those nations' abilities to feed and educate their people.

to Pakistan, Iran, and various Central Asian republics. However, overall the greatest portion of Third World emigrants have journeyed to developed countries.

While most industrialized nations have long welcomed immigrants (with Japan being the notable exception), they are increasingly troubled by the millions of illegal immigrants who now cross their borders (often at great personal risk). The question of how to deal with illegal and legal immigration has taken center stage in U.S. politics. Western European nations have generally had a more permissive attitude toward illegal immigrants, but growing popular resentment of recent immigrants (both legal and illegal) has spawned large, far-right-wing political parties in nations such as France, Austria, and Belgium. Americans who advocate cracking down on illegal immigration argue that: undocumented workers are taking jobs away from U.S. citizens; they increase the crime rate; and they put a strain on public services such as the schools. Some people also warn that undocumented workers constitute a threat to American culture and unity because many of them have not learned English or otherwise integrated themselves into American society as well as earlier, legal immigrants did.[7] The primary targets of such criticisms in the U.S. are illegal Hispanic immigrants, especially Mexicans. Similar arguments are raised against Third World immigrants to Europe, including North African Muslims in France and Spain, as well as Indians, Pakistanis and Africans in the United Kingdom.

Those who favor a more receptive attitude toward immigration argue that efforts to build border fences or to otherwise keep out illegal aliens are largely doomed to failure. Therefore, primary effort should focus on better integrating both legal and illegal immigrants into the national culture. They maintain that most illegal immigrants are not taking jobs away from American workers (though some of them undoubtedly are), but instead, they are primarily doing jobs—such as picking crops—which few Americans are willing to do. Were the U.S. (or Europe) able to cut off most illegal immigration, they contend, there would be serious labor shortages in a number of fields. This argument is particularly persuasive in Europe and Japan, whose aging and declining populations face serious labor shortages in the near future. Finally, many analysts reject the contention that illegal aliens have raised the crime rate. For example, a recent study indicates that among males aged 18–39 (the group responsible for most crime), "the incarceration rate of native-born men . . . (3.5 percent) was *5 times higher* than the incarceration rate of foreign-born men (0.7 percent)."[8]

Efforts to prevent illegal immigration have been tempered by Western worries about the migrants' civil liberties—concerns that were not an important part of the political discussion during nineteenth- and early twentieth-century waves of immigration. In both the U.S. and Europe, a variety of church and human rights groups have organized to protect immigrants' rights and provide them with material assistance. Interestingly, despite the frequently heard argument that those who entered the country illegally should not be granted amnesty, a surprisingly high percentage of Americans believe that illegal aliens should be given a path to citizenship under certain conditions. In 2007 the Gallup Poll asked a national sample of Americans the following question:

> *Which comes closest to your view about what government policy should be toward illegal immigrants currently residing in the United States? Should the government 1) deport all illegal immigrants back to their home country, 2) allow illegal immigrants to remain in the United States in order to work, but only for a limited amount of time, or 3) allow illegal immigrants to remain in the United States and become U.S. citizens, but only if they meet certain requirements over a period of time?*

Almost three out of five Americans (59%) favored the third option—allowing illegal immigrants to stay and become citizens. Only one-fourth (24%) favored deporting them.[9]

The American debate over illegal immigration does not always divide people along party lines. For example, while Republicans generally are far more likely than Democrats to favor deporting illegal immigrants and are less likely to be willing to grant them citizenship, many business owners (an important Republican constituency) favor a more open policy, including guest worker programs, because their industries depend on immigrant labor. The industries most likely to support more open immigration policies include agriculture, food packing and processing, and construction. In 2008, when President Bush proposed landmark immigration reform to the U.S. Senate, including a path to citizenship for millions of illegal aliens, over two-thirds of the Democrats supported his proposal, but almost three-fourths of the Republican senators opposed it.*

Nor do attitudes toward immigration divide predictably across ethnic lines. Although legal Hispanic immigrants tend to favor easing the path to citizenship for illegal immigrants, U.S.-born Latinos support tougher border controls and stringent citizenship requirements. In fact, the attitudes of U.S.-born Latinos toward illegal immigration basically mirror those of non-Hispanic U.S. citizens.[10]

Regardless of what policies the United States or Western European nations adopt, powerful economic forces will continue to draw illegal immigrants to developed nations, and it will be difficult to halt that trend. For example, despite enormous efforts to tighten the U.S.-Mexican border, an estimated 97 percent of Mexicans trying to cross illegally eventually make it through, either on their first try or on subsequent attempts.[11] Other efforts to stem the tide focus on penalizing employers who hire illegal aliens. But this is an issue that is unlikely to go away unless developing nations are able to narrow the vast income gap that separates them from the developed world. That is particularly challenging on the U.S.-Mexican frontier, where the income disparity between those two neighbors is greater than across any other border in the world.

RUSSIA AND THE WEST: A NEW COLD WAR?

After the fall of the Soviet Union, Russia seemed to enter a new era of good feelings toward the United States and its NATO (North Atlantic Treaty Organization) partners. While the Clinton and Yeltsin administrations did not always see eye to eye, relations between the two governments were generally amicable. This new bond produced several bilateral nuclear arms reduction treaties (see Chapter 18) and cooperation in a number of areas, including the War on Terror and restraining the North Korean nuclear weapons program. In 1998 the members of what was then called the G7 (the "Group of Seven" leading industrial democracies) welcomed Russia into its fold, thereby becoming the G8.† While that organization has no formal

---

* The bill was a compromise worked out between the Bush administration and leading Democrats (especially Senator Ted Kennedy). But it died when over half the senators present refused to cut off an opposition filibuster. Senator John McCain originally supported the bill, but subsequently backed away from it somewhat during the Republican presidential primaries.

† The original members of the G6, founded in the mid-1970s, were the United States, the United Kingdom, West Germany, Japan, France, and Italy. Canada was soon invited to join and the group changed its name to the G7. Finally, two decades later, Russia was welcomed in.

Russian tanks roll into the Republic of Georgia to prevent the Georgian military from forcibly re-annexing the breakaway provinces of Abkhazia and South Ossetia.

policy-making powers, its prime ministers and presidents hold an annual summit meeting in which they discuss mutual concerns and announce areas of policy agreement to the world's highly attentive news media. These summits, then, have great symbolic importance as demonstrations of growing world interdependence and as forums for demonstrating mutual commitments and generating greater cooperation between G8 members.[12] Russia's admission signaled its acceptance by the major Western powers and Japan, and seemed to drive the final nail into the Cold War's coffin. Several years later (2001), when America's new president, George W. Bush, met with Vladimir Putin (then Russia's relatively new president) for the first time, the two leaders appeared to get along famously. The Russian president said that he considered the U.S. a partner and Bush offered his famous evaluation of Putin:

> I looked the man in the eye. I found him to be very straight-forward and trustworthy and we had a very good dialogue. . . . I was able to get a sense of his soul.[13]

Following the 9/11 attacks on the World Trade Center and the Pentagon, Russia, facing its own Islamic terrorist threat (see Chapter 13), cooperated with the U.S. in the War on Terror. Indeed, Putin was the first head of state to call President Bush after 9/11 to offer his condolences and support.

Since that time, however, relations between Russia and the other G8 nations, particularly the United States, have deteriorated badly. The West has been dismayed by the demise of Russia's budding democracy (see Chapter 13) and by that country's increasingly confrontational foreign policy. While the two nations continue to co-operate in some areas, they have often been at loggerheads. For example, Russia has used its veto power in the Security Council to water down threatened UN sanctions against Iran's nuclear program.

While Vladimir Putin's heavy-handed expressions of Russian nationalism and his country's occasional paranoia bear much of the responsibility for renewed East-West tensions, some analysts maintain that the West, particularly the Clinton and Bush administrations, has needlessly provoked the Russians at times. The West often failed to understand the Russian population's humiliation in the 1990s as their country declined from a superpower to a nation with little international influence and a collapsing economy. Consequently, when Russia's economy rebounded dramatically after 2000—based on its petroleum wealth—most Russians supported Putin's more belligerent foreign policy, including his attempts to bully Ukraine, Georgia, and other nations in the "near abroad" (the term used by Russians to describe other former Republics of the Soviet Union that are now independent countries).

Several Western policies particularly irritated the Russian leadership. First, it took offense when NATO bombed Russia's ally, Serbia, to protect the secessionist province of Kosovo from Serbian assaults. Second, Russia felt threatened when NATO extended membership to a number of ex-communist Eastern and Central European nations (including Hungary, Poland, the Czech Republic, Romania and Bulgaria) and to three former Soviet Republics (Estonia, Latvia, and Lithuania), bringing the Western military alliance up to Russia's doorstep.* A number of foreign policy experts—including George Kennan, the father of America's containment policy toward the Soviets during the Cold War—criticized Clinton's decision to extend NATO into Eastern Europe and Bush's intensification of that policy. Given Russia's weakened state, they maintained that the West could adequately protect those countries from any attack, without bringing them into NATO and that their inclusion into the military pact needlessly provoked Moscow. Most recently, Kremlin leaders have been particularly dismayed by the Bush administration's plans to install defensive missiles in Poland and to build a support base in the Czech Republic. While the U.S. insists that these missiles are being installed to defend Europe against a potential missile attack from a rogue state (presumably Iran), Moscow views them as an additional Western military build-up in Russia's front yard. Finally, Russia was particularly dismayed over NATO's announced plans to consider Ukraine and Georgia (both former Soviet Republics) for membership.

Since Putin became president, Russia's petroleum wealth and its associated economic boom (2000–2008) have restored the country's self confidence and given it the economic power (and added military hardware) to support a more aggressive foreign policy. Moscow's relations with the Republic of Georgia (on Russia's southern flank) had been particularly tense since that country's "Rose Revolution" (2003) brought a pro-Western, democratic government to power. The Georgian revolution helped inspire Ukraine's "Orange Revolution" (2004) and Kyrgyzstan's "Tulip Revolution" (2005). Each of those countries had been part of the Soviet Union and years after their secession from the USSR each of them had peaceful "revolutions," in which relatively bloodless, mass demonstrations ousted Soviet-era presidents and replaced them with pro-Western democrats. Georgia's and Ukraine's plans to join NATO further convinced Moscow that the West was ganging up on it.

---

* NATO was created early in the Cold War (1949) and until the demise of the Soviet Union its main purpose was protecting Europe, North America, and Turkey from possible Soviet aggression. Since the 1990s its focus has shifted elsewhere, but the Russians still view it as a hostile force.

When the USSR disintegrated in 1991 and Georgia declared its independence, two small ethnic enclaves on Georgia's border with Russia—South Ossetia and Abkhazia—wanted to secede. Though no country recognized these regions' claims to independence, Russia has supported them and has used its military power to keep the Georgian army out of both areas. On August 8, 2008 (the day the 2008 Summer Olympics opened in Beijing), the Georgian armed forces bombed and invaded South Ossetia in an attempt to regain control of the region. Georgia President Mikheil Saakashvili badly miscalculated, believing that Russia would not intervene for fear of possible Western retaliation. Instead, Moscow sent its troops across the border to reinforce its "peacekeepers" already in South Ossetia, easily driving out the Georgian troops and occupying substantial parts of Georgia for a few weeks.* Subsequent to its pull-back, Russia became the first country in the world to recognize South Ossetian and Abkhazian independence. Secretary of State Rice hinted that Moscow's behavior might eventually lead the U.S. to propose removing Russia from the G8 and could end Russian military cooperation with NATO (Moscow quickly ended its NATO links on its own).

But NATO's Western European members feel that it is not worth confronting Russia over Georgia's secessionist enclaves. Undoubtedly, they were mindful that Europe currently receives 30 percent of its oil and 40 percent of its natural gas from Russia.[14] Recalling how Russia had briefly cut off Ukraine's natural gas supply in 2007 after the two countries had quarreled, most Western European nations are reluctant to confront Moscow. Even before the Russian confrontation over South Ossetia, Germany and France had opposed NATO membership for Georgia or Ukraine. Recent events have only reinforced that opposition.

In the end, there was no real winner in the conflict between Russia and Georgia. Moscow was able to flex its muscles, but at the cost of antagonizing the U.S. and the Europeans, especially the East Europeans. While most Poles initially opposed stationing U.S. missiles in their country, public opinion turned sharply after the Russian invasion of Georgia. The Polish government quickly signed a treaty with the U.S. permitting the missile installations. For its part, Georgia grossly miscalculated the Russian response. It has no realistic prospect of recovering South Ossetia, and probably has now lost any chance of entering NATO soon. The United States, though it had warned President Saakashvili not to invade South Ossetia, had clearly not done so convincingly enough. After Russia's military incursion into Georgia, Secretary of State Condoleezza Rice repeatedly warned Moscow about the negative consequences of continued occupation. But the U.S. was not in a position to do much about it.

To be sure, the current stand-off between Russia and the U.S., which extends well beyond the confrontation in Georgia, is less threatening to world peace than the Cold War with the Soviets was. But it undoubtedly will be a troublesome issue for American and European policy makers for years to come.

THE ASIAN CENTURY?

Throughout the nineteenth century, the center of world military, economic, and political power lay in Europe, with countries such as France, Germany (or Prussia), and, especially, the United Kingdom (whose empire encompassed nearly one-fourth of the

---

* Russia subsequently withdrew its soldiers from the rest of Georgia, but retained troops in both South Ossetia and Abkhazia.

The skyline of downtown Kuala Lumpur, Malaysia symbolizes Asia's dramatic modernization. The Petronas Towers on the right were the two tallest buildings in the world when they were built in 1998. They were surpassed in 2004 by the Taipei 101 Tower (Taiwan) and the Shanghai World Financial Center (China) in 2008. All of these buildings are in East or Southeast Asia.

world's population). Historians often call that era "the British Century" (or, perhaps "the European Century"). During the twentieth century, particularly after World War I, the United States emerged as the world's most powerful economic, military, and political force. Despite challenges from Nazi Germany and the Soviet Union, that was clearly "the American Century."[15]

While the U.S. continues to be the most powerful nation on earth, many journalists, political leaders, and futurists believe that in time the twenty-first century will be known as "the Asian Century." Currently, the combined population of just Asia's two largest nations—China and India—exceeds 2.4 billion people, representing more than one out of three people on Earth. Asia's entire population now accounts for nearly 60 percent of the world's total. That proportion will probably hold steady through the year 2050, but the number of Asians who are economically highly productive will grow substantially. At the same time, Europe's share of the world's population, which stood at 21 percent in 1950, will fall to only 7 percent by 2050.[16] Clearly, large populations do not necessarily make nations more economically developed or militarily powerful. However, Asia's vast population coupled with rapid economic growth will make that continent far more politically and militarily influential in the future.

In 2007, American military spending nearly equaled the combined military expenditures of the rest of the world. U.S military outlays were about ten times higher than spending in any of the next four largest competitors (Britain, China, France, and Japan).[17] There is no likelihood that any single country or any continent will match the U.S. military outlays in the near future. Still, Asian nations already have some of the world's largest military budgets, including China (3rd in the world), Japan (5th), India (10th), and South Korea (11th).[18] Furthermore, in addition to their large conventional armies, China, India, Pakistan, and North Korea all have or may have nuclear weapons.*

But it is in the world's economy that Asian nations will exert the most influence in this century. In recent decades, China, South Korea, and Singapore have enjoyed spectacular economic growth. As we have seen (Chapter 14), China has had the fastest growing economy in the world and it continued to have phenomenal "real" growth (i.e., controlled for inflation) of more than 10 percent in 2008. It is already the world's largest manufacturer and, depending on which measure of GDP we use, it is either already the world's second largest economy or will soon pass Japan for that position. Many economists believe its economy will surpass the United States by about 2050.† The motor for rapid economic growth in Asia's newly industrialized countries (China, Hong Kong, India, Indonesia, Malaysia, Singapore, South Korea, Taiwan, and Thailand) has been exports (particularly manufactured exports). Between 1990 and 2006, Asia's percentage of total world trade rose from 21 percent to 34 percent.[19] That share is almost certain to grow substantially during the remainder of this century. Perhaps the major economic consequence of Asia's dramatic economic growth has been that hundreds of millions of people have climbed out of poverty. The World Bank estimates that the number of Chinese living in extreme poverty fell from 835 million in 1981 to 207 million in 2005. In India, the proportion of the population living in extreme poverty fell from 60 percent in 1981 to 42 percent in 2005.[20]

But, despite China's economic boom, millions of peasants and urban migrants have been left behind or have even lost ground. The situation is far worse in India and Indonesia. And, as of 2005, fully 1.5 billion people—nearly two-thirds—of India and China's combined population of 2.3 billion people—were living on less than $2 a day.[21] Furthermore, most of the continent's rapidly expanding economies are in East and Southeast Asia, while much of South Asia has not joined in the growth (including Afghanistan, Bangladesh, and Pakistan). To some extent, Asia's continued emergence as an economic superpower and its continued progress toward democracy will hinge on its ability to extend its economic miracle to its rural and urban poor.

As is frequently the case, economic growth has helped stimulate the spread of democracy in the region. As many Asian economies have grown, so too has the size of the middle and working classes, both of whom have historically supported democratic governance in other parts of the word. In recent decades, the Philippines, Taiwan, South Korea, Pakistan, and Nepal have all embraced democracy. On the other hand, the correlation between economic and political development is by no means perfect. Thus, Singapore, China, and Malaysia—all rapidly growing economies—have retained authoritarian governments and movement toward democracy has been very uneven in Thailand and the Philippines. At the same time, two of the poorest countries in the continent—Nepal and Afghanistan—have made tentative progress toward democratic rule.

* North Korea claimed to have tested a nuclear device in October of 2006 and, based on scientific evidence, both Western and Russian intelligence agencies were inclined to believe them.

† Long-term predictions of this type are quite fallible, and economists disagree about China's prospects of becoming the world's largest economy. Of course, China's population is currently over four times larger than the U.S. So, no matter which estimates on the size of *total* GDP are correct, China's *per capita* income will remain a fraction of America's.

Along with its obvious benefits, rapid Asian economic growth, like all major changes, also has potentially damaging consequences. Rapid industrialization, particularly in the Asian giants of China and India, has contributed substantially to greenhouse gas emissions and global warming. China has recently passed the United States as the world's largest producer of greenhouses gases and India is a major contributor as well. Finally, Asia' economic surge presents challenges to the U.S. and other developed economies. Western nations have already made difficult adjustments as many of their manufacturing industries have folded in the face of competition from low-wage nations in Asia. Just as India has developed call centers for an increasing number of American computer software and airline companies, English-speaking countries such India and Singapore will likely compete with American workers for service sector jobs as well employment in manufacturing.

CONCLUSION

In a span of less than sixty years, the earth's population has more than doubled from some 2.5 billion people in 1950 to 6.7 billion in late 2008.[22] At the same time, a huge percentage of the scientists and technicians who have ever lived on Earth are alive today. At the start of the twentieth century most of the world had never been transported other than by their own feet or with the help of horses or other animals. By the end of that century, man had been to the moon and traveled on Earth in supersonic airplanes. At the start of the twentieth century aircraft had never been used in warfare. By the middle of that century aircraft had dropped atomic bombs that had obliterated whole cities. Small wonder that political, economic, and social practices, attitudes, and values have changed enormously and continue to do so rapidly.

As we have seen throughout this text, the world has become enormously interconnected: China exports a large percentage of the consumer goods purchased in the United States; the U.S. exports food and technology to much of the world; waves of migration bring Latin Americans to the United States as well as Africans and Asians to Europe; multinational banks, petroleum companies, and pharmaceutical firms dominate world markets; and McDonalds and Starbucks have numerous franchises in China, Mexico, and other parts of the developing world.

In many ways this interconnectedness has benefited the world, raising living standards and life expectancy. But it has also produced new problems and exacerbated old ones. Immigration from the developing world has contributed to racial and ethnic tensions and a political backlash in Europe and the United States. Urbanization, migration, and population growth within countries such as Kenya, Uganda, and India have often produced tribal, religious, and ethnic conflicts. The spread of American and other Western popular culture—including movies, TV, music, sports, and t-shirts—has proven irresistible to much of the Third World's youth. But at the same time, it has provoked an enormous cultural backlash in parts of the developing world, most notably on the so-called Arab street, where many religious leaders and ordinary citizens object to the perceived immorality of Western society and feel victim to its "cultural imperialism."

All of these problems—and opportunities—pose an enormous challenge to the world's citizens and their political leaders. University students and other young adults throughout the world face a particular challenge to study and better understand these issues.

Notes _____

1. The National Academy of Sciences, representing the major American scientific, engineering, and medical associations, offers scientific advice to the government and the public. See, for example, the "Joint Science Academies' Statement: Global Response to Climate Change," issued by the American National Academy of Sciences and the academies of Canada, France, Germany, Italy, Japan, the United Kingdom, Brazil, India, Russia, and China, http://royalsociety.org/displaypagedoc.asp?id=13618.

2. "U.S. Drivers Traveled 20 Billion Fewer Miles In April," *Treehugger*, (June 2008) http://www.treehugger.com/files/2008/06/americans-drove-fewer-miles-april-2008.php. Even though this seemingly represents a significant change in driver habits, the Department of Transportation predicted a drop in driving mileage of only 2–3 percent for 2008.

3. "Weekly Retail Premium Gasoline Prices" (1996–2008), http://www.eia.doe.gov/emeu/international/gas1.html.

4. "Dust-Up: The New Scarcity?" *Los Angeles Times* (May 5, 2008). http://www.chicagotribune.com/topic/la-op-gardner-clark5may05,0,6490625,full.story. This article features a debate between Gary Gardner of the Worldwatch Institute and Gregory Clark of the University of California-Davis.

5. All of the statistics in this section come from The Population Reference Bureau, 2007 *World Population Data Sheet*, http://www.prb.org/pdf07/07WPDS_Eng.pdf.

6. Ibid.

7. This last argument is central to a controversial book on recent immigration to the U.S. by Samuel Huntington, a highly influential political scientist. See his, *Who Are We?: the Challenges to America's National Identity* (New York: Simon & Schuster, 2004).

8. Ruben Rumbaut and Walter Ewing, "The Myth of Immigrant Criminality," *Border Battles: The U.S. Immigration Debates* Social Science Research Council (SSRC), May 2007, http://borderbattles.ssrc.org/Rumbault_Ewing/index1.html. This research drew on U.S. census data.

9. "Public Still Supports Path to Citizenship for Illegal Immigrants," *USA Today*/Gallup Poll, March 2–4, 2007, *Gallup News Service*, http://www.gallup.com/poll/26875/Public-Still-Supports-Path-Citizenship-Illegal-Immigrants.aspx.

10. Rodolfo O. de la Garza, "Understanding Contemporary Immigration Debates: The Need for a Multidimensional Approach," *Border Battles: The U.S. Immigration Debates*, Social Science Research Council (SSRC), July 2006, http://borderbattles.ssrc.org/de_la_Garza/.

11. Interview with Wayne Cornelius (Director of the University of California, San Diego's Center for Comparative Immigration Studies) for *Frontline/World*, a PBS investigative journalism show, http://www.pbs.org/frontlineworld/stories/mexico704/interview/cornelius.html. The UCSD Center has conducted the most comprehensive research on Mexican immigration.

12. Martin Weiss, "The Group of Eight Summits: Evolution and Possible Reform," *CRS (Congressional Research Service) Report for Congress* (March 17, 2006), http://italy.usembassy.gov/pdf/other/RS22403.pdf.

13. "Bush and Putin: Best of Friends," *BBC News* (June 16, 2001), http://news.bbc.co.uk/2/hi/europe/1392791.stm.

14. Andrei Konoplyanik, "Uncertainty Surrounds Russia-to-Europe Gas Agreements," *Oil and Gas Financial Journal*, 2, no. 10 (December 2005), http://www.ogfj.com/Articles/Article_Display.cfm?Article_ID=243369.

15. That term was coined in 1941 in an article by Henry Luce, the publisher of *Time* and *Life* magazines, two of America's most influential publications at that time. Luce's article called on the U.S. to abandon its isolationist tendencies and assume leadership in a worldwide battle for democracy.

16. *Geohive*. These statistics are drawn from the U.S. Bureau of the Census, http://www.geohive.com/earth/his_proj_continent.aspx.

17. Stockholm International Peace Research Institute (SIPRI), "The 15 Major Spender Countries in 2007," http://www.sipri.org/contents/milap/milex/mex_major_spenders.pdf. SIPRI is supported by the Swedish government and is the most respected source of data on military spending.

18. Ibid.

19. Paul Gruenwald and Masahiro Hori, "Intra-Regional Trade Key to Asia's Export Boom," *IMF Survey Magazine* (February 6, 2008), http://www.imf.org/external/pubs/ft/survey/so/2008/CAR02608A.htm.

20. "World Bank Finds that Adjustment Places More in Steep Poverty," *New York Times* (August 27, 2008). The *Times* article explains that the World Bank has just changed its definition of "extreme poverty" from anyone living on less that $1.00 a day to anyone living on less that $1.25 a day. That redefinition raised the number of people living in extreme poverty worldwide from 1 billion to 1.4 billion. The data cited here showing poverty reductions in China and India are based on a definition of $1.25 a day (adjusted for inflation) in both 1981 and 2005.

21. World Bank data quoted in Pranab Bardhan, "China, India Superpowers? Not so Fast!" *Yale Global on Line* (25 October, 2005), http://yaleglobal.yale.edu/display.article?id=6407.

22. Population Reference Bureau, "How Many People Have Ever Lived on Earth?" http://www.prb.org/Articles/2002/HowManyPeopleHaveEverLivedonEarth.aspx?p=1 and U.S. Census Bureau, *U.S. and World Population Clocks—POP Clocks*, http://www.census.gov/main/www/popclock.html.

For Further Reading ─────────

Boxhill, Bernard, ed. *Race and Racism*. New York: Oxford University Press, 2001.

Carment, David and Patrick James, eds. *Wars in the Midst of Peace: The International Politics of Ethnic Conflict*. Pittsburgh: University of Pittsburgh Press, 1997.

Friedman, Thomas. *The World is Flat: A Short History of the Twenty-First Century*. New York: Farrar, Straus, and Giroux, 2006.

Friedman, Thomas. *Hot, Flat and Crowded: Why We Need A Green Revolution—and How It Can Renew America*. New York: Farrar, Straus, and Giroux, 2008.

Krugman, Paul R. *The Conscience of a Liberal*. New York: W. W. Norton and Company, 2007.

Levitt, Steven D. and Stephen J. Dubner. *Freakonomics: A Rogue Economist Explores the Hidden Side of Everything*. New York: William Morrow, 2005.

Olson, Mancur, Jr. *The Rise and Decline of Nations*. New Haven, CT: Yale University Press, 1982.

Stiglitz, Joseph E. *Making Globalization Work*. New York: W. W. Norton and Company, 2006.

GLOSSARY

Absolutism The concentration of tremendous political power in a single source, such as an absolute monarch. (**Ch. 13**)

Adversarial Democracy The kind of democratic politics created by the use of a single-member-district electoral system. Since the winning party receives all of the representation from each district, there is usually no need to form a coalition with minority parties. *See also* Consensual Democracy. (**Ch. 4**)

Adversarial System A legal system in which an independent judge (sometimes with a jury) hears arguments presented by two opposing sides before rendering a decision. (**Ch. 9**)

Agents of Political Socialization Individuals, groups, and institutions—such as the family, schools, churches, or labor unions—that transmit political values to each generation. (**Ch. 3**)

Allocation of Resources The distribution of a society's wealth among its members. Resources may be allocated authoritatively, by government action, or by the workings of a free market system. (**Ch. 1**)

Anarchism The opposition to government in all forms. The advocates of this ideology believe that government is unnecessary and inevitably harmful and divisive, and that people would coexist peacefully without it. (**Ch. 2**)

Appellate Courts Courts that hear appeals from decisions made by trial courts. Normally, appellate courts do not hear new evidence, but instead respond to claims that a trial court misinterpreted the law or made a procedural error. (**Ch. 9**)

Aristocracy The most prestigious echelon of a stratified society. In Great Britain aristocratic families have a royal title, often dating back centuries. (**Ch. 12**)

Articles of Confederation The basic agreement among the former British colonies in America ("states") that governed the relations among them and the powers of the national congress until the Constitution was ratified in 1789. (**Ch. 11**)

Authoritarian Systems Non-democratic (dictatorial) government that exercises extensive control or authority over society. (**Chs. 1, 5, 13, 14, 15, 16**)

Balance of Power The relative levels of military strength among potential adversaries. Many "realist" theorists of international relations feel that the balance of power is the most important factor in explaining the outbreak of war. (**Ch. 17**)

Basic Law A body of law that supersedes other laws; for example, the U.S. Constitution is basic law in that statutes that contradict it are invalid. (**Ch. 9**)

Behavioralism An approach to political research that emphasizes observation of individual political behavior, as contrasted with approaches that focus on political documents and laws. (**Ch. 1**)

Belief System An ordering of opinions and attitudes held together by some broader ideological theme or pattern; not a random assortment of beliefs. (**Ch. 4**)

Bicameralism The division of the legislature into two chambers, or "houses." (**Chs. 7, 11**)

Bolsheviks The Marxist faction in the Russian Revolution headed by Vladimir Lenin. The Bolsheviks evolved into the Soviet Communist Party. (**Ch. 13**)

Budget Formulation The process of forming a proposal for a government's budget, including plans for both revenues and expenditures. (**Ch. 8**)

Bureaucracy The government organizations, usually staffed with officials selected on the basis of expertise and experience, that implement (and sometimes make) public policy. (**Ch. 10**)

Bureaucrat A person working for the public sector who is appointed on the basis of training and experience; usually applied to an official with a specified realm of authority. (**Ch. 10**)

Caciques Mexico's regional political bosses or strongmen. (**Ch. 16**)

Cadre In China, the term means a public official holding a full time, responsible position in the Communist Party or the government. (**Ch. 14**)

Candidate Evaluation The personal appeal of an electoral candidate. Candidate evaluation may be positive or negative, and where it is a strong factor, it may exert greater influence on vote choices than party identification or voters' opinions about issues. (**Ch. 4**)

Capitalism An ideology advocating private property and minimal government. Also, the third stage of "prehistory" in Marxist ideology; in this stage, ownership of capital becomes the basis for political power and industrial workers are exploited by those who own factories. (**Ch. 2**)

Cárdenas, Lázaro Mexico's most revered recent leader, President Cárdenas introduced a series of economic and political reforms in the 1930s that benefited the nation's poor and strengthened the role of the state in the economy. (**Ch. 16**)

Catchall Parties Parties that try to appeal to a wide range of social classes and groups and, hence, have a relatively poorly defined policy program or ideology. The Democratic and Republican parties in the United States have fit in this category in the past, but are becoming more well defined. (**Ch. 5**)

Charismatic Authority The ability to evoke allegiance and loyalty from citizens or subordinates by virtue of image, speaking skills, and the generation of emotional responses. (**Ch. 8**)

Checks and Balances The principle, associated most prominently with U.S. government, holding that arbitrary, irresponsible government power is best prevented by establishing a system in which each part of the government can check the actions of the others. (**Ch. 11**)

Chief Administrator An individual who manages and coordinates the implementation of programs through administrative agencies; one of the primary roles of modern chief executives. (**Ch. 8**)

Christian Democrats Political parties and their supporters who profess a political doctrine usually linked to the Catholic Church. Important in Latin America and Europe, these parties range from right of center to left of center ideologically. (**Ch. 5**)

Citizen Participation The practice of involving citizens in the bureaucratic decision-making process. (**Ch. 10**)

Civil Law The body of law pertaining to efforts by private parties to gain compensation for injuries inflicted by other private parties; for example, one person suing another for damages arising from libelous statements is a civil law matter. (**Ch. 9**)

Civil Society The network of groups such as labor unions, business associations, church groups, and the like that can influence the political system but are independent of government control. (**Ch. 13**)

Class Consciousness A Marxist term used to describe a given socioeconomic class's awareness of its common self-interest. A socio-economic class, most particularly the working class, needs class consciousness if it is to act cohesively to pursue its interests. (**Ch. 2, 13**)

Classical Political Philosophy A body of political philosophy based on the ideas of Plato (427–347 BCE) and his student Aristotle (384–322 BCE), associated with a distrust of democracy and efforts to envision the just state. (**Ch. 1**)

Coalition Government A government formed, usually when no single party has a majority in Parliament, from a coalition of parties. In countries such as India and Israel, where frequently no single party wins a majority in Parliament, national elections are followed by negotiations between possible coalition partners since the prime minister must have the backing of a parliamentary majority. (**Ch. 12**)

Coercive Authority The authority that a leader enjoys by virtue of possessing the power to force compliance with his or her demands. (**Ch. 8**)

Cold War The period of tensions and confrontation between the world's major military powers, the United States and the Soviet Union, lasting from the mid-1940s until the collapse of the Soviet Union. (**Ch. 18**)

Collectives A term used to describe cooperatively owned factories and other enterprises. These are neither state-owned nor private enterprises. (**Ch. 14**)

Collectivization The process, common to many leftist revolutionary societies, of bringing private farm plots under the control of large, collectively administered units. Although collective farms are technically run by the farmers who belong to the unit, they are generally under some degree of state control. Often collectivization involves considerable repression of peasants and landowners. This was especially true in the Soviet Union under Stalin, where millions died. (**Ch. 13**)

Command Economy A highly centralized, communist economy in which key decisions on production, employment, and the like are made by a powerful state and party bureaucracy. (**Ch. 13**)

Committee System The way in which committees are empowered in a legislature. Committees in some systems are quite powerful, independently determining which bills become law, whereas in other systems committees normally have little influence. (**Ch. 7**)

Common Law A set of principles first developed centuries ago by British courts in efforts to establish a basic code of fairness for situations in which no statutory law applied. (**Ch. 9**)

Communalism The first stage of "prehistory" in Marxist ideology; in this stage, society's productive capacity is so undeveloped that each person must consume everything he or she produces to survive, making slavery or other forms of exploitation economically impractical; sometimes termed "primitive communism." (**Ch. 2**)

Communes Highly collectivized agricultural units that were introduced to China in the late 1950s and subsequent decades. Because the commune system involved enormous state intrusion in their lives, the peasantry generally resented them. (**Ch. 14**)

Communism The stage in Marxist ideology in which "true" human history begins; in this stage, technological development has advanced to the point at which scarcity of resources no longer exists, and there is no class conflict or exploitation. (**Ch. 2**)

Conflictual and Consensual Political Cultures In consensual political cultures, citizens tend to agree on basic political procedures as well as the values and general goals of the political system. Conversely, conflictual political cultures are highly polarized by fundamental differences over those issues. (**Ch. 3**)

Connecticut Compromise The decision made, in drafting the U.S. Constitution, to divide the legislative power into two chambers, with the upper chamber designed so that each state would have two members in it regardless of population. Smaller states had been reluctant to support the Constitution if all legislative power were to be placed in a single chamber with districts allotted to states on the basis of population. (**Ch. 11**)

Consensual Democracy The kind of democratic politics created by the use of proportional representation electoral systems. Since a party does not have to win a majority of the votes in any state or district to gain parliamentary representation, this arrangement is said to force several parties to form an inclusive coalition and to govern in a more consensual manner. *See also* Adversarial Democracy. (**Ch. 4**)

Conservatism An approach to political life that sees traditional values as important in solving social problems. Edmund Burke (1729–1797) produced a landmark statement of conservatism in his criticism of the French Revolution, arguing that it destroyed aristocratic and religious traditions and would destabilize and coarsen French society. (**Ch. 2**)

Constituent Service Activities by legislators to obtain information, favors, and exceptions to regulations for their constituents, normally by making requests of administrative officials. (**Ch. 7**)

(The) Core A term used by dependency theorists to refer to the highly developed, capitalist nations that dominate the world economy. (**Ch. 15**)

Corporatism A political system in which citizens are represented in government by major interest groups. In its most advanced form, it involves the organization of the population into officially sanctioned interest groups based on occupational or other socioeconomic lines. (**Ch. 16**)

Council Housing Public housing built for the poor by the local government council. (**Ch. 12**)

Coup d'État (or **Coup**). An irregular, nonconstitutional removal of a head of state by a small group. A rapid takeover of the government, usually by the military (**Ch. 8, 15**)

Criminal Law The body of law pertaining to the prosecution and punishment of those accused of crimes. (**Ch. 9**)

Cult of Personality An effort, commonly encountered in totalitarian political systems such as Stalin's Soviet Russia or Nazi Germany, to glorify a political leader and develop a cult following behind him. Cults of personality developed around Joseph Stalin and Mao Zedong, for example. (**Ch. 13**)

Cultural Revolution Mao Zedong's effort (1966–1976) to revitalize China's revolutionary spirit and to cleanse the nation of real or alleged antirevolutionary cultural aspects. It involved a reign of terror in which hundreds of thousands, perhaps millions, were killed. (**Ch. 14**)

Debt Crisis The severe economic downturn suffered in the 1980s by nations in Latin America and Africa, arising from their inability to repay outstanding international debts. (**Chs. 16, 18**)

Declaration of Independence The formal statement, written primarily by Thomas Jefferson and adopted by the Second Continental Congress on July 4, 1776, that the 13 American colonies were independent of British control. (**Ch. 11**)

Defendant The person accused of a crime or sued by a plaintiff in a civil action. (**Ch. 9**)

Delegate Model An approach to representation in which the representative acts in accordance with the expressed preferences of the constituency that elected him or her. (**Ch. 7**)

Democracy A system of government in which government is ultimately accountable to the citizens. Although democracy literally means "government by the people," in practice it normally means that the people can select and remove those that govern them. (**Ch. 1**)

Democratic Peace The idea that something about the nature of democratic government makes it very unlikely that democratic states will go to war with other democracies. (**Ch. 17**)

Democratic Revolutionary Party *See* Party of the Democratic Revolution (PRD).

Deng Xiaoping Leader of the Chinese political system from the 1970s to 1997 and architect of the nation's transformation to a more market-based economy. (**Ch. 14**)

Dependency Theory A theory once supported by many scholars that suggested that the Third World's underprivileged position was attributable to the control that powerful capitalist nations held over them. Dependency involves a measure of economic and political control by developed nations (the core) over less-developed ones (the periphery). (**Ch. 15**)

Deregulation A movement in public policy, most widespread in the United States and Great Britain in the 1980s, that involved removing or reducing regulations on private-sector activity, generally on the assumption that much government regulation is wasteful, counterproductive, and unnecessary. (**Ch. 2**)

Devolution The transfer of political power from a central government to regional or local government. (**Ch. 12**)

Diplomacy The communications and negotiations among national leaders regarding matters of foreign policy. (**Ch. 8**)

Disadvantage Theory The idea that the organized interests that use litigation as a strategy of influence do so because they are disadvantaged relative to other interests when trying to influence legislative and executive institutions. The classic example used to illustrate disadvantage theory was the successful effort of the groups working in the U.S. to stop racial segregation in public schools: facing virtually no chance of changing policy by lobbying state legislatures, these groups brought suit in federal court to change policy. (**Ch. 6**)

Dual Democratic Legitimacy A characteristic of presidential systems; the fact that the chief executive and the legislature are separately elected means that both institutions can claim to represent the people, and when these institutions disagree over policy, gridlock can ensue. In parliamentary systems, only the Parliament can claim democratic legitimacy, and the chief executive (prime minister) is elected from that body. (**Ch. 7**)

Dual Transition A simultaneous transition from a command economy to a free market and from a communist political system to democracy. (**Ch. 13**)

Duma The lower house of the current Russian parliament. (**Ch. 13**)

Economic Austerity A set of government economic policies, often imposed as the result of pressure from the international financial community, designed to reduce inflation, trade deficits, and budget deficits, and to facilitate repayment of the country's external debt. Such policies, at least in the short run, generally lead to reduced living standards, especially for the poor. At the same time, they may be necessary to restore a nation's economic health. Hence, the precise form that they take is subject to heated debate. (**Ch. 16**)

Economic Determinism The idea that economic forces govern changes in the nature of societies; largely, but not exclusively, associated with Marxism. (**Ch. 2**)

Economic Internationalism (Liberalism) An approach to international political economy that emphasizes the benefits of free trade among nations. It is associated with classical liberal economics; often termed "liberalism" in this context. (**Ch. 17**)

Economic Nationalism An approach to international political economy that focuses on the importance of national interest and national power, holding these to be more important than the economic efficiency gains that may be obtained through free trade; also termed "mercantilism." (**Ch. 17**)

Economic Structuralism An approach to international political economy associated with Marxist-Leninist thinking; it emphasizes the persistent economic inequalities separating poor and rich countries, and focuses on how state economic systems produce a structure of dependency and inequality. (**Ch. 17**)

Electoral Democracy A political system that features competitive (free and fair) government elections but may not respect fundamental civil liberties. *See* Liberal Democracy. (**Ch. 15**)

Elite Theory The idea that a single, generally unified elite dominates society; typically contrasted with pluralism. (**Ch. 6**)

Emergency Leadership The effort by a chief executive to initiate, coordinate, and energize governmental activities in time of crisis. (**Ch. 8**)

Environmentalism An ideology holding that the issues pertaining to the state of the physical environment, and policies directed toward it, are of primary importance. The most intense advocates of this ideology argue that environmental problems sometimes supersede other issues, such as economic development, poverty, and international relations. (**Ch. 2**)

Ethnicity A type of group identification in which individuals identify with people like themselves (and set themselves apart from other people) on the basis of race, religion, culture, language, nationality, and the like. Examples of ethnicities in the United States include Irish-Americans, Afro-Americans, Catholics, Italian-Americans, Jews, and Gypsies. (**Ch. 15**)

European Union (EU) The Western European trade and economic organization that binds together 27 of the region's nations. It is the successor to the European Community (EC) but involves a more intensive and geographically extensive union. (**Chs. 12, 18**)

Evolutionary Change A process of gradual, interrelated change, as distinguished from more rapid, and often disruptive, revolutionary change. (**Ch. 12**)

Expert Faction That faction of Chinese Communist Party leadership in the 1960s and 1970s that favored assigning management positions to trained experts even when they were not the most ideologically "correct" citizens. (**Ch. 14**)

Extended Republic The idea, associated with James Madison, that political disputes would be less violent and destabilizing if the political system were extended to comprise all the states (rather than continuing to resolve most political disputes independently in each of the states). (**Ch. 11**)

Falun Gong A Chinese spiritual sect stressing meditation and exercises. The government has repressed the movement, with hundreds of members allegedly dying while in police custody. (**Ch. 14**)

Fascism An ideology that emphasizes extreme appeals to national unity, hatred of foreigners and ethnic minorities, and complete obedience to the state. (**Ch. 2**)

Feminism An ideology that advocates equal rights for females. Some versions of feminism also identify specific feminine traits, such as compassion and sharing, that proponents claim will improve society as women achieve more leadership positions. (**Ch. 2**)

Feudalism The second stage of "prehistory" in Marxist ideology; in this stage, land ownership becomes the basis for political power and farm workers are exploited by those who own the land. (**Ch. 2**)

Fixed Jurisdictions The bureaucratic principle holding that agency officials should have clearly established areas of activity or specialization, making it possible to determine who is responsible for any given decision or program. (**Ch. 10**)

Folkways The norms and traditions observed in a legislature pertaining to the way members treat one another and expect to be treated. (**Ch. 7**)

Formal-Legal Analysis An approach to political science that emphasizes the study of laws, constitutions, and official institutions. (**Ch. 1**)

Free-Market Economy (also known as a Market Economy). An economic system in which production and commerce are largely in private hands and in which production strategies and prices are determined by the forces of supply and demand with limited or no government intervention. Often the term is used synonymously with "capitalism." (**Ch. 15**)

Free-Rider An individual who enjoys the benefits of a collective effort without contributing to it. (**Ch. 6**)

Free Trade A trade system in which the export and import of goods and services internationally is relatively unimpeded by tariffs, quotas, or other government-created barriers. (**Ch. 18**)

FSB The Federal Security Service of the Russian Federation. The primary successor to the Soviet KGB, the FSB is primarily concerned with internal security operations. Its first director was Vladimir Putin, who then moved on to be Prime Minister, then President, and then Prime Minister again. While not as feared or repressive as the KGB, it may be a more powerful force in Russian politics than its predecessor was in Soviet politics. (**Ch. 13**)

Fundamentalism A belief among some Christians, Hindus, and Muslims that their holy book must be accepted literally and that traditional religious values must be protected against the intrusions of the modern world. *See* Islamic Fundamentalism. (**Ch. 15**)

Fundamentalist Somebody who believes in religious fundamentalism. *See* Fundamentalism *and* Islamic Fundamentalism. (**Ch. 15**)

Gender Empowerment Measure (GEM) A statistical measure of how much gender equality or inequality exists in a country or set of countries in terms of economic and political power. (**Ch. 15**)

Gender Gap A difference between men as a group and women as a group with respect to some specific criterion, such as support for a given political party. (**Ch. 4**)

Gender-Related Development Index (GDI) A composite index that compares women's life expectancy, educational level, and income to the levels for men in the same society. It compares the Human Development Index (HDI) of women to that of men. *See also* Human Development Index. (**Ch. 15**)

Generation Y The generation of young people who were born in the last two decades of the twentieth century (in the United States and other affluent democracies) and have or will come of age politically in the early decades of the twenty-first century. (**Ch. 3**)

Glasnost The opening up of Soviet politics under Mikhail Gorbachev's government. *Glasnost* allowed greater media freedom and freedom of speech in an attempt to remedy the faults of Soviet communism through more honest discussion. (**Ch. 13**)

Globalization The spread of economic activity, political interactions, mass culture, and ideas across national borders, often in de facto defiance of national sovereignty. (**Ch. 18**)

Glorious Revolution The removal of King James II by the British Parliament in 1688, firmly establishing parliamentary dominance over the monarch at a time when royalty elsewhere in Europe still based their authority on divine right. (**Ch. 12**)

Government The people or organizations that make, enforce, and implement political decisions for a society. (**Ch. 1**)

Government Functions The basic tasks that governments perform in healthy, developed political systems. (**Ch. 1**)

Grand Jury A group of citizens who determine whether there is sufficient evidence to charge (or indict) a person or persons with a crime. (**Ch. 9**)

Great Leap Forward China's ultimately disastrous effort (1958–1961) to rapidly accelerate industrial and agricultural production through the use of mass mobilization and other radical techniques. (**Ch. 14**)

Green Party A party with a platform primarily devoted to protecting the environment. Taking a strong stand on ecological issues such as global warming and pollution, these parties have been most successful in Western Europe but exist in other regions as well. (**Ch. 18**)

Gulag The extensive network of prison camps to which millions of Soviet citizens were sent under Stalin. (**Ch. 13**)

Hierarchical Political or social system in which people have clearly understood ranks, from a governing elite down to the lowest ranks of society. (**Ch. 5**)

Hierarchy The bureaucratic principle holding that clear lines of super- and subordinate status should exist in organizations. (**Ch. 10**)

Homogeneous Societies Societies that lack sharp class, racial, regional, or ethnic divisions. (**Ch. 12**)

Honor Killings Murders committed by male family members against female relatives who have allegedly dishonored the family. The women are accused of committing adultery, engaging in extra-marital sex, marrying someone who is unacceptable to her family, rejecting an arranged marriage, or even being the victim of rape. As many as 7,000 women are murdered annually in honor killings, mostly in the developing world. Many of them had not even committed the "sins" of which they are accused. (**Ch. 18**)

Human Development Index (HDI) A composite measure of life expectancy, school enrollment, literacy rate, and per capita income used to evaluate living standards. (**Ch. 15**)

Human Rights The principle that all people, regardless of their culture, their level of economic development, or the type of political system in which they live, are entitled to certain fundamental freedoms and privileges. (**Ch. 1**)

Human Rights Act Legislation passed by Parliament in 1998 that gave Britain its first written Bill of Rights drawn from the European Union's Convention on Human Rights. (**Ch. 12**)

ICT *See* Information and Communications Technology. (**Ch. 3**)

Idealism An approach to international relations holding that wars are caused by evil and ignorance and that they can be avoided by nurturing a spirit of international community and justice. (**Ch. 17**)

Ideology A more or less coherent system of political thinking. A vision of society as it should be. (**Ch. 2**)

Income Distribution A measure of how the wealth of a society is shared among its members. Often we examine and measure the *equality* or *inequality* of income distribution. (A highly equal income distribution is one in which the difference in income between the poorest and the richest segments of the population is not great.) (**Chs. 1, 14, 15, 16**)

Incumbency Advantage The political advantages enjoyed by those in office over challengers. These advantages include the ability to manipulate news coverage, free mail privileges, and the power to grant favors to constituents. (**Ch. 11**)

Individualism A way of thinking that emphasizes individual interests, needs, and rights in contrast to social or communal interests, needs, and rights. (**Ch. 2**)

Industrial Democracies Highly industrialized nations or societies with a democratic political system. (**Ch. 12**)

Information and Communications Technology (ICT) The wide array of new, electronic information and communications innovations, including the Internet, podcasts, text messaging and the like. These are particularly important to young adults as sources of political information and opinion. (**Ch. 3**)

Inquisitorial System A system of criminal law in which the judge acts as a representative of the state, seeking information from the person or persons accused of a crime in an effort to determine guilt or innocence. (**Ch. 9**)

Institutional Coups Military takeovers carried out by the armed forces as a unified institution rather than a coup led by a single military strongman. Such coups tend to have some motivating ideology or plan of action. (**Ch. 15**)

Institutional Revolutionary Party (PRI) The party that ruled Mexico continuously from that party's formation in 1929 until 2000. (**Ch. 16**)

Interest Articulation The process of expressing concerns and problems as demands for governmental action. (**Ch. 1**)

Interest Group An organization that attempts to influence public policy in a specific area of importance to its members. (**Ch. 6**)

International Criminal Court Established in 2002, the International Criminal Court draws its authority from a treaty (the "Rome Statute") ratified by 106 nations. The U.S., Russia, China, and Israel are not among the ratifying nations, however. The countries that ratified the ICC agreed to allow it to prosecute persons "accused of the most serious crimes of international concern, namely genocide, crimes against humanity and war crimes." (**Ch. 17**)

International Law The body of law consisting of treaties (both bilateral and general) and traditionally recognized rights and duties pertaining to the relations among states. (**Ch. 17**)

International Organization An organization whose members are individual nation-states. Such organizations may be general, dealing with a wide range of issues, or they may be designed to address only a single set of problems. (**Ch. 17**)

Iron Triangles The idea that interest groups, legislative committees, and bureaucratic agencies in a given policy area engage in continuing interaction, and that they act together to perpetuate policies and programs, resisting change and control. (**Ch. 10**)

Islamic Fundamentalism An extremely devout movement within the Islamic religion whose members believe in a traditional and literal interpretation of the Quran, the Muslim holy book. They reject many aspects of modern life and reject such Western cultural influences as Hollywood movies, rock music, and "immodest dress" as corrupt threats to traditional, conservative Islamic values. Some fundamentalist Muslims support the use of violence to advance their cause; others do not. (**Chs. 2, 3**)

Judicial Activism The principle holding that judges should follow their own values in deciding how to interpret statutes and provisions of basic law. (**Ch. 9**)

Judicial Restraint The principle holding that judges should be reluctant to overturn legislative or executive laws and decisions, doing so only when absolutely necessary. (**Ch. 9**)

Judicial Review The power of courts to overturn or void actions or laws that they feel are unlawful or inconsistent with basic law. (**Ch. 9**)

Justice The quality of being righteous, fair, and deserved. (**Ch. 9**)

Just War The philosophical tradition that attempts to define the conditions under which war is just and those under which it is not. (**Ch. 17**)

KGB The Committee for State Security (KGB) was the last of a series of Soviet security agencies dating back to 1917 (the end of the Russian Revolution). It combined overseas espionage activities (like those of the American CIA), internal security operations, combating crime, maintaining internal security (like the FBI), and extensive spying on Soviet citizens. Its ruthless repression of real or suspected dissent made it greatly feared. It was dissolved in 1991 and replaced by Russia's FSB. (**Ch. 13**)

The Kremlin A historic fortified complex in Moscow which has served as the seat of (and symbol of) national political power under both the Soviet Union and the Russian Federation. The term "the Kremlin" was used to mean the Soviet government and is now often used to represent the Russian government as well, just as "the White House" is used to mean the U.S. government. (**Ch. 13**)

Kuomintang (KMT) The Chinese nationalist party that toppled the imperial government but, following a prolonged civil war, was overthrown nearly forty years later by the Chinese Communists. (**Ch. 14**)

"Law of 1/n" An idea, drawn from rational choice theory, predicting that legislatures with a larger number of legislators will spend more on public policies than legislatures with fewer legislators. A given legislator's constituents will only have to pay $1/n$ of the tax revenue for a given project (where "n" is the number of legislative districts), although they will receive the majority of the benefits from any policies or programs targeted for that district. Since all legislators face the same situation, they all have an incentive to favor decisions that are wasteful for the country as a whole, because they are still a net benefit to their constituents. The "law" suggests that this incentive is more potent in larger legislatures. (**Ch. 7**)

Leadership Recruitment The process through which a political system attracts its leadership. In most countries, political parties play a critical role in this process. (**Ch. 5**)

Leftist (Left-Wing) Political Parties Political parties that support substantial reform of the current political and economic systems. To varying degrees they support active government involvement in the economy in order to redistribute some of the nation's wealth from the well-off to the more needy sectors of society and create a safety net. (**Ch. 5**)

Legitimacy A government's or a state's basis for claiming authenticity, the right to rule. (**Ch. 15**)

Leninist (Party or Ideology) V. I. Lenin, the leader of the 1917 communist revolution in Russia, argued that in a revolutionary society, the Communist Party must have absolute power and that strict Party discipline within the Party must commit its members to support all the leadership's decisions. At least until 1989, all ruling Communist parties adhered to these principles, and even most Communist parties that were not in power enforced Leninist unity within the party itself. (**Ch. 5, 13, 14**)

Less-Developed Countries (LDCs) Countries in Africa, Asia, Latin America, and the Middle East that have less-developed economic and political systems including greater poverty and more conflictual politics. (**Ch. 15**)

Liberal Democracy A political system characterized by both free and fair elections (electoral democracy) *and* respect for civil liberties, including a free press (media), free speech, and freedom of religion. (**Ch. 15**)

Liberalism (1) A political ideology stressing tolerance for diverse lifestyles and opinions and demanding public assistance for those in need. (2) An approach to international political economy holding that trade barriers are counterproductive and wasteful. Synonymous with "economic internationalism" in this context. (**Chs. 2, 17**)

Libertarianism An ideology advocating minimum government and maximum individual liberty. (**Ch. 2**)

Lobbying Efforts by groups or individuals to influence public officials through formal and informal contacts with them. (**Ch. 6**)

Long March The PLA's difficult 6,000-mile trek fleeing the KMT in 1934–1935. Though they suffered enormous losses in the march, the Chinese Communists planted the seeds of their eventual victory. (**Ch. 14**)

Macho (Machista) Culture A culture, common in many parts of Latin America, in which men display and are expected to display an assertive, sexist attitude and accompanying behavior. Men dominate personal relationships and public life. (**Ch. 16**)

Majority Rule A decision-making principle that holds that when individuals disagree about which alternative is best, the choice taken will be that which the larger number of individuals prefer. (**Ch. 1**)

Malapportionment A condition in which legislative districts are of very different sizes, making the vote of a citizen in a district with a large population effectively less influential than the vote of a citizen in a district with a small population. (In the United States, the Supreme Court required states to correct malapportionment in the 1962 *Baker v. Carr* decision.) (**Ch. 4**)

Mao Zedong The leader and theoretician of the communist revolution in China. Mao's stress on the role of the peasantry in Third World revolutions and his belief that underdeveloped nations could experience communist revolutions had a profound impact on Marxist thinking and on revolutionary movements in Africa, Asia, and Latin America. (**Ch. 14**)

Marbury v. Madison The U.S. Supreme Court case from 1803 that, for the first time, held an act of Congress unconstitutional. Most historians believe that the opinion in this case established much of the power of the Supreme Court. (**Ch. 11**)

Marginal Seats Legislative seats won by a small electoral margin; incumbents in these seats cannot be confident that they will be reelected. (**Ch. 11**)

Market Economy or Market System *See* Free-Market Economy.

Marxism A comprehensive political and economic ideology based heavily on the writings of Karl Marx (1818–1883). It offers an explanatory theory of historical development and calls for class struggle (political struggle, either peaceful or violent) between the working class and the capitalists. Marxist thought is the basis of communist and radical socialist ideology. (**Ch. 2**)

Mass Parties Parties growing out of the working class movement, usually with a socialist orientation. (**Ch. 5**)

Member of Parliament (MP) A Member of the British Parliament (House of Commons). Also used to describe members of parliament in other countries. (**Ch. 12**)

Mercantilism An approach to international political economy holding that states pursue their national interests in making international economic policies, especially those pertaining to trade. (**Ch. 17**)

Mexican Economic Miracle The period of dramatic economic growth and industrialization from the 1940s until the 1982 debt crisis and the country's subsequent deep recession. (**Ch. 16**)

Military Coup A sudden seizure of full government power by the armed forces. The word *coup* is a shortened version of "coup d'état," which means "a blow at the state." (**Ch. 15**)

Missouri Plan An approach for selecting judges. Adopted by Missouri in 1940, the plan allows the governor to select judges from a list of candidates compiled by a nominating commission made up of legal experts and citizens. (**Ch. 9**)

Modernization Theory A popular academic theory that attributes a country's political and socioeconomic underdevelopment to the Third World's traditional cultural values and weak political and economic institutions. To modernize, the theory suggests, Third World nations must borrow (and possibly adapt) Western values and institutions. Modern values are transmitted through urbanization, increased education and literacy, as well as through greater exposure to the mass media. (**Ch. 15**)

Modern Political Philosophy A body of political philosophy associated with Machiavelli (1469–1527), Hobbes (1588–1679), Locke (1632–1704), and others. In contrast to "classical" political philosophy, modern political philosophy places greater emphasis on individualism and on pragmatic concerns about how government works. (**Ch. 1**)

Multiculturalism The idea that cultural diversity is valuable and that measures should be taken to ensure that cultural traditions other than the dominant one are preserved and respected. (**Ch. 2**)

National Action Party (PAN) One of Mexico's major parties (along with the PRI and PRD), it now holds the presidency. It is a conservative, pro-Catholic party with close links to the business community. Its strong stance against government corruption and in favor of democratic reform helped it gain power. (**Ch. 16**)

Nationalist Party (KMT, Guomindang) China's first important, modern political party. Led by reformist elements and traditional warlords, it rose to power with the overthrow of the old imperial dynasty. (**Ch. 14**)

Nationalization The process whereby the government takes control of an economic enterprise, as when Great Britain nationalized the railroads and steel mills after World War II. (**Ch. 12**)

Natural Law A moral or ethical standard grounded in some concept of nature or divinity. (**Ch. 9**)

Neofascist Parties Political parties that support a modified, and usually toned down, form of fascism with an emphasis on supernationalism, ethnic prejudice, and, in Europe, a commitment to limiting or ending further immigration. (**Ch. 5**)

New Labour The title that Prime Minister Tony Blair and his supporters gave the Labour Party after it largely abandoned socialism and converted to a more centrist political ideology. (**Ch. 12**)

Newly Industrialized Country (NIC) Countries in East Asia and Latin America—including Taiwan, South Korea, Hong Kong, Mexico, and Brazil—that have expanded their industrial capacities dramatically in recent decades and have become important international economic actors. (**Chs. 15, 18**)

New World Order (NWO) A concept proposed by President George Bush following the end of the cold war and the Allied victory over Iraq in the 1991 Gulf War. As envisioned by its proponents, it would entail close cooperation among the world's major powers to deter future aggression and would maintain international stability based on the rule of law and collective security. The vision has largely faded since it was of little utility during the conflicts in Bosnia and Iraq. In the 21st century, America's European allies have often differed with Washington over many international issues, including the best way to combat terrorism, the invasion of Iraq, politics toward Iran, and global warming. (**Ch. 18**)

NICs *See* Newly Industrialized Country

Nomenklatura The list of positions (some one million) within the Soviet Communist Party, the government bureaucracy, the military, state-owned business enterprises, labor unions, the media, cultural organizations, and professional groups for which appointment required party approval. The term more commonly referred to the hundreds of thousands who held important posts, constituting a tremendously powerful and privileged elite. (**Ch. 13**)

Nondecisions Problems and issues not addressed by a political system. Elite theorists often point to nondecisions as evidence that elite forces successfully steer government away from actions that would threaten elite interests. (**Ch. 6**)

Nongovernmental Organizations (NGOs) Organizations that are active and often influential in areas such as education, health care, the environment, and promoting the needs of the poor, but have no formal links to government. They can be very influential in developing nations. (**Ch. 18**)

No-Party Regimes A political system in which there are no organized political parties, often because the government has banned them. (**Ch. 5**)

North Atlantic Treaty Organization (NATO) A defense community established by the United States and many of its Western European allies during the cold war. Its purpose was to defend Europe against a possible attack by the Soviet Union and its Eastern European allies in the Warsaw Pact. It has survived the end of the Cold War. (**Ch. 18**)

North–South Relations Economic and political relations between the more economically developed nations of the world (the North) and the developing nations of the South. (**Ch. 18**)

Nuclear Proliferation The spread of nuclear weapons or of the capacity to produce nuclear weapons to additional countries, most notably in the developing world. (**Ch. 18**)

Nuclear Terror The idea that the prospects of nuclear war are so horrible that nations avoid it, even when their national interests would have led to war in the absence of nuclear weapons. (**Ch. 17**)

Oligarchy The relatively small group of multi-millionaire or billionaire businessmen in Russia who often gained their wealth illicitly after the fall of communism and who now control most of the economy. Individually they are known as oligarchs, and collectively they are called the oligarchy. (**Ch. 13**)

Ombudsman A person who attempts (or an office that attempts) to resolve the problems that individual citizens have with administrative agencies and programs. (**Ch. 7**)

One-Child Policy A Chinese government population-control policy that penalizes urban families that have more than one child and most rural families that have more than two children. (**Ch. 14**)

Open-Door Policy Deng Xiaoping's policy of opening up China to economic, trade, and cultural exchange with the West and then with Japan, Hong Kong, and Taiwan. (**Ch. 14**)

PAN *See* National Action Party.

Parliament The entire British national legislature consisting of the elected House of Commons and the House of Lords (with inherited or appointed seats). In common usage, however, *Parliament* refers only to the far more influential House of Commons. (**Ch. 12**)

Parliamentary Supremacy The idea that the Parliament enjoys sovereign power, and that no court or executive can abrogate its decisions. (**Ch. 9**)

Parliamentary System A system of executive–legislative relations in which the legislature elects the chief executive. (**Ch. 7**)

Party Discipline The capacity of a party to have its legislative representatives vote as a unified bloc. (**Ch. 12**)

Party Identification A citizen's sense of attachment to a political party. (**Ch. 4**)

Party of the Democratic Revolution (PRD) A coalition of Mexico's leftist, nationalist parties originally headed by Cuauhtémoc Cárdenas, the son of the legendary former president, Lázaro Cárdenas. In 1988, heading a predecessor coalition to the PRD, Cárdenas mounted a formidable challenge to the ruling PRI. In a symbolically important election, the PRD gained control of Mexico City in 1997, led by Cuauhtémoc Cárdenas, who became the first popularly elected mayor of the giant metropolis in more than 70 years. The PRD is one of Mexico's two major opposition parties (along with the PRI) that now control the Chamber of Deputies. It expresses the unhappiness felt by many of Mexico's poor over their country's severe economic setbacks in recent years. (**Ch. 16**)

Party Platform The set of policy orientations officially held by a political party. (**Ch. 5**)

Patronage The practice of selecting bureaucratic officials on the basis of their political support for the elected official with the power to appoint them; contrasted with appointment on the basis of neutral competence or expertise. (**Ch. 10**)

Patron-Client Relations Relations between a politically or economically powerful figure (the patron) and a less powerful individual, often a fairly dependent person such as a Third World peasant (the client). The patron (such as a local political party boss) gives the client services or goods that he or she needs (a job in the civil service, financial credit, or a welfare payment, for example) and, in return, the client agrees to vote for or even campaign for the patron's political party. (**Ch. 5**)

People's Liberation Army (PLA) China's Red army, which, under Mao Zedong's leadership, carried out the communist revolution. (**Ch. 14**)

Perestroika The restructuring of Soviet political and, especially, economic institutions introduced by Communist Party Secretary Mikhail Gorbachev. The goal was to make communism more humane and more efficient. (**Ch. 13**) This term is also used to designate a movement created by a group of contemporary political scientists who oppose what they see as the domination of the discipline by rational choice theory and quantification. (**Ch. 1**)

Personal Coups Coups led by a single military strongman, such as Somoza in Nicaragua, with little in the way of long-term goals other than increasing the power and wealth of the leader. (**Ch. 15**)

Personalistic Party A political party whose primary purpose is to further the political career of one person, the party leader. Sometimes the party is actually named or nicknamed after that leader, as, for example, the Peronist party in Argentina (nicknamed after its founding leader, Juan Perón). (**Ch. 5**)

PLA *See* People's Liberation Army.

Plaid Cymru A Welsh nationalist political party. (**Ch. 12**)

Plaintiff The person who brings a legal action against another person for damages in a civil suit; the "complaining party." (**Ch. 9**)

Pluralism The idea that there are many centers of political power in society (typically contrasted with elite theory or other views holding that a single class or group dominates society). Also, the condition of having many centers of power in a society. (**Ch. 6**)

Policy Initiation The first steps taken to make or change policy. Executives and administrators have increasingly taken over this function in industrial democracies. (**Ch. 7**)

Politburo The highest-ranking decision-making body of the now-defunct Soviet Communist Party. Its roughly 12 to 16 members represented the power elite of the party and made most key political and economic decisions until it was stripped of much of its power shortly before the fall of the Soviet Union. Other ruling communist parties (such as China, Vietnam, and Cuba) also had politburos at their helms. (**Ch. 13**)

Political Action Committees (PACs) Organizations established to gather and disburse campaign contributions to candidates in the United States. (**Ch. 11**)

Political Aggregation The process through which a political system reduces the multitude of conflicting societal demands to a manageable number of alternatives. Frequently this is done through programmatically oriented political parties. (**Ch. 5**)

Political Culture The pattern of individual attitudes and orientations toward politics among the members of a political system. (**Ch. 3**)

Political Development The idea that nations become modern by acquiring certain capacities and capabilities. The term is sometimes considered controversial because it implies that traditional (or "underdeveloped") nations will change along a known path to become similar to the Western industrial democracies. (**Chs. 1, 15**)

Political Economy The study of the impact of government on economic conditions, including analysis of alternative public policies and different systems of government. (**Ch. 1**)

Political Liberalization The process of loosening authoritarian controls over society and allowing a higher degree of political freedom, but not a transition to democracy. (**Ch. 14**)

Political Party An organization that unites people in an effort to win government office and thereby influence or control government policies. (**Ch. 5**)

Political Resocialization The active effort by government to transform society's political culture. Political resocialization is common during radical revolutions (such as Maoist China's) or after a mobilized country has suffered a defeat in war (as in the postwar de-Nazification efforts in Germany). (**Ch. 3**)

Political Socialization The process of creating a shared political culture among the members of a political system, typically from one generation to another. It may also entail changes over time that lead to a gradual transformation of the culture. (**Chs. 1, 3**)

Political Subcultures The distinct political orientations of a region, a class, an ethnicity, or a race found within a larger political culture. (**Ch. 3**)

Political Underdevelopment A condition marked by lack of state and national autonomy, weak government institutions, weak political parties, limited opportunities for popular political participation and articulation, and instability. (**Ch. 15**)

Politico Model An approach to representation in which the legislator alternately represents constituents in accordance with the delegate model and the trustee model (see definitions), depending on the nature of the issue and the degree of public concern about it. (**Ch. 7**)

Politics The process of making collective decisions in a community, society, or group through the application of influence and power. (**Ch. 1**)

Popular Consultation A regularized process through which citizens can make known their preferences regarding governmental policies and decisions; a key component of democracy. (**Ch. 1**)

Populist (Parties) Political parties that try to build a broad electoral coalition of working-class, middle-class, and, sometimes, business-community voters, often by promising a wide range of government programs that would benefit each sector of the coalition. (**Ch. 5**)

Positive Law Laws made by governments; normally contrasted with "natural" law. (**Ch. 9**)

Postmaterialism A somewhat distinctive set of political orientations common to many individuals in industrial democracies who were politically socialized during the era of postwar affluence. Postmaterialists tend to be somewhat less concerned with ideology and with economic issues and more concerned with issues such as civil liberties, grassroots political participation, the environment, and civil liberties. (**Ch. 3**)

Postmodernism Advocates of postmodernism can be found in many disciplines. In political science, postmodernism is a reaction to what its advocates see as excessive faith in the certainty and objectivity of scientific method. Believing that all researchers "construct" their own reality as they analyze data, postmodernists

argue that scientific methods can only rarely generate useful findings. (**Ch. 1**)

Postwar Settlement An unspoken agreement between Europe's labor or socialist parties and allied labor unions, on the one hand, and conservative parties and the business community, on the other. The right agreed to accept a welfare state in return for the left's agreement to abide by the ground rules of the free-market system. (**Ch. 12**)

Power Elite The name given to the set of forces that, in C. Wright Mills's interpretation, dominates American society; it consists of the leaders of the military, corporate, and political establishments. (**Ch. 6**)

PRD *See* Party of the Democratic Revolution.

Presidential "Character" Developed in the study of the U.S. presidency, the idea that the behavior of individual presidents is largely determined by basic elements of their personalities and character. (**Ch. 11**)

Presidentialism Concentration of political power in the hands of the national president. (**Ch. 16**)

Presidential System A system of executive–legislative relations in which the chief executive is elected independently of the members of the legislature. (**Ch. 7**)

President's Cabinet The secretaries of the cabinet-level departments in the executive branch of the U.S. government. (**Ch. 11**)

PPP (Parity Purchasing Power) A calculation of each country's Gross Domestic Product, computed by converting the GDP into purchasing power parity (PPP), that is by calculating what that GDP could buy in that country. This method is considered a more accurate measure of a country's economic size and its per capita income than the traditional calculation based on currency exchange rates. (**Ch. 15**)

PRI *See* Institutional Revolutionary Party.

Primaries Elections held to select candidates for a general election. (**Ch. 11**)

Princelings Children of high-ranking Chinese government and Communist Party officials who use their connections and privileged position to enrich themselves and gain power in the growing private sector. (**Ch. 14**)

Privatization The process whereby the government transfers state-owned enterprises (such as petroleum companies or electric power) to the private sector through the sale of stock. (**Chs. 12, 13, 15, 16**)

Proletariat The Marxist word used to describe the working class. The proletariat were viewed by Karl Marx as the greatest victims of capitalist exploitation and, hence, the ones who would bring the communist revolution to fruition. (**Ch. 13**)

Proportional Representation (PR) An electoral system in which parties receive seats in the legislature in proportion to the share of the popular vote they receive. Voters choose between party lists in larger, multi-member districts, rather than choosing a particular candidate. **(Ch. 4)**

Public Opinion Polls Data on the opinions, demographic characteristics, and vote choices of citizens; nearly always estimated by gathering information about a sample of the larger population of citizens. **(Ch. 4)**

Public Schools The term used to describe Great Britain's most elite private schools (pre-university). The meaning of term *public* here is totally different from its meaning in reference to U.S. schools. **(Ch. 12)**

Rational Choice An approach to political theory distinguished by its application of economic principles, particularly the assumption that individuals seek their own interests in making political decisions. **(Chs. 1, 6)**

Rational-Legal Authority The authority that a leader enjoys when his or her actions are consistent with established legal principles. **(Ch. 8)**

Realism An approach to international relations that emphasizes the role of national interest in explaining the causes of war and conflict. **(Ch. 17)**

Red Faction That faction of Chinese Communist Party leadership in the 1960s and 1970s that favored assigning all leadership and management positions in society to those individuals who proved themselves most committed to Maoist, communist ideology. *See* Reds versus Experts. **(Ch. 14)**

Red Guards Young people who became the shock troops of China's Cultural Revolution and helped enforce its terror. **(Ch. 14)**

Redistricting The process of redrawing the boundaries of legislative districts; necessary to avoid malapportionment as populations grow at different rates in different areas. **(Ch. 4)**

Reds versus Experts The name given to a debate in the 1960s between those Chinese leaders who favored maximizing the use of Maoist ideology as a driving force in society (the Reds) and those who felt that concessions needed to be made to pragmatism and technical expertise (the Experts). **(Ch. 14)**

Representative Authority The authority that a leader enjoys when it is perceived that he or she is representative of the "people" or the "majority." **(Ch. 8)**

Representative Bureaucracy The idea that non-elected bureaucrats may be, in practice, more closely representative of the citizens than elected legislators or executives. **(Ch. 10)**

Responsibility System The program giving China's peasantry control over their own family plots. It was the opening step in the conversion of the nation's collective farms to private holdings. **(Ch. 14)**

Responsible Parties Parties that can demand discipline from members elected to a legislature, who almost always vote in accordance with the party platform. **(Ch. 7)**

Routines Patterns of bureaucratic activity that become established. **(Ch. 10)**

Right-Wing (Rightist) Political Parties Parties that are more likely to support the existing political and economic systems and to defend traditional values such as religion. **(Ch. 5)**

Rule Adjudication The process of applying governmental rules to individual cases. **(Ch. 1)**

Rule Execution The process of implementing or carrying out policy decisions. **(Ch. 1)**

Rule Making The process of establishing laws, orders, edicts, regulations, and other authoritative acts by government. **(Ch. 1)**

Self-Help The idea that in the international system, states cannot rely on protection provided by a higher power (as citizens can rely on government to protect them from criminals). **(Ch. 17)**

Shays's Rebellion An uprising in Massachusetts in 1786–1787 challenging the foreclosures of farm mortgages and demanding government action to improve the position of debtors. **(Ch. 11)**

Siloviki This group is widely considered the most powerful of several contending factions within the Kremlin's inner circle. Composed primarily of former officers from the KGB, the FSB (the KGB's successor), and the military, many of its leaders were colleagues of Vladimir Putin in the KGB and/or come from Putin's home city of St. Petersburg. **(Ch. 13)**

Shock Therapy Drastic government measures designed to reduce rampant inflation, large budget deficits, and troublesome trade deficits. Typically, shock treatment involves currency devaluation, slashes in public spending, layoffs of public employees, restraints on wages, and other painful measures that, at least in the short run, reduce popular living standards. **(Ch. 13)**

Single-Member Districts An electoral system in which each electoral district has one representative in the legislature; sometimes called "winner-take-all" because, in contrast to proportional representation systems, parties receiving fewer votes than the winner get no representation from that district. **(Ch. 4)**

Social Capital The density of associational involvement (belonging to groups ranging from church choirs to the League of Women Voters) in a town, region, or country, and the norms and social trust that these group activities produce. **(Ch. 3)**

Social Class *See* Socioeconomic Status.

Social Democrats Political parties and their supporters who adhere to a non-Marxist, moderate form of socialism. **(Ch. 5)**

Social Movements Broad mobilizations of ordinary people [seeking] a particular goal or goals. **(Ch. 5)**

Socialism The fourth and final stage of "prehistory" in Marxist ideology; in this stage, following a revolution by the workers exploited under capitalism, the state is governed in the interests of the workers; also an ideology advocating social equality, public ownership of industry, and a lesser role for private property. In the non-communist world (especially Europe) socialism has a different, more moderate meaning. *See* Socialist (Party) and Social Democrats **(Ch. 2)**

Socialist (Parties) In Western Europe where socialist parties are most influential and often govern, the terms *socialist* and *socialism* have shed the Marxist meaning found in the previous definition of socialism. Instead, they have become left-of-center, democratic parties that favor working class and middle-class economic interests and a somewhat more active state. Often used interchangeably with the label *social democratic*. **(Ch. 5)**

Socioeconomic Status (SES) A person's position in society, with regard to income, educational attainment, and occupational status. **(Ch. 4)**

SOEs (State-Owned Enterprises) Firms, primarily in industrial manufacturing, still owned by the communist government. The term is used especially regarding Chinese firms of this kind. **(Ch. 14)**

State Capitalism An economic system in which most of the economy is owned and managed by private enterprise but the state controls important segments (such as Mexico's giant petroleum industry) and uses its economic wealth and political power to help direct the economy. **(Ch. 16)**

State Duma *See* Duma.

Statist Favoring a large role for the government (the state) in national life, especially the economy. Statist parties generally favor extensive government programs for welfare, economic development, and the like, whereas anti-statists prefer a more limited government role. **(Ch. 5)**

Statutes Laws passed by a legislature. **(Ch. 7)**

Statutory Interpretation The process of deciding how statutes apply to particular contexts; normally a task of courts. **(Ch. 9)**

Statutory Law The body of law created by acts of the legislature; distinct from provisions in constitutional law, law made by judges, and administrative regulations. **(Ch. 9)**

Suffrage The right to vote or the exercise of that right. **(Ch. 12)**

Superpowers States whose military strength is of a higher order than that of all but the other superpowers. **(Ch. 17)**

Symbolic Leader One who serves as the unifying symbol of the nation; a key function of modern chief executives. **(Ch. 8)**

Technical Responsibility The idea that bureaucrats may be controlled by their own sense of professional standards, even when public control is weak or absent. **(Ch. 10)**

Technocrats Highly trained bureaucrats, often with graduate degrees in the social sciences (frequently from a developed country). In recent years many modernizing societies, such as Mexico, have increased the technocrats' power at the expense of that of elected politicians in the belief that technocrats can render more impartial, scientifically informed administrative decisions. **(Ch. 16)**

Techno-Enthusiasts Analysts who believe that the ICT revolution (the Internet, text messaging, YouTube etc.) has had a beneficial effect on the political socialization of young adults in the United States and other advanced democracies. The term is also used to describe people who are enthusiastic about other new technologies. **(Ch. 3)**

Term Limits The idea that legislators should be allowed to serve only a limited number of terms. A movement to enact term limits gained momentum in the United States in the early 1990s. **(Ch. 11)**

Thatcherism The philosophy of the British Conservative Party's right wing as espoused by former Prime Minister Margaret Thatcher. Thatcherites rejected much of the welfare state and sought substantial reductions of state intervention in the free market. **(Ch. 12)**

Third Generation The new generation of Chinese political leadership, led by President Jiang Zemin, that took over after Deng Xiaoping's death. This generation began to turn power over to a fourth generation of leaders at the 2002 party congress. **(Ch. 14)**

Third Way An approach to governing that blends policies associated with modern liberalism with some conservative principles. The term is most closely associated with former British Prime Minister Tony Blair, although former U.S. Presidents Bill Clinton and George W. Bush may also be seen as "third way" leaders. **(Ch. 2)**

Third World A category of nations in Africa, Asia, Latin America, and the Middle East that share two primary characteristics: they are politically and/or economically less developed; and they are neither industrialized democracies (the First World) nor former members of the Soviet–Eastern European bloc of communist nations (the Second World). The term "Third World" is used interchangeably with "developing nations" and "less-developed countries" (LDCs). (Ch. 15)

Tiananmen Square Located near Beijing's imperial Heavenly City, it has been the locale of major political gatherings in communist China. In 1989 it was the center of student pro-democracy demonstrations, and the June 4 massacre there made it a symbol of China's ongoing political repression. (Ch. 14)

Tories Members or supporters of the British Conservative Party. (Ch. 12)

Totalitarian Government (Regime) A form of authoritarian (non-democratic) government in which the government exercises near-total control over all forms of political activity and organized societal activity. Such extreme control is very rare and perhaps only Nazi Germany, the USSR under Stalin, and China under Mao exercised it. (Chs. 1, 5, 13, 14)

Traditional Authority The authority that derives from a leader's embodiment of long-standing, widely accepted social and political traditions. (Ch. 8)

Traditional Society A society that tends to stress long-standing beliefs; evaluations of individuals based on their ethnicity, class, or other innate qualities rather than on their abilities; and other pre-modern social values. (Ch. 15)

Transnational Corporations (TNCs) Large corporations with holdings in many nations and in some cases corporate ownership in more than one country. Also referred to as multinational corporations. (Ch. 18)

Trial and Appellate Courts The two basic levels of courts in most judicial systems. The evidence pertaining to a case is presented in trial courts, whereas appellate courts normally rule on claims that trial courts made errors of law or procedure. (Ch. 9)

Trustee Model An approach to representation in which the representative acts in accordance with his or her independent judgment, regardless of the wishes of the constituency that elected him or her. (Ch. 7)

Two-and-One-Half-Party System A national party system in which two parties are predominant but a third party presents a significant challenge, as in Great Britain. (Ch. 5)

Vanguard Party A term used by Vladimir Lenin to describe the Communist Party as an enlightened elite acting in the best interests of the working class. (Ch. 13)

Vertical Power Russian President Vladimir Putin's efforts to concentrate political power in the hands of the federal government and, in turn, in his own hands. (Ch. 13)

Vote of No Confidence A vote by the Parliament expressing its unwillingness to support the prime minister and his or her cabinet. (Ch. 12)

Voter Turnout A measure of how many voters actually vote in a given election. (Ch. 4)

Warlords Regional military leaders who exercised much of the local power in the Chinese imperial order. (Ch. 14)

Watergate Refers to the wide-ranging patterns of illegal and abusive activities of the Nixon administration during 1972–1974. The Watergate is the name of an office and apartment building in Washington, DC, in which a burglary associated with the Nixon reelection effort took place. (Ch. 11)

Wave of Democracy One of three periods in world history since 1828 when a substantial number of countries were making a transition to democracy. (Ch. 15)

Welfare State The arrangement of public services, regulations, and programs of income redistribution that are established to provide a basic standard of living to all members of society. (Chs. 2, 12)

Zapatista A member of the contemporary revolutionary group in the Mexican state of Chiapas known as the EZLN (Zapatista Army of National Liberation). They were named after the legendary hero of the Mexican Revolution (1910-1920), Emiliano Zapata. (Ch. 16)

Zipper-Style Quota An electoral system for a legislature or parliament that is based on proportional representation and the introduction of quotas for women or other underrepresented groups. Women candidates are given a guaranteed share (often 30 percent) of candidates on the party list and are alternated from the top of the list (those who are most likely to win seats) to the bottom in accordance with that quota. *See also* Proportional Representation. (Ch. 5)